THE OFFICIAL®
PRICE GUIDE
TO
WATCHES

By **Cooksey Shugart** and **Tom Engle**

Edited by **Walter Presswood**

TENTH EDITION

HOUSE OF COLLECTIBLES • NEW YORK

THE OFFICIAL®
PRICE GUIDE
TO
WATCHES

Copyright © 1990 by Cooksey Shugart

All rights reserved under International and Pan-American Copyright Conventions.

Published by: The House of Collectibles
201 East 50th Street
New York, New York 10022

Distributed by Ballantine Books, a division of Random House, Inc., New York and simultaneously in Canada by Random House of Canada Limited, Toronto.

Manufactured in the United States of America

Library of Congress Catalog Card Number: 88-641146

ISBN 0-876-37808-4
Tenth Edition: March 1990
10 9 8 7 6 5 4 3 2 1

TABLE OF CONTENTS

ACKNOWLEDGMENTS

I am especially appreciative of Bob Overstreet, author of **The Official® Overstreet Comic Book Price Guide**, for his encouragement.

To Walter Presswood, who is the editor of **The Official® Price Guide to Watches**.

To my wife Martha, for her complete understanding and assistance in compiling this book.

To the NAWCC Museum, Hamilton Watch Co., and Bowman Technical School, for allowing us to photograph their watches.

To Christie's, Osvaldo Patrizzi and Muller & Joseph for photographs of watches.

And to the following people whose help was invaluable and will be long remembered: Frank Irick, John Cubbins, Harold Harris, Paul Gibson, Robert L. Ravel, M.D., William C. Heilman Jr., M.D., Thomas McEntyre, Paul Morgan, Bill Selover, Oscar Laube, Ed Kieft, Charles Wallace, Bob Walters, Jack Warren, Howard Schroeder, Edward M. McGinnis, James Gardner, Paul Zuercher, Irving E. Roth, Don Bass, Stephen Polednak, Dick Stacy, Ernest J. Lewis, Herbert McDonald, David Steger, Fred Favour, Ralph Warner, Estus Harris, Charles Cleves, Tom McIntyre, Ralph Ferone, Arnold C. Varey, Jeffrey Ollswang, Tom Rohr, Leon Beard, Glenn Smith, Kenneth Vergin, Thomas Rumpf, Frank Diggs, Tom Thacker, Bob Lavoie, Norman Howard, Constantin Tanasecu, Rod Minter, Ernest Lueman, Mike Kirkpatrick, Clint B. Geller, Art W. Rontree, Denford Jones Photographics; and a special thanks to Peter Kushnir, Dr. J. Mauss, Robert D. Gruen, Jeff Hess, Col. R. A. Mulholland, Dick Ziebell, Jack Warren, Ron Starnes, Dick Flaute, Ralph Vinge, Edward Fletcher, Richard Walker, Alex Wolanguk, Carl Goetz, Miles Sandler, Dave Mycko (comic characters), and Martin Cullen.

*   *   *

Send only corrections, additions, deletions and comments to Cooksey Shugart, 780 Church St. N.E., Cleveland, TN 37311. When corresponding, please send a self-addressed, stamped envelope.

Special consultants:

Dan Crawley

David Searles

Paul A. Duggan

Geoff White

Dennis Nichinson

Jeff Cohen

ACKNOWLEDGMENTS

INTRODUCTION

This book is dedicated to all watch collectors who we hope will find it an enjoyable and valuable reference to carry on buying trips or to trace the lost history of that priceless family heirloom.

The origin of this book began when I was given a pocket watch which had been in our family for many years. After receiving the prized heirloom I wanted to know its complete history, and thus the search began. Because of the lack of a comprehensive reference on American pocket watches the venture took me through volume after volume. Over the course of ten years many hours were accumulated in running down the history of this one watch. But the research sparked my interest in the pocket watch field and pointed to the need for a book such as this one. We hope it will provide the information that you are looking for.

— The Authors

Watches are unique collectibles. Since the beginning of civilization when man scooped up a handful of sand and created the hourglass, portable timepieces have held a fascination that demanded the attention of the wealthy and poor alike. Man has sought constantly to improve his time-measuring instruments and has made them with the finest metals and jewels. The pocket watch, in particular, became an ornamentation and a source of pride, and this accounts for its value among families for generation after generation.

The watch has become precious and sentimental to so many because it is one of the true personal companions of the individual night and day. Mahatma Gandhi, the father of India and one of the rare people in history who was able to renounce worldly possessions, was obsessed with the proper use of his time. Each minute, he held, was to be used in the service of his fellowman. His own days were ordered by one of his few personal possessions, a sixteen-year-old, eight-shilling Ingersoll pocket watch that was always tied to his waist with a piece of string.

Another factor that has made watches unique collectibles is the intricate artisanship with which they are put together. Many of the watches of yesteryear, which were assembled with extreme accuracy and fine workmanship, continue to be reliable timepieces today. They stand out as unique because that type of watch is no longer manufactured. In today's world of mass production, the watch with individual craftmanship containing precious jewels and metals can rarely be found—and, if found, it is rarely affordable.

The well-made watch is a tribute to man's skills, artisanship and craftsmanship at their finest level. That is why the watch holds a special place in the collectible field.

In America, there are about 80,000 avid watch collectors. About 5 million people own two or more watches, and an untold number possess at least one of these precious heirlooms.

The Official® Price Guide to Watches does not attempt to establish or fix values or selling prices in the pocket watch trade market.

It does, however, *reflect* the trends of buying and selling in the collector market. Prices listed in this volume are based on data collected and analyzed from dealers and shops all over the country.

These prices should serve the collector as a guide only. The price you pay for any watch will be determined by the value it has to you. The intrinsic value of any particular watch can be measured only by you, the collector, and a fair price can be derived only after mutual agreement between both the buyer and the seller.

It is our hope that this volume can help make your watch collecting venture both pleasurable and profitable.

Information contained herein may not necessarily apply to every situation. Data is still being found, which may alter statements made in this book. These changes, however, will be reflected in future editions.

Hopefully, everyone interested in horology will research the American pocket watch and add to his library on the subject.

COLLECTAMANIA

Hobby — Business — Pastime — Entertainment

Just name it. More than likely someone will want to buy or sell it: books, coins, stamps, bottles, beer cans, gold, glassware, baseball cards, guns, clocks, pocket watches, comics, art, cars, and . . . . the list goes on and on.

Most Americans seem to be caught up in *collectamania*. More and more Americans are spending hour after hour searching through antique shops, auctions, flea markets and yard sales for those rare treasures of delight that have been lying tucked away for generations just waiting to be found.

This sudden boom in the field of collecting may have been influenced by fears of inflation or disenchantment with other types of investments. But more people are coming into the field because they gain some degree of nostalgic satisfaction from these new tangible ties with yesteryear. Collecting provides great fun and excitement. The tales of collecting and the resultant "fabulous finds" could fill volumes and inspire even the non-collector to embark upon a treasure hunt.

Collecting for the primary purpose of investment may prove to have many pitfalls for the amateur. The lack of sufficient knowledge is the main cause of disappointment. The inability to spot fakes or flawed merchandise can turn excitement into disappointment. And, in many fields, high-class forgers are at work, doing good and faithful reproductions in large quantities that can sometimes fool even the experts the first time they see them.

Collecting for fun and profit can be just that if you observe a fair amount of caution. Always remember, amidst your enthusiasm, that an object may not be what it would first appear. Below are a few guidelines that may be helpful to you:

1. **Make up your mind** as to what you want to collect and concentrate in this area. Your field of collecting should be one that you have a genuine liking for, and it helps if you can use the objects. It may help also to narrow your field even further, for instance, in collecting watches, to choose only one company or one type of pocket watch.

2. **Gain all the knowledge you can** about the objects you collect. The more knowledge you have the more successful you will be in finding valuable, quality pieces. Amassing the knowledge required to be a good collector is easier if you have narrowed your scope of interest. Otherwise, it may take years to become an "expert." Don't try to learn everything there is to know about a variety of fields. This will end in frustration and disappointment. Specialize.

3. **Buy the best you can afford**, assuming the prices are fair. The advanced collector may want only mint articles; but the novice collector may be willing to accept something far less than mint condition due to caution and economics. Collectible items in better condition continue to rise in value at a steady rate.

4. **Deal with reputable dealers** whom you can trust. Talk with the dealer; get to know the seller; get a business card; know where you can contact the dealer if you have problems, or if you want the dealer to help you find something else you may be looking for.

HOROLOGICAL PUZZLE

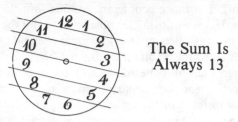

The Sum Is
Always 13

HOW TO USE THIS BOOK

The Official® Price Guide to Watches is a simple reference, with clear and carefully selected information. The first part of the book is devoted to history, general information, and a how-to section. The second part of the guide consists mainly of a listing of watch manufacturers, identification guides, and prices. This is a unique book because it is designed to be taken along as a handy pocket reference for identifying and pricing watches. With the aid of this book, the collector should be able to make on-the-spot judgments as to identification, age, quality, and value. This complete guide and a pocket magnifying glass will be all you need to take on your buying trips.

*　　　　*　　　　*

Watch collecting is fast growing as a hobby and business. Many people collect for the enjoyment and profit. The popularity of watches continues to rise because watches are a part of history. The American railroad brought about the greatest watch of that time—the railroad pocket watch. Since that time America has produced some of the best quality pocket watches that money could buy. The gold-filled cases made in America have never been surpassed in quality or price in the foreign market. With the quality of movement and cases being made with *guaranteed* high standards as well as beauty, the American pocket watch became very desirable. Because they are no longer being made in the U. S. A., pocket watches continue to rise in value.

The watch is collected for its beauty, quality in movement and case, and the value of metal content. Solid gold is the top of the line; platinum and silver are also very desirable. (Consider that some watches in the early 1900s sold between $700 and $1,000. This is equal to or greater

5-A

than the price of a good car of the same period.)

As with limited edition prints, a watch of supreme excellence is also limited and will increase in value. There is universal appeal and excitement in owning a piece of history, and your heirloom is just that. At one time pocket watches were a status symbol. Everyone competed for beauty and quality in the movement and case. Solid gold cases were adorned with elaborate engravings, diamonds, and other precious jewels. The movements were beautiful and of high quality. Manufacturers went to great lengths to provide movements that were both accurate and lovely. Fancy damaskeening on the back plates of nickel with gold lettering, 26 jewels in gold settings, and a solid gold train (gears) were features of some of the more elaborate timepieces. The jewels were red rubies, or diamond-end stones, or sapphires for the pallet stones. There were gold timing screws, and more. The faces were made by the best artisans of the day— hand-painted, jewel-studded, with fancy hands and double-sunk dials made of enamel and precious metals.

*   *   *

HOW TO DETERMINE MANUFACTURER

When identifying a watch, look on the face or dial for the name of the company and then refer to the alphabetical list of watch companies in this book. If the face or dial does not reveal the company name you will have to seek information from the movement's back plate. The company name or the town where it was manufactured will likely be inscribed there. The name engraved on the back plate is referred to as the "signature." After locating the place of manufacture, see what companies manufactured in that town. This may require reading the histories of several companies to find the exact one. Use the process of elimination to narrow the list.

Note: Some of the hard-to-identify watches are extremely collectible and valuable. Therefore, it is important to learn to identify them.

HOW TO DETERMINE AGE

After establishing the name of the manufacturer, you may be interested in the age of the watch. This information can be obtained by using the serial number inscribed on the back movement plate and referring to the production table. It is often difficult to establish the exact age, but this method will put you within a two- or three-year period of the date of the manufacture.

The case that houses the movement is not necessarily a good clue to the origin of the movement. It was a common practice for manufacturers to ship the movements to the jewelers and watchmakers uncased. The customer then married the movement and case. That explains why an expensive movement can be found in a cheaper case or vice versa.

If the "manufacturer's" name and location are no help, the inscription could possibly be that of a jeweler and his location. Then it becomes obvious there is no quick and easy way to identify some American-made watches. However, the following steps may be helpful. Some watches can be identified by comparing the models of each company until the correct model is found. Start by sizing the watch and then comparing the varied plate shapes and styles. The cock or bridge for the balance may also be a clue. The general arrangement of the movement as to jeweling, whether it is an open face or hunting case, and style of regulators may help to find the correct identification of the manufacturer of the movement.

Numbers on a watch case should not be considered as clues to the age of the movement because cases were both American- and foreign-made, and many of the good watches were re-cased through the years.

APPRAISING WATCHES

Watch collecting is still young when compared to fields of the standard collectibles: coins and stamps. The watch collecting field is growing but information is still scarce, fragmented, and sometimes unreliable. To be knowledgeable in any field, one must spend the time required to study it.

The value of any collectible is determined first by demand. Without demand there is no market. In the watch trade, the law of supply and demand is also true. The supply of the American watches has stopped and the demand among collectors continues to rise. There are many factors that make a watch desired or in demand. Only time and study will tell a collector just which pieces are most collectible. After the collector or investor finds out what is desirable, then a value must be placed on it before it is sold. If it is priced too high, the watch will not sell; but, on the other hand, if it is priced too low, it will be hard to replace at the selling price. The dealer must arrive at a fair market price that will move the watch.

There are no two watches alike. This makes the appraising more difficult and oftentimes arbitrary. But there are certain guidelines one can follow to arrive at a fair market price. When watches were manufactured, most companies sold the movements to a jeweler, and the buyer had a choice of dials and cases. Some high-grade movements were placed in a low-grade case and vice versa. Some had hand-painted multicolored dials; some were plain. The list of contrasts goes on. Conditions of watches will vary greatly, and this is a big factor in the value. The best movement in the best original case will bring the top price for any type of watch.

Prices are constantly changing in the watch field. Gold and silver markets affect the price of the cases. Scarcity and age also affect the value. These prices will fluctuate regularly.

APPRAISING GUIDELINES

Demand, supply, condition, and **value** must be the prime factors in appraising an old watch.

Demand is the most important element. Demand can be determined by the number of buyers for the particular item. A simple but true axiom is that value is determined by the price someone is willing to pay.

In order to obtain a better knowledge in appraising and judging watches, the following guidelines are most useful. Consider all these factors before placing a value on the watch. (There is no rank or priority to the considerations listed.)

1. Demand: Is it high or low?
2. Availability: How rare or scarce is the watch? How many of the total production remain?
3. Condition of both the case and movement **(very important)**.
4. Low serial numbers: The first one made would be more valuable than later models.
5. Historical value.
6. Age.
7. Is it an early handmade watch?
8. Type of case: beauty and eye appeal; value of metal content.
9. Is it in its original case? **(very important)**.
10. Complications: Repeaters, for example.

11. Type of escapement.
12. Size, number of jewels, type of plates (¾, full and bridge), type of balance, type of winding (key-wind, lever-set, etc.), number of adjustments, gold jeweled settings, damaskeening, gold train.
13. What grade of condition is it? Pristine, Mint, Extra Fine, Average, Fair, or Scrap?
14. Identification ability.
15. Future potential as an investment.
16. Quality (high or low grade), or low cost production watches (dollar watch).
17. How much will this watch scrap for?

GRADING WATCHES

Pricing in this book is based on the following grading system:

PRISTINE MINT (G-10): Absolutely factory new; sealed in factory box with wax paper still intact.

MINT PLUS (G-9): Still in factory box; has had paper removed for inspection only; has never been used.

MINT (G-8): Same as factory new but with very little use; no faint scratches; is original in every way—crystal, hands, dial, case, movement; used briefly and stored away; may be in box.

NEAR MINT (G-7): Completely original in every way; faint marks may be seen with a loop only; expertly repaired; movement may have been cleaned and oiled.

EXTRA FINE (G-6): May or may not be in factory box; looks as though watch was used very little; crystal may have been replaced; original case, hands, dial, and movement. If watch has been repaired, all original replacement parts have been used. Faint case scratches are evident but hard to detect with the eye. No dents and no hairline on dial are detectable.

FINE (G-5): May have new hands and new crystal, but original case, dial and movement; faint hairline in dial; no large scratches on case; slight stain on movement; movement must be sharp with only minor scratches.

AVERAGE (G-4): Original case, dial and movement; movement may have had a part replaced, but part was near to original; slight brass showing through on gold-filled case; no rust or chips in dial; may have hairlines in dial that are hard to see. All marks are hard to detect, but may be seen without a loop.

FAIR (G-3): Hairlines in dial and small chips; brass can be seen through worn spots on gold-filled case; rust marks in movement; a small dent in case; wear in case, dial, and movement; well used; may not have original dial or case.

POOR (G-2): Watch may not run; needs new dial; case well worn, with many dents; hands may be gone; replacement crystal may be needed.

SCRAP (G-1): Not running; bad dial; rusty movement; brass showing badly; may not have case; some parts not original; no crystal or hands. Good for parts.

Below is an example of how the price is affected by the different grades of the same watch:

Hamilton 992B

G-10	$290
G-9	$255
G-8	$225
G-7	$200
G-6	$175
G-5	$160
G-4	$150
G-3	$70
G-2	$45
G-1	$35

The value of a watch can only be assessed after the watch has been carefully inspected and graded. It may be difficult to evaluate a watch honestly and objectively, especially in the rare or scarce models.

If the watch has any defects, such as a small scratch on it, it can not be Pristine. It is important to realize that older watches in grades of Extra Fine or above are extremely rare and may never be found.

COLLECTING ON A LIMITED BUDGET

Most collectors are always looking for that sleeper, which *is* out there waiting to be found. One story goes that the collector went into a pawn shop and asked the owner if he had any gold pocket watches for sale. The pawn broker replied, "No, but I have a 23J silver cased pocket watch at a good price." Even though the pocket watch was in a cheaper case, the collector decided to further explore the movement. When he opened the back to look at the movement, there he saw engraved on the plates 24J Bunn Special and knew immediately he wanted to buy the pocket watch. The movement was running, and looked to be in first grade shape. The collector asked the price. The broker said he has been trying to get rid of the pocket watch, but had no luck and if he wanted it, he would sell it for $35. The collector took the pocket watch and replaced the bent-up silver case for a gold-filled J. Boss case, and sold it a month later for $400. He had a total of $100 invested when he sold it, netting a cool $300 profit.

Most collectors want a pocket watch that is in mint or near-mint condition and original in every way. But consider the railroad pocket watches such as the Bunn Special in a cheaper case. The railroad man was compelled to buy a watch with a quality movement, even though he may have only been able to afford a cheap case. The railroad man had to have a pocket watch that met certain standards set by the railroad company. A watch should always be judged on quality and performance and not just on its appearance. The American railroad pocket watch was unsurpassed in reliability. It was durable and accurate for its time, and that accounts for its continuing value today.

If you are a limited-budget collector, you would be well advised not to go beyond your means. But watch collecting can still be an interesting, adventurous, and profitable hobby. If you are to be successful in quadrupling your purchases that you believe to be sleepers, you must first be a hard worker, have perserverence and let shrewdness and skill of knowledge take the place of money. A good starting place is to get a working knowledge of how a pocket watch works. Learn the basic skills such as cleaning, mainspring and staff replacement. One does not have to be a watchmaker, but should learn the names of parts and what they do. If a watch that you are considering buying does not work, you should know how and what it takes to get it in good running order or pass it by. Stay away from pocket watches that do not wind and set. Also avoid "odd" movements that you hope to be able to find a case for. Old watches with broken or missing parts are expensive and all but impossible to have repaired. Some parts must be made by hand. The odd and low-cost production watches are fun to get but hard to repair. Start out on the more common basic-jeweled lever pocket watches. The older the watch, the harder it is to get parts. Buy an inexpensive pocket watch movement that runs and play with it. Get the one that is newer and for which parts can be bought; and get a book on watch repairing.

You will need to know the history and demand of a watch. Know what collectors are looking for in your area. If you cannot find a buyer, then, of course, someone else's stock has become yours.

1989 MARKET REPORT

The eyes of the horological world turned on Geneva, Switzerland on April 9, 1989, as Habsburg, Feldman presented an auction of "The Art of Patek Philippe." Under the expert supervision of Osvaldo and Madeleine Patrizzi and Jean-Claude Sabrier, the gallery offered 301 of the finest products of this maker to commemorate the 150th anniversary of the founding of Patek Philippe in 1839.

The sale took place at the fashionable Hotel des Bergues which is situated in the heart of Geneva by the lake, at a short distance from the Patek Philippe showroom. The preview was no less than splendid, the watches were carefully displayed in numerous and well attended glass showcases, with white-coated watchmakers from the factory present to assist in opening and inspecting the timepieces. The spacious sale was later transformed into the main auction room of three, which housed the more than one thousand reserved seat spectators, who enjoyed an exquisite Sunday brunch prior to the sale. The atmosphere was filled with excitement, and the first lots shot to stunning levels at twice the catalogue estimates.

This set the tone for an afternoon of record prices that made the gallery gasp, and on occasion spontaneously applaud. Not since the Belin sale in 1979 has so much interest galvanized the watch community, but the two sales hardly compare. The Patek Philippe sale grossed almost 6 times the Belin take, achieving a staggering 25 million Swiss francs, or 15 million dollars.

Highlighting the sale was the "Calibre 89," by far the most complicated mechanical timepiece ever created, which fetched a stunning price of 4.5 million Swiss francs, or 2.727 million dollars. The Calibre

The most complicated portable time piece every made. The Calibre 89 has 33 complications divided into five main catagories-time keeping, the calendar, the chronograph, the chime and the operational functions. The movement has a diameter of 71.5 mm; thickness of 28.05 mm; weighs 19.29 oz. The Calibre 89 has two noteworthy watch making achievements: The first is a perpetual calendar that registers the fact that century years are only leap years every 400 years. The second feature is the date-of-Easter indicator. The watch is an open face clock watch with two dials in a bassine-style, 18 carat gold case with 126 jewels and driven by a single mainspring barrel and regulated by a tourbillon regulator. The Calibre 89 contains 1278 parts and the entire movement is configured on three plates.

89, measuring 88 mm in total diameter and weighing over 35 ounces, was designed in 1980 and was manufactured specifically for this occasion. With 33 horological complications, and dials both front and back, the watch was splendid and massive in appearance; it was displayed at the preview within a mirrored and alarmed spotlighted podium, while video presentations in various languages demonstrated the multiple functions as well as the specifics of the mechanism. Spectators craned their necks to glimpse the three bidders as Patrizzi slowly took the offers. The gallery came to its feet with the hammer.

Other record prices (in U.S. dollars) included: An outstanding "Grande Complication" clockwatch at $515,000; a tourbillon wrist watch at just under $400,000; a unique chronometer escapement tourbillon pocket watch at $485,000; a superb minute repeating wrist watch at $315,000; a rare "carre cambre" enamel dial split-seconds wrist watch with left hand wind at $254,000; and a rare perpetual calendar clock watch with wind indicators at $454,000.

More common styles of wrist watches brought generally 20-40% more than in other recent sales. In particular, stainless steel wrist watches were very strong, owing to the twin factors of rarity and Japanese interest. Perpetual calendar wrist watches of later manufacture conformed to market expectations, as did the perpetual calendar repeater pocket watches, with one exception. Other pocket watches were extremely high, particularly those of technical horological interest, although many were extremely rare or unique pieces. Ladies' enamel pendant watches sold reasonably at the market, while certain wrist models fetched very strong prices relative to their typical levels.

What's next? Another sale of a major maker, soon to be announced.

SELLING AT CHRISTIE'S

Christie, Manson & Woods International, Inc. is an auction house of superior reputation, known thoughout the world for its sales of the finest works of art and collectibles. Frequently in the news for record breaking sales in the art market, Christie's is respected in the watch world for its professional presentation and sale of the best in pocket and wrist watches.

Under the expert direction of Christie's Vice-President Jonathan Snellenburg, the New York gallery's watch sales have enjoyed great success. The catalogues are reliable, estimates sensible and attractive to bidders, and the merchandise selected for sale is both original and excellent.

Those interested in selling fine watches at auction may contact Mr. Snellenburg who will then evaluate the watches and their suitability for auction, as well as discuss timetables, sales strategy, photos and commission rates. Typical commission rates on goods over $7,500 are 10% and 6% to the trade. Insurance is also available, as well as certain repair services. Should an agreeable arrangement be made, a contract is drawn up and the goods are prepared for cataloguing and marketing. Clients examine the goods at a preview and may leave **order** bids or attend the sale by phone or in person. The seller, if successful, then receives payment within the contracted period, usually 35 days.

One of the keys to successful sales lies in establishing reasonable estimates and reserves (minimum selling price acceptable to seller), so as to attract competition and obtain the best price. Overestimation alienates prospective buyers, while underestimation may jeopardize the seller. The art is to find the right balance, which is where Mr. Snellenburg's experience pays off.

THAT GREAT AMERICAN
RAILROAD POCKET WATCH

It was the late nineteenth century in America. The automobile had not yet been discovered. The personal Kodak camera was still not on the market. Women wore long dresses, and the rub board was still the most common way to wash clothes. Few homes had electricity, and certainly the radio had not yet invaded their lives. Benjamin Harrison was president. To be sure, those days of yesteryear were not quite as nostalgically simple as most reminiscing would have them be. They were slower, yes, because it took longer to get things done and longer to get from one place to another. The U.S. mail was the chief form of communication linking this country together, as America was inching toward the Twentieth Century.

The tremendous impact of the railroad on the country during this era should not be underestimated. Most of the progress since the 1830s had chugged along on the back of the black giant locomotives that belched steam and fire, up and down the countryside. In fact, the trains brought much life and hope to the people all across the country, delivering their goods and food, bringing people from one city to another, carrying the U.S. mail, and bringing the democratic process to the people by enabling candidates for the U.S. Presidency to meet and talk with people in every state.

Truly the train station held memories for most everyone and had a link with every family.

In 1891, the country had just eased into the period that historians would later term the "Gay Nineties." It was on April 19 of that year that events occurred near Cleveland, Ohio, that clearly pointed out that the nation's chief form of transportation was running on timepieces that were not reliable. The time had come for strict standards for pocket watches used by the railroaders. From the ashes of this smoldering

Ohio disaster rose the phoenix in the form of the great American railroad pocket watch, a watch unrivaled in quality and reliability.

That April morning the fast mail train, known as No. 4, was going East. On the same track an accommodation train was going West. It was near Elyria, about 25 miles from Cleveland, Ohio, that the engineer and conductor of the accommodation train were given written orders to let the fast mail train pass them at Kipton, a small station west of Oberlin.

As the accommodation train was leaving the station at Elyria, the telegraph operator ran to the platform and verbally cautioned the engineer and conductor, "Be careful, No. 4 is on time." The conductor replied, "Go to thunder. I know my business."

The train left Elyria on time according to the engineer's watch. What was not known was that the engineer's watch had stopped for four minutes and then started up again. Had the conductor looked at his own watch, the impending disaster could have been avoided.

The two trains met their destiny at Kipton; the accommodation train was under full brakes, but the fast mail was full speed ahead. Both engineers were killed as well as nine other people. The railroad companies (Lake Shore Railroad and Michigan Southern Railway) sustained great losses in property as did the U.S. Post Office.

Following this disaster, a commission was appointed to come up with standards for timepieces that would be accepted and adopted by all railroads. The commission learned that, up to the time of the Kipton crash, conductors on freight trains were depending on cheap alarm clocks. The railroading industry had grown, fast new trains were now in service, and the same lines were used by several different railways. Very often, in only a short space of time, two trains would cover the same track. The industry now had to demand precision in its timekeeping.

By 1893 the General Railroad Timepiece Standards were adopted, and any watch being used in rail service—by railroaders responsible for schedules—was required to meet the following specifications:

> Be open faced, size 18 or 16, have a minimum of 17 jewels, adjusted to at least five positions, keep time accurately to within a gain or loss of only 30 seconds a week, adjusted to temperatures of 34 to 100 degrees Fahrenheit, have a double roller, steel escape wheel, lever set, micrometric regulator, winding stem at 12 o'clock, grade on back plate, use plain Arabic numbers printed bold and black on a white dial, and have bold black hands.
>
> Some also wanted a Breguet hairspring, adjusted to isochronism and 30 degrees Fahrenheit with a minimum of 19 jewels.

The railroad man was compelled to buy a timepiece more accurate than many scientific instruments of precision used in laboratories. The American pocket watch industry was compelled to produce just such an instrument—which it did. The railroad watch was a phenomenal timekeeper and durable in long life and service. It had the most minute adjustments, no small feat because watchmaking was rendered far more difficult than clockmaking, due to the fact that a clock is always in one position and watches must be accurate from several positions.

The 1893 railroad pocket watch standards were adopted by almost every railroad line. While each company had its individual standards, most all of them included the basic recommendations of the commission.

The key figure in developing the railroad watch standards was Webb C. Ball of Cleveland, Ohio, the general time inspector for over 125,000 miles of railroad in the U.S., Mexico, and Canada. Ball was authorized by railroad officials to establish the timepiece inspection system. After Ball presented his guidelines, most American manufacturers set out to meet those standards and a list of the different manufacturers producing watches of the grade that would pass inspection, was soon available.

According to the regulations, if a watch fell behind or gained 30 seconds in 7 to 14 days, it must be sent in for adjustment or repair. Small cards were given to the engineers and conductors—the railroad timekeepers—and a complete record of the watch's performance was written in ink. All repairs and adjustments were conducted by experienced and approved watchmakers; inspections were conducted by authorized inspectors.

Because this system was adopted universally and adhered to, and because American watch manufacturers produced a superior railroad watch, the traveling public was assured of increased safety and indeed the number of railroad accidents occurring as a result of faulty timepieces was minimized.

Prior to the 1891 collision, some railroad companies had already initiated standards and were issuing lists of those watches approved for railroad use. Included were the Waltham 18s, 1883 model, Crescent Street Grade, and the B.W. Raymond, 18s, both in open and hunter cases with lever set or pendant set.

By the mid 1890s hunter cases were being turned down as well as pendant set. Watches meeting approval then included Waltham, 18s, 1892 model; Elgin, 7th model; and Hamilton, 17j, open face, lever set.

Hamilton Grade 992, 17 size, 21 jewels, nickel ¾ plate movement, lever set only, gold jewel settings, gold center wheel, steel escape wheel, micrometric regulator, compensating balance. Adjusted to temperature, isochronism and 5 positions.

By 1900 the double roller sapphire pallets and steel escape wheels with a minimum of five positions were required.

The early Ball Watch Co. movements, made by Howard, used initials of railroad labor organizations such as "B. of L.E. Standard" and "B. of L.F. Standard." Ball also used the trademark "999" and "Official Railroad Standard." Some watches may turn up that are marked as "loaners." These were issued by the railroad inspectors when a watch had to be kept for repairs.

By 1920 the 18 size watch had lost popularity with the railroad men and by 1950 most railroad companies were turning them down all together.

In 1936 duties on Swiss watches were lowered by 50 percent, and by 1950 the Swiss imports had reached a level of five million a year.

In 1969 the last American railroad pocket watch was sold by Hamilton Watch Co.

RAILROAD GRADE WATCH ADJUSTMENTS

The railroad watch, as well as other fine timepieces, had to compensate for several factors in order to be reliable and accurate at all times. These compensations, called adjustments, were for heat and cold, isochronism, and five to six different positions. These adjustments were perfected only after experimentation and a great deal of careful hand labor on each individual movement.

All railroad grade watches were adjusted to a closer rate to compensate for heat and cold. The compensation balance has screws in the rim of the balance wheel which can be regulated by the watchmaker. The movement was tested in an ice box and in an oven, and if it did not keep the same time in both temperature extremes, as well as under average conditions, the screw in the balance wheel was shifted or adjusted until accuracy was achieved.[1]

The isochronism adjustment maintained accuracy of the watch both when the mainspring was fully wound up and when it was nearly run down. This was achieved by selecting a hairspring of exact proportions to cause the balance wheel to give the same length of arc of rotation regardless of the amount of the mainspring that had been spent.

Railroad watches were adjusted to be accurate whether they were laying on their face or back, or being carried on their edges with pendants up or down, or with the three up or the nine up. These adjustments were accomplished by having the jewels, in which the balance pivots rest, of proper thickness in proportion to the diameter of the pivot and, at the same time, equal to the surface on the end of the

---

[1]Railroad grade watches had a compensation balance made of brass and steel. Brass was used on the outside rim and steel on the inside. Brass is softer than steel, and steel is more sensitive to temperature changes. The rim on the balance was cut to form two pieces and had two arms. Each piece was independent of the other so the rim was free to be influenced through expansion or contraction. (A small balance wheel with the same hairspring would run faster than a large balance wheel.) At a high temperature the entire balance wheel would expand in bulk and thus run slower. That is why a compensation balance was necessary. When the bulk of the balance wheel expands, the expansion of the brass on the outside of the rim is greater than that of the steel on the inside; thus it throws the loose ends of the rim toward the center. Consequently this makes the circumference smaller and therefore compensation for the increased volume is achieved.

pivot which rests on the cap jewel. To be fully adjusted for positions, the balance wheel and the pallet and escape wheel must be perfectly poised. Perfect poise is achieved when the pivots can be supported on two flat surfaces, perfectly smooth and polished and when the wheel is placed in any position, it will remain exactly as it is placed. If it is not perfectly poised, the heaviest part of the wheel will always turn to the point immediately under the lines of support.

The micrometric regulator or the patent regulator is a device used on all railroad grade and higher grade watches for the purpose of assisting in the finer manipulation of the regulator. It is arranged so that the regulator can be moved the shortest possible distance without fear of moving it too far. There is always a fine graduated index attached which makes it possible to determine just how much the regulator has been moved.

E. Howard Watch Co. Railroad Chronometer, Series 11, 16 size, 21 jewels, expressly designed for the railroad trade.

The hairspring used on the so-called ordinary and medium-grade watches is known as the flat hairspring. The Breguet hairspring was an improvement over the flat hairspring and was used on railroad and high-grade watches. The inside coil of any hairspring is attached to a collet on the balance staff and the end of the outside coil of the hairspring is attached to a stud which is held firmly by a screw in the balance wheel bridge. Two small curb pins are fastened to the regulator. These pins clasp the outer side of the hairspring a short distance from the hairspring stud. If the regulator index is moved toward the "S," the curb pins will move, allowing the hairspring to lengthen and the balance wheel to make a longer arc of rotation. This causes the watch to run slower because it requires a longer time for the wheel to perform the longer arc.

When the regulator is moved toward the "F" these curb pins are moved from the stud which shortens the hairspring and makes shorter arcs of the balance wheel, thus causing the movement to run faster. Sometimes, after a heavy jolt, the coil next to the outside one will catch between these curb pins and this will shorten the length of the hairspring just one round, causing a gaining rate of one hour per day. When this occurs, the hairspring can be easily released and will resume its former rate.

The Breguet hairspring, which is used on railroad grade movements, prevented the hairspring from catching on the curb or guard pins and protected against any lateral or side motion of the balance wheel ensuring equal expansion of the outside coil.

Railroad grade watches also used the patent or safety pinion which was developed to protect the train of gears from damage in the event of breakage of the mainspring.

Some railroad grade watches had non-magnetic movements. This was achieved by the use of non-magnetic metals for the balance wheel, hairspring, roller table and pallet. Two of the metals used were iridium and paladium, both very expensive.

Rockford Grades 805-Hunting & 905-Open Face, 18 size, 21 extra fine ruby jewels in gold settings, beautifully damaskeened nickel plates, gold lettering, adjusted to temperature, isochronism and 5 positions, Breguet hair spring, double roller escapement, steel escape wheel, sapphire pallets, micrometric regulator, compensating balance in recess.

RAILROAD WATCH DIALS

Railroad watch dials are distinguished by their simplicity. A true railroad watch dial contained no fancy lettering or beautiful backgrounds. The watches were designed to be functional and in order to achieve that, the dials contained bold black Arabic numbers against a white background. This facilitated ease of reading the time under even the most adverse conditions.

True railroad watches had the winding stem at the 12 o'clock position. The so-called "side winder," that winds at the 3 o'clock position, was not approved for railroad use. (The side winder is a watch movement designed for a hunter case but one that has been placed in an open-faced case.)

One railroad watch dial design was patented by a Mr. Ferguson. On this dial, the five minute numbers were much larger than the hour numbers which were on the inside. This dial never became very popular.

About 1910 the Montgomery dials began to appear. The distinguishing feature of the Montgomery dial is that each minute is numbered around the hour chapter. The five-minute divisions were in red, and the true Montgomery dial has the number "6" inside the minute register. These dials were favored by the railroad men.

The so-called Canadian dial had a 24-hour division inside the hour chapter.

The double-time hands are also found on some railroad grade watches. One hour hand was in black and the other was in red, one hour apart, to compensate for passing from one time zone to another.

Ball Watch Co. Motto: "Carry a Ball and Time Them All." This case is an example of Ball's patented Stirrup Bow. With the simple easy-to-read dial, this watch was a favorite among railroad men.

RAILROAD WATCH CASES

Open face cases were the only ones approved for railroad use. Railroad men sought a case that was tough and durable; one that would provide a dust-free environment for the movement. The swing-out case offered the best protection against dust, but the screw-on back and bezel were the most popular open-face cases.

The lever-set was a must for railroad-approved watches and some of the case manufacturers patented their own styles of cases, most with a heavy bow. One example is the Stirrup Bow by the Ball Watch Co. Hamilton used a bar above the crown to prevent the stem from being pulled out. Glass was most commonly used for the crystal because it was not as likely to scratch.

RAILROAD GRADE OR
RAILROAD APPROVED WATCHES

Note: Not all watches listed here are railroad approved, even though all are railroad grade. See Ball Watch Co. for railroad standards.

BALL

All official R.R. standard with 19, 21, & 23J, hci5p, 18 & 16S, open face.

COLUMBUS WATCH CO.

Columbus King, 21, 23, 25J; Railway King, 17-25J; Time King, 21-25J, 18S; Ruby Model, 16S.

ELGIN

1. "Pennsylvania Railroad Co." on dial, 18S, 15J & 17J, key wind and set, first model "B. W. Raymond."
2. "No. 349," 18S, seventh model, 17-21J.
3. Veritas, B. W. Raymond, or Father Time, 18S, 21-23J.
4. Grades 162, 270, 280, or 342 marked on back plate, 16S, 17-21J.
5. Veritas, Father Time, or Paillard Non-Magnetic, 16S, 19-23J.
6. 571, 21J or 572, 16S, 19J.
7. All wind indicator models.

HAMILTON

1. Grade 946, 23J, 18S.
2. Grades 940, 942, 21J, 18S.
3. Grade 944, 19J, 18S.
4. Grades 924, 926, 934, 936, 938, 948, 17J, 18S.
5. Grades 950, 950B, 950E, 23J, 16S.
6. Grades 992, 992B, 992E, 954, 960, 970, 994, 990, 21J, 16S.
7. Grade 996, 19J, 16S.
8. Grades 972, 968, 964, 17J, 16S.

HAMPDEN

1. Special Railway, 17J, 21J, 23J; New Railway, 23J & 17J; North Am. RR, 21J; Wm. McKinley, 21J; John Hancock, 21J & 23J; John C. Duber, 21J, 18S.
2. 105, 21J; 104, 23J; John C. Duber, 21J; Wm. McKinley, 17, 21, & 23J; New

Railway, 21J; Railway, 19J; Special Railway, 23J, 16S.

E. HOWARD & CO.
1. All Howard models marked "Adjusted" or deer symbol.
2. Split plate models, 18S or N size; 16S or L size.

HOWARD WATCH CO.
All 16S with 19, 21, & 23J.

ILLINOIS
1. Bunn 15J marked "Adjusted," and Stuart, 15J marked "Adjusted," 18S.
2. Benjamin Franklin, 17-26J; Bunn 17, 19, 21, 24J; Bunn Special, 21-26J; Chesapeake & Ohio Sp., 24J; Interstate Chronometer, 23J;Lafayette, 24J; A. Lincoln, 21J; Paillard W. Co., 17-24J; Trainsmen, 23J; Pennsylvania Special 17-26J; The Railroader & Railroad King, 18S.
3. Benjamin Franklin, 17-25J; Bunn, 17-19J; Bunn Special, 21-23J; Diamond Ruby Sapphire, 21 & 23J; Interstate Chronometer, 23J; Lafayette, 23J; A. Lincoln, 21J; Paillard Non-Magnetic W. Co., 17 & 21J; Pennsylvania Special, 17, 21, & 23J; Santa Fe Special, 21J; Sangamo, 21-26J; Sangamo Special, 19-23J; Grades 161, 161A, 163, 163A, 187, and 189, 17J, 16S.

PEORIA WATCH CO.
15 & 17J with a patented regulator, 18S.

ROCKFORD
1. All 21 or more jewels, 16-18S, and wind indicators.
2. Grades 900, 905, 910, 912, 918, 945, 200, 205, 18S.
3. Winnebago, 17-21J, 505, 515, 525, 535, 545, 555, 16S.

SETH THOMAS
Maiden Lane, 21-28J; Henry Molineux, 20J; 260 Model, 18S.

SOUTH BEND
1. Studebaker 329, Grade Nos. 323, and 327, 17-21J, 18S.
2. Studebaker 229, Grade Nos. 223, 227, 293, 295, 299, 17-21J, 16S.
3. Polaris.

UNITED STATES WATCH CO., MARION
United States, 19J, gold train.

U. S. WATCH CO., WALTHAM
The President, 17J, 18S.

WALTHAM

1. 1857 KW with Pennsylvania R.R. on dial, Appleton Tracy & Co. on movement.
2. Crescent Street, 17-23J; 1883 & 1892 Models; Appleton Tracy & Co., 1892 Model; Railroader, 1892 Model; Pennsylvania Railroad; Special Railroad, Special RR King, Vanguard, 17-23J, 1892 Model; Grade 845, 18S.
3. American Watch Co., 17-21J, 1872 Models; American Watch Co., 17-23J, Bridge Models; Crescent Street, 17-21J, 1899 & 1908 Models; Premier Maximus; Railroader; Riverside Maximus, 21-23J; Vanguard, 19-23J; 645, 16S.
4. All wind indicators.

American Waltham Watch Co. Vanguard, 16 size, 19-23 jewels, winding indicator which alerts user to how far up or down the mainspring is wound. This watch was made to promote new sales in the railway industry.

Hamilton Watch Co. A Favorite raiload style case by Hamilton. Note the Montgomery style dial as well as the bar above the crown.

CANADIAN PACIFIC SERVICE RAILROAD APPROVED WATCHES 1899

WALTHAM

Vanguard, 18-16S, 19-21-23 jewels
Crescent St., 18S, 19J; 18-16S, 21J
Appleton-Tracy 17J; also No. 845, 21J
Riverside 16S, 19J; Riverside Maximus, 16S, 23J; and 16S, No. 645, 21J
C. P. R. 18-16S, 17J; also C. T. S. 18-16S, 17J

ELGIN
Veritas, 18-16S, 21-23J
B. W. R. 18-16S, 17-19-21J
Father Time 18-16S, 21J
Grade 349, 18S, 21J

HAMILTON
18S, 946, 23J; 940-942, 21J; 944, 19J; 936-938, 17J
16S, 950, 23J; 960-990-992, 21J; 952, 19J; 972, 17J

SOUTH BEND
18S, 327-329, 21J; 323, 17J
16S, 227-229, 21J; 223, 17J

BALL
All Balls 18S, 16S, 17-19-21-23J

ILLINOIS
Bunn Special, 18-16S, 21-23J; also Bunn 18-16S, 17-19J
A. Lincoln, 18-16S, 21J
Sangamo Special, 16S, 19-21-23J

SETH THOMAS
Maiden Lane, 18S, 25J; No. 260, 21J; No. 382, 17J

E. HOWARD WATCH CO.
16S Series, 0-23J, 5-19J, 2-17J, 10-21J; also No. 1, 21J

ROCKFORD
18S, Grade 918-905, 21J; Winnebago, 17J; also Grade 900, 24J
16S, Grades 545, 525, 515, 505, 21J; 655 W.I., 21J; and Grade 405, 17J

LONGINES
18S, Express Monarch, 17-19-21-23J
16S, Express Monarch, 17-19-21-23J

BRANDT-OMEGA
18S, D.D.R., 23J; C.C.C.R., 23J; C.D.R., 19J; C.C.R., 19J

AMERICAN RAILROAD APPROVED WATCHES—1930

The following requirements for railroad approved watches are outlined by Mr. R. D. Montgomery, General Watch Inspector of the Santa Fe Railway System:

"The regulation watch designated as of 1930 to be standard is described as follows:"

"16 size, American, lever-setting, 19 jewels or more, open face, winding at '12,' double-roller escapement, steel escape wheel, adjusted to 5 positions, temperature and isochronism, which will rate within a variation not exceeding 6 seconds in 72 hour tests, pendant up, dial up and dial down, and be regulated to run within a variation not exceeding 30 seconds per week."

"The following listed makes and grades meet the requirements and comprise a complete list of watches acceptable. Watches bearing the name of jewelers or other names not standard trade marks or trade numbers will not be accepted:"

American Waltham Watch Co. (16 Size)		Elgin Watch Co. (16 Size)		Howard Watch Co. (16 Size)	
23J	Premier Maximus	23J	Veritas	All 23J	
23J	Riverside Maximus	21J	Veritas	All 21J	
23J	Vanguard 6 position winding indicator	21J	B. W. Raymond	All 19J	
		21J	Father Time		
		21J	No. 270	**Illinois Watch Co. (16 Size)**	
23J	Vanguard 6 position			23J	Sangamo Special
21J	Crescent Street	**Hamilton Watch Co. (16 Size)**		23J	Sangamo
21J	No. 645	23J	No. 950	23J	Bunn Special
19J	Vanguard	21J	No. 990	21J	Bunn Special
19J	Riverside	21J	No. 992	21J	Sangamo
		19J	No. 952	21J	A. Lincoln
Ball Watch Co. (16 Size)		19J	No. 996	19J	Bunn
23J	Official R.R. Standard	**Hampden Watch Co. (16 Size)**		**South Bend Watch Co. (16 Size)**	
21J	Official R.R. Standard	23J	Special Railway	21J	No. 227
19J	Official R.R. Standard	21J	New Railway	21J	No. 229
		19J	Railway	21J	No. 295
				19J	No. 293

APPROVED POCKET WATCHES IN CP RAIL SERVICE AS OF FEBRUARY 1, 1957

Waltham (16 Size)		Hamilton (16 Size)		Zenith (16 Size)	
23J	Vanguard No. 29, 634, 001 and up	23J	No. 950B	21J	Extra RR 56
		21J	No. 992B		
Elgin (16 Size)		**Ball (16 Size)**			
21J	B.W.R.	21J	(Hamilton) No. 992C		
21J	No. 571	21J	No. 435C		

APPROVED WRIST WATCHES IN CP RAIL SERVICE

Cyma		Longines		Zenith	
17J	RR 2852 M	17J	RR 280	18J	RR 120 T
25J	RR 2872 A				
Girard Perregaux		**Universal**			
17J	CP 307H.F.	19J	RR 1205		

APPROVED WRIST WATCHES IN
CP RAIL SERVICE
BATTERY POWERED

Bulova Accutron	**Rodania**	**Wittnauer**
17J 214	13J RR 2780 Calendar	13J RR 12 WT Calendar
17J 218 Calendar		

APPROVED WRIST WATCHES SEMI-MECHANICAL
QUARTZ ANALOG BATTERY POWERED
IN CP RAIL SERVICE AS OF 1978

Cyma	**Rodania**	**Wyler**
7J Calendar RR 9361 Q	6J Calendar 9952.111RR	7J Calendar RR 9361 Q
6J Calendar RR 960 Q	7J Calendar RR 9361 Q	
		Wittnauer
Bulova	**Rotary**	7J Calendar RR 2 Q 115 C
7J Calendar RR 9362 Q	7J Calendar RR 9366 Q	
6J Calendar RR 960.111Q		

ADJUSTMENTS

There are nine basic adjustments for watch movements. They are:

heat ... 1	positions ... 6
cold ... 1	TOTAL ... 9
isochronism ... 1	

THE SIX POSITION ADJUSTMENTS ARE:

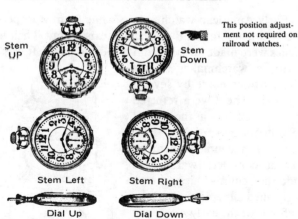

Stem UP

Stem Down

This position adjust-
ment not required on
railroad watches.

Stem Left   Stem Right

Dial Up   Dial Down

A watch with eight adjustments (the most common) will be listed
in this book as: "Adj.5P" (heat, cold, isochronism, 5 positions).

The total number of pocket watches made for the railroad industry was small in comparison to the total pocket watches produced. Generally, watches defined as "Railroad Watches" fall into five categories:

1. **Railroad Approved**—Grades and Models approved by the railway companies.[1]
2. **Railroad Grade**—Those advertised as being able to pass railroad inspection.[2]
3. **Pre-Commission Watches**—Those used by the railroads before 1893.[3]
4. **Company Watches**—Those with a railroad logo or company name on the dial.[4]
5. **Train Watches**—Those with a locomotive painted on the dial or inscribed on the case.[4]

---

[1]Not all railroad employees were required to purchase or use approved watches, just the employees that were responsible for schedules. But many employees did buy the approved watches because they were the standard in reliability.

[2]These were used primarily by those railroaders who were not required to submit their watches for inspection.

[3]There were many watches made for railroad use prior to 1893. Some of the key wind ones, especially, are good quality and highly collectible.

[4]Some manufacturers inscribed terms such as railroader, special railroad, dispatcher, etc. on the back plates of the movements.

COLONIAL WATCHMAKERS

Early American watchmakers came from Europe; little is known about them, and few of their watches exist today. Their hand-fabricated watches were made largely from imported parts. It was common practice for a watchmaker to use rough castings made by several craftsmen. These were referred to as "movements in the gray." The watchmaker finished these parts and assembled them to make a complete watch. He would then engrave his name on the finished timepiece.

Some of the early American watchmakers designed the cases or other parts, but most imported what they needed. The early colonial watchmakers showed little originality as designers and we can only guess how many watches were really made in America.

These early hand-made watches are almost non-existent; therefore, only the name of the watchmaker will be listed. This compilation comes from old ads in newspapers and journals and other sources. It is not considered to be complete.

Because of the rarity and condition of these early watches, prices may vary widely from $400 to $2,000.

Example of watch paper placed inside a pair-cased watch by a watch maker. This was a form of advertisement placed in the watch after repair was made.

Ephraim Clark, 18 size, non-jeweled, made between 1780-1790; a good example of a colonial watch. These early watches usually included chain driven fusees, verge type escapements, hand pierced balance cock, key wind & set; note the circular shaped regulator on the far left side of the illustrated example.

Nath. Hawxhurst, N.Y., 18 size, non-jeweled, ca. 1770-1780, chain driven fusee, verge type escapement, notice hand-pierced cock.

J.F. Bartlett, Clinton, Mass. Example of watch paper placed inside a pair-cased watch by the watch maker, ca. 1850.

EARLY AMERICAN WATCHMAKERS
(With Location and Approximate Date)

Adams, Nathan (Boston, MA, 1800)
Adams, William (Boston, MA, 1810)
Aldrich, Jacob (Wilmington, DE, 1802)
Allebach, Jacob (Phila., PA, 1825-1840)
Atherton, Nathan (Phila., PA, 1825)
Atkinson, James (Boston, MA, 1745)
Backhouse, John (Lancaster, PA, 1725)
Bagnall, Benjamin (Phila., PA, 1750)
Bailey, John (Boston, MA, 1810)
Bailey, William (Phila., PA, 1820)
Baker, Benjamin (Phila., PA, 1825)
Banks, Joseph (Phila., PA, 1790)
Barnhill, Robert (Phila., PA, 1775)
Barrow, Samuel (Phila., PA, 1771)
Barry, Standish (Baltimore, MD, 1785)
Basset, John F. (Phila., PA, 1798)
Belknap, William (Boston, MA, 1815)
Bell, William (Phila., PA, 1805)
Benedict, S. W. (New York, NY, 1835)
Bigger & Clarke (Baltimore, MD, 1783)
Billion, C. (Phila., PA, 1775-1800)
Bingham & Bricerly (Phila., PA, 1778-1799)
Birnie, Laurence (Phila., PA, 1774)
Blundy, Charles (Charleston, SC, 1750)
Blunt & Nichols (New York, NY, 1850)
Bond, William (Boston, MA, 1800-1810)
Bonnaud (Phila., PA, 1799)
Bower, Michael (Phila., PA, 1790-1800)
Bowman, Joseph (Lancaster, PA, 1821-1844)
Boyd & Richards (Phila., PA, 1808)
Boyter, Daniel (Lancaster, PA, 1805)
Brands & Matthey (Phila., PA, 1799)
Brandt, Aime (Phila., PA, 1820)
Brant, Brown & Lewis (Phila., PA, 1795)
Brazier, Amable (Phila., PA, 1795)
Brearley, James (Phila., PA, 1790-1800)
Brewer, William (Phila., PA, 1785-1791)
Brewster & Ingraham (Bristol, CT, 1827-1839)
Brown, Garven (Boston, MA, 1767)
Brown, John (Lancaster, PA, 1840)
Brownell, A. P. (New Bedford, MA)
Burkelow, Samuel (Phila., PA, 1791-1799)
Bush, George (Easton, PA, 1790-1800)
Campbell, Charles (Phila., PA, 1796)
Campbell, William (Carlisle, PA, 1765)
Capper, Michael (Phila., PA, 1799)
Carey, James (Brunswick, ME, 1830)
Carrell, John (Phila., PA, 1791-1793)
Carter, Jacob (Phila., PA, 1805)
Carter, Thomas (Phila., PA, 1823)
Carver, Jacob (Phila., PA, 1790)

Carvill, James (New York, NY, 1803)
Chandlee, John (Wilmington, DE, 1795-1810)
Chaudron (Phila., PA, 1799)
Chaudron & Joseph Ives (Bristol, CT, 1825)
Chauncey & Joseph Ives (Bristol, CT, 1825)
Cheney, Martin (Windsor, VT, 1800)
Chick, M. M. (Concord, NH, 1845)
Clark, Benjamin (Wilmington, DE, 1737-1750)
Clark, Ephraim (Phila., PA, 1780-1800)
Clark, John (New York, NY, 1770-1790)
Clark, John (Phila., PA, 1799)
Clark, Thomas (Boston, MA, 1764)
Claudon, John-George (Charleston SC, 1773)
Cook, William (Boston, MA, 1810)
Crow, George (Wilmington, DE, 1740-1770)
Crow, John (Wilmington, DE, 1770-1798)
Crow, Thomas (Wilmington, DE, 1770-1798)
Currier & Trott (Boston, MA, 1800)
Curtis, Solomon (Phila., PA, 1793-1795)
Dakin, James (Boston, MA, 1795)
Davis, Samuel (Boston, MA, 1820)
Delaplaine, James K. (New York, NY, 1786-1800)
DeVacht, Joseph & Frances (Gallipolis, OH, 1792)
Dix, Joseph (Phila., PA, 1770)
Downes, Anson (Bristol, CT, 1830)
Downes, Arthur (Charleston, SC, 1765)
Downes, Ephriam (Bristol, CT, 1830)
Droz, Hannah (Phila., PA, 1840)
Droz, Humbert (Phila., PA, 1793-1799)
Duffield, Edward W. (Whiteland, PA, 1775)
Dunheim, Andrew (New York, NY, 1775)
Dupuy, John (Phila., PA, 1770)
Dupuy, Odran (Phila., PA, 1735)
Dutch, Stephen, Jr. (Boston, MA, 1800-1810)
Eberman, George (Lancaster, PA, 1800)
Eberman, John (Lancaster, PA, 1780-1820)
Ellicott, Joseph (Buckingham, PA, 1763)
Elsworth, David (Baltimore, MD, 1780-1800)
Embrec, Effingham (New York, NY, 1785)
Evans, David (Baltimore, MD, 1770-1773)
Fales, James (New Bedford, MA, 1810-1820)
Ferris, Tiba (Wilmington, DE, 1812-1850)
Fessler, John (Phila., PA, 1785-1820)
Feton, J. (Phila., PA, 1825-1840)
Filder, John (Lancaster, PA, 1810-1825)
Fister, Amon (Phila., PA, 1794)
Fix, Joseph (Reading, PA, 1820-1840)
Fowell, J & N (Boston, MA, 1800-1810)
Frances, Basil & Alexander Vuille
    Baltimore, MD, 1766)

Galbraith, Patrick (Phila., PA, 1795)
Gibbons, Thomas (Phila., PA, 1750)
Goodfellow, William (Phila., PA, 1793-1795)
Goodfellow & Son, William (Phila., PA, 1796-1799)
Gooding, Henry (Boston, MA, 1810-1820)
Green, John (Phila., PA, 1794)
Groppengeiser, J. L. (Phila., PA, 1840)
Grotz, Issac (Easton, PA, 1810-1835)
Hall, Jonas (Boston, MA, 1848-1858)
Harland, Theodore (Norwich, CT, 1750-1790)
Harland, Thomas (Norwich, CT, 1802)
Harrison, James (Shrewbury, MA, 1805)
Hawxhurst, Nath. (New York, NY, 1784)
Heilig, Jacob (Phila., PA, 1770-1824)
Heilig, John (Germantown, PA, 1824-1830)
Hepton, Frederick (Phila., PA, 1785)
Heron, Isaac (New York, NY, 1770-1780)
Hodgson, William (Phila., PA, 1785)
Hoff, John (Lancaster, PA, 1800)
Hoffner, Henry (Phila., PA, 1791)
Howard, Thomas (Phila., PA, 1789-1791)
Howe, Jubal (Shrewbury, MA, 1800)
Huguenail, Charles (Phila., PA, 1799)
Hunt, Hiram (Robbinston, ME, 1800)
Hutchins, Abel (Concord, MA, 1785-1818)
Hutchins, Levi (Concord, MA, 1785-1815)
Hyde, John E. (New York, NY, 1805)
Hyde & Goodrich (New Orleans, LA, 1850)
Ingersoll, Daniel B. (Boston, MA, 1800-1810)
Ingold, Pierre Frederick (NY, NY, 1845-1850)
Ives, Chauncy & Joseph (Bristol, CT, 1825)
Jacob, Charles & Claude (Annapolis, MD, 1775)
Jackson, Joseph H. (Phila., PA, 1802-1810)
Jessop, Jonathan (Park Town, PA, 1790)
Jounit, Joseph (Meadville, PA, 1763)
Johnson, David (Boston, MA, 1690)
Johnson, John (Charleston, SC, 1763)
Jones, George (Wilmington, DE, 1815-1835)
Jones, Low & Ball (Boston, MA, 1830)
Keith, William (Shrewbury, MA, 1810)
Kennedy, Patrick (Phila., PA, 1795-1799)
Kincaid, Thomas (Christiana Bridge, DE, 1775)
Kirkwood, John (Charleston, SC, 1761)
Launy, David F. (Boston & New York, 1800)
Leavenworth, Mark (Waterbury, CT, 1820)
Leavenworth, Wm. (Waterbury, CT, 1810)
Leslie & Co., Baltimore, MD, 1795)
Leslie & Price (Phila., PA, 1793-1799)
Leslie, Robert (Baltimore, MD, 1788-1791)
Levely, George (Phila., PA, 1774)
Levi, Michael & Issac (Baltimore, MD, 1785)

Limeburner, John (Phila., PA, 1790)
Lind, John (Phila., PA, 1791-1799)
Lowens, David (Phila., PA, 1785)
Ludwig, John (Phila., PA, 1791)
Lufkins & Johnson (Boston, MA, 1800-1810)
Lukins, Isaac (Phila., PA, 1825)
MacDowell, Robert (Phila., PA, 1798)
MacFarlane, John (Boston, MA, 1800-1810)
Mahve, Matthew (Phila., PA, 1761)
Manross, Elisha (Bristol, CT, 1827)
Martin, Patrick (Phila., PA, 1830)
Maunroe & Whitney (Concord, MA, 1805-1825)
Maus, Frederick (Phila., PA, 1785-1793)
Maynard, George (New York, NY, 1702-1730)
McCabe, John (Baltimore, MD, 1774)
McDowell, James (Phila., PA, 1795)
McGraw, Donald (Annapolis, MD, 1767)
Mends, James (Phila., PA, 1795)
Merriman, Titus (Bristol, CT, 1830)
Merry, Charles F. (Phila., PA, 1799)
Meters, John (Fredricktown, MD, 1795-1825)
Miller, Abraham (Easton, PA, 1810-1830)
Mitchell & Atkins (Bristol, CT, 1830)
Mitchell, Henry (New York, NY, 1787-1800)
Mohler, Jacob (Baltimore, MD, 1773)
Moir, J & W (Waterbury, CT, 1790)
Montandon, Julien (Shrewbury, CT, 1812)
Moollinger, Henry (Phila., PA, 1794)
Morgan, Thomas (Phila. & Balti., 1774-1793)
Moris, William (Grafton, MA, 1765-1775)
Mulford, J. H. (Albany, NY, 1845)
Mulliken, Nathaniel (Boston, MA, 1765)
Munroe & Whitney (Concord, MA, 1820)
Narney, Joseph (Charleston, SC, 1753)
Neiser, Augustine (Phila., PA, 1739-1780)
Nicholls, George (New York, NY, 1728-1750)
Nicollette, Mary (Phila., PA, 1793-1799)
O'Hara, Charles (Phila., PA, 1799)
Oliver, Griffith (Phila., PA, 1785-1793)
Ormsby, James (Baltimore, MD, 1771)
Palmer, John (Phila., PA, 1795)
Palmer, John Peter (Phila., PA, 1795)
Park, Seth (Parktown, PA, 1790)
Parke, Solomon (Phila., PA, 1791-1795)
Parke, Solomon & Co. (Phila., PA, 1799)
Parker, James (Cambridge, OH, 1790)
Parker, Thomas (Phila., PA, 1783)
Parry, John J. (Phila., PA, 1795-1800)
Patton, Abraham (Phila., PA, 1799)
Patton, David (Phila., PA, 1800)
Payne, Lawrence (New York, NY, 1732-1755)
Pearman, W. (Richmond, VA, 1834)
Perkins, Thomas (Phila., PA. 1785-1800)

Perry, Marvin (New York, NY, 1770-1780)
Perry, Thomas (New York, NY, 1750-1775)
Phillips, Joseph (New York, NY, 1713-1735)
Pierret, Mathew (Phila., PA, 1795)
Pope, Joseph (Boston, MA, 1790)
Price, Philip (Phila., PA, 1825)
Proctor, Cardan (New York, NY, 1747-1775)
Proctor, William (New York, NY, 1737-1760)
Proud, R. (Newport, RI, 1775)
Purse, Thomas (Baltimore, MD, 1805)
Quimby, Phineas & William (Belfast, ME, 1825)
Reily, John (Phila., PA, 1785-1795)
Rich, John (Bristol, CT, 1800)
Richardson, Francis (Phila., PA, 1736)
Ritchie, George (Phila., PA, 1785-1790)
Roberts, John (Phila., PA, 1799)
Roberts, S & E (Trenton, NJ, 1830)
Rode, William (Phila., PA, 1785)
Rodger, James (New York, NY, 1822-1878)
Rodgers, Samuel (Plymouth, MA, 1790-1804)
Russell, George (Phila., PA, 1840)
Saxton & Lukens (Phila., PA, 1828)
Schriner, Martin (Lancaster, PA, 1790-1830)
Schriner, M & P (Lancaster, PA, 1830-1840)
Seddinger, Margaret (Phila., PA, 1846)
Severberg, Christian (NY, NY, 1755-1775)
Sherman, Robert (Wilmington, DE, 1760-1770)
Sibley, O. E. (New York, NY, 1820)
Smith, J. L. (Middletown, CT, 1830)
Smith & Goodrich (Bristol, CT, 1827-1840)
Soloman, Henry (Boston, MA, 1820)
Souza, Sammuel (Phila., PA, 1820)
Sprogell, John (Phila., PA, 1791)

Spurck, Peter (Phila., PA, 1795-1799)
Stanton, Job (New York, NY, 1810)
Stein, Abraham (Phila., PA, 1799)
Stever & Bryant (Wigville, CT, 1830)
Stillas, John (Phila., PA, 1785-1793)
Stinnett, John (Phila., PA, 1769)
Stokel, John (New York, NY, 1820-1840)
Store, Marmaduke (Phila., PA, 1742)
Strech, Thomas (Phila., PA, 1782)
Syderman, Philip (Phila., PA, 1785)
Taf, John James (Phila., PA, 1794)
Taylor, Samuel (Phila, PA, 1799)
Tonchure, Francis (Baltimore, MD, 1805)
Townsend, Charles (Phila., PA, 1799)
Townsend, David (Boston, MA, 1800)
Trott, Andrew (Boston, MA, 1800-1810)
Turrell, Samuel (Boston, MA, 1790)
Voight, Henry (Phila., PA, 1775-1793)
Voight, Sebastian (Phila., PA, 1775-1799)
Voight, Thomas (Henry's son) (Phila., PA, 1811-1835)
Vuille, Alexander (Baltimore, MD, 1766)
Warner, George T. (New York, NY, 1795)
Weller, Francis (Phila., PA, 1780)
Wells, George & Co. (Boston, MA, 1825)
Wells, J.S. (Boston, MA, 1800)
Wetherell, Nathan (Phila., PA, 1830-1840)
Wheaton, Caleb (Providence, RI, 1800)
White, Sebastian (Phila., PA, 1795)
Whittaker, William (NY, NY, 1731-1755)
Wood, John (Phila., PA, 1770-1793)
Wright, John (New York, NY, 1712-1735)
Zahm, G.M. (Lancaster, PA, 1865)

Baldwin Jones, Boston, 18 size, early American key wind watch with date calendar, verge chain driven fusee, ca. 1800.

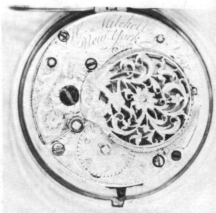

H. Mitchell, New York, 18 size, verge chain driven fusee; note regulator below hand-pierced cock, ca. 1790.

MILLIMETERS

10 20 30 40 50 60 70 80 90 100 110

AMERICAN MOVEMENT SIZES
LANCASHIRE GAUGE

Size	Inches	Inches	mm	Lignes	Size	Inches	Inches	mm	Lignes
18/0	18/30	.600	15.24	6 3/4	2	1 7/30	1.233	31.32	13 7/8
17/0	19/30	.633	16.08	7 1/8	3	1 8/30	1.266	32.16	14 1/4
16/0	20/30	.666	16.92	7 1/2	4	1 9/30	1.300	33.02	14 7/8
15/0	21/30	.700	17.78	7 7/8	5	1 10/30	1.333	33.86	15 1/8
14/0	22/30	.733	18.62	8 1/4	6	1 11/30	1.366	34.70	15 3/8
13/0	23/30	.766	19.46	8 5/8	7	1 12/30	1.400	35.56	15 3/4
12/0	24/30	.800	20.32	9 1/8	8	1 13/30	1.433	36.40	16 1/8
11/0	25/30	.833	21.16	9 3/8	9	1 14/30	1.466	37.24	16 1/2
10/0	26/30	.866	22.00	9 3/4	10	1 15/30	1.500	38.10	16 7/8
9/0	27/30	.900	22.86	10 1/8	11	1 16/30	1.533	38.94	17 1/4
8/0	28/30	.933	23.70	10 1/2	12	1 17/30	1.566	39.78	17 5/8
7/0	29/30	.966	24.54	10 7/8	13	1 18/30	1.600	40.64	18 1/8
6/0	1	1.000	25.40	11 1/4	14	1 19/30	1.633	41.48	18 3/8
5/0	1 1/30	1.033	26.24	11 5/8	15	1 20/30	1.666	42.32	18 3/4
4/0	1 2/30	1.066	27.08	12 1/8	16	1 21/30	1.700	43.18	19 1/8
3/0	1 3/30	1.100	27.94	12 3/8	17	1 22/30	1.733	44.02	19 1/2
2/0	1 4/30	1.133	28.78	12 3/4	18	1 23/30	1.766	44.86	19 7/8
0	1 5/30	1.166	29.62	13 1/8	19	1 24/30	1.800	45.72	20 1/4
1	1 6/30	1.200	30.48	13 1/2	20	1 25/30	1.833	46.56	20 3/4

SWISS MOVEMENT SIZES
Lignes With Their Equivalents in Millimeters and Decimal Parts of an Inch

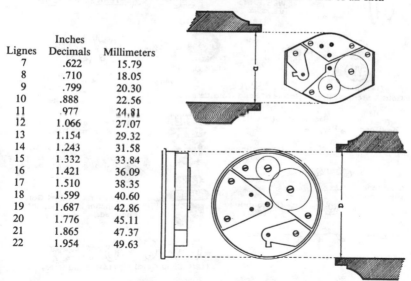

Lignes	Inches Decimals	Millimeters
7	.622	15.79
8	.710	18.05
9	.799	20.30
10	.888	22.56
11	.977	24.81
12	1.066	27.07
13	1.154	29.32
14	1.243	31.58
15	1.332	33.84
16	1.421	36.09
17	1.510	38.35
18	1.599	40.60
19	1.687	42.86
20	1.776	45.11
21	1.865	47.37
22	1.954	49.63

GAUGES FOR MEASURING YOUR WATCH SIZE

The size of a watch is determined by measuring the outside diameter of the dial side of the lower pillar plate. The gauges below may be placed across the face of your watch to calculate its approximate size.

AMER. MOVEMENT SIZES

26/0 21/0 20/0 16/0 12/0 10/0 8/0 5/0 6/0 10 16
18/0   6/0 4/0 0   8 12 14 18

SWISS MOVEMENT SIZES
LIGNES
2 4 6 8 10 12 14 16 18 20
3 5 7 9 11 13 15 17 19

SOLID GOLD MARKS

GOLD-FILLED CASES

The first patent for gold-filled cases was given to J. Boss on May 3, 1859.

Gold-filled cases are far more common than solid gold cases. Only about 5 percent of the cases were solid gold. In making the gold-filled case, the following process was used: two bars of gold, 12" long, 2" wide, and ½" thick were placed on either side of a bar of base metal. The bar of base metal was ¾" thick and the same length and width as the gold bars. These three bars were soldered together under pressure at high temperature. The bars were sent through rolling mills under tremendous pressure; this rolling was repeated until the desired thickness was reached. The new sandwich-type gold was now in a sheet. Discs were punched out of the sheet and pressed in a die to form a dish-shaped cover. Finally the lip, or ridge, was added. The bezel, snap, and dust caps were added in the finishing room. Gold-filled cases are usually 10k or 14k gold. The cases were marked ten-year, fifteen-year, twenty-year, twenty-five-year, or thirty-year. The number of years indicated the duration of guarantee that the gold on the case would not wear through to the base metal. The higher the number of years indicates that more gold was used and that a higher original price was paid.

In 1924 the government prohibited any further use of the guarantee terms of 5, 10, 15, 20, 25, or 30 years. After that, manufacturers marked their cases 10k or 14k Gold-Filled and 10k Rolled Gold Plate. Anytime you see the terms "5, 10, 15, 20, 25 and 30-year" this immediately identifies the case as being gold-filled. The word "guaranteed" on the case also denotes gold-filled.

Rolled Gold

Rolled gold involved rolling gold into a micro thinness and, under extreme pressure, bonding it to each sheet of base metal. Rolled gold carried a five-year guarantee. The thickness of the gold sheet varied and had a direct bearing on value, as did the richness of the engraving.

Gold Gilding

Brass plates, wheels and cases are often gilded with gold. To do this, the parts are hung by a copper wire in a vessel or porous cell of a galvanic battery filled with a solution of offerro-cyanid of potassium, carbonate of soda, chloride of gold, and distilled water. An electric current deposits the gold evenly over the surface in about a six-minute period. One ounce of gold is enough for heavy gilding of six hundred watches. After gilding, the plates are polished with a soft buff using powdered rouge mixed with water and alcohol. The older method is fire-gilt which uses a gold and mercury solution. The metal is subjected to a high temperature so the mercury will evaporate and leave the gold plating. This is a very dangerous method, however, due to the harmful mercury vapor.

GOLD-FILLED MARKS

The following gold-filled and rolled gold plate marks are not complete, but if you have any doubt that the case is solid gold, pay only the gold-filled price.

GOLD FILLED MARKS

☆ 10 K ROLLED GOLD PLATE

BEE HIVE

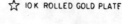

FAHYS

(14K. Filled.)

(Jas. Boss 10K. Filled. 20 Years.)

CROWN 14K. FILLED
(25 Years.)

(Keystone Extra, Substitute for All-Gold Case.)

CROWN 10K. FILLED
(20 Years.)

(Rolled Gold.)

(Jas. Boss 14K. Filled. 25 Years.)

EMPRESS
(Gold Filled, 10 Years.)

FORTUNE
(Gold Filled, 20 Years.)

(14K. Filled.)

(10 Years.)

PREMIER
(Gold Filled, 25 Years.)

XV.

THE BELL 14K.
(25 Years.)

CASHIER
(Gold Filled, 25 Years.)

V.

(15 Years.)

XX.

THE COMET
(10 Years.)

(10K. Gold Filled.)

(5 Years.)

(20 Years.)

(25 Years.)

SILVER CASE MARKS

DUEBER STERLING

925

(Discontinued.)   *(Discontinued.)*

A.W.W.CO.
COIN.

NEWPORT COIN

DUEBER COIN

(Coin Silver with Albata Cap) (Coin Silver with Silver Cap)
(Discontinued.)   *(Discontinued.)*

CHAMPION COIN.

N.A.W.Co. STERLING
(Sterling Silver.)

STAR W.C.CO

STERLING 925/1000 FINE

DUEBER STERLING

925

DUEBER COIN

(Coin Silver, with Silver Caps, Gold Joints and Crowns.)

Sterling Silver

SILVER CASE MARKS

  STERLING
SILVER
UNITED STATES
ASSAY
925./1000
FINE.

(Sterling Silver.)

 ILLINOIS
W.C.CO,
ELGIN
STERLING

HUNTING CASES

A hunting case is identified by a cover over the face of the watch. The case is opened by pressing the stem of the watch. The cover was used for dress and protection and the hunter case was carried by men of status.

How To Handle A Hunting Case Watch

Hold the watch in right hand with the bow or swing ring between the index finger and thumb. Press on the stem with the right thumb to release the cover exposing the face.

When closing, don't snap the front cover. Press the crown to move the catch in, close the cover, then release the crown. This will prevent wear to the soft gold on the rim and catch.

Above: Example of a hunting case

Right: Example of a swing-out case

SWING-OUT MOVEMENTS

On some watches the movement swings out from the front. On these watches the movement can be swung out by unscrewing the crystal and pulling the stem out to release the movement. See example above.

Demi-Hunting case

Example of a 14 carat gold boxed hinged case, selling for $94 in 1890.

Below: Example of a reversible case to either hunting or open face.

Left: Example of a screw bezel and screw back case.

Note: The screw on bezel was invented by E. C. Fitch in 1886.

CASE PRICES

Case prices are for complete cases with bezel, crystal, stem, crown and bow. Hunting case must have workable lift spring.

SILVEROID CASES

Size	Avg	Ex-Fn	Mint
18S, OF, SW	$10	$15	$25
18S, OF, KW	15	20	35
18S, HC, SW	20	25	40
18S, HC, KW	22	30	50
16S, OF	8	12	18
16S, HC	10	15	22
12S, OF	3	4	6
12S, HC	5	7	10
6S, OF	3	4	6
6S, HC	5	7	10

COIN CASES

Size	Avg	Ex-Fn	Mint
18S, OF, SW	$15	$22	$35
18S, OF, KW	25	35	50
18S, HC, SW	20	27	40
18S, HC, KW	30	43	60
16S, OF	12	18	25
16S, HC	15	20	35
12S, OF	5	6	8
12S, HC	5	6	8
6S, OF	5	6	8
6S, HC	8	10	13

GOLD-FILLED CASES

Size and Style	Avg	Ex-Fn	Mint
18S, OF, Plain	$55	$65	$95
18S, OF, Fancy	65	75	115
18S, HC, Plain	75	85	135
18S, HC, Fancy	85	95	155
16S, OF, Plain	50	60	90
16S, OF, Fancy	55	65	95
16S, HC, Plain	65	75	120
16S, HC, Fancy	70	80	135
12S, OF, Plain	15	20	30
12S, OF, Fancy	20	25	35
12S, HC, Plain	25	30	45
12S, HC, Fancy	30	40	55
6S, OF, Plain	10	20	30
6S, OF, Fancy	15	25	35
6S, HC, Plain	25	30	45
6S, HC, Fancy	30	40	55

Note: Plain enamel single sunk dial brings $15 to $30.

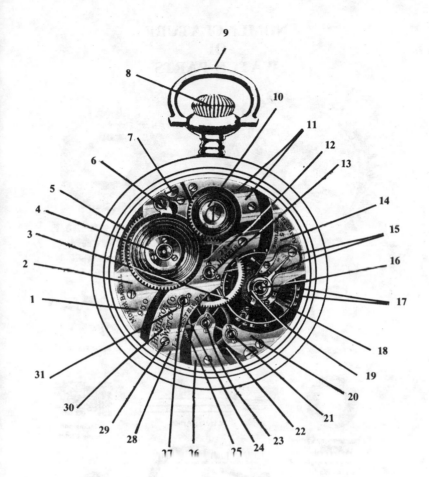

MOVEMENT IDENTIFICATION

1. Grade Number. **2.** Nickel Motor Barrel Bridge. **3.** Center Wheel (2nd Wheel). **4.** Winding Wheel with Jewel Setting. **5.** First Barrel Wheel. **6.** Winding Click. **7.** Case Screw. **8.** Pendant Crown. **9.** Pendant Bow or Swing Ring. **10.** Crown Wheel with Screw. **11.** Damaskeening-horizontal pattern. **12.** Number of Jewels. **13.** Center Wheel Jewel with Setting. **14.** Adjusted to Heat, Cold, Isochronism & 5 Positions. **15.** Patented Regulator with Index & Spring. **16.** Balance End Stones (Diamonds, Rubies, & Sapphires were used). **17.** Balance Screws. **18.** Compensating Balance Wheel. **19.** Hairspring. **20.** Escapement Bridge. **21.** Escapement Wheel Jewel with Setting (Diamonds, Rubies, & Sapphires were used). **22.** Escapement Wheel. **23.** Fourth Wheel Jewel with Setting. **24.** Third Wheel. **25.** Fourth Wheel. **26.** Fourth Wheel Bridge. **27.** Third Wheel Jewel with Setting. **28.** Center & Third Wheel Bridge. **29.** Bridge Screw. **30.** Manufacturers Name & Location. **31.** Jewel Setting Screw.

NOMENCLATURE
OF
WATCH PARTS

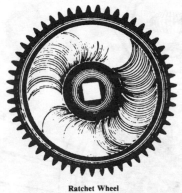

Ratchet Wheel

Crown or Main Wheel

Click Spring

Setting Cam

Bevel Pinion

Crown or Main
Screw Washer

Winding Arbor

Winding and
Setting Clutch

Setting
Lever

Setting Spring

Click

Setting
Spring Cam

Winding Sleeve

Clutch Lever

NOMENCLATURE
OF
WATCH PARTS

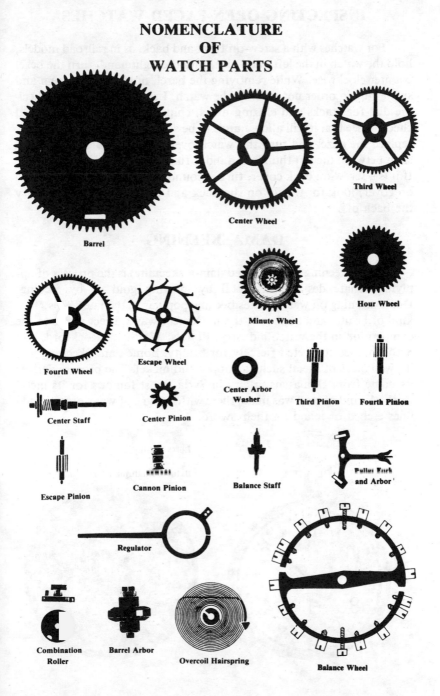

Barrel

Center Wheel

Third Wheel

Minute Wheel

Hour Wheel

Fourth Wheel

Escape Wheel

Center Arbor Washer

Third Pinion

Fourth Pinion

Center Staff

Center Pinion

Escape Pinion

Cannon Pinion

Balance Staff

Pallet Fork and Arbor

Regulator

Combination Roller

Barrel Arbor

Overcoil Hairspring

Balance Wheel

INSPECTING OPEN-FACED WATCHES

For watches with a screw-on front and back, as in railroad models, hold the watch in the left hand and, with the right hand, turn the bezel counter clockwise. While removing the bezel, hold onto the stem and swing ring in order not to drop the watch. Lay the bezel down, check the dial for cracks and crazing nicks, chips, etc. Look for lever and check to see that it will allow hands to be set. After close examination, replace the bezel and turn the watch over. Again, while holding the stem between the left thumb and index finger, remove the back cover. If it is a screw-on back cover, turn it counter clockwise. If it is a snap-on cover, look for the lip on the back and use a pocket knife to pry the back off.

DAMASKEENING

Damaskeening (pronounced dam-a-skeening) is the process of applying ornate designs on metal by inlaying gold or by etching. Damaskeening on watch plates became popular in the late 1870s. This kind of beauty and quality in the movement was a direct result of the competition in the watch industry. Illinois, Waltham, Rockford, and Seth Thomas competed fiercely for beauty. Some damaskeening was in two colors of metal such as copper and nickel. The process derives its name from Damascus, a city in Syria, most famous for its metal work. A kind of steel was made there with designs of wavy or varigated lines etched or inlaid on their swords.

Left: Example of open face case

Below: Example of Damaskeening

DISPLAY CASE WATCHES

Display case watches were used by salesmen and in jewelry stores to show the customer the movement. Both front and back had a glass crystal. These are not rare, but they are nice to have in a collection to show off a nice watch movement.

WATCH CASE PRODUCTION

Before the Civil War, watchmaking was being done on a very small scale, and most of the companies in business were making their own movements as well as their own cases. After the War, tradesmen set up shops specializing exclusively in cases, while other artisans were making the movements. The case factories, because of mass production, could supply watch manufacturers with cases more economically than the manufacturers could produce their own.

A patent was granted to James Boss on May 3, 1859, and the first gold-filled watch cases were made from sandwich-type sheets of metal. Boss was not the first to use gold-filled, but he did invent a new process that proved to be very successful, resulting in a durable metal that Boss sold with a 20-year **money-back** guarantee.

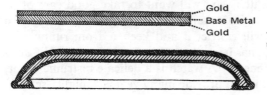

The illustration at left is a sandwiched type gold-filled case.

GOLD CASE
WEIGHTS BY SIZE

Size & Style of Case	Ex. Heavy	Heavy	Medium	Light	Ex. Light
18 size Hunting Case	60 to 65	50 to 55	45 to 50	40 to 45	35
16 size Hunting Case	55 to 60	45 to 50	40 to 45	35 to 40	32
18 size Open Face Case		40 to 45	38	35	
16 size Open Face Case		40	36	30	
12 size Open Face Case (Thin)					14
6 size Hunting Case	24	22	20	18	
0 size Hunting Case					14 to 16

Pennyweights (DWT)

An 18 size movement with a full plate weighs 50 DWT; a 16 size movement with a ¾ plate weighs 35 DWT. These weights do not include the case.

CARE OF WATCHES

To some people a watch is just a device that keeps time. They do not know the history of its development nor how it operates. They have no appreciation for improvements made over the years. That the watch is a true miracle of mechanical genius and skill, is seldom more than a fleeting thought. The average person will know it must be wound to run, that it has a mainspring and possibly a hairspring. Some even realize there are wheels and gears and, by some strange method, these work in harmony to keep time. If for some reason the watch should stop, the owner will merely take it to a watch repair shop and await the verdict on damage and cost.

To be a good collector one must have some knowledge of the components of a watch and how they work and the history of the development of the watch. To buy a watch on blind faith is indeed risky, but many collectors do it every day because they have limited knowledge.

How does a watch measure time and perform so well? Within the case one can find the fulcrum, lever, gear, bearing, axle, wheel, screw, and the spring which overcomes nature's law of gravity. All these parts harmonize to provide an accurate reading minute by minute. A good collector will be able to identify all of them.

After acquiring a watch, you will want to take good care of it. A watch should be cleaned inside and out. Dirt will wear it out much faster, and gummy oil will restrict it and keep it from running all together. After the watch has been cleaned it should be stored in a dry place. Rust is the No. 1 enemy. A watch is a delicate instrument but, if it is given proper care, it will provide many years of quality service. A pocket watch should be wound at regular intervals—about once every 24 hours, early each morning—so the mainspring has its full power to withstand the abuse of daily use. Do not carry a watch in the same pocket with articles that will scratch or tarnish the case. A fully wound watch can withstand a jar easier than a watch that has been allowed to run down. Always wind a watch and leave it running when you ship it. If you are one who enjoys carrying a watch be sure to have it cleaned at least once every two years.

EXAMINATION AND INSPECTION OF A WATCH BEFORE PURCHASING

The examination and inspection of a watch before purchasing is of paramount importance. This is by no means a simple task for there are many steps involved in a complete inspection.

The first thing you should do is to listen to a watch and see how it sounds. Many times the trained ear can pick up problems in the escapement and balance. The discriminating buyer will know that sounds cannot be relied on entirely because each watch sounds different, but the sound test is worthwhile and is comparable to the doctor putting the stethescope to a patient's heart as his first source of data.

Check the bow to see if it is securely fastened to the case and look at the case to see if correction is necessary at the joints. The case should close firmly at both the back and front. (Should the case close too firmly, rub the rim with beeswax which will ease the condition and prolong the life of the rim.)

Take note of the dents, scratches, wear and other evidences of misuse. Does the watch have a generally good appearance? Check the bezel for proper fit and the crystal to see if it is free of chips.

Remove the bezel and check the dial for chips and hairline cracks. Look for stains and discoloration; and check to see if the dial is loose. It is important to note that a simple dial with only a single sunk dial is by nature a stronger unit due to the fact that a double sunk dial is constructed of three separate pieces.

If it is a stem-winder, try winding and setting. Problems in this area can be hard to correct. Parts are hard to locate and may possibly have to be handmade. If it is a lever set, pull the lever out to see if it sets properly into gear. Also check to see that the hands have proper clearance.

Now that the external parts have been inspected, open the case to view the movement. Check to see that the screws hold the movement in place securely. Note any repair marks and any missing screws. Make a visual check for rust and discoloration, dust, dirt and general appearance. If the movement needs cleaning and oiling, this should be deducted from the price of the watch, as well as any repair that will have to be made.

Note the quality of the movement. Does it have raised gold jewel settings or a gold train (center wheel or all gears)? Are the jewels set in or pressed in? Does it have gold screws in the balance wheel? Sapphire pallets? Diamond end stones? Jeweled motor barrel? How many adjustments does it have? Does it have overall beauty and eye appeal?

Examine the balance for truth. First look directly down upon the balance to detect error truth in the roundness. Then look at it from the side to detect error in the flat swing or rotation. It should be smooth in appearance.

Examine the hairspring in the same manner to detect errors in truth. When a spring is true in the round, there will be no appearance of jumping when it is viewed from the upper side. The coils will appear to uniformly dilate and contract in perfect rhythm when the balance is in motion. Check the exposed portion of the train wheels for burred, bent, or broken teeth. Inspect pinions and pivots for wear. If a watch has complicated features such as a repeater, push the slides, plungers, and buttons to see that they are in good working order.

After the movement and case have been examined to your satisfaction and all the errors and faults are found, talk to the owner as to the history and his personal thoughts about the watch. Is the movement in the original case? Is the dial the original one? Just what has been replaced?

Has the watch been cleaned? Does it need any repairs? If so, can the seller recommend anyone to repair the watch?

Finally, see if the seller makes any type of guarantee, and get an address and phone number. It may be valuable if problems arise, or if you want to buy another watch in the future.

WATCH MOVEMENT PARTS

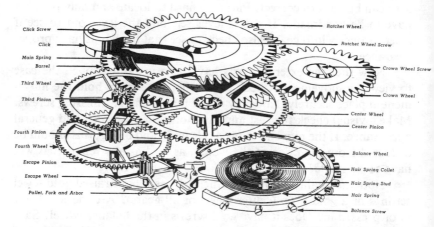

Mechanical watches are small engines powered by a spring, which keeps the balance in motion. The uniformity of this motion relies on the balance; the durability rests on the quality of material and construction of the complete movement.

HOW A WATCH WORKS

There are five basic components of a watch:
1. The **mainspring**, and its winding mechanism, which provides power.
2. The **train** which consists of gears, wheels and pinions that turn the hands.
3. The **escapement** consisting of the escape wheel and balance which regulates or controls.
4. The **dial and hands** which tell the time.
5. The **housing** consisting of the case and plates which protect.

The motion of the balance serves the watch the same as a pendulum serves a clock. The balance wheel and roller oscillate in each direction moving the fork and lever by means of a ruby pin. As the lever moves back and forth it allows the escape wheel to unlock at even intervals (about 1/5 sec.) and causes the train of gears to move in one direction under the power of the mainspring. Thus, the mainspring is allowed to be let down or unwind one pulse at a time.

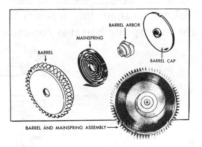

Power unit for modern watch showing the various parts.

Early style watch with a stackfreed (tear shaped cam).
Note the balance is dumbell shaped.

THE MAINSPRING

Watches were developed from the early portable clocks. The coiled spring or mainspring provided the drive power. The first coiled springs were applied to clocks about 1435. For the watch, coiled springs were first used about 1510. The power from a mainspring is not consistent and this irregular power was disastrous to the first watches. The Germans' answer to irregular power was a device called a **stackfreed**. Another apparatus employed was the **fusee**. The fusee proved to be the best choice. At first catgut was used between the spring barrel and fusee. By around 1660 the catgut was replaced by a chain. Today, the fusee is still used in naval chronometers. One drawback to the fusee is the amount of space it takes up in the watch. Generally, the simplest devices are best.

The mainspring is made of a piece of hardened and tempered steel about 20 inches long and coiled in a closed barrel between the upper and lower plates of the movement. It is matched in degree of strength, width, and thickness most suitable for the watch's need or design. It is subject to differing conditions of temperature and tensions (the wound-up position having the greatest tension). The lack of uniformity in the mainspring affects the timekeeping qualities of a watch.

The power assembly in a watch consists of the mainspring, mainspring barrel, arbor, and cap. The mainspring furnishes the power to run the watch. It is coiled around the arbor and is contained in the mainspring barrel, which is cylindrical and has a gear on it which serves as the first wheel of the train. The arbor is a cylindrical shaft with a hook for the mainspring in the center of the body. The cap is a flat disk which snaps into a recess in the barrel. A hook on the inside of the mainspring barrel is for attaching the mainspring to the barrel.

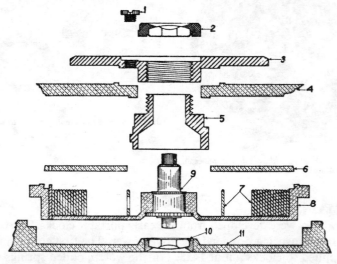

Jeweled Motor Barrel Unit: 1. Barrel top jewel screw. 2. Barrel top jewel and setting. 3. Ratchet wheel. 4. Barrel bridge. 5. Barrel hub. 6. Barrel head. 7. Mainspring (in barrel). 8. Barrel. 9. Barrel arbor (riveted to barrel). 10. Barrel lower jewel and setting. 11. Pillar plate.

The mainspring is made of a long thin strip of steel, hardened to give the desired resiliency. Mainsprings vary in size but are similar in design; they have a hook on the outer end to attach to the mainspring barrel, and a hole in the inner end to fasten to the mainspring barrel arbor.

By turning the crown clockwise, the barrel arbor is rotated and the mainspring is wound around it. The mainspring barrel arbor is held stationary after winding by means of the ratchet wheel and click. As the mainspring uncoils, it causes the mainspring barrel to revolve. The barrel is meshed with the pinion on the center wheel, and as it revolves it sets the train wheels in motion. Pocket and wrist watches, in most cases, will run up to 36 hours on one winding.

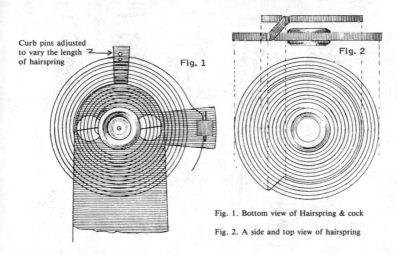

Curb pins adjusted to vary the length of hairspring

Fig. 1

Fig. 2

Fig. 1. Bottom view of Hairspring & cock

Fig. 2. A side and top view of hairspring

THE HAIRSPRING

The hairspring is the brain of the watch and is kept in motion by the mainspring. The hairspring is the most delicate tension spring made. It is a piece of flat wire about 12 inches long, 1/100th of an inch wide, 2½/1,000th of an inch thick, and weighs only about 1/9,000th of a pound. Thousands of these hairsprings can be made from one pound of steel. The hairspring controls the action of the balance wheel. The hairspring steel is drawn through the diamond surfaces to a third the size of a human hair. There are two kinds of hairsprings in the watches of later times, the flat one and the Breguet. The Breguet (named for its French inventor) is an overcoil given to the spring. There are two methods for overcoil, the oldest is the way the spring is bent by hand; and with the other method the overcoil is bent or completed in a form

REGULATORS
Identification

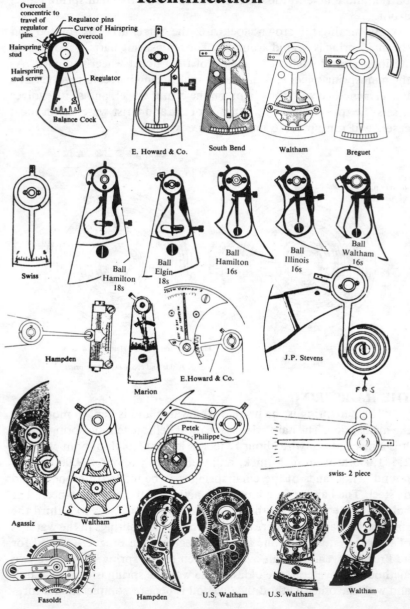

Overcoil concentric to travel of regulator pins
Regulator pins
Curve of Hairspring overcoil
Hairspring stud
Hairspring stud screw
Regulator
Balance Cock

E. Howard & Co.

South Bend

Waltham

Breguet

Swiss

Ball Hamilton 18s

Ball Elgin 18s

Ball Hamilton 16s

Ball Illinois 16s

Ball Waltham 16s

Hampden

Marion

E. Howard & Co.

J.P. Stevens

F S

Agassiz

Waltham

Petek Philippe

swiss- 2 piece

Fasoldt

Hampden

U.S. Waltham

U.S. Waltham

Waltham

REGULATORS
Identification

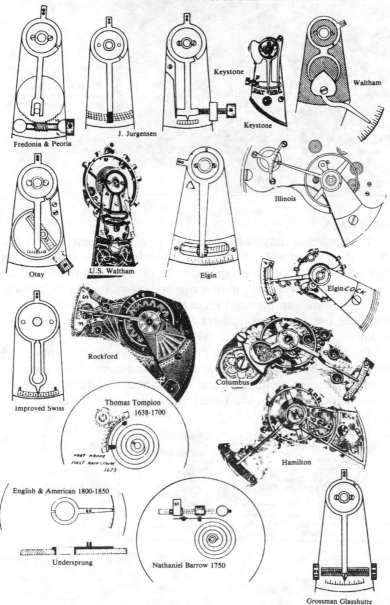

Fredonia & Peoria

J. Jurgensen

Keystone

Keystone

Waltham

Otay

U.S. Waltham

Elgin

Illinois

Elgin COCK

Improved Swiss

Rockford

Columbus

Thomas Tompion
1638-1700

Hamilton

English & American 1800-1850

Undersprung

Nathaniel Barrow 1750

Grossman Glasshutte

at one end and at the same time is hardened and tempered in the form. The hairspring contracts and expands 432,000 times a day.

A modern style **Regulator**. Note triangular shaped hairspring stud which is located on the balance bridge between the screw and curb pin.

THE TRAIN

The time train consists of the mainspring barrel, center wheel and pinion, third wheel and pinion, fourth wheel and pinion, and escape wheel which is part of the escapement. The function of the time train is to reduce the power of the mainspring and extend its time to 36 hours or more. The mainspring supplies energy in small units to the escapement, and the escapement delays the power from being spent too quickly.

The long center wheel arbor projects through the pillar plate and above the dial to receive the cannon pinion and hour wheel. The cannon pinion receives the minute hand and the hour wheel the hour hand. As the mainspring drives the barrel, the center wheel is rotated once each hour.

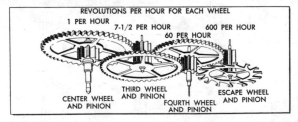

Actual alignment of **Train Unit**

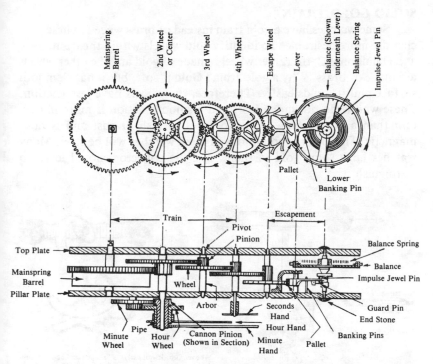

The second or center wheel of the watch turns once every hour. It is the largest wheel in the train, and the arbor or post of the center wheel carries the minute hand. The center wheel pinion is in mesh with the mainspring barrel (pinions follow and the wheel supplies the power). The center wheel is in mesh with the third wheel pinion (the third wheel makes eight turns to each turn of the center wheel). The third wheel is in mesh with the fourth wheel pinion, and the fourth wheel pinion is in mesh with the escape wheel pinion. The fourth wheel post carries the second hand and is in a 1:60 ratio to the center wheel (the center wheel turns once every hour and the fourth wheel turns 60 turns every hour). The escape wheel has 15 teeth (shaped like a flat foot) and works with two pallets on the lever. The two pallet jewels lock and unlock the escape wheel at intervals (1/5 sec.) allowing the train of gears to move in one direction under the influence of the mainspring. The lever (quick train) vibrates 18,000 times to one turn of the center wheel (every hour). The hour hand works from a motion train. The mainspring barrel makes about five turns every 36 hours.

SOLID GOLD TRAIN

Some watches have a gold train instead of brass wheels. These watches are more desirable. To identify gold wheels within the train, look at a Hamilton 992; the center wheel is made of gold and the other wheels are made of brass. Why a gold train? Gold is soft, but it has a smooth surface and it molds easily. Therefore, the wheels have less friction. These wheels do not move fast, and a smooth action is more important than a hard metal. Gold does not tarnish or rust and is non-magnetic. The arbors and pinions in these watches will be steel. Many watches have some gold in them, and the collector should learn to distinguish it.

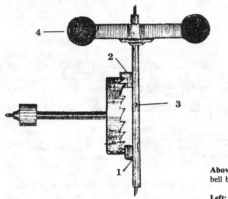

Above: Top view of early "s" shaped cock. Note dumbbell balance and cock is pinned to the plate.

Left: Early verge style escapement with dumbbell balance. 1. Lower pallet. 2. Upper pallet. 3. Verge. 4. Dumbbell balance.

TYPES OF ESCAPEMENTS

The verge escapement is the earliest form of escapement. It was first used in clocks as far back as the early 1300s. The verge escapement consists of a crown escape wheel, a verge which has two flags called pallets, and a balance. Early German watches had a balance shaped like a dumbbell, called a "foliot." Later most other watches used a balance shaped like a wheel. The crude weights of the foliot could be adjusted closer to or farther from the center of the balance for better timekeeping. Another design from that period was the circular balance. The circular balance was used by Christiaan Huygens in 1675 when he introduced the hairspring. This remarkable invention was used from that time onward.

The verge escapement was used by Luther Goddard in America as well as most of the Colonial watchmakers.

About 1725 the cylinder escapement was invented by George Graham, an Englishman. His cylinder escapement was a great im-

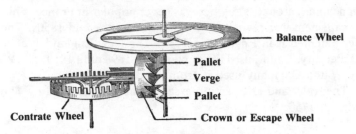

A later style Verge Escapement with a more common balance wheel.

provement over the verge. Even so, the cylinder escapement was not popular until Abraham Louis Breguet adopted the idea about 1765. This escapement wears out rather rapidly, unfortunately.

Note: *We have never seen a Colonial watch that used a cylinder escapement in a movement. If you have one or know where one is, please contact the author.*

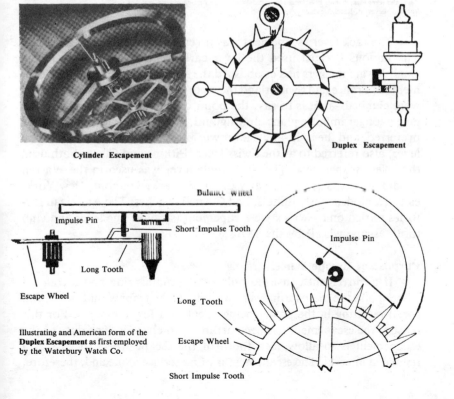

Cylinder Escapement

Duplex Escapement

Illustrating and American form of the **Duplex Escapement** as first employed by the Waterbury Watch Co.

The duplex escapement is accredited generally to Pierre LeRoy, a Frenchman, around 1750, but was never popular in France. This type of escapement was favored in England up to the mid 1850s. Thomas Tyrer patented it in England in 1782. The New England Watch Co. of Waterbury, Conn., used the duplex from 1898 until 1910. The Waterbury Watch Company used it from 1880 to 1898.

The roller and lever action escapement was invented by Thomas Mudge in 1750.

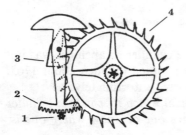

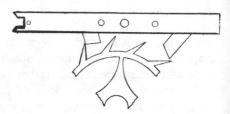

Rack and lever escapement. 1. Balance wheel pinion. 2. Rack. 3. Lever. 4. Ratchet escape wheel.

English style right angle lever which was used in earlier American made watches.

The rack lever escapement was invented by Hautefeuille in 1722. The famous Breguet used the lever early in the 1800s. By 1830 the English watchmakers had established the superiority of the lever escapement. In France and Switzerland the teeth of the lever escapement wheel were clubbed—that is to say, the point of the teeth were cut away to give a longer impulse plane. In England, pointed or ratchet teeth were preferred, and the right-angle lever was preferred over the straight line lever, also referred to as the Swiss lever. Pitkins and Custer both used the lever escapements. The right-angle lever was used in the Warren & Samuel Curtis as well as early Elgin, Newark, Tremont, New York, early Hampden, early Illinois, and Cornell watches. The American factories settled on a Swiss style escapement (straight line lever and club tooth escape wheel) by the 1870s.

Purpose of Escape Wheel

If a movement consisted only of the mainspring and a train of wheels, and the mainspring were would up, the train would run at full speed resulting in the power being spent in a few moments. For this reason, the escapement has been arranged to check it. The duty of the escapement is to allow each tooth of the escape wheel to pass at a regulated interval. The escapement is of no service alone and, therefore, must have some other arrangement to measure and regulate these intervals. This is accomplished by the balance assembly.

The escape wheel is in most cases made of steel and is staked on a pinion and arbor. It is the last wheel of the train and connects the train with the escapement. It is constructed so that the pallet jewels move in and out between its teeth, allowing but one tooth to escape at a time. The teeth are "club-shaped" because of the addition of impulse faces to the end of the teeth.

The pallet jewels are set at an angle to make their inside corners reach over three teeth and two spaces of the escape wheel. The outside corners of the jewels will reach over two teeth and three spaces of the escape wheel with a small amount of clearance. At the opposite end of the pallet, directly under the center of the fork slot, is a steel or brass pin called the guard pin. The fork is the connecting link to the balance assembly.

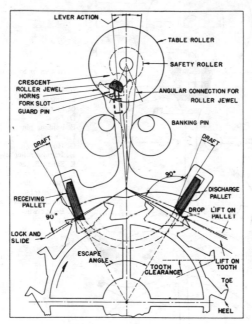

BALANCE AND HAIRSPRING

The rotation of the balance wheel is controlled by the hairspring. The inner end of the hairspring is pinned to the collet, and the collet is held friction-tight on the staff above the balance wheel. The outer end of the hairspring is pinned to a stud which is held stationary on the balance cock by the stud screw. The roller jewel is cemented in the large roller assembly, which is mounted on the staff directly under the balance wheel. Under the first roller is a smaller one which acts as a safety roller. This is necessary because of the crescent cut out in the roller table which allows the guard pin of the escapement assembly to pass through.

The balance wheel rotates clockwise and counterclockwise on its axis by means of the impulse it receives from the escapement. The motion of the balance wheel is constant due to the coiling and uncoiling of the hairspring. The impulse, transmitted to the roller jewel by

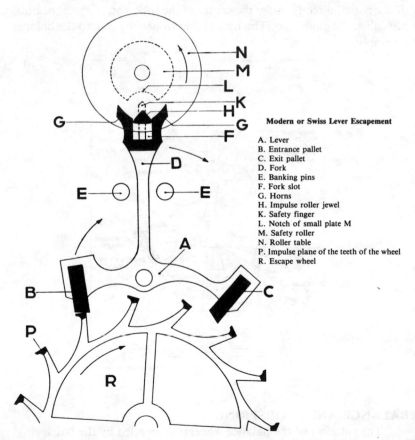

Modern or Swiss Lever Escapement

A. Lever
B. Entrance pallet
C. Exit pallet
D. Fork
E. Banking pins
F. Fork slot
G. Horns
H. Impulse roller jewel
K. Safety finger
L. Notch of small plate M
M. Safety roller
N. Roller table
P. Impulse plane of the teeth of the wheel
R. Escape wheel

the swinging of the pallet fork to the left, causes the balance to rotate in a counterclockwise direction. The position of the fork allows the roller jewel to move out of the slot of the fork freely and in the same direction. The fork continues on until it reaches the banking pin. Meanwhile the balance continues in the same direction until the tension of the hairspring overcomes the momentum of the balance wheel. When this occurs the balance returns to its original position, which causes the roller jewel to again enter the slot of the fork.

Pallet and Escape Tooth Action. The momentum that has been built up during the return of the balance, causes the roller pin to impart an impulse on the inside of the fork slot. This impulse is great enough to push the fork away from its position against the banking pin. As the fork is pushed away, it causes the pallet stone to slide on the toe of the escape wheel tooth. When the pallet stone has slid down to its edge, it frees the escape wheel tooth, thereby unlocking the escape wheel. The escape wheel, being impelled by the force of the mainspring, starts to rotate. As the escape wheel turns, the tooth glides along the impulse face of the pallet jewel, forcing it to move out of the way. The moving pallet carries the fork with it and imparts the impulse to the roller jewel. The right pallet stone intercepts a tooth of the escape wheel to lock it, as the fork moves toward the banking pin. Having a short "run" left to the banking pin, the pressure of the escape wheel tooth against the locking face of the pallet jewel draws the stone deeper into the escape wheel and, therefore, causes the fork to complete its run and holds it against the banking pin. Meanwhile the balance continues in a clockwise direction until the tension of the hairspring overcomes the momentum of the balance and returns it to its original position.

Rate of Escape Tooth Release. Through the motion of the escapement, the mainspring keeps the balance vibrating, and the balance regulates the train. The escape wheel has 15 teeth and is allowed to revolve 10 turns per minute. Thus, 150 teeth glide over each pallet stone in 1 minute. The gliding of the escape wheel teeth over the impulse faces of the pallet stones will cause the balance to vibrate 300 vibrations or beats per minute. These vibrations will continue until the force of the mainspring is spent.

SCREWS

Screws used in watches are very small and precise. These screws measure 254 threads to the inch and 47,000 of them can be put into a thimble. The screws were hardened and tempered and polished to a cold hard brilliance. By looking at these screws through a magnifying glass one can see the uniformity.

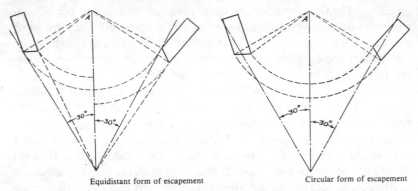

Equidistant form of escapement   Circular form of escapement

EQUIDISTANT ESCAPEMENT

The term Equidistant Escapement is a form of lever escapement. The locking of each pallet takes place at the same distance from the pallet arbor. A similar form of escapement is the circular pallet with the circular form of escapement. The impulses are given at equal distance from the center line. The Swiss preferred the equidistant while the Americans preferred the circular. There is little difference in performance between these two types of escapement.

THE PLATES

The movement of a watch has two plates and the works are sandwiched in between. The plates are called the top plate and the pillar plate. The top plate fully covers the movement. The ¾ plate watch and the balance bridge are flush and about ¼ of a full plate is cut out to allow for the balance, thus the ¾ plate. The bridge watch has two or three fingers to hold the wheels in place and together are called a bridge, just as the balance is called the balance bridge. The metal is generally brass, but on better grade watches, nickel is used. The full plate is held apart by four pillars. In older watches the pillars were very fancy, and the plates were pinned, not screwed, together. The plates can be gilded or engraved when using brass. Some of the nickel plates have damaskeening. There are a few watches with plates made of gold. The plates are also used to hold the jewels, settings, etc. Over 30 holes are drilled in each plate for pillars, pivots, and screws.

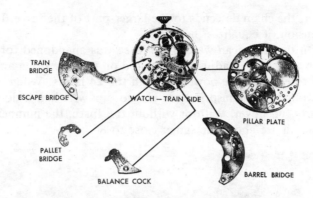

TRAIN BRIDGE

ESCAPE BRIDGE

WATCH – TRAIN SIDE

PILLAR PLATE

PALLET BRIDGE

BALANCE COCK

BARREL BRIDGE

The plates and bridges which hold all the parts in proper relation to each other.

The pinion is the smaller of the two wheels that exist on the shaft or arbor. They are small steel gears and usually have six teeth called leaves. Steel is used wherever there is great strain, but where there is much friction, steel and brass are used together; one gear of brass, and a pinion of steel. After the leaves have been cut, the pinions are hardened, tempered, and polished.

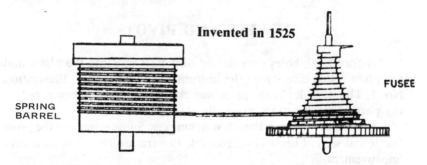

Invented in 1525

FUSEE

SPRING BARREL

THE FUSEE

A mainspring gives less and less power as it lets down. To equalize the power a fusee was first used. Fusee leverage increases as the mainspring lets down. A fusee is smaller at the top for a full mainspring. When the chain is at the bottom, the mainspring is almost spent, and the fusee has more leverage. Leonardo da Vinci is said to have invented the fusee.

When the mainspring is fully wound, it also pulls the hardest. At that time the chain is at the small end of the fusee. As the spring grows weaker, the chain descends to the larger part of the fusee. In shifting the tension, it equalizes the power.

On the American watch, the fusee was abandoned for the most part in 1850 and an adjustment is used on the hairspring and balance wheel to equalize the power through the 24 hours. When a watch is first wound the mainspring has no more power than it does when it is nearly run down. With or without the fusee, the number of parts in a watch are about the same: close to 800.

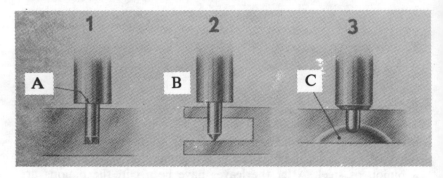

1. Illustration of pivot before 1700. 2. Pivot used in early 1700s. 3. Pivot used in late 1700s to present

JEWELS AND PIVOTS

Before 1700, holes were drilled only part way into the plates and the pivot rested directly on the bottom of the hole, as in Illustration No. 1. The shoulder of the pivot was above the plate, however, reducing part of the function, as in Illustration No. 1A.

In the early 1700s, a French watchmaker, Sully, improved the pivot friction as seen in Illustration No. 2B. Illustration No. 3 shows a later improvement.

N. F. de Duiller of Geneva, in conjunction with Peter and Jacob Debaufre, French immigrants living in London, developed a method of piercing jewels. This method was patented in 1704; however, it was not until around 1800 that holed jewels started to appear in watch movements and then only in high grade watches.

In the mid-1800s experiments were already being made for artificial rubies. In 1891 Fremy solved the problem and by the early 1900s the synthetic ruby was popular.

SHOCK ABSORBERS

When a watch is dropped or subjected to a hard shock, the balance and pivots usually suffer the most.

A shock-resisting device was invented by Breguet in 1789; he called it a parachute. This device was a spring steel arm supporting the end-stone. The parachute gives a cushioning effect to the balance staff.

The American pocket watch industry tried to find a device to protect pocket watch pivots, but it was the Swiss who perfected the devices for wristwatches around 1930.

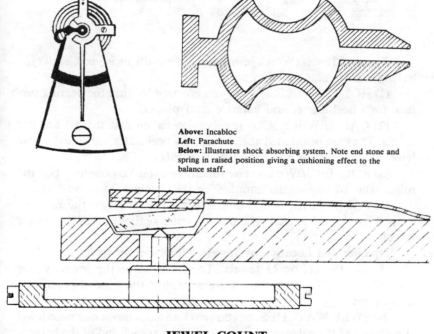

Above: Incabloc
Left: Parachute
Below: Illustrates shock absorbing system. Note end stone and spring in raised position giving a cushioning effect to the balance staff.

JEWEL COUNT

Jewels are used as bearings to reduce metal-to-metal contacts which produce friction and wear. They improve the performance and accuracy of the watch, and materially prolong its usefulness. The materials used for making watch jewels are diamonds, sapphires, rubies, and garnets. The diamond is the hardest but is seldom used except for cap jewels. The sapphire is the next in hardness and is the most commonly used because of its fine texture. Garnets are softer than sapphires and rubies.

They add to the outward appearance of the watch but do not have the fine texture of the sapphire jewel.

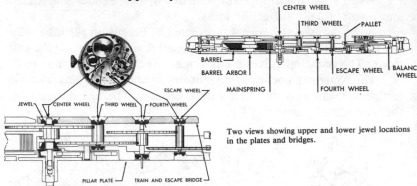

Two views showing upper and lower jewel locations in the plates and bridges.

Types of Jewels. Watch jewels are of four distinct types, each type having a particular function.

(1) HOLE JEWELS. Hole jewels are used to form the bearing surface for wheel arbors and balance staff pivots.

(2) CAP JEWELS. Cap jewels (also called end stones) are flat jewels. They are positioned at the ends of wheel staffs, outside the hole jewels, and limit the end thrust of the staff.

(3) ROLLER JEWELS. The roller jewel (pin) is positioned on the roller table to receive the impulse for the balance from the fork.

(4) PALLET JEWELS. The pallet jewels (stones) are the angular-shaped jewels positioned in the pallet to engage the teeth of the escape wheel.

Number and Location of Jewels. Most watches have either 7, 9, 11, 15, 17, 19, 21, or 23 jewels. The location of the jewels varies somewhat in different makes and grades, but the general practice is as follows:

7-JEWEL WATCHES. Seven-jewel watches have: one hole jewel at each end of the balance staff; one cap jewel at each end of the balance staff; one roller jewel; and two pallet jewels.

9-JEWEL WATCHES. These have the seven jewels mentioned in 7-jewel watches, with the addition of a hole jewel at each end of the escape wheel.

11-JEWEL WATCHES. In these, seven are used in the escapement as in 7-jewel watches. In addition, the four top pivots (the third wheel, the fourth wheel, the escape wheel, and the pallet) are jeweled.

15-JEWEL WATCHES. These watches have the nine jewels found

in 9-jewel watches, with the addition of the following: one hole jewel at each end of the pallet staff; one hole jewel at each end of the fourth-wheel staff; and one hole jewel at each end of the third-wheel staff.

17-JEWEL WATCHES. The 15 jewels in 15-jewel watches are used with the addition of one hole jewel located at each end of the center wheel staff.

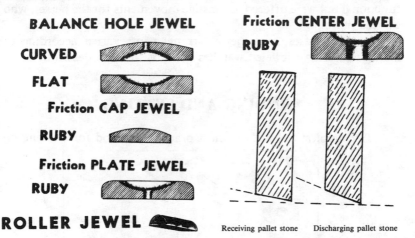

BALANCE HOLE JEWEL

CURVED

FLAT

Friction CAP JEWEL

RUBY

Friction PLATE JEWEL

RUBY

ROLLER JEWEL

Friction CENTER JEWEL

RUBY

Receiving pallet stone   Discharging pallet stone

19-JEWEL WATCHES. In these watches, the jewels are distributed as in the 17-jewel watch, with the addition of one for each pivot of the barrel or mainspring.

21-JEWEL WATCHES. The jewels in these are distributed as in the 17-jeweled grade, with the addition of two cap jewels each for the

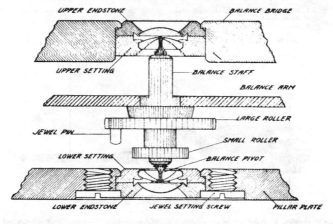

Location of jewels in balance

pallet and escape wheel.

23-JEWEL WATCHES. The jewels are distributed as in the 21-jewel watch, with the addition of one for each pivot of the barrel or mainspring.

24-, 25-, and 26-JEWEL WATCHES. In all of these watches, the additional jewels were distributed as cap jewels. These were not very functional but were offered as prestige movements for the person who wanted more.

In many cases, these jewel arrangements varied according to manufacturer. All jeweled watches will not fit these descriptions.

WINDING AND SETTING

The simplest but not the most practical method for winding up

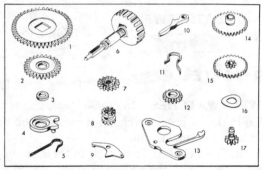

WINDING & SETTING PARTS

1. Ratchet Wheel	6. Stem and Crown	10. Clutch Lever	14. Hour Wheel
2. Crown Wheel	7. Winding Pinion	11. Clutch Lever Spring	15. Minute Wheel
3. Crown Wheel Center	8. Clutch Wheel	12. Setting Wheel	16. Dial Washer
4. Click	9. Setting Lever	13. Yoke	17. Cannon Pinion
5. Click Spring			

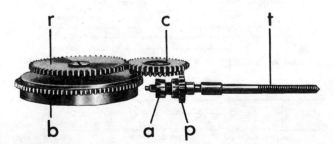

Winding Mechanism. a—Winding and setting clutch. p—Winding pinion. b—Barrel. r—Ratchet wheel. c—Crown or main wheel. t-Winding arbor.

the mainspring of a pocket watch was to wind the barrel staff by means of a key, but then it is necessary to open up the watch case. And the key method of winding proved unpopular, as oftentimes the key became lost.

The modern principle of the winding of the mainspring and hand-setting by pulling on the crown, dates back to 1842. We owe this combination to Adrian Philippe, associate of Patek, of Geneva.

The winding and setting mechanism consists of the stem, crown, winding pinion, clutch wheel, setting wheel, setting lever, clutch lever, clutch spring, crown wheel, and ratchet wheel. When the stem is pushed in, the clutch lever throws the clutch wheel to winding position. Then, when the stem is turned clockwise, it causes the winding pinion to turn the crown and ratchet wheels. The ratchet wheel is fitted on the square of the mainspring arbor and is held in place with a screw. When the stem and crown are turned, the ratchet wheel turns and revolves the arbor which winds the mainspring, thereby giving motive power to the train. Pulling the stem and crown outward pushes the setting lever against the clutch lever, engaging the clutch wheel with the setting wheel. The setting wheel is in constant mesh with the minute wheel; therefore, turning the stem and crown permits setting the hands to any desired time.

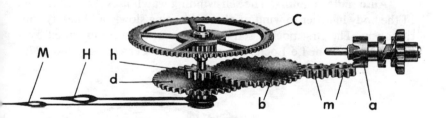

Setting Mechanism. Clutch **a** meshes with **m** and the minute works wheel **b**. The minute works wheel meshes with the cannon pinion **h**. The hour cannon **d** bears the hour hand **H**. **C**—Center wheel. **M**—Minute hand.

The dial train consists of the cannon pinion, minute, and hour wheels. The cannon pinion is a hollow steel pinion which is mounted on the center wheel arbor. A stud which is secured in the pillar plate holds the minute wheel in mesh with the cannon pinion. A small pinion is attached to the minute wheel which is meshed with the hour wheel.

The center arbor revolves once per hour. A hand affixed to the cannon pinion on the center arbor would travel around the dial once per hour. This hand is used to denote minutes. The hour wheel has a pipe that allows the hour wheel to set over the cannon pinion. The hour wheel meshes with the minute wheel pinion. This completes the train of the cannon pinion, minute wheel, and hour wheel. The ratio between the cannon pinion and the hour wheel is 12 to 1; therefore, the hand affixed to the hour wheel is to denote the hours. With this arrangement, time is recorded and read.

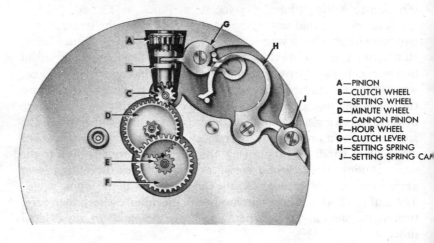

A—PINION
B—CLUTCH WHEEL
C—SETTING WHEEL
D—MINUTE WHEEL
E—CANNON PINION
F—HOUR WHEEL
G—CLUTCH LEVER
H—SETTING SPRING
J—SETTING SPRING CAM

Automatic Winding. The self-winding watch uses the movements of the body in order to wind up the mainspring slowly and nearly continuously. The first pocket self-winding watches were executed by a watchmaker from Le Locle, Abraham-Louis Perrelet, around 1770.

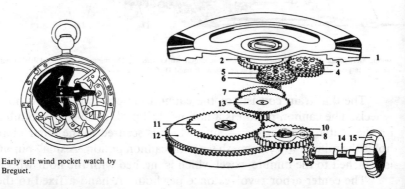

Early self wind pocket watch by Breguet.

Eterna-Matic Automatic Winding Mechanism. 1—Oscillating weight. 2—Oscillating gear. 3—Upper wheel of auxiliary pawl-wheel. 4—Lower wheel of auxiliary pawl-wheel. 5—Pawl-wheel with pinion. 6—Lower wheel of pawl-wheel with pinion. 7—Transmission-wheel with pinion. 8—Crown-wheel yoke. 9—Winding pinion. 10—Crown-wheel. 11—Ratchet-wheel. 12—Barrel. 13—Driving runner for ratchet-wheel. 14—Winding stem. 15—Winding button.

They were improved soon after by Abraham-Louis Breguet. In the case of the pocket watch, the movements causing the winding of the watch were essentially the result of walking. This system of winding was never widely adopted. The watch was a fancy model and not a really useful one. Herman von der Heydt was the only maker in America to work with the self-winding pocket watch. However, inventors always kept the idea of the self-winding watch in mind.

In 1923, the British firm Harwood took up once again the solution of the problem of automatic winding, for wrist watches. This was the spark which rapidly resulted in research to improve and simplify this type of mechanism. A company was formed in London to manufacture Harwood's watch, and before long over 500 jewelers in the United Kingdom were selling his automatic watch. A second company was formed in France, and a third in the United States. The business flourished about two and one-half years. Then, in 1931, these companies were liquidated.

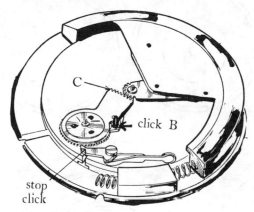

Illustration of Self Winding mechanism used by Harwood.

This 1931 wrist watch made by Perpetual Self-Winding Watch Co. of America originally sold for $29.75.

THE BALANCE ARC OF VIBRATION

If the watch is to function with any degree of satisfaction, the proper arc of motion of a balance must be no less than 225 degrees in a single vibration direction. Wind up the watch, stop the balance; upon releasing the balance, carefully observe the extent of the swing or vibration. After 30 seconds it should have reached its maximum. If it takes longer, the full power of the mainspring is not being communicated strongly enough. With the watch fully wound, the balance should vibrate between 225 degrees and 315 degrees in a single vibration direction.

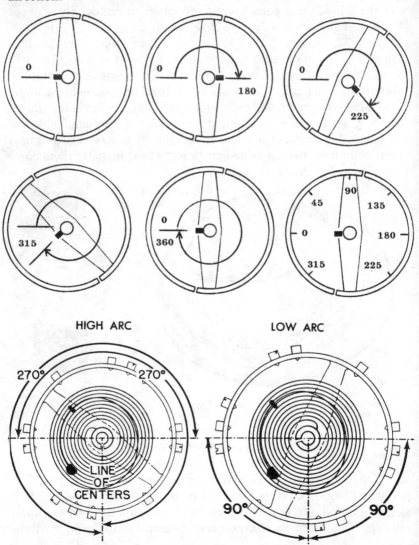

HIGH ARC   LOW ARC

COTTAGE INDUSTRY WATCHMAKING
IN COLONIAL AMERICA

The cottage industry (pre-1700s to 1800s) consisted of organized, skilled craftsmen having separate divisions for the purpose of producing watches. The movements were handmade using manpowered tools. The parts generally were not given a final finish. The cottage industries were in most countries including France, England, Switzerland, Germany, and others, but not in America. Each skilled parts maker specialized in a specific part of the watch. There were fusee makers, wheel makers, plate and cock makers, spring makers, case makers and enamelers, to name a few. In the cottage industry each maker became an expert in his field. Expenses and overhead were less because fewer tools and less labor were required. Because all components were produced separately, a larger volume of watches resulted.

The enterprising colonial watchmaker in America would order all the parts and assemble them to complete a finished movement. This finisher, or watchmaker, would detail the parts, such as filing them to fit, polishing and gilding the parts, fitting the movement to a case, installing a dial, and adjusting the movement to perform. The finisher would then engrave his name and town of manufacture to the movement or dial. The finisher determined the timekeeping quality of the completed watch, thus gaining a good reputation for some watchmakers.

Most watchmakers used this system during this period; even, to some extent, Abram Breguet. A colonial watchmaker or finisher could produce about 50 watches a year. There were few colonial watchmakers because only the wealthy could afford such a prized possession as a watch. Most colonial watchmakers struggled financially, and supplemented their businesses with repair work on European-made watches. Since most of them understood the verge escapement, and imported this type of part from England to produce watches, many colonial watches have the verge escapement. Few colonial watches survive today.

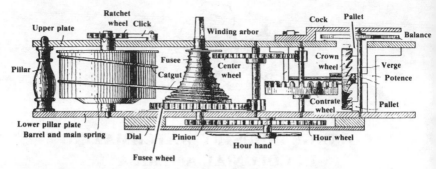

Side-view of 17th Century single-hand movement with fusee and catgut line to barrel. This three-wheel movement normally ran from 15 to 16 hours between windings. Also note the balance has no hairspring.

EBAUCHES

The stamping out of plates and bridges began with Frederic Japy of Beaucort, France, around 1770. At first, ebauches consisted of two plates with barrel and train bridges, the cock and fusee, pillars, and the clicks and assembly screws. The ebauches were stamped-out or rough movements. Japy invented machinery a common laborer could operate, including a circular saw to cut brass sheets into strips, a machine for cutting teeth in a wheel, a machine for making pillars, a press for the balance, and more. These machines were semi-automatic and hard to keep in alignment or register. But, with the aid of these new machines the principal parts of the movement could be produced in a short period of time with some precision. However, the parts of watches at this time were not interchangeable. These movements in the rough or "grey" were purchased by finishers. The finisher was responsible for fitting and polishing all parts and seeing to the freedom and depth of these working parts. He had to drill the holes to fit the dial and hands. The plates, cock and wheel, after being fitted and polished, were gilded. After the parts were gilded, the movement would be reassembled, regulated for good timekeeping, and placed in a case. The finisher had to be a master watchmaker.

In England, during the 1800s, Lancashire became the center of the movement trade. One of the better known English ebauche makers was Joseph Preston & Sons of Prescot. The movements were stamped J. P. Some Swiss ebauches would imitate or stylize the movement for the country in which they were to be sold, making it even harder to identify the origin.

As the watch industry progressed, the transformation of the ebauche to a more completed movement occurred. Automation eventually made possible the watch with interchangeable parts, standard sizing, and precision movements that did not need retouching. This automation began about 1850 with such talented mechanics as Pierre-Fredric Ingold, the Pitkins Brothers, A. L. Dennison, G. A. Leschot

Five typical Ebauches. Three with bar movements, one with a three-quarter plate, one with a half plate. Four with lever escapements, one with a cylinder escapement. The age ranges from 1860 to 1890.

with Vacheron and Constantin, Patek Philippe, and Frederic Japy of Beaucourt (still in business today as Japy Freres). The pioneers in the 1850s who set the standards for modern watchmaking included the Pitkin Brothers, Dennison, Howard, and Jacob Custer. By 1880 most other countries had begun to follow the lead of America in the manufacture of the complete pocket watch with interchangeable parts.

EBAUCHES S.A.

Ebauches S.A. with its main office in Neuchatel, Switzerland, consists of 17 affiliated firms:

A. Schild S.A., Grenchen

Fabrique d'Horlogerie de Fontainemelon, fontainemelon

Eta S.A., Fabrique d'Ebauches, Grenchen

Fabrique d'Horlogerie de Fontainemelon, Succursale du Landeron, Le Landeron

A. Michel S.A., Grenchen

Felsa S.A., Grenchen

Fabriques d'Ebauches Bernoises S.A., Etablissement Aurore, Villeret

Fabrique d'Ebauches Venus S.A., Moutier

Fabrique d'Ebauches Unitas S.A., Tramelan

Fabrique d'Ebauches de Fleurier S.A., Fleurier

Fabrique d' Ebauches de Peseux S.A., Peseux

Fabriques d'Ebauches Reunies Arogno S.A., Arogno

Fabriques d'Ebauches de bettlach, Bettlach

Fabrique d'Ebauches de Chezard S.A., Chezard

Derby S.A., La Chaux-de-Fonds

Nouvelle Fabrique S.A., Tavannes

Valjoux S.A., Les Bioux

Examples of four ebauches: **Upper left:** Example of a Chinese duplex. **Lower left:** An ebauche circa 1900-1930. **Upper right:** A three-finger bridge movement, circa 1890-1910. **Lower right:** Bridge movement, circa 1885-1900.

WORM GEAR ESCAPEMENT

This oddity was advertised as "The Watch With a Worm in It."

Robert J. Clay of Jersey City was given a patent on October 16, 1886. Mr. Clay said, "The principal object of my invention is to provide a watch movement which is very simple and has but few parts." The worm gear or continuous screw was by no means simple. Mr. Clay and William Hanson of Brooklyn revamped the original worm gear and obtained another patent on January 18, 1887.

The first watch containing a worm gear escapement reached the market in 1887. However, the New York Standard Watch Co. soon converted to a more conventional lever escapement. About 12,000 watches with the worm gear were made, but few survived.

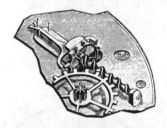

Enlarged worm gear escapement. Note endless screw was referred to by the New York Watch Co. as "a watch with a worm in it."

Movement with top plate removed.

DIAL MAKING

Watch dials were basically hand produced. The base is copper and the coating is generally enamel. In the process the copper plate is covered with a fine white enamel, spread with a knife to a thickness of 3/100ths of an inch. It is then allowed to dry at which time it is placed on a plate and inserted into a red hot furnace. The dial is turned frequently with a pair of long tongs. The copper would melt if it were not coated with the enamel. After the dial has been in the furnace for one minute it is removed and the resulting enamel is soft. The dial is now baked onto the copper plate or "set." The surface is rough after cooling, and it is sanded smooth with sandstone and emery, then baked again. The dial is now ready for the painter, who draws six lines across the dial using a lead pencil. Then, with a pencil of black enamel, he traces the numbers, finishing the ends to make them symmetrical. Then the minute marks are made. Lastly, the name of the watch company is painted onto the dial. The dial is glazed and fired again, then polished. The dial artist used a magnifying glass and a fine camelhair brush to paint the dials and produced about one dozen per hour.

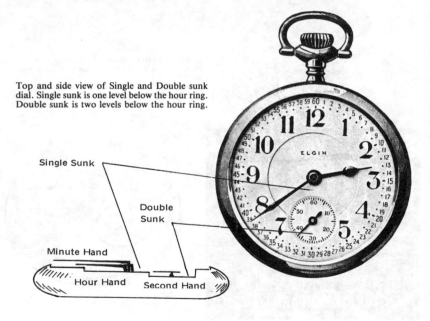

Top and side view of Single and Double sunk dial. Single sunk is one level below the hour ring. Double sunk is two levels below the hour ring.

Single Sunk

Double Sunk

Minute Hand

Hour Hand

Second Hand

FIRST DIALS

Henri Foucy was the first man to make enamel dials in America. He came to New York from Geneva, Switzerland, in 1856 and was employed by the American Watch Factory.

CRAZING

The word "craze" means a minute crack in the glaze of the enamel. This is not a crack in the dial because the dial has a backing of copper. Crazing does little damage to the structure of the enamel, even though it may go all the way through to the copper.

ENAMEL

Enamel may be transparent or colored. Enamel acts as a protective surface on the metals. It is resistant to acid, corrosion, and weather. Enamel is made of feldspar, quartz, silica, borax, lead, and mineral oxides. These materials are ground into a fine powder and then fired at a temperature of about 1500 degrees Fahrenheit. The heat melts the enamel powder and unites it with the surface of the metal.

PIN LEVER ESCAPEMENT (DOLLAR WATCHES)

The pin lever escapement is sometimes erroneously referred to as "Roskopf escapement" and watches with pin lever escapements are sometimes referred to as "Roskopf watches."

The original Roskopf watch, which was publicly exhibited at the Paris Exposition in 1867, was a rugged "poor man's watch." It had one less wheel than the conventional pocket watch. The mainspring bar-

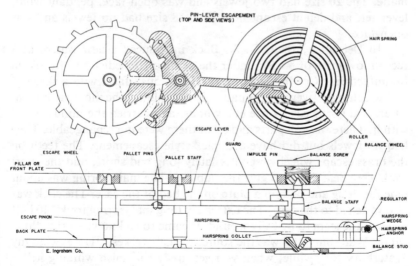

PIN-LEVER ESCAPEMENT
(TOP AND SIDE VIEWS)

HAIR SPRING

ESCAPE LEVER

GUARD

ROLLER

BALANCE WHEEL

ESCAPE WHEEL

PALLET PINS

PALLET STAFF

IMPULSE PIN

BALANCE SCREW

PILLAR OR
FRONT PLATE

BALANCE STAFF

REGULATOR

ESCAPE PINION

HAIRSPRING

HAIRSPRING
WEDGE

BACK PLATE

HAIRSPRING
ANCHOR

HAIRSPRING COLLET

BALANCE STUD

E. Ingraham Co.

rel was placed in the center of the watch, and the minute wheel and pinion fastened to it friction tight. In effect, the center wheel was thereby eliminated. The watch also incorporated a pin-lever escapement, which is also used in spring-wound clocks such as alarm clocks. Watches of this type have no provision for repair or adjustments and cannot be accurately regulated. The service charge of a fine watch repairman was usually higher than the initial cost of this type watch. As a result, most of the pin lever watches were discarded after they would no longer run. Some fakes use the name "Rosskopf."

LOW COST PRODUCTION WATCHES (DOLLAR WATCHES)

Jason R. Hopkins hoped to produce a watch that would sell for no more than 50 cents as early as the 1870s. He had a plan for which he received a patent (No. 161513) on July 20, 1875. It was a noble idea even though it was never fully realized. In 1876, Mr. Hopkins met a Mr. Fowle who bought an interest in the Hopkins watch. The movement was developed by the Auburndale Watch Co., and the Auburndale Rotary Watch was marketed in 1877. It cost $10, and 1,000 were made. The 20 size had two jewels and was open-face, pendant wind, lever set, and detent escapement. The 18 size had no jewels and was open-face.

In December, 1878, D. A. Buck introduced a new watch, at a record low price of $3.50, under the name of Benedict and Burnham Manufacturing Co. It was a rotary watch, open-face, with a skeleton dial which was covered with paper and celluloid. The movement turned around in the case, once every hour, and carried the minute hand with it. There were 58 parts and all of them were interchangeable. They had no jewels but did have a duplex style escapement. The teeth on the brass escape wheel were alternately long and short, and the short teeth were bent down to give the impulse. The main spring was about nine feet long and laid on a plate on the bed of the case. The click was also fastened to the case. The extremely long mainspring took 140 half turns of the stem to be fully wound. It came to be known as the "long wind" Waterbury and was the source of many jokes, "Here, wind my Waterbury for awhile; when you get tired, I'll finish winding it."

In 1892 R. H. Ingersoll ordered 1,000 watches produced at a cost of 85 cents each. He offered the watch for sale in his mail-order catalog

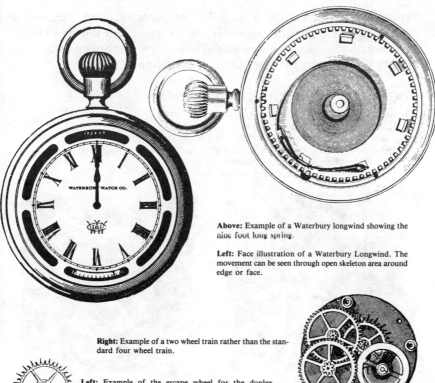

Above: Example of a Waterbury longwind showing the nine foot long spring.

Left: Face illustration of a Waterbury Longwind. The movement can be seen through open skeleton area around edge or face.

Right: Example of a two wheel train rather than the standard four wheel train.

Left: Example of the escape wheel for the duplex escapement.

for $1 each and advertised it as, "The Watch that Made the Dollar Famous." These watches were thick, sturdy and noisy and were wound from the back like a clock. The wages in 1892 were about 8 cents per hour, so it took some 13 hours of work to buy a Dollar Watch.

The E. N. Welch Manufacturing Co. was the next low cost production watch manufacturer. Then came the New York City Watch Co., who in 1895, produced a watch with a unique pendant crank to wind the movement. In 1899 came the Western Clock Mfg. Co., which later became the Westclox Corporation.

Also, among the low cost production watches were the "comic character" watches. They have become prime collectibles in recent years.

About 70 percent of the watches sold in the U. S. were Dollar-type. These watches were characterized by the pin lever, non-jeweled (for the most part), and with a face of paper or other inexpensive material. These watches were difficult to repair and the repairs cost more than the price of a new one. Thus they were thrown away, and today it is hard to find one in good condition.

DOLLAR WATCH CHARACTERISTICS:

1. Sold at a price that almost everyone could afford.
2. Used pin lever or duplex escapement.
3. Stamped or pressed out parts; also used fewer parts overall.
4. Were non-jeweled (except for a few) but rugged and practical.
5. Dial made of paper or other inexpensive material.
6. Case and movement were sold as one unit.

Personalized watch movement by Rockford. Engraved on movement. "W.G. Gane, Special Railway, 17j, Adj, serial No. 344551." To identify, see the Identification of Movement section of all watch companies, noting plate design & screw locations to determine that it is a **Rockford** Model No. 8.

Personalized watch movement by **Hamilton**. Engraved on movement, "Mayer, Chattanooga, Tenn., Adjusted, 21 jewels, serial No. 254507." To identify, see the Identification of Movement section of all watch companies, noting plate design & screw locations to determine that it is an 18 size, open face **Hamilton** model. Then by using the serial number, the grade can be determined.

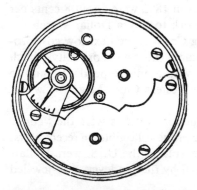

Model 8, 18 size, Rockford, full plate, hunting, lever set. This illustration from the identification section matches the model above.

Grade 936, 18 size, Hamilton, open face. This matches the model above.

PERSONALIZED WATCHES

It was common practice for some watch manufacturers to personalize watches for jobbers, jewelry firms, and individuals. This was done either by engraving the movement or painting on the dial. Probably the Ball Watch Co. did more of this than any other jobber.

Each manufacturer used its own serial number system even though there may have been a variety of names on the movements and/or dials. Knowledge of this will aid the collector in identifying watches as well as determining age.

"**Remington Watch Co.**"-marked on movement and case, made by N.Y. Standard Watch Co., 16 size, 11 jewels.

"**E.F. Randolph**"-marked on movement, made by Illinois Watch Co., 23j, hunting, model No. 4.

16 size, No. 390, made by New York Standard Watch Co. Watch. Same model as above.

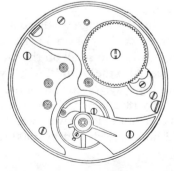

Model 4, 16 size, made by Illinois Watch Co. Same model as above.

In order to establish the true manufacturer of the movement, one must study the construction, taking note of the shape of the balance, shape of the plates, location of jewels, etc. Compare each company in this volume until the manufacturer is located. The best place to start is at the Hamilton and Illinois sections because these two companies made most of the personalized watches.

After the correct manufacturer has been determined, the serial number can be used to determine the age. Taking the age, grade, size, and manufacturer into consideration, the approximate value can be determined by comparing similar watches from the parent company. If a jeweler's name and location are on the watch, this particular watch will command a higher price in that area.

SWISS IMPORTED FAKES

Before 1871 a flood of pocket watches were made which had names strikingly similar to many well-known American watches. These were made in foreign countries—as well as in America—and looked and sounded like high quality watches. But they were fakes, inferior in quality.

These key-wind imitations of American pocket watches are a fascinating and inexpensive watch type that would make a good collection. The watches closely resembled the ones they were intended to emulate. Names such as "Hampton Watch Company" might fool the casual buyer into thinking he had purchased a watch from Hampden. "Rockville Watch Co." could easily be mistaken for the American Rockford Watch Co. Initials were also used such as H. W. Co., R. W. Co., and W. W. Co., making it even harder to determine the true identity.

In 1871 Congress passed a law requiring all watches to be marked with the country of origin. The Swiss tried to get around this by printing "Swiss" so small on the movement that it was almost impossible to see. Also the word "Swiss" was printed on the top of the scroll or on a highly engraved area of the movement, making it difficult to spot.

By 1885 these Swiss imitations were of better quality and resembled even more closely what was popular in America. But the Swiss fakes did not succeed, and by 1900 they were no longer being sold here.

Example of a Swiss imported fake. Note misspelled signature "P.S. Barrett." The authentic American Waltham watch is spelled "P.S. Bartlett."

Example of a Swiss imported fake. Note similarity to E. Howard & Co. watches.

HOW TO IDENTIFY A SWISS FAKE

1. At first they were keywind and keyset; then they became stem wind, full plate, about 18 size, large jewels on the plate side, and used Roman numerals.

2. Most had American-sounding names so close to the original that it looks merely like a misspelling.

3. The material was often crudely finished with very light gilding.

4. The dial used two feet; American watches used three.

5. The balance wheel was made to look like a compensated balance, but it was not.

6. The large flat capped jewels were blue in color.

These characteristics are not present with all imported fakes. Some or none of these factors may be present. The later the date, the more closely the fake resembled the American watch.

AMERICAN
POCKET WATCHES

AMERICAN LISTINGS
Pricing at Retail Level
(Complete Watches Only)

Watches listed in this book are priced at the retail level and as complete watches, having an original 14k gold-filled case with an original white enamel single sunk dial. The entire original movement is in good working order with no repairs needed, unless otherwise noted. Watches listed as 14k and 18k are solid gold cases. Coin or silveroid-type and stainless steel cases will be listed as such. Keywind and keyset watches are listed as having original coin silver cases. Dollar-type watches or low cost production watches are listed as having a base metal type case and a composition dial. Wrist watches are priced as having original gold-filled case with the movement being all original and in good working order, and the wrist watch band being made of leather except where bracelet is described.

Many of the watch manufacturers were commissioned to put jewelers' or jobbers' names on their movements in place of their own. Due to this practice, the true manufacturers of these movements are difficult to identify. These watch models are listed under the original manufacturer and can be identified by comparison with the model sections under each manufacturer. See "Personalized Watches" for more detailed information.

The prices shown were averaged from dealers' lists just prior to publication and are an indication of the retail level or what collectors will pay. Prices are provided in three categories: average condition, extra fine, and mint condition, and are shown in whole dollar amounts only. The values listed are a guide for the retail level and are provided for your information only. Dealers will not necessarily pay full retail price. Prices listed are for watches with **original** cases and dials.

Note: Descriptions and serial number ranges listed for early watches cannot be considered 100 percent accurate due to the manner in which records were kept by these companies.

WARNING: It has been reported to us that 24 Jeweled watches are being faked, especially in Illinois and Rockford watches. One method known is the altering of the number 21 on the movement to a 24. Before buying a 24 Jewel watch, compare the movement with a known 24 Jewel.

INFORMATION NEEDED—We are interested in any facts and information you might have that should possibly be considered for future editions. Documented facts are needed, so please send photo or sources of information. Send to: Cooksey Shugart, 780 Church Street N.E., Cleveland, Tennessee 37311. (When corresponding, please include a self-addressed, stamped envelope.)

ABBREVIATIONS USED
IN
THE OFFICIAL® PRICE GUIDE TO WATCHES

★ ★ ★ ★—Extremely rare; less than 20 known to exist.
★ ★ ★—Rare; less than 100 known to exist.
★ ★—Scarce; less than 500 known to exist.
★—Uncommon; less than 2,500 known to exist.
ADJ—Adjusted (to temperature, heat and cold, also isochronism)
BASE—Base metal used in cases; e.g., silveroid
BC—Box case
BRG—Bridge plate design movement
COIN—Coin silver
DB—Double back
DES—Diamond end stones
DMK—Damaskeened
DS—Double sunk dial
DR—Double roller
DWT—Penny weight: 1/20 Troy ounce
ETP—Estimated total production
EX—Extra nice; far above average
FULL—Full plate design movement
    ¾—¾ plate design movement
    1F brg—One finger bridge design and a ¾ plate (see Illinois 16s M#5)
    2F brg—Two finger bridge design
    3F brg—Three finger bridge design
GF—Gold filled
GJS—Gold jewel settings
G#—Grade number
GT—Gold train (gold gears)
GCW—Gold center wheel
GRO—Good running order
HC—Hunter case
HCI_P—Adjusted to heat, cold, isochronism, and positions; e.g., HCI5P
HL—Hairline crack
J—Jewel (as 21J)
K—Karat (as 14k solid gold—not gold filled)
KS—Key set
KW—Key wind
KW/SW—(Key wind/stem wind) transition

LS—Lever set
MCBC—Multi-color box case
MCC—Multi-color case
MCD—Multi-color dial
MD—Montgomery type dial
M#—Model number
Mvt. Only—Dial and movement only; no case
NI—Nickel plates or frames
OF—Open face
P—Position (5 positions adj)
PS—Pendant set
RGP—Rolled gold plate
RR—Railroad
RRA—Railroad approved
RRG—Railroad grade
S—Size
SBB—Screw back and bezel
SRC—Swing ring case
SS—Stainless steel
SW—Stem wind
S#—Serial number
TEMP—Temperature
TP—Total production
2T—Two-tone
WGF—White gold filled
WI—Wind indicator (also as up and down indicator)
WW—Wrist watch
YGF—Yellow gold filled

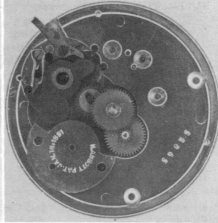

Abbott Stem Wind Attachment. Left: Normal view of an Illinois watch movement with 'hidden' Abbott Stem Wind Attachment (pat. Jan., 18th, 1881). Right: Same watch with dial removed exposing the Abbott Stem Wind Attachment. Serial number 52045. Add $100 to $250 to value of watch with this attachment.

ABBOTT'S STEM WIND
HENRY ABBOTT

Henry Abbott first patented his stem wind attachment on June 30, 1876. The complete Abbott's stem wind mechanism is arranged in such a way as to convert key wind to stem wind. He also made a repeater-type slide mechanism for winding. On January 18, 1881, he received a patent for an improved stem wind attachment. On the new model the watch could be wound with the crown. Abbott sold over 50,000 of these stem-wind attachments, and many of them were placed on Waltham, Elgin, and Illinois watches.

ABBOTT WATCH CO.
(MADE BY HOWARD WATCH CO.)
1908 - 1912

Abbott Sure Time Watches were made by the E. Howard Watch Co. (Keystone), and are similar to Howard Watch Co. 1905 model. These watches sold for $8.75 and had 17 jewels. The open face watches are actually hunting case models without the second bits register.

Description	Avg	Ex-Fn	Mint
Abbott Sure Time, 16S, 17J, ¾, OF, GF Case	$150	$225	$300
Abbott Sure Time, 16S, 17J, ¾, HC, GF Case	200	275	350
Abbott Sure Time, 16S, 17J, ¾, OF or HC, Coin	175	250	325
Abbott Sure Time, 16S, 17J, ¾, Silveroid...............	100	175	250
Abbott Sure Time, 16S, 17J, ¾, 18K, HC	450	500	600
Abbott Sure Time, 16S, 17J, ¾, 14K, HC	550	600	700

Example of **Abbott Watch Co.**, 16 size, 17 jewels, gold jeweled settings, hunting case. Note similarity to the Howard Watch Co. model 1905. Serial number 993932.

Example of **Abbott Watch Co.**, 16 size, 17 jewels, gold jeweled settings, open face. Note similarity to the Howard Watch Co. series 9.

ADAMS AND PERRY WATCH MANUFACTURING CO.
Lancaster, Pennsylvania
1874 - 1877

This company, like so many others, did not have sufficient capital to stay in business for long. The first year was spent in setting up and becoming incorporated. The building was completed in mid-1875, and watches were being produced by September. The first watches were limited to three grades, and the escapement and balance were bought from other sources. By December 1875, the company was short of money and, by the spring of 1876, they had standardized their movements to 18 size. The first movement went on sale April 7, 1876. The next year the company remained idle. In August 1877 the company was sold to the Lancaster Watch Company, after making only about 800 to 1,000 watches. In 1892 Hamilton acquired the assets.

Description		Avg	Ex-Fn	Mint
20S, 20J, GJS, PS, KW, 18K original case .... ★ ★ ★		$2,000	$2,500	$3,000
18S, 20J, GJS, PS............................. ★ ★ ★		1,000	1,500	2,000
18S, 17J, GJS, PS................................ ★ ★		700	1,200	1,700
18S, 17J, GJS, PS, Coin, Original .... ★ ★		700	1,200	1,700

Example of **Adams & Perry Watch Co.**movement. This basic model consists of 19 jewels, gold jeweled settings, key wind and pendant set, serial number 1681.

Example of **Adams & Perry Watch Co.** movement. This model consists of 20 jewels, gold jeweled settings, stem wind with micrometric regulator, 20 size.

J. H. ALLISON
Detroit, Michigan
1853 - 1890

The first watch J. H. Allison made was in 1853; it was a chronometer with full plate and a fusee with chain drive. The balance had time screws and sliding weights. In 1864, he made a ¾ plate chronometer with gold wheels. He also damaskeened the nickel movement. He produced only about 25 watches, of which 20 were chronometers. By 1883 he was making ¾ plate movements with a stem wind of his own design. Allison made most of his own parts and designed his own tools. He also altered some key wind watches to stem wind. Allison died in 1890.

Description		Avg	Ex-Fn	Mint
Full Plate & ¾ Plate, GT, NI, DMK .... ★ ★		$1,500	$1,800	$2,500
Detent Chronometer Escapement, 21J, KW/KS, GJS ★ ★ ★		3,000	3,500	4,500

AMERICAN REPEATING WATCH CO.
Elizabeth, New Jersey
1885 - 1892

Around 1675, a repeating mechanism was attached to a clock for the first time. The first repeating watch was made about 1687 by Thomas Tompion or Daniel Quare. Five-minute, quarter-hour and half-hour repeaters were popular by 1730. The minute repeater became common about 1830.

Fred Terstegen applied for a patent on August 21, 1882, for a repeating attachment that would work with any American key-wind or stem-wind watch. He was granted three patents: No. 311,270 on January 27, 1885; No. 3,421,844 on February 18, 1890; and No. 3,436,162 in September 1890. Waltham was the only watch company to fabricate repeating watches in America. It is not known how many repeaters were made, but it is estimated to be from 1,300 to 3,000.

Add $1,000 to $2,000 to value of a watch with this attachment.

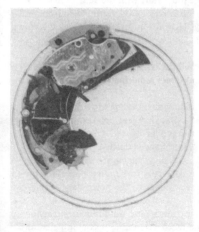 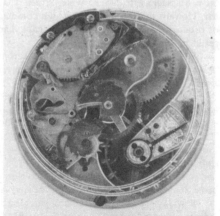

American Repeating Attachment. Illustration at left shows Terstegen's patented repeating attachment only. Illustration at right shows attachment as normally found on movement. The two outside circles on left illustration are wire gongs. The hammer can be seen at upper right.

THE AMERICAN WALTHAM WATCH CO.
1851 - 1957

   To trace the roots of the Waltham family one must start with the year 1850 in Roxbury, Massachusetts, No. 34 Water Street. That fall David Davis, a Mr. Dennison, and Mr. Howard together formed a watch company. Howard and Dennison had a dream of producing watches with interchangeable parts that were less expensive and did not result in less quality.

   Howard served an apprenticeship to Aaron Willard Jr. in about 1829. Several years later, in 1842, Howard formed a clock and balance scale manufacturing company with Davis.

   Howard and Dennison combined their ideas and, with financing provided by Samuel Curtis, the first of their watches was made in 1850. But they had problems. They were trying out ideas such as using jewels, making dials, and producing steel with mirror finishes. This required all new machinery and resulted in a great financial burden. They discovered, too, that although all watches were produced on the same machines and of the same style, each watch was individual with its own set of errors to be corrected. This they had not anticipated. It took months to adjust the watches to the point they were any better than any other timepieces on the market.

   But Howard had perfected and patented many automatic watchmaking machines that produced precision watch parts. In 1851 the factory building was completed and the name American Horologe Company was chosen. It was not until late 1852 that the first watches were completed bearing the signature "The Warren Mfg. Co.," after a famed Revolutionary War hero. The first 17 watches were not placed on the market but went to officials of the company. Watches numbered 18 through 110 were marked "Warren...Boston;" the next 800 were marked "Samuel Curtis;" a few were marked "Fellows & Schell" and sold for $40.

The name was changed to the Boston Watch Company in September 1853, and a factory was built in Waltham, Massachusetts, in October 1854. The movements that were produced here carried serial numbers 1,001 to 5,000 and were marked "Dennison, Howard & Davis," "C. T. Parker," and "P. S. Bartlett."

Boston Watch Company failed in 1857 and was sold at a sheriff's auction to Royal E. Robbins. In May 1857, it was reorganized as the Appleton, Tracy & Co., and the watches produced carried serial numbers 5,001 to 14,000, model 1857. The first movements were marked Appleton, Tracy & Co. The C. T. Parker was introduced as model 1857 and sold for $12. 399 of these models were made. Also 598 chronodrometers were produced and in January 1858 the P. S. Bartlett watch was made.

Example of a **Warren** model, 18 size, 15 jewels, serial number 44. Note: This movement was made for an English case and will not fit a standard 18 size American case.

Example of a **Samuel Curtis** model, 18 size, 15 jewels, serial number 112. This movement was also made for an English case.

In January 1859 the Waltham Improvement Co. and the Appleton, Tracy & Co. merged to form the American Watch Company. In 1860, as Lincoln was elected president and the country was in Civil War, the American Watch Co. was faced with serious problems. The next year, business came to a standstill. There seemed to be little hope of finding a market for watches, and bankruptcy again seemed close at hand. At this point it was decided to cut expenditures to the lowest possible figure and keep the factory in operation.

American horology owes much to members of the Waltham Watch group such as Bacon, Church, Dennison, Fogg, Howard Marsh, Webster, and Woerd, who contributed much to its development and success.

In early 1861, the name "J. Watson" appeared on model 1857 (first run: Nos. 23,601 to 24,300—total production 1,200).

The next model 1857 was the "R. E. Robbins" of which 2,800 were made.

The William Ellery, marked "Wm. Ellery," (model 1857) was then introduced with the first serial number of 46,201. It was key wind and key set and had 7 to 15 jewels.

A size 10 woman's watch was marketed with first serial numbers of 44,201. It was key wind and key set, ¾ plate, 13 to 15 jewels. Some were marked "P S Bartlett" and a 15 jewel was marked "Appleton, Tracy & Co."

A special model, 10 size, serial numbers of 45,801 to 46,200, is extremely rare.

The first stem wind, beginning with serial number 410,698, was produced in 1868. By 1880 all watches were quick train.

The last key wind was serial No. 22,577,000, about 1919, 18 size, 1883 model, 7J, sterling, produced for export.

WALTHAM ESTIMATED SERIAL NUMBERS AND PRODUCTION DATES

Date	Serial No.	Date	Serial No.	Date	Serial No.
1852	50	1888	3,800,000	1924	24,550,000
1853	400	1889	4,200,000	1925	24,800,000
1854	1,000	1890	4,700,000	1926	25,200,000
1855	2,500	1891	5,200,000	1927	26,100,000
1856	4,000	1892	5,800,000	1928	26,400,000
1857	6,000	1893	6,300,000	1929	26,900,000
1858	10,000	1894	6,700,000	1930	27,100,000
1859	15,000	1895	7,100,000	1931	27,300,000
1860	20,000	1896	7,450,000	1932	27,550,000
1861	30,000	1897	8,100,000	1933	27,750,000
1862	45,000	1898	8,400,000	1934	28,100,000
1863	65,000	1899	9,000,000	1935	28,600,000
1864	110,000	1900	9,500,000	1936	29,100,000
1865	180,000	1901	10,200,000	1937	29,400,000
1866	260,000	1902	11,100,000	1938	29,750,000
1867	330,000	1903	12,100,000	1939	30,050,000
1868	410,000	1904	13,500,000	1940	30,250,000
1869	460,000	1905	14,300,000	1941	30,750,000
1870	500,000	1906	14,700,000	1942	31,050,000
1871	540,000	1907	15,500,000	1943	31,400,000
1872	590,000	1908	16,400,000	1944	31,700,000
1873	680,000	1909	17,600,000	1945	32,100,000
1874	730,000	1910	17,900,000	1946	32,350,000
1875	810,000	1911	18,100,000	1947	32,750,000
1876	910,000	1912	18,200,000	1948	33,100,000
1877	1,000,000	1913	18,900,000	1949	33,500,000
1878	1,150,000	1914	19,500,000	1950	33,560,000
1879	1,350,000	1915	20,000,000	1951	33,600,000
1880	1,500,000	1916	20,500,000	1952	33,700,000
1881	1,670,000	1917	20,900,000	1953	33,800,000
1882	1,835,000	1918	21,800,000	1954	34,100,000
1883	2,000,000	1919	22,500,000	1955	34,450,000
1884	2,350,000	1920	23,400,000	1956	34,700,000
1885	2,650,000	1921	23,900,000	1957	35,000,000
1886	3,000,000	1922	24,100,000		
1887	3,400,000	1923	24,300,000		

The above list is provided for determining the approximate age of your watch. Match serial number with date.

20 SIZE
MODEL 1862,-20-KW
T. P. 3,500

Grade or Name — Description	Avg	Ex-Fn	Mint
American Watch Co., 19J, KW, 18K, HC, all original ★★	$3,500	$4,000	$5,500
American Watch Co., 15 & 17J, KW, KS, ¾, vibrating hairspring stud, silver case...................★★	700	1,000	1,500
American Watch Co., 15 & 17J, KW, KS, ¾, vibrating hairspring stud, 18K HC, all original...........★★	3,500	4,000	5,500
American Watch Co., 15 & 17J, ¾, KW, ADJ........★	300	500	750
American Watch Co., 19J, ¾, KW, ADJ...........★★	2,000	2,500	3,000
American Watch Co., 19J, ¾, KW, ADJ, with Maltese cross stopwork, all original...................★★	2,500	3,000	3,600
American W. Co., 15J, ¾, KW.....................★	300	450	600
American W. Co., 7-11J, ¾, KW...................★	250	400	550
American W. Co., 19J, ¾, KW, Stratons Pat. Barrel ★★	2,000	2,500	3,500
American W. Co., Nashua S# under dial, below 51,000 ....★★★	3,500	4,500	5,500
American W. Co., Woerd's Pat., Cam Reg........★★★	2,200	2,500	3.300
Am'n W. Co., 15J, KW, ¼, coin case...............★	300	375	450
Am'n W. Co., 15J, KW, ¾, Mvt. only................	100	125	175
Appleton, Tracy & Co., 15J, ¾, KW, with Maltese cross stopwork, all original...........................★	500	600	750
Appleton, Tracy & Co., 15 & 17J, ¾, KW, ADJ, gold balance...★	450	550	700
Appleton, Tracy & Co., 15 & 17J, ¾, KW..............	250	400	550
Appleton, Tracy & Co., 15 & 17J, ¾, KW, vibrating hairspring stud, silver case........................★★	600	900	1,400
Appleton, Tracy & Co., 15 & 17J, ¾, KW, vibrating hairspring stud, 18K HC........................★★★	1,800	2,300	2,800
Appleton Tracy & Co., 15J, KW, ¾, Mvt. only.........	100	125	175
Appleton Tracy & Co., 15J, KW, Vibrating hairspring stud, Straton barrel, Fuggs Pat.................★★	600	1,000	1,200

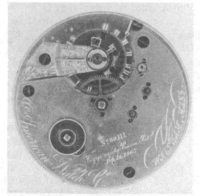

American Watch Co., Model 1862, 20 size, 17 jewels, gold balance and escape wheel, gold jeweled settings, key wind, key set from back, serial number 80111.

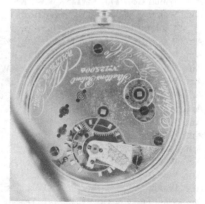

Appleton Tracy & Co., Model20KW, 20 size, 15 jewels, serial number 125004. Note vibrating hairspring stud.

American Watch Co., Model 18KW, 17 jewels, reversible center pinion, patented Nov. 30th, 1858, serial number 36369.

Model 1857, 18 size, 16 jewels, "Chronodrometer" on dial, "Appleton Tracy & Co." or "P.S. Bartlett on back plate, key wind & set.

18 SIZE
MODELS 1857, 18KW, 1862, 1870, 1877, 1879, 1883, 1892

Grade or Name — Description	Avg	Ex-Fn	Mint
American Watch Co., 17J, ¾, KW, M#18KW ..... ★★★	$1,400	$1,700	$2,200
American Watch Co., 19J, M#18KW, ¾ .... ★★	1,600	1,900	2,400
American Watch Co., 19J, M#1883, HC, silver ...... ★★	800	1,000	1,400
American Watch Co., 17J, M#1883....................	75	100	150
American Watch Co., 21J, M#1883, ADJ, GJS	125	150	225
American Watch Co., 15J, M#18KW, ¾, Pat. Nov. 30, 1858, reverse pinion, original silver case...... ★★★	3,000	3,500	4,000
American Watch Co., 17j, M–18KW, ¾, KW, Fitts Pat. Reversing Pinion, Originial 18K case................	4,000	5,000	6,000
American Watch Co., 15J, M#1870, KW................	200	250	350
Am. Watch Co., 15J, M#1857, KW, KS	75	100	150
Am. Watch Co., 17J, M#1857, KW, KS .... ★	200	250	350
Am. Watch Co., 14K, HC, heavy box hinged, multi-color, (4 colors).....................................	2,000	2,200	2,800
Am. Watch Co., 11J, thin model, KW, ¾ plate .... ★	175	275	400
Am. Watch Co., 15 & 17J, M#1870, KW, ADJ	150	200	300
Am. Watch Co., 11J, M#1883, SW or KW..............	50	75	125
Am. Watch Co., 17J, M#1892, LS	75	100	150
Am. Watch Co., 17J, M#1892, PS	75	100	150
Am. Watch Co., 21J, M#1892, LS	100	125	200
Am. Watch Co., 21J, M#1892, PS	100	125	200
Am. Watch Co., 7J, M#1877	50	75	100
Am. Watch Co., 7J, M#1883, KW	75	100	150
Am. Watch Co., 11J, M#1877	50	75	100
Am. Watch Co., 11J, M#1883, KW	75	100	150
Am. Watch Co., 15J, M#1857, SW.................... ★	200	300	450
Appleton, Tracy & Co., 15J, M#1857, SW	100	125	175
Appleton, Tracy & Co., 7-11J, KW, M#1857	125	150	200

Grade or Name—Description	Avg	Ex-Fn	Mint
Appleton, Tracy & Co., 15J, M#18KW, ¾, reverse pinion, Pat. Nov. 30, 1858, orig. silver case ... ★★★	$1,000	$1,200	$1,500
Appleton, Tracy & Co., KW, ¾ .... ★	275	350	450
Appleton, Tracy & Co., 11J, thin model, KW, ¾ ...... ★	225	350	450
Appleton, Tracy & Co., 15J, ¾, KW, with vibrating hairspring stud, Fuggs Pat., coin case .... ★★★★	1,250	1,500	1,800
Appleton, Tracy & Co., 15J, ¾, KW, with vibrating hairspring stud, orig. 18K case .... ★★★	1,200	1,500	2,000
Appleton, Tracy & Co., Sporting,(Chronodrometer) M#1857, 16J, KW, KS, orig. case, with stop feature ★★	1,500	2,000	2,500
Appleton, Tracy & Co., 15J, ¾, KW, Fitts Pat., pinion .... ★★	400	500	600
Appleton, Tracy & Co., 15J, ¾, KW .... ★	150	200	285
Appleton, Tracy & Co., 15J, M#1857, KW, 18K	600	700	1,000
Appleton, Tracy & Co., 15J, M#1857, KW	100	125	175
Appleton, Tracy & Co., 11J, M#s 1877, 1879, SW	50	75	100
Appleton, Tracy & Co., 17J, M#1892, SW, Premiere	75	100	150
Appleton, Tracy & Co., 15J, M#1892, SW, OF	60	85	100
Appleton, Tracy & Co., 17J, M#1892, SW, OF	70	95	125
Appleton, Tracy & Co., 19J, M#1892, SW, OF	85	115	150
Appleton, Tracy & Co., 21J, M#1892, SW, OF	90	125	175
Appleton, Tracy & Co., 15J, M#1883, SW, OF	50	65	90
Appleton, Tracy & Co., 15J, M#1877, KW	60	75	110
Appleton, Tracy & Co., 15J, M#1879, SW, OF	50	65	90
Appleton, Tracy & Co., 17J, M#1883, OF	60	80	100
Appleton, Tracy & Co., 17J, M#1892, SW, HC..........	75	100	150
Appleton, Tracy & Co., 19J, M#1892, SW, HC..........	100	125	175
Appleton, Tracy & Co., 21J, M#1892, SW, HC..........	100	125	175
Appleton, Tracy & Co., 15J, M#1883, SW, HC..........	75	100	150
Appleton, Tracy & Co., 15J, M#1879, SW, HC..........	75	100	150
Appleton, Tracy & Co., 17J, M#1883, SW, HC..........	75	100	150

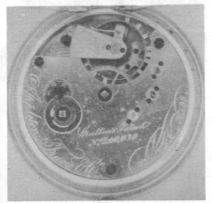

Appleton, Tracy & Co. 18 size, 15 jewels, with vibrating hairspring stud, key wind & set from back, serial number 140030.

P.S. Bartlett, Model 18KW, 18 size, 11 jewels, key wind & set from back, serial number 41597.

Grade or Name—Description	Avg	Ex-Fn	Mint
A. W. W. Co., 7J, M#1883, SW, OF	$35	$45	$75
A. W. W. Co., 11J, M#1883, SW, OF	35	45	75
A. W. W. Co., 7J, M#1883, KW, OF	50	75	125
A. W. W. Co., 11J, M#1879, OF	35	45	75
A. W. W. Co., 15J, M#1879, OF	50	60	90
A. W. W. Co., 11J, M#1883, OF	35	45	75
A. W. W. Co., 15J, M#1883, OF	45	55	85
A. W. W. Co., 17J, M#1892, LS, OF	80	90	135
A. W. W. Co., 17J, M#1892, PS, OF	70	80	125
A. W. W. Co., 17J, M#1892, HC	75	100	150
A. W. W. Co., 19J, M#1892	90	115	160
A. W. W. Co., 21J, M#1892	100	125	175
A. W. W. Co., 17J, "for R.R. Service" on dial	200	250	350
A. W. W. Co., 15J, OF	50	60	90
A. W. W. Co., 15J, 14K multi-color boxcase HC	1,500	2,000	2,500
A. W. W. Co., 11J, LS, HC	75	100	150
A. W. W. Co., 15J, HC	75	100	150

P.S. Bartlett, 18 size, 15 jewels, Model 1857, Engraved on back "4 PR. Jewels." Serial number 13446.

Canadian Railway Time Service, Model 1892, 18 size, 17 jewels, serial number 22,017,534.

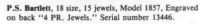

Grade or Name—Description	Avg	Ex-Fn	Mint
P. S. Bartlett, 7J, M#1857, KW, 1st Run	$200	$225	$325
P. S. Bartlett, 11J, M#1857, KW, 1st Run	200	225	325
P. S. Bartlett, 11J, M#1857, KW, 2nd-3rd Run	75	100	125
P. S. Bartlett, 15J, M#1857, KW, 2nd-3rd Run	100	125	150
P. S. Bartlett, 11J, LS, HC, 14K	550	650	850
P. S. Bartlett, 15J, M#1857, KW, below S#5000	200	225	325
P. S. Bartlett, 11J, M#1879, KW	50	75	125
P. S. Bartlett, 11J, M#1857, KW, Eagle inside case lid	125	150	175
P. S. Bartlett, 15J, M#1879, KW	75	100	150

Grade or Name—Description	Avg	Ex-Fn	Mint
P. S. Bartlett, 15J, M#1879, SW	$55	$65	$80
P. S. Bartlett, 11-15J, M#1870, SW	75	85	100
P. S. Bartlett, 11-15J, M#1877, KW	100	125	175
P. S. Bartlett, 11J, M#1883, SW	50	70	100
P. S. Bartlett, 15J, M#1883, KW......................	75	100	150
P. S. Bartlett, 17J, M#1883, SW	50	70	100
P. S. Bartlett, 15J, M#1883, SW	50	70	100
P. S. Bartlett, 11J, M#18KW, ¾, thin model, KS from back	275	350	450
P. S. Bartlett, 11J, M#18KW, ¾, Pat. Nov. 30, 1858	400	500	675
P. S. Bartlett, 15J, pinned plates, KW	300	350	425
P. S. Bartlett, 15J, M#1892, SW	65	75	100
P. S. Bartlett, 17J, M#1892, SW, OF, LS	75	85	110
P. S. Bartlett, 17J, M#1892, SW, HC	125	150	175
P. S. Bartlett, 17J, M#1892, SW, OF, PS	75	80	110
P. S. Bartlett, 17J, M#1892, SW, 2-Tone	85	95	120
P. S. Bartlett, 19J, M#1892, SW	95	105	130
P. S. Bartlett, 21J, M#1892, SW	95	105	140
P. S. Bartlett, 21J, M#1892, SW, 2-Tone	100	115	150
Broadway, 7J, M#1857, KW, HC	75	100	150
Broadway, 11J, M#1857, KW, HC	75	100	150
Broadway, 11J, M#1877, KW, SW, NI, HC	75	100	150
Broadway, 7J, M#1883, KW, HC	75	100	150
Broadway, 11J, M#1883, KW, HC	75	100	150
Broadway, 11J, M#1883, SW, HC......................	75	100	150
Canadian Railway Time Service, 17J, M#1892, Adj.5P ...	300	375	450
Central Park, 15J, M#1857, KW	150	175	225
Champion, 15J, M#1877, OF	50	75	100
Crescent Park, 15J M#1857............................	150	175	225
Crescent Street, 15J, M#1870, KW	150	200	225
Crescent Street, 17J, M#1870, KW .... ★	275	375	500

Crescent Street, Model 1870, 18 size, 15 jewels, series A, Key wind & set from back, serial number 520,206.

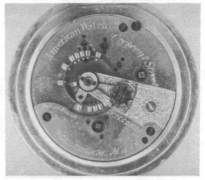

Crescent Street, Model 1870, 18 size, 15 jewels, series B, Key wind & set from back, serial number 552,526.

Grade or Name—Description	Avg	Ex-Fn	Mint
Crescent Street, 15J, M#1870, SW......................	$125	$150	$200
Crescent Street, 15J, M#1883, SW, non-magnetic, OF	100	150	200
Crescent Street, 15J, M#1883, SW, non-magnetic, HC	100	125	175
Crescent Street, 15J, M#1883, SW, 2-Tone	100	125	175
Crescent Street, 17J, M#1883, SW, OF	75	100	150
Crescent Street, 17J, M#1883, SW, HC	100	125	175
Crescent Street, 19J, M#1883 .... ★	200	275	325
Crescent Street, 17J, M#1892, SW, GJS.................	100	125	175
Crescent Street, 17J, M#1892, SW, OF	75	100	135
Crescent Street, 17J, M#1892, SW, HC	100	125	175
Crescent Street, 19J, M#1892, SW, Adj.5P, GJS	100	125	175
Crescent Street, 21J, M#1892, SW, Adj.5P, GJS	100	125	175
Crescent Street, 21J, M#1892, Wind Indicator	800	1,000	1,300
Crescent Street, 19J, M#1899, SW, OF	75	100	150
Crescent Street, 19J, M#1899, SW, HC	100	125	175
Crescent Street, 21J, M#1899, GJS, OF	100	125	175
Crescent Street, 21J, M#1899, GJS, HC.................	125	150	200
Samuel Curtis, 11-15J, M#1857, KW, S# less than 200, original 17S silver case .... ★★	2,500	3,000	4,000
Samuel Curtis, 11-15J, M#1857, KW, S# less than 400, original 17S silver case .... ★★	2,300	2,800	3,800
Samuel Curtis, 11-15J, M#1857, KW, S# less than 600, original 17S silver case .... ★★	2,000	2,500	3,500
Samuel Curtis, 11-15J, M#1857, KW, S# less than 1,000, original 17S silver case .... ★★	1,700	2,200	3,200
(Samuel Curtis not in original silver case, deduct $800 to $1,000 from value)			
Dennison, Howard, Davis, 7J, M#1857, KW, orig. case. ★	500	700	1,000
Dennison, Howard, Davis, 11J, M#1857, KW, orig. case ★	700	900	1,200
Dennison, Howard, Davis, 15J, M#1857, KW, orig. case ★	800	1,000	1,300
Dennison, Howard, Davis, 15J, M#1857, KW, S# less than 2,000, original case .... ★★	900	1,100	1,400
Denver & Rio Grande, 21J, M#1892, GJS, Adj.3P	900	1,200	1,500
Dominion Railway, 15J, M#1883, OF, SW, train on dial..	800	1,000	1,200
Wm. Ellery, 7-11J, M#1857, Boston, Mass.	75	100	125
Wm. Ellery, 7-11J, M#1857, KW......................	65	90	110
Wm. Ellery, 7-11J, M#KW, ¾	150	175	250
Wm. Ellery, 15J, KW, ¾	320	380	450
Wm. Ellery, 7-11J, M#18KW, KW-KS from back, 18K HC	1,000	1,200	1,500
Wm. Ellery, 7J, M#1857, KW, KS from back	175	200	275
Wm. Ellery, 15J, M#1857, KW	75	100	150
Wm. Ellery, 15J, M#1857, SW....................... ★	200	300	450
Wm. Ellery, 7-11J, M#1877, KW, M#1879, KW	75	100	150
Wm. Ellery, 11-15J, M#1877, SW	50	75	100
Wm. Ellery, 7-11J, M#1883	50	75	100
Excelsior, M#1877, KW	80	95	140
Export, 7-11J, M#1877.............................	50	75	120
Export, 7-11J, M#1883, KW	75	100	150
Favorite, 15J, M#1877	75	100	150

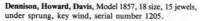

Dennison, Howard, Davis, Model 1857, 18 size, 15 jewels, under sprung, key wind, serial number 1205.

Howard & Rice, Model 1857, 18 size, 15 jewels, under sprung, serial number 6003.

Grade or Name—Description	Avg	Ex-Fn	Mint
Fellows & Schell, 15J, KW, KS .... ★ ★ ★	$1,500	$1,700	$2,000
Franklin, 7J, M#1877, SW	125	150	200
Home Watch Co., 7-11J, M#1857, KW	75	100	125
Home Watch Co., 7J, M#1877, KW	75	100	125
Home Watch Co., 7-11J, M#1879, SW	75	100	125
Howard, Davis & Dennison, S#1-17 .... ★ ★ ★ ★	30,000	40,000	50,000
Howard & Rice, 15J, M#1857, KW, KS (serial numbers range from 6000 to 6500)...................... ★ ★	1,200	1,400	1,700
E. Howard & Co., Boston (on dial & mvt.), English style escape wheel, upright pallets, 15J, M#1857, KW, KS, S#s about 6,400 to 6,500 .... ★ ★ ★	2,500	2,800	3,500
Martyn Square, 7-11J, M#1857, KW, SW (exported)	125	150	200
Mermod, Jaccard & King—Paragon Timekeeper, 23J, M#1892, Vanguard, LS, GJS, HC..................	200	250	300

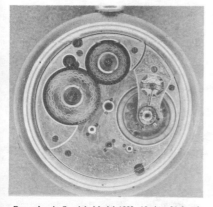

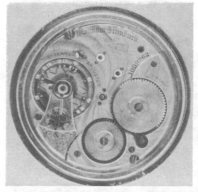

Pennsylvania Special, Model 1892, 18 size, 21 jewels, serial number 14,000,015.

Railroad, Model 1892, 18 size, 19 jewels, Adj5P, open face, note engine & coal car engraved on movement, serial number 10,099,625.

Grade or Name—Description	Avg	Ex-Fn	Mint
Non-Magnetic, 15J, SW, LS, NI	$100	$125	$175
Non-Magnetic, 17J, M#1892, SW, LS..................	125	150	200
Paragon, 15J, M#1883, HC	100	125	175
C. T. Parker, 7J, M#1857, KW, 14K, HC.......... ★ ★	1,200	1,400	1,800
Pennsylvania R.R. on dial, Appleton, Tracy & Co. on Mvt.,			
KW, KS...................................... ★ ★	400	500	700
Pennsylvania Special, 21J, M#1892, HC.......... ★ ★ ★	1,400	1,700	2,000
Pennsylvania Special, 21J, M#1892, OF .... ★ ★ ★	1,200	1,500	1,800
Pioneer, 7J, M#1883..................................	50	75	100
Premier, 17J, M#1892, LS, OF	125	150	175
Railroad, 17J, M#1892, LS	200	250	350
Railroad, 21J, M#1892, LS	250	300	400
Railroader, 17J, M#1892, LS .... ★ ★	500	600	800
Railroad King, 15J, M#1883, LS	200	250	350
Railroad King, 15J, M#1883, 2-Tone	250	300	400
Railroad King, 17J, Special, M#1883, LS...............	250	300	400
Railroad Watches with R.R. names on dial and movement			
as follows:			
Canadian Pacific R.R., 17J, M#1883	225	275	325
Canadian Pacific R.R., 17J, M#1892	350	450	550
Canadian Pacific R.R., 21J, M#1892	400	500	600
Santa Fe Route, 17J, M#1883.....................	350	450	550
Santa Fe Route, 17J, M#1892.................... ★	500	600	750
Riverside, 7J, M#1857	100	125	175
Riverside, 17J, M#1892 .... ★	300	350	450
Roadmaster, 17J, M#1892, LS .... ★	300	350	450
R. E. Robbins, 11J, M#1857, KW.................... ★	400	450	550
R. E. Robbins, 15J, M#1877, KW.....................	200	250	350
R. E. Robbins, 13J, M#1883..........................	100	125	175

Sidereal, model –1892, 17j, 24 hour dial used by astronomers.

Vanguard, Model 1892, 18 size, 23 jewels, diamond end stone, gold jewel settings, exposed winding gears, serial number 10,533,465.

Grade or Name—Description	Avg	Ex-Fn	Mint
Sol, 7J, M#1883, OF	$50	$75	$100
Sol, 17J, OF, PS	75	100	125
Special Railroad, 17J, M#1883, LS, OF	300	350	450
Special R. R. King, 15J, M#1883	300	350	450
Sterling, 7J, M#1857, KW, Silver	100	125	150
Sterling, 7-11J, M#1877, M#1879	50	75	100
Sterling, 7-11J, M#1883, KW	50	75	100
Sterling, 11J, M#1883, SW	50	75	100
Tourist, 11J, M#1877	50	75	100
Tourist, 7J, M#1877	50	75	100
Tracy, Baker & Co., 15J, 18K original A.W.W. Co. case ★★★★	3,000	3,500	4,500
Vanguard, 17J, M#1892, GJS, HC ★★★	400	500	650
Vanguard, 17J, M#1892, LS, Adj.5P, DR, GJS, OF.. ★★	300	400	550
Vanguard, 17J, M#1892, Wind Indicator, Adj.5P, DR, GJS	800	1,000	1,200
Vanguard, 19J, M#1892, LS, Adj.5P, Diamond end stones	125	150	200
Vanguard, 19J, M#1892, LS, Adj.5P, DR, GJS, OF	125	150	200
Vanguard, 19J, M#1892, Wind Indicator, LS, Adj.5P, DR, GJS	1,000	1,200	1,400
Vanguard, 19J, M#1892, Adj.5P, GJS, HC ★	250	350	450
Vanguard, 21J, M#1892, Adj.5P, PS	100	125	175
Vanguard, 21J, M#1892, HC, GJS, Adj.5P	200	250	300
Vanguard, 21J, M#1892, LS, Adj.5P, DR, GJS, OF	100	125	175
Vanguard, 21J, M#1892, LS, Adj.5P, Diamond end stone.	125	150	200
Vanguard, 21J, M#1892, Wind Indicator, LS, Adj.5P, DR, GJS ★	1,000	1,200	1,400
Vanguard, 23J, M#1892, LS, Adj.5P, DR, GJS, OF	175	250	350
Vanguard, 23J, M#1892, LS, Adj.5P, DR, GJS, HC	250	325	425
Vanguard, 23J, M#1892, LS, Adj.5P, DR, GJS, Diamond end stone	200	275	375

American Waltham Watch Co., Model 1883, 18 size, 15 jewels, serial number 3,093,425.

845, Model 1892, 18 size, 21 jewels, railroad grade, Adj5p, serial number 15,097,475.

Grade or Name—Description	Avg	Ex-Fn	Mint
Vanguard, 23J, M#1892, PS, Adj.5P, DR, GJS, OF......	$175	$250	$350
Vanguard, 23J, M#1892, Wind Indicator, LS, Adj.5P, DR, GJS .... ★	1,100	1,300	1,600
Warren, 15J, M#1857, KW, KS, S#18-29, original 17S silver case .... ★ ★ ★	18,000	23,000	28,000
Warren, 15J, M#1857, KW, KS, S#30-60, original 17S silver case .... ★ ★ ★	10,000	15,000	18,000
Warren, 15J, M#1857, KW, KS, S#61-90, original 17S silver case .... ★ ★ ★	8,000	13,000	16,000
Warren, 15J, M#1857, KW, KS, S#91-110, original 17S silver case .... ★ ★ ★	6,000	11,000	14,000
(Warren not in original silver case, deduct $1,000 to $2,500)			
George Washington, M#1857, KW	150	175	225
J. Watson, 7J, M#1857, KW, KS, "Boston" .... ★	500	700	1,000
J. Watson, 7-11J, M#1857, KW, KS, "London" .... ★	500	700	1,000
45, 19J, GJS, 2-Tone, HC........................ ★ ★	500	600	800
845, 21J, M#1892, OF	100	125	175
845, 21J, M#1892, HC	200	250	300
820, 825, M#1883	50	75	100
836, 17J, DR, Adj.4P, LS, OF	75	100	125
M#1892, 19J, Sidereal, OF .... ★ ★ ★	1,200	1,500	2,000
M#1892, 17J, Astronomical Sidereal .... ★ ★ ★	1,000	1,300	1,800

Note: Some grades are not included. Their values can be determined by comparing with similar models and grades listed.

American Watch Co., Model 16KW, 16 size, 11-15 jewels, key wind and set from back, serial number 330,635.

American Watch Co., Model 1888, 16 size, 19 jewels, gold jeweled settings, gold train, hunting case. Waltham's highest grade; serial number 5,000,297.

Note: Watches listed in this book are priced at the retail level, as complete watches having an original 14k gold-filled case, an original white enamel single sunk dial, and with the entire original movement in good working order with no repairs needed.

16 SIZE
MODELS 16KW, 1868, 1872, 1888,
1899, 1908, BRIDGE MODEL

Grade or Name — Description	Avg	Ex-Fn	Mint
Am. Watch Co., 11J, M#16KW, KW & KS from back, original silver case .... ★ ★	$400	$450	$575
Am. Watch Co., 15J, M#16KW, KW & KS from back ★ ★	400	450	575
Am. Watch Co., 11J, M#1868, ¾, KW	175	200	250
Am. Watch Co., 15-17J, M#1868, ¾, KW	200	225	275
Am. Watch Co., 15J, M#1872, ¾, SW	100	125	175
Am. Watch Co., 16-17J, M#1872, ¾, SW	150	175	225
Am. Watch Co., 19J, M#1872, ¾, SW	400	500	650
Am. Watch Co., 7-11J, M#1888, ¾, SW	50	75	100
Am. Watch Co., 15J, M#1888, ¾, SW	50	75	100
Am. Watch Co., 17J, M#1899	75	100	125
Am. Watch Co., 7-11J, M#1899	50	75	100
Am. Watch Co., 13J, M#1899	50	75	100
Am. Watch Co. 15-16J, M#1899, HC..................	100	125	175
Am. Watch Co., 15J, M#1899, SW, HC	100	125	175

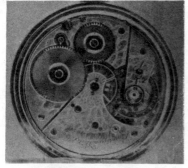

American Watch Co., Model 1888, 16 size, 21 jewels, gold train, note tadpole regulator.

American Watch Co., Bridge Model, 16 size, 23 jewels, gold train, Adj5p.

Grade or Name—Description	Avg	Ex-Fn	Mint
Am. Watch Co., 15J, M#1899, SW, OF	$50	$75	$100
American Watch Co., 19J, M#16KW, Maltese cross stopwork, all original 1860 Model, 18K .... ★ ★	1,500	1,800	2,200
American Watch Co., 17-19J, M#16KW, ¾, KW & KS from back, vibrating hairspring stud, 1860 Model, 18K ★ ★ ★	1,200	1,500	1,900
American Watch Co., 19J, M#16KW, ¾, KW & KS from back, 1860 Model, original case, 18K .... ★ ★ ★	2,000	2,500	3,000
American Watch Co., 15J, M#1868, ¾, KW, Silver .. ★ ★	300	350	475
American Watch Co., 17J, M#1868, ¾, KW, ADJ, Silver ★ ★	400	450	550
American Watch Co., 19J, M#1868, SW, Silver .... ★ ★ ★	450	500	600

Grade or Name—Description	Avg	Ex-Fn	Mint
American Watch Co., 17J, M#1872, ¾, SW, HC, 14K . ★	$900	$1,100	$1,250
American Watch Co., 19J, M#1872, ¾, SW . . . . . . ★ ★ ★	600	700	900
American Watch Co., 19J, M#1872, ¾, GJS, Woerd's Pat. sawtooth balance, all original . . . . ★ ★ ★	2,000	2,500	3,200
American Watch Co., 21J, M#1872, ¾, SW . . . . ★ ★	1,200	1,400	1,550
American Watch Co., 21J, M#1872, ¾, SW, 18K . . ★ ★ ★	1,500	1,800	2,200
American Watch Co., 19J, M#1888, 14K . . . . ★ ★	700	900	1,050
American Watch Co., 19J, M#1888 . . . . ★	300	400	550
American Watch Co., 21J, M#1888, NI, ¾ . . . . ★ ★	400	500	650
American Watch Co., 23J, BRG, Adj.5P, GT, GJS, 14K original case . . . . ★ ★ ★	1,500	2,000	2,500
American Watch Co., 23J, BRG, Adj.5P, GT, GJS, 18K original case . . . . ★ ★ ★	1,800	2,300	2,800
American Watch Co., 23J, BRG, Adj.5P, GT, GJS . . . . ★	900	1,200	1,600
American Watch Co., 21J, BRG, Adj.5P, GT, GJS . . . . ★	500	550	650
American Watch Co., 19J, BRG, Adj.5P, GT, GJS . . . . ★	400	450	550
American Watch Co., 17J, BRG, Adj.5P, GT, GJS . . . . ★	300	350	450
Appleton, Tracy & Co., 15J, M#16KW, ¾, KW & KS from back, all original	400	450	575
Appleton, Tracy & Co., 15J, M#1868, ¾, KW	300	350	450
Appleton, Tracy & Co., 15J, ¾, KW, with vibrating hairspring stud, all original, silver case . . . . ★ ★	600	700	900
Appleton, Tracy & Co., 15J, ¾, KW, with vibrating hairspring stud, 18K, original case . . . . ★ ★	1,200	1,400	1,800
A. W. Co., 7J, M#1872, SW, HC	100	125	175
A. W. Co., 11J, M#1872, SW, HC	100	125	175
A. W. Co., 17J, M#1872, SW, DMK, GJS, DES, HC	200	300	450
A. W. Co., 7J, M#1899, SW DMK	35	45	65
A. W. Co., 9J, SW, NI	40	50	75
A. W. Co., 11J, M#1899, SW	40	50	75
A. W. W. Co., 7J, SW, M#1888	35	45	65
A. W. W. Co., 11J, M#1888	40	50	75

P.S. Bartlett, Model 1899, 16 size, 17 jewels, serial number 10,014,478.

Crescent Street, Model 1899, 16 size, 21 jewels, Adj5p, serial number 16,179,418.

Grade or Name—Description	Avg	Ex-Fn	Mint
A. W. W. Co., 13J, M#1888, OF	$40	$50	$75
A. W. W. Co., 15J, M#1899, OF	40	50	75
A. W. W. Co., 15J, M#1888, SW, HC	50	60	95
A. W. W. Co., 16J, M#1888, SW, OF.................	55	65	100
A. W. W. Co., 16J, M#1899, SW, DMK, HC	65	80	125
A. W. W. Co., 17J, M#1899, SW, OF.................	75	85	100
P. S. Bartlett, 17J, M#1899, OF	55	65	80
P. S. Bartlett, 17J, M#1899, HC	100	125	175
P. S. Bartlett, 17J, M#1908, OF	50	75	100
Bond St., 7J, M#1888	35	45	65
Bond St., 11J, M#1888	55	75	100
Bond St. 15J, M#1888	55	75	100
Bond St., 7J, M#1899	35	45	65
Canadian Railway Time Service, M#1908.............. ★	400	500	650
Crescent St., 19J, M#1899, Adj.5P, LS, OF	75	100	150
Crescent St., 19J, M#1899, Adj.5P, PS, OF	75	100	150
Crescent St., 19J, M#1899, Adj.5P, LS, HC...........	125	150	200
Crescent St., 19J, M#1899, Adj.5P, PS, HC...........	125	150	200
Crescent St., 21J, M#1899, Adj.5P, PS, OF	100	125	150
Crescent St., 21J, M#1899, Adj.5P, LS, OF	100	125	150
Crescent St., 21J, M#1899, Adj.5P, PS, HC...........	125	150	200
Crescent St., 19J, M#1908, Adj.5P, LS, OF	100	125	150
Crescent St., 19J, M#1908, Adj.5P, PS, OF	100	125	150
Crescent St., 21J, M#1908, Adj.5P, LS, OF	100	125	150
Crescent St., 21J, M#1908, Adj.5P, PS, OF	100	125	150
Crescent St., 21J, M#1908, Adj.6P, LS, OF	100	125	150
Crescent St., 21J, M#1908, Adj.5P, PS, HC...........	125	150	200
Crescent St., 21J, M#1908, Adj.5P, LS, Wind Indicator ..	350	400	450
Crescent St., 21J, M#1912, Adj.5P, LS, Wind Indicator ..	350	400	450
Chronometro Superior, 21J, M#1899, LS, OF	125	150	250
Chronometro Victoria, 21J, M#1899, HC	150	175	275
Chronometro Victoria, 15J, M#1899, PS, OF...........	75	100	125
Diamond Express, 17J, M#1888, PS, OF, Diamond End			
Stones .... ★	400	450	525
Electric Railway, 17J, OF, LS, Adj.3P.................	100	125	150
Equity, 7-11J, PS, OF, 16½ Size.....................	45	55	65
Equity, 7-11J, PS, HC, 16½ Size	40	50	75
Equity, 15-17J, PS, OF, 16½ Size....................	55	65	75
Equity, 15-17J, PS, HC, 16½ Size	65	75	90
Hillside, 7J, M#1868, ADJ	100	125	175
Hillside, 7J, M#1868, sweep sec. .... ★ ★	250	300	475
Marquis, 15J, M#1899, PS	65	75	100
Marquis, 15J, M#1908, PS	65	75	100
Non-Magnetic, 15J, NI, HC	135	155	185
Park Road, 16-17J, M#1872, PS	100	120	150

Note: Some grades are not included. Their values can be determined by comparing with similar models or grades listed.

Premier Maximus, "Premier" on movement. "Maximus" on dial, 16 size, 23 jewels (two diamond end stones), open face, pendant set, serial number 17,000,014.

American Waltham Watch Co., 5 minute repeater, 16 size, 16 jewels, ¾ plate, grade 1888, adj, 2 gongs, ca. 1900.

Grade or Name—Description	Avg	Ex-Fn	Mint
Park Road, 11-15J, M#1872, PS	$90	$110	$135
Premier, 9J, M#1908, PS, OF	35	45	70
Premier, 11J, M#1908	40	50	75
Premier, 15J, M#1908, LS, OF	70	85	100
Premier, 17J, M#1908, PS, OF	75	90	105
Premier, 17J, M#1908, PS, OF, Silveroid	45	60	70
Premier, 21J, M#1908, Silveroid	55	75	80
Premier, 21J, M#1908, LS, OF	75	95	125
Premier Maximus, 23J, M#1908, GT, gold case, LS, GJS, Adj.6P, WI, DR, 18K Maximus case, box & papers ★ ★	8,000	9,000	10,000
Premier Maximus, 23J, M#1908, GT, gold case, LS, GJS, Adj.6P, WI, DR, 18K Maximus case, no box.... ★ ★	7,000	8,000	9,000
Premier Maximus, 23J, M#1908, GT, gold case, LS, GJS, Adj.6P, WI, DR, 18K Maximus case, sterling box and papers, extra crystal & mainspring.............. ★ ★	9,000	10,000	11,000
Premier Maximus, 23J, M#1908, GT, YGF recased ... ★ ★	2,000	2,500	3,000
Railroader, 17J, M#1888, LS, NI.................... ★ ★	300	350	535
Railroad King, 17J, 2-Tone......................... ★	195	240	375
Railroad Watches with R. R. names on dial and movement, such as Canadian Pacific RR, Santa Fe Route, etc., M#s 1888, 1899, 1908 .... ★	255	450	750
Repeater, 16J, M#1872, original coin case, 5 min..... ★ ★	2,000	2,500	3,000
Repeater, 16J, M#1888, 5 Min., 14K	2,500	2,800	3,200
Repeater, 16J, M#1872, 5 min., 18K................ ★ ★	3,000	4,000	5,500
Repeater, 16J, M#1872, 5 min., chronograph with register, 18K	4,000	5,000	6,500
Repeater, 1 min. moon phase, M#1872, Perpetual Cal., 18K case, all original .... ★ ★ ★ ★	30,000	35,000	45,000

(Prices are with gold filled cases except where noted.)

Grade or Name—Description	Avg	Ex-Fn	Mint
Riverside, 15J, M#1872, PS, NI, OF....................	$75	$100	$125
Riverside, 15J, M#1872, PS, gilted, OF	75	100	125
Riverside, 16-17J, M#1888, NI, OF, 14K	400	475	600
Riverside, 16-17J, M#1888, NI, OF.....................	75	100	125
Riverside, 17J, M#1888, gilded, OF.....................	75	100	125
Riverside, 15J, M#1888, gilded, OF.....................	75	100	125
Riverside, 17J, M#1888, checker goldtone DMK, raised gold jewel settings, OF...........................	150	175	225
Riverside, 17J, M#1899, LS, DR, OF	75	100	125
Riverside, 17J, M#1899, LS, DR, HC...................	100	125	150
Riverside, 19J, M#1899, LS, DR, OF	100	125	150
Riverside, 19J, M#1899, PS, DR, OF	100	125	150
Riverside, 21J, M#1899, LS, DR, OF	100	125	150
Riverside, 19-21J, M#1908, Adj.5P, LS, DR	100	125	150
Riverside, 19J, M#1908, Adj.5P, PS, DR, OF	100	125	150
Riverside Maximus, 21J, M#1888, LS, ADJ, GJS, GT, DR, HC, GF...................................★★	600	700	850
Riverside Maximus, 21J, M#1888, LS, ADJ, GJS, GT, DR, HC, 14K...................................★★	1,000	1,100	1,250
Riverside Maximus, 21J, M#1899, PS, Adj.5P, GJS, GT, DR	300	400	550
Riverside Maximus, 21J, M#1899, LS, Adj.5P, GJS, GT, DR	350	450	600
Riverside Maximus, 23J, M#1899, LS, Adj.5P, GJS, GT, DR	400	500	650
Riverside Maximus, 23J, M#1908, PS, Adj.5P, GJS, GT, DR	400	500	650
Riverside Maximus, 23J, M#1908, LS, Adj.5P, GJS, GT, DR	400	500	650
Riverside Maximus, 23J, M#1908, PS, Adj.5P, GJS, GT, DR, HC, GF ....★	500	600	750
Riverside Maximus, 23J, M#1908, PS, Adj.5P, GJS, GT, DR, 14K, HC................................★	1,000	1,100	1,250
Riverside Maximus, 21J, M#1888, LS, GT, Diamond end stones, OF ....★★	500	600	750

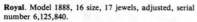

Royal. Model 1888, 16 size, 17 jewels, adjusted, serial number 6,125,840.

Vanguard, Model 1908, 16 size, 23 jewels, diamond end stone, gold jewel settings, exposed winding gears, serial number 11,012,533.

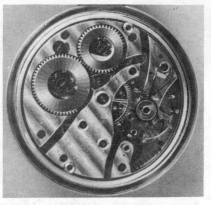

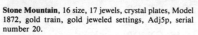

Stone Mountain, 16 size, 17 jewels, crystal plates, Model 1872, gold train, gold jeweled settings, Adj5p, serial number 20.

Vanguard, 16 size, 23 jewels, Adj6p, note pressed-in jewels rather than gold jewel settings. c. 1945.

Grade or Name—Description	Avg	Ex-Fn	Mint
Riverside Maximus, 21J, M#1899,LS,GT,Diamond end stone, OF .... ★	$375	$475	$625
Riverside Maximus, 21J, M#1899, LS, GT, Diamond end stone, HC .... ★	500	600	750
Riverside Maximus, 23J, M#1908, LS, Adj.5P, Wind Indicator .... ★ ★	2,500	3,000	3,500
Roadmaster, 17J, M#1899, LS, OF GJS .... ★	200	250	350
Royal, 15J, M#1872, PS, OF	70	95	120
Royal, 17J, M#1888, PS, OF	75	100	125
Royal, 17J, M#1888, PS, HC	100	125	150
Royal, 17J, M#1899, Adj.3P, OF	65	85	110
Royal, 17J, M#1899, LS, Adj.5P	75	100	125
Royal, 17J, M#1899, PS, Adj.5P	70	95	120
Royal Special, 17J, M#1888	100	125	175
Sol, 7J, M#1888	50	75	100
Sol, 7J, M#1908	50	75	100
Stone Mountain, 17J, M#1872, GT, Crystal plates . ★ ★ ★	5,500	6,000	7,000
Traveler, 7J, M#1888, 1899, 1908	40	50	60
Vanguard, 19J, M#1899, PS, LS, Adj.5P, GJS, DR, OF..	100	125	170
Vanguard, 19J, M#1899, PS, LS, Adj.5P, GJS, DR, HC .	150	175	225
Vanguard, 21J, M#1899, Adj.5P	100	125	175
Vanguard, 23J, M#1899, Adj.5P, HC...................	250	275	350
Vanguard, 23J, M#1899, Adj.6P, OF	175	200	250
Vanguard, 23J, M#1899, LS, Adj.5P, GJS, DR, OF......	150	175	200
Vanguard, 23J, M#1899, PS, Adj.5P, GJS, DR, OF......	150	175	200
Vanguard, 23J, M#1899, PS, Wind Indicator, Adj.5P, GJS, DR...	350	400	450
Vanguard, 19J, M#1908, LS & PS, Adj.5P, GJS, DR	100	125	175

Grade or Name—Description	Avg	Ex-Fn	Mint
Vanguard, 21J, M#1908, Adj.5P, GJS, DR, Diamond end stone	$125	$150	$175
Vanguard, 21J, M#1908, Adj.5P, GJS, DR, PS, LS, OF	75	100	125
Vanguard, 21J, M#1908, Adj.5P, GJS, DR, PS, LS, HC	125	175	200
Vanguard, 23J, M#1908, LS, Adj.5P, GJS, DR, OF	150	175	200
Vanguard, 23J, M#1908, LS, Adj.5P, GJS, DR, HC	250	275	300
Vanguard, 23J, M#1908, PS, Adj.5P, GJS, DR	150	175	200
Vanguard, 23J, M#1908, Adj.5P, Wind Indicator, GJS, DR	350	400	450
Vanguard, 23J, M#1908, Adj.5P, GJS, Diamond end stone	150	175	200
Vanguard, 23J, M#1908, Adj.5P, GJS, HC	275	300	400
Vanguard, 23J, OF, LS or PS, 14K	500	550	675
Vanguard, 23J, M#1908, Adj.6P, Wind Indicator, GJS, DR	360	400	450
Vanguard, 23J, M#1908, Adj.6P, Wind Indicator, Lossier, GJS, DR	350	400	450
Vanguard, 23J, M#1912, Press Jewels	100	125	150
Vanguard, 23J, M#1912, PS, military (case), Wind Indicator	400	385	475
George Washington, 11J, M#1857	125	150	200
Weems, 23j, Navigation watch, Wind Indicator ★★	500	600	700
M#665, 19J, GJS, BRG, HC ★★	600	700	800
M#1888, G #s 650, 640	60	70	85
M#1899, G #s 610, 615, 618, 620, 625, 628, 630	60	70	85
M#1908, G #s 610, 611, 613, 614, 618, 620, 621, 623, 625, 628, 630, 635, 636, 637, 640, 641, 642	60	70	85
M#645, 21J, GCW, OF, LS	85	110	145
M#645, 19J, OF, LS	80	105	130
M#16-A, 22J, Adj.3P, 24 hr. dial	100	125	150
M#16-A, 17J, Adj.5P	65	75	80
M#1621, 21J, Adj.5P	85	110	145
M#1623, 23J, Adj.5P	150	175	200

Weems Navigation watch, 21j, Weems pat. seconds dial, pusher for seconds scale setting, ca. 1942.

Grade 645, Model 1899, 16 size, 21 jewels, Adj5p, gold center wheel.

14 SIZE
MODELS 14KW, 1874, FULL PLATE
1884, 1895, 1897, COLONIAL-A

Grade or Name — Description	Avg	Ex-Fn	Mint
Adams Street, 7J, M#14KW, ¾, KW, Coin	$100	$125	$175
Adams Street, 11J, M#14KW, ¾, KW, Coin	100	125	175
Adams Street, 15J, M#14KW, ¾, KW	100	125	175
A. W. Co., 7J, M#14KW, ¾, KW	50	75	100
A. W. W. Co., 7J, M#1874, SW, LS, HC	75	100	125
A. W. Co., 15-16J, M#1874, ¾, SW	50	65	85
A. W. Co., 7-11J, M#s FP, 1884, & 1895	40	50	65
A. W. Co., 13J, M#1884............................	40	50	65
A.W.Co., 19J, GJS, GCW	65	75	95
Am. Watch Co., 7-11J, KW, ¾	35	45	60
Am. Watch Co., 13J, M#1874, ¾, SW	65	75	95
Am. Watch Co., 15J, M#1874, ¾.....................	70	80	100
Am. Watch Co., 16J, M#1874, ¾, SW	70	80	100
Am. Watch Co., 7-11J, M#FP, KW	50	65	85
Am. Watch Co., 16J, M#1884, ¾, SW	55	75	95
Am. Watch Co., 15J, M#1897, SW....................	40	60	90
Bond St., 7J, M#1895, ¾, SW........................	40	55	75
Bond St., 9J, M#1884, ¾, KW	75	100	125
Bond St., 7J, M#1884, ¾, SW, PS....................	50	60	90
Beacon, 15J, M#1897, ¾, SW	50	60	90
Chronograph, 13J, M#1884, 14K, OF, Am. W. Co. case..	600	800	1,000
Chronograph, 13J, M#1884, 14K, HC, Am. W. Co. case .	700	900	1,100
Chronograph, 13J, M#1884, 18K, HC, Am. W. Co. case★	1,000	1,200	1,400
Chronograph, 13J, M#1884, 14K OF with register, Am. W. Co. case	750	950	1,150

Chronograph, Model 1874, split-second, 14 size. Note two split second hands on dial.

Bond St., 14 size, 7 jewels, stem wind, open face, note pin set, serial number 2,437,666. c. 1884.

Grade or Name—Description	Avg	Ex-Fn	Mint
Chronograph, 13J, M#1884, 14K HC with register, Am. W. Co. case	$850	$950	$1,350
Chronograph, 13J, M#1884, 18K HC with register, Am. W. Co. case	1,200	1,400	1,600
Chronograph, 13J, M#1884	175	225	300
Chronograph, 15J, M#1884	185	250	335
Chronograph, 17J, M#1884	195	270	365
Chronograph, 17J, M#1874, split second, Am. W. Co. case ★	350	425	550
Chronograph, 15J, M#1874, split second, 14K, HC... ★ ★	1,200	1,400	1,600
Chronograph, 15J, M#1874, split second, min. register, 14K Am. W. Co. HC ★ ★	1,400	1,600	1,800
(Above in 18K case, add $250 to $400 to value)			
Chronograph, 16J, double dial, M#1874, 18K, Am. W. Co. case ★ ★	2,000	2,500	3,500
Chronometro Victoria, 15J, M#1897, ¾	65	75	95
Church St., 7J, M#1884, ¾	40	60	75
Crescent Garden, 7-11J, M#14KW, KW	60	75	100
Crescent Garden, 7J, M#FP, KW	60	75	90
Wm. Ellery, 7J, M#1874, SW	35	45	75
Gentleman, 7J, M#1884, SW	35	45	75
Hillside, 7-15J, M#1874, SW	35	45	75
Hillside, 7-11J, M#FP, SW	35	45	75
Hillside, 7-13J, M#1884, ¾, KW	35	45	75
Hillside, 11J, M#1884, ¾, KW	35	45	75
Hillside, 15J, M#1884, ¾, SW	65	75	100
Maximus, 21J, Colonial A	145	185	275
Maximus, 21J, Colonial A, 14K	300	400	575
Night Clock, 7J, M#1884, KW	50	70	95
Repeater (5 min.), 16J, M#1884, SW, LS, 14K	3,500	4,000	5,000
Repeater (5 min.), 16J, M#1884, SW, LS, 18K ★	3,800	4,800	6,300

Chronograph, Model 1874-double dial, 14 size, 15 jewels, hunting. case.

Chronogrpah, Model 1874-Split Second, 14 size, 15 jewels, open face, gold escape wheel, gold train, serial number 303,094.

Five Minute Repeater, Model 1884, 14 size, 13-15 jewels, hunting case, slide actuated, serial number 2,809,551.

Grade or Name—Description	Avg	Ex-Fn	Mint
Repeater (5 min.), 16J, M#1884, split second chronograph, 18K case	$5,000	$6,000	$7,500
Repeater (5 min.), 16J, M#1884, SW, LS, chronograph with register, 14K Am. W. Co. case	3,500	4,000	5,000
Repeater (5 min.), 16J, M#1884, SW, LS, chronograph with register, 18K Am. W. Co. case	4,000	4,500	6,000
Repeater (5 min.), 16J, M#1884, SW, LS, Coin, original	2,000	2,500	3,000
Repeater (5 Min.), 18K, HC ★ ★	3,000	4,000	5,500
Repeater (1 Min.), perpetual calendar, moon phase, 18K ★ ★ ★	30,000	35,000	45,000
Riverside, 11-15J, M#s 1874, HC ★	150	175	250
Riverside, 15J, M#1884, OF	55	60	80
Riverside, 19-21J, Colonial A, OF ★ ★	150	175	250
Royal, 11-13J, M#s 1874, 1884	40	55	65
Seaside, 7-11J, M#1884, SW	40	55	65
Special, 7J, M#1895, HC	75	100	125
Sterling, 7J, M#1884	40	55	65
Stone Movement, 16J, M#1874, crystal top & bottom plates, 14K ★ ★ ★	4,500	5,000	7,000
Waltham, Mass., 7J, Full Plate, KW	75	100	125

12 SIZE
MODELS KW, 1894, BRIDGE, COLONIAL SERIES

Grade or Name — Description	Avg	Ex-Fn	Mint
A. W. W. Co., 7J, M#1894, 14K, OF	$200	$225	$275
A. W. W. Co., 11J, M#1894, Colonial	40	50	60
A. W. W. Co., 15J, M#1894, Colonial	40	50	60
A. W. W. Co., 15J, M#1894, Colonial, 14K, HC	250	275	350
A. W. W. Co., 17J, M#1894, Colonial	40	50	60
A. W. W. Co., 17J, M#1894, Colonial, 14K OF	200	225	275
P. S. Bartlett, 19J, M#1894, 14K, HC	275	300	375
P. S. Bartlett, 19J, M#1894	50	60	70
Bond St., 7J, M#1894	40	50	60

Actual size illustration of a cushion style shaped watch depicting thinness with emphasis on style and beauty. This watch was popular in the 1930s.

Grade or Name—Description	Avg	Ex-Fn	Mint
Bridge Model, 19J, GJS, Adj.5P, GT..................	$75	$100	$125
Bridge Model, 19J, GJS, Adj.5P, GT, 18K, HC	500	550	575
Bridge Model, 21J, GJS, Adj.5P, GT, OF	75	100	125
Bridge Model, 21J, GJS, Adj.5P, GT, HC, 14K ..... ★ ★	600	700	850
Bridge Model, 23J, GJS, Adj.5P, GT..................	125	150	175
Duke, 7-15J, M#1894	40	50	70
Digital Hour & Second Window, 17J	75	100	125
Elite, 17J, OF	40	50	70
Ensign, 7J, OF......................................	25	35	45
Martyn Square, 7-11J, M#KW	100	125	175
Maximus, 21J, GJS, GT	200	250	325
Premier, 17-19J, M#1894............................	65	80	100
Premier, 21J, M#1894	65	80	100
Riverside, 17-19J, M#1894, Colonial	60	70	80
Riverside, 19-21J, M#1894, Colonial	70	80	90

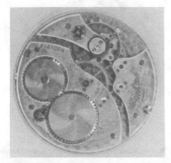

A.W.W.Co., Model 1894, 12 size, 7-11 jewels, open face, serial number 7,565,004.

Riverside, Colonial series, 12 size, 19 jewels, open face or hunting, Adj5p, double roller.

Grade or Name—Description	Avg	Ex-Fn	Mint
Riverside, 19-21J, M#1894, Colonial, 14K, HC	$225	$275	$375
Riverside Maximus, 21J, M#1894, Colonial, GT, GJS, 14K	400	475	575
Riverside Maximus, 21J, M#1894, Colonial, GT, GJS	175	225	325
Riverside Maximus, 23J, M#1894, Colonial, GT, GJS .. ★	225	275	375
Riverside Maximus, 23J, M#1894, Colonial, GT, GJS, 14K	425	475	575
Royal, 17J, OF, PS	45	55	65
Royal, 19J, OF, PS	55	65	75

10 SIZE
MODEL KW, 1861, 1874

NOTE: These watches (excluding Colonial) are usually found with solid gold cases, and are therefore priced accordingly. Without cases, these watches have very little value due to the fact that the cases are difficult to find. Many of the cases came in octagon, decagon, hexagon, cushion and triad shapes.

Grade or Name — Description	Avg	Ex-Fn	Mint
Am. W. Co., 7-15J, M#1874, KW, 14K.................	$200	$250	$350
American Watch Co., 11-15J, M#1874, 14K, HC	275	325	425
Appleton, Tracy & Co., 15J, M#1861 or 1874, 14K	200	250	350
Appleton, Tracy & Co., 15J, M#1861, 18K multi-color box case	650	750	900
P. S. Bartlett, 11J, M#1861, KW, 14K.................	275	300	375
P. S. Bartlett, 13J, M#KW, gold balance, 1st S#45,801, last 46,200, 14K, Pat. Nov. 3, 1858.............★ ★	300	375	525
P. S. Bartlett, 13J, M#KW, gold balance, 1st S#45,801, last 46,200, 18K...................................	400	475	625
P. S. Bartlett, 13J, M#1861, KW, 14K.................	200	250	300
Crescent Garden, 7J, M#1861, KW, 14K	200	250	300
Wm. Ellery, 7,11,15J, M#1861, KW, 14K	200	250	300
Home W. Co., 7J, M#1874, KW, 14K	200	250	300
Martyn Square, 7-11J, M#1861, 14K...................	200	250	300
Maximus "A", 21J, 14K.........................★ ★	400	475	600

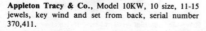

Appleton Tracy & Co., Model 10KW, 10 size, 11-15 jewels, key wind and set from back, serial number 370,411.

Am. W. Co., Model 1873, 8 size, 15 jewels, serial number 691,001.

Grade or Name — Description	Avg	Ex-Fn	Mint
Maximus "A", 23J, 14K .... ★ ★	$425	$500	$600
Riverside, 19J, HCI5P, GF	65	75	100
Riverside Maximus, 19-21J, Adj.5P, GJS, GF	125	200	275
Riverside Maximus, 19-21J, Adj.5P, GJS, 18K..........	450	525	625
Riverside Maximus, 23J, Adj.5P, GJS, GF	200	250	375
Royal, 15J, Adj.5P, GF..............................	55	65	80

8 SIZE
MODEL 1873

NOTE: Collectors usually want solid gold cases in small watches. The gold case value must be added to price listed.

Grade or Name — Description	Avg	Ex-Fn	Mint
Am. W. Co., 15J, M#1873, 14K, Multi-Color Box Hinge Case..	$500	$700	$900
Am. W. Co., 15J, M#1873	65	75	85
P. S. Bartlett, 15-16J, M#1873	40	50	60
Wm. Ellery, 7-11J, M#1873	40	50	60
Wm. Ellery, 7J, 14K, HC	200	275	350
Riverside, 7-11J, M#1873, 18K, HC	325	400	475
Riverside, 7-11J, M#1873............................	65	75	85
Royal, 7-13J, M#1873...............................	40	50	60

Wm. Ellery, Model 1873, 8 size, 7 jewels, ¾ plate, serial number 2,679,907.

Riverside, Model 1873, 8 size, 7 jewels, serial number 931,395.

6 SIZE
MODEL 1873, 1889

Grade or Name — Description	Avg	Ex-Fn	Mint
A,B,C,D,E,F,G,H,J,K	$65	$70	$85
A,B,C,D,E,F,G,H,J,K, 14K, HC......................	200	275	325
A. W. W. Co., 19J, 18K, HC	325	400	475
A. W. W. Co., 19J, 14K, Multi-Color gold case	450	600	800
A. W. W. Co., 7J, M#1873	40	45	55

Grade or Name—Description	Avg	Ex-Fn	Mint
A. W. W. Co., 15J, multi-color GF HC	$175	$200	$275
A. W. W. Co., 11J, HC, LS	75	100	150
Am. W. Co., 7J, M#1889	40	45	55
American W. Co., 7J, KW & KS from back, 10K, HC ...	175	225	275
Wm. Ellery, 7J, M#1873	40	50	70
Lady Waltham, 16J, M#1873, Demi, HC, 14K	275	300	350
Lady Waltham, 16J, M#1873, 18K	300	325	375
Riverside Maximus, 21J, GT, DR	225	250	300
Riverside, 15-17J, PS	50	75	100
Seaside, 7J, M#1873	40	45	55

American Watch Co., Model 1889, 6 size 7 jewels, serial number 4,700,246.

Stone Movement, Crystal Plate, size 4, 16 jewels, gold train, open face, serial number 28.

4 SIZE

Grade or Name — Description	Avg	Ex-Fn	Mint
Stone Movement, 4 size, crystal, 16 ruby jewels in gold settings, gold train, exposed pallets, compensation balance adjusted to temperature, isochronism, position, Breguet hairspring, and crystal top plate, 14K . ★ ★ ★	$3,500	$4,500	$6,000

NOTE: Watches listed in this book are priced at the retail level, as complete watches having an original 14k gold-filled case, an original white enamel single sunk dial, and with the entire original movement in good working order with no repairs needed, unless otherwise noted.

0 SIZE
MODELS 1882, 1891, 1900, 1907

Grade or Name — Description	Avg	Ex-Fn	Mint
A.W.Co., 7-15J, multi-color 14K HC	$350	$475	$600
A. W. Co., 7J, 14K, HC	175	275	350
A. W. Co., 7J, SW, 14K, GF, OF	50	60	70
A. W. Co., 11J, ¾, SW, HC	75	100	150
American Watch Co., 15J, ¾, SW, OF & HC	75	100	150

Lady Waltham, Model 1900, 0 size, 16 jewels, open face or hunting, adjusted, stem wind, pendant set.

A.W. Co., Model 1891, 0 size, 7 jewels, stem wind, originally sold for $13.00.

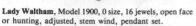

Grade or Name—Description	Avg	Ex-Fn	Mint
American Watch Co., 15J, ¾, SW, 14K, HC	$175	$275	$350
P. S. Bartlett, 11J, M#1891, OF, 14K	125	150	175
P. S. Bartlett, 16J, 14K, HC	175	275	350
Lady Waltham, 15J, ¾, SW, 14K, HC	175	275	350
Lady Waltham, 15-16J, ¾, SW, HC	100	125	175
Maximus, 19J, ¾, SW, HC	100	125	175
Riverside, 15,16,17J, ¾, SW, HC	100	125	175
Riverside, 15,16,17J, ¾, SW, HC, 14K	175	275	350
Riverside Maximus, 21J, GT, multi-color gold HC, 14K ★ ★	500	675	850
Riverside Maximus, 21J, ¾, GT	125	150	175
Riverside Maximus, 19J, ¾, SW, HC	150	175	250
Riverside Maximus, 19J, ¾, HC, 14K ★	275	350	475
Royal, 16J, ¾, SW, HC	75	100	125
Seaside, 15J, ¾, SW, HC, 14K	175	275	350
Seaside, 11J, ¾, SW, OF, multi-color dial, no chips	125	175	200
Seaside, 11J, ¾, SW, HC	75	100	125
Seaside, 7J, ¾, HC	65	75	100
Seaside, 7J, ¾, HC, 14K	175	275	350
Special, 11J, M#1891, OF, 14K	125	175	200

Riverside, Jewel Series, 6/0 size, 17 ruby jewels, raised gold settings, gold center wheel.

Ruby, Jewel Series, 6/0 size, 15 jewels, adjusted to temperature, open face or hunting.

JEWEL SERIES 6/0

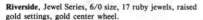

Grade or Name — Description	Avg	Ex-Fn	Mint
Riverside J Size, 17J, HC, 14K	$200	$250	$300
Ruby J Size, 15J, OF, 14K	150	200	250
Sapphire, 15J, OF, 14K	150	200	250
Diamond, 15J, HC, 14K	200	250	300

AMERICAN WALTHAM WATCH CO.
IDENTIFICATION OF MOVEMENTS
BY MODEL NUMBER

How to Identify Your Watch: Compare the movement of your watch with the illustrations in this section. Upon matching the movement exactly, the model number and size can be determined. When comparing, note the location of the balance, jewels, screws, gears and type of back plate (Full, ¾, Bridge) which will be clues to identifying the movement you have. Having determined the size and model number, you can now find your watch in the main price listing by name or number (which is engraved on the movement).

20 size, 1862 or KW 20 model. Note vibrating hairspring stud. 1st serial number 50,001

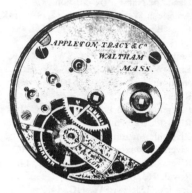

18 size, key wind model 1st serial number 28,821

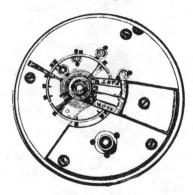

Model 1857, KW, KS. 1st serial number 1,001

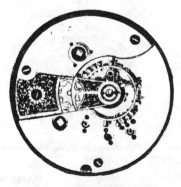

Model 1870, KW, KS from back 1st serial number 500,001

Model 1877, 18 size

Model 1879, 18 size

Model 1883, hunting
1st serial number 2,354,001

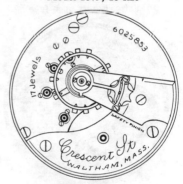

Model 1883, open face

Model 1892, open face

Model 1892, hunting.
1st serial number 6,026,001

16½ size, Equity open face

Model 1868 or Model 16KW,
16 size

Model 1872, 16 size

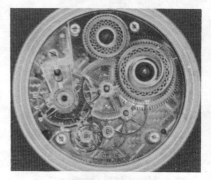

Stone Mountain crystal plates,
16 size

Model 1888, 16 size, hunting

Bridge Model, 16 size

**Model 1899 or Model 1908,
16 size, open face**

**Model 1899 or Model 1908,
16 size, hunting**

**Model 1899 or Model 1908,
16 size, open face**

Model 16-A, 16 size

**Model 1622, Deck Watch
16 size, sweep second**

Model 1874 & 1884, 14 size

Model 1874, 14 size, hunting

Model 1884, 14 size, open face

5 Minute Repeater, 14 size

5 Minute Repeater, 14 size

Model 1874, 14 size

Model 1884, 14 size

**Model 1895, 14 size,
open face**

Model 1897, 14 size

Colonal A Model, 14 size

Colonial Series, 14 size

Model 1924, The Colonial

Model 1894, 12 size

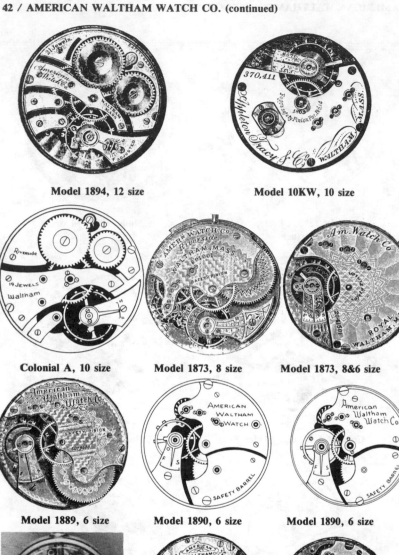

Model 1894, 12 size

Model 10KW, 10 size

Colonial A, 10 size

Model 1873, 8 size

Model 1873, 8&6 size

Model 1889, 6 size

Model 1890, 6 size

Model 1890, 6 size

Stone Mtn, 4 size

Model 1882, 1 size

Model 1891, 0 size

Model 1900, 0 size   **Model 1907, 0 size**   **Jewel Series**

Model 1900, 0/3 size,   **Model 1907, 0/3 size,**   **Model 1898 & 1912,**
open face   **hunting**   **0/6 size, hunting**

Model 1898 & 1912,   **10½ ligne**   **10 ligne**
0/6 size, open face

ANSONIA CLOCK CO.
Brooklyn, New York
1904 - 1929

The Ansonia Watch Co. was owned by the Ansonia Clock Company in Ansonia, Connecticut. Ansonia started making clocks in about 1850 and began manufacturing watches in 1904. They produced about 10,000,000 dollar-type watches. The company was sold to a Russian investor in 1930. "Patented April 17, 1888," is on the back plate of some Ansonia watches.

Ansonia Watch Company. Example of a basic movement, 16 size, stem wind.

Ansonia Watch Co., Sequi-Centennial model.

Grade or Name—Description	Avg	Ex-Fn	Mint
Ansonia White Dial	$40	$50	$70
Ansonia Radium Dial	45	55	75
Ansonia in NI case, Black Dial	40	45	60
Ascot	40	55	75
Bonnie Laddie Shoes	60	95	115
Dispatch	30	40	60
Faultless	40	45	55
Guide	40	55	70
Lenox	35	40	50
Mentor	35	45	55
Picadilly	45	60	75
Rural	35	47	70
Sesqui-Centennial	250	275	350
Superior	45	60	75
Tutor	45	60	75

APPLETON WATCH CO.
(REMINGTON WATCH CO.)
Appleton, Wisconsin
1901 - 1903

In 1901, O. E. Bell bought the machinery of the defunct Cheshire Watch Company and moved it to Appleton, Wisconsin, where he had organized the Remington Watch Company. The first watches were shipped from the factory in February 1902; production ceased in mid-1903 and the contents were sold off before the end of that year. Most movements made by this firm were modified Cheshire movements and were marked "Appleton Watch Company." Advertisements for the firm in 1903 stated that they made 16 and 18 size movements with 11, 15, or 17 jewels. Serial numbers range from 90,000 to 104,950. During the two years they were in business, the company produced about 2,000 to 3,000 watches.

Appleton Watch Co., 18 size, 7 jewels, "The Appleton Watch Co." on dial. Engraved on movement "Appleton Watch Co., Appleton, Wis." Note that the stem is attached to movement. Serial number 93,106.

Description	Avg	Ex-Fn	Mint
18S, 7J, OF, NI, ¾, DMK, SW, PS, stem attached ★ ★ ★	$500	$600	$750
18S, 7J, OF, NI, ¾, DMK, SW, PS, Coin, OF . . . . ★ ★ ★	450	550	700
18S, 15J, NI, LS, SW, ¾, M#2 . . . . ★ ★ ★ ★	600	700	850
16S, 7-11J, ¾, stem attached . . . . ★ ★ ★	500	600	750

Note: Prices are for watches with original cases. This case is difficult to find.

AUBURNDALE WATCH CO.
Auburndale, Massachusetts
1876 - 1883

This company was the first to attempt an inexpensive watch. Jason R. Hopkins was issued two patents in 1875 covering the "rotary design." The rotary design eliminated the need of adjusting to various positions, resulting in a less expensive watch. The company was formed about 1876, and the first watches were known as the "Auburndale Rotary." In 1876, equipment was purchased from the Marion Watch Co., and the first rotary designed watches were placed on the market for $10 in 1877. Auburndale produced about 3,230 watches before closing in 1883.

Auburndale Timer, 18 size, 7 jewels, stem wind, 10 minute, ¼ second jump timer.

Auburndale Rotary, 20 size, 2 jewels, lever set, stem wind, detent escapement.

Grade or Name — Description	Avg	Ex-Fn	Mint
Auburndale Rotary, 20S, 2J, LS, SW, NI case, detent ★ ★	$1,500	$1,900	$2,500
Auburndale Rotary, 18S, 2J, SW, LS, NI case, lever . ★ ★	1,000	1,300	2,000
Bentley, 18S, 7J, LS, NI case, SW, ¾ .... ★ ★	600	800	1,100
Lincoln, 18S, 7J, LS, NI case, KW, ¾ .... ★ ★	600	800	1,100
Auburndale Timer, 18S, 7J, SW, NI case, 10 min. timer, ¼ sec. jump, Chronograph........................	200	250	375
Auburndale Timer, 18S, 7J, KW, NI case, 10 min. timer, ¼ sec. jump with split seconds, Chronograph .... ★	375	425	550

Bentley, 18 size, 7 jewels, ¾ plate, stem wind, serial number 2.

Auburndale Rotary, 18 size, 2 jewels, stem wind, lever set, serial number 448.

AURORA WATCH CO.
Aurora, Illinois
1883 - 1892

Aurora Watch Co. was organized in mid-1883 with the goal of getting one jeweler in every town to handle Aurora watches. The first movements were 18S, full plate, and were first sold in the fall of 1884. There were several watches marked No. 1. The total

production was about 215,000; over 100,000 were 18S, and some were 6S ladies' wat
ches. For the most part Aurora produced medium to low grade; and at one time made
about 150 movements per day. The Hamilton Watch Co. purchased the company on
June 19, 1890.

AURORA WATCH CO.
Estimated Serial Nos. and Production Dates

1884 - 10,001	1887 - 160,000	1889 - 215,000
1885 - 60,000	1888 - 200,000	1891 - 230,901
1886 - 110,000		

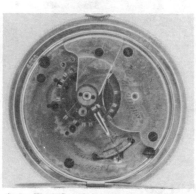

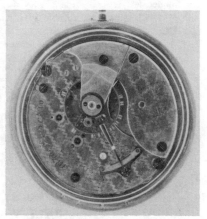

Aurora Watch Co., 18 size, 15 jewels, serial number 142,060. Made for railroad service. New model.

Aurora Watch Co., 18 size, 15 jewels, Adj, engraved on movement "Made expressly R.J.A.," serial number 73,529.

Description	Avg	Ex-Fn	Mint
18S, 7J, KW, KS, Gilded, OF	$125	$150	$175
18S, 7J, KW, KS, Gilded, HC	135	165	195
18S, 7J, 5th pinion, Gilded, LS, SW, OF	135	165	195
18S, 7J, LS, SW, Gilded, new model, HC	200	250	325
18S, 11J, KW, KS, Gilded, HC	135	165	195
18S, 11J, KW, KS, Gilded, OF	135	165	195
18S, 11J, 5th pinion, LS, SW, Gilded, new model, OF	150	185	225
18S, 11J, 5th pinion, LS, SW, NI, GJS, OF	140	170	200
18S, 11J, 5th pinion, LS, SW, NI, GJS, new model, OF	160	190	230
18S, 11J, LS, SW, Gilded, HC, made expressly for the guild	150	185	225
18S, 11J, 5th pinion, LS, SW, NI, OF, made expressly for the guild	170	190	240
18S, 15J, KW, KS, NI, GJS, DMK, OF or HC .... ★	225	275	350
18S, 15J, 5th pinion, LS, SW, Gilded, OF	200	250	325
18S, 15J, 5th pinion, LS, SW, NI, GJS, DMK, ADT, OF.	225	275	350
18S, 15J, 5th pinion, LS, SW, NI, GJS, DMK, ADJ, new model, OF	300	350	400
18S, 15J, LS, SW, NI, GJS, DMK, ADJ, new model, HC	300	350	400
18S, 15J, LS, SW, NI, GJS, ADJ, 2 Tone DMK, checkerboard or snowflake HC	325	375	425

Size and Description	Avg	Ex-Fn	Mint
18S, 15J, LS, SW, NI, GJS, DMK, ADJ, Railroad Time Service or Caufield Watch, new model, HC .... ★	$400	$550	$675
18S, marked 15 Ruby Jewels but has 17J, 5th pinion, LS, SW, NI, GJS, 2 Tone, ADJ, OF .... ★ ★	600	700	900
18S, marked 15 Ruby Jewels, only 15J, LS, SW, NI, GJS, 2 Tone DMK, ADJ, HC	350	400	475
18S, marked 15 Ruby Jewels, only 15J, LS, SW, NI, GJS, ADJ, 2 Tone DMK, OF...................... ★	400	475	550
18S, 15J, Chronometer, LS, SW, NI, DMK, ADJ, new model, HC .... ★ ★	400	475	550
18S, 15J, Chronometer, LS, SW, NI, GJS, DMK, ADJ, HC .... ★	375	450	650
18S, 15J, LS, SW, NI, DMK, HC, made expressly for the guild...	200	250	325
18S, 15J, 5th pinion, LS, SW, Gilded, OF, made expressly for the guild..................................	250	300	375
18S, 15J, LS, SW, Gilded, HC, made expressly for the "RJA" (Retails Jeweler's Assoc.)	225	265	350
6S, 11-15J, LS, SW, Gilded, ¾, HC	125	150	200
6S, 11-15J, LS, SW, NI, GJS, DMK, ¾, HC	150	175	225
6S, 11-15J, LS, SW, ¾ plate, 14K, HC.................	250	300	400

BALL WATCH CO.
Cleveland, Ohio
1879 - 1969

The Ball Watch Company did not manufacture watches but did help formulate the specifications of watches used for railroad service. Webb C. Ball of Cleveland, Ohio, was the general time inspector for over 125,000 miles of railroad in the U. S., Mexico, and Canada. In 1891 there was a collision between the Lake Shore and Michigan Southern Railways at Kipton, Ohio. The collision was reported to have occurred because an engineer's watch had stopped, for about four minutes, then started running again. The railroad officials commissioned Ball to establish the timepiece inspection system. Ball knew that the key to safe operations of the railroad was the manufacturing of sturdy, precision timepieces. He also knew they must be able to withstand hard use and still be accurate. Before this time, each railroad company had its own rules and standards. After Ball presented his guidelines, most American manufacturers set out to meet these standards and soon a list was made of the manufacturers that produced watches of the grade that would pass inspection. Each railroad employee had a card that he carried showing the record of how his watch performed on inspection. Ball was also instrumental in the formation of the Horological Institute of America.

A 1902 advertisement for Ball Watch Company read, "We do not sell movements or cases separately."

200,000 railroad watches, plus 150,000 non-railroad grade watches, were made and sold by the Ball Watch Co., totaling approximately 350,000.

ESTIMATED SERIAL NUMBERS AND PRODUCTION DATES
FOR RAILROAD GRADE WATCHES

Hamilton		Waltham		Elgin
Date	**Serial No.**	**Date**	**Serial No.**	**Date**
1895	13,000	1900	060,700	1904 - 1906
1897	20,500	1905	202,000	S# range:
1900	42,000	1910	216,200	11,853,000 - 12,282,000
1902	170,000	1915	250,000	
1905	462,000	1920	260,000	**E. Howard & Co.**
1910	600,000	1925	270,000	
1915	603,000			**Date**
1920	610,000	**Illinois W. Co.**		1893 - 1895
1925	620,000			S# range:
1930	637,000	**Date**	**Serial No.**	226,000 - 308,000
1935	641,000	1929	800,000	
1938	647,000	1930	801,000	**Hampden**
1939	650,000	1931	803,000	
1940	651,000	1932	804,000	**Date**
1941	652,000			1890 - 1892
1942	654,000			S# range:
				626,750 - 657,960 -
				759,720

BALL—AURORA
18 SIZE

Description		Avg	Ex-Fn	Mint
17J, OF, marked Ball . . . . ★ ★		$1,500	$1,750	$2,000

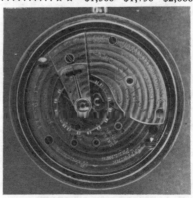

Ball-Elgin, Grade 333, 18 size, 17 jewels, rare hunting case model, serial number 11,958,002.

Ball-Elgin, Grade 333, 18 size, 17 jewels, open face model, serial number 11,856,801.

BALL—ELGIN
18 SIZE G. F. CASES

Description		Avg	Ex-Fn	Mint
16J, G#327, OF, LS . . . . ★		$275	$350	$475
17J, G#328, OF, LS . . . . ★		300	375	500

Description	Avg	Ex-Fn	Mint
17J, G#328, Coin, OF, LS .... ★	$250	$325	$450
17J, G#329, NI, Adj.5P, LS, HC .... ★	1,200	1,500	1,800
21J, G#330, LS, official RR std., HC .... ★ ★ ★ ★	2,000	2,500	3,000
16J, G#331, NI, OF, Adj.5P, PS, Commercial Std. .. ★ ★	375	400	550
17J, G#331, NI, OF, Adj.5P, PS......................	165	255	325
17J, G#332, OF, PS .... ★	300	350	400
17J, G#333, NI, OF, Adj.5P, LS......................	175	200	275
17J, G#333, NI, HC, Adj.5P, LS .... ★ ★	1,300	1,600	1,900
21J, G#333, NI, OF, Adj.5P, LS......................	200	250	325
21J, G#334, NI, OF, Adj.5P, LS......................	325	375	425

Note: 18 Size Ball watches in hunting cases are scarce.

BALL—HAMILTON
18 SIZE G. F. CASES

Description	Avg	Ex-Fn	Mint
17J, M#999, Commercial Standard .... ★	$300	$400	$505
17J, M#999, NI, OF, Adj.5P, LS, Coin................	150	200	275
17J, M#999, NI, OF, Adj.5P, LS	150	200	275

Ball-Hamilton, Grade 999, 18 size, 17 jewels, serial number 458,623.

Ball-Hamilton, Grade 999, 18 size, 17 jewels, marked "Railroad Watch Co." serial number 20,793.

Description	Avg	Ex-Fn	Mint
17J, M#999, NI, OF, Adj.5P, marked "Loaner" on case .	$200	$275	$375
19J, M#999, NI, OF, Adj.5P, LS	175	225	300
21J, M#999, NI, OF, Adj.5P, LS	225	275	375
23J, M#999, NI, OF, Adj.5P, LS .... ★ ★ ★	6,000	7,500	10,000
23J, M#999, NI, HC, Adj.5P, LS .... ★ ★ ★ ★	7,000	9,000	12,000
Ball & Co., 17J, SR, Coin	450	600	800
Brotherhood of Locomotive Engineers, 17J, OF	400	500	650
Brotherhood of Locomotive Engineers, 19J, OF	500	600	750

Ball Watch Co., Brotherhood of RR trainmen, 18 size, 17 jewels; movement made by Hamilton, serial number 13,020.

Ball Watch Co. (Hamilton). Grade 999, 18 size, 21 jewels, sun ray damaskeening, serial number 548,157, c.1906.

Description	Avg	Ex-Fn	Mint
Brotherhood of Locomotive Engineers, 21J, OF	$600	$700	$850
Brotherhood of Locomotive Firemen, 17J, OF	400	500	650
Brotherhood of Locomotive Firemen, 19J, OF	500	600	750
Brotherhood of Locomotive Firemen, 21J, OF	600	700	850
Brotherhood of Railroad Trainsmen, 17J, OF	400	500	650
Brotherhood of Railroad Trainsmen, 19J, OF	500	600	750
Brotherhood of Railroad Trainsmen, 21J, OF	600	700	850
Order of Railroad Conductors, 17J, OF.................	400	500	650
Order of Railroad Conductors, 19J, OF.................	500	600	750
Order of Railroad Conductors, 21J, OF.................	600	700	850
Order of Railroad Telegraphers, 17J, OF................	400	500	650
Order of Railroad Telegraphers, 19J, OF................	500	600	750
Order of Railroad Telegraphers, 21J, OF................	600	700	850
Railroad Watch Co., 16J, OF, LS, marked dial ...... ★★	900	1,200	1,750
Railroad Watch Co., 17J, OF, LS, marked dial ...... ★★	1,000	1,300	1,850
17J, Off. Ball marked jewelers name on dial & mvt., OF★	350	450	575
17J, M#999, adjusted "A," OF .... ★	400	500	650

BALL—DeLONG ESCAPEMENT
16 SIZE

Description	Avg	Ex-Fn	Mint
21J, 14K OF Case..................................	$2,000	$2,500	$3,000

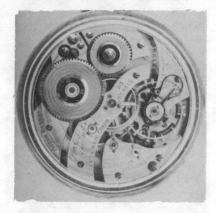

Ball-Hamilton, Model 998 Elinvar, 16 size, 23 jewels, with center bridge.

BALL—HAMILTON
16 SIZE G. F. CASES

Description	Avg	Ex-Fn	Mint
16J, M#976, 977, NI, OF, LS.............................	$125	$150	$200
17J, M#974, NI, OF, LS	125	150	200
17J, Official RR Standard, OF..........................	150	175	225
19J, Official RR Standard, OF..........................	300	350	425
19J, M#999, NI, OF, LS	150	175	225
21J, M#999, NI, OF, LS	175	200	250
21J, M#999B (marked), NI, OF, LS, Adj.6P	300	350	400
21J, M#999, Coin case	150	175	225
21J, M#999 Loaner, marked case........................	175	200	250
23J, M#999B, NI, OF, LS, Adj.6P	500	600	700
23J, M#998 Elinvar, Adj.6P	475	575	650
23J, M#999, NI, OF, LS	450	550	650
21J, M#992-B, NI, OF, LS, Webb C. Ball .... ★★★	600	750	1,000
Brotherhood of Locomotive Engineers, OF	300	350	500
Brotherhood of Locomotive Firemen, OF	300	350	500
Brotherhood of Railroad Trainmen, OF..................	300	350	500
Order of Railroad Conductors, OF	300	350	500

BALL—HAMPDEN
18 SIZE

Description	Avg	Ex-Fn	Mint
17J, LS, SW, OF, marked "Superior Grade"...... ★★★	$1,250	$1,400	$1,850
17J, LS, SW, OF, **not** marked "Superior Grade" .... ★★	1,000	1,200	1,600
15J, LS, SW, OF .... ★	200	250	300
15J, LS, SW, HC .... ★★★	400	500	650

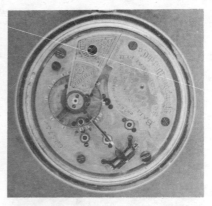

Ball-Hampden, 18 size, 17 jewels, serial number 759,728.

Ball-Hampden, marked "Superior Grade," 18 size, 17 jewels, serial number 626,754.

BALL—E. HOWARD & CO.
18 SIZE

Description	Avg	Ex-Fn	Mint
17J, ¾, HC, PS, GJS, 18K, VII, orig. gold HC ... ★ ★ ★	$4,000	$5,000	$6,500
17J, ¾, OF, PS, GJS, 14K, VIII, orig. gold OF case. ★ ★	2,500	3,000	5,000
17J, ¾, OF, PS, GJS, 14K, VIII, Brotherhood of Locomotive Engineers	3,000	4,000	6,000

Ball & Co. (E. Howard & Co.), Series VIII, 18 size, 17 jewels. Order of Railway Conductors, serial number 307,488. c.1900.

Ball-E. Howard Watch Co., 16 size, 21 jewels (Keystone). This watch believed to be one-of-a-kind prototype, serial number 982,201.

BALL—E. HOWARD WATCH CO.
16 SIZE

Description		Avg	Ex-Fn	Mint
17J, OF, GJS		$2,000	$2,500	$3,500
21J, OF, GJS	★ ★ ★	2,500	3,000	4,000

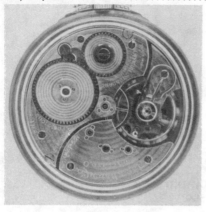

Ball Watch Co., Illinois Model, 16 size, 23 jewels. To identify, note back plates that circle around balance wheel, serial number B801,758.

BALL—ILLINOIS
16 SIZE

Description		Avg	Ex-Fn	Mint
23J, ¾, LS, OF, GJS	★ ★	$800	$1000	$1,200
23J, ¾, LS, OF, GJS, marked 60 hr	★ ★	1,200	1,400	1,600

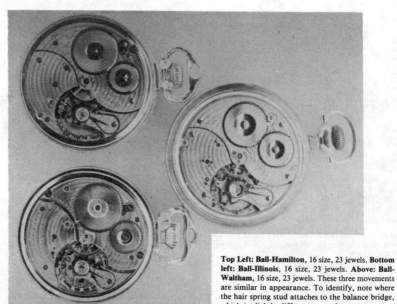

Top Left: Ball-Hamilton, 16 size, 23 jewels. Bottom left: Ball-Illinois, 16 size, 23 jewels. Above: Ball-Waltham, 16 size, 23 jewels. These three movements are similar in appearance. To identify, note where the hair spring stud attaches to the balance bridge, which is slightly different on each movement.

BALL—SETH THOMAS
18 SIZE

Description		Avg	Ex-Fn	Mint
17J, M#3, LS, OF, ¾, GJS .... ★★★		$1,500	$2,000	$2,800

BALL—WALTHAM
18 SIZE

Description		Avg	Ex-Fn	Mint
1892, 15J, OF, LS, SW, marked Webb C. Ball, Cleveland .... ★★		$1,300	$1,500	$2,000

BALL—WALTHAM
16 SIZE

Description		Avg	Ex-Fn	Mint
15J, HC, GCW .... ★★		$325	$400	$550
17J, OF, LS, ¾, Adj.5P, Multi-color case, GF		250	300	400
17J, OF, LS, ¾, Adj.5P		150	200	275
17J, official RR std., HC .... ★★		800	1,000	1,300
17J, commercial std., OF		75	100	150

Ball-Waltham, 16 size, 19 jewels, ORC (Order of Railroad Conductors), serial number B204,475.

Description	Avg	Ex-Fn	Mint
19J, BLF&E	$450	$500	$650
21J, Brotherhood, marked ORC, BOFLE	500	600	750
19J, Hunting case .... ★★	900	1,100	1,400
19J, OF, LS, 14K	575	650	750
19J, OF, LS, stirrup style case	150	200	225

Description	Avg	Ex-Fn	Mint
19J, OF, LS, Coin	$100	$125	$175
19J, OF, LS, ¾, Adj.5P............................	150	200	275
19J, OF, LS, ¾, Adj.5P, Wind Indicator .... ★ ★	2,500	3,000	4,000
21J, OF, LS, ¾, Adj.5P............................	225	250	300
21J, LS, OF, Adj.5P, marked Loaner	250	275	350
23J, LS, OF, Adj.5P, NI, GJS .... ★	550	650	850

Ball Watch Co. by Waltham, 12 size, 19 jewels, open face, digital seconds

12 SIZE
(Not Railroad Grade)

Description	Avg	Ex-Fn	Mint
19J, Illinois, OF, PS.................................	$135	$175	$250
19J, Illinois, HC, PS	200	300	450
19J, Waltham, OF, PS, rotating digital sec	150	200	275

0 SIZE
(Not Railroad Grade)

Description	Avg	Ex-Fn	Mint
17-19J, Waltham, OF, PS	$225	$275	$375
19J, HC, PS, "Queen" in Ball case	350	400	550

FOR CANADA R.R. SERVICE

Description	Avg	Ex-Fn	Mint
16S, ¾, LS, OF, GJS	$500	$600	$750

RAILROAD INSPECTOR'S OR JEWELRY CO. NAME
ON DIAL AND MOVEMENT

Description	Avg	Ex-Fn	Mint
18S, 17J, Adj.5P, OF.................................	$700	$850	$1,000

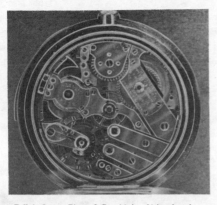

Ball-Audemars Piguet & Co., 14 size, 31 jewels, minute repeater, open face, serial number 4,220.

Ball-Vacheron & Constantin, 43mm, 18 jewels, hunting; note wolf-teeth winding.

BALL—SWISS
16 SIZE

Description	Avg	Ex-Fn	Mint
21J, M#435-B, OF, LS, Adj.6P, Ball case, stirrup bow ...	$175	$225	$275
21J, M#435-C, OF, LS, Adj.6P, Ball case, stirrup bow ...	175	225	275
21J, M#477-B, Adj.6P (BXC-Record Watch Co.)	150	175	225
17J, "Garland"	100	125	175
40mm Audemar Piguet, min. repeater, jeweled thru hammers, 18K, OF, triple signed Webb C. Ball	6,000	7,500	9,500
43mm Vacheron & Constantin, 18J, HC, 18K	800	900	1,100

BANNATYNE WATCH CO.
1905 - 1911

Mr. Bannatyne had previously worked for Ansonia, in charge of watch production. Bannatyne made non-jeweled watches that sold for about $1.50. Ingraham bought this company in 1912.

ESTIMATED SERIAL NUMBERS AND PRODUCTION DATES

Date	Serial No.	Date	Serial No.	Date	Serial No.
1906	40,000	1908	140,000	1910	250,000

Description		Avg	Ex-Fn	Mint
18S, OF, SW, NI case .... ★		$500	$600	$800

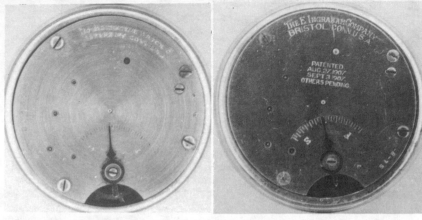

Bannatyne Watch Co. (left), **Ingraham Watch Co.** (right). Note similarity of movements. Both patented Aug. 27th, 1907 & Sept. 3rd, 1907.

BENEDICT & BURNHAM MFG. CO.
Waterbury, Connecticut
1878 - 1880

This name will be found on the dial of the first 1,000 "long wind" Waterbury watches made in 1878. These watches had skeleton type movements with open dials that made the works visible. They contained 58 parts and were very attractive. The company was reorganized in March 1880 as the Waterbury Watch Co. and in 1886 became the New England Watch Co.

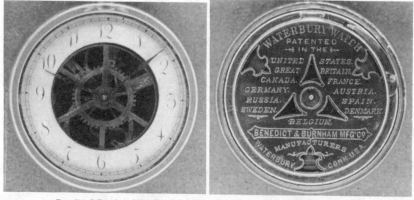

Benedict & Burnham Mfg. Co. dial & movement, 18 size, long wind, skeletonized dial.

Description		Avg	Ex-Fn	Mint
18S, long wind, NI case .... ★ ★		$700	$800	$1,000

BOWMAN WATCH CO.
Lancaster, Pennsylvania
1877 - 1882

In March 1879, Ezra F. Bowman, a native of Lancaster, Pa., opened a retail jewelry and watch business. He employed William H. Todd to supervise his watch manufacturing. Todd had previously been employed by the Elgin and Lancaster Watch companies. Bowman made a 17S, ¼ plate, fully-jeweled movement. The escape wheel was a star-tooth design, fully capped, similar to those made by Charles Frodsham, an English watchmaker. They were stem wind with dials made by another company. Enough parts were made and bought for 300 watches, but only about 50 watches were completed and sold. Those performed very well. The company was sold to J. P. Stevens of Atlanta, Ga.

Description	Avg	Ex-Fn	Mint
18S, 17J, Hamilton 928, OF, marked E. F. Bowman	$300	$400	$550
17S, 19-21J, ¼, GJS, NI, LS, SW .... ★ ★ ★	8,000	11,000	16,000
16S, 21J, Hamilton 960, OF, marked E. F. Bowman	300	400	550

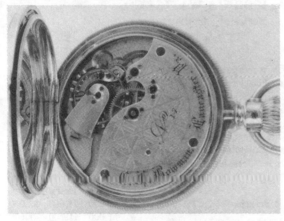

Bowman Watch Co., 16-18 size, 17 jewels, ¼ plate, gold jewel settings, lever set, stem wind. Note free sprung balance. Serial number 17, c.1880.

ROBERT BROWN & SON
1833 - 1856
J. R. BROWN & SHARPE
1856
Providence, Rhode Island

Description		Avg	Ex-Fn	Mint
18S, KW, KS, FULL .... ★ ★ ★		$2,000	$2,500	$3,500

California Watch Co., 18 size, 15 jewels, full plate.

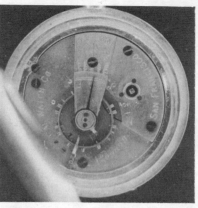

California Watch Co., 18 size, 7 jewels, full plate, serial number 29,029.

CALIFORNIA WATCH CO.
Berkeley, California
1876 - 1877

The Cornell Watch Co. was reorganized in early 1876 as the California Watch Co. The new company bought machinery to make watch cases of gold and silver. In a short time the company was in bad financial trouble and even paid its employees with watches. The business closed in the summer of 1876. Albert Troller bought the unfinished watches that were left. In about four months, he found a buyer in San Francisco. The factory was then closed and sold to the Independent Watch Co. Only about 5,000 watches were made by the California Watch Company. Serial numbers range from 25,115 to 30,174. Inscribed on the movements is "Berkeley."

Description		Avg	Ex-Fn	Mint
18S, 15J, FULL, KW, KS, "Berkeley" .... ★ ★		$1,300	$1,600	$2,000
18S, 11J, FULL, KW, KS .... ★		1,000	1,200	1,600

CHESHIRE WATCH CO.
Cheshire, Connecticut
1883 - 1890

In October 1883, the Cheshire Watch Company was formed by George J. Capewell with D. A. Buck (designer of the long-wind Waterbury) as superintendent. Their first movement was 18S, ¾ gilt plate, stem wind, stem set, with the pendant attached to the movement. It fit into a nickel case which was also made at the Cheshire factory. The first watches were completed in April 1885. A new 18S nickel movement with a second hand was made to fit standard size American cases, and was introduced in 1887. By that date production was at about 200 watches per day. Serial numbers range from 201 to 89,650. All Cheshire watches were sold through L. W. Sweet, general selling agent, in New York City. The factory closed in 1890, going into receivership. The receiver had 3,000 movements finished in 1892. In 1901 O. E. Bell bought the machinery and had it shipped to Appleton, Wisconsin, where he had formed the Remington Watch Company. The watches produced by Remington are marked "Appleton Watch Co." on the movements.

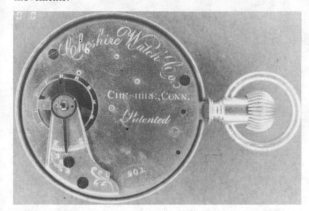

Cheshire Watch Co., 18-20 size, 4 jewels, model number 1. Note stem attached and will not fit standard size case, serial number 201.

Description	Avg	Ex-Fn	Mint
20S, 4-7J, FULL, OF, SW, NI case, stem attached, 1st model, closed top plate .... ★ ★ ★	$450	$550	$700
18S, 4-7J, ¾, SW, OF, NI case, stem attached, 2nd model ★	300	350	450
18S, 7J, OF, fits standard case....................... ★	250	300	375
18S, 11J, OF, SW, standard case, 3rd model .... ★	275	325	400
18S, 15J, OF, NI, ADJ, standard case, 3rd model ..... ★	300	350	450
18S, 21J, OF, SW, Coin, standard case, 3rd model... ★ ★	400	450	550
6S, ¾, OF, SW, NI case............................ ★	200	275	350

Cheshire Watch Co., 18 size, 4-7 jewels. This model number 2 was manufactured with the stem attached and requires a special case.

Cheshire Watch Co., 18 size, 4-7 jewels. This model fits standard 18 size cases. Model number 3.

Chicago Watch Co., 18 size, 15 jewels, open face, nickel movement, serial number 209,145.

CHICAGO WATCH CO.
Chicago, Illinois
1895 - 1903

The Chicago Watch Company's watches were 18S, 7J, open-faced, had silveroid type cases, and were produced at low cost. They are believed to have been made by another manufacturer and sold by Chicago Watch Co.

Description	Avg	Ex-Fn	Mint
18S, 7J, OF	$100	$150	$200
18S, 7-11J, HC or OF, Swiss fake......................	40	50	65
18S, 11J, KW...	325	375	450
18S, 15J, OF, SW.....................................	175	200	300
Columbus, 18S, 15J, SW, NI, HC .... ★ ★	200	225	325
Illinois, 18S, 11J, SW, NI .... ★ ★	200	225	325
Waltham, 18S, 15J .... ★ ★	200	225	325
12S, 15J, OF	100	150	200
12S, 15J, YGF, HC	200	225	325

COLUMBIA WATCH CO.
Waltham, Massachusetts
1896 - 1899

The Columbia Watch Company was organized in 1896 by Edward A. Locke, formerly General Manager of the Waterbury Watch Company. The firm began manufacturing an 0-size, 4-jewel gilt movement with duplex escapement in 1897. These movements were marked "Columbia Watch Co./Waltham, Mass." The firm also made movements marked "Hollers Watch Co./Brooklyn, NY," as well as nickeled movements marked "Cambridge Watch Co./New York."

Locke turned the business over to his son-in-law, Renton Whidden, in 1898, and the firm changed to an 0-size, 7-jewel nickel movement with lever escapement called the Suffolk. The firm name was not changed until early 1901.

Description	Avg	Ex-Fn	Mint
0S, 4J, SW, OF, HC, Duplex, gilded	$50	$60	$75
0S, 7J, SW, OF, lever escapement	60	75	85

Columbia Watch Co., 0 size, 4 jewels, stem wind, open face and hunting, duplex escapement.

COLUMBUS WATCH CO.
Columbus, Ohio
1882 - 1903

The Columbus Watch Co. grew from the Columbus Watch Mfg. Co. which was started in 1876 by D. Gruen and W. J. Savage. The company finished Swiss-imported movements in 8, 16, and 18 sizes to fit American-made cases. They continued to import movements until Nov. 18, 1882, at which time a factory was built. By Aug. 18, 1883, the first movements had been produced. There are several features that separate the Columbus from other American watches. The train is different because the barrel has 72 teeth, the center wheel 72, center pinion 11, third wheel 11 leaves. No cases were made by the company, and the mainsprings and hairsprings, as well as the jewels, were imported. The company started making its own dials in 1884. They were producing watches at the rate of 150 a day in 1888. Serial numbers range from 20,000 to 383,000 for standard grade movements. In 1894 a block of numbers from 500,000 to 505,800 was assigned to some higher grade movements. Also in that year some movements bore the name "New Columbus Watch Co." In 1903 the Columbus Watch Co. was sold to the South Bend Watch Co.

18 SIZE

Grade or Name — Description	Avg	Ex-Fn	Mint
Champion, 15J, NI, FULL, HC	$125	$150	$185
Champion, 15J, gilt, FULL, HC	125	150	185
Champion, 15J, gilt, FULL, Coin, OF..................	100	125	175
Champion, 16J, NI, ADJ, FULL, DMK, OF	85	110	140
Columbus W. Co., 15J, OF, LS	85	110	140
Columbus W. Co., 16J, OF, LS	95	120	150
Columbus W. Co., 17J, OF, LS	100	125	175
Columbus W. Co., 17J, OF, LS, 2-Tone	135	160	200
Columbus W. Co., 16J, KW, KS, HC .... ★ ★ ★	400	550	775

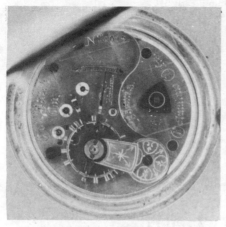 

Columbus Watch Co., 18 size, 15 jewels, key wind and set, "Ohio Watch Co." on dial, "Col. Watch Co." on movement.

Columbus Watch Co., Railway King, 18 size, 23 jewels, with choo choo dial.

Grade or Name—Description	Avg	Ex-Fn	Mint
Columbus W. Co., 11-15J, KW, KS, HC	$200	$300	$450
Columbus W. Co., 15J, KW, KS, 18K, HC	700	800	950
Columbus W. Co., 15J, HC, LS, KW/SW Trans.	125	150	200
Columbus W. Co., 15J, Multi-color 14K box hinge HC	1,600	1,800	2,500
Columbus W. Co., 15J, Coin	75	100	125
Columbus W. Co., 15J, "New Columbus W. Co." on mvt.	75	100	125
Columbus W. Co., 11J, Coin	75	100	125
Columbus W. Co., 11J, HC, LS	125	150	200
Columbus W. Co., 13J, HC, LS	125	150	200
Columbus W. Co., 17J, HC, LS, Trans.	125	150	200
Columbus King, 17J, HC	250	275	350
Columbus Watch Co., 17J, NI, 14K Multi-color box hinge HC	1,600	1,800	2,200
Columbus King, 21J, HC	275	300	375
Columbus King, 23J, HC	700	1,000	1,350
Columbus King, 25J, HC ★ ★	2,000	2,500	3,500
Jay Gould, 15J, OF	200	275	375
Jackson Park, 15J, NI, ADJ, OF	200	275	375
North Star, 11J, NI, FULL, HC	75	100	125
North Star, 11J, gilt, FULL, HC	75	100	125
North Star, 15J, gilt, FULL, Coin, HC	85	110	140
North Star, 15J, NI, FULL, HC	85	110	140
Ohio Watch Co., 13J, OF, KW, KS ★ ★	300	375	475
Ohio Watch Co., 11-13J, OF, transition KW/KS to SW/LS ★	200	275	375

Grade or Name—Description	Avg	Ex-Fn	Mint
Railroad Monarch, 17J, ADJ, OF	$200	$275	$375
Railway King, 16J, ADJ, GJS, 2-Tone, Choo Choo dial, HC	250	325	425
Railway King, 17J, ADJ, GJS, Choo Choo dial, HC	250	325	425
Railway King, 17J, 2-Tone, HC.........................	175	225	300
Railway King, 19J, GJS, Adj.5P, HC .... ★ ★	500	600	700
Railway King, 19J, GJS, Adj.5P, OF .... ★ ★	500	600	700
Railway King, 21J, GT, Adj.6P, DMK, GJS, HC........	200	275	375
Railway King, 21J, GT, Adj.6P, DMK, GJS, 2-Tone, HC	225	275	375
Railway King, 23J, Adj.6P, DMK, GJS, HC .... ★	800	1,100	1,450
Railway King, 25J, GT, Adj.6P, DMK, GJS, OF .... ★ ★	2,000	2,500	3,500
Railway King, 25J, GT, Adj.6P, DMK, GJS, HC .. ★ ★ ★	2,500	3,000	4,000
Railway King Special	200	275	375
R. W. K. Special, 17J, OF, LS, 2-Tone.................	225	275	375
R. W. K. Special, 19J, HC, LS, 2-Tone................	250	325	425
Railway Regulator, 17J, OF	200	250	350
Railway Time Service, 17J, OF, NI....................	175	225	300
Time King, 17J, 2-Tone, OF...........................	150	175	200
Time King, 21J, GT, Adj.6P, DMK, GJS, 2-Tone, HC ...	225	275	375
Time King, 23J, GT, Adj.6P, DMK, GJS, HC	800	1,100	1,450
Time King, 25J, GT, Adj.6P, DMK, GJS .... ★ ★	2,000	2,500	3,500
G#18, 16J, HC, Adj.6P, GJS, DMK, NI.................	150	175	200
G#20-21, 7-11J, HC	100	125	175
G#28, 16J, HC, FULL, ADJ, GJS, DMK	125	150	175
G#34, 15J, HC, FULL, NI	125	150	175
G#32, 15J, HC, FULL, gilded	125	150	175
G#90, 7J, gilt, OF, FULL	75	100	125
G#90, 7J, gilt, OF, Coin	75	100	125
G#93, 15J, gilt, OF, FULL	85	110	140
G#94, 15J, NI, OF, FULL	85	110	140

Columbus King, 18 size, 25 jewels, hunting case, stem wind, serial number 503,094.

Railway King, 18 size, 23 jewels, adjusted, stem wind, open face, serial number 503,315.

Grade or Name—Description	Avg	Ex-Fn	Mint
G#95, 15J, NI, OF, FULL, ADJ, GJS.................	$75	$100	$125
G#98, 16J, NI, OF, FULL, ADJ, GJS, DMK	85	110	140
G#99, 16J, NI, OF, FULL, Adj.6P, GJS, DMK	100	125	150
G#105, 19J, GJS, 2-Tone, HC .... ★	1,000	1,200	1,500
Swiss-made 18S, 7J, HC, SW, LS, ¾ Plate	75	100	125
Swiss-made 18S, 11J, HC, SW, LS, ¾ Plate	75	100	125
Swiss-made 18S, 15J, HC, SW, LS, ¾ Plate	85	110	140
Swiss-made 18S, 16J, HC, SW, LS, ¾ Plate	85	110	140

Columbus Watch Co., 16 size, 17 jewels, gold train, serial number 228,188.

Columbus Watch Co., Ruby Model, 16 size, 21 jewels, three quarter plate, gold jewel settings, gold train, Adj6p.

16 SIZE

Grade or Name — Description	Avg	Ex-Fn	Mint
New Columbus Watch Co., 11J, ¾, OF	$50	$75	$100
New Columbus Watch Co., 15J, ¾, OF	50	75	100
New Columbus Watch Co., 16J, ¾, OF	50	75	100
New Columbus Watch Co., 17J, 14K, Multi-color HC....	1,000	1,200	1,500
New Columbus Watch Co., 17J, 2-Tone	75	100	125
Ruby Model, 21J, ¾, NI, GJS, GT, OF, 2-tone ..... ★ ★	525	600	725
Ruby Model, 21J, ¾, NI, GJS, Adj.6P, GT, HC ...... ★	425	500	625
G#41, 11J, gilt, ¾, HC	75	100	125
G#43, 11J, NI, ¾, HC	75	100	125
G#44, 15J, NI, GJS, ADJ, ¾, HC....................	85	110	140
G#45, 19J, GJS, 2-Tone, HC .... ★ ★	800	1,000	1,300
G#46, 15J, NI, GJS, ADJ, ¾, HC....................	75	100	125
G#47, 16J, NI, ADJ, GJS, ¾, HC....................	85	110	140
G#81, 11J, OF, gilt, ¾	50	75	100
G#83, 11J, OF, NI, ¾	50	75	100
G#84, 15J, OF, NI, GJS, ADJ, ¾	50	75	100
G#86, 15J, OF, NI, GJS, ADJ, ¾	75	100	125
G#87, 16J, OF, Adj.3P, GJS, ¾, NI, DMK.............	85	110	140
G#88, 16J, OF, Adj.6p, 14K, GJS, ¾, DMK, NI	475	500	600

Grade or Name—Description	Avg	Ex-Fn	Mint
Swiss-made 16S, 15J, SW, LS, OF	$50	$75	$100
Swiss-made 16S, 15J, SW, LS, HC	75	100	125
Swiss-made 16S, 16J, SW, LS, OF	50	75	100
Swiss-made 16S, 16J, SW, LS, HC	85	110	140

Columbus Watch Co., 6 size, 15 jewels, ¼ plate, stem wind, serial number 377,489

New Columbus Watch Co. Example of a basic model for 6 size. ¼ plate, 7-16 jewels, gilded and nickel.

6 SIZE

Grade or Name — Description	Avg	Ex-Fn	Mint
G#102-G#50, 7J, gilded, HC...........................	$75	$100	$125
G#101-G#51, 11J, gilded, HC...........................	75	100	125
G#53, 11J, NI, HC.....................................	75	100	125
G#55, 15J, GJS, NI, 18K, HC	375	425	575
G#55, 15J, GJS, NI, HC	75	100	125
G#104-G#57, 16J, GJS, DMK, NI, HC	75	100	125
Swiss made 6S, 11-15J, SW, LS, HC	50	75	100

4 SIZE

Grade or Name—Description	Avg	Ex-Fn	Mint
Columbus Watch Co., 15J, HC, gilt mvt.	$100	$150	$200
Columbus Watch Co., 15J, HC, nickel mvt..............	110	160	220

COLUMBUS
ESTIMATED SERIAL NUMBERS AND PRODUCTION DATES

Date	Serial No.	Date	Serial No.	Special Block of Serial Nos.	
1883	23,000	1893	207,000		
1884	30,000	1894	229,000		
1885	40,000	1895	251,000	**Date**	**Serial No.**
1886	53,000	1896	273,000	1894	500,001
1887	75,000	1897	295,000	1896	501,500
1888	97,000	1898	317,000	1898	503,000
1889	119,000	1899	339,000	1900	504,500
1890	141,000	1900	361,000	1902	505,800
1891	163,000	1901	383,000		
1892	185,000				

CORNELL WATCH CO.
Chicago, Illinois
1870 - 1874
San Francisco, California
1875 - 1876

The Cornell Watch Co. bought the Newark Watch Co. and greatly improved the movements being produced. In the fall of 1874, the company moved to San Francisco, Calif., with about 60 of its employees. The movements made in California were virtually the same as those made in Chicago. The company wanted to employ Chinese who would work cheaper, but the skilled employees refused to go along and went on strike. The company stayed alive until 1875 and was sold to the California Watch Co. in January 1876. But death came a few months later.

The Chronology of the Development of Cornell Watch Co.:
Newark Watch Co. 1864-1870; S#s 6901-12,000
Cornell Watch Co., Chicago, Ill. 1870-1874; S#s 12,001 to 25,000;
Cornell Watch Co., San Francisco, Calif. 1874-Jan. 1876; S#s 25,001 to 35,000;
California Watch Co., Jan. 1876-mid 1876.

 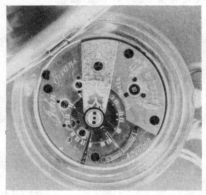

Cornell Watch Co., J.C. Adams, 18 size, 11 jewels, key wind & set, made in Chicago, Ill, serial number 13,647.

Cornell Watch Co., 18 size, 15 jewels, key wind & set, marked "John Evans," serial number 16,868.

18 SIZE

Grade or Name — Description		Avg	Ex-Fn	Mint
J. C. Adams, 11J, KW	★	$400	$500	$650
C. T. Bowen, FULL, KW	★	350	450	600
C. M. Cady, 15J, SW	★	300	400	550
Cornell, 7J, San Francisco on mvt., KW	★	900	1,100	1,400
Cornell, 11J, KW		300	400	550
Cornell, 11J, San Francisco on mvt., KW		900	1,100	1,400
Cornell, 15J, KW	★	350	450	600
Cornell W. Co., 15J, San Francisco on mvt., KW	★	1,100	1,300	1,600

Grade or Name—Description		Avg	Ex-Fn	Mint
Cornell W. Co., 15J, San Francisco on mvt., SW .. ★ ★ ★		$1,200	$1,400	$1,800
Paul Cornell, 19J, GJS, HCI5P, SW .... ★ ★		1,500	1,800	2,500
John Evans, 15J, KW .... ★		350	450	600
Excelsior, 15J, FULL, KW, KS		300	400	550
H. N. Hibbard, 11J, KW, ADJ .... ★		350	450	600
George F. Root, 15J, KW .... ★		350	450	600
George Waite, 7J, (Hyde Park), KW .... ★		400	550	650
E. J. Williams, 7J, KW .... ★		350	450	600
Ladies Stemwind .... ★		150	200	300
Eugene Smith, 17J .... ★		350	450	600

JACOB D. CUSTER
Norristown, Pennsylvania
1840 - 1845

At the age of 19, Jacob Custer repaired his father's watch. He was then asked to repair all the watches within his community. Custer was basically self-taught and had very little formal education and little training in clocks and watches. He made all the parts except the hairspring and fusee chains. The watches were about 14 size, and only 12 to 15 watches were made. The 14S fusee watches had lever escapement, ¾ plate and were sold in his own gold cases. He made a few chronometers, one with a helical spring.

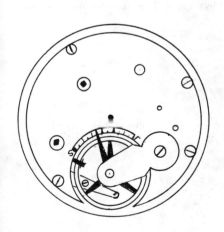

J. D. Custer, 11 12 also, engraved on movement J.D. Custer, Morristown, Pa. Patented Feb. 4, 1843.

Description	Avg	Ex-Fn	Mint
14S, OF, engraved on mvt. "J. D. Custer, Patented Feb. 4, 1843, #2,939" .... ★ ★ ★			
	$8,500	$12,000	$18,000

DUDLEY WATCH CO.
Lancaster, Pennsylvania
1920 - 1925

William Wallace Dudley became interested in watches and horology at the age of 13 and became an apprentice making ship chronometers in Canada. When he moved to America, he worked for the South Bend and Illinois Watch companies and the Trenton Watch Co. before going to Hamilton Watch Co. in Lancaster. He left Hamilton at age 69 to start his own watch company. In 1922 his first watches were produced; they were 14S, 19J, and were labeled Models 1894 and 1897. Watch parts, dials and hands were Swiss made. The winding mechanism was made at the Dudley factory. The cases came from Wadsworth Keystone and the Star Watch Case Co. Dudley also made a 12S, 19J watch. By 1924, the company was heavily in debt, and on February 20, 1925, a petition for bankruptcy was filed. The Masonic Watch was his most unusual.

Dudley Watches

				Total Production
Dudley Watch Co.	1920-1925	Model No. 1	S# 500-1,900	1,400
P. W. Baker Co.	1925-1935	Model No. 2	S# 2,001-4,800	1,600
XL Watch Co., N.Y.	1935-1976	Model No. 3	S# 4,801-6,500	1,000
			Total	4,000

Model No. 1, 14S, 19J, OF, can be distinguished by the "Holy Bible" engraved on the winding arbor plate.

Model No. 2, 12S, 19J, used the 910 and 912 Hamilton wheels and escapement, has a flat silver-colored Bible.

Model No. 3, 12S, can be distinguished by the silver Bible which was riveted in place and was more three-dimensional.

Dudley Watch Co., Model 1, 14 size, 19 jewels, open face, flip back, serial number 1232.

12 SIZE - 14 SIZE
"MASONS" MODEL

Grade or Name—Description	Avg	Ex-Fn	Mint
14S, Dudley, 19J, 14K, flip open back, Serial #1 (made 5 experimental models with Serial #1)........... ★ ★ ★	$5,000	$7,000	$10,000
14S, M#1, 19J, OF, 14K, flip open back .... ★	3,000	3,200	3,500
12S, M#1, 19J, OF, 14K, flip open back, w/box & papers ★	3,500	3,800	4,000
12S, M#2, 19J, OF, flip open back, GF .... ★	1,600	1,800	2,200
12S, M#2, 19J, OF, 14K, flip open back case.......... ★	2,000	2,200	2,600
12S, M#2, 19J, OF, 14K display case .... ★	1,850	2,200	2,400
12S, M#3, 19J, OF, display case, GF .... ★	1,600	1,800	2,200
12S, M#3, 19J, OF, 14K flip open case .... ★	2,000	2,200	2,600

Dudley Watch Co., Model 2, 12 size, 19 jewels, open face, serial number 2,420.

Dudley Watch Co., Model 3, 12 size, 19 jewels, open face.

ELGIN WATCH CO.
(NATIONAL WATCH CO.)
Elgin, Illinois
1864 - 1964

This was the largest watch company in terms of production; in fact, Elgin produced half of the total number of pocket watches (dollar-type not included). Some of the organizers came from Waltham Watch Co., including P. S. Bartlett, D. G. Currier, Otis Hoyt, Charles H. Mason and others. The idea of beginning a large watch company for the mid-West was discussed by J. C. Adams, Bartlett and Blake. After a trip to Waltham, Adams went back to Chicago and approached Benjamin W. Raymond, a former mayor of Chicago, to put up the necessary capital to get the company started. Adams and Raymond succeeded in getting others to pledge their financial support also. The National Watch Co. (Elgin) was formed in August 1864. The factory site was in Elgin, Illinois, where the city had donated 35 acres of land. The factory was completed in 1866, and the first movement was a B. W. Raymond, 18S, full plate design. The first watches were put on the market in 1867, selling for about $115, and all were quick train. The first stem wind model was an H. L. Culver with serial No. 155,001, lever set and quick train. In 1874 the name was changed to the Elgin National Watch Co. and they produced watches into the 1950s.

The first wrist watch made by Elgin was sold in 1910. This watch, Serial No. 101, sold for $12,000 in 1988.

Elgin Movements

	1st App.	1st S#		1st. App.	1st. S#
18S B. W. Raymond	April 1867	101	10S Lady Elgin	Jan. 1869	40,001
18S H. L. Culver	July 1867	1,001	10S Frances Rubie	Aug. 1870	50,001
18S J. T. Ryerson	Oct. 1867	5,001	10S Gail Borden	Sept. 1871	185,001
18S H. H. Taylor	Nov. 1867	25,001	10S Dexter Street	Dec. 1871	201,001
18S G. M. Wheeler	Nov. 1867	6,001	First Stem Wind	June 1873	
18S Matt Laflin	Jan. 1868	9,001	1st Nickel Movement	Aug.15, 1879	
18S Father Time	No date	2,300,001	Convertible	Fall 1878	
18S Veritas	No date	8,400,001			

Some Serial Nos. have the first two numbers replaced by a letter; i.e., 39,482,000 would be X482,000.

X—39	V—46
C,E,T&Y—42	H—47
L—43	N—48
U—44	F—49
J—45	S—50

ELGIN ESTIMATED SERIAL NUMBERS
AND PRODUCTION DATES

Date	Serial #	Date	Serial #	Date	Serial #
1867	10,000	1897	7,100,000	1926	29,100,000
1868	35,000	1898	7,550,000	1927	30,050,000
1869	65,000	1899	8,200,000	1928	31,500,000
1870	95,000	1900	9,000,000	1929	32,000,000
1871	120,000	1901	9,250,000	1930	32,500,000
1872	155,000	1902	9,700,000	1931	33,000,000
1873	170,000	1903	10,100,000	1932	33,800,000
1874	210,000	1904	10,900,000	1933	35,100,000
1875	320,000	1905	11,900,000	1934	35,000,000
1876	390,000	1906	12,600,000	1935	35,750,000
1877	475,000	1907	12,900,000	1936	36,200,000
1878	500,000	1908	13,550,000	1937	37,100,000
1879	580,000	1909	14,000,000	1938	37,900,000
1880	750,000	1910	14,900,000	1939	38,200,000
1881	900,000	1911	15,900,000	1940	39,100,000
1882	1,000,000	1912	16,500,000	1941	40,200,000
1883	1,300,000	1913	17,200,000	1942	41,100,000
1884	1,500,000	1914	17,900,000	1943	42,200,000
1885	1,700,000	1915	18,400,000	1944	42,600,000
1886	2,000,000	1916	19,500,000	1945	43,200,000
1887	2,400,000	1917	20,100,000	1946	43,800,000
1888	2,900,000	1918	21,000,000	1947	44,200,000
1889	3,400,000	1919	22,000,000	1948	45,100,000
1890	3,900,000	1920	23,000,000	1949	46,000,000
1891	4,500,000	1921	24,050,000	1950	47,000,000
1892	4,800,000	1922	25,100,000	1951	48,000,000
1893	4,900,000	1923	26,050,000	1952	49,000,000
1894	5,550,000	1924	27,000,000	1953	50,000,000
1895	5,900,000	1925	28,050,000	1956	55,000,000
1896	6,550,000				

Some collectors seek out low serial numbers and will usually pay a premium for them. The lower the number, the more desirable the watch. The table shown below lists the first serial number of each size watch made by Elgin.

Size	1st Serial Nos.	Size	1st Serial Nos.
18	101	10	40,001
17	356,001	6	570,001
16	600,001	0	2,889,001
14	351,001		

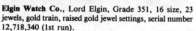

Elgin Watch Co., Lord Elgin, Grade 351, 16 size, 23 jewels, gold train, raised gold jewel settings, serial number 12,718,340 (1st run).

Father Time, 18 size, 21 jewels, model –8 with wind indicator, free sprung model, serial number 22,888,020

18 SIZE

Grade or Name — Description	Avg	Ex-Fn	Mint
Advance, 11J, gilded, KW, HC, FULL	$75	$100	$125
Age, 7J, gilded, KW, FULL, HC	75	100	125
Atlas Watch Co., 7J, HC, LS, FULL	75	100	125
California Watch, 15J, gilded, HC, KW, KS, FULL......	125	150	200
Chief, 7J, gilded, KW, FULL, HC	75	100	125
Convertible, 7J, G#98................................	75	100	125
H. L. Culver, 15J, gilded, KW, KS, FULL, HC, ADJ, low S#	200	250	325
H. L. Culver, 15J, gilded, KW, KS, FULL, HC, ADJ	125	150	200
H. L. Culver, 15J, KW, KS, 14K, HC	525	550	600
H. L. Culver, 15J, gilded, KW, KS, FULL, HC	100	125	175
H. L. Culver, 15J, gilded, SW, FULL, HC..............	75	100	125
H. L. Culver, 15J, gilded, KW, FULL, LS, HC	75	100	125
Elgin W. Co., 7J, OF, SW	50	75	100
Elgin W. Co., 7J, KW, gilded, HC....................	75	100	125
Elgin W. Co., 11J, KW, LS	50	75	100
Elgin W. Co., 11J, LS, SW, HC, 9K-10K	325	375	475
Elgin W. Co., 11J, LS, SW, HC, Silveroid	40	50	65
Elgin W. Co., 11J, LS, , SW, OF	50	70	100
Elgin W. Co., 13J, SW, PS/LS, Silveroid	40	50	65
Elgin W. Co., 13J, SW, PS/LS	50	75	100

California Watch, 18 size, 15 jewels, gilded, key wind & set, serial number 200,700.

Convertible, 18 size, 21 jewels, converts to either hunting or open face.

Grade or Name—Description	Avg	Ex-Fn	Mint
Elgin W. Co., 15J, KW, LS, HC	$75	$100	$150
Elgin W. Co., 15J, SW, LS, OF	50	75	100
Elgin W. Co., 15J, SW, LS, YGF, Multi-color box	300	325	500
Elgin W. Co., 15J, SW, LS, OF, Silveroid	50	60	75
Elgin W. Co., 15J, SW, LS, HC	75	100	125
Elgin W. Co., 15J, KW, hidden key	125	150	175
Elgin W. Co., 17J, SW, LS, Silveroid	50	60	75
Elgin W. Co., 17J, SW, LS or PS, OF	50	75	100
Elgin W. Co., 17J, SW, Multi-color, 14K, HC	1,500	1,800	2,200
Elgin W. Co., 21J, SW, LS or PS, OF	100	125	175
Elgin W. Co., 21J, SW, LS, box case, GF	175	200	275
Elgin W. Co., 21J, LS, HC, 14K	575	600	675
Elgin W. Co., 21J, SW, LS, Silveroid	60	70	90
Elgin W. Co., 21J, SW, LS, HC	125	150	175

Elgin W. Co., Grade 297, 18 size, 15 jewels.

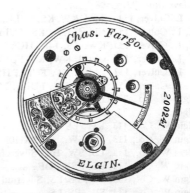

Charles Fargo, 18 size, 7 jewels, gilded, key wind & set, hunting case.

 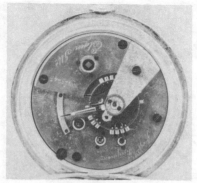

Pennsylvania Railroad Co. on dial. **B.W. Raymond** on movement. One of the first railroad watches commissioned by Penn. RR Co., 18 size, 15 jewels, key wind and set, serial number 123,245, c. 1874.

Grade or Name—Description	Avg	Ex-Fn	Mint
Elgin W. Co., 21J, Wind Indicator	$600	$800	$1,000
Elgin W. Co., 21J, Wind Indicator, free sprung	600	800	1,000
Charles Fargo, 7J, gilded, KW, HC	150	175	200
J. V. Farwell, 11J, gilded, KW, HC .... ★	250	300	375
Father Time, 17J, NI, KW, FULL, HC, DMK......... ★	250	350	450
Father Time, 17J, NI, FULL, OF, DMK................	100	125	175
Father Time, 17J, SW, OF, Silveroid	50	60	80
Father Time, 17J, SW, HC...........................	125	150	200
Father Time, 20J, NI, SW, FULL, HC, DMK .... ★	250	300	375
Father Time, 21J, NI, SW, FULL, OF, GJS, DMK	150	175	200
Father Time, 21J, NI, SW, ¾, GJS, DMK, HC	125	150	200
Father Time, 21J, NI, SW, ¾, OF, GJS, DMK	125	150	200
Father Time, 21J, GJT, HCI5P, Diamond end stone	125	150	200
Father Time, 21J, NI, SW, ¾, OF, GJS, Wind Indicator .	800	1,000	1,300
Father Time, 21J, SW, ¾, GJS, wind indicator, HC	1,000	1,200	1,500
Father Time, G#367, 21J, NI, SW, ¾, OF, GJS, military wind indicator, free sprung, 602 sterling case	1,200	1,400	1,700
W. H. Ferry, 15J, gilded, KW, HC	125	150	175
W. H. Ferry, 11J, gilded, KW, HC	125	150	175
Mat Laflin, 7J, gilded, KW, HC	125	150	175
National W. Co., 7J, KW, KS.......................	75	100	125
National W. Co., 11J, KW, KS......................	75	100	125
National W. Co., 15J, KW, KS......................	85	110	135
M. D. Ogden, 15J, KW, HC	125	150	175
M. D. Ogden, 11J, gilded, KW, HC.................	225	150	175
Overland, 17J, NI, KW, HC, DMK	150	175	200
Overland, 17J, NI, SW, HC, DMK...................	100	125	175
Pennsylvania Railroad Co. on dial, B. W. Raymond on mvt., 15J, KW, KS (1st RR watches)............... ★★★	600	700	900
Railway Timer, 15J, FULL, HC .... ★	300	350	400

B.W. Raymond, 18 size, 23 jewels, wind indicator. Note small winding indicator gear next to crown wheel.

H.H. Taylor, 18 size, 15 jewels, key wind & set, serial number 288,797.

Grade or Name—Description	Avg	Ex-Fn	Mint
B. W. Raymond, 15-17J, KW, low S# under 1000	$400	$500	$650
B. W. Raymond, 15J, gilded, KW, FULL, HC	125	150	175
B. W. Raymond, 17J, gilded, KW, FULL, HC	125	150	175
B. W. Raymond, 15J, SW, HC	75	100	125
B. W. Raymond, 17J, NI, FULL, OF	50	75	100
B. W. Raymond, 17J, Silveroid	40	60	80
B. W. Raymond, 17J, NI, FULL, HC	100	125	175
B. W. Raymond, 15J, box case, 14K	700	800	1,200
B. W. Raymond, 17J, gilded, NI, SW, FULL, ADJ	75	100	125
B. W. Raymond, 19J, NI, ¾, SW, OF, GJS, DMK, GT..	75	100	150
B. W. Raymond, 19J, NI, ¾, SW, OF, GJS, Wind Indicator, DMK	500	600	850
B. W. Raymond, 19J, ¾, GJS, GT, Diamond end stone..	75	100	125
B. W. Raymond, 21J, ¾, GJS, GT, Diamond end stone, OF	125	150	175
B. W. Raymond, 21J, SW, Silveroid	75	100	125
B. W. Raymond, 21J, SW, GJS, GT, DES, HC	175	200	250
B. W. Raymond, 21J, NI, ¾, SW, GJS, DMK, GT	100	125	175
B. W. Raymond, 21J, NI, ¾, SW, GJS, Wind Indicator, DMK	650	750	950
J. T. Ryerson, 7J, gilded, FULL, KW, HC..............	75	100	125
Solar W. Co., 15J, Multi-color dial	75	100	150
Standard, 17J, OF, LS...............................	100	125	150
Sundial, 7J, SW, PS.................................	50	60	75
H. H. Taylor, 15J, gilded, FULL, KW, HC	100	125	175
H. H. Taylor, 15J, NI, FULL, KW, HC, DMK	100	125	175
H. H. Taylor, 15J, NI, FULL, SW, HC, DMK, quick train	100	125	175
H. H. Taylor, 15J, SW, Silveroid	40	50	65
H. H. Taylor, 15J, SW, slow train	60	70	85
Veritas, 21J, SW, PS, HC............................	175	225	300
Veritas, 21J, SW, LS, GJS, GT, HC	175	225	300

Veritas, 18 size, 23 jewels, solid gold train, gold jewel settings, diamond end stone, serial number 9,542,678.

G.M. Wheeler, Grade 369, 18 size, 17 jewels, open face, gold jewel settings, serial number 14,788,315

Grade or Name—Description	Avg	Ex-Fn	Mint
Veritas, 21J, ¾, NI, GJS, OF, DMK, GT	$100	$125	$175
Veritas, 21J, ¾, GJS, GT, Diamond end stones	100	125	175
Veritas, 21J, ¾, GJS, GT, Diamond end stones, HC	175	225	300
Veritas, 21J, ¾, NI, GJS, OF, Wind Indicator, DMK	1,000	1,100	1,300
Veritas, 21J, ¾, NI, GJS, HC, Wind Indicator, DMK	1,000	1,200	1,400
Veritas, 23J, ¾, NI, GJS, OF, DMK, GT	175	225	300
Veritas, 23J, ¾, GJS, HC, GT	250	275	350
Veritas, 23J, ¾, NI, GJS, OF, DMK, GT, Diamond end stone	200	225	300
Veritas, 23J, ¾, Wind Indicator, GJS, OF, DMK, GT, 14K	1,400	1,600	2,000
Veritas, 23J, G#214, ¾, NI, GJS, OF, Wind Indicator, DMK	800	1,000	1,300
Veritas, 23J, G#214, SW, OF	125	150	200
Veritas, 23J, SW, NI, GJS, GT, LS, HC	250	275	350
Veritas, 23J, SW, OF, 14K	550	575	650
G. M. Wheeler, 11J, gilded, KW, HC	75	100	150
G. M. Wheeler, 13-15J, gilded, FULL, KW	75	100	150
G. M. Wheeler, 15J, NI, FULL, KW, DMK, HC	75	100	150
G. M. Wheeler, 15J, SW, NI, FULL, DMK, OF	50	75	100
G. M. Wheeler, 17J, KW, NI, FULL, DMK, OF	100	125	175
G. M. Wheeler, 17J, SW, NI, FULL, DMK, OF	50	75	125

MOVEMENTS WITH NO NAME

	Avg	Ex-Fn	Mint
No. 5 & No. 17, 7J, gilded, FULL, HC	$50	$75	$125
No. 23 & No. 18, 11J, gilded, FULL, HC	50	75	125
No. 69, 15J, M#1, KW, quick train, HC	50	75	125
No. 316, 15J, NI, FULL, HC, DMK	75	100	150
No. 317, 15J, NI, FULL, ADJ, OF, DMK	75	100	150

Grade or Name—Description	Avg	Ex-Fn	Mint
No. 316 & No. 317, 15J, Silveroid	$40	$50	$65
No. 326, 15J, OF	60	70	80
No. 327, 15J, HC	75	100	150
No. 335, 17J, HC	75	100	150
No. 336, 17J, NI, FULL, OF, DMK	50	75	150
No. 345, 19J, GJS, 2-Tone, HC .... ★	600	700	900
No. 348, 21J, NI, FULL, HC, GJS, DMK	100	125	175
No. 349, 21J, OF	50	75	150
No. 378, 19J, NI, FULL, HC, DMK	75	100	150
No. 379, 19J, OF	50	75	125

Elgin Watch Co., 17 size, 11 jewels, key wind & set, made for English market, serial number 418,220.

Elgin Watch Co., 17 size, 7 jewels, key wind & set, serial number 199,076. Made for Kennedy & Co.

17 SIZE

Grade or Name — Description	Avg	Ex-Fn	Mint
Avery, 7J, gilded, KW, FULL, HC....................	$75	$100	$150
Leader, 7J, gilded, KW, FULL, HC..................	75	100	150
Leader, 7J, gilded, KW, FULL, HC, early movement	75	100	150
Sunshine, 15J, KW, KS from back	100	125	175
M#11, 14, 15, 51, 59: 7J, gilded, KW, FULL, HC	100	125	175
17 Size, KW, Silveroid	50	60	75

16 SIZE

Grade or Name — Description	Avg	Ex-Fn	Mint
Blind Man's Watch, 17J, HC	$75	$100	$150
Convertible Model, 13J, BRG, OF	50	75	125
Convertible Model, 15J, BRG, ADJ, 14K, HC...........	450	475	525
Convertible Model, 15J, ADJ, DMK, 3F BRG, HC	75	100	150
Convertible Model, 15J, ¾, ADJ, DMK, GJS	75	100	150

Elgin Watch Co., 16 size, 21 jewels, converts to open face or hunting case, serial number 607,061.

Elgin W. Co., 16 size, 21 jewels, three-fingered bridge model, adjusted, gold jewel settings, gold train, serial number 6,469,814.

Grade or Name—Description	Avg	Ex-Fn	Mint
Convertible Model, 15J, Silveroid	$50	$60	$90
Convertible Model, 15J, 3F BRG, OF	50	75	125
Convertible Model, 21J, 3F BRG	900	1,100	1,450
Convertible Model, 21J, G#72, ¾, ADJ, DMK, GJS, 14K	1,000	1,200	1,500
Convertible Model, 21J, G#91, 3F BRG, 14K	1,600	1,800	2,100
Doctors Watch, 15J, 4th Model, NI, GT, sweep second hand, GF case	150	175	225
Doctors Watch, 15J, 4th Model, gilded, sweep second hand, coin silver case	125	150	200
Doctors Watch, 15J, 4th Model, sweep second hand, 14K	525	550	600
Elgin W. Co., 7J, OF	50	75	125
Elgin W. Co., 7J, HC	75	100	150

Doctors Watch, 16 size, 15 jewels, fourth model, gold jewel settings, gold train, sweep second hand, serial number 926,458.

Grade or Name—Description	Avg	Ex-Fn	Mint
Elgin W. Co., 9J, OF..............................	$50	$75	$125
Elgin W. Co., 11J, OF.............................	50	75	125
Elgin W. Co., 11J, HC	75	100	150
Elgin W. Co., 13J, OF............................	50	125	125
Elgin W. Co., 13J, OF, Silveroid	40	50	70
Elgin W. Co., 13J, HC	75	100	150
Elgin W. Co., 15J, HC	75	100	150
Elgin W. Co., 15J, OF, Silveroid	40	50	70
Elgin W. Co., 15J, OF............................	50	75	125
Elgin W. Co., 15J, HC, 14K	400	450	550
Elgin W. Co., 17J, OF............................	50	75	125
Elgin W. Co., 17J, 14K, HC	400	450	550
Elgin W. Co., 17J, G#280, 9th model, ADJ5P......	100	125	175
Elgin W. Co., 17J, HC	100	125	175
Elgin W. Co., 19J, OF, LS........................	75	100	150
Elgin W. Co., 21J, HC	150	175	225
Elgin W. Co., 21J, OF, Silveroid	50	60	75
Elgin W. Co., 21J, OF............................	100	125	175
Elgin W. Co., 17J, LS, multi-color HC, GF..........	250	300	400
Elgin W. Co., 17J, multi-color HC, 14K	1,000	1,200	1,600
3F Bridge Model, 15J, NI, DMK....................	50	75	125
3F Bridge Model, 17J, Adj.3P, NI, DMK, GJS.......	50	75	125
3F Bridge Model, 17J, Adj.5P, NI, DMK, GJS, GT....	75	100	150
3F Bridge Model, 21J, Adj.5P, NI, DMK, GJS, GT....	200	250	325
Father Time, 17J, ¾, NI, OF, GJS, DR, DMK........	100	125	175
Father Time, 21J, ¾, NI, HC, GJS, DR, DMK	175	200	275
Father Time, 21J, ¾, NI, OF, GJS, DR, Wind Indicator .	400	450	500
Father Time, 21J, Silveroid.......................	60	70	80
Father Time, 21J, NI, GJS, DR, OF	100	125	175
Lord Elgin, 21J, GJS, DR, Adj.5P, 3F BRG, 14K ...★ ★	1,200	1,500	2,000

Father Time, 16 size, 21 jewels, gold train; Note up and down wind indicator.

Father Time, 16 size, 21 jewels, gold train; Note up and down wind indicator, serial number 18,106,465.

Lord Elgin, 16 size, 23 jewels, gold train, raised gold jewel settings, serial number 12,718,340.

B.W. Raymond, 16 size, 19 jewels, gold jewel settings, serial number 17,822,991.

Grade or Name—Description	Avg	Ex-Fn	Mint
Lord Elgin, 23J, GJS, DR, Adj.5P, ¾, 14K, OF .... ★ ★	$1,000	$1,200	$1,400
B. W. Raymond, 17J, ¾, GJS, 14K, OF................	475	525	650
B. W. Raymond, 17J, ¾, GJS, SW, HC................	200	275	350
B. W. Raymond, 17J, 3F BRG .... ★ ★	400	500	650
B. W. Raymond, 17J, M#8, LS, NI, Wind Indicator	300	350	400
B. W. Raymond, 17J, GJS, SW, OF	150	200	250
B. W. Raymond, 17J, ¾, GJS, DR, Adj.5P, DMK	175	225	275
B. W. Raymond, 19J, ¾, GJS, DR, Adj.5P, DMK, OF ..	75	100	150
B. W. Raymond, 19J, OF, 14K, 30 DWT	400	450	500
B. W. Raymond, 19J, ¾, GJS, DR, HCI5P, DMK, Wind Indicator	350	400	450
B. W. Raymond, 19J, M#8, G#240, OF, Adj.5P	75	100	150
B. W. Raymond, 19J, GJS, Adj.5P, HC................	150	175	225
B. W. Raymond, 21J, 14K, OF......................	425	475	525
B. W. Raymond, 21J, G#389, OF	100	125	175
B. W. Raymond, 21J, G#571, ¾, Adj.5P, OF...........	100	125	175
B. W. Raymond, 21J, ¾, GJS, DR, Adj.5P, HC	175	225	275
B. W. Raymond, 21J, ¾, GJS, DR, Adj.5P, DMK, OF ..	100	125	175
B. W. Raymond, 21J, ¾, GJS, DR, Adj.5P, DMK, Wind Indicator	350	400	450
B. W. Raymond, 22J, WWII Model, sweep second hand..	125	150	175
B. W. Raymond, 23J, ¾, GJS, DR, Adj.5P, DMK	250	300	375
B. W. Raymond, 23J, ¾, GJS, DR, Adj.5P, DMK, Wind Indicator	475	525	600
B. W. Raymond, 23J, ¾, GJS, DR, Adj.5P, DMK, Wind Indicator, military style.....................	425	475	550
Repeater, Terstegen, 5 min., 21J, 2 gongs .... ★ ★	2,500	3,000	4,500
Veritas, 21J, 3F brg, GJS .... ★	225	275	350
Veritas, 21J, GJS, DR, Adj.5P, DMK, ¾, HC	250	300	375

Veritas, 16 size, 23 jewels, solid gold train, gold jeweled settings, Adj5p, serial number 16,678,681.

Grade 340, 16 size, 17 jewels, three-fingered bridge model, open face.

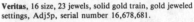

Grade or Name—Description	Avg	Ex-Fn	Mint
Veritas, 21J, GJS, DR, Adj.5P, DMK, ¾, Wind Indicator	$550	$600	$700
Veritas, 21J, GJS, SW, Grade 360 .... ★	375	400	475
Veritas, 21J, GJS, SW, Adj.5P, OF, Grade 270.........	125	150	200
Veritas, 23J, GJS, Adj.5P, 14K, OF....................	575	675	800
Veritas, 23J, GJS, Adj.5P, HC	300	400	500
Veritas, 23J, GJS, DR, Adj.5P, DMK, ¾, OF, Grade 376 ★	350	400	500
Veritas, 23J, GJS, DR, Adj.5P, DMK, ¾, Diamond end stone, Grade 350 .... ★	375	425	525
Veritas, 23J, GJS, DR, Adj.5P, DMK, ¾, Wind Indicator	600	650	750
G. M. Wheeler, 17J, DR, Adj.3P, DMK, ¾	50	75	90
G. M. Wheeler, 17J, 3F BRG.........................	50	75	90
G. M. Wheeler, 17J, HC, 14K	450	475	525
WWII Model, 17J, OF...............................	100	125	175
WWII Model, 21J, OF...............................	125	150	200
M#13, 9J, HC	75	85	100
M#48, 13J, HC	75	100	150

(Add $50 to hunting case models listed as open face)

MODELS WITH NO NAMES

	Avg	Ex-Fn	Mint
Grade #72-91, 21J, 3F BRG .... ★ ★	$450	$550	$700
Grade #145, 19J, GJS, BRG, HC .... ★ ★	650	750	900
Grade #156, 21J, ¾, NI, DR, DMK, GT, GJS, OF	150	175	225
Grade #156, 21J, ¾, NI, DR, DMK, GT, GJS, HC, 14K .	475	500	625
Grade #162, 21J, SW, PS, NI, GJS, GT	225	275	350
Grade #270, 21J, 3F BRG, GJS, marked mvt.	150	175	225
Grade #280, 17J, marked on mvt......................	125	150	200
Grade #290 & #291, 7J, OF, ¾, NI, DMK	50	75	90

Grade or Name—Description	Avg	Ex-Fn	Mint
Grade #291, 7J, ¾, HC, 14K	$400	$450	$550
Grade #312 & #313, 15J, ¾, NI, DR, DMK, OF	50	75	90
Grade #372, 19J, M#15, LS, OF, Adj.5P	250	300	375
Grade #374, 21J, M#15, LS, OF, Adj.5P	275	325	400
Grade #381 & #382, 17J, ¾, NI, DR, DMK, OF	65	85	125
Grade #391, 21J, M#15, LS, OF, Adj.5P	300	350	450
Grade #145, 19J, GJS, BRG, HC .... ★ ★	900	1,000	1,200
Grade #156, 21J, ¾, NI, DR, DMK, GT, GJS, HC	175	200	250
Grade #156, 21J, ¾, NI, DR, DMK, GT, GJS, HC, 14K .	475	500	550
Grade #162, 21J, SW, PS, NI, GJS, GT, OF	200	250	325
Grade #72, 21J, ADJ, ¾, HC .... ★	400	450	525
Grade #91, 21J, 3F BRG, HC .... ★ ★	700	800	1,000
Grade #571, 21J, Adj.5P, OF	100	125	175

14 SIZE

Grade or Name — Description	Avg	Ex-Fn	Mint
Lord Elgin, 17J, SS, ¾, OF	$200	$225	$275
7J, ¾, M#1, gilded, KW, 14K, HC	300	350	400
7J, ¾, M#1, gilded, KW, YGF, HC....................	75	100	150
11J, ¾, M#1, gilded, KW, YGF, HC...................	75	100	150
11J, ¾, M#1, gilded, KW, YGF, OF	50	60	85
13J, ¾, M#1, gilded, KW, OF........................	50	60	85
15J, ¾, M#1, gilded, KW, OF........................	50	60	85
7J, ¾, M#2, SW, OF.................................	50	60	85
15J, ¾, M#2, SW, OF................................	60	75	100
15J, ¾, M#2, SW, 14K, HC	275	325	375

12 SIZE

Grade or Name — Description	Avg	Ex-Fn	Mint
Eight Day, 21J, 8-Day Wind Indicator, BRG .... ★ ★ ★ ★	$2,000	$2,500	$3,000

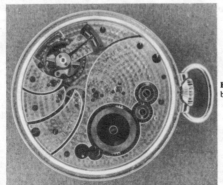

Elgin Eight Day, 12 size, 21 jewels, wind indicator, bridge movement, open face, serial number 12,345,678.

Example of a 12 size 17 jewel Elgin with a personalized logo on dial.

Lord Elgin, 12 size, 21 jewels, gold train, gold jewel settings, serial number 24,999,947.

Grade or Name—Description	Avg	Ex-Fn	Mint
Elgin W. Co. #30, 7J, ¾, gilded, KW, OF	$45	$55	$85
Elgin W. Co. #189, 19J, HC, ¾, NI	75	100	150
Elgin W. Co. #190-194, 23J, OF, GJS, ¾, Adj.5P, NI, DMK, GT	125	150	200
Elgin W. Co. #190-194, 23J, HC, GJS, ¾, Adj.5P, NI, DMK, GT	150	175	225
Elgin W. Co. #236 & #237, 21J, OF, GJS, ¾, Adj.5P, NI, DMK, GT	75	100	150
Elgin W. Co. #236 & #237, 21J, HC, GJS, ¾, Adj.5P, NI, DMK, GT	100	125	175
Elgin W. Co. #301 & #302, 7J, ¾, HC, NI	50	60	85
Elgin W. Co. #314 & #315, 15J, ¾, HC, NI	50	60	85
Elgin W. Co. #383 & #384, 17J, ¾, HC, NI	60	70	95
Elgin W. Co., 15J, 14K, Multi-color...................	500	600	750
Elgin W. Co., 15J, OF, GF	50	60	75
Elgin W. Co., 15J, HC, 14K	300	350	425
Elgin W. Co., 17J, OF, 14K........................	275	300	350
Elgin W. Co., 19J, HC, 14K	325	375	450
Elgin W. Co., 19J, 14K, OF.........................	275	300	350
C. H. Hulburd, 19J, thin BRG model, 14K case .... ★	800	1,000	1,200
C. H. Hulburd, 19J, thin BRG model, 18K .... ★	1,000	1,200	1,400
Lord Elgin, 23J, HC, GJS, DR, Adj.5P, DMK, NI	175	200	275
Lord Elgin, 17J, HC	75	100	150
Lord Elgin, 19J, HC	75	100	150
Lord Elgin, 21J, 14K, OF	275	300	375
Lord Elgin, 21J, HC	75	100	150

Lord Elgin, 12 size, 23 jewels, gold jewel settings, Adj5p, originally sold for $110.00.

G.M. Wheeler, 12 size, 17 jewels, Adj3p, originally sold for $27.00.

Grade or Name—Description	Avg	Ex-Fn	Mint
B. W. Raymond, 19J, HC, ¾, GJS, Adj.5P, DR, DMK, NI	$75	$100	$125
G. M. Wheeler, 17J, ¾, DR, Adj.5P, DMK, NI, OF	40	60	75
G. M. Wheeler, 17J, ¾, DR, Adj.5P, DMK, NI, HC	65	90	110

Frances Rubie, Grade 23, 10 size, 15 jewels, key wind & set.

Gail Borden, Grade 22, 10 size, 11 jewels, key wind & set, serial number 947,696.

10 SIZE
(HC)

Grade or Name — Description	Avg	Ex-Fn	Mint
Dexter St., 7J, KW, HC, 14K	$200	$275	$325
Dexter St., 7J, KW, HC, 18K	250	325	375
Dexter St., 7J, ¾, gilded, KW, HC, gold filled	50	75	125
Frances Rubie, 15J, ¾, gilded, KW, HC, 14K ★	550	600	700
Frances Rubie, 15J, KW, HC, 18K ★★	600	650	750

Grade or Name—Description	Avg	Ex-Fn	Mint
Gail Borden, 11J, ¾, gilded, KW, HC, 14K.............	$200	$275	$325
Gail Borden, 11J, ¾, KW, HC, gold filled..............	50	75	125
Gail Borden, 11J, KW, HC, 18K.......................	250	325	375
Lady Elgin, 15J, ¾, gilded, KW, HC, 14K..............	200	275	325
Lady Elgin, 15J, KW, HC, 18K........................	250	325	375
21 or 28, 7J, ¾, gilded, KW, HC, gold filled	50	75	125
Elgin, multi-color case, gold filled, HC	200	225	275
Elgin, 15J, Silveroid, HC	30	40	50
Elgin, 15J, YGF, HC	50	75	125

Elgin W. Co., Grade 121, 6 size, 15 jewels, hunting, serial number 4,500,445.

Elgin W. Co., Grade 67, 6 size, 11 jewels, serial number 1,149,615.

6 SIZE
(HC Only)

Grade or Name — Description	Avg	Ex-Fn	Mint
Atlas, 7J, HC...	$50	$75	$125
Elgin W. Co. #286, 7J, HC, ¾, DMK, NI	50	75	125
Elgin W. Co. #295, 15J, HC, ¾, DMK, NI	50	75	125
Elgin W. Co., 7J, HC, 10K	150	175	225
Elgin W. Co., 7J, HC, ¾, 14K	175	225	300
Elgin W. Co., 15J, SW, HC, Enamel case, 18K..........	800	1,000	1,300
Elgin W. Co., 15J, YGF, HC.........................	50	75	125
Elgin W. Co., 15J, HC, ¾, 14K	175	225	300
Elgin W. Co., 15J, HC, ¾, 10K	150	175	225
Elgin W. Co., 15J, HC, ¾, 18K	250	325	375
Elgin W. Co., 15J, HC, GF multi-color case	200	225	275
Elgin W. Co., 11J, HC, 14K	175	225	300
Elgin W. Co., 15J, demi-HC	75	100	150
Elgin W. Co., 15J, 14K, Multi-color HC...............	450	500	650

Elgin W. Co., 6 size, 15 jewels

Elgin W. Co., Grade 201-HC, 205-OF, 0 size, 19 jewels, gold train.

Elgin W. Co., Grade 200-HC, 204-OF, 0 size, 17 jewels, gold jewel settings.

0 SIZE

Grade or Name — Description	Avg	Ex-Fn	Mint
Atlas W. Co., 7J, HC	$75	$100	$150
Elgin W. Co., 7J, NI, ¾, DR, DMK, OF	35	40	50
Elgin W. Co., 15J, NI, ¾, DR, DMK, OF	40	45	55
Elgin W. Co., 15J, NI, ¾, DR, DMK, HC	75	100	150
Elgin W. Co., 17J, NI, ¾, DR, DMK, ADJ, OF	50	60	80
Elgin W. Co., 19J, NI, ¾, DR, DMK, GJS, ADJ, OF ...	55	65	85
Elgin W. Co., 15J, HC, 14K	175	225	300
Elgin W. Co., 15J, HC, multi-color GF.................	175	200	250
Elgin W. Co., 15J, OF, multi-color dial	100	125	175
Elgin W. Co., 11J, HC, 14K	175	225	300
Elgin W. Co., 7J, HC, 10K	150	175	225
Elgin W. Co., 15J, 14K, Multi-color...................	400	450	525
Elgin W. Co., 15J, 14K, Multi-color + diamond	500	550	625
Frances Rubie, 19J, HC............................★	200	225	300

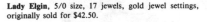

Lady Elgin, 5/0 size, 17 jewels, gold jewel settings, originally sold for $42.50.

Lady Raymond, 5/0 size, 15 jewels, originally sold for $24.20.

3/0 and 5/0 SIZE
(HC ONLY)

Grade or Name—Description	Avg	Ex-Fn	Mint
Lady Elgin, 15J, PS, HC.............................	$75	$100	$150
Lady Elgin, 15J, 14K, HC...........................	200	225	275
Lady Raymond, 15J, PS, HC.........................	75	100	150
Elgin W. Co., 7J, HC	75	100	150

ELGIN NATIONAL WATCH CO.
IDENTIFICATION OF MOVEMENTS
BY MODEL NUMBER

How to Identify Your Watch: Compare the movement of your watch with the illustrations in this section. Upon matching the movement exactly, the model number and size can be determined. While comparing, note the location of the balance, jewels, screws, gears and type of back plate (Full, ¾, Bridge) which will be clues in identifying the movement you have. Having determined the size and model number, you can now find your watch in the main price listing by name or number (which is engraved on the movement).

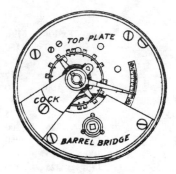

Model 1, 18 size, full plate, hunting, key wind & set, first serial number 101, Apr., 1867.

Model 2-4, 18 size, full plate, hunting, lever set, first serial number 155,001, June, 1873.

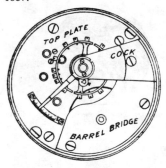

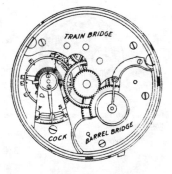

Model 5, 18 size, full plate, open face, pendant set, first serial number, 2,110,001, Grade 43, Dec., 1885.

Model 6, 18 size, three-quarter plate, hunting, open face, pendant set.

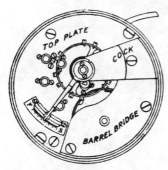

Model 7, 18 size, full plate, open face, lever set, first serial number 6,563,821, Grade 265, Apr., 1897.

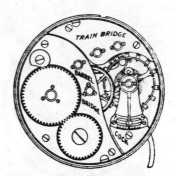

Model 8, 18 size, three-quarter plate, open face, lever set, first serial number 8,400,001, Grade 214, Dec., 1900.

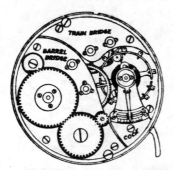

Model 8, 18 size, three-quarter plate, open face, lever set with winding indicator.

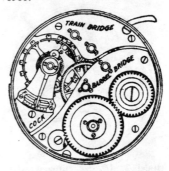

Model 9, 18 size, three-quarter plate, hunting, lever set, first serial number 9,625,001, Grade 274, May, 1904.

Model 9, 18 size, three-quarter plate, hunting, lever set with winding indicator.

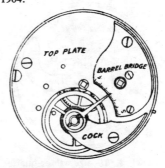

Model 1, 17 size, full plate, hunting, key wind and set.

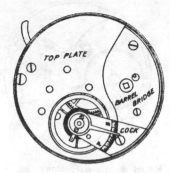

Model 2, 17 size, full plate, hunting, lever set.

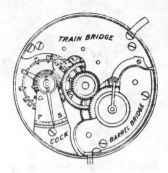

Model 1, 16 size, three-quarter plate, hunting & open face, lever set.

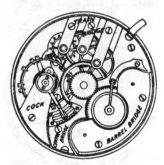

Model 2, 16 size, three-quarter plate, bridge, hunting & open face, lever set.

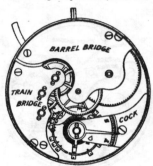

Model 3, 16 size, three-quarter plate, hunting, lever set, first serial number 625,001, Grade 1, Feb., 1879.

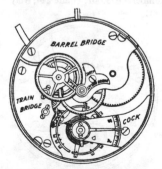

Model 4, 16 size, three-quarter plate, sweep second, hunting & open face, lever set.

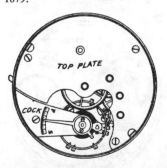

Model 5, 16 size, three-quarter plate, open face, pendant set.

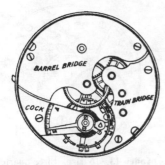

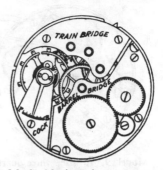

Model 5, 16 size, three-quarter plate, open face, pendant set, first serial number 2,811,001, Grade 105, Oct., 1887.

Model 6, 16 size, three-quarter plate, hunting, pendant set, first serial number 6,458,001, Grade 151, Aug., 1895.

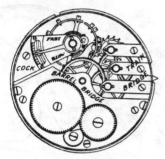

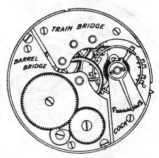

Model 6, 16 size, three-quarter plate, bridge, hunting, pendant set, first serial number 6,463,001, Grade 156, May, 1896.

Model 7, 16 size, three-quarter plate, open face, pendant set, first serial number 6,464,001. Grade 157, Sept., 1895.

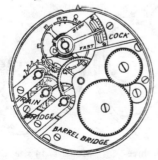

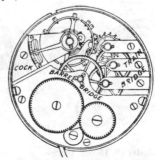

Model 7, 16 size, three-quarter plate, bridge, open face, pendant set, first serial number 6,469,001, Grade 162, Apr., 1896.

Model 8, 16 size, three-quarter plate, bridge, hunting, lever set, serial number 12,283,001, Grade 341, Jan., 1907.

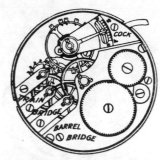

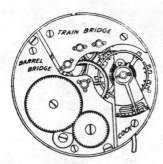

Model 9, 16 size, three-quarter plate, bridge, open face, lever set, first serial number 9,250,001, Grade 270, July, 1902.

Model 13, 16 size, three-quarter plate, open face, lever set, first serial number 12,717,001, Grade 350, June, 1908.

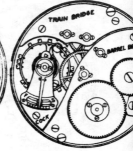

Model 14, 16 size, three-quarter plate, hunting, lever set.

Model 15, 16 size, three-quarter plate, open face, lever set.

Model 17, 16 size, three-quarter plate, hunting, lever set.

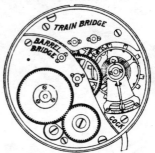

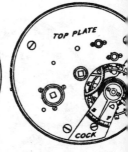

Model 19, 16 size, three-quarter plate, open face, lever set with winding indicator.

Model 20, 16 size, three-quarter plate, open face, Grades 571, 572, 573, 574, 575, 616.

Model 1, 14 size, three-quarter plate, hunting, key wind and set.

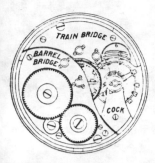

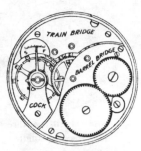

Model 2, 14 size, three-quarter plate, open face, pendant set.

Model 1, 12 size, three-quarter plate, hunting, key wind and set.

Model 2, 12 size, three-quarter plate, hunting, pendant set, first serial #7,410,001, Grade 188, Dec., 1897.

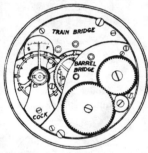

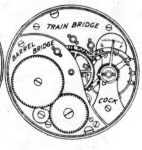

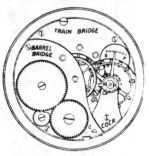

Model 2, 12 size, three-quarter plate, spread to 16 size, hunting, pendant set.

Model 3, 12 size, three-quarter plate, open face, pendant set, serial number 7,423,001, Grade 192, May 1898.

Model 3, 12 size, three-quarter plate, spread to 16 size, open face, pendant set.

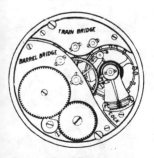

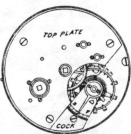

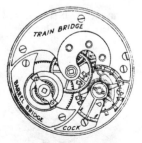

Model 4, 12 size, three-quarter plate, open face, pendant set, serial number 16,311,001, Grade 392, July, 1912.

Model 1, 10 size, three-quarter plate, style 1, hunting, key wind and set.

Model 2, 10 size, three-quarter plate, hunting, key wind and set.

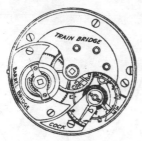

Model 3, 10 size, three-quarter plate, hunting.

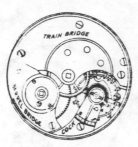

Model 4, 10 size, three-quarter plate, hunting.

Model 5 & 6, 10 size, three-quarter plate.

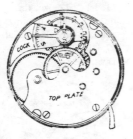

Model 1, 6 size, three-quarter plate, hunting.

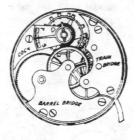

Model 1, 6 size, three-quarter plate, hunting.

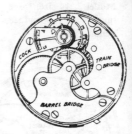

Model 2, 6 size, three-quarter plate, hunting.

Model 1, 0 size, three-quarter plate, hunting.

Model 2, 0 size, three-quarter plate, hunting.

Model 2, 0 size, three-quarter plate, hunting.

Model 3, 0 size, three-quarter plate, open face.

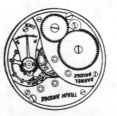

Model 3, 0 size, three-quarter plate, open face.

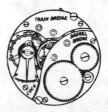

Model 2, 3-0 size, three-quarter plate, hunting.

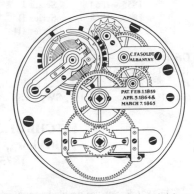

Charles Fasoldt, 18-20 size, 16 jewels, gold jewel settings, key wind & set, bar movement, serial number 90.

Charles Fasoldt, 18-20 size, 16 jewels, key wind & set, bar movement; note patented regulator, series II.

CHARLES FASOLDT WATCH CO.
Rome, New York
1849 - 1861
Albany, New York
1861 - 1878

Charles Fasoldt came to the United States in 1848. One of his first watches, Serial No. 27, was for General Armstrong and was an eight-day movement. At about that same time, he made several large regulators and a few pocket chronometers. He displayed some of his work at fairs in Utica and Syracuse and received four First-Class Premiums and two diplomas. In 1850, he patented a micrometric regulator (generally called the Howard Regulator because Howard bought the patent). He also patented a chronometer escapement in 1855-1865, a watch regulator in 1864, and a hairspring stud in 1877. He was also known for his tower clocks, for which he received many awards and medals. He made about 500 watches in Albany and about 50 watches in Rome.

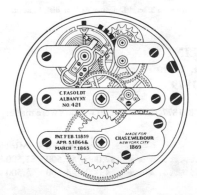

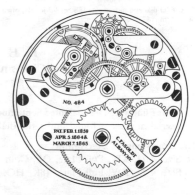

Charles Fasoldt, 18-20 size, 16 jewels, stem wind, key set, bar movement, series III.

Charles Fasoldt, 18-20 size, 16 jewels, stem wind, key set, bar movement, series III.

Year	Model	Style	Serial # Range
1855 - 1864	Series I	KW, ½ plate	5- 40
1865 - 1868	Series II	KW, Bar	41-330
1868 - 1878	Series III	SW, Bar	331-540

Grade or Name — Description	Avg	Ex-Fn	Mint
18—20 SIZE, 16J, GJS, KW, KS .... ★ ★ ★	$8,000	$10,000	$14,500
10—12 SIZE, 16J, GJS, KW & SW, KS, 14K............	3,500	4,000	5,000
Otto H. Fasoldt, 18S, 15J, SW, Swiss made or American .	175	200	250

FITCHBURG WATCH CO.
Fitchburg, Massachusetts
1875 - 1878

In 1875 S. Sawyer decided to manufacture watches. He hired personnel from the U. S. Watch Company to build the machinery, but by 1878 the company had failed. It is not known how many, if any, watches were made. The equipment was sold to Cornell and other watch companies.

 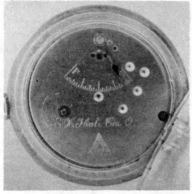

E.H. Flint dial and movement, 18 size, 4-7 jewels, open face, key wind & set, "Lancaster Pa." on dial, "Patented Sept. 18th, 1877" on movement.

E. H. FLINT
Cincinnati, Ohio
1877 - 1879

The Flint watch was patented September 18, 1877, and about 50 watches were made. The serial number is found under the dial.

Grade orName — Description	Avg	Ex-Fn	Mint
18 Size, 4-7J, KW, Full Plate, OF, Coin .... ★ ★ ★	$2,000	$2,500	$3,500
18 Size, 4-7J, KW, Full Plate, 18K, HC........... ★ ★ ★	4,000	4,500	5,500

Fredonia Watch Co., 18 size, 15 jewels, signature on movement "Cyrus N. Gibbs, Mas," key wind & set, serial number 4403.

Fredonia Watch Co., 18 size, 15 jewels, adjusted, serial number 8,368.

FREDONIA WATCH CO.
Fredonia, New York
1883 - 1885

This company sold the finished movements acquired from the Independent Watch Co. These movements had been made by other companies. The Fredonia Watch Company was sold to the Peoria Watch Co. in 1885, after having produced approximately 20,000 watches.

Chronology of the Development of Fredonia:

Independent Watch Co.	1880-1883
Fredonia Watch Co.	1883-1885
Peoria Watch Co.	1885-1895

Fredonia Watch Co., with a reversible case; changes to either hunting or open face.

Grade or Name — Description	Avg	Ex-Fn	Mint
18S, 7J, SW, OF	$100	$125	$175
18S, 7J, SW, HC	125	150	200
18S, 9J, SW, OF	100	125	175
18S, 9J, SW, HC	125	150	200
18S, 11J, SW, OF	100	125	175
18S, 11J, KW, KS, HC, Coin	125	150	200
18S, 15J, SW, Multi-color, 14K, HC	1,600	1,800	2,200
18S, KW, Reversible case	300	350	450
18S, 15J, SW, LS, Gilt, OF	100	125	175
18S, 15J, straight line escapement, NI	300	350	450
18S, 15J, HC, low serial number	300	350	450
18S, 15J, personalized mvt.	200	250	350
18S, 15J, KW, HC, marked Lakeshore W. Co.	250	300	400

FREEPORT WATCH CO.
Freeport, Illinois
1874 - 1875

Probably less than 20 watches made by Freeport have survived. Their machinery was purchased from Mozart Co., and a Mr. Hoyt was engaged as superintendent. The building erected was destroyed by fire on Oct. 21, 1875. A safe taken from the ruins contained 300 completed movements which were said to be ruined.

Grade or Name — Description		Avg	Ex-Fn	Mint
18S, 15J, KW, KS, gold train, 18K case	★ ★ ★	$4,500	$5,000	$6,000

Freeport Watch Co.. Example of a basic movement, 18 size, 15 jewels, key wind & set, pressed jewels, gold train, high grade movement, serial number 11.

SMITH D. FRENCH
Wabash, Indiana
1866 - 1878

On August 21, 1866, Mr. French was issued a patent for an improved escapement for watches. The escape wheel has triangular shaped pins and the lever has two hook-shaped pallets. The pin wheel escapement was probably first used by Robert Robin, about 1795, for pocket watches. Antoine Tavan also used this style escape wheel around 1800. Mr. French's improved pin wheel and hook shaped lever (about 70 total production) can be seen through a cutout in the plates of his watches.

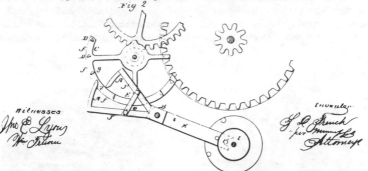

Illustration from the patent office, patent number 57,310, patented Aug. 21, 1866. Note pin wheel escapement with adjustable hook shaped lever.

Grade or Name — Description	Avg	Ex-Fn	Mint
18S, 15J, ¾, KW, KS, gilt, pin wheel escapement, Silver ....★ ★ ★ ★	$3,000	$3,500	$4,500
18S, 15J, ¾, KW, KS, gilt, pin wheel escapement, 18K ....★ ★ ★ ★	4,000	5,000	6,000

S.D. French, about 18 size, 15 jewels, gilt ¾ movement, key wind & set, with pin wheel escapement, engraved on movement "S.D. French, Walbash Ind., Aug. 21. 1866, No. 24."

L. Goddard, 55mm, 7 jewels, full plate movement with solid cock, chain driven fusee, flat steel balance, serial number 235, ca. 1809-1817.

LUTHER GODDARD
Shrewsbury, Massachusetts
1809 - 1825

The first significant attempt to produce watches in America was made by Luther Goddard. William H. Keith, who became president of Waltham Watch Co. (1861-1866) and was once apprenticed to Goddard, said that the hands, dials, round and dove-tail brass, steel wire, mainsprings and hairsprings, balance verge, chains, and pinions were all imported. The plates, wheels, and brass parts, however, were cast at the Goddard shop. He also made the cases for his movements which were of the usual style—open faced, double case—and somewhat in advance of the prevalent style of thick bull's eye watches of the day. About 600 watches were made that were of high quality and more expensive than the imported type. The first watch was produced about 1812 and was sold to the father of ex-governor Lincoln of Worcester, Massachusetts. In 1820 his watches sold for about $60.

D. Goddard, 18-20 size, 15 jewels, "Worcester, Mass." on movement, key wind & set, solid balance, under sprung, serial number 8.

L. Goddard & Co., 16-18 size, pair case, open face-thick bulls-eye type, and of high quality for the time.

About 1870 Goddard built a shop one story high with a hip roof about 18' square, and a lean-to at the back for casting. The building was intended for making clocks, but a need for watches developed and Goddard made watches there. He earned the distinction of establishing the first watch factory in America.

His movements were marked as follows: L. Goddard, L. Goddard & Co., Luther Goddard & Son, P. Goddard, L & P Goddard, D. P. Goddard & Co., P. & D. Goddard.

Frank A. Knowlton purchased the company and operated it until 1933.

Chronology of the Development of Luther Goddard:

Luther Goddard,		D. Goddard & Son	1842-1850
"L Goddard,"		Luther D. Goddard	1850-1857
Luther Goddard & Son	1809-1825	Goddard & Co.	1857-1860
L Goddard & Co.	1817-1825	D. Goddard & Co.	
P & D Goddard	1825-1842	(also Benjamen Goddard)	1860-1872

NOTE: Watches listed below are with original silver cases.

Grade or Name — Description	Avg	Ex-Fn	Mint
Benjamin Goddard	$1,000	$1,200	$1,500
Luther Goddard, S#1-35 with eagle on balance bridge ★ ★ ★	5,000	6,000	7,500
Luther Goddard, without eagle on cock .... ★	2,500	3,000	3,500
Luther Goddard, L. Goddard, Luther Goddard & Son.. ★	2,000	2,500	3,000

L. Goddard & Son. Example of basic movement, about 18 size, open face, pair case; most of the parts are made in America but resemble the English style.

L. Goddard & Son, about 18 size, pair case, verge escapement, engraved on movement "L. Goddard & Son, Shrewsbury," serial number 460.

Grade or Name—Description	Avg	Ex-Fn	Mint
L. Goddard & Co., P & D Goddard, D. Goddard & Son ★	$1,000	$1,200	$1,500
Luther D. Goddard, Goddard & Co., D. Goddard & Co. .... ★	1,000	1,200	1,500
P. Goddard, with eagle on cock .... ★	1,000	1,200	1,500

JONAS G. HALL
Montpelier, Vermont
1850 - 1870
Millwood Park, Roxbury, Vermont
1870 - 1890

Jonas G. Hall was born in 1822 in Calais, Vermont. He opened a shop in Montpelier where he sold watches, jewelry, silverware, and fancy goods. While at this location, he produced more than 60 full plate, lever style watches. Hall later established a business in Roxbury where he manufactured watch staking tools and other watchmaking tools. At Roxbury, he made at least one watch which was a three-quarter plate model. He also produced a few chronometers, about 20-size with a fusee and detent escapement and a wind indicator on the dial.

Hall was employed by the American Waltham Watch Co. for a short time and helped design the first lady's model. He also worked for Tremont Watch Co., E. Howard & Co., and the United States Watch Co. of Marion, New Jersey.

Style or Name—Description	Avg	Ex-Fn	Mint
18S, 15J, full plate, KW, KS	$1,000	$1,500	$2,200
18S, 15J, ¾, gilt, KW, KS	2,000	2,500	3,000
20S, 15J, Detent Chronometer, KW, KS	4,000	5,000	7,500

J.G. Hall, 18 size, 15 jewels, full plate, key wind & set, engraved on movement "J.G. Hall, Montpelier, VT.," serial number 25, ca. 1857.

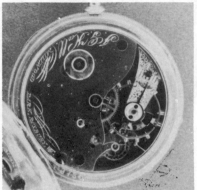

J.G. Hall, 18 size, 15 jewels, ¾ plate, key wind and set, engraved on movement "J.G. Hall, Millwood Park, Roxbury, VT," no serial number, ca. 1880.

HAMILTON WATCH CO.
Lancaster, Pennsylvania
December 14, 1892 - Present

Hamilton's roots go back to the Adams & Perry Watch Manufacturing Co. On Sept. 26, 1874, E. F. Bowman made a model watch, and the first movement was produced on April 7, 1876. It was larger than an 18S, or about a 19S. The movement had a snap-on dial and the patented stem-setting arrangement. They decided to start making the watches a standard size of 18, and no more than 1,000 of the large-size watches were made. Work had commenced on Sept. 1, 1877, at the Lancaster Watch Co. The watches were designed to sell at a cheaper price than normal. It had a one-piece top ¾ plate and a pillar plate that was fully ruby-jeweled (4½ pairs). It had a gilt or nickel movement and a new stem-wind device designed by Mosely & Todd. By mid-1878, the Lancaster Watch Co. had made 150 movements. Four grades of watches were produced: Keystone, Fulton, Franklin, and Melrose. In September 1879 the company had manufactured 334 movements. In 1880 some 1,250 movements had been made. In mid-1882, about 17,000 movements had been assembled. All totaled, about 20,000 movements were made.

Grade 936, 18 size, 17 jewels, serial number 1. c. 1893.   Grade 936, 18 size, 17 jewels, serial number 2, c. 1893.

The first Hamilton movement to be sold was No. 15 to W. C. Davis on January 31, 1893. The No. 1 movement was finished on April 25, 1896, and was never sold. The No. 2 was finished on April 25, 1893, and was shipped to Smythe & Ashe of Rochester, N. Y. Nos. 1 & 2 are at the N.A.W.C.C. museum.

Chronology of the Development of Hamilton:

Adams & Perry Watch Co.	Sept. 1874-May 1876
Lancaster, Pa., Watch Co.	Aug. 1877-Oct. 1887
Lancaster, Pa., Watch Co.	Nov. 1877-May 1879
Lancaster Watch Co.	May 1883-1886
Keystone Standard Watch Co.	1886-1890
Hamilton Watch Co.	Dec. 14, 1892-1969

In 1893 the first watch was produced with the Hamilton label. The watches became very popular with railroad men and by 1923 some 53 percent of Hamilton's production were railroad watches. The 940 model watch was discontinued in 1910. Most Hamilton

Grade 937, 18 size, 17 jewels, hunting case. Note serial number 1047. Hunting case models began with 1001.   Hamilton Watch Co., 18 size, 7 jewels, serial number 2934.

movements were fitted with a 42-hour mainspring. The Elinvar hairspring was patented in 1931 and used in all movements thereafter. On October 15, 1940, Hamilton introduced the 992B which were fitted with the Elinvar hairspring. Elinvar and Invar are tradenames and are the same 36 percent nickel steel. Although the Hamilton Watch Co. is still in business today making modern type watches, they last produced American-made watches in 1969.

HAMILTON ESTIMATED SERIAL NUMBERS AND PRODUCTION DATES

Date	Serial No.	Date	Serial No.	Date	Serial No.	Date	Serial No.
1893	1-2,000	1906	590,000	1919	1,700,000	1932	2,500,000
1894	5,000	1907	756,000	1920	1,790,000	1933	2,600,000
1895	10,000	1908	921,000	1921	1,860,000	1934	2,700,000
1896	14,000	1909	1,087,000	1922	1,900,000	1935	2,800,000
1897	20,000	1910	1,050,500	1923	1,950,000	1936	2,900,000
1898	30,000	1911	1,290,500	1924	2,000,000	1937	3,000,000
1899	40,000	1912	1,331,000	1925	2,100,000	1938	3,200,000
1900	50,000	1913	1,370,000	1926	2,200,000	1939	3,400,000
1901	90,000	1914	1,410,500	1927	2,250,000	1940	3,600,000
1902	150,000	1915	1,450,500	1928	2,300,000	1941	3,800,000
1903	260,000	1916	1,517,000	1929	2,350,000	1942	4,025,000
1904	340,000	1917	1,580,000	1930	2,400,000		
1905	425,000	1918	1,650,000	1931	2,450,000		

NOTE: The serial numbers and dates listed above are only close approximations. The actual date of your watch could vary 2 to 3 years from the listed date.

The Hamilton Masterpiece

The adjoining illustration shows the Masterpiece in a platinum case. The dial is sterling silver with raised gold numbers and solid gold hands. This watch sold for $685.00 in 1930. All 922 MP Models included the following: 23 jewels, were adjusted to heat, cold, isochronism, and five positions, with a motor barrel, solid gold train, steel escape wheel, double roller, sapphire pallets and a micrometric regulator.

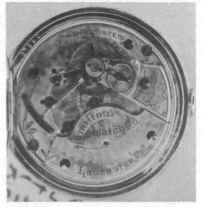

Grade **925**, 18 size, 17 jewels, hunting case, serial number 101,495.

Grade **932**, 18 size, 16 jewels, open face, serial number 6,888.

HAMILTON
18 SIZE

Grade or Name — Description		Avg	Ex-Fn	Mint
7J, OF, LS, FULL	★ ★	$600	$700	$900
11J, HC, LS, FULL	★ ★ ★	1,200	1,400	1,700
11J, OF, LS, FULL	★ ★ ★ ★	1,500	1,700	2,000
922, 15J, OF	★	375	450	575
923, 15J, HC	★	475	550	675
924, 17J, NI, OF, DMK		50	75	100
925, 17J, NI, HC, DMK		100	125	175
926, 17J, NI, OF, DMK, ADJ		50	75	100
927, 17J, NI, HC, DMK, ADJ		100	125	175
928, 15J, NI, OF		125	150	200
929, 15J, NI, HC, 14K		500	600	750
929, 15J, NI, HC		175	225	300
930, 16J, NI, OF		150	200	275
931, 16J, NI, HC		200	250	325
932, 16J, NI, OF	★ ★	400	450	525
932 *(S#s less than 400 up to $1,200)*				
933, 16J, NI, HC	★ ★	500	550	625
933 *(S#s less than 1,300 up to $1,400)*				
934, 17J, NI, OF, DMK, DR, Adj.5P		100	125	175
934, 17J, NI, OF, Adj.5P, Coin		75	100	150
935, 17J, NI, HC, DMK, DR, Adj.5P	★	250	300	375
936, 17J, NI, OF, DMK, DR		75	100	150
936 *(Early S#s less than 400 up to $1,200)*				
937, 17J, NI, HC, DMK, DR		150	200	275
937 *(S#s less than 1,300 up to $1,200)*				

Grade or Name—Description	Avg	Ex-Fn	Mint
938, 17J, NI, OF, DMK, DR ....★★	$500	$600	$775
939, 17J, NI, HC, DMK, DR ....★★	600	700	875
940, 21J, NI, OF, Mermod Jaccards St. Louis Paragon Time Keeper & an hour glass on mvt.	275	325	400
940, 21J, NI, OF, DMK, DR, Adj.5P, GJS	125	175	250
940, 21J, NI, OF, 2-Tone	150	200	275
940, 21J, NI, OF, Extra.............................	175	225	300
940, 21J, NI, OF, Coin	75	100	150
940, 21J, NI, OF, Special	175	225	300
941, 21J, NI, HC, GJS, Marked	125	175	250
941, 21J, NI, HC, GJS, Special......................	275	350	450
941, 21J, NI, HC, DMK, DR, Adj.5P, GJS	200	275	375
942, 21J, NI, OF, DMK, DR, Adj.5P, GJS	175	250	300
943, 21J, NI, HC, DMK, DR, Adj.5P, GJS ....★	225	300	350
943, Burlington Special, 21J	550	650	800
944, 19J, NI, OF, DMK, DR, Adj.5P, GJS	150	200	275
945, 19J, GJS, 2-Tone, HC......................★★	1,000	1,200	1,500
946, Anderson (jobber name on movement), 14K	800	1,000	1,300
946, 23J, Extra, OF, GJS	500	550	625
946, 23J, "Loaner" on case	425	475	575
946, 23J, NI, OF, DMK, DR, Adj.5P, GJS	400	450	525
946, 23J, NI, OF, DMK, Adj.5P, GJS, unmarked	300	350	425
947, 23J, NI, HC, DMK, DR, Adj.5P, GJS, 14K, HC, not marked "947" ....★	3,500	4,000	5,000

Note: Some movements are marked with grade numbers, some are not. Add $25 to $75 for a marked movement. The first **hunting case** was a Model number 937 which begins with serial number 1001.

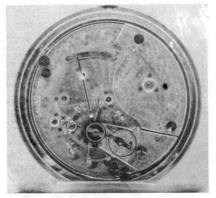

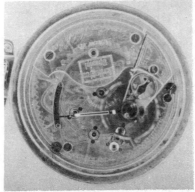

Grade 947 (marked), 18 size, 23 jewels, gold jewel settings, hunting case, Adj6p, serial number 163,219.

Burlington Special, 18 size, 21 jewels, Grade 943, open face, serial number 121,614.

NOTE: Watches listed in this book are priced at the retail level, as complete watches having an original 14k gold-filled case, an original white enamel single sunk dial, and with the entire original movement in good working order with no repairs needed, unless otherwise noted.

Grade or Name—Description	Avg	Ex-Fn	Mint
947, 23J, NI, HC, Adj.5P, GJS, 14K, HC, marked "947" .... ★ ★	$4,500	$5,500	$6,500
947, 23J, Extra, NI, GJS, marked 947, 14K, HC... ★ ★ ★	5,000	6,000	7,500
948, 17J, NI, OF, DMK, DR, Adj.5P, GJS .... ★	300	350	425
948, 17J, NI, DMK, DR, Adj.5P, GJS, OF, Coin...... ★	300	350	425
The Banner, 928, 15J, NI, OF	125	150	200
The Banner, 940, 21J, NI, OF	150	175	225
The Banner, 941, 21J, NI, HC.......................	200	225	275
The Banner, 17J, M#927, HC, ADJ	125	150	200
Burlington Special, 17J, Adj.5P, OF.................	200	250	325
Burlington Special, 17J, Adj.5P, HC	250	300	375
Burlington Special, 21J, Adj.5P, OF.................	300	350	425
Burlington Special, 21J, Adj.5P, HC	350	400	475
Inspectors Standard, 21J, OF	300	350	475
The Union, 17J	125	150	200
The Union Special, 17J	125	150	200
The Union, 17J, G#925, HC.........................	200	225	275

Grade 950, 16 size, 23 jewels, pendant set, gold train, gold jewel settings, serial number 1,020,650.

Grade 961, 16 size, 21 jewels, gold train, gold jewel settings, serial number 81,848.

16 SIZE

Grade or Name — Description	Avg	Ex-Fn	Mint
950, 23J, LS, DR, GT, 14K	$700	$775	$900
950, 23J, LS, DR, OF, BRG, GJS, Adj.5P, NI, GT......	325	375	450
950, 23J, PS, DR, OF, GJS, BRG, Adj.5P, NI, GT......	350	400	475
950B, 23J, LS, OF, Adj.5P, NI, DR, BRG..............	350	400	450
950E, 23J, LS, OF, Adj.5P, NI, DR, BRG..............	325	375	425
951, 23J, LS, Adj.5P, NI, GT, GJS, DR, HC ..... ★ ★ ★	3,500	4,000	5,000
951, 23J, PS, HC, Adj.5P, NI, GT, GJS, DR ..... ★ ★ ★	3,500	4,000	5,000
951, 23J, PS, HC, Adj.5P, NI, GT, GJS, DR, 14K ★ ★ ★	4,000	4,500	5,500
952, 19J, LS or PS, OF, BRG, Adj.5P, NI, GJS, DR	175	200	275
952, 19J, LS or PS, Adj.5P, OF, 14K	475	525	600
953, 19J, LS or PS, HC, GJS, GT .... ★ ★	2,000	2,500	3,000

Grade or Name — Description	Avg	Ex-Fn	Mint
954, 17J, LS or PS, OF, ¾, DR, Adj.5P	$75	$100	$150
956, 17J, PS, OF, ¾, DR, Adj.5P	75	100	150
960, 21J, PS, OF, BRG, GJS, GT, DR, Adj.5P .... ★	300	325	400
960, 21J, LS, OF, BRG, GJS, GT, DR, Adj.5P .... ★	325	350	425
961, 21J, PS & LS, HC, BRG, GJS, GT, DR, Adj.5P .. ★	400	450	500
962, 17J, PS, OF, BRG .... ★ ★	500	650	600
963, 17J, PS, HC, BRG .... ★ ★	550	600	700
964, 17J, PS, OF, BRG .... ★ ★	650	700	800
965, 17J, PS, HC, BRG .... ★ ★	500	550	650
966, 17J, PS, OF, ¾ .... ★ ★	600	650	750
967, 17J, PS, HC, ¾ .... ★ ★	625	675	775
968, 17J, PS, OF, ¾ .... ★	325	375	475
969, 17J, PS, HC, ¾ .... ★	425	450	500
970, 21J, PS, OF, ¾	150	175	225
971, 23J, Adj.5P, Swiss made	75	100	135
971, 21J, PS, HC, ¾	175	200	250
972, 17J, PS & LS, OF, ¾, NI, GJS, DR, Adj.5P, DMK .	100	125	175
973, 17J, PS & LS, HC, ¾, NI, DR, Adj.5P	150	175	225
974, 17J, LS, OF, ¾, NI, Adj.3P	50	75	100
974, 17J, OF, PS, Adj.3P	50	75	100
974, 17J, OF, 2-tone	125	150	200
2974B, 17J, OF, Adj.3P	100	125	175
975, 17J, PS & LS, HC, ¾, NI, Adj.3P	75	100	150
976, 16J, PS, OF, ¾	150	175	225
977, 16J, PS, HC, ¾	150	175	225
978, 17J, LS, OF, ¾, NI, DMK	50	75	100
990, 21J, LS, OF, GJS, DR, Adj.5P, DMK, NI, ¾, GT ..	150	175	225
991, 21J, LS, HC, ¾, GJS, Adj.5P, DMK, NI, GT	175	200	250
992, 21J, OF, ¾, LS, GJS, Adj.5P, DR, NI, DMK	100	125	175
992, 21J, OF, ¾, PS & LS, GJS, Adj.5P, DR, NI, DMK, 2-Tone	150	175	225
992, 21J, Extra, OF, ¾, PS & LS, GJS, Adj.5P, DR, NI, DMK	150	175	225

Grade 992B, 16 size, 21 jewels, Adj5p.   **Grade 4992B**, 16 size, 22 jewels, Adj6p.

Grade 996, 16 size, 19 jewels, open face, gold jewel settings, serial number 152,060.

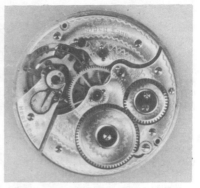

Hayden W. Wheeler, 16 size, 17 jewels, adjusted to heat & cold, serial number 76,029.

Grade or Name—Description	Avg	Ex-Fn	Mint
992, 21J, ¾, PS, GJS, Adj.5P, OF	$100	$150	$200
992, 21J, Elinvar, ¾, GJS, Adj.5P	150	175	200
992, 21J, Special, OF, ¾, PS & LS, GJS, Adj.5P, DR, NI, DMK, 'Adj. for RR Service' on dial	350	400	500
992B, 21J, 2-Tone	200	250	300
992B, 21J, LS, OF, ¾	150	175	225
992B, 21J, OF, ¾, silver case	75	100	175
3992B, 22J, Adj.6P, 12 hr. dial ★	150	200	275
4992B, 22J, LS, OF, ¾, Adj.6P, 24-hour dial, Greenwich Civil Time	125	150	200
993, 21J, PS, HC, GJS, Adj.5P, DR, NI, DMK	200	225	275
993, 21J, LS, HC, GJS, Adj.5P, DMK, DR, NI	175	200	250
993, 21J, LS, HC, GJS, Adj.5P, DMK, DR, NI, 14K	550	600	700

Grade 994, 16 size, 21 jewels, pendent set, gold train, gold jewel settings, serial number 1,153,431.

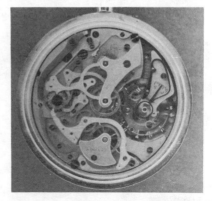

Chronograph, Grade 23, 16 size, 19 jewels, start-stop-reset to 0.

Grade or Name—Description	Avg	Ex-Fn	Mint
993, 21J, LS, HC, GJS, Adj.5P, DMK, DR, NI, GF multicolor case	$275	$325	$400
994, 21J, BRG, OF, GJS, GT, DR, Adj.5P, DMK, PS . ★	600	750	900
994, 21J, BRG, OF, GJS, GT, DR, Adj.5P, DMK, LS . ★	700	850	950
995, 19J, GJS, BRG, HC .... ★ ★	900	1,000	1,200
996, 19J, LS, OF, ¾, GJS, DR, Adj.5P, DMK..........	125	150	200
DeLong Escapement, 21J, 992-B .... ★ ★ ★	1,000	1,100	1,300
Electric Interurban, 17J, G#974, OF....................	50	75	100
Official Standard, 17J, OF	175	200	275
Union Special, 17J	100	125	200
Hayden W. Wheeler, 17J, OF .... ★	400	500	650
Hayden W. Wheeler, 17J, HC .... ★	450	550	700
Hayden W. Wheeler, 21J............................ ★	600	700	850
Hayden W. Wheeler, 21J, 14K H.W.W. case	1,000	1,100	1,300
Swiss Mfg., 17J, Adj.2P, GF case....................	85	100	145

CHRONOGRAPH
Grade 23

Grade or Name — Description	Avg	Ex-Fn	Mint
16S, 19J, start-stop-reset to 0	$175	$200	$300

12 SIZE

(Some cases were octagon, decagon, cushion, etc.)

Grade or Name — Description	Avg	Ex-Fn	Mint
900, 19J, BRG, DR, Adj.5P, GJS, OF, 14K.............	$275	$300	$375
900, 19J, BRG, DR, Adj.5P, GJS, OF	75	100	175
902, 19J, BRG, DR, Adj.5P, GJS.....................	100	125	200

 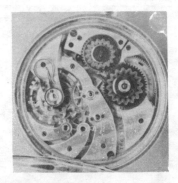

Grade 918, 12 size, 19 jewels, Adj3p, serial number 3,136,257.

Grade 920, 12 size, 23 jewels, gold train, gold jewel settings, serial number 1,863,381.

Grade or Name—Description	Avg	Ex-Fn	Mint
902, 19J, BRG, DR, Adj.5P, GJS, 14K	$300	$325	$375
904, 21J, BRG, DR, Adj.5P, GJS, GT	100	125	175
910, 17J, ¾, DR, ADJ	40	50	70
912, 17J, Digital model, rotating seconds, OF	50	60	80
912, 17J, ¾, DR, ADJ	40	50	70
914, 17J, ¾, DR, Adj.3P, GJS	40	50	70
914, 17J, ¾, DR, Adj.3P, GJS, 14K	225	250	300
916, 17J, ¾, DR, Adj.3P	40	50	70
916, 17J, Adj.3P, silver case	30	40	60
918, 19J, Adj.3P, WGF	75	100	150
918, 19J, ¾, DR, Adj.3P, GJS, OF	75	100	150
920, 23J, BRG, DR, Adj.5P, GJS, GT, OF	200	250	325
920, 23J, BRG, DR, Adj.5P, GJS, GT, 14K	400	450	525
922, 23J, BRG, DR, Adj.5P, GJS, GT, 14K	400	450	525
922, 23J, BRG, DR, Adj.5P, GJS, GT, OF	200	250	325
922 MP, 18K case	800	900	1,100
922 MP, GF, Hamilton case	300	400	550
400, 21J, ¾, ADJ ★	300	400	550

Grade 922MP, 12 size, 23 jewels, serial number 3,013,390, c. 1930.

Grade 912, 12 size, 17 jewels, with Secometer dial, originally sold for $88.70.

10 SIZE

Grade or Name — Description	Avg	Ex-Fn	Mint
917, 17J, ¾, DR, Adj.3P	$40	$50	$70
917, 17J, ¾, DR, Adj.3P, 14K	200	225	300
921, 21J, BRG, DR, Adj.5P	60	70	90
923, 23J, BRG, DR, Adj.5P	150	175	250
923, 23J, M.P.G.F.	275	300	375
923, 23J, M.P., 18K, and box	600	700	900
945, 23J, Adj.5P	125	150	225

0 SIZE

Grade or Name — Description	Avg	Ex-Fn	Mint
981, 17J, ¾, Adj.3P, DR, 18K, HC	$275	$300	$350
983, 17J, Adj.3P, DR, GJS, 18K, HC	275	300	350
985, 19J, BRG, Adj.3P, DR, GJS, GT, 18K, HC	300	325	375
Lady Hamilton, 14K case, OF	200	225	300

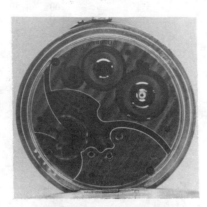

Top: **Pocket Chronometer,** 36 size, 21 jewels, gold jewel settings, Adj5p, serial number 1,260,382.

Right: **Chronometer** in gimbles and box, 35 size, wind indicator.

CHRONOMETER

Grade or Name — Description	Avg	Ex-Fn	Mint
35S, M#22, 21J, Wind Indicator, Adj.6P, in gimbles and box, lever	$500	$600	$700
35S, M#22, 21J, Wind Indicator, Adj.6P, in a large base metal OF case	400	500	600
36S, M#36, 21J, Wind Indicator, in gimbles and box	1,200	1,400	1,600
36S, M#36, 21J, Wind Indicator, in Hamilton sterling pocket watch case with bow	1,500	1,700	2,000
85S, M#21, 14J, KW, KS, Fusee, Detent Escapement with boxes	1,300	1,500	1,800

HAMILTON WATCH COMPANY
IDENTIFICATION OF MOVEMENT
BY MODEL NUMBER

How to Identify Your Watch: Compare the movement with the illustrations in this section. While comparing, note the location of the balance, jewels, screws, gears, and back plate (Full, ¾, Bridge) which will be clues in identifying the movement you have. Having determined the size, the Grade can also be found by looking up the serial number of your watch in the Hamilton Serial Number and Grades list.

Grade 936, 18 size

Open face, 17 jewels, single roller before No. 426,001, double roller after No. 426,000.

Grade 925, 18 size

Hunting, 17 jewels, single roller

Grade 971, 16 size

Hunting, 21 jewels, ¼ plate movt.

Grade 992, 16 size

Open face, ¾ plate movt., 21 jewels, single roller berfore No. 377,001, double roller after No. 379,000.

Grade 992B, 16 size
Open face, ¾ plate movt., 21 jewels, double roller

Grade 950, 16 size
Open face, bridge movt., 23 jewels, double roller

Grade 950B, 16 size
Open face, bridge movt., 23 jewels, double roller

Grade 902, 12 size
Open face, bridge movt., 19 jewels, double roller

Grade 912, 12 size
Open face, ¾ plate movt., 17 jewels, double roller

Grade 918, 12 size
Open face, ¾ plate movt., 19 jewels, double roller

Grade 922, 12 size
Open face, bridge movt., 23 jewels, double roller

Grade 917, 10 size
Open face, ¼ plate movt., 17 jewels, double roller

Grade 921, 10 size
Open face, bridge movt., 21 jewels, double roller

Grade 923, 10 size
Open face, bridge movt., 23 jewels, double roller

Grade 983, 0 size
Hunting, bridge movt., 17 jewels, double roller

Grade 979,6/0 size
Hunting, ¼ plate movt., 19 jewels, double roller

Grade 986, 6/0 size
Open face, ¼ plate movt., 17 jewels, double roller

HAMPDEN WATCH CO.
(DUEBER WATCH CO.)
Springfield, Massachusetts
Canton, Ohio
1876 - 1930

The New York Watch Co. preceded Hampden, and before that Don J. Mozart (1864) produced his three-wheel watch. Mozart was assisted by George Samuel Rice of New York and, as a result of their joint efforts, the New York Watch Co. was formed in 1866 in Providence, Rhode Island. It was moved in 1867 to Springfield, Massachusetts. Two grades of watches were decided on, and the company started with a 18S, ¾ plate engraved "Springfield." They were sold for $60 to $75. The 18S, ¾ plate were standard production, and the highest grade was a "George Walker" that sold for about $200 and a 16S, ¾ plate "State Street" which had steel parts and exposed balance and escape wheels that were gold plated.

John C. Dueber started manufacturing watch cases in 1864 and bought a controlling interest in a company in 1886. At about this time a disagreement arose between Elgin, Waltham, and the Illinois Watch companies. Also, at this time, an anti-trust law was passed, and the watch case manufacturers formed a boycott against Dueber. Dueber was faced with a major decision, whether to stay in business, surrender to the watch case companies or buy a watch company. He decided to buy the Hampden Watch Co. of Springfield, Mass. By 1889 the operation had moved to Canton, Ohio. By the end of the year the company was turning out 600 watches a day. The first 16 size watch was produced in 1890. In 1894 Hampden introduced the first 23J movement made in America.

HAMPDEN ESTIMATED SERIAL NUMBER
AND PRODUCTION DATES

Date	Serial No.	Date	Serial No.	Date	Serial No.
1877	60,000	1893	775,000	1909	2,536,000
1878	91,000	1894	833,000	1910	2,664,000
1879	122,000	1895	888,500	1911	2,792,000
1880	153,000	1896	944,000	1912	2,920,000
1881	184,000	1897	1,000,000	1913	3,048,000
1882	215,000	1898	1,128,000	1914	3,176,000
1883	250,000	1899	1,256,000	1915	3,304,000
1884	300,000	1900	1,384,000	1916	3,432,000
1885	350,000	1901	1,512,000	1917	3,560,000
1886	400,000	1902	1,642,000	1918	3,680,000
1887	450,000	1903	1,768,000	1919	3,816,000
1888	500,000	1904	1,896,000	1920	3,944,000
1889	555,500	1905	2,024,000	1921	4,072,000
1890	611,000	1906	2,152,000	1922	4,200,000
1891	666,500	1907	2,280,000	1923	4,400,000
1892	722,000	1908	2,408,000	1924	4,600,000

Chronology of the Development of Hampden Watch Co.:

Issued 1890

The Mozart Watch Co., Providence, R. I. — 1864-1866
New York Watch Co., Providence, R. I. — 1866-1867
New York Watch Co., Springfield, Mass. — 1867-1875
New York Watch Mfg. Co., Springfield, Mass. — 1875-1876
Hampden Watch Co., Springfield, Mass. — 1877-1886
Hampden-Dueber Watch Co., Springfield, Mass. — 1886-1888

Issued 1892

Hampden Watch Co., Canton, Ohio — 1888-1923
Dueber Watch Co., Canton, Ohio — 1888-1923
Dueber-Hampden Watch Co., Canton, Ohio — 1923-1931
Amtorg, U.S.S.R. — 1930-Present

Issued 1895

Dueber Watch Co., 18 size, 15 jewels, nickel movement.
Model 3, hunting case.

Dueber Grand, 18 size, 17 jewels, open face, originally
sold for $20.00.

HAMPDEN
18 SIZE

Grade or Name — Description	Avg	Ex-Fn	Mint
Anchor, 17J, ADJ, GJS, DMK, OF	$75	$100	$150
"3" Ball, 17J, ADJ, NI, DMK, OF	100	125	175
Champion, 7J, ADJ, FULL, gilded, NI, OF	50	75	125
Correct Time, 15J, HC	125	150	200
Dueber, 16J, gilded, DMK, OF	75	100	150
Dueber, 17J, gilded, DMK, OF	75	100	150
John C. Dueber, 15J, gilded, DMK, OF	75	100	150
John C. Dueber, 17J, gilded, ADJ, DMK, OF	75	100	150
John C. Dueber, Sp., 17J, gilded, ADJ, DMK, OF	75	100	150
John C. Dueber, 17J, HC	100	125	175
Dueber Grand, 17J, OF	75	100	150
Dueber Grand, 17J, ADJ, HC	100	125	175
Dueber Grand, 21J, ADJ, DMK, NI, HC	150	175	225
Dueber W. Co., 11J, OF	75	100	125
Dueber W. Co., 15J, DMK, OF	75	100	135
Dueber W. Co., 16J	750	100	150
Dueber W. Co., 17J, DMK, ADJ, OF	75	100	150
Dueber W. Co., 17J, Gilded	75	100	150
Dueber W. Co., 17J, DMK, ADJ, HC	100	125	175
Dueber W. Co., 19J, ADJ, GJS, HC ★	400	475	550
Dueber W. Co., 21J, Adj.5P, GJS, OF	100	125	175

John C. Dueber Special, 18 size, 17 jewels, serial number 949,097.

Oriental, 18 size, 15 jewels, open face, serial number 117,825.

Grade or Name—Description	Avg	Ex-Fn	Mint
Dueber W. Co., 21J, GJS, Adj.5P, HC	$150	$175	$225
Homer Foot, gilded, KW, OF (Early)	150	175	225
Gladiator, KW, OF	75	100	150
Gladiator, 11J, NI, DMK, OF	75	100	150
Gulf Stream Sp., 21J, OF, LS	200	250	325
Hampden W. Co., 7J, KW, KS, OF	75	100	150
Hampden W. Co., 7J, SW, OF	50	75	100
Hampden W. Co., 11J, OF, KW	75	100	135
Hampden W. Co., 11J, HC, KW	100	125	150
Hampden W. Co., 11J, OF, SW	75	100	135
Hampden W. Co., 11J, HC, SW	100	125	175
Hampden W. Co., 15J, OF, KW	75	100	150
Hampden W. Co. 15J, HC, KW	100	125	175
Hampden W. Co., 15J, HC, SW	100	125	175
Hampden W. Co., 15J, SW, Gilded, OF	75	100	150
Hampden W. Co., 15J, SW, NI, OF	75	100	150
Hampden W. Co., 15J, Multi-color, 14K, HC	1,600	1,800	2,200
Hampden W. Co., 16J, OF	75	100	150
Hampden W. Co., 17J, SW, Gilded	75	100	150
Hampden W. Co., 17J, SW, NI, OF	75	100	150
Hampden W. Co., 17J, HC, SW	100	125	175
Hampden W. Co., 17J, LS, HC, 14K	500	550	625
Hampden W. Co., 17J, LS, HC, 10K	350	400	475
Hampden W. Co., 21J, OF, HC, SW	150	125	225
John Hancock, 17J, GJS, Adj.3P, OF	75	100	150
John Hancock, 21J, GJS, Adj.3P, OF	125	150	200
John Hancock, 23J, GJS, Adj.5P, OF	200	250	325
Hayward, 15J, KW	100	125	200
Hayward, 11J, SW	75	100	125

Menlo Park, 18 size, 17 jewels, serial number 1,184,116.

New Railway, 18 size, 23 jewels, open face only, gold jewel settings, originally sold for $50.00, Model 2.

Grade or Name—Description	Avg	Ex-Fn	Mint
Lafayette, 11J, NI	$75	$85	$125
Lafayette, 15J, NI, KW	125	150	200
Lafayette, 15J, NI	100	125	175
Lakeside, 15J, NI, SW	100	125	175
M. J. & Co. Railroad Watch Co., 15J, HC	300	400	525
Menlo Park, 17J, NI, ADJ, OF	100	125	175
Mermod, Jaccard & Co., 15J, KW, HC	125	150	200
Metropolis, 15J, NI, SW, OF	75	100	150
Wm. McKinley, 17J, Adj.3P, OF	75	100	150
Wm. McKinley, 21J, GJS, Adj.5P	125	150	200
New Railway, 17J, GJS, Adj.5P, OF	75	100	150
New Railway, 19J, GJS, Adj.5P, OF	150	175	225
New Railway, 19J, GJS, Adj.5P, HC	150	175	225

Railway, 18 size, 17 jewels, key wind & set; early railroad watch.

Special Railway, 18 size, 23 jewels, Adj5p, serial number 3,357,284.

Grade or Name—Description	Avg	Ex-Fn	Mint
New Railway, 21J, GJS, Adj.5P, HC	$125	$150	$200
New Railway, 21J, GJS, Adj.5P, OF	100	125	175
New Railway, 23J, GJS, Adj.5P	175	225	300
New Railway, 23J, GJS, Adj.5P, 14K, OF	550	575	625
North Am. RR, 21J, GJS, Adj.5P, OF, LS	125	150	200
North Am. RR, 21J, GJS, Adj.3P, HC, PS	150	175	225
Pennsylvania Special, 17J, GJS, Adj.5P, DR, NI .... ★ ★	700	900	1,200
J. C. Perry, 15J, KW, gilded, HC	125	150	200
J. C. Perry, 15J, NI, SW, OF	70	80	95
J. C. Perry, 15J, gilded, SW, OF	75	100	150
Railway, 15J, gilded, OF	75	100	150
Railway, 17J, NI, OF	75	100	150
Railway, 15J, KW, marked on mvt., HC ★ ★	400	500	650
Railroad with R.R. names on dial and movement:			
Canadian Pacific RR, 17J, OF ★	275	300	400
Canadian Pacific RR, 21J, OF ★	375	400	500
Special Railway, 17J, GJS, Adj.5P, NI, DR, OF	75	100	150
Special Railway, 21J, GJS, Adj.5P, NI, DR, 2-Tone, OF .	125	150	200
Special Railway, 23J, GJS, Adj.5P, NI, DR, 2-Tone, OF .	200	275	375
Special Railway, 23J, Adj.5P, HC	225	300	400
Special Railway, 23J, 14K, HC	625	675	750
Springfield, 7-11J, KW, gilded, HC	100	125	175
Springfield, 7-11J, SW, NI, HC	100	125	175
Standard, 15J, gilded, HC	100	125	175
State Street, 15J, NI, LS, (Early KW)	150	175	225
Theo. Studley, 15J, KW, KS, HC	125	150	200
Tramway Special, 17J, NI	125	150	200
Woolworth, 11J, KW	100	125	175
Grade 45 HC & 65 OF, 11J	75	100	150
Grade 60, 15J, LS, OF	75	100	150
Grade 80 & 81, 17J, ADJ, OF	75	100	150
Grade 85, 19J, GJS, 2-Tone, HC ★ ★	500	600	750
Grade 95, 21J, GJS, OF	100	125	175
Grade 125, 21J, Adj.3P, OF	125	150	200

16 SIZE

Grade or Name — Description	Avg	Ex-Fn	Mint
Champion, 7J, NI, ¾, gilded, coin, OF	$50	$75	$100
Champion, 7J, NI, ¾, gilded, OF	50	75	100
Champion, 7J, NI, ¾, gilded, HC	100	125	175
Chronometer, 21J, NI, Adj.3P, GJS	150	175	225
John C. Dueber, 17J, GJS, NI, Adj.5P, ¾	75	100	150
John C. Dueber, 21J, GJS, NI, Adj.5P, ¾	100	125	175
John C. Dueber, 21J, GJS, NI, Adj.5P, DR, BRG	125	150	200
Dueber Watch Co., 17J, ADJ, ¾	75	100	150

Hampden W. Co., Bridge Model, 16 size, 23 jewels, 2-tone movement, serial number 1,899,430.

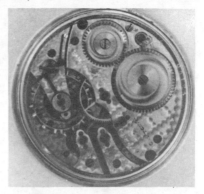

Hampden W. Co., 16 size, 17 jewels, gold jewel settings, serial number 3,075,235.

Grade or Name—Description	Avg	Ex-Fn	Mint
Hampden W. Co., 7J, SW, OF	$30	$75	$125
Hampden W. Co., 7J, SW, HC	75	100	150
Hampden W. Co., 11J, SW, OF	50	75	125
Hampden W. Co., 11J, SW, HC	75	100	150
Hampden W. Co., 15J, SW, OF	50	75	125
Hampden W. Co., 15J, SW, HC	75	100	150
Hampden W. Co., 17J, SW, OF	50	75	125
Hampden W. Co., 17J, 14K, Multi-color, HC	1,200	1,400	1,600
Hampden W. Co., 17J, SW, HC	75	100	150
Hampden W. Co., 21J, SW, HC	125	150	200
Hampden W. Co., 21J, SW, OF	100	125	175
Hampden W. Co., 23J, Adj.5P, GJS, ¾	200	225	300
Hampden W. Co., 23J, Series 2, HC "Freesprung", GJS, GT ★ ★	375	450	550
Masonic Dial, 23J, GJS, 2-Tone porcelain dial	350	400	500

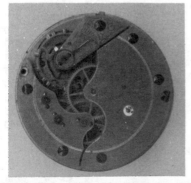

Hampden W. Co., Series I, 16 size, 15 jewels, stem wind, open face.

Railway, 16 size, 17 jewels, Adj5p, serial number 2,271,866.

Grade 104, 16 size, 23 jewels, gold jewel settings, gold train, Adj5p, serial number 2,801,184.

Grade 108, 16 size, 17 jewels, open face and hunting, serial number 1,042,051.

Grade or Name—Description	Avg	Ex-Fn	Mint
Wm. McKinley, 17J, GJS, Adj.5P, NI, DR, ¾	$75	$100	$150
Wm. McKinley, 21J, GJS, Adj.5P, NI, DR, ¾	100	125	175
Wm. McKinley, 21J, GJS, Adj.5P, NI, DR, ¾, Coin	75	100	150
Wm. McKinley, 21J, GJS, Adj.5P, NI, DR, BRG........	100	125	175
New Railway, 21J, GJS, Adj.5P	100	125	175
New Railway, 23J, GJS, Adj.5P, LS, HC..............	250	300	375
Ohioan, 21J, Adj.3P, GJS, ¾	150	175	225
Railway, 19J, GJS, Adj.5P, BRG, DR.................	125	150	175
Special Railway, 23J, Adj.5P, NI, BRG, DR	225	275	350
Gen'l Stark, 15J, DMK, BRG	75	100	150
Gen'l Stark, 17J, DMK, BRG	75	100	150
95, 21J, marked "95", GJS	125	150	175
97 HC, 98 HC, & 108 OF, 17J, Adj.3P, NI, ¾, DMK ...	75	100	150
99, 15J, ¾, HC....................................	100	125	175
103, 21J, GJS, Adj.5P, NI, BRG, DR	100	125	175
104, 23J, GJS, Adj.5P, NI, BRG, DR, DMK..........	225	275	350
105, 21J, GJS, Adj.5P, NI, ¾, DR, DMK	100	125	175
106, 107 OF, & 108, 17J, SW, NI	75	100	150
109, 15J, ¾, OF	75	100	150
110, 11J, ¾	60	70	85
115-120, 21J, SW, NI, OF..........................	100	125	175
340, 17J, SW, NI	75	100	150
440, 15J, 2-tone..................................	100	125	175
555, 21J, GT, GJS, Chronometer on dial & mvt.	200	250	325
600, 17J, SW, NI	75	100	150

12 SIZE

Grade or Name — Description	Avg	Ex-Fn	Mint
Champion, 7J, SW	$40	$50	$75

Dueber Grand, 12 size, 17 jewels, gold jewel settings, hunting case, serial number 1,737,354.

Dueber Grand, 12 size, 17 jewels, gold jewel settings, open face, pin set, serial number 1,732,255.

Grade or Name—Description	Avg	Ex-Fn	Mint
Dueber Grand, 17J, BRG	$40	$50	$75
Hampden W. Co., 7J, SW, OF	40	50	75
Hampden W. Co., 17J, 14K, Multi-color, HC	700	800	1,000
John Hancock, 21J, BRG	55	65	85
Gen'l Stark, 15J, BRG	40	50	75
Gen'l Stark, 15J, pin set	40	50	75
207-300 HC & 302 OF, 7J, ¾ (add $25 for HC)	40	50	75
304 HC & 306 OF, 15J, ¾ (add $25 for HC)	40	50	75
305-308 HC & 310 OF, 17J, ¾	40	50	75
307, 17J	40	50	75
312 HC & 314 OF, 21J, ¾, Adj.5P (add $25 for HC)	50	75	125
31 OF, 17J, SW, 14K	275	325	400

Paul Revere. Example of Hampden Watch Co.'s thin series showing face and movement, 12 size, 17-19 jewels, Adj5p.

12 SIZE (THIN MODEL)

Grade or Name — Description	Avg	Ex-Fn	Mint
Aviator, 17J, Adj.4P	$40	$50	$75
Aviator, 19J, Adj.4P	45	60	85
Beacon, 17J	40	50	75
Nathan Hale, 15J	40	50	75
Minuteman, 17J	50	60	85
Paul Revere, 17J, 14K, OF	275	325	400
Paul Revere, 17J	50	60	85
Paul Revere, 19J	60	70	95

Note: Some 12 Sizes came in cases of octagon, decagon, hexagon, triad, and cushion shapes, and these usually bring slightly higher prices.

6 SIZE

Grade or Name — Description	Avg	Ex-Fn	Mint
200, 7J (add $25 for HC)	$40	$50	$75
206, 11J (add $25 for HC)	40	50	75
213, 15J (add $25 for HC)	40	50	75
220, 17J (add $25 for HC)	40	50	75
Hampden W. Co., 15J, multi-color GF, HC	150	200	275
Hampden W. Co., 15J, Multi-color, 14K, HC	375	425	500

Molly Stark, 000 size, 7 jewels, hunting or open face, originally sold for $12.00.

000 SIZE

Grade or Name — Description	Avg	Ex-Fn	Mint
Diadem, 15J, 14K, OF Case	$100	$150	$200
Diadem, 15J, HC, 14K	200	250	325
Diadem, 15J, HC	100	125	175
Molly Stark, 7J, HC	100	125	175
Molly Stark, 7J, 14K, HC	200	250	325
Molly Stark, 7J, Pin Set, OF	50	75	125
Four Hundred, 11, 15, 16, & 17J, HC	100	125	175
14K Multi-color, HC	375	425	500

HAMPDEN WATCH CO.
IDENTIFICATION OF MOVEMENTS

How to Identify Your Watch: Compare the movement of your watch with the illustrations in this section. While comparing, note the location of the balance, jewels, screws, gears, and type of back plate (Full, ¾, Bridge) which will be clues in identifying the movement you have.

Series I, 18 size
Hunting or open face, key wind & set

Series II, 18 size
Hunting, stem wind, pendant or lever set

Series III, 18 size
Hunting, stem wind, pendant or lever set

Series IV, 18 size
Open face, stem wind, lever set

Series 1, 16 size
Open face, stem wind, pendant or lever set

Series II, 16 size
Hunting, stem wind, pendant or lever set

Series III, 16 size
Open face, stem wind, pendant set

Series IV, 16 size
Hunting, stem wind, pendant or lever set

Series V, 16 size
Open face, stem wind, pendant or lever set

Series VI, 16 size
Hunting, stem wind, pendant set

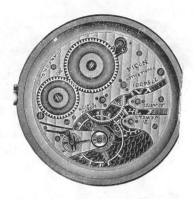

Series VII, 16 size
Open face, stem wind, pendant set

Series III, 12 size
Open face, stem wind, pendant set

Series I, 12 size
Hunting, stem wind, lever set

Series II, 12 size
Open face, stem wind, lever set

Series IV, 12 size
Open face, stem wind, pendant

Series V, 12 size
Open face, stem wind, pendant
set

Series I, 6 size
Open face, stem wind

Series I, 3/0 size
Hunting, stem wind

Series II, 3/0 size
Open face, stem wind, pendant set

Series III, 3/0 size
Hunting, lever or pendant set

Series IV, 3/0 size
Hunting, stem wind, pendant or lever set

HERMAN VON DER HEYDT
Chicago, Illinois
1883

Herman von der Heydt patented a self-winding watch on Feb. 19, 1884. A total of 35 watches were hand-made by von der Heydt. The watches were 18S, full plate, lever escapement and fully-jeweled. The wind mechanism was a gravity type made of heavy steel and shaped like a crescent. The body motion let the heavy crescent move which was connected to a ratchet on the winding arbor, resulting in self-winding. Five movements were nickel and sold for about $90; the gilded model sold for about $75.

Grade or Name — Description		Avg	Ex-Fn	Mint
18S, 19J, FULL, NI	★ ★ ★	12,000	$14,000	$16,000
18S, 19J, FULL, gilded	★ ★ ★	10,000	12,000	14,000

Example of **Herman Von Der Heydt**, 18 size self winding watch. "Chicago S.W. Co." on dial.

Herman Von Der Heydt, 18 size, 19 jewels; America's only self winding pocket watch. Note crescent shaped winding weight.

E. HOWARD & CO.
Boston (Roxbury), Massachusetts
December 11, 1858 - 1903

After the failure of the Boston Watch Company (1853-57), Edward Howard decided to personally attempt the successful production of watches using the interchangeable machine-made parts system. He and Charles Rice, his financial backer, were unable to buy out the defunct watch company in Waltham, however, they did remove (per a prior claim) the watches in progress, the tools and the machinery to Howard and Davis' Roxbury factory (first watch factory in America), in late 1857. During their first year, the machinery was retooled for the production of a revolutionary new watch of Howard's design. Also, the remaining Boston Watch Co. movements were completed (E. Howard & Co. dials, Howard & Rice on the movement). By the summer of 1858, Edward Howard had produced his first watch. On December 11, 1858 the firm of E. Howard & Co. was formed for the manufacture of high-grade watches. Howard's first model was entirely different from any watch previously made. It introduced the more accurate "quick beat" train to American watchmaking. The top plate was in two sections and had six pillars instead of the usual four pillars in a full plate. The balance was gold or steel at first, then later it was a compensation balance loaded with gold screws. Reed's patented barrel was used for the first time. The size, based on the Dennison system, was a little larger than the regular 18 size. In 1861, a ¾ plate model was put on the market. Most movements were being stamped with "N" to designate Howard's 18 size. On February 4, 1868 Howard patented a new steel motor barrel which was to supersede the Reed's, but not before some 28,000 had been produced. Also, in 1868 Howard introduced the stemwinding movement and was probably the first company to market such a watch in the U. S. By 1869, Howard was producing their "L" or 16 size as well as their first nickel movements. In 1870, G. P. Reed's micrometer regulator was patented for use by E. Howard & Co. The Reed style "whiplash" regulator has been used in more pocket watches, worldwide, than any other type. In 1878, the manufacturing of keywind movements was discontinued. Mr. Howard retired in 1882, but the company continued to produce watch movements of the grade and style set by him until 1903. This company was the first to adjust to all six positions. Their dials were always a hard enamel and always bore the name "E. Howard & Co., Boston." In 1903, the company transferred all rights to use the name "Edward Howard," in conjunction with the production of watches, to the Keystone Watch Case Co. Most of their models were stamped "Howard" on the dial and "E. Howard Watch Co., Boston. U.S.A." on the movement. Edward Howard's company never produced its own watch cases, the great majority of which were solid gold or silver. Keystone, however, produced complete watches, many of which were gold filled.

CHRONOLOGICAL DEVELOPMENT OF E. HOWARD & CO.:
Howard, Davis & Dennison, Roxbury, Mass., 1850
American Horologue Company, Roxbury, Mass., 1851
Warren Manufacturing Company, Roxbury, Mass., 1851-53
Boston Watch Co., Roxbury, Mass. — 1853-1854/Waltham, Mass., 1854-57
Howard & Rice, Roxbury, Mass., 1857-58 (E. Howard & Co. on dials)
E. Howard & Co., Roxbury, Mass. — 1858-1903
Keystone Watch Case Co. (Howard line), Jersey City, N. J., 1903-30

E. HOWARD & CO.
15 JEWELS
APPROXIMATE DATES, SERIAL NOS., AND TOTAL PRODUCTION

Serial Number	Date	Series	Total Prod.
131-1,800	-1860	I (18S)	1,800
1,801-3,000	1860-1861	II (18S)	1,200
3,001-3,200	1861	K(14S)	100
3,201-3,400	1861	i(10S)	100
3,501-28,000	1861-1871	III (18S)	24,500
30,001-50,000	1868-1882	IV (18S)	20,000
50,001-71,000	1869-1899	V (16S)	21,000
100,001-105,500	1869-1899	VI (6S)	5,500
200,001-227,000	1880-1899	VII (18S)	27,000
*228,001-231,000	1895	VII (18S)	3,000
300,001-309,000	1884-1899	VIII (18S)	9,000
*309,001-310,000	1895	VIII (18S)	1,000
400,001-405,000	1890-1895	IX (18S)	5,000
500,001-501,500	1890-1899	X (12S)	1,500
*600,001-601,500	1896	XI (16S)	1,500
*700,001-701,500	1896	XII (16S)	1,500

* ¾ Split Plates with 17 Jewels

E. HOWARD & CO. WATCH SIZES

Letter	Inches	Approx. Size
N	1 13/16	18
L	1 11/16	16
K	1 10/16	14
J	1 9/16	12
I	1 8/16	10
H	1 7/16	8
G	1 6/16	6
F	1 5/16	4
E	1 4/16	2
D	1 3/16	0

Standard Escapement

Deer — Adjusted to Hcl6P

Horse — Adjusted to HCI-No positions

Hound — Unadjusted

Coles Escapement

NOTE: E. Howard & Co. movements will not fit standard cases properly.

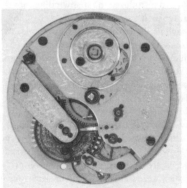

18 or N size, 15 jewels, right angle lever escapement, experimental model, serial number 3,122.

10 or I size, 15 jewels; note cut-out to view escape wheel, experimental model, serial number 3,472.

E. HOWARD & CO.
N SIZE (18)
(In Original Cases)

Series or Name — Description	Avg	Ex-Fn	Mint
E. Howard & Co. on dial and movement, 1857 Model, upright pallets, English style escape wheel, KW & KS, silver case ★ ★	$1,600	$2,000	$2,500
I, II or III, Isochronism, 15J, gilded, KW, helical hairspring ★ ★ ★	5,000	6,000	8,000

Series 1, 18 size, 15 jewels, note the compensating balance on this early movement, serial number 133.

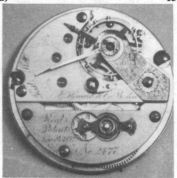

Series II, 18 size, 15 jewels, key wind & set, serial number 2,477.

Grade or Name—Description	Avg	Ex-Fn	Mint
I, 15J, with serial # below 100	$5,000	$6,000	$7,500
I, 15J, with serial # below 200	2,000	3,000	4,500
I, 15J, with serial # below 300	1,000	2,000	3,000
I, 15J, gilded, KW, 18K, HC or OF, upright pallets .. ★ ★	2,200	2,800	3,500
I, 15J, gilded, KW, 18K, HC or OF, horizontal pallets . ★	1,800	2,000	2,500
I, 15J, gilded, KW, silver HC........................ ★	1,000	1,200	1,400
I, 15J (movement only) .... ★	350	400	500
II, 15J, gilded, KW, 18K, HC or OF .... ★	1,600	1,800	2,000
II, 15J, gilded, KW, silver HC....................... ★	800	1,000	1,200
II, 15J (movement only) .... ★	200	250	325
III, 15J, gilded, KW, 18K, HC	1,300	1,500	1,800
III, 15J, gilded, KW, silver case.....................	600	800	1,000
III, 15J, nickel, KW, silver case.....................	700	900	1,100
III, 15J, gilded, KW, 18K, Mershon's Patent	1,500	1,800	2,200
III, 15J, gilded, KW, 18K, Coles Escapement .... ★ ★	1,600	1,900	2,300
III, 15J, NI, Private label	800	1,000	1,200
III, 15J (movement only)............................	150	175	225
IV, 15J, gilded or nickel, KW, 18K, HC	1,200	1,400	1,700
IV, 15J, gilded or nickel, SW, 18K, HC	1,000	1,200	1,400

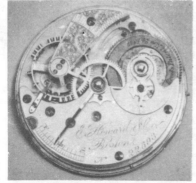

Series III, 18 size, 15 jewels, note center wheel rack regulator, serial number 22,693.

Series III, 18 size, 15 jewels, note high balance wheel over center wheel, serial number 7,000.

Series IV, 18 size, 15 jewels, key wind and set, serial number 37,893.

Series VII, 18 size, 15 jewels, nickel movement, note running deer on movement, "adjusted" on bridge, serial number 219,304.

Series or Name—Description		Avg	Ex-Fn	Mint
IV, personalized with jobber's name, silver	★ ★	$500	$600	$800
IV, 15J, gilded, Cole's Escapement	★ ★ ★	1,500	1,600	1,700
IV, 15J (movement only)		90	110	150
VII, 15J, gilded or nickel, SW, 14K, HC		1,000	1,200	1,500
VII, 17J, nickel, split plate, SW, 14K, HC	★	1,200	1,400	1,700
VII, 17J, nickel, split plate, SW, silver, HC	★	600	700	900
VII, 19J, nickel, split plate, SW, 14K HC	★ ★ ★	2,500	3,000	4,000
VII, 15J (movement only)		90	100	115
VII, Ball, 17J, nickel, SW, 14K, HC	★ ★ ★	3,500	4,000	6,000
VII, Ball, 17J, nickel, SW, GF, HC	★ ★ ★	2,200	2,800	3,500
VIII, 15J, gilded or nickel, SW, 14K, OF		900	1,000	1,400
VIII, 17J, nickel, split plate, SW, 14K, OF	★	1,200	1,400	1,700
VIII, 17J, nickel, split plate, SW, silver, OF	★	425	525	650
VIII, 15J (movement only)		80	90	100
VIII, Ball, 17J, nickel, SW, 14K, OF	★ ★	3,000	3,500	4,000
VIII, Ball, 17J, nickel, SW, GF, OF	★ ★	1,000	1,500	2,000

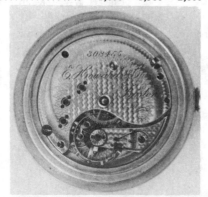

Series VII, 18 size, 17 jewels, ¾ split plate, serial number 228,055.

Series VIII, 18 size, 15 jewels, serial number 308,455.

Series VIII, 18 size, 17 jewels, split plate model, gold jewel settings, serial number 309,904.

Series IX, 18 size, 15 jewels, hunting. This series is guilded only and hound grade exclusively, serial number 402,873.

Series or Name—Description	Avg	Ex-Fn	Mint
IX, 15J, gilded, SW, 14K, HC	$900	$1,100	$1,400
IX, 15J, gilded, SW, silver, HC	425	525	650
IX, 15J (movement only)	75	85	100

L SIZE (16)
(In Original Cases)

Series or Name — Description	Avg	Ex-Fn	Mint
V, 15J, gilded, KW, 18K, HC	$1,000	$1,200	$1,500
V, 15J, gilded, KW, 18K, Coles Escapement ★	1,300	1,500	1,800
V, 15J, gilded or nickel, SW, 14K, HC	800	1,000	1,300
V, 15J, gilded, SW, 14K, Coles Escapement ★	1,100	1,300	1,600

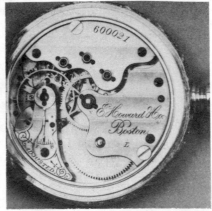

Series V, 16 or L size, Prescott Model, 15 jewels, hunting, serial number 50,434.

Series XI, 16 size, 17 jewels, split plate model, nickel movement, gold jewel settings, serial number 600,021.

Series XII, L-16 size, 21 jewels, split plate model, nickel movement, gold lettering, gold jewel settings, serial number 700,899.

Series K, 14 or K size, 15 jewels, key wind & set, serial number 3,005.

Series or Name—Description				Avg	Ex-Fn	Mint
V, 15J (movement only)				$90	$100	$125
XI, 17J, nickel, split plate, SW, 14K, HC			★	1,100	1,300	1,600
XI, 17J, nickel, split plate, SW, silver, HC			★	400	500	650
XI, 17J (movement only)				200	300	450
XII, 17J, nickel, split plate, SW, 14K, OF			★	1,000	1,200	1,500
XII, 17J, nickel, split plate, SW, silver, OF			★	375	475	625
XII, 17J (movement only)				100	150	175
XII, 21J, nickel, split plate, SW, 14K OF	★	★	★	2,500	3,000	4,000

K SIZE (14)
(In Original Cases)

Series or Name — Description				Avg	Ex-Fn	Mint
K, 15J, gilded, KW, 18K, HC	★	★	★	$2,500	$3,000	$4,000

J SIZE (12)
(In Original Cases)

Series or Name — Description			Avg	Ex-Fn	Mint
X, 15J, nickel, hound, SW, 14K, OF		★	$700	$900	$1,200
X, 15J, nickel, horse, SW, 14K, OF		★	800	1,000	1,300
X, 15J, nickel, deer, SW, 14K, OF		★	900	1,100	1,400
X, 15J, hound (movement only)		★	200	250	300

Series X, 12 or J size, 15 jewels, note deer on movement, serial number 501,361.

I size (10 size), 15 jewels, guilded, key wind, serial number 3,404.

I SIZE (10)
(In Original Cases)

Series or Name — Description		Avg	Ex-Fn	Mint
I, 15J, gilded, KW, 18K HC...................... ★ ★ ★		$2,500	$3,000	$4,000

G SIZE (6)
(In Original Cases)

Series or Name — Description		Avg	Ex-Fn	Mint
VI, 15J, gilded, KW, 18K, HC...................... ★ ★		$1,400	$1,800	$2,400
VI, 15J, gilded or nickel, SW, 18K, HC		1,000	1,200	1,500
VI, 15J, gilded or nickel, SW, 14K, HC		800	1,000	1,300
VI, 15J (movement only).............................		175	200	300

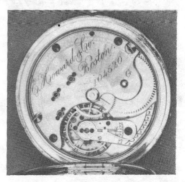

Series VI, 6 or G size, 15 jewels, stem wind.

Series VI, 6 or G size, 15 jewels, stem wind, serial number 104,520.

E. HOWARD WATCH CO.
Waltham, Massachusetts
1902 - 1930

The Howard name was purchased by the Keystone Watch Case Co. in 1902. The watches are marked "E. Howard Watch Co. Boston, U. S. A." There were no patent rights transferred, just the Howard name. The "Edward Howard" chronometer was the highest grade, 16 size, and was introduced in 1912 for $350.

Keystone Howard gained control of U. S. Watch Co. of Waltham and N. Y. Standard Watch Co.

ESTIMATED SERIAL NUMBERS AND PRODUCTION DATES

Date	Serial No.
1902	850,000
1903	900,000
1909	980,000
1912	1,100,000
1915	1,285,000
1917	1,340,000
1921	1,400,000
1930	1,500,000

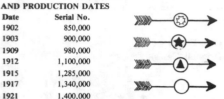

The arrows denote number of jewels and adjustments in each grade.

Cross—23 jewel, 5 positions

Star—21 jewel, 5 positions

Triangle—19 jewel, 5 positions

Circle—17 jewel, 3 positions

Series 1905, 16 size, 17 jewels. This model can be identified by the slant parallel damaskeening. This represents the middle grade.

Series 9, 16 size, 17 jewels. This model can be identified by the checkerboard damaskeening. This represents the top grade.

Series 3, 16 size, 17 jewels. This model can be identified by the circular damaskeening. This represents the lowest grade of the three.

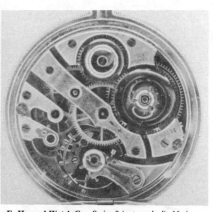

E. Howard Watch Co., Series 0, 16 size, 23 jewels, in original E. Howard Watch Co. swing-out movement Keystone Extra gold filled OF case.

E. Howard Watch Co., Series 0 (not marked), 16 size, 23 jewels, HC.

E. HOWARD WATCH CO.
(KEYSTONE)
16 SIZE

Series or Name — Description	Avg	Ex-Fn	Mint
No. 0, 23J, BRG, Adj.5P, DR, OF	$425	$500	$600
Series 0, 23J, BRG, Adj.5P, DR, Ruby banking pins	425	500	600
Series 0, 23J, BRG, Adj.5P, DR, jeweled barrel	450	525	625
Series 0, 23J, BRG, Adj.5P, DR, OF, 14K	700	900	1,200
Series 0, 23J, BRG, Adj.5P, DR, HC, 14K	750	950	1,250
No. 1, 21J, BRG, Adj.5P, DR......................★	275	300	375
Series 1, 21J, BRG, Adj.5P, DR	275	300	375
Series 2, 17J, BRG, Adj.5P, DR, HC	175	200	250

Note: Add $75-$100 for original box and papers. Add $50 for hunting case models listed as open face.

Series II, Railroad Chronometer, 16 size, 21 jewels, Adj5p, serial number 1,217,534.

Edward Howard Model, 16 size, 23 blue sapphire jewels, frosted gold bridge, wolfteeth wind, serial number 77. c.1914.

E. Howard Watch Co., 16 size, 23 jewels, by Waltham, raised gold jewel settings, Adj5p, hunting case, bridge style movement.

E. Howard Watch Co., 16 size 19 jewels, by Waltham, gold jewel settings, Adj3p, hunting case, ¾ plate movement.

Series or Name—Description	Avg	Ex-Fn	Mint
Series 2, 17J, BRG, Adj.5P, DR, OF	$125	$150	$175
Series 3, 17J, ¾, Adj.3P, circular DMK	100	125	150
Series 3, 17J, OF, Adj.3P, 14K, circular DMK	500	525	550
No. 5, 19J, GJS, BRG, HC ★	400	425	450
Series 5, 19J, BRG, Adj.5P, DR, 14K	550	575	600
Series 5, 19J, BRG, Adj.5P, DR, 1907 Model	200	225	275
1905, 17J, ¾, Adj.5P, DR, RGJS, slant parallel DMK, OF	125	150	175
1905, 17J, ¾, Adj.5P, DR, RGJS, slant parallel DMK, HC	175	200	250
Series 9, 17J, ¾, Adj.5P, DR, LS, checkerboard DMK	175	200	250
Series 9, 17J, ¾, Adj.5P, DR, 14K, checkerboard DMK (railroad grade)	475	500	550
Series 10, 21J, BRG, Adj.5P, DR	250	300	375
No. 10, 21J, BRG, Adj.5P, DR	250	300	375
Series 11, 21J, R.R. Chrono., Adj.5P, DR	300	350	425
"Edward Howard," 23 blue sapphire J, Adj.6P, GJS, GT, DR — Serial numbers below 300, without box ★★	8,000	9,000	10,000
"Edward Howard," 23 blue sapphire J, Adj.6P, GJS, GT, DR — Serial numbers below 300, with original box and papers, 18K the Edward Howard case ★★★	9,000	10,000	11,000
23J, E. Howard W. Co. on movement (mfg. by Waltham), 14K, Brg model ★★	1,200	1,400	1,700
23J, E. Howard W. Co. on movement (mfg. by Waltham), OF, gold filled	500	600	700
23J, E. Howard W. Co. on movement (mfg. by Waltham), HC, gold filled	600	700	800
21J, Waltham Model, ¾, OF	275	300	350
19J, Waltham Model, ¾, OF	275	300	350

Series or Name—Description	Avg	Ex-Fn	Mint
17J, Waltham Model, ¾, OF	$225	$250	$300
Unmarked, 23J, BRG, Adj.5P, DR, OF	425	450	500

Note: Add $100 for original wood box and papers on 16 size watches.

12 SIZE

Series or Name — Description	Avg	Ex-Fn	Mint
Series 6, 19J, BRG, DR, Adj.5P, 1908 Model, 14K, HC ..	$300	$350	$425
Series 6, 19J, BRG, DR, Adj.5P, 14K, OF	200	250	325
Series 6, 19J, BRG, DR, Adj.5P, OF	75	90	125
Series 7, 17J, BRG, DR, Adj.3P, 14K, OF	200	250	325
Series 7, 17J, BRG, DR, Adj.3P, OF	75	90	125
Series 8, 21J, BRG, DR, Adj.5P, OF	85	100	150
Series 8, 23J, BRG, DR, Adj.5P, 14K, OF	350	400	475
Series 8, 23J, BRG, DR, Adj.5P, OF	100	150	200
Series 8, 23J, BRG, DR, Adj.5P, 14K, HC	450	500	575

NOTE: Add $25 for gold filled hunting case.

Series 8, 12 size, 21 jewels, open face, stop works, extra thin.

E. Howard Watch Co., 10 size, 17 jewels, Adj3p, serial number 61,230. (Serial numbers started at about 1,001 on this model.)

10 SIZE

Series or Name — Description	Avg	Ex-Fn	Mint
Thin Model, 21J, ADJ, 14K case, OF	$250	$275	$325
Thin Model, 19J, ADJ, 14K case, OF	225	250	300
Thin Model, 17J, ADJ, 14K case, OF	200	225	275

NOTE: Serial numbers start at about 1,001 on this model.

ILLINOIS WATCH CO.
Springfield, Illinois
1869 - 1927

The Illinois Watch Company was organized mainly through the efforts of J. C. Adams. The first directors were J. T. Stuart, W. B. Miller, John Williams, John W. Bunn, George Black and George Passfield. In 1879 the company changed all its watches to a quick train movement by changing the number of teeth in the fourth wheel. The first mainspring made by the company was used in 1882. The next year soft enamel dials were used.

The Illinois Watch Co. used more names on its movements than any other watch manufacturer. To identify all of them requires extensive knowledge by the collector plus a good working knowledge of watch mechanics. Engraved on some early movements, for example, are "S. W. Co." or "I. W. Co., Springfield, Ill." To the novice these abbreviations might be hard to understand, thus making Illinois watches difficult to identify. But one saving clue is that the location "Springfield, Illinois" appears on most of these watches. It is important to learn how to identify these type watches because some of them are extremely collectible. Examples of some of the more valuable of these are: the Benjamin Franklin (size 18 or 16, 25 or 26 jewels), Paillard's Non-Magnetic, Pennsylvania Special, C & O, and B & O railroad models.

The earliest movements made by the Illinois Watch Co. are listed below. They made the first watch in early 1872, but the company really didn't get off the ground until 1875. Going by the serial number, the first watch made was the Stuart. Next was the Mason, followed by the Bunn, the Miller, and finally the Currier. The first stem-wind was made in 1875.

The Illinois Watch Company was sold to Hamilton Watch Co. in 1927. The Illinois factory continued to produce Illinois watches under the new management until 1932. After 1933 Hamilton produced watches bearing the Illinois name in their own factory until 1939.

Illinois Watch Co., Bates Model, 18 size, 7 jewels, key wind & set, serial number 43,876, c.1874.

Bunn, 18 size, 16 jewels, hunting case, serial number 1,185,809.

CHRONOLOGY OF THE DEVELOPMENT OF ILLINOIS WATCH CO.:

Illinois Springfield Watch Co. 1869-1879
Springfield Illinois Watch Co. 1879-1885
Illinois Watch Co. 1885-1927
Illinois Watch Co. was sold to Hamilton Watch Co. in 1927.

ILLINOIS ESTIMATED SERIAL NUMBERS
AND PRODUCTION DATES

Date	Serial No.	Date	Serial No.	Date	Serial No.
1872	5,000	1893	1,120,000	1914	2,600,000
1873	20,000	1894	1,160,000	1915	2,700,000
1874	50,000	1895	1,220,000	1916	2,800,000
1875	75,000	1896	1,250,000	1917	3,000,000
1876	100,000	1897	1,290,000	1918	3,200,000
1877	145,000	1898	1,330,000	1919	3,400,000
1878	210,000	1899	1,370,000	1920	3,600,000
1879	250,000	1900	1,410,000	1921	3,750,000
1880	300,000	1901	1,450,000	1922	3,900,000
1881	350,000	1902	1,500,000	1923	4,000,000
1882	400,000	1903	1,650,000	1924	4,500,000
1883	450,000	1904	1,700,000	1925	4,700,000
1884	500,000	1905	1,800,000	1926	4,800,000
1885	550,000	1906	1,840,000	1927	5,000,000
1886	600,000	1907	1,900,000	(Sold to Hamilton)	
1887	700,000	1908	2,100,000	1928	5,200,000
1888	800,000	1909	2,150,000	1929	5,350,000
1889	900,000	1910	2,200,000	1930	5,400,000
1890	1,000,000	1911	2,300,000	1931	5,500,000
1891	1,040,000	1912	2,400,000	1932	5,600,000
1892	1,080,000	1913	2,500,000		

(See **Illinois Identification of Movements** section located at the end of the Illinois price section to identify the movement, size and model number of your watch.)

(Prices are with gold filled cases except where noted.)

ILLINOIS
18 SIZE

Grade or Name — Description	Avg	Ex-Fn	Mint
Alleghany, 11J, KW, gilded, OF	$50	$75	$125
Alleghany, 11J, M#1, NI, KWM#	100	125	175
Alleghany, 11J, M#2, NI, Transition	100	125	175
America, 7J, M#3, Silveroid	50	65	95
America, 7J, M#1-2, KW, FULL.....................	100	125	175
America Special, 7J, M#1-2, KW, FULL	150	175	225
Army & Navy, 19J, GJS, Adj.5P, FULL	225	250	300
Army & Navy, 21J, GJS, Adj.5P, FULL	275	300	350
Baltimore & Ohio R.R. Special, 17J, GJS, ADJ	500	600	750
Baltimore & Ohio R.R. Special, 21J, GJS, NI, ADJ......	800	900	1,050
Baltimore & Ohio R.R. Standard, 24J, GJS, ADJ........	1,300	1,400	1,550
Bates, 7J, M#1-2, KW, FULL	125	150	185
Benjamin Franklin U.S.A., 17J, ADJ, NI	500	600	750

Illinois Watch Co., 18 size, railroad watch with a Ferguson dial.

Army and Navy, 18 size, 19 jewels, engraved on movement "Washington Watch Co.," serial number 1,606,612.

Grade or Name—Description	Avg	Ex-Fn	Mint
Benjamin Franklin U.S.A., 21J, GJS, Adj.6P, NI...... ★	$900	$1,000	$1,150
Benjamin Franklin U.S.A., 21J, GJS, Adj.5P, NI...... ★	800	900	1,050
Benjamin Franklin U.S.A., 24J, GJS, Adj.6P, FULL, NI, DMK .... ★	2,000	2,500	3,000
Benjamin Franklin U.S.A., 25J, GJS, Adj.6P, FULL, NI, DMK .... ★ ★ ★	6,000	6,500	7,500
Benjamin Franklin U.S.A., 26J, GJS, Adj.6P, FULL, DR, NI, DMK .... ★ ★ ★	5,000	5,500	7,000
Bunn, 15J, M#1, KW, KS, FULL, OF	500	600	775
Bunn, 15J, M#1, KW, KS, ADJ, FULL	550	650	825
Bunn, 15J, KW/SW transition	375	400	500
Bunn, 15J, M#1, KW, Coin	500	600	775
Bunn, 15J, KW, M#1, HC	550	650	825
Bunn, 16J, KW, OF	500	600	775
Bunn, 16J, KW, HC.................................	550	650	825
Bunn, 17J, SW, M#1, HC....................... ★	650	750	925
Bunn, 17J, M#2, SW, NI, FULL, HC	150	200	275
Bunn, 17J, SW, NI, Coin	125	150	200
Bunn, 17J, SW, M#3, 5th pinion, gilded, OF	350	400	475
Bunn, 17J, M#4, SW, NI, FULL, OF	125	150	200
Bunn, 17J, M#5, SW, NI, FULL, HC	150	200	275
Bunn, 17J, M#6, SW, NI, FULL, OF	125	150	200
Bunn, 19J, SW, NI, FULL, OF, DR, LS, GJS, Adj.5P, J. barrel	250	300	325
Bunn, 19J, SW, OF, Adj.6P, DR, J. barrel	300	350	425
Bunn, 19J, SW, GJS, FULL, HC, DR, Adj.5P, J. barrel .... ★	350	400	475
Bunn Special, 21J, SW, Coin	150	175	225
Bunn Special, 21J, GJS, ADJ, HC	300	350	400

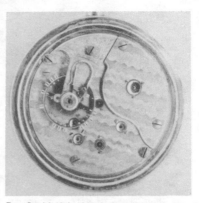

Bunn Special, 18 size, 24 jewels, adjusted, serial number 1,413,435

Bunn Special, 18 size, 26 Ruby jewels, "J. Home & Co." on dial, adjusted to six positions, gold jewel settings, serial number 2,019,415.

Grade or Name—Description	Avg	Ex-Fn	Mint
Bunn Special, 21J, GJS, ADJ, DR, OF	$150	$175	$225
Bunn Special, 21J, GJS, DR, Adj.5P, OF	155	180	230
Bunn Special, 21J, GJS, DR, Adj.6P, OF	160	185	235
Bunn Special, 21J, GJS, Adj.5P, HC, 14K	700	750	825
Bunn Special, 21J, GJS, ADJ, 2-Tone	175	200	250
Bunn Special, 21J, GJS, Adj.5P, DR	175	200	250
Bunn Special, 21J, Extra, GJS	275	300	350
Bunn Special, 23J, GJS, ADJ, DR, OF	350	375	425
Bunn Special, 23J, GJS, Adj.6P, DR, OF	375	400	450
Bunn Special, 23J, GJS, Adj.6P, DR, 2-Tone, OF	375	400	450
Bunn Special, 23J, GJS, ADJ, DR, HC . . . . ★	1,800	2,200	2,500
Bunn Special, 24J, GJS, Adj.5P, DR, HC	600	700	850
Bunn Special, 24J, GJS, Adj.5P, DR, 14K, HC	1,300	1,400	1,600
Bunn Special, 24J, GJS, Adj.5P, DR, OF	475	525	600
Bunn Special, 24J, GJS, Adj.6P, DR, OF	500	600	700
Bunn Special, 24J, GJS, Adj.5P, single roller	425	475	550
Bunn Special, 25J, GJS, Adj.6P, DR . . . . ★ ★ ★	5,000	5,500	6,500
Bunn Special, 26J, GJS, Adj.6P, DR . . . . ★ ★	4,500	5,000	6,000
Central Truck Railroad, 15J, KW, KS	350	400	475
Chesapeake & Ohio, 17J, ADJ, OF	300	350	425
Chesapeake & Ohio Special, 21J, GJS, 2-Tone . . . . ★	900	1,100	1,400
Chesapeake & Ohio Special, 24J, NI, ADJ, GJS . . . . ★	1,600	1,800	2,100
Chronometer, 15J, M#2, HC	150	175	225
Columbia, 11J, M#3, 5th Pinion	100	125	175
Columbia, 11J, M#1 & 2, FULL, KW	100	125	175
Columbia, 11J, M#1 & 2, Silveroid	75	100	150
Columbia Special, 11J, M#1-2-3, FULL, KW	100	125	175
Columbia Special, 11J, M#1-2-3, FULL, KW, transition . .	75	100	125
Comet, 11J, M#3, OF, LS, SW	75	100	125

Diurnal, 18 size, 7 jewels, key wind & set, only one run, total production 2,000, serial number 86,757.

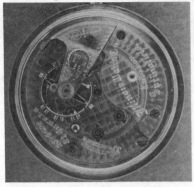

Emperor, 18 size, 21 jewels, Adj3p, serial number 2,396,628.

Grade or Name—Description	Avg	Ex-Fn	Mint
Commodore, 17J, HC	$150	$175	$225
Currier, 11J, KW, FULL, OF	100	125	175
Currier, 11J, KW, FULL, Coin	100	125	175
Currier, 11J, KW, HC	125	175	225
Currier, 11J, KW/SW, HC	100	150	200
Currier, 11J, transition, OF	75	100	125
Currier, 11J, M#3, OF	75	100	125
Currier, 13J, M#3, OF	75	100	125
Dauntless, 11J	75	100	125
Dean, 15J, M#1, KW, FULL, HC....................	150	175	225
Diurnal, 7J, KW, KS, HC, Coin .... ★	200	250	325
Dominion Railway, with train on dial.................	800	900	1,150
Eastlake, 11J, SW, KW, Transition.....................	100	125	175
Emperor, 21J, M#6, LS, SW, ADJ.....................	150	175	225
Enterprise, M#2, ADJ	100	125	175
Eureka, 11J	100	125	175
Forest City, 11J, SW, LS, HC	125	150	200
General Grant or General Lee, 11J, M#1, KW	225	250	300
Hoyt, 9-11J, M#1-2, KW, FULL	75	100	150
Illinois Watch Co., 11J, M#1-2, KW, FULL.............	75	100	125
Illinois Watch Co., 11J, M#3	50	75	100
Illinois Watch Co., 13J, M#1-2, KW, FULL.............	100	125	175
Illinois Watch Co., 15J, M#1-2, KW, FULL.............	100	125	175
Illinois Watch Co., 15J, G#106, KW, ADJ, FULL, NI ...	125	150	200
Illinois Watch Co., 17J, M#3, 5th Pinion	200	225	275
Illinois Watch Co., 15J, SW, ADJ, DMK, NI	75	100	125
Illinois Watch Co., 15J, transition....................	50	75	100
Illinois Watch Co., 15J, SW, Silveroid..................	50	60	75
Illinois Watch Co., 15J, SW, 9K, HC	300	400	550
Illinois Watch Co., 17J, SW, Silveroid..................	50	60	75

Ill. W. Co., 18 size, 17 jewels, adjusted, 2-tone movement, serial number 1,404,443.

Miller, 18 size, 17 jewels, 5th pinion model which changes hunting case to open face.

Grade or Name—Description	Avg	Ex-Fn	Mint
Illinois Watch Co., 17J, SW, ADJ	$75	$100	$125
Illinois Watch Co., 17J, transition	75	100	125
Illinois Watch Co., 19J, OF	150	175	225
Illinois Watch Co., 21J, OF	150	175	225
Illinois Watch Co., 21J, HC	175	200	250
Interior, 7J, KW, FULL	100	125	175
Interior, 7J, M#3	75	100	150
Interstate Chronometer, 17J, HC	400	500	650
Interstate Chronometer, 17J, OF	300	400	550
Interstate Chronometer, 23J, Adj.5P, GJS, NI, OF	850	950	1,150
Interstate Chronometer, 23J, Adj.5P, GJS, NI, HC	950	1,050	1,250
Iowa W. Co., 7J, M#1-2, KW, FULL	175	200	250
Iowa W. Co., 11J, M#1-2, KW	175	200	250
King of the Road, 16&17J, NI, OF & HC, LS, FULL, ADJ ★	400	500	625
Lafayette, 24J, GJS, Adj.6P, NI, SW, OF	950	1,050	1,250
Lakeshore, 17J, OF, LS, NI, FULL, SW	100	125	175
Landis W. Co., 7-11J	75	100	150
Liberty Bell, 17J, NI, SW, FULL	100	125	175
Liberty Bell, 17J, Silveroid	75	100	150
A. Lincoln, 21J, Silveroid	75	100	150
A. Lincoln, 21J, Adj.5P, NI, DR, GJS, HC	250	300	375
A. Lincoln, 21J, Adj.5P, NI, FULL, DR, OF, GJS	150	175	225
Maiden Lane, 17J, 5th Pinion	400	475	600
Manhatten, 11J, HC, NI, FULL, KW, LS	125	150	200
Mason, 7J, KW, KS, HC, FULL	125	150	200
Miller, 15J, Silveroid	75	100	125
Miller, 15J, M#1, HC, KW, FULL	150	175	225
Miller, 15J, M#1, HC, KW, FULL, ADJ	175	200	250
Miller, 15J, KW, FULL, OF	125	150	200

Paillard Non-Magnetic W. Co., 18 size, 24 jewels, gold jewel settings, serial number 1,397,812.

Pennsylvania Special, 18 size, 26 jewels, Adj6p, 2-tone movement, serial number 1,742,913.

Grade or Name—Description	Avg	Ex-Fn	Mint
Miller, 17J, 5th Pinion, ADJ	$275	$300	$375
Monarch W. Co., 17J, NI, ADJ, SW, FULL	125	150	200
Montgomery Ward, 17J, OF, GJS	125	150	200
Montgomery Ward, 21J	150	175	225
Montgomery Ward Timer, 21J, Silveroid	125	150	200
Montgomery Ward, 24J, OF	950	1,050	1,250
Montgomery Ward, 24J, HC ★	1,200	1,400	1,700
Muscatine W. Co., 15J, LS, NI, HC	150	175	225
The National, 11J, SW, LS, OF	75	100	135
Non-Magnetic W. Co., 21J, OF	225	275	350
Paillard Non-Magnetic W. Co., 15J, NI, OF	75	100	150
Paillard Non-Magnetic W. Co., 17J, GJS, NI, Adj.5P, OF	100	125	155
Paillard Non-Magnetic W. Co., 21J, GJS, NI, Adj.5P, OF	200	250	325
Paillard Non-Magnetic W. Co., 23J, GJS, NI, Adj.5P, OF	850	900	1,150
Paillard Non-Magnetic W. Co., 24J, GJS, NI, Adj.5P, OF	950	1,050	1,250
Pennsylvania Special, 17J, GJS, Adj.3P ★	600	750	900
Pennsylvania Special, 21J, DR, Adj.5P ★	1,200	1,400	1,800
Pennsylvania Special, 24J, DR, GJS, ADJ ★	1,800	2,000	2,400
Pennsylvania Special, 25J, DR, GJS, ADJ, NI ★ ★ ★ ★	5,000	5,500	6,500
Pennsylvania Special, 26J, DR, GJS, ADJ, NI ★ ★	4,500	5,000	6,000
Pierce Arrow, 17J, "automaker logo"	350	425	575
Plymouth W. Co., 17J, SW, FULL	75	100	135
Potomac, 17J, OF, FULL, ADJ, NI	125	150	200
The President, 15J, FULL, NI, OF	125	150	200
The President, 17J, DMK, FULL, 14K gold case	600	700	850
Railroad Construction, 17J, OF	200	250	325
Railroad Dispatcher Extra, 17J, OF	200	250	325
Railroad King, 15-17J, FULL, NI, ADJ	300	350	425
The Railroader, 15J, OF, FULL, ADJ, NI	250	300	375
Railway Engineer, 15J	250	300	375

The President, 18 size, 17 jewels, chalmer patented regulator, serial number 1,240,909.

Railroad King, 18 size, 17 jewels, Fifth Pinion Model, adjusted. Note chalmer patented regulator, serial number 1,160,836.

Grade or Name—Description	Avg	Ex-Fn	Mint
Railway Regulator, 15J, KW, KS, gilt	$400	$500	$675
S. W. Co., 15J, M#1, KW, HC	125	150	200
Sears & Roebuck Special, 17J, GJS, NI, DMK, ADJ	125	150	200
Senate, 17J, NI, DMK, FULL	125	150	200
Southern R.R. Special, 21J, LS, ADJ, OF .... ★	800	1,000	1,250
Southern R.R. Special, 21J, M#5, LS, ADJ, HC .... ★	1,200	1,400	1,650
Star Light, 17J, 5th pinion, Chalmers Reg. OF	175	225	300
J. P. Stevens, 17J, SW. FULL, NI	600	700	850
Stuart, 15J, M#1, KW, KS	500	600	750
Stuart, 15J, M#1, KW, KS, transition .... ★	300	350	450
Stuart, 15J, M#1, KW, KS, marked ADJ .... ★★	500	650	825
Stuart, ADJ, KW, Abbotts Conversion, 18K, HC .... ★★	1,500	1,700	2,000
Stuart, 15J, M#1, KW, KS, Coin.................. ★★	500	600	775

Sears & Roebuck Special, 18 size, 17 jewels, serial number 1,481,879.

Washington Watch Co., Lafayette model, 18 size, 24 Ruby jewels, gold jewel settings, adjusted, serial number 3,392,897.

Vault Time Lock for Mosler Lock Co., Covington, Ky. Movement is 18 size, 15 jewels, open face, Model number 6, serial number 4,576,540. Note 72 hour dial. Strong arm rooms first used vault time locks in the 1870s.

Grade or Name—Description		Avg	Ex-Fn	Mint
Stuart, 17J, M#3, 5th Pinion	★ ★	$300	$400	$475
Stuart, 17J, M#3, 5th Pinion, ADJ	★ ★	375	425	500
Transition Models, 17J, OF		100	125	155
Time King, 17J, OF, LS, FULL, NI		150	175	250
Time King, 21J, OF, LS, FULL		175	200	275
Vault Time Lock for Mosler, 15J, 72 hr.		100	125	155
Washington W. Co. (See Army & Navy, Liberty Bell, Lafayette, Senate)				
65, 15J, HC, LS, M#2		75	100	135
101, 11J, FULL, SW, KW, OF		75	100	135
101, 11J, SW, KW, Silveroid		40	60	85
101, 11J, SW, KW, HC		75	100	150
102, 13J, SW, KW, Silveroid		40	60	85
102, 13J, SW, KW, OF		75	100	135
102, 13J, FULL, SW, KW, HC		100	125	155
104, 15J, M#2, HC	★ ★	250	300	375
104, 17J, M#3, OF	★ ★ ★	300	350	425
105, 17J, M#3, OF	★ ★ ★	300	350	425
105, 15J, M#2, GJS, ADJ, FULL, KW, KS, HC	★ ★	275	325	400
106, 15J, ADJ, FULL, KW, KS		100	125	155
444, 17J, OF, NI, ADJ, FULL		50	75	135
445, 19J, GJS, 2-Tone, HC	★ ★	1,000	1,200	1,500
1905 Special, 21J, OF, NI, Adj.5P		300	400	550

NOTE: Watches listed in this book are priced at the retail level, as complete watches having an original 14k gold-filled case, an original white enamel single sunk dial, and with the entire original movement in good working order with no repairs needed, unless otherwise noted.

ILLINOIS
16 SIZE

Note: Bunn Special original cases were marked Bunn Special except for Elinvars (Hamilton cased).

Grade or Name — Description	Avg	Ex-Fn	Mint
Adams Street, 17J, ¾, SW, NI, DMK, HC	$175	$225	$300
Adams Street, 21J, 3F brg, NI, DMK	250	300	375
Ak-Sar-Ben (Nebraska backward), 17J, OF, GCW	150	175	225
Ariston, 11J, OF.....................................	50	75	125
Ariston, 15J, OF.....................................	50	75	125
Ariston, 17J, 3F brg, HC	175	225	300
Ariston, 17J, Adj.3P, OF	150	175	225
Ariston, 19J, Adj.3P, OF	150	175	225
Ariston, 21J, GJS, Adj.6P, OF	300	375	450
Ariston, 23J, GJS, Adj.6P, OF	500	600	750
Ariston, 23J, GJS, Adj.6P, HC......................	700	800	950
Arlington Special, 17J, OF	75	100	135
Arlington Special, 17J, OF, Silveroid	50	75	125
Army & Navy, 19J, GJS, Adj.5P, NI, 1F brg	200	250	325
Army & Navy, 21J, GJS, Adj.5P, 1F brg	250	300	375
B & M Special, 17J, BRG, Adj.4P	200	250	325
B & O Standard, 21J	350	400	525
Benjamin Franklin, 17J, ADJ, DMK, ¾	300	325	400
Benjamin Franklin, 21J, GJS, Adj.5P, DR, GT, ¾	500	550	625
Benjamin Franklin, 25J, GJS, Adj.6P, DR, GT, ¾, OF★★	3,000	3,500	4,000
Benjamin Franklin, 25J, GJS, Adj.6P, DR, GT, ¾, HC★★★	3,500	4,000	4,500
Bunn, 17J, LS, OF, NI, ¾, GJS, Adj.5P	100	125	155
Bunn, 17J, LS, NI, ¾, Adj.5P, HC...................	450	500	575
Bunn, 19J, LS, OF, NI, ¾, GJS, Adj.5P	100	125	155

Ben Franklin, 16 size, 25 jewels, gold jewel settings, gold train, serial number 2,242,138.

Bunn Special, Model 163, 16 size, 23 jewels, gold jewel settings, gold train, 60 hour movement, serial number 5,421,504.

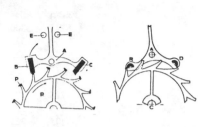

Left: Standard style escapement. **Right:** DeLong style escapement.

Illinois Watch Co., 16 size, 25 jewels, three-fingered bridge, gold train, hunting, note serial number S731,870.

Grade or Name—Description	Avg	Ex-Fn	Mint
Bunn, 19J, LS, NI, ¾, Adj.5P, HC .... ★ ★	$500	$700	$1,000
Bunn, 19J, LS, OF, NI, ¾, GJS, Adj.5P, 60 hour	300	350	425
Bunn, 19J, marked Jeweled Barrel	175	200	250
Bunn Special, 19J, LS, OF, NI, ¾, Adj.6P, GT	125	150	200
Bunn Special, 19J, LS, OF, NI, ¾, Adj.6P, GT, 60 hour .	300	350	425
Bunn Special, 21J, NI, GJS, HC .... ★	400	450	525
Bunn Special, 21J, LS, OF, NI, ¾, GJS, Adj.6P, GT	125	150	175
Bunn Special, 21J, LS, OF, NI, ¾, GJS, Adj.6P, GT, 60 hour	200	225	275
Bunn Special, 21J, LS, OF, NI, ¾, GJS, Adj.6P, GT, 60 hr. Elinvar....................................	275	300	375
Bunn Special, 21J, 60 hr., 14K, OF, Bunn Special case . ★	675	725	800
Bunn Special, 23J, LS, OF, NI, ¾, GJS, Adj.6P, GT	300	375	425
Bunn Special, 23J, LS, OF, NI, ¾, GJS, Adj.6P, GT, 60 hour	350	425	475
Bunn Special, 23J, LS, OF, NI, ¾, GJS, Adj.6P, GT, with 23J 60-hour on dial	450	475	525
Bunn Special, 23J, LS, NI, GJS, HC .... ★	1,200	1,300	1,500
161 Bunn Special, 21J, ¾, Adj.6P, 60 hour	250	300	375
161A Bunn Special, 21J, ¾, Adj.6P, 60 hour (Elinvar signed under balance or on top plate)	325	375	450
161 Elinvar Bunn Special, 21J, ¾, Adj.6P, 60 hour (Elinvar signed at bottom of bridge)	375	425	500
161B, Bunn Special, 21J, 60 hour, pressed jewels .. ★ ★ ★	1,000	1,200	1,500
163 Bunn Special, 23J, GJS, Adj.6P, ¾, 60 hour	400	475	575
163 Elinvar Bunn Special, 23J, GJS, Adj.6P, 60 hour (Elinvar signed at bottom of bridge) .... ★	900	950	1,050

Grade or Name—Description	Avg	Ex-Fn	Mint
163A Elinvar Bunn Special, 23J, GJS, Adj.6P, ¾, 60 hour (Elinvar signed under balance)	$800	$850	$950
163A Elinvar Bunn Special, 23J, Adj.6P, ¾, 60 hour (Elinvar signed on top plate)	800	850	950
Burlington, 15J, OF	50	75	125
Burlington, 15J, HC	125	150	200
Burlington, 17J, OF	50	75	125
Burlington, 17J, HC	125	150	200
Burlington W. Co., 19J, ¾, NI, Adj.3P	75	100	135
Burlington W. Co., 19J, BRG, NI, Adj.3P	75	100	135
Burlington W. Co., 19J, ¾, HC	125	150	200
Burlington W. Co., 19J, 3F brg, NI, Adj.3P	75	100	125
Burlington W. Co., 21J, ¾, NI, Adj.3P	100	125	150
Burlington W. Co., 21J, Adj.6P, GJS ★★	200	225	275
Burlington, Bull Dog, 21J, SW, LS, GJS, GT	200	275	350
C & O Special, 21J, ¾, NI, ADJ	600	700	900
Capitol, 19J, OF, ¾, NI, Adj.5P	100	125	150
Central, 17J, SW, PS, OF	50	75	125
Craftsman, 17J, OF	50	75	125
DeLong Escapement, 21J, GJS, Adj.6P, 14K OF ★★★	1,500	1,600	1,800
Diamond, Ruby, Sapphire, 21J, GJS, GT, Adj.6P, NI, BRG, DR ★	800	900	1,100
Diamond, Ruby, Sapphire, 23J, GJS, GT, Adj.6P, NI, BRG, DR ★★	1,500	1,700	2,000
Diamond, Ruby, Sapphire, 23J, GJS, GT, Adj.6P, NI,DR, ¾ plate	900	1,000	1,200
Dispatcher, 19J, Adj.3P	50	75	125
Forest City, 17J, KW/SW, gilted, FULL	150	175	225
Franklin Street, 15J, ¾, NI, ADJ	75	100	150
Getty Model, 21J	150	175	225
Getty Model, 17J	75	100	135

Interstate Chronometer, 16 size, 23 jewels, one-fingered bridge, serial number 2,327,614.

A. Lincoln, 16 size, 21 jewels, gold jewel settings, gold train, Adj5p, serial number 2,237,406.

Grade or Name—Description	Avg	Ex-Fn	Mint
Great Northern Special, 17J, BRG, ADJ	$250	$275	$325
Great Northern Special, 19J, BRG, ADJ	275	300	350
Great Northern Special, 21J, BRG, ADJ, Adj.3P	300	325	375
Illinois Central, 17J, 2-Tone, GT......................	100	125	150
Illinois Watch Co., 7J, M#1-2-3........................	50	75	125
Illinois Watch Co., 11J, M#1-2-3.......................	80	75	125
Illinois Watch Co., 11J, ¾, OF........................	50	75	125
Illinois Watch Co., 11J, M#7, ¾, OF	50	75	125
Illinois Watch Co., 11J, M#6, ¾, HC	100	125	175
Illinois Watch Co., 15J, M#2, OF......................	50	75	125
Illinois Watch Co., 15J, M#1, HC	100	125	175
Illinois Watch Co., 15J, M#3, OF......................	50	75	125
Illinois Watch Co., 15J, ¾, ADJ	50	75	125
Illinois Watch Co., 15J, 3F brg, GJS	50	75	125
Illinois Watch Co., 17J, 14K, HC	400	450	525
Illinois Watch Co., 17J, M#2-3, SW, OF................	50	75	125
Illinois Watch Co., 17J, M#6, SW, HC	100	125	175
Illinois Watch Co., 17J, M#7, OF	75	100	135
Illinois Watch Co., 17J, M#5, ¾, ADJ, HC.............	100	125	150
Illinois Watch Co., 17J, M#4, 3F brg, GJS, Adj.5P, HC .	100	125	150
Illinois Watch Co., 19J, M#1, ¾, GJS, Adj.5P	75	100	135
Illinois Watch Co., 19J, ¾, BRG, Adj.3P	75	100	135
Illinois Watch Co., 21J, ADJ, OF.....................	175	200	250
Illinois Watch Co., 21J, GJS, HC.....................	150	175	225
Illinois Watch Co., 21J, ¾, GJS, Adj.5P	100	125	150
Illinois Watch Co., 21J, 3F brg, GJS, Adj.5P	125	150	200
Illinois Watch Co., 23J, GJS	250	300	375
Illinois Watch Co., 25J, 3F brg, GJS, Adj.5P .... ★ ★	3,000	3,500	4,000
Imperial Sp, 17J, SW, LS, Adj.4P, OF	75	100	135
Interstate Chronometer, 17J, GCW, Adj.5P, HC	275	300	325
Interstate Chronometer, 17J, GCW, Adj.5P, OF	250	275	300
Interstate Chronometer, 23J, 1F brg, ADJ, OF	600	700	850
Interstate Chronometer, 23J, 1F brg, ADJ, HC	900	1,000	1,150
Lafayette, 23J, 1F brg, GJS, Adj.5P, GT	750	850	1,000
Lakeshore, 17J, OF	75	100	135
Lakeshore, 17J, HC	150	175	225
Landis W. Co., 15J	75	100	135
Liberty Bell, 17J	100	125	150
A. Lincoln, 21J, ¾, GJS, Adj.5P	125	150	200
Marine Special, 21J, ¾, Adj.3P	250	275	325
Monroe, 17J, NI, ¾, OF (Washington W. Co.)..........	100	125	150
Monroe, 15J, ¾, OF (Washington W. Co.)	75	100	150
Our No. 1, 15J, HC, M#1............................	150	200	275
Paillard Non-Magnetic Watch Co., 11J, ¾	75	100	135
Paillard Non-Magnetic Watch Co., 15J, ¾	75	100	135
Paillard Non-Magnetic Watch Co., 17J, ¾, Adj.5P, DMK	100	125	175

Sangamo, 16 size, 23 jewels, Adj6p, gold jewel settings, gold train, serial number 2,222,797.

Sangamo Special, 16 size, 19 jewels, 60 hour movement, Adj6p, gold jewel settings, gold train, serial number 4,720,522.

Grade or Name—Description	Avg	Ex-Fn	Mint
Paillard Non-Magnetic Watch Co., 21J, ¾, GJS, Adj.5P, DMK	$300	$325	$375
Pennsylvania Special, 23J, ¾, GJS, Adj.5P	1,200	1,300	1,450
Plymouth W. Co., 17J, OF (Add $25 for HC)	75	100	125
Precise, 21J, OF, LS, Adj.3P	125	150	200
Quincy Street, 17J, ¾, NI, DMK, ADJ	75	100	125
Railroad Dispatcher, 11J, HC	150	175	225
Railroad King, 17J, HC	200	225	275
Railroad Official, 23J, 3F brg ★ ★	800	900	1,050
Railway King, 17J, OF	150	175	225
Sangamo, 21J, GJS, HC	275	300	350
Sangamo, 21J, GJS, Adj.5P, OF	150	175	225
Sangamo, 21J, ¼, GJS, DR, Adj.6P, OF	150	175	225
Sangamo, 23J, ¾, GJS, DR, Adj.6P, OF	250	275	325
Sangamo, 23J, ¾, GJS, DR, Adj.6P, HC	425	475	550
Sangamo, 25J, M#5, ¾, GJS, DR, Adj.6P ★ ★ ★	4,000	5,000	6,500
Sangamo, 26J, M#5, ¾, GJS, DR, Adj.6P ★ ★ ★	5,000	6,000	7,500
Sangamo Extra, 21J, ¾, GJS, DR, Adj.6P	400	500	650
Sangamo Special, 19J, BRG, GJS, GT, Adj.6P	350	375	425
Sangamo Special, 19J, BRG, GJS, GT, Adj.6P, 60 hour	450	475	525
Sangamo Special, 19J, BRG, GJS, GT, Adj.6P, HC	800	850	950
Sangamo Special, 21J, M#7, OF	325	375	450
Sangamo Special, 21J, M#8, BRG, HC ★ ★ ★	700	800	950
Sangamo Special, 21J, M#9, BRG, GJS, GT, Adj.6P, OF	325	375	450
Sangamo Special, 21J, BRG, GJS, GT, Diamond end cap.	350	400	475
Sangamo Special, 23J, M#9-10, BRG, GJS, GT, Adj.6P, Sangamo Special case	400	450	525

Grade or Name—Description	Avg	Ex-Fn	Mint
Sangamo Special, 23J, BRG, GJS, GT, Adj.6P, Diamond end stone, screw back, Sangamo Special case	$400	$450	$525
Sangamo Special, 23J, BRG, GJS, GT, Adj.6P, marked 60 hour, rigid bow, Sangamo Special case	700	750	825
Sangamo Special, 23J, BRG, GJS, GT, Adj.6P, *not* marked 60 hour, rigid bow, Sangamo Special case	450	550	575
Sangamo Special, 23J, M#8, BRG, GJS, GT, Adj.6P, HC .... ★ ★ ★	1,000	1,200	1,500
Santa Fe Special, 17J, BRG, Adj.3P.....................	150	175	225
Santa Fe Special, 21J, ¾, Adj.5P, OF.................	275	300	350
Santa Fe Special, 21J, ¾, Adj.5P, HC	450	500	575
Sears, Roebuck & Co. Special, 17J, ADJ	75	100	135
Senate, 17J, OF, NI, ¾..............................	75	100	135
Standard, 15J.......................................	50	75	125
Sterling, 19J, SW, PS, Adj.3P, OF....................	50	75	125
Stewart, 17J	50	75	125
Stewart Special, 17J	50	75	125
Time King, 17J, OF	75	100	135
Time King, 19J, Adj.3P, M#p	80	100	145
Victor, 21J, ¾, Adj.5P	75	100	135

Grade 163, 16 size, 23 jewels, adjusted to 6 positions, motor barrel, 60 hour model, serial number 5,421,504.

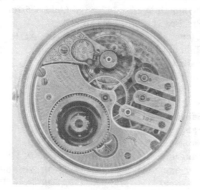

Grade 187, 16 size, 17 Ruby jewels, three-fingered bridge model, gold jewel settings, gold train, Adj5p, serial number 2,487,510.

Grade or Name—Description	Avg	Ex-Fn	Mint
161 through 163A—See Bunn Special			
167L, 17J, marked	$125	$150	$175
167, 17J..	50	75	125
169, 19J, Adj.3P, OF................................	100	125	150
174, 23J, LS, GJS, Adj.5P, OF, marked .... ★ ★	675	725	800
175, 19J, GJS, BRG, HC .... ★	900	975	1,100
177, 19J, SW, LS, 60 hour, Adj.5P, OF	400	500	650

Grade or Name—Description	Avg	Ex-Fn	Mint
179, 21J, HC, 3F brg, marked Ruby Jewels .... ★	$300	$400	$550
187, 17J, 3F brg, Adj.5P, GJS, GT, HC	225	275	350
189, 21J, 3F brg, Adj.6P, GJS, GT, DR, marked Ruby Jewels, HC................................	400	450	525
333, 15J, HC	100	125	175
555, 17J, ¾, ADJ.....................................	75	100	135
777, 17J, ¾, ADJ.....................................	75	100	135
900, 19J, LS, Adj.3P	100	125	150

Illinois Watch Co., 14 size, 16 jewels, Adj5p.

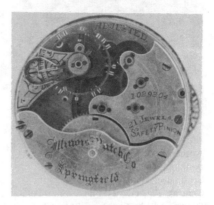

Illinois Watch Co., 14 size, 21 jewels, adjusted, nickel movement, gold jewel settings, serial number 1,029,204.

ILLINOIS
14 SIZE

Grade or Name — Description	Avg	Ex-Fn	Mint
Illinois Watch Co., 7J, M#1-2-3, SW, OF	$40	$50	$65
Illinois Watch Co., 11J, M#1-2-3, SW, OF	50	60	75
Illinois Watch Co., 15J, M#1-2-3, SW, OF	60	70	90
Illinois Watch Co., 16J, M#1-2-3, SW, OF	75	80	115
Illinois Watch Co., 21J, M#1-2-3, SW, OF	90	110	135
Illinois Watch Co., 21J, Silveroid	60	70	90

NOTE: Add $25 for above watches in hunting case.

ILLINOIS
12 SIZE and 13 SIZE

Grade or Name — Description	Avg	Ex-Fn	Mint
Aristocrat, 19J, OF.................................	$40	$50	$70
Ariston, 11-17J, OF	60	70	85
Ariston, 19J, OF	75	100	150
Ariston, 21J, OF	85	110	160
Ariston, 23J, OF	175	200	250

Ben Franklin, 12 size, 17 jewels, open face, gold train, serial number 2,366,286.

Illini, 12 size, 21 jewels, bridge model, serial number 3,650,129. Note five tooth click.

Grade or Name—Description	Avg	Ex-Fn	Mint
Autocrat, 17J, Adj.3P, ¾	$60	$70	$85
Autocrat, 19J, Adj.3P, ¾	65	75	95
Benjamin Franklin, 17J, OF	200	250	325
Burlington W. Co., 21J, OF	60	70	85
Central, 17J, OF, 2-Tone	40	50	70
Diamond Ruby Sapphire, 21J, Adj.5P, GJS	300	350	425
Elite, 19J, OF	60	70	85
Illini, 13 Size, 21J, Adj.5P, 14K, HC	275	325	400

Example of Illinois Thin Model, 12 size, 17 jewels, adjusted to 3 positions.

Maiden America, 12 size, 17 jewels, serial number 2,820,499.

Santa Fe Special, 12 size, 21 jewels, three-quarter plate, serial number 3,414,422.

Grade or Name—Description	Avg	Ex-Fn	Mint
Illini, 13 Size, 21J, Adj.5P, BRG, GJS	$75	$100	$135
Illini Extra, 13 Size, 21J, Adj.5P, OF	75	100	135
Illini, 13 Size, 23J, Adj.5P, BRG, GJS	125	150	200
Illinois Watch Co., 15J, OF	40	50	70
Illinois Watch Co., 17J, OF, 14K	250	275	325
Illinois Watch Co., 17J, HC, GF......................	75	100	135
Illinois Watch Co., 19J, OF	60	70	85
Illinois Watch Co., 21J, OF	70	80	95
Illinois Watch Co., 21J, HC	100	125	150
Interstate Chronometer, 21J, GJS, OF	150	175	225
Interstate Chronometer, 21J, GJS, HC.................	200	225	275
A. Lincoln, 19J, Adj.5P, GJS, DR, ¾, marked on mvt...	60	70	85
A. Lincoln, 21J, Adj.5P, DR, GJS.....................	70	80	95
Maiden America, 17J, ADJ	60	70	85
Marquis Autocrat, 17J, OF	60	70	85
Master, 21J, GT, GJS, OF	70	80	95
Masterpiece, 19J, Adj.3P, OF	65	75	100
Plymouth Watch Co., 15-17J, OF, HC	50	60	75
Railroad Dispatch Special, 17J, SW, GT	70	80	95
Santa Fe Special, 21J	75	100	135
Sterling, 17J, OF....................................	40	50	65
Stewart Special, 17J, SW, Adj.3P	50	60	75
Stewart Special, 19J, SW, OF, GT	55	65	80
Time King, 19J, SW, Adj.3P	60	70	85
Time King, 21J, SW, Adj.3P	70	80	95
Transit, 19J, OF, PS	60	70	85
Vim, 17J, ADJ, BRG, GJS, DR, OF	50	60	75
Washington W. Co., 11J, HC	100	125	150
Washington W. Co., Army & Navy, 19J	100	125	150
Washington W. Co., Senate, 17J, M#2, PS, HC	60	70	85

Grade or Name—Description	Avg	Ex-Fn	Mint
121, 21J, Adj.3P	$70	$85	$95
127, 17J, ADJ	60	70	85
129, 19J, Adj.3P	60	70	85
219, 11J, M#1	50	60	75
403, 15J, BRG	60	70	85
405, 17J, BRG, ADJ, OF	60	70	85
409, 21J, BRG, Diamond, Ruby, Sapphire, Adj.5P, GJS	275	325	400
410, 23J, BRG, GJS, Adj.6P, DR	150	200	275
410, 23J, BRG, GJS, Adj.6P, DR, 14K, OF	250	300	375

ILLINOIS
8 SIZE

Grade or Name — Description	Avg	Ex-Fn	Mint
Arlington, 7J, ¾ ★	$125	$150	$200
Rose LeLand, 13J, ¾ ★★	225	250	300
Stanley, 7J, ¾ ★★★	250	300	350
Mary Stuart, 15J, ¾ ★★	200	250	300
Sunnyside, 11J, ¾ ★	150	200	250
151, 7J, ¾	40	50	65
152, 11J, ¾	50	60	75
155, 11J, ¾	60	70	85
155, 11J, ¾, Coin	30	40	55

Note: Add $10 more for above watches in hunting case.

Illinois Watch Co., 8 size, 7 jewels

Grade 144, 6 size, 15 jewels, serial number 5,902,290.

ILLINOIS
6 SIZE

Grade or Name — Description	Avg	Ex-Fn	Mint
Illinois W. Co., 7J, LS, HC, 14K	$200	$225	$300
Illinois W. Co., 7J, HC	50	75	125

Grade or Name—Description	Avg	Ex-Fn	Mint
Illinois W. Co., 7J, OF, Coin	$35	$45	$60
Illinois W. Co., 11J, OF, HC....................	50	75	125
Illinois W. Co., 15J, OF, HC, 14K	200	250	325
Illinois W. Co., 17J, OF, HC......................	50	75	125
Illinois W. Co., 19J, OF, HC......................	75	100	150
Plymouth Watch Co., 17J, OF HC....................	50	60	75
Washington W. Co., 15J, HC, Liberty Bell	125	150	200

ILLINOIS
4 SIZE

Grade or Name — Description	Avg	Ex-Fn	Mint
Illinois W. Co., 7J, LS, HC........................	$50	$55	$95
Illinois W. Co., 11J, LS, HC.......................	50	75	125
Illinois W. Co., 15J, LS, HC.......................	50	75	125

ILLINOIS
0 SIZE

Grade or Name — Description	Avg	Ex-Fn	Mint
Illinois W. Co., 7J, LS, HC, 14K	$175	$225	$300
201, 11J, BRG, NI	75	100	150
203, 15J, BRG, NI	75	100	150
204, 17J, BRG, NI	75	100	150
Interstate Chronometer, 15J, HC, SW	175	200	275
Interstate Chronometer, 17J, HC, SW	185	210	285
Plymouth Watch Co., 15J, HC	50	60	75
Washington W. Co., Liberty Bell, 15J, ADJ	150	175	250
Washington W. Co., Mt. Vernon, 17J, ADJ	160	185	275

Grade 201, 0 size, 11 jewels, originally sold for $8.10.

Grade 203, 0 size, 15 jewels, originally sold for $10.40

Grade 204, 0 size, 17 jewels, originally sold for $12.83.

ILLINOIS SPRINGFIELD WATCH CO.
IDENTIFICATION OF MOVEMENTS
BY MODEL NUMBER

How to Identify Your Watch: Compare the movement of your watch with the illustrations in this section. Upon matching the movement exactly, the model number and size can be determined. While comparing, note the location of the balance, jewels, screws, gears, and type of back plate (Full, ¾, Bridge) which will be clues in identifying the movement you have. Having determined the size and model number, you can now find your watch in the main price listing by name or number (which is engraved on the movement).

THE ILLINOIS WATCH CO. GRADE AND MODEL CHART

Size	Model	Plate Design	Setting	Hunting or Open Face	Type Barrel	Started w/ Serial No.	Remarks
18	1	Full	Key	Htg	Reg	1	Course train
	2	Full	Lever	Htg	Reg	38,901	Course train
	3	Full	Lever	OF	Reg	46,201	Course train, 5th pinion
	4	Full	Pendant	OF	Reg	1,050,001	Fast train
	5	Full	Lever	Htg	Reg	1,256,101	Fast train, RR Grade
	6	Full	Lever	OF	Reg	1,144,401	Fast train, RR Grade
16	1	Full	Lever	Htg	Reg	1,030,001	Thick model
	2	Full	Pendant	OF	Reg	1,037,001	Thick model
	3	Full	Lever	OF	Reg	1,038,001	Thick model
	4	¾ & brg	Lever	Htg	Reg	1,300,001	Getty model
	5	¾ & brg	Lever	OF	Reg	1,300,601	Getty model
	6	¾ & brg	Pendant	Htg	Reg	2,160,111	DR & Improved RR model
	7	¾ & brg	Pendant	OF	Reg	2,160,101	DR & Improved RR model
	8	¾ & brg	Lever	Htg	Reg	2,523,101	DR & Improved RR model
	9	¾ & brg	Lever	OF	Reg	2,522,001	DR & Improved model
	10	Cent brg	Lever	OF	Motor	3,178,901	Also 17S Ex Thin RR gr 48 hr
	11	¾	Lever & Pen	OF	Motor	4,001,001	RR grade 48 hr
	12	¾	Lever & Pen	Htg	Motor	4,002,001	RR grade 48 hr
	13	Cent brg	Lever	OF	Motor	4,166,801	Also 17S RR grade 60 hr
	14	¾	Lever	OF	Motor	4,492,501	RR grade 60 hr
	15	¾	Lever	OF	Motor	5,488,301	RR grade 60 hr Elinvar
14	1	Full	Lever	Htg	Reg	1,009,501	Thick model
	2	Full	Pendant	OF	Reg	1,000,001	Thick model
	3	Full	Lever	OF	Reg	1,001,001	Thick model
13	1	brg	Pendant	OF	Motor		Ex Thin gr 538 & 539
12	1	¾	Pendant	OF	Reg	1,685,001	
Thin	2	¾	Pendant	Htg	Reg	1,748,751	
	3	Cent brg	Pendant	OF	Reg	2,337,011	Center bridge
	4	Cent brg	Pendant	Htg	Reg	2,337,001	Center bridge
	5	Cent brg	Pendant	OF	Motor	3,742,201	Center bridge
	6	Cent brg	Pendant	Htg	Motor	4,395,301	Center bridge
12T	1	True Ctr brg	Pendant	OF	Motor	3,700,001	1 tooth click, Also 13S
	2	True Ctr brg	Pendant	OF	Motor	3,869,301	5 tooth click
	3	¾	Pendant	OF	Motor	3,869,201	2 tooth click
8	1	Full	Key or lever	Htg	Reg	100,001	Plate not recessed
	2	Full	Lever	Htg	Reg	100,101	Plate is recessed
6	1	¾	Lever	Htg	Reg	552,001	
4	1	¾	Lever	Htg	Reg	551,501	
0	1	¾	Pendant	OF	Reg	1,815,901	
	2	¾	Pendant	Htg	Reg	1,749,801	
	3	Cent brg	Pendant	OF	Reg	2,644,001	
	4	Cent brg	Pendant	Htg	Reg	2,637,001	

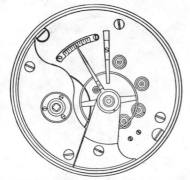

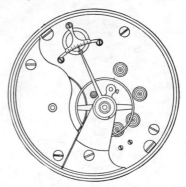

Model 1, 18 size, hunting, key wind & set.

Model 2, 18 size, hunting, lever set, coarse train.

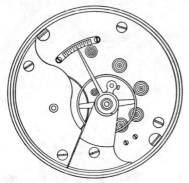

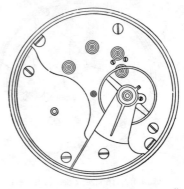

Model 3, 18 size, open face, lever set, coarse train, with fifth pinion.

Model 4, 18 size, open face, pendant set, fine train.

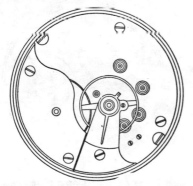

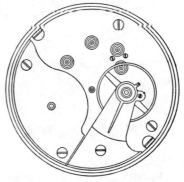

Model 5, 18 size, hunting, lever set, fine train.

Model 6, 18 size, open face, lever set, fine train.

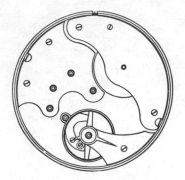

Model 1, 16 size, hunting, lever set.

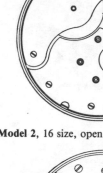

Model 2, 16 size, open face, pendant set.

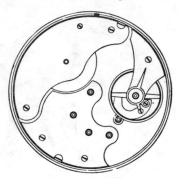

Model 3, 16 size, open face, lever set

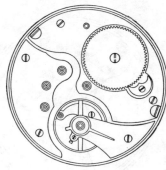

Model 4, 16 size, three-quarter plate, hunting, lever set.

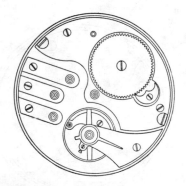

Model 4, 16 size, three-quarter plate, bridge, hunting, lever set.

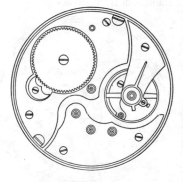

Model 5, 16 size, three-quarter plate, open face, lever set.

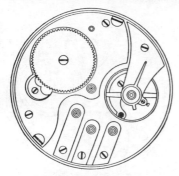

Model 5, 16 size, three-quarter plate, bridge, open face, lever set.

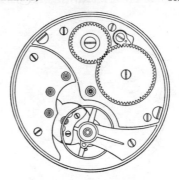

Model 6, 16 size - Pendant set
Model 8, 16 size - Lever set
hunting, three-quarter plate

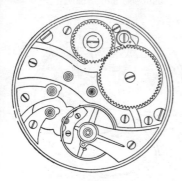

Model 6, 16 size - Pendant set
Model 8, 16 size - Lever set
hunting, bridge model

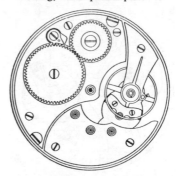

Model 7, 16 size - Pendant set
Model 9, 16 size - Lever set
open face, three-quarter plate

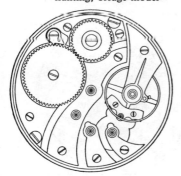

Model 7, 16 size - Pendant set
Model 9, 16 size - Lever set
open face, bridge model

Model 10, 16 size, bridge, extra thin, open face, lever set, motor barrel.

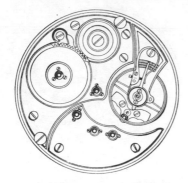

Model 11, 16 size, three-quarter plate, open face, pendant set, motor barrel.

Model 12, 16 size, three-quarter plate, hunting, pendant set, motor barrel.

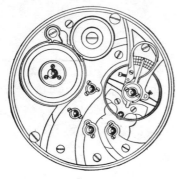

Model 13, 16 size, bridge, open face, lever set, motor barrel.

Model 14, 16 size, three-quarter plate, open face, lever set, 60-hour motor barrel.

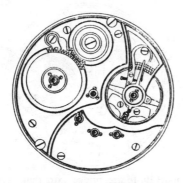

Model 15, 60 Hr. Elinvar.

Model B, 16 size, hunting case.

Model C, 16 size, open face

Model D, 16 size, open face

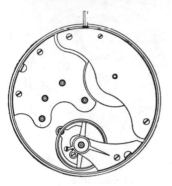

Model 1, 14 size, hunting, lever set.

Model 2, 14 size, open face, pendant set.

Model 3, 14 size, open face, lever set.

Model 1, 13 size, bridge, extra thin, open face, pendant set, motor barrel.

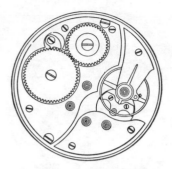

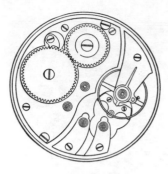

Model 1, 12 size, three-quarter plate, open face, pendant set.

Model 1, 12 size, three-quarter plate, bridge, open face, pendant set.

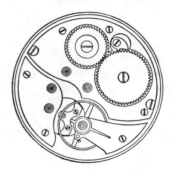

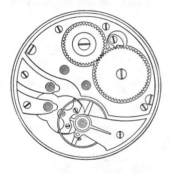

Model 2, 12 size, three-quarter plate, hunting, pendant set.

Model 2, 12 size, three-quarter plate, bridge, hunting, pendant set.

Model 3, 12 size, **Model 4**, 12 & 14 size, bridge, open face, pendant set.

Model 4, 12 size, bridge, hunting, pendant set.

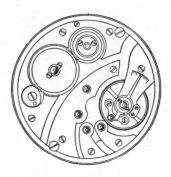

Model 5, 12 size, bridge, open face, pendant set, motor barrel.

Model 1, 12 size, extra thin, bridge, open face, pendant set, motor barrel.

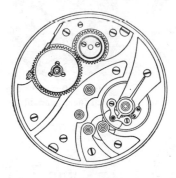

Model 2, 12 size, extra thin, bridge, open face, pendant set, motor barrel.

Model 3, 12 size, extra thin, three-quarter plate, open face, pendant set, motor barrel.

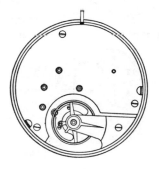

Model A, 12 size, bridge, open face.

Model 1, 8 size, hunting, key or lever set.

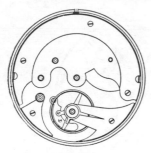

Model 2, 8 size, hunting, lever set.

Model 1, 6 size, hunting, lever set.

Model 1, 4 size, hunting, lever set.

Model 1, 0 size, three-quarter plate, open face, pendant set.

Model 2, 0 size, three-quarter plate, hunting, pendant set.

Model 3, 0 size, bridge, open face, pendant set.

Model 4, 0 size, bridge, hunting, pendant set.

Model 3, 3/0 size, bridge, open face, pendant set.

Model 4, 3/0 size, bridge, hunting, pendant set.

Model 1, 6/0 size, three-quarter plate, open face, pendant set.

Model 2, 6/0 size, bridge, open face, pendant set.

INDEPENDENT WATCH CO.
Fredonia, New York
1880 - 1885

The California Watch Company was idle for two years before it was purchased by brothers E. W. Howard and C. M. Howard. They had been selling watches by mail for sometime and started engraving the Howard Bros. name on them and using American-made watches. Their chief supply came from Hampden Watch Co., Illinois, U. S. Watch Co. of Marion, and Cornell Watch Co. The brothers formed the Independent Watch Co. in 1880, but it was not a watch factory in the true sense. They had other manufacturers engrave the Independent Watch Co. name on the top plates and on the dials of their watches. These watches were sold by mail order and sent to the buyer C. O. D. The names used on the movements were "Mark Twain," "Howard Bros.," "Independent Watch Co.," "Fredonia Watch Co.," and "Lakeshore Watch Co., Fredonia, N. Y."

The company later decided to manufacture watches and used the name Fredonia Watch Co. But they found that selling watches two different ways was no good. The business survived until 1885 at which time the owners decided to move the plant to a new location at Peoria, Illinois. Approximately 350,000 watches were made that sold for $16.

CHRONOLOGY OF THE DEVELOPMENT OF INDEPENDENT WATCH CO.:

Independent Watch Co.	1880-1883
Fredonia Watch Co.	1883-1885
Peoria Watch Co.	1885-1895

Grade or Name — Description		Avg	Ex-Fn	Mint
18S, 7J, KW, KS, OF, by U.S. W. Co. Marion, with butterfly cutout	★	$450	$550	$675
18S, 11J, KW, KS, by Hampden		200	250	325
18S, 11J, KW, KS, Coin		150	175	225
18S, 11J, KW, KS		150	175	225
18S, 15J, KW, KS		160	185	235

Independent Watch Co., 18 size, 11 jewels, key wind & set, made by Hampden Watch Co. (Model Number 1), serial number 170,844.

Independent Watch Co., 18 size, 15 jewels, key wind, made by U.S. Marion Watch Co., note butterfly cuttout, serial number 192,661.

Grade or Name—Description	Avg	Ex-Fn	Mint
18S, Howard Bros., 11J, KW, KS	$250	$300	$375
18S, Independent W. Co., 11J	150	175	225
18S, Lakeshore W. Co., 15J, KW, HC, by N.Y. W. Co.	200	250	325
18S, Mark Twain, 11J, KW, KS	350	400	475

ROBERT H. INGERSOLL & BROS.
New York, New York
1892 - 1922

In 1892 this company published a catalog for the mail order trade. It listed men's watch chains and a "silverine" watch for $3.95. It was not a true Ingersoll but a "Universal," introduced that same year to the dealers. The first $1 watches were jeweled; "Reliance" had seven jewels. In 1916, Ingersoll's production was 16,000 a day. The slogan was "The Watch that Made the Dollar Famous." The first 1,000 watches were made by Waterbury Clock Co. By 1922 the Ingersoll line was completely taken over by Waterbury. U. S. Time Corp. acquired Waterbury in 1944 and continued to use the Ingersoll name on certain watches.

ESTIMATED SERIAL NUMBERS
AND PRODUCTION DATES

Date	Serial No.	Date	Serial No.	Date	Serial No.
1892	150,000	1905	10,000,000	1918	47,500,000
1893	310,000	1906	12,500,000	1919	50,000,000
1894	650,000	1907	15,000,000	1920	55,000,000
1895	1,000,000	1908	17,500,000	1921	58,000,000
1896	2,000,000	1909	20,000,000	1922	60,500,000
1897	2,900,000	1910	25,000,000	1923	62,000,000
1898	3,500,000	1911	30,000,000	1924	65,000,000
1899	3,750,000	1912	38,500,000	1925	67,500,000
1900	6,000,000	1913	40,000,000	1926	69,000,000
1901	6,700,000	1914	41,500,000	1927	70,500,000
1902	7,200,000	1915	42,500,000	1928	71,500,000
1903	7,900,000	1916	45,500,000	1929	73,500,000
1904	8,100,000	1917	47,000,000	1930	75,000,000
				1944	95,000,000

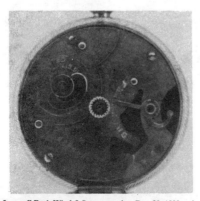

Ingersoll Back Wind & Set, patent date Dec. 23, 1890 and Jan. 13, 1891, c. late 1890s.

Ingersoll Blind Man's Watch.

INGERSOLL
DOLLAR TYPE

NOTE: Prices are for complete watch in good running order. In some specialty markets, the comic character watches may bring higher prices in top condition.

Grade or Name — Description	Avg	Ex-Fn	Mint
Ingersoll Back Wind .... ★	$100	$125	$175
Admiral Dewey, "Flagship Olympia" on back of case	125	150	200
American Pride	75	100	125
Are U My Neighbor	35	45	65
B. B. H. Special, Backwind	65	75	95
Blind Man Pocket Watch	40	50	60
Buck..	25	30	40
Champion (many models)	50	75	125
Chancery..	50	75	125
Chicago Expo. 1933	175	200	275
Climax..	40	45	65
Clock Watch, pat. 1878-90-91........................	65	75	95
Cloverine...	60	70	85
Colby...	20	25	35
Columbus	45	60	85
Columbus (3 ships on back of case), 1893	200	275	350
Connecticut W. Co.	30	40	50
Cord..	20	30	45
Crown	20	25	35
Dan Dee	25	35	50
Defiance	30	40	55
Delaware W. Co......................................	25	30	40
Devon Mfg. Co.	20	25	35

Scout watch (Be prepared)

Yankee watch with bicycle on dial.

Ingersoll Premium, early back wind & set.

Ingersoll Triumph, note pin for setting.

Grade or Name—Description	Avg	Ex-Fn	Mint
Eclipse (many models)	$25	$30	$40
Eclipse Radiolite	30	35	40
Ensign	30	35	40
Escort	25	30	40
Fancy Dials unfaded to be mint	100	145	200
Freedom	30	35	40
Gotham	15	20	35
Graceline	45	50	65
Gregg	15	25	35
Junior (several models)................................	15	25	35
Junior Radiolite	35	40	55
Kelton	10	15	25
Lapel Watches	25	45	65
Leeds	15	20	25
Liberty U.S.A., backwind	75	100	150
Liberty Watch Co.	35	45	75
Limited, lever set.....................................	40	50	60
Major...	10	15	20
Maple Leaf	25	30	40
Master Craft..	10	15	20
Midget (several models)	25	40	55
Monarch	20	25	30
New West	30	45	65
New York World's Fair, 1939.........................	275	325	425
Overland	35	40	50
Pan American Expo., Buffalo	200	275	350
Paris World Expo., 1900	250	325	400
Patrol..	35	45	65
Perfection	35	45	55
Pilgram	40	50	55
Premier, back wind, eagle on back, c. 1894	70	100	120

Left: **Ingersoll Back Wind**, c. 1895. Right: **Yankee Back Wind**, c. 1893.

Grade or Name—Description	Avg	Ex-Fn	Mint
Premium Back Wind and Set	$50	$75	$100
Progress, 1933 World's Fair Chicago	200	275	350
Puritan	35	50	75
Quaker	40	45	60
Radiolite	30	35	45
Reliance, 7J	35	45	85
Remington W. Co. USA	60	75	95
Rotary International, c. 1920	40	45	65
Royal	10	15	25
St. Louis World's Fair (two models)	225	250	300
St. Louis World's Fair, 1904	100	150	200
The Saturday Post	150	175	225
Scout "Be Prepared"	250	300	375
Senator	35	40	50
Senior	25	30	40
Sir Leeds	25	30	40
Solar	25	30	40
Souvenir Special	35	45	60
Sterling	35	40	50
Ten Hune	60	70	85
Traveler with Bed Side Stand	35	45	65
Triumph	75	85	100
Triumph Penset	150	175	225
True Test	25	30	40
Trump	35	45	55
USA (two models)	50	75	100
Universal, 1st model	200	250	300
Uncle Sam	40	50	60
George Washington	150	175	225
Waterbury (several models)	40	60	90

Grade or Name—Description	Avg	Ex-Fn	Mint
Waterbury Back Wind, 35 Size..........................	$100	$150	$200
Winner...	20	25	35
Winner with S.B.B...................................	40	45	55
Yankee Backwind	85	95	150
Yankee Bicycle Watch (sold for $1.00 in 1896)...........	150	175	225
Yankee Radiolite.....................................	40	55	75
Yankee Radiolite with S.B.B.	45	50	60
Yankee Special (many models)	75	100	150
Yankee, Perpetual calendar on back of case	75	100	150

 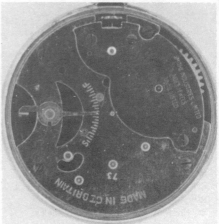

Exmple of an Ingersoll moveable calendar for years 1929-1951 located on back of case.

Example of an Ingersoll watch made in Great Britain.

INGERSOLL LTD.
(GREAT BRITAIN)

Grade or Name — Description	Avg	Ex-Fn	Mint
Ingersoll Ltd. (many models)	$50	$75	$100
Coronation, Elizabeth II on watch	175	200	250
Coronation, June 2, 1953 on dial	175	200	250
16S, 7J, 3F Brg	55	60	85
16S, 15J, 3F Brg	75	85	110
16S, 17J, 3F Brg, ADJ...............................	115	145	175
16S, 19J, 3F Brg, Adj5P	200	250	350
12S, 4J	25	30	45

Example of an Ingraham movement.

New York to Paris, airplane model commemorating Lindbergh's famous flight.

E. INGRAHAM CO.
Bristol, Connecticut
1912 - 1968

The E. Ingraham Co. purchased the Bannatyne Co. in 1912. They produced their first American pocket watch in 1913. A total of about 65 million American-made pocket watches and over 12 million wrist watches were produced before they started to import watches in 1968.

Grade or Name — Description	Avg	Ex-Fn	Mint
Ingraham W. Co. (many models)	$25	$35	$50
Aristocrat Railroad Sp.	25	30	40
Autocrat	15	20	25
Beacon	15	20	25
Biltmore	10	15	20
Biltmore Radium	10	15	20
Bristol	15	20	25
Clipper	20	25	35
Comet	15	20	25
Companion, sweep second hand	15	20	30
Cub	15	20	25
Demi-hunter cover	20	30	45
Dixie	10	15	20
Dot	10	20	25
Endura	10	15	20
Everbrite (all models)	15	25	30
Ingraham USA	10	15	20

Grade or Name—Description	Avg	Ex-Fn	Mint
Jockey	$15	$20	$25
Laddie	25	30	40
Laddie Athlete	40	45	55
Lady's Purse Watch, with fancy bezel	45	50	65
Lendix Extra	25	30	40
Master	10	15	20
Miss Ingraham	25	30	40
New York to Paris	200	250	300
Overland	30	35	45
The Pal	20	30	45
Pastor, stop watch	45	50	65
Pathfinder, compass on pendant	65	75	95
Patriot	125	150	250
Peerless	30	35	55

Example of **Path Finder** showing compass in crown.   Printed on dial, "Unbreakable crystal," ca. 1924.

Grade or Name—Description	Avg	Ex-Fn	Mint
Pilot	$30	$40	$55
Pocket Pal	15	20	25
Pony	25	30	40
Pride	20	25	35
Princess	20	30	45
Pup	25	30	40
Reliance	45	50	65
Rex	15	20	25
Rite Time	25	30	40
St. Regis	15	20	25
Secometer	20	25	35
Sentinel	15	20	25
Sentinel Click	20	25	35
Sentinel Fold Up Travel	45	50	65
Sentry	25	30	35
Seven Seas, 24 hr. dial & nautical dial	45	50	65
Silver Star	15	25	30
Sterling	20	25	35
Sterling W. Co. Stop Watch, fly back to zero	45	50	65
Sturdy	10	15	20

Grade or Name—Description	Avg	Ex-Fn	Mint
Target	$10	$15	$20
Time Ball	25	30	40
Time & Time	30	40	55
Top Flight	20	25	35
Top Notch	35	45	50
Tower	15	20	25
Trail Blazer	150	200	275
Unbreakable Crystal	45	50	65
Uncle Sam (all models)	50	75	95
Uncle Sam Backwind & Set	85	110	145
Viceroy	20	25	35
Victory	25	30	55
Zep	150	200	275

Left: Example of a basic **International Watch Co.** movement with patent dates of Aug. 19, 1902, Jan. 27, 1903 & Aug. 11, 1903. Right: Example of a **Highland.**

INTERNATIONAL WATCH CO.
Newark City, New Jersey
1902 - 1907

This company produced only non-jeweled or low-cost production type watches that were inexpensive and nickel plated. Names on their watches include: Berkshire, Madison, and Mascot.

Grade or Name — Description		Avg	Ex-Fn	Mint
Berkshire, OF	★	$75	$100	$150
Highland	★	65	90	140
Madison, 18S, OF	★	75	100	150
Mascot, OF	★	50	75	125

KANKAKEE WATCH CO.
Kankakee, Illinois
1900

This company reportedly became the McIntyre Watch Co. Little other information is available.

Grade or Name — Description		Avg	Ex-Fn	Mint
16S, BRG, NI .... ★ ★ ★		$5,500	$6,000	$7,000

Kelly Watch Co., 16 size, aluminum movement, straight line lever, quick train, porcelain dial, stem set, reversible ratchet stem wind, originally sold for $2.20, c. 1900.

KELLY WATCH CO.
Chicago, Illinois
c. 1900

Grade or Name — Description	Avg	Ex-Fn	Mint
16S, aluminum movement and OF case	$50	$75	$125

KEYSTONE STANDARD WATCH CO.
Lancaster, Pennsylvania
1886 - 1890

Abram Bitner agreed to buy a large number of stockholders' shares of the Lancaster Watch Co. at 10 cents on the dollar; he ended up with 5,625 shares out of the 8,000 that were available. Some 8,900 movements had been completed but not sold at the time of the shares purchase. The company Bitner formed assumed the name of Keystone Standard Watch Co. as the trademark but in reality existed as the Lancaster Watch Co. The business was sold to Hamilton Watch Co. in 1891. Total production was 48,000.

Grade or Name — Description		Avg	Ex-Fn	Mint
18S, 20J, ¾, LS, HC	★ ★	$500	$550	$650
18S, 7-15J, OF, KW		50	75	125
18S, 15J, dust proof, ADJ		125	150	200
18S, 15J, dust proof, OF		100	125	175
18S, 15J, dust proof, HC		150	175	225
18S, West End, 15J, HC		75	125	175
18S, 11J, dust proof		100	125	175
18S, 7-15J, OF, SW, ¾, LS		50	75	125
6S, 7-10J, HC		100	125	175

Keystone Watch Co., dust proof model, 18 size, 15 jewels, serial number 352,766.

Example of a basic **Knickerbocker** movement, 16-18 size, 7 jewels, duplex escapement.

KNICKERBOCKER WATCH CO.
New York, New York
1890 - 1930

This company imported and sold Swiss and low-cost production American watches.

Grade or Name — Description	Avg	Ex-Fn	Mint
6S, Duplex	$40	$50	$65
10S, Barkley "8 Day"	75	100	125
12S, 7J, OF	45	55	85
18S, 7J, OF, PS, NI, duplex escapement	50	60	80
16S, 7J	45	55	75

LANCASTER WATCH CO.
Lancaster, Pennsylvania
1877 - 1886

Work commenced on Sept. 1, 1877, at the Lancaster Watch Co. The watches produced there were designed to sell at a cheaper price than normal. They had a solid top, ¾ plate, and a pillar plate that was fully ruby-jeweled (4½ pairs). They had a gilt and nickel movement and a new stem-wind device, modeled by Mosly & Todd. By mid-1878 the Lancaster Watch Co. had produced 150 movements. Four grades of watches were made: Keystone, Fulton, Franklin, and Melrose. In September 1879 the company had made 334 movements. In 1880 the total was up to 1,250 movements, and by mid-1882 about 17,000 movements had been produced. All totaled, about 20,000 watch movements were made.

About 75 8-size ladies' watches were also made.

CHRONOLOGY OF THE DEVELOPMENT OF THE LANCASTER WATCH CO.:
Adams and Perry Watch Mfg. Co. — 1874-1876
Lancaster Watch Co. — 1877-1878
Lancaster Pa. Watch Co. — 1878-1879
Lancaster Watch Co. — 1879-1886
Keystone Standard Co. — 1886-1890
Hamilton Watch Co. — 1892-1958

LANCASTER
18 SIZE
(All ¾ Plate)

Grade or Name — Description	Avg	Ex-Fn	Mint
Chester, 7J, KW, gilded	$125	$150	$200
Comet, 7J, NI	125	150	200
Delaware, 20J, ADJ, SW, gilded	300	375	450
Denver, 7J, gilded	75	100	125
Denver, 7J, gilded, Silveroid	40	50	65
Elberon, 7J, dust proof	125	150	200
Ben Franklin, 7J, KW, gilded	250	300	375
Ben Franklin, 11J, KW, gilded	300	350	425
Fulton, 7J, ADJ, KW, gilded	125	150	200
Fulton, 11J, ADJ, KW, gilded	125	150	200
Girard, 15J, ADJ, gilded	100	150	200
Hoosac, 11J, OF	125	175	225
Keystone, 15J, ADJ, gilded, GJS, dust proof	100	125	175
Keystone, 15J, ADJ, gilded, GJS, Silveroid	50	60	75
Lancaster, 7J, SW	40	50	65
Lancaster, 15J, SW, Silveroid	50	60	75
Lancaster, 15J, OF	75	100	150
Lancaster Pa., 20J, ADJ, NI ★★	400	500	650

Lancaster Watch Co., 18 size, 20 jewels, gold jeweled settings, stem wind & pendant set, serial number 1747.

Stevens Model, 18 size, 15 jewels, adjusted, dust proof model, swing-out movement, c.1886.

Grade or Name—Description	Avg	Ex-Fn	Mint
Lancaster Watch, 20J, DR, ADJ, NI, GJS, 14K HC . ★ ★	$700	$800	$950
Malvern, 7J, gilded	50	60	75
Melrose, 15J, NI, ADJ, GJS	100	125	175
Nation Standard American Watch Co., 7J, HC	200	225	275
New Era, 7J, gilded, KW, HC	75	100	150
New Era, 7J, gilded, KW, Silveroid	40	60	90
Paoli, 7J, NI	50	75	125
Wm. Penn, 20J, ADJ, NI, dust proof	400	500	650
Radnor, 7J, gilded	100	125	175
Record, 7J, Silveroid	40	50	65
Record, 15J, NI	75	100	150

West End, 18 size, 15 jewels, key wind & set, serial number 158,080, c. 1878.

Example of a basic Lancaster movement, 8-10 size, 15 jewels, serial number 317,812.

Grade or Name—Description	Avg	Ex-Fn	Mint
Ruby, 16J, NI	$275	$325	$400
Sidney, 15J, NI	100	125	150
Stevens, 15J, ADJ, NI, dust proof	150	175	225
West End, 19J, HC, KW, gilded .... ★ ★	450	500	550
West End, 15J, HC, KW, KS...........................	175	200	250
West End, 15J, SW	175	200	250
West End, 15J, SW, Silveroid	40	60	85

8 SIZE

Grade or Name — Description	Avg	Ex-Fn	Mint
Flora, gilded...	$75	$100	$150
Lady Penn, 20J, GJS, ADJ, NI.......................	300	350	425
Lancaster W. Co., 7J................................	75	100	125

Manhattan Watch Co., Chronograph, 18-16 size, note two buttons on top; one sets hands, the other starts and stops watch, serial number 117,480.

Manhattan Watch Co., 18 size, Chronograph. Note two buttons on top; one sets hands, the other starts and stops watch.

MANHATTAN WATCH CO.
New York, New York
1883 - 1891

The Manhattan Watch Co. made mainly low cost production watches. A complete and full line of watches was made, and most were cased and styled to be sold as a complete watch. The watches were generally 16S with full plate movements. The patented winding mechanism was different. These watches were in both the hunter and open-face cases and later had a sweep second hand. Total production was 160,000 or more watches.

16 SIZE

Grade or Name — Description		Avg	Ex-Fn	Mint
OF, with back wind	★	$250	$300	$400
OF, stop watch	★	200	250	350
7J, 2 button, sweep sec., OF	★	125	175	225
7J, 2 button, sweep sec., HC	★	200	250	300
Stallcup, 7J, OF	★	150	200	250

12 SIZE

Grade or Name — Description		Avg	Ex-Fn	Mint
12S	★	$125	$200	$275

MANISTEE WATCH CO.
Manistee, Michigan
1908 - 1912

The Manistee watches, first marketed in 1909, were designed to compete with the low-cost production watches. Dials, jewels, and hairsprings were not produced at the factory. The first movement was 18S, 7J, and sold for about $5. Manistee also made 5J, 15J, 17J, and 21J watches in cheap cases in sizes 16 and 12. Estimated total production was 60,000. Most were sold by Star Watch Case Co.

18 TO 12 SIZE

Grade or Name — Description		Avg	Ex-Fn	Mint
18S, 7J, ¾, LS, HC	★	$325	$375	$425
18S, 7J, ¾, LS, OF	★	275	325	375
16S, 15J, HC	★	225	250	325
16S, 7J, OF	★	200	250	325

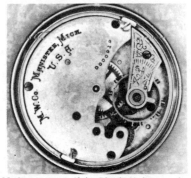

Manistee movement, 18 size, 7 jewels, ¾ plate, open face, serial number 919.

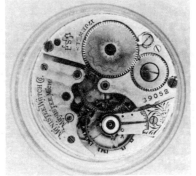

Manistee movement, 16 size, 17 jewels, ¾ plate, open face, serial number 39,052.

Grade or Name—Description		Avg	Ex-Fn	Mint
16S, 15-17J, OF..	★	$225	$250	$325
16S, 19J, HC..	★	300	350	425
16S, 21J, OF..	★	325	375	450
12S, 15J..	★	150	175	225

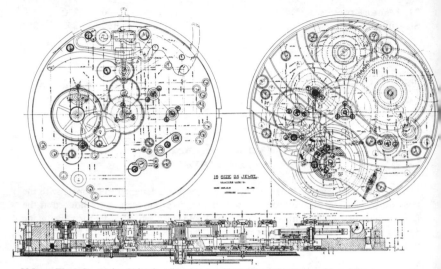

McIntyre Watch Co., 16 size, 25 jewels, adjusted to 5 positions with wind indicator, with equidistant escapement, manufactured about 1909. Above illustration taken from a blue print.

McINTYRE WATCH CO.
Kankakee, Illinois
1905 - 1911

This company probably bought the factory from Kankakee Watch Co. In 1908 Charles DeLong was made master watchmaker, and he designed and improved the railroad watches. Only a few watches were made, estimated total production being about eight watches.

Grade or Name — Description		Avg	Ex-Fn	Mint
16S, 21J, BRG, NI, WI........................	★ ★ ★	$4,500	$5,000	$6,500
16S, 25J, BRG, NI, WI, Adj.5P, equidistant escapement................................	★ ★ ★	5,500	6,000	7,500
12S, 19J, BRG................................	★ ★ ★	2,000	2,500	3,500

MELROSE WATCH CO.
Melrose, Massachusetts
1866 - 1868

Melrose Watch Co. began as Tremont Watch Co. and imported the expansion balances and escapements. Dials were first made by Mr. Gold and Mr. Spear, then later by Mr. Hull and Mr. Carpenter. Tremont had hoped to produce 600 sets of trains per month. They were 18S, key wind, fully jeweled movements and were engraved "Tremont Watch Co." In 1866 the company moved, changed its name to Melrose Watch Co., and started making complete watch movements, including a new style 18S movement engraved "Melrose Watch Co." About 3,000 were produced. Some watches are found with "Melrose" on the dial and "Tremont" on the movement. Serial numbers start at about 30,000.

Example of a basic **Melrose Watch Co.** movement, 18 size, 15 jewels, key wind & set.

Grade or Name — Description		Avg	Ex-Fn	Mint
18S, 7J, KW, KS	★ ★	$300	$350	$425
18S, 11J, KW, KS, OF	★ ★	325	375	450
18S, 15J, KW, KS	★ ★	350	400	475
18S, 15J, KW, KS, Silveroid	★ ★	250	300	375

Note: Add $25.00 to values of above watches in hunting case.

MOZART WATCH CO.
Providence, Rhode Island
Ann Arbor, Michigan
1864 - 1870

In 1864 Don J. Mozart started out to produce a less expensive three-wheel watch in Providence, R. I. Despite his best efforts, the venture was declared a failure by 1866. Mozart left Providence and moved to Ann Arbor, Mich. There, again, he started on a three-wheel watch and succeeded in producing thirty. The three-wheel watch was not a new idea except to American manufacturers. Three-wheel watches were made many decades before Mozart's first effort, but credit for the first American-made three-wheel watch must go to him. The size was about 18 and could be called a ¾ or full plate movement. The balance bridge was screwed on the top plate, as was customary. The round bridge partially covered the opening in the top plate and was just large enough for the balance to oscillate. The balance was compensated and somewhat smaller in diameter than usual. Mozart called it a chronolever, and it was to function so perfectly it would be free from friction. That sounded good but was in no way true. The watch was of the usual thickness of the American watches of 18S. The train had a main wheel with the usual number of teeth and a ten-leaf center pinion, but it had a large center wheel of 108 teeth and a third wheel of 90 teeth, with a six-leaf third (escape) pinion. The escape wheel had 30 teeth and received its impulse directly from the roller on the staff, while the escape tooth locked on the intermediate lever pallet. The escape pinion had a long pivot that carried the second hand, which made a circuit of the dial, once in 12 seconds. The total number of Mozart watches produced was 165, and about 30 of these were the three-wheel type.

Grade or Name — Description	Avg	Ex-Fn	Mint
18S, ¾, KW, KS, 3-wheel . . . . ★ ★ ★			
	$11,000	$15,000	$20,000
18S, ¾, KW, KS . . . . ★ ★	6,000	7,000	8,000

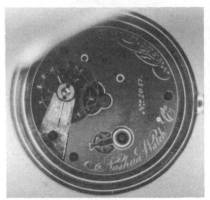

Example of a basic **Mozart Watch Co.** movement, 18 size, three-quarter plate, key wind & set, three-wheel train, "Patent Dec. 24th, 1868" engraved on back plate.

Nashua Watch Co. (marked), 20 size, 19 jewels, key wind & set from back, serial number 1,057.

NASHUA WATCH CO.
Nashua, New Hampshire
1859 - 1862

One of the most important contributions to the American Watch industry was made by the Nashua Watch Co. of Nashua, New Hampshire. Founded in 1859 by B. D. Bingham, the company hired some of the most innovative and creative watchmakers in America and produced an extremely high grade American pocket watch.

His company included N. P. Stratton, C. V. Woerd, Charles Moseley, James H. Gerry, and James Gooding, among others. Most of the people connected with the Nashua Watch Company became famous for various advances in watch manufacture, at one time or another. Many had extremely important American patents on various inventions that came to be regarded as a benchmark of the best watches America was capable of making at the time.

The Nashua Watch Co. is important for many reasons. It was the first American company to produce a truly superior high grade movement; the ¾ plate design used by Nashua became the standard for over 40 years in the American marketplace. Perhaps most importantly, the watches designed by the Nashua Watch Co., and later by the Nashua division of the American Watch Co., became the leaders in the production of the highest quality watches made in America and forced the entire Swiss watch industry to change their technology to compete with the Nashua designs.

Nashua continually won awards for their various models of watches both here and in Europe. By virtue of their sheer technical superiority and classical elegance, Nashua became known universally as the most innovative producer of watches America ever knew.

The original Nashua company produced material for about 1,000 movements but, except for a handful, almost the entire production was finished by the American Watch Company at Waltham, Mass., after R. E. Robbins took over Nashua in 1862 when the company was in grave financial difficulty. Robbins was very happy about the arrangement since he got back almost all the watchmaking geniuses who had left him in 1859 to join Nashua. Robbins incorporated the Nashua Division into the American Watch Company as its high grade experimental division.

Over the years, many of the major advances were made by the Nashua division of Waltham, including the 1860 model 16-size keywind keyset, the 1862 model 20-size keywind keyset, the 1870 model 18-size keywind keyset, pin set, and lever set (which became the first American advertised Railroad watch), the 1868 model 16-size stemwind, and the 1872 model 17-size stemwind. The Nashua division also greatly influenced the 1888 model and the 1892 model by Waltham.

Since almost all the production material made by Nashua from 1859 until its incorporation into the American Watch Co. in 1862 was unfinished by Nashua, only about four examples of the 20-size keywind keyset from the back signed Nashua Watch Co. are known to exist.

Grade or Name — Description		Avg	Ex-Fn	Mint
Nashua (marked), 19J, KW, KS, ¾, 18K . . . . . . ★ ★ ★	$18,000	$22,000	$28,000
Nashua (unmarked), 15J, KW, KS, ¾, silver case . . . . ★ ★	3,000	4,000	5,000

NEWARK WATCH CO.
Newark, New Jersey
1864 - 1870

Arthur Wadsworth, one of the designers for Newark Watch Co., patented an 18 Size full plate movement. The first movements reached the market in 1867. This company produced only about 4,000 watches before it was sold to the Cornell Watch Co.

CHRONOLOGY OF THE DEVELOPMENT OF NEWARK WATCH CO.:
Newark Watch Co. 1864-1870; S#s 6,901 to 12,000;

Cornell Watch Co., Chicago, Ill. 1870-1874; S#s 12,001 to 25,000;
Cornell Watch Co., San Francisco, Calif. 1874-Jan. 1876; S#s 25,001 to 35,000;
California Watch Co., Jan. 1876-mid 1876.

Newark Watch Co. Robert Fellows movement, 18 size, 15 jewels, key wind & set, serial number 12, 044.

Grade or Name — Description		Avg	Ex-Fn	Mint
18S, 15J, KW, KS, HC	★ ★	$350	$400	$500
18S, 15J, KW, KS, OF	★ ★	300	350	425
18S, 7J, KW, KS	★ ★	300	350	425
J. C. Adams, 11J, KW, KS	★ ★	350	400	475
J. C. Adams, 11J, KW, KS, Coin	★ ★	350	400	475
Edward Biven, 15J, KW, KS	★ ★	350	400	475
Robert Fellows, KW, KS	★ ★	400	450	525
Keyless Watch Co., 15J, LS, SW		300	350	425
Newark Watch Co., 7-15J, KW, KS	★ ★	350	400	475
Arthur Wadsworth, SW	★ ★	300	350	425
Arthur Wadsworth, 18S, 15J, 18K, HC ("Arthur Wadsworth, New York" on dial; "Keyless Watch, Patent #3655, June 19, 1866" engraved on movement)	★ ★	800	1,000	1,250

NEW ENGLAND WATCH CO.
Waterbury, Connecticut
1898 - 1914

The New England Watch Co., formerly the Waterbury Watch Co., made a watch with a duplex escapement, gilt, 16S, open faced. Watches with the skeletonized movement are very desirable. The company later became Timex Watch Co.

Grade or Name — Description		Avg	Ex-Fn	Mint
16S, OF, duplex, skeleton, good running order	★	$200	$250	$325
12S, 16S, 18S, OF, pictures on dial: ladies, dogs, horses, trains, flags, ships, cards, etc.		100	125	150
12S, 16S, 18S, OF, duplex escapement, good running order		30	40	60
12S, 16S, 18S, OF, pin lever escapement, good running order		15	25	45

Front and back view of a skeletonized New England Watch Co. movement. This watch is fitted with a glass back and front, making the entire movement and wheels visible, 4 jewels, silver hands, black numbers, originally sold for $10-13.

Grade or Name—Description	Avg	Ex-Fn	Mint
6S, duplex	$35	$40	$55
Addison	35	40	55
Alden	35	40	55
Ambassador, 12S, duplex	25	30	40
Americus, duplex	20	25	30
Avour, duplex escapement	35	40	55
Berkshire, duplex, 14K, GF	60	70	85

New England Watch co., 16 size, 7 jewels, open face, double roller, Dan Patch stop watch.

New England Watch Co., Scout, about 16 size, 4 jewels, duplex escapement, New England base metal case.

New England Watch Co., multi-colored paper dials, showing an assorted selection. Watches complete with these type dials bring $125 - $175.00.

Grade or Name—Description	Avg	Ex-Fn	Mint
Cadish, duplex escapement	$35	$40	$55
Cavour	45	50	60
Columbian	15	20	30
Cruiser, duplex	45	50	69
Dan Patch, 7J ★	275	350	425
Excelsor, 7J	65	70	95
Fancy dial, "unfaded"	100	145	200
Gabour	65	70	85
General	20	30	45
Hale, 7J	25	30	45
Jockey, duplex	55	60	75
Oxford	15	20	30
Padishah, duplex	45	50	65
Putnam	65	70	85
Rugby, stop watch	65	70	85
Scout, 12 Size, duplex escapement, HC	40	45	60
Senator, duplex escapement	40	45	55
Trump, duplex	15	20	30
Tuxedo	15	20	35

NEW HAVEN CLOCK AND WATCH CO.
New Haven, Connecticut
1853 - 1956

The company started making watches in early 1880 in New Haven and produced the regular 16S, lever watch. These sold for $3.75. The company soon reached a production of about 200 watches per day, making a total of some 40 million watches.

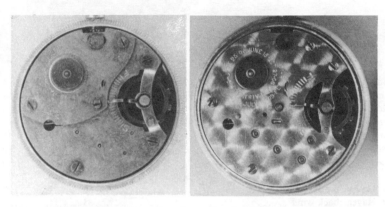

New Haven Clock & Watch Co., Angelus, with rotating dials, patented Jan 23, 1900.

Example of a New Haven movement.

Grade or Name — Description	Avg	Ex-Fn	Mint
Always Right	$45	$55	$75
Angelus, 2 rotating dials	45	55	75
Babe Ruth	125	175	245
Beardsley—Radiant	45	50	65
Buddy	35	40	45
Bull Dog	40	45	60
Captain Scout	85	100	150
Chronometer	45	85	100
Elite	30	40	55
Fancy dials, no fading	100	145	200
Football Timer	45	55	75
Ford Special	75	85	100
Hamilton	35	45	60
Handy Andy	40	45	50
Jerome USA	35	40	50
Kaiser Wilhelm ★ ★	175	250	325

Example of **Kaiser Wilhelm**.

Example of **Traveler**.

Grade or Name—Description	Avg	Ex-Fn	Mint
Kermit	$40	$45	$55
Laddie	25	30	40
Leonard Watch Co.	25	40	50
Leonard	25	35	45
Mastercraft Rayolite	35	45	60
Miracle	25	30	40
Nehi	45	60	75
New Haven, pin lever, SW	50	75	100
New Haven, back wind	85	115	165
Panama Official Souvenir, 1915	200	250	350
Pastor Stop Watch	65	85	100
Playing cards on dial	100	175	300
Ships Time & Franklin dial	50	60	75
Sports Timer	65	75	95
Surity	15	20	30
Tip Top	15	20	30
Tip Top Jr.	15	20	30
Tommy Ticker	30	35	40
Traveler, with travel case	40	45	60
True Time Teller Tip Top	40	45	60
USA	30	35	40

NEW HAVEN WATCH CO.
New Haven, Connecticut
1883 - 1887

This company was organized October 16, 1883 with the intention of producing W. E. Doolittle's patented watch; however, this plan was soon abandoned. They did produce a "Model A" watch, the first was marketed in the spring of 1884. Batch or lot numbers were used instead of serial numbers, and watches can be found bearing the same batch number. Estimated total production was 2,000 to 3,000. The original capital became absorbed by Trenton Watch Co.

Example of a basic **New Haven Watch Co.** movement with batch or lot number 65. Note this is not a serial number.

Grade or Name — Description		Avg	Ex-Fn	Mint
"A" Model, about 18S, pat. Dec. 27, '81 . . . . ★ ★ ★		$200	$275	$475
Alpha Model, pat. Dec. 27, '81 . . . . ★ ★ ★		200	275	475

New York City Watch Co., 20 size, "Lever Winder" on dial. This watch is wound by cranking the pendant, pin lever escapement, patent number 526,871.

NEW YORK WATCH CO.
and
NEW YORK CITY WATCH CO.
New York, New York
1890 - 1897

This company manufactured the Dollar-type watches, which had a pendant-type crank. The patent number 526,871, dated October 1894, was held by S. Schisgall.

Grade or Name — Description	Avg	Ex-Fn	Mint
20S, no jewels, "Lever Winder" .... ★ ★ ★ ★	$450	$600	$850

N.Y. Chronograph Watch Co., dial and movement, 16 size, 7 jewels, open face, sweep second hand, serial number 174,484.

NEW YORK CHRONOGRAPH WATCH CO.
New York, New York
1883 - ?

This company sold about 18,000 watches marked "New York Chronograph Watch Co," manufactured by Manhattan Watch Co. They used a sweep second hand.

Grade or Name — Description	Avg	Ex-Fn	Mint
18S, 7J, HC	$100	$175	$250
18S, 7J, OF .... ★	100	175	250
16S, 7J, SW, OF .... ★	100	175	250
16S, 9J, SW, OF .... ★	100	175	250
16S, 9J, SW, OF, time only sweep sec.	100	175	250

New York Chronograph Watch Co. dial and movement, 7 jewels, open face, buttons at the top of case set hands and stop watch.

NEW YORK STANDARD WATCH CO.
Jersey City, New Jersey
1885 - 1929

The first watch reached the market in early 1888 and was a 18S. The most interesting feature was a straight line lever with a "worm gear escapement." This was patented by R. J. Clay. All watches were quick train and open-faced. The company also made its own cases and sold a complete watch. A prefix number was added to the serial number after the first 10,000 watches were made. Estimated total production was 7,000,000.

Chronograph, 16-18 size, 7 jewels, stem wind, second hand start-stop and fly back, three-quarter plate, serial number 5,334,322.

Example of a basic New York Standard movement, 18 size, 7 jewels, stem wind, serial number 296,893.

N. Y. STANDARD
16 AND 18 SIZE

Grade or Name — Description	Avg	Ex-Fn	Mint
18S, 7J, N. Y. Standard, KW, KS	$250	$300	$375
18S, 7J, N. Y. Standard, SW	40	60	85
18S, 15J, N. Y. Standard, SW, LS, HC	100	125	175
Chronograph, 7J, ¾, NI, DMK, SW, second hand stop, and fly back	125	175	250
Chronograph, 13J, sweep sec., stop & fly back	135	185	260
Chronograph, 15J, ¾, NI, DMK, SW, second hand stop, and fly back	150	200	275
Columbus, 7J	40	60	85
Crown W. Co., 7J, OF or HC	40	60	85
Crown W. Co., 15J, HC	50	75	100
Dan Patch, 7J, stop watch ★	275	350	425
Dan Patch, 17J, stop watch ★ ★	375	450	525
Edgemere, 7J, OF & HC	40	60	85
Excelsior, 7J, OF or HC	40	60	85

New York Standard, with worm gear (located under cut-out star), 18 size, 7 jewels, serial number 31,138.

Remington W. Co. (marked on movement & case), 16 size, 11 jewels, 2-tone damaskeening, serial number CC021,331.

Grade or Name—Description	Avg	Ex-Fn	Mint
Hi Grade	$40	$60	$85
Ideal	40	60	85
New Era, 7J, OF or HC, skeletonized (Poor Man's Dudley)	250	275	325
New York Standard W. Co., 11J, ¾	50	75	100
New York Standard, 7J, ¾	50	75	100
New York Standard, 15J, BRG	75	100	125
New York Standard, with worm gear ★	300	350	425

Grade or Name—Description	Avg	Ex-Fn	Mint
Pan American, 7J, OF	$50	$75	$100
Perfection, 7J, OF or HC	40	60	85
Perfection, 15J, OF or HC, NI	50	75	100
Remington W. Co., 11J, marked mvt. & case	75	100	135
Solar W. Co., 7J	40	60	85
18S Tribune USA, 23J, HC or OF, Pat. Reg. Adj.	150	175	225
Wilmington	40	60	85

Note: For watches with O'Hara Multi-Color Dials, add $75 to value in mint condition; add $5 for Hunting Cases.

12 SIZE

Grade or Name — Description	Avg	Ex-Fn	Mint
N. Y. Standard, 7J, OF	$25	$30	$45
N. Y. Standard, 7J, HC, Multi-Color dial	100	125	175

New York Standard Watch Co., 12 size, 7 jewels, open face, serial number 1021224.

6 SIZE AND 0 SIZE

Grade or Name — Description	Avg	Ex-Fn	Mint
Empire State W. Co., 7J	$40	$50	$65
Standard USA, 7J	40	50	65
6S, Columbia, 7J, HC	60	70	85
6S, N. Y. Standard, 7J, HC	60	70	85
6S, Orient, SW	30	40	55
6S, Progress, 7J, YGF	40	50	65
0S, Ideal, 7J, HC	60	70	85
0S, N. Y. Standard, 7J, HC	60	70	85

NOTE: Watches listed in this book are priced at the retail level, as complete watches having an original 14k gold-filled case, an original white enamel single sunk dial, and with the entire original movement in good working order with no repairs needed, unless otherwise noted.

NEW YORK STANDARD WATCH CO.
IDENTIFICATION OF MOVEMENTS

How to Identify Your Watch: Compare the movement of your watch with the illustrations in this section. Upon matching the movement exactly, the model number and size can be determined. While comparing, note the location of the balance, jewels, screws, gears, and type of back plate (Full, ¾, Bridge) which will be clues in identifying the movement you have. Having determined the size and model number, you can now find your watch in the main price listing by name or number (which is engraved on the movement).

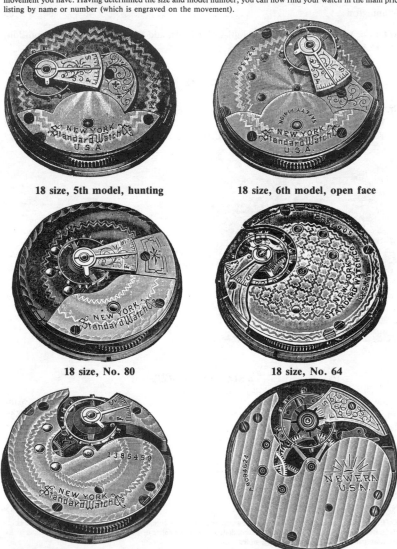

18 size, 5th model, hunting

18 size, 6th model, open face

18 size, No. 80

18 size, No. 64

18 size, No. 360

18 size, No. 60

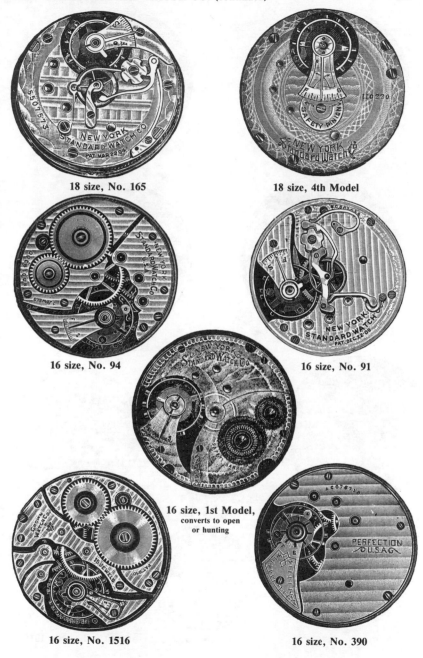

18 size, No. 165

18 size, 4th Model

16 size, No. 94

16 size, No. 91

16 size, 1st Model,
converts to open
or hunting

16 size, No. 1516

16 size, No. 390

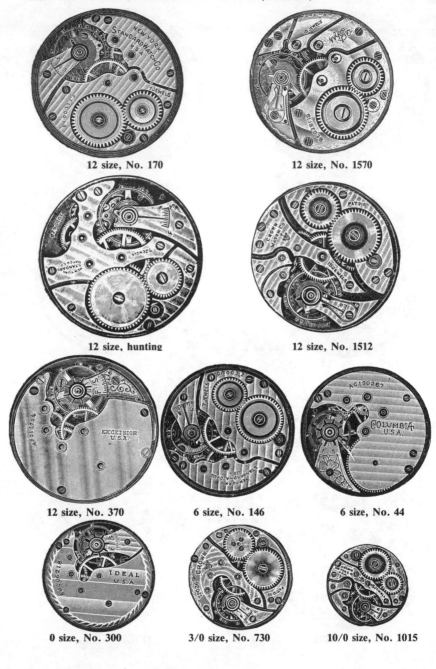

12 size, No. 170

12 size, No. 1570

12 size, hunting

12 size, No. 1512

12 size, No. 370

6 size, No. 146

6 size, No. 44

0 size, No. 300

3/0 size, No. 730

10/0 size, No. 1015

NEW YORK SPRINGFIELD WATCH CO.
Springfield, Massachusetts
1866 - 1876

The New York Watch Co. had a rather difficult time getting started. The name of the company was changed from the Mozart Watch Co. to the New York Watch Co., and it was located in Rhode Island. Before any watches had been produced, they moved to Springfield, Mass., in 1867. A factory was built there, but only about 100 watches were produced before a fire occurred on April 23, 1870. Shortly after the fire, in 1870, a newly-designed watch was introduced. The first movements reached the market in 1871, and the first grade was a fully-jeweled adjusted movement called "Frederick Billings." The standard 18S and the Swiss Ligne systems were both used in gauging the size of these watches. The New York Watch Co. used full signatures on its movements. The doors closed in the summer of 1876.

In January 1877, the Hampden Watch Co. was organized and commenced active operation in June 1877.

CHRONOLOGY OF THE DEVELOPMENT OF NEW YORK WATCH CO.

The Mozart Watch Co., Providence, R. I. — 1864-1866
New York Watch Co., Providence, R. I. — 1866-1867
New York Watch Co., Springfield, Mass. — 1867-1875
New York Watch Mfg. Co., Springfield, Mass. — 1875-1876
Hampden Watch Co., Springfield, Mass. — 1877-1886
Hampden-Dueber Watch Co., Springfield, Mass. — 1886-1888
Hampden Watch Co., Canton, Ohio — 1888-1923
Dueber Watch Co., Canton, Ohio — 1888-1923
Dueber-Hampden Watch Co., Canton, Ohio — 1923-1931
Amtorg, U.S.S.R. — 1930-

NEW YORK WATCH CO.—SPRINGFIELD
ESTIMATED SERIAL NUMBERS
AND PRODUCTION DATES

Date	Serial No.	Date	Serial No.
1866	1,000	1871	20,000
1867	3,000	1872	30,000
1868	5,000	1873	40,000
1869	7,000	1874	50,000
1870	10,000	1875	60,000

N. Y. W. SPRINGFIELD
18 TO 20 SIZE

Grade or Name — Description		Avg	Ex-Fn	Mint
Aaron Bagg, 7J, KW, KS .... ★		$200	$250	$325
Frederick Billings, 15J, KW, KS .... ★		200	250	325
E. W. Bond, 15J, ¾ .... ★ ★		300	350	425
J. A. Briggs, 11J, KW, KS, from back .... ★ ★		300	350	425

E.W. Bond movement, 18 size, 7 jewels, three-quarter plate.

Chas. F. Hayward, 18 size, 15 jewels, key wind & set, serial number 18,733.

Grade or Name—Description	Avg	Ex-Fn	Mint
Albert Clark, 15J, KW, KS, from back, ¾ .... ★ ★	$300	$350	$425
Homer Foot, 15J, KW, KS, from back, ¾ .... ★ ★	300	350	425
Herman Gerz, 11J, KW, KS .... ★	200	250	325
John Hancock, 7J, KW, KS	100	200	275
John Hancock, 7J, KW, KS, Silveroid	75	100	125
John Hancock, 7J, KW, KS, Coin	150	200	275
Chas. E. Hayward, 15J, KW, KS, long balance cock	150	200	275
Chas. E. Hayward, 15J, KW, KS, Coin................	150	200	275
John L. King, 15J, KW, KS, from back, ¾ .... ★ ★	300	350	425
New York Watch Co., 7J, KW, KS .... ★	150	200	275
New York Watch Co., 15J, KW, KS, (Serial #s below 75).	1,300	1,500	1,800
New York Watch Co., 15J, KW, KS, Wolf's Teeth winding, all original .... ★ ★ ★	1,000	1,200	1,500
New York Watch Co., 11J, KW, KS .... ★ ★	300	350	375
H. G. Norton, 15J, KW, KS, from back, ¾ .... ★ ★	300	350	425

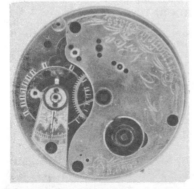

H.G. Norton, 18 size, 15 jewels, three-quarter plate, gold escape wheel, serial number 6592.

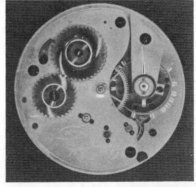

New York Watch Co., 18 size, 15-19 jewels, stem wind, hunting, note wolf teeth winding, serial number 978.

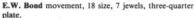

State Street movement, 18 size, 11 jewels, three-quarter plate.

Theo E. Studley movement, 18 size, 15 jewels, key wind & set, full plate.

Grade or Name—Description	Avg	Ex-Fn	Mint
J. C. Perry, 15J....................................★	$150	$200	$275
J. C. Perry, 15J, Silveroid..........................★	100	125	175
Railway, 15J, KW, FULL, Coin ....★	600	650	725
Railway, 15J, KW, KS, FULL ....★	600	650	725
Geo. Sam Rice, 7J, KW, KS.........................★	300	350	425
Springfield, 19J, KW, KS, from back, ADJ, Wolfsteeth wind, serial Nos. below 1,000................★★★	1,300	1,500	1,800
State Street, 11J, ¾, SW...........................★	250	275	325
State Street, 11J, ¾, SW, Silveroid...................★	200	225	275
Theo E. Studley, 15J, KW, Coin......................	100	125	175
Theo E. Studley, 15J, KW, KS	100	125	175
George Walker, 17J, KW, ¾, ADJ....................	250	275	325
Chester Woolworth, 15J, KW, KS....................	100	125	175
Chester Woolworth, 11J, KW, KS....................	100	125	175
Chester Woolworth, 11J, KW, KS, Silveroid............	50	65	95
Chester Woolworth, 11J, KW, KS, ADJ	150	175	225
#4, 15J, ADJ, KW, KS	125	150	200
#5, 15J, KW, KS.................................	100	125	175
#6, 11J, KW, KS.................................	100	125	175
#6, 11J, KW, KS, Silveroid.........................	50	65	95

NOTE: Some KW, KS watches made by the New York Watch Co. have a hidden key. If you unscrew the crown, and the crown comes out as a key, add $100 to the listed value.

NOTE: Watches listed in this book are priced at the retail level, as complete watches having an original 14k gold-filled case, an original white enamel single sunk dial, and with the entire original movement in good working order with no repairs needed, unless otherwise noted.

NON-MAGNETIC WATCH CO.
Geneva and America
1887 - 1905

The Non-Magnetic Watch Co. sold and imported watches from the Swiss as well as contracted watches made in America. Geneva Non-Magnetic marked watches appear to be the oldest type of movement. This company sold a full line of watches, high grade to low grade, as well as repeaters and ladies watches. An advertisement appeared in the monthly journal of "Locomotive Engineers" in 1887. The ad states that the "Paillard's patent non-magnetic watches are uninfluenced by magnetism of electricity." Each watch contains the Paillard's patent non-magnetic, inoxydable compensation balance and hairspring. An ad in 1888 shows prices for 16 size Swiss style watches as low as $15 for 7 jewels and as high as $135 for 20 jewels.

18 SIZE
(must be marked Paillard's Patent)

Grade or Name — Description	Avg	Ex-Fn	Mint
Elgin, 17J, FULL, SW, LS, OF	$100	$125	$175
Elgin, 17J, FULL, SW, LS, HC	125	150	225
Elgin, 15J, FULL, SW, LS, OF	75	100	150
Elgin, 15-17J, FULL, SW, LS, HC	100	125	175
Illinois, 24J, GJS, NI, Adj.5P, OF	800	850	925
Illinois, 24J, GJS, NI, Adj.5P, HC	900	950	1,025
Illinois, 23J, GJS, NI, Adj.5P, OF	700	750	925
Illinois, 23J, GJS, NI, Adj.5P, HC ★★★	1,600	1,800	2,100
Illinois, 21J, GJS, NI, Adj.5P, OF	200	250	325
Illinois, 21J, GJS, NI, Adj.5P, HC	250	300	325
Illinois, 17J, NI, ADJ, OF	100	125	175
Illinois, 17J, NI, ADJ, HC	125	150	225
Illinois, 15J, NI, OF	75	100	150
Illinois, 15J, NI, HC	100	125	175
Illinois, 11J, OF	75	100	150

Non-Magnetic Watch Co., 18 size, 15 jewels, gold jewel settings, Adj.5p, by Peoria Watch Co.

Non-Magnetic Watch Co., 18 size, 21 Ruby jewels, Adj.5p, note "Paillard" engraved on movement.

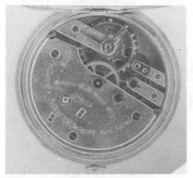

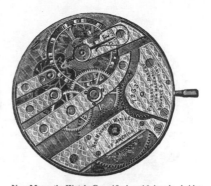

Non-Magnetic Watch co., 18 size, 16 jewels, ½ plate, hunting, note "Geneva" engraved on movement, serial number 6113.

Non-Magnetic Watch Co., 18 size, 16 jewels, bridge model, example of a Swiss Ebauche.

Grade or Name—Description	Avg	Ex-Fn	Mint
Illinois, 11J, HC	$100	$125	$175
Peoria, 17J, FULL, SW, LS, OF.......................	325	350	400
Peoria, 15J, FULL, SW, LS, OF.......................	300	325	375
Peoria, 15J, FULL, SW, LS, HC	400	425	475
Peoria, 11J, FULL, SW, LS, OF	100	125	175
Peoria, 11J, FULL, SW, LS, HC	175	200	250
Swiss, 16J, ½ plate, SW, LS, OF	60	70	85
Swiss, 16J, ½ plate, SW, LS, HC....................	75	100	150
Swiss, 15J, bar bridge, SW, LS, OF	55	65	80
Swiss, 15J, bar bridge, SW, LS, HC.................	75	100	150
Swiss, 11J, ½ plate, SW, LS, OF, HC................	75	100	150
Swiss, 11J, bar bridge, SW, LS, OF, HC	75	100	150

Non-Magnetic Watch Co., 16 size, 21 Ruby jewels, adjusted, made by Illinois Watch Co.

Non-Magnetic Watch Co., 16 size, 20 jewels in gold jewel settings, stem wind, open or hunting. Swiss made.

16 SIZE
(must be marked Paillard's Patent)

Grade or Name — Description	Avg	Ex-Fn	Mint
Illinois, 21J, GJS, ¾, DR, Adj.6P, OF	$200	$250	$325

Non-Magnetic Watch Co., 16 size, three-quarter plate, 15 jewels, adjusted.

Non-Magnetic Watch Co., 16 size, three-quarter plate, 15 jewels, note "Paillard's Patent, Balance And Spring" engraved on movement.

Grade or Name—Description	Avg	Ex-Fn	Mint
Illinois, 21J, GJS, ¾, DR, Adj.6P, HC	$300	$350	$425
Illinois, 17J, ¾, DR, ADJ, OF	75	100	150
Illinois, 17J, ¾, DR, ADJ, HC	100	125	175
Illinois, 15J, HC	75	100	125
Illinois, 15J, OF	55	80	135
Illinois, 11J, OF	50	75	125
Illinois, 11J, HC	75	100	150
Swiss, 20J, GJS, DR, Adj.6P, NI, OF	75	100	150
Swiss, 20J, GJS, DR, Adj.6P, NI, HC	100	125	175
Swiss, 18J, GJS, DR, Adj.6P, NI, OF	75	100	150
Swiss, 18J, GJS, DR, Adj.6P, NI, HC	100	125	175
Swiss, 16J, GJS, DR, Adj.6P, NI, OF	75	100	150
Swiss, 16J, GJS, DR, Adj.6P, NI, HC	75	100	150
Swiss, 15J, DR, NI, OF	75	100	150
Swiss, 15J, DR, NI, HC	100	125	175
Swiss, 11J, NI, OF	60	70	95
Swiss, 11J, NI, HC	100	125	175
Swiss, 7J, OF & HC	50	60	85

OTAY WATCH CO.
Otay, California
1889 - 1894

This company produced about 1,000 watches with a serial number range of 1,000 to 1,500 and 30,000 to 31,000. The company was purchased by a Japanese manufacturer in 1894. Names on Otay movements include: Golden Gate, F. A. Kimball, Native Sun, Overland Mail, R. D. Perry, and P. H. Wheeler.

Otay Watch Co. Dial; note hunting case style and lever for setting hands.

Otay Watch Co., F.A. Kimball, 18 size, 15 jewels, lever set, hunting, serial number 1,264.

18 SIZE

Grade or Name — Description		Avg	Ex-Fn	Mint
California, 15J, LS, HC, NI	★ ★ ★	$2,000	$2,200	$2,500
Golden Gate, 15J, LS, HC, OF, NI	★ ★ ★	1,800	2,000	2,300
F. A. Kimball, 15J, LS, HC, Gilt	★ ★	1,200	1,400	1,700
Native Son, 15J, LS, HC, NI	★ ★	1,600	1,800	2,100
Overland Rail, 15J, LS, HC, NI	★ ★	1,800	2,000	2,300
R. D. Perry, 15J, LS, HC, Gilt	★ ★	1,200	1,400	1,700
P. H. Wheeler, 15J, LS, HC, Gilt	★ ★	1,200	1,400	1,700

D. D. PALMER WATCH CO.
Waltham, Massachusetts
1864 - 1875

In 1858, at age 20, Mr. Palmer opened a small jewelry store in Waltham, Mass. Here he became interested in pocket chronometers. At first he bought the balance and jewels from Swiss manufacturers. In 1864 he took a position with the American Watch Co. and made the chronometers in his spare time (only about 25 produced). They were 18S, ¾ plate, gilded, key wind, and some were nickel. At first they were fusee driven, but he mainly used going barrels. About 1870, Palmer started making lever watches and by 1875 he left the American Watch Co. and started making a 10S keywind, gilded-movement, and a 16S, ¾ plate, gilt and nickel, and a stem wind of his own invention (a vibrating crown wheel). In all he made about 1,500 watches. The signature appearing on the watches was "Palmer W. Co. Wal., Mass."

He basically had three grades of watches: Fine—Solid Nickel; Medium—Nickel Plated; and Medium—Gold Gilt. They were made in open-face and hunter cases.

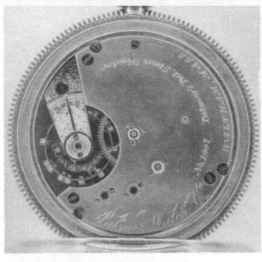

D.D. Palmer Watch Co., 18 size, 15 jewels, "Palmer's Pat. Stem Winder" on movement, serial number 1,007.

Grade or Name — Description		Avg	Ex-Fn	Mint
18S, 15-17J, ¾ Plate, KW, Chronometer .... ★ ★ ★	$4,000	$4,500	$6,000
16S, 17J, NI, OF, 18K .... ★ ★	1,500	1,800	2,200

PEORIA WATCH CO.
Peoria, Illinois
1885 - 1895

The roots of this company began with the Independent Watch Co. (1880-1883). These watches marked "Marion" and "Mark Twain" were made by the Fredonia Watch Co. (1883-1885). Peoria Watch Co. opened Dec. 19, 1885, and made one model of railroad

Peoria Watch Co., 18 size, 15 jewels, nickel damaskeening plates, hunting, note patented regulator, serial number 11,532.

watch in 1887. They were 18S, quick train, 15 jewel, and all stem wind. These watches are hard to find, as only about 3,000 were made. Peoria also made railroad watches for A. C. Smith's Non-Magnetic Watch Co. of America, from 1884-1888. The 18S watches were full plate, adjusted, and had whiplash regulator.

The Peoria Watch Co. closed in 1889, having produced about 47,000 watches.

Grade or Name — Description	Avg	Ex-Fn	Mint
18S, 11J, SW, OF	$125	$150	$225
18S, 15J, SW, personalized name	150	175	250
18S, Peoria W. Co., 15J, SW, OF	175	200	275
18S, Peoria W. Co., 15J, SW, HC	225	250	325
18S, Peoria W. Co., 15J, SW, low S#	325	350	400
18S, Anti-Magnetic, 15J, SW	325	350	400
18S, Non-Magnetic Watch Co. of America, 15J, NI, SW, GJS, Adj.5P, OF	350	375	425
18S, 15J, Non-Magnetic Watch Co. of America, NI, SW, GJS, Adj.5P, HC	400	425	475
18S, Made for Railway Service, 15J, NI, GJS, Adj.5P, OF	300	350	425
18S, Made for Railway Service, NI, GJS, Adj.5P, HC....	350	400	475

PHILADELPHIA WATCH CO.
Philadelphia, Pennsylvania
1874 - 1886

Eugene Paulus organized the Philadelphia Watch Co. about 1874. Most all the parts were made in Switzerland, and finished and cased in this country. The International Watch Co. is believed to have manufactured the movements for Philadelphia Watch Co. Estimated total production of the company is 12,000 watches.

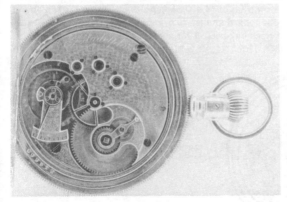

Philadelphia Watch Co., 16 size, 15 jewels, gold jewel settings, hunting case model. "Paulus Patents 1868. Aug. 25th, Nov. 3rd" on movement, serial number 5,751.

Grade or Name — Description		Avg	Ex-Fn	Mint
18S, 15J, SW, HC	★	$350	$450	$575
18S, 15J, KW, KS	★	275	375	500
18S, 15J, SW, OF	★	325	425	525
18S, HC, KW, KS, 18K original case marked				
Philadelphia Watch Co.	★	1,200	1,400	1,800
18S, 11J, KW, KS	★	150	175	225
16S, 15J, KW, KS	★	150	175	225
16S, 19J, KW, KS, GJS	★	375	475	600
8S-6S, 11J, HC	★	150	175	225
8S-6S, 15J, HC	★	150	175	225
8S-6S, Paulus, 19J, KW, KS	★	225	300	400
000S, 7J, HC, PS	★	125	200	300

JAMES & HENRY PITKIN
Hartford, Connecticut
New York, New York
1838 - 1852

Henry Pitkin was the first to attempt to manufacture watches by machinery. The machines were of Pitkin's own design and very crude, but he had some brilliant ideas. His first four workers were paid $30 a year plus their board. After much hardship, the first watches were produced in the fall of 1838. The watches had going barrels, not the fusee and chain, and the American flag was engraved on the plates to denote they were American made and to exemplify the true spirit of American independence in watchmaking.

The first 50 watches were stamped with the name "Henry Pitkin." Others bore the firm name "H & J F Pitkin." The movements were about 16S and ¾ plate. The plates were rolled brass and stamped out with dies. The pinions were lantern style with tight leaves. The movement had a slow train of 14,400 beats per hour. Pitkin's first plan was to make the ends of the pinions conical and let them run in the ends of hardened steel screws, similar to the Marine clock balances. A large brass setting was put in the plates and extended above the surface. Three screws, with small jewels set in their ends, were

Example of a basic **Henry Pitkin** movement, 16 size, key wind & set.

inserted so that they closed about the pivot with very small end shake. This proved to be too expensive and was used in only a few movements. Next, he tried to make standard type movements extend above the plates with the end shake controlled by means of a screw running down into the end of the pivots, reducing friction. This "capped jewel train" was used for a while before he adopted the standard ways of jeweling. The escape wheels were the star type, English style. The balance was made of gold and steel. These movements were fire gilded and not interchangeable. The dials, hands, mainsprings and hairsprings were imported. The rounded pallets were manufactured by Pitkin,and the cases for his watches were made on the premises. As many as 900 watches could have been made by Pitkin.

Grade or Name — Description	Avg	Ex-Fn	Mint
Henry Pitkin S#1-50 . . . . ★ ★ ★ ★	$15,000	$20,000	$25,000
H. & J. F. Pitkin & Co., S#50-377 . . . . ★ ★ ★	10,000	15,000	20,000
Pitkin & Co., New York, S#378-900 . . . . ★ ★ ★	4,500	6,000	7,500
W. Pitkin, Hartford, Conn., S# approx. 40,000, fusee lever,			
KW, Coin . . . . ★ ★	450	500	600

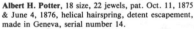

Albert H. Potter, 18 size, 22 jewels, pat. Oct. 11, 1875 & June 4, 1876, helical hairspring, detent escapement, made in Geneva, serial number 14.

A.H. Potter Watch Co., Boston, 18 size, about 6 jewels, detent escapement, note similarity to E.H. Howard & Co. early watches, serial number 5.

ALBERT H. POTTER WATCH CO.
New York, New York
1855 - 1875

Albert Potter started his apprenticeship in 1852. When this was completed he moved to New York to take up watchmaking on his own. He made about 35 watches in all that sold for $225 to $350. Some were chronometers, some were lever escapements, key wind, gilded movements, some were fusee driven, both bridge and ¾ plate. Potter was a contemporary of Charles Fasoldt and John Mulford, both horological inventors from Albany, N. Y. Potter moved to Cuba in 1861 but returned to New York in 1868. In 1872 he worked in Chicago and formed the Potter Brothers Company with his brother William. He moved to Geneva about 1876. His company produced a total of about 600 watches, but only about 40 of those were made in the U. S.

Grade or Name — Description	Avg	Ex-Fn	Mint
18S, 29J, 18K HC, 1 min. repeater, Geneva	$6,000	$7,000	$8,000
18S, BRG lever, Chronometer, signed A. H. Potter, New York, 18K Potter case, U.S. mfg. . . . . ★ ★ ★ ★	10,000	12,000	16,000
18S, BRG lever with wind indicator, 18K Potter case ★ ★ ★	5,000	6,000	7,000
18S-20S, Tourbillion, signed A. H. Potter, Boston, gilded, 18K Potter case, U.S. mfg. . . . . ★ ★ ★ ★	15,000	17,000	20,000
16S-18S, 22J, helical spring, detent chronometer escapement, Geneva, 18K	4,000	5,000	6,500
4S, 21J, ¼ hour repeater, Geneva, 18K Potter HC	3,000	3,500	4,500

George P. Reed, 18 size, 15 jewels, key & stem wind, key & lever set, lever escapement, 48 hour up and down wind indicator, serial number 262.

George P. Reed, 18 size, 15 jewels, key & stem wind, key & lever set, lever escapement, 48 hour up and down wind indicator, serial number 5.

GEORGE P. REED
Boston, Massachusetts
1865 - 1885

In 1854, George P. Reed entered the employment of Dennison, Howard and Davis, in Roxbury, Mass., and moved with the company to Waltham, Mass. Here he was placed in charge of the pinion finishing room. While there he invented and received a patent for the mainspring barrel and main timing power combination. This patent was dated February 18, 1857. Reed returned to Roxbury with Howard who purchased his patented barrel. He stayed with the Howard factory as foreman and adjuster until 1865, when he left for Boston to start his own account.

He obtained a patent on April 7, 1868, for an improved chronometer escapement which featured simplified construction. He made about 100 chronometers with his improved escapement, to which he added a stem-wind device. His company turned out about 100 watches the first three years. Most, if not all, of his watches run for two days and have up and down indicators on the dial. They are both 18S and 16S, ¼ plate, nickel, and are artistically designed. Reed experimented with various combinations of lever and chronometer escapements. One was a rotary watch he made in 1862 and called the "Monitor." It was the first rotary watch made in America. In all, Reed made a total of about 550 watches, and these are valuable to collectors.

Grade or Name — Description	Avg	Ex-Fn	Mint
18S, 15J, LS, OF or HC, Wind Indicator, chronometer escapement, 18K case .... ★ ★ ★ ★	$9,000	$11,500	$15,000
16S, 15J, LS, OF or HC, **not** chronometer, 18K case ★ ★ ★	6,500	7,000	9,000
16S, 15J, LS, OF, 31 day calendar, 18K case ...... ★ ★ ★	6,500	7,000	9,000

ROCKFORD WATCH CO.
Rockford, Illinois
1873 - 1915

The Rockford Watch Company's equipment was bought from the Cornell Watch Co., and two of Cornell's employees, C. W. Parker and P. H. Wheeler, went to work for Rockford. The factory was located 93 miles from Chicago on the Rock River. The first watch was placed on the market on May 1, 1876. They were key wind, 18S, full plate expansion balance. By 1877 the company was making ¾ plate nickel movements that fit standard size cases. Three railroads came through Rockford, and the company always advertised to the railroad men—and was very popular with them. The company had some problems in 1896, and the name changed to Rockford Watch Co. Ltd. It closed in 1915.

ROCKFORD ESTIMATED SERIAL NUMBERS
AND PRODUCTION DATES

Date	Serial No.	Date	Serial No.	Date	Serial No.	Date	Serial No.
1876	5,000	1886	110,000	1896	290,000	1906	620,000
1877	15,000	1887	125,000	1897	320,000	1907	650,000
1878	25,000	1888	140,000	1898	350,000	1908	690,000
1879	35,000	1889	150,000	1899	385,000	1909	730,000
1880	50,000	1890	165,000	1900	415,000	1910	765,000
1881	60,000	1891	175,000	1901	450,000	1911	820,000
1882	70,000	1892	195,000	1902	480,000	1912	850,000
1883	80,000	1893	200,000	1903	515,000	1913	880,000
1884	90,000	1894	230,000	1904	550,000	1914	930,000
1885	100,000	1895	260,000	1905	580,000	1915	1,000,000

(See Rockford Watch Co. **Identification of Movements** section located at the end of the Rockford price section to identify the movement, size, and model number of your watch.)

(Prices are with gold filled cases except where noted.)

NOTE: Some grades are not included. Their values can be determined by comparing with similar models or grades listed.

ROCKFORD
18 SIZE

Grade or Name — Description	Avg	Ex-Fn	Mint
Belmont USA, 21J, LS, OF, NI, M#7	$200	$250	$325
Chronometer, 17J, ADJ, OF, G925	275	350	500
Dome Model, 9J, brass plates........................ ★	150	175	225

Rockford Watch Co., 18 size, 11 jewels, hunting, Model number 6, exposed escapement, serial number 190,564.

Special Railway, 18 size, 17 jewels, hunting, Model number 8, serial number 344,551.

Grade or Name—Description	Avg	Ex-Fn	Mint
King Edward, Plymouth W. Co., 21J, 14K HC	$700	$800	$975
King Edward (Sears), 21J, GJS, ADJ, NI, OF	275	350	475
King Edward (Sears), 21J, GJS, ADJ, NI, HC...........	300	325	500
Pennsylvania Special, 25J, LS, Adj.6P, OF....... ★ ★ ★	3,000	4,000	6,000
Railway King, 21J, OF................................	475	600	750
The Ramsey Watch, 11J, NI, KW or SW	100	125	150
The Ramsey Watch, 15J, NI, KW or SW	100	125	150
The Ramsey Watch, M#7, 21J, OF, NI, ADJ...........	350	375	450
Rockford Early KW-KS, M#1-2, with low Serial #s less than 500................................... ★	400	500	675
Rockford Early KW-KS, M#1-2, with low Serial #s less than 500, Coin .... ★	400	500	675
Rockford Early KW-KS, M#1-2, with reversible case	275	325	400
Rockford Early KW-KS, M#1-2, S#s less than 100.... ★ ★	1,000	1,400	2,000
Rockford, 7J, SW, FULL, OF..........................	70	85	135
Rockford, 7J, KW, FULL, OF	70	85	135
Rockford, 7J, KW, FULL, Silveroid...................	40	60	85
Rockford, 9J, SW, FULL, HC	100	125	175
Rockford, M#1, 9J, KW, FULL, HC...................	150	175	225
Rockford, 11J, SW, FULL, OF........................	75	100	150
Rockford, M#1-2, 11J, KW, FULL.....................	150	175	225
Rockford, M#1-2, 11J, transition case, FULL	100	125	175
Rockford, 11J, KW, Coin HC	150	175	225
Rockford, 11-15J, KW, HC, M#5, ¾ Plate, Coin...... ★	275	350	550
Rockford, 13J, HC....................................	100	125	175
Rockford, 15J, SW, FULL	75	100	150
Rockford, 15J, KW, FULL, multi-color dial.............	275	350	425
Rockford, 15J, SW, 2-Tone movement.................	100	125	175

Rockford movement, 18 size, 7 jewels, model 5, hunting, lever set, three-quarter plate.

Grade 900, 18 size, 24 jewels, Adj5p. **Warning:** 24 jewel fakes have been made from 21 jewel movements. The fakes are missing the eliptical jewel setting on the barrel bridge.

Grade or Name—Description	Avg	Ex-Fn	Mint
Rockford, 15J, KW, FULL, ADJ	$175	$225	$350
Rockford, 15J, KW/SW	100	150	200
Rockford, 15J, KW/SW, Silveroid	60	70	85
Rockford, 15J, M#6, exposed escapement wheel, FULL, HC, LS, nickel mvt...............................	275	300	350
Rockford, 15J, M#6, exposed escapement wheel, FULL, HC, LS, gilded mvt...............................	175	200	250
Rockford, 15J, M#6, exposed wheel, nickel mvt., Coin ...	175	200	250
Rockford, M#1, 15J, KW, FULL	100	125	175
Rockford, 16J, GJS, NI, DMK, SW....................	75	100	150
Rockford, 16J, GJS, NI, DMK, SW, Silveroid...........	50	60	90
Rockford, 16J, GJS, NI, DMK, SW, Coin	75	100	150
Rockford, 17J, NI, DMK, SW, OF.....................	75	100	150
Rockford, 17J, GJS, NI, DMK, SW, Adj.5P	100	125	175
Rockford, 17J, GJS, NI, SW, 2-Tone, OF	125	150	200
Rockford, M#1-2, 19J, KW, FULL, GJS, ADJ .. ★ ★ ★ ★	1,500	1,700	2,000
Rockford, 19J, transition, HC, GJS .... ★	400	500	650
Rockford, 21J, SW, Silveroid.......................	75	100	150
Rockford, 21J, GJS, OF, Adj.5P, wind indicator .... ★ ★	2,500	3,000	3,500
Rockford, 21J, SW, DMK, ADJ, HC	275	325	400
Rockford, 21J, NI, DMK, ADJ, OF....................	175	225	300
Rockford, 21J, GJS, NI, DMK, Adj.5P, marked "RG" ..	200	250	325
Rockford, 24J, GJS, SW, LS, Adj.5P, marked "RG," OF	800	1,000	1,200
Rockford, 24J, GJS, SW, LS, Adj.5P, marked "RG," HC .... ★	1,200	1,400	1,600
Rockford, 25J, GJS, SW, LS, Adj.5P, NI, DMK .... ★ ★	3,500	5,000	6,500
Rockford, 26J, GJS, SW, LS, Adj.5P, NI, DMK .. ★ ★ ★	8,000	10,000	16,000

Rockford Watch Co., 18 size, 15 jewels, ¾ plate, key & stem wind.

Rockford Watch Co., 18 size, 15 jewels, model 4, open face, lever set, serial number 227,430.

Grade or Name—Description	Avg	Ex-Fn	Mint
Special Railway, 17J, ADJ, 2-tone, SW, HC	$300	$400	$550
The Syndicate Watch Co., M#7, 15J, LS, NI, HC	150	200	275
Winnebago, 17J, LS, GJS, Adj.5P, DR, NI, DMK.......	150	175	225
Winnebago, 17J, LS, GJS, Adj.5P, DR, NI, DMK, Silveroid	100	125	175
24 Hour Dial, 15J, SW or KW	150	175	225
40, 15J, M#3, HC................................★ ★	250	300	375
43, 15J, M#3, HC, 2-Tone	100	125	175
66, 11J, M#7, OF	75	100	150
66, 11J, M#7, OF, Silveroid	35	45	60
66, 11J, M#7, HC...................................	75	100	150
81, 9J, M#3, HC, Gilt	100	125	175
82, Special, 21J, SW...........................★ ★	400	500	650
83, 15J, M#8, HC, 2-Tone	125	150	200
86, 15J, M#7, OF, NI	50	75	125
93, 9J, M#8, HC, Gilt	100	125	175
94, 9J, M#7, OF	50	75	125
200-205, 17J, M#9, OF, NI, LS	75	100	150
245, 19J, HC, GJS, 2-Tone.........................★	1,000	1,200	1,400
800, 24J, GJS, DR, Adj.5P, DMK, HC...............★	1,200	1,400	1,600
805, 21J, GJS, Adj.5P, NI, DMK, HC, marked "RG" ...	200	250	325
810, 21J, NI, DMK, ADJ, HC........................	250	300	375
820, 17J, HC, SW..............................★ ★	300	350	425
825, 17J, HC, FULL	125	150	200
830, 17J, HC, FULL	100	125	175
835, 17J, HC, FULL	100	125	175
835, 17J, HC, FULL, Silveroid	50	75	125
845, 21J, HC, GJS, FULL ....★	400	475	550
870, 7J, HC, FULL	75	100	150

Grade or Name—Description	Avg.	Ex-Fn	Mint
900, 24J, GJS, DR, Adj.5P, OF, NI, DMK .... ★★	$1,000	$1,200	$1,500
900, 24J, GJS, DR, Adj.5P, 14K, OF case .... ★★	1,400	1,600	1,900
905, 21J, GJS, DR, Adj.5P, OF, NI, DMK	250	275	350
910, 21J, NI, DMK, 1 ADJ, OF	150	175	250
912, 21J, OF .... ★★	425	475	600
915, 17J, M#9, OF, SW........................ ★★★	450	500	625
918, 21J, OF, NI, GJS, Adj.5P, DR	150	175	225
918, 21J, OF, NI, GJS, Adj.5P, DR, Silveroid	100	125	175
918, 21J, OF, NI, GJS, Adj.5P, DR, Coin	125	175	225
930, 17J, OF	175	225	275
935, 17J, OF	75	100	135
945, 21J, M#9, OF, SW.............................	150	175	225
950, 21J, OF, NI, GJS, Adj.5P, DR, Wind Indicator. ★★	2,500	3,000	4,000
970, 7J, OF	60	70	90
970, 7J, OF, Silveroid	40	50	70

16 SIZE

Grade or Name — Description	Avg	Ex-Fn	Mint
Commodore Perry, 21J, OF, GJS, GT, marked "RG" ...	$350	$450	$600
Cosmos, 17J, OF, GJS, LS, DMK, marked dial & mvt. ..	225	350	500
Doll Watch Co., 23J, marked dial & mvt.......... ★★★	1,000	1,200	1,500
Dome Model, 15J	60	75	100
Dome Model, 17J	65	80	120
Dome Model, 17J, 2-tone, HC........................	200	250	325
Iroquois, 17J, DR, 14K, HC.........................	525	575	675
Iroquois, 17J, DR	150	175	225
Peerless, 17J, OF, NI, LS, DMK......................	75	100	125
Pocahontas, 17-21J, GJS, Adj.5P, DR.................	225	250	375
Prince of Wales (Sears), 21J	225	250	375
Prince of Wales (Sears), 21J, 14K	525	550	675

Grade 103, 16 size, 17 jewels, Model 1, hunting.

Example of a **Cosmos** movement, 16 size, 17 jewels, open face, gold jewel settings.

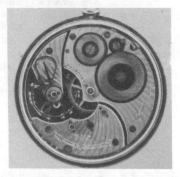

Example of a Rockford movement, 16 size, 21 jewels, three-quarter plate, serial number 842,520.

Grade 500-HC, 505-OF, 16 size, 21 jewels, gold jewel settings, gold train, Adj6p, marked "RG," originally sold for $100.00

Grade or Name—Description	Avg	Ex-Fn	Mint
Rockford 7J, ¾, HC	$100	$125	$175
Rockford, 9J, ¾, SW, OF	40	60	85
Rockford, 9J, SW, Silveroid........................	30	40	60
Rockford, 9J, SW, HC	100	125	175
Rockford, 11J, SW, Silveroid........................	40	60	85
Rockford, 11J, ¾, HC	100	125	175
Rockford, 15J, ¾, ADJ, OF	75	100	135
Rockford, 15J, ¾, ADJ, Silveroid	40	60	85
Rockford, 15J, ¾, ADJ, HC	100	125	175
Rockford, 16J, ¾, SW, Silveroid	40	60	85
Rockford, 16J, ¾, ADJ, NI, DMK	75	100	135
Rockford, 17J, ¾	75	100	135
Rockford, 17J, ¾, 2-Tone, marked "RG"	125	150	200
Rockford, 17J, BRG, Adj.3P, DR	100	125	175
Rockford, 17J, GJS, Adj.5P, DR, Wind Indicator	400	450	525
Rockford, 17J, BRG, Silveroid	40	60	85
Rockford, 17J, ¾, Silveroid..........................	40	60	85
Rockford, 21J, ¾, SW, Silveroid	75	100	135
Rockford, 21J, BRG, SW, Silveroid	75	100	135
Rockford, 21J, ¾, GJS, Adj.5P	125	150	200
Rockford, 21J, BRG, GJS, Adj.5P, GT, DR	150	175	225
Rockford, 21J, GJS, Adj.5P, DR, Wind Indicator	500	600	750
Winnebago, 17J, BRG, GJS, Adj.5P, NI	150	175	225
Winnebago, 21J, BRG, GJS, Adj.5P, NI	175	200	275
100, 16J, M#1, HC, ¾, 2-Tone	175	200	250
100S, 21J, Special, HC, ¾, LS	200	250	325
102, 15J, HC, M#1 ....★	125	150	200
103, 17J, HC, M#1 ....★ ★	250	300	375
104, 11J, HC, M#1	40	50	65
115-125, 17J, Special, HC ....★ ★ ★	500	600	750
120-130, 17J, HC ....★ ★ ★	400	500	650

Pocahontas, 16 size, 21 jewels, hunting case, bridge model, Adj.5pserial number 670,203.

Rockford movement, 16 size, 17 jewels, ¾ plate, hunting, lever set, serial number 556,064.

Grade or Name—Description	Avg	Ex-Fn	Mint
400 & 405, 17J, NI, Adj.5P, GJS, DR, BRG	$100	$125	$175
445, 19J, HC, GJS, BRG . . . . ★ ★	850	1,000	1,200
500, 21J, BRG, NI, GJS, Adj.5P, GT, HC . . . . ★ ★	500	550	625
501, 21J, GJS, HC . . . . ★ ★ ★	900	1,100	1,250
505, 21J, BRG, NI, GJS, Adj.5P, GT, OF . . . . ★ ★	400	500	650
510, 21J, BRG, NI, GJS, Adj.5P, GT, HC . . . . ★	300	400	550
515 & 525, 21J, OF, ¾	150	175	225
520, 21J, HC, ¾	200	250	325
520, 21J, BRG, NI, GJS, Adj.5P, HC . . . . ★	400	450	525
530, 21J, HC, GJS, Adj.5P, marked "RG" . . . . ★	300	350	425
535, 21J, OF, ¾ . . . . ★	225	275	350
537, 21J, OF, GJS, Adj.5P . . . . ★ ★	500	600	775
545, 21J, OF	150	175	225
561, 17J, BRG	125	150	200
566, 17J, BRG	125	150	200
572, 17J, BRG, NI, GJS, Adj.5P	75	100	135
573, 17J, BRG, NI	75	100	135
578-579, 17J, PS, GJS . . . . ★ ★	300	350	475
584 & 585, 15J, ¾, NI	40	60	85
620-625, 21J, HC, ¾ . . . . ★	300	400	525
655, 21J, OF, Wind Indicator, marked 655 . . . . ★	500	600	750

12 SIZE
All ¾ Bridge

Grade or Name — Description	Avg	Ex-Fn	Mint
Iroquois, 17J, BRG, DR, ADJ	$60	$70	$100
Pocahontas, 21J, GJS, Adj.5P, BRG, DR	100	125	125

Rockford Watch co., 12 size, 15 jewels, model 1, hunting, pendant set.

Rockford Watch Co., 12 size, 15 jewels, model 2, open face, pendant set.

Grade or Name—Description	Avg	Ex-Fn	Mint
Rockford, 15J, BRG	$35	$40	$55
Rockford, 17J, BRG, NI, DR, ADJ	50	60	75
Rockford, 21J, BRG, NI, DR, ADJ	70	80	110
Rockford, 21J, BRG, NI, DR, ADJ, Silveroid	40	60	85
Winona, 15J, BRG	45	55	80
300, 23J, ¾, HC, GJS, Adj.5P ★ ★ ★	300	350	425
305, 23J, BRG, NI, GJS, Adj.5P, GT, OF ★ ★ ★	300	350	425
310(HC)-315(OF), 21J, BRG, NI, GJS, Adj.5P	75	100	150
320(HC)-325(OF), 17J, BRG, NI, ADJ, DR	40	60	85
330, 17J, BRG, NI, DR, OF	40	60	85
335, 17J, BRG, NI, DR, HC	40	60	85
340(HC)-345(OF), 21J, M#1 ★	200	225	300
350, 17J, OF	40	60	85
355, 17J, HC	40	60	85

Note: Add $10 to above watches with hunting case.

8 SIZE

Grade or Name — Description	Avg	Ex-Fn	Mint
15J, ¾, HC, LS, 14K, 40 DWT	$375	$400	$475
15J, ¾, HC, LS	100	125	175

6 SIZE

Grade or Name — Description	Avg	Ex-Fn	Mint
9J, HC, NI	$60	$70	$85

Rockford movement, 6 size, 17 jewels, quick train, straight line escapement, compensating balance, adjusted to temperature, micrometric regulator, three-quarter damaskeened plates.

Grade or Name—Description	Avg	Ex-Fn	Mint
15J, ¾, NI	$40	$60	$85
16J, ¾, NI	70	90	115
17J, ¾, ADJ, NI	80	100	125

0 SIZE

Grade or Name — Description	Avg	Ex-Fn	Mint
Plymouth Watch Co., 15J, HC	$200	$225	$275
7J, BRG, HC	100	120	155
11J, BRG, NI, DR, HC	110	130	165
15J, BRG, NI, DR, HC	125	135	175
17J, BRG, NI, DR, HC	180	205	255
17J, BRG, NI, DR, in marked Rockford HC in dust cover ring	325	350	375

ROCKFORD WATCH CO.
IDENTIFICATION OF MOVEMENTS
BY MODEL NUMBER

How to Identify Your Watch: Compare the movement of your watch with the illustrations in this section. Upon matching the movement exactly, the model number and size can be determined. While comparing, note the location of the balance, jewels, screws, gears, and type of back plate (Full, ¾, Bridge) which will be clues in identifying the movement you have. Having determined the size and model number, you can now find your watch in the main price listing by name or number (which is engraved on the movement).

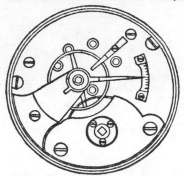

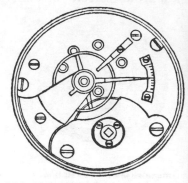

Model 1, 18 size, full plate, hunting, key wind & set.

Model 2, 18 size, full plate, hunting, lever set.

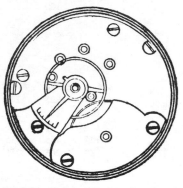

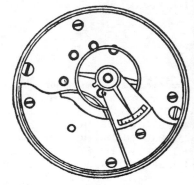

Model 3, 18 size, full plate, hunting, lever set.

Model 4, 18 size, full plate, open face, lever set.

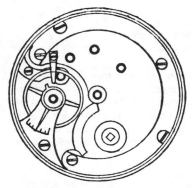

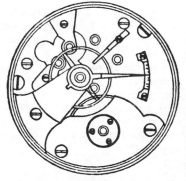

Model 5, 18 size, three-quarter plate, hunting, lever set.

Model 6, 18 size, full plate, hunting, lever set, exposed escapement.

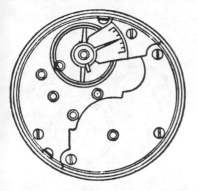

Model 7, 18 size, full plate, open face, lever set.

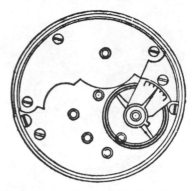

Model 8, 18 size, full plate, hunting, lever set.

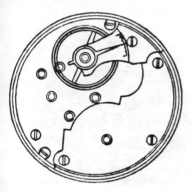

Model 9, 18 size, full plate, open face, lever set.

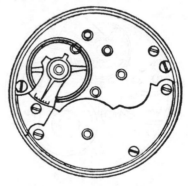

Model 10, 18 size, full plate, hunting, lever set.

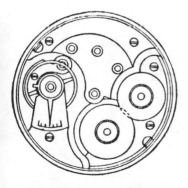

Model 1, 16 size, three-quarter plate, hunting, lever set.

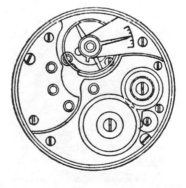

Model 2, 16 size, three-quarter plate, open face, pendant & lever set.

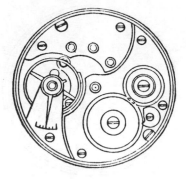

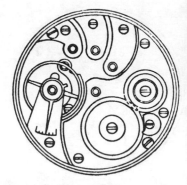

Model 3, 16 size, three-quarter plate, hunting, pendant & lever set.

Model 4, 16 size, three-quarter plate, bridge, hunting, pendant & lever set.

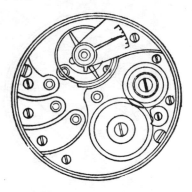

Model 5, 16 size, three-quarter plate, bridge, open face, pendant & lever set.

Model 1, 12 size, three-quarter plate bridge, hunting, pendant set.

Model 2, 12 size, three-quarter plate bridge, open face, pendant set.

Model 1, 6 & 8 size, three-quarter plate, hunting, lever set.

Model 2, 6 size, three-quarter plate, hunting, lever set.

Model 1, 0 size, three-quarter plate, bridge, hunting, pendant set.

Model 2, 0 size, three-quarter plate, bridge, open face, pendant set.

SAN JOSE WATCH CO.
San Jose, California
1891

Very few watches were made by the San Jose Watch Co., and very little is known about them.

Grade or Name — Description		Avg	Ex-Fn	Mint
16S, SW .... ★ ★ ★		$1,500	$2,000	$2,500

Example of a basic **M.S. Smith & Co.** movement, 18 size, 15 jewels, three-quarter plate, key wind & set.

M. S. SMITH & CO.
Detroit, Michigan
1870 - 1874

Eber B. Ward purchased the M. S. Smith & Co. which was a large jewelry firm. These watches carried the Smith name on them. A Mr. Hoyt was engaged to produce these watches and about 100 were produced before the Freeport Watch Co. purchased the small firm.

Grade or Name — Description	Avg	Ex-Fn	Mint
18S, 15J, ¾, KW, KS, 18K case	$2,500	$3,000	$3,600
18S, 15J, ¾, KW, KS .... ★ ★ ★	1,200	1,500	2,300
6S, 15J, SW, 18K case............................	700	800	1,000
6S, 15J, SW .... ★ ★	400	500	700

SOUTH BEND WATCH CO.
South Bend, Indiana
March 1903 - December 1929

Three brothers, George, Clement and J. M. Studebaker, purchased the successful Columbus Watch Co. The first South Bend watches were full plate and similar to the Columbus watches. The serial numbers started at 380,501 whereas the Columbus serial numbers stopped at about 500,000. The highest grade watch was a "Polaris," a 16S, ¾ plate, 21 jewels, and with an open face. This watch sold for about $100. The 227 and 229 were also high grade. The company identified its movements by model numbers 1, 2, and 3, and had grades from 100 to 431. The even numbers were hunting cases, and the odd numbers were open-faced cases. The lowest grade was a 203, 7J, that sold for about $6.75. The company closed on Dec. 31, 1929.

SOUTH BEND ESTIMATED SERIAL NUMBERS
AND PRODUCTION DATES

Date	Serial No.	Date	Serial No.	Date	Serial No.	Date	Serial No.
1903	380,501	1910	620,000	1917	865,000	1924	1,110,000
1904	410,000	1911	655,000	1918	900,000	1925	1,145,000
1905	445,000	1912	690,000	1919	935,000	1926	1,180,000
1906	480,000	1913	725,000	1920	970,000	1927	1,215,000
1907	515,000	1914	760,000	1921	1,005,000	1928	1,250,000
1908	550,000	1915	795,000	1922	1,040,000	1929	1,275,000
1909	585,000	1916	825,000	1923	1,075,000		

SOUTH BEND
18 SIZE (Lever set)

Grade or Name — Description	Avg	Ex-Fn	Mint
South Bend, 15J, OF	$75	$100	$150
South Bend, 15J, HC................................	100	125	175
South Bend, 17J, OF	75	100	150
South Bend, 17J, HC................................	100	125	175
South Bend, 21J, OF	150	175	225
South Bend, 21J, HC, 14K	550	600	675
South Bend, 21J, OF, HC, Silveroid...................	75	100	125
South Bend, 21J, SW, HC	200	225	275
The Studebaker, G#323, 17J, OF, GJS, NI, Adj.5P	200	250	325
The Studebaker, G#328, 21J, HC, GJS, NI, FULL, Adj.5P	275	325	400
The Studebaker, G#329, 21J, OF, GJS, NI, FULL, Adj.5P	225	275	350
304, 15J, HC	100	125	175

South Bend movement, 18 size, 17 jewels, stem wind, hunting, serial number 426,726.

The Studebaker, 18 size, 21 jewels, gold jewel settings, stem wind.

Grade or Name—Description	Avg	Ex-Fn	Mint
305, 15J, OF	$75	$100	$150
305, 15J, OF, Silveroid	40	50	65
309, 17J, OF	75	100	150
312, 17J, HC, NI, ADJ	100	125	175
313, 17J, OF, NI, ADJ, marked 313 ....★	200	250	325
315, 17J, OF, NI, Adj.3P	75	100	150
327, 21J, OF, Adj.5P	125	150	200
327, 21J, OF, Adj.5P, Silveroid	75	100	150
330, 15J, M#1, LS, HC ....★ ★	300	350	425
331, 15J, M#1, LS, OF ....★ ★	275	325	400
332, 15J, HC ....★ ★	275	325	400
333, 15J, OF	75	100	150
337, 17J, OF	75	100	150
340, 17J, M#1, Adj.3P, NI, HC	125	150	200
341, 17J, M#1, ADJ, NI, Adj.3P, OF	100	125	175
342, 17J, M#1, LS	75	100	150
343, 17J, M#1, LS, OF	75	100	150
344, 17J, HC, NI, Adj.3P ....★ ★	300	350	425
345, 17J, OF, NI, Adj.3P ....★ ★	275	325	400
346, 17J, HC, NI ....★ ★	300	350	425
347, 17J, OF, NI	75	100	125
355, 19J, GJS, 2-Tone, HC ....★ ★	1,000	1,200	1,500

(Prices are with gold filled cases except where noted.)

NOTE: Some grades are not included. Their values can be determined by comparing with similar models or grades listed.

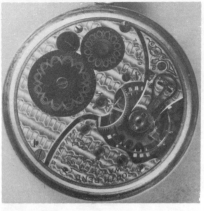

Grade 211, 16 size, 17 jewels, three-quarter plate, serial number 703,389.

Grade 295, 16 size, 21 jewels, first model, gold jewel settings, gold train, open face, serial number 518,022.

16 SIZE
M#1 Lever set

Grade or Name — Description	Avg	Ex-Fn	Mint
Polaris, 21J, M#1, Adj.5P, ¾, NI, DR, GJS, GT, 14K			
South Bend case with Polaris dial .... ★ ★	$1,500	$1,800	$2,200
South Bend, 7J, OF	50	75	125
South Bend, 7J, HC	75	100	150
South Bend, 9J, OF	50	75	125
South Bend, 9J, HC	75	100	150
South Bend, 15J, OF	50	75	125
South Bend, 15J, HC	75	100	150
South Bend, 15J, OF, Silveroid	40	60	85
South Bend, 17J, OF	50	75	125
South Bend, 17J, HC, ADJ	100	125	175
South Bend, 17J, 14K HC	475	500	575
South Bend, 21J, OF	100	125	175
South Bend, 21J, HC, ADJ	200	250	325
The Studebaker 223, M#2, 17J, Adj.5P, BRG, GJS, DR, GT	275	300	375
The Studebaker 229, 21J, M#2, Adj.5P, BRG, GJS, DR, GT	300	325	400
Studebaker, 21J, OF, PS, Adj.5P	125	150	200
203, 7J, ¾, NI, OF	50	75	125
204, 15J, ¾, NI, HC	75	100	150
207, 15J, OF, PS...................................	50	75	125
209, 9J, M#2, OF, PS	50	75	125
211, 17J, M#2, ¾, NI, OF	50	75	125
212, 17J, M#2, HC, LS, heat & cold	100	125	175
215, 17J, M#2, OF, LS, heat & cold.................	50	75	125

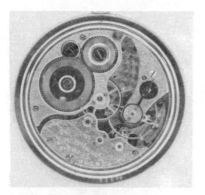
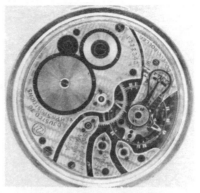

South Bend Watch Co., Polaris, 16 size, 21 jewels, model number 1, Adj5p, gold jewel settings, gold train, open face, serial number 518,236.

Grade 227, 16 size, 21 jewels, gold jewel settings, Adj5p, serial number 1,222,843.

Grade or Name—Description	Avg	Ex-Fn	Mint
215, 17J, M#2, OF, Silveroid	$40	$50	$65
217, 17J, M#2, OF, BRG, NI, DR, Adj.3P..............	75	100	150
219, 19J, M#2, OF, NI, PS, BRG, DR, Adj.4P..........	100	125	175
223, 17J, M#2, OF, LS, Adj.5P........................	50	75	125
227, 21J, M#2, BRG, NI, LS, OF, DR, Adj.5P..........	125	150	200
229, 21J, M#2, BRG, GJS, ADJ, OF .... ★★	300	350	425
245, 19J, GJS, BRG, HC .... ★★	600	700	850
260, 7J, M#1, HC...................................	75	100	125
261, 7J, M#1, OF	50	75	100
280, 15J, M#1, HC..................................	80	100	150
281, 15J, M#1, OF	50	75	125
290, 17J, M#1, LS, Adj.3P, HC .... ★★	200	250	325
291, 17J, M#1, OF, Adj.3P .... ★★	175	200	275
292, 19J, M#1, HC, ¾, GJS, NI, DR, Adj.5P .... ★	250	300	375
293, 19J, M#1, OF, ¾, GJS, NI, DR, Adj.5P .... ★	175	225	275
294, 21J, M#1, Adj.5P, GJS, GT, HC, marked 294 .. ★★	300	350	475
295, 21J, M#1, OF, LS, Adj.5P, GJS, GT, marked 295 ★	250	300	425
298, 17J, M#1, HC, Adj.3P .... ★★	200	250	325
299, 17J, M#1, OF, Adj.3P .... ★★	175	225	275

12 SIZE
(OF Only)

Grade or Name — Description	Avg	Ex-Fn	Mint
Chesterfield, 15J, BRG, NI, DR, G#407	$50	$60	$75
Chesterfield, 17J, BRG, NI, GJS, DR, Adj.3P, G#419....	60	70	85
Chesterfield, 21J, BRG, NI, GJS, DR, Adj.5P, G#431....	75	100	125
Digital, 21J, GJS, DR, BRG, Adj.5P .... ★★	200	250	325

Grade 411., 12 size, 17 jewels, open face, double roller.

Chesterfield, 12 size, 21 jewels, open face only, bridge, gold jewel settings, pendant set, double roller, Adj5p.

Grade or Name—Description	Avg	Ex-Fn	Mint
South Bend, 15J	$35	$45	$60
South Bend, 17J	40	50	65
South Bend, 17J, Silveroid	30	40	55
South Bend, 19J	60	70	85
South Bend, 21J	70	80	95
Studebaker, 21J, ¾, NI, Adj.5P, GJS	125	150	200
407, 15J, Silveroid.................................	30	35	45
407, 15J..	35	45	60
411, 17J, DR, GJS	40	50	65
415, 17J, ADJ to temp............................★ ★	125	150	200
419, 17J, Adj.3P ....★ ★	125	150	200
429, 19J, Adj.4P, GT, GJS..........................★	100	125	175
431, 21J, Adj.5P, DR, GJS ....★ ★	125	150	200
431, 21J, Adj.5P, Silveroid	40	50	65

6 SIZE

Grade or Name — Description	Avg	Ex-Fn	Mint
South Bend, 11J, G#160, HC	$75	$85	$100
South Bend, 15J, G#170, HC	100	125	175
South Bend, 17J, G#180, HC	100	125	175
South Bend, 17J, G#180, 14K.........................	200	250	325

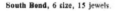

South Bend, 6 size, 15 jewels.

Grade 120-HC, 121-OF, 0 size, 17 jewels, bridge, nickel, double roller, pendant set.

0 SIZE

Grade or Name — Description	Avg	Ex-Fn	Mint
South Bend, 15J, OF, PS	$50	$60	$75
Grade 100 HC & 101 OF, 7J, PS	75	100	150
Grade 110 HC & 111 OF, 15J, 3F Brg, DR .... ★	100	125	150
Grade 120 HC & 121 OF, 17J, BRG, NI, DR, PS.... ★ ★	125	150	200
Grade 150 HC & 151 OF, 17J, BRG, NI, PS .... ★ ★	125	150	200

Note: Add $20 to above watches with hunting case; add $40 for hunting cases marked South Bend.

SOUTH BEND WATCH CO.
IDENTIFICATION OF MOVEMENTS
BY MODEL NUMBER

How to Identify Your Watch: Compare the movement of your watch with the illustrations in this section. Upon matching the movement exactly, the model number and size can be determined. While comparing, note the location of the balance, jewels, screws, gears, and type of back plate (Full, ¾, Bridge) which will be clues in identifying the movement you have. Having determined the size and model number, you can now find your watch in the main price listing by name or number (which is engraved on the movement).

18 SIZE—MODEL 1
Open Face and Hunting. Lever Set
Grade Numbers and Description of Movements

No. 341—Open Face, 17 Jewels, Lever Set, Adjusted to Temperature & 3 Positions.

No. 340—Hunting, 17 Jewels, Lever Set, Adjusted to Temperature & 3 Positions.
No. 343—Open Face, 17 Jewels, Lever Set.
No. 331—Open Face, 15 Jewels, Lever Set.

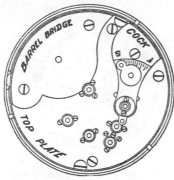
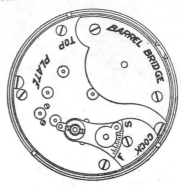

Model 1, Full Plate, Open face.   **Model 1** , Full Plate, Hunting

18 SIZE—MODEL 2
Open Face and Hunting. Lever Set
Grade Numbers and Description of Movements

No. 329—21J, Open Face, "Studebaker," Adjusted to Temperature and 5 Positions.
No. 328—21J, Hunting, Adjusted to Temperature and 5 Positions.
No. 327—21J, Open Face, Adjusted to Temperature and 5 Positions.
No. 323—17J, Open Face, "Studebaker," Adjusted to Temperature and 5 Positions.
No. 345—17J, Open Face, Adjusted to Temperature and 3 Positions.
No. 344—17J, Hunting, Adjusted to Temperature and 3 Positions.
No. 313—17J, Open Face, Adjusted to Temperature.
No. 312—17J, Hunting, Adjusted to Temperature.

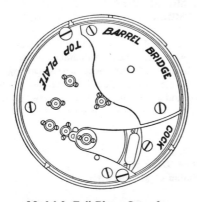
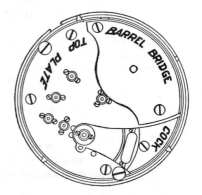

Model 2, Full Plate, Open face.   **Model 2,** Full Plate, Hunting.

Nos. 309, 337, 347—17J, Open Face.
No. 346—17J, Hunting.
Nos. 333, 305—15J, Open Face.
Nos. 332, 304—15J, Hunting.

16 SIZE—MODEL 1
Open Face and Hunting. Lever Set
Grade Numbers and Description of Movements

No. 295—Open Face, 21 Jewels, Adjusted to Temperature and 5 Positions.
No. 294—Hunting, 21 Jewels, Adjusted to Temperature and 5 Positions.
No. 293—Open Face, 19 Jewels, Adjusted to Temperature and 5 Positions.
No. 292—Hunting, 19 Jewels, Adjusted to Temperature and 5 Positions.
No. 299—Open Face, 17 Jewels, Adjusted to Temperature and 3 Positions.
No. 298—Hunting, 17 Jewels, Adjusted to Temperature and 3 Positions.
No. 291—Open Face, 17 Jewels, Adjusted to Temperature and 3 Positions.
No. 290—Hunting, 17 Jewels, Adjusted to Temperature and 3 Positions.
No. 281—Open Face, 15 Jewels.
No. 280—Hunting, 15 Jewels.
No. 261—Open Face, 7 Jewels.
No. 260—Hunting, 7 Jewels.

Model 1, ¾ Plate, Open Face.   **Model 1,** ¾ Plate, Hunting.

16 SIZE—MODEL 2
Open Face and Hunting. Pendant and Lever Set.
Grade Numbers and Description of Movements

No. 229—21J, Open Face, Lever Set, "Studebaker," Adjust. to Temp. and 5 Positions.
No. 227—21J, Open Face, Lever Set, Adjusted to Temperature and 5 Positions.
No. 219—19J, Open Face, Pendant Set, Adjusted to Temperature and 4 Positions.
No. 223—17J, Open Face, Lever Set, "Studebaker," Adjust. to Temp. and 5 Positions.

No. 217—17J, Open Face, Lever Set, Adjusted to Temperature and 3 Positions.
No. 215—17J, Open Face, Pendant Set, Adjusted to Temperature.
No. 212—17J, Hunting, Lever Set, Adjusted to Temperature.
No. 211—17J, Open Face, Pendant Set.
No. 207—15J, Open Face, Pendant Set.
No. 204—15J, Hunting, Lever Set.
No. 209— 9J, Open Face, Pendant Set.
No. 203— 7J, Open Face, Pendant Set.

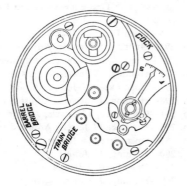

Model 2, ¾ Plate, Hunting.   **Model 2,** ¾ Plate, Open Face.

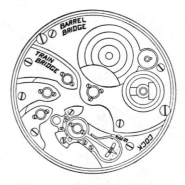

Model 2, Bridges, Open Face.

12 SIZE—MODEL 1
Chesterfield Series
and Grade 429 Special

Made in Pendant Set, Open Face Only
Grade Numbers and Description of Movements

No. 431—21J, Adjusted to Temperature and 5 Positions.
No. 429—19J, Adjusted to Temperature and 4 Positions.

No. 419—17J, Adjusted to Temperature and 3 Positions.
No. 415—17J, Adjusted to Temperature.
No. 411—17J.
No. 407—15J.

Model 1, Bridges, Open Face

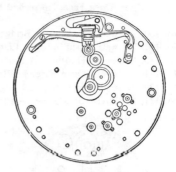

Model 1, Lower Plate, Dial Side

6 SIZE—MODEL 1
Hunting
Grade No. 180, 17 Jewels
Grade No. 170, 15 Jewels
Grade No. 160, 11 Jewels

Serial Number Range
380,501 to 389,900

Model 1, ¼ Plate, 6
size

0 SIZE—MODEL 1
Open Face, No second hand, Hunting has second hand

Model 1, Open Face, ¼ Plate, 7 jewels.

Model 1, Hunting, Bridges, 15-17 jewels.

Model numbers 1 & 2 serial numbers under 659,700. All open face and hunting parts for this model except dial and fourth pinion are interchangeable.

0 SIZE—MODEL 2
Open Face, No second hand, Hunting has second hand

No. 100, 7 Jewels, Hunting, ¾ Bridge.
No. 101, 7 Jewels, Open Face, ¾ Plate.
No. 110, 15 Jewels, Hunting, ¾ Bridge.
No. 111, 15 Jewels, Open Face, ¾ Plate.
No. 120, 17 Jewels, Hunting, ¾ Bridge.
No. 121, 17 Jewels, Open Face, ¾ Plate.

Model 2, Open Face, ¾ Plate.   **Model 2**, Hunting, ¾ Bridge.

0 SIZE—MODEL 3
Both Open Face and Hunting have second hand
Grade Numbers and Description of Movements

No. 151—21J, Open Face, Bridge Model.
No. 150—21J, Hunting, Bridge Model.
No. 121—17J, Open Face, Bridge Model.
No. 120—17J, Hunting, Bridge Model.

Model 3, Open Face, Bridges.   **Model 3**, Hunting, Bridges.

Example of a basic original **J. P. Stevens** movement, 18 size, 15 jewels, note patented eccentric style regulator, serial number 65.

J.P. Stevens Watch Co. movement by Waltham, 18 size, 11 jewels, serial number 1,240,058.

J. P. STEVENS & CO.
Atlanta, Georgia
1882 - 1887

In mid-1881 J. P. Stevens bought part of the Springfield Watch Co. of Massachusetts; and some unfinished watch components from E. F. Bowman. He set up his watchmaking firm above his jewelry store in Atlanta, Ga., and started to produce the Bowman unfinished watches which were 16 size and 18 size, to which was added the "Stevens Patent Regulator." This regulator is best described as a simple disc attached to the plate which has an eccentric groove cut for the arm of the regulator to move in. This regulator is a prominent feature of the J. P. Stevens, and only the top is jeweled. These watches were 16S, ¾ plate, stem wind and had a nickel plate with damaskeening. The pallets were equidistant locking and needed greater accuracy in manufacturing. About 50 of these watches were made. A line of gilt movements was added. The pallet and fork are made of one piece aluminum. The aluminum was combined with 1/10 copper and formed an exceedingly tough metal which will not rust or become magnetized. The lever of this watch is only one-third the weight of a steel lever. The aluminum lever affords the least possible resistance for overcoming inertia in transmitting power from the escape wheel to the balance. In 1884, the company was turning out about ten watches a day at a price of $20 to $100 each. In the spring of 1887 the company failed. Only 174 true Stevens watches were made, but other watches carried the J. P. Stevens name.

16 TO 18 SIZE

Grade or Name — Description		Avg	Ex-Fn	Mint
Original Model, Serial Nos. 1 to 174 . . . . ★ ★ ★		$2,000	$2,500	$3,000

Grade or Name—Description	Avg	Ex-Fn	Mint
Original Model, Serial Nos. 1 to 174 with original J. P. Stevens 18K case	$2,700	$3,200	$4,000
Aurora, 17J .... ★	350	400	525
Chronograph, 17J, Swiss made	500	600	700
Columbus W. Co., 17J .... ★	400	450	575
Elgin, 17J .... ★	300	350	425
Hamilton, 17J .... ★	400	450	525
Hampden, 17J .... ★	300	350	425
Illinois, 17J...................................... ★	600	650	725
N. Y. W. Co., 17J, Full Plate, S#s range in 500s	700	750	825
N. Y. W. Co. "Bond" Model, S#s range in 500s .... ★ ★	850	950	1,100
A. Potter, 14K case, Swiss made	2,000	3,000	4,000
Rockford, 15J, Full Plate, HC...................... ★	400	450	625
16S Swiss, 17J, Longines .... ★	175	200	250
Waltham, 17J.................................... ★	400	450	625

J.P. Stevens movement made by **Hampden**, 18 size, 17 jewels, note eccentric style regulator, serial number 1695.

J.P. Stevens Watch Co., 6 size, 11 jewels, exposed winding gears.

6 SIZE

Grade or Name — Description	Avg	Ex-Fn	Mint
Ladies Model, 15J, LS, HC, 14K .... ★	$500	$575	$650
Ladies Model, 15J, LS, GF case, HC.................. ★	225	275	350
Ladies Model, 15J, LS, GF cases, OF .... ★	200	250	325
Ladies Model, 15J, LS, GF cases, Swiss made	175	225	325

SUFFOLK WATCH CO.
Waltham, Massachusetts
c. 1899 - 1901

The Suffolk Watch Company officially succeeded the Columbia Watch Company in March 1901. However, the Suffolk 0-size, 7-jewel nickel movement with lever escapement was being manufactured in the Columbia factory before the end of 1899. More than 25,000 movements were made. The factory was closed after it was purchased by the Keystone Watch Case Company on May 17, 1901. The machinery was moved to the nearby factory of the United States Watch Company (purchased by Keystone in April 1901), where it was used to make the United States Watch Company's 0-size movement, introduced in April 1902.

Both the Columbia Watch Company and the Suffolk Watch Company made 0-size movements only.

Suffolk Watch Co., 0 Size, 7 jewels, serial number 216,841.

Grade or Name — Description	Avg	Ex-Fn	Mint
0S, 7J, NI, HC .... ★ ★	$400	$450	$550

SETH THOMAS WATCH CO.
Thomaston, Connecticut
1883 - 1915

Seth Thomas is a very prominent clock manufacturer, but in early 1883, the company made a decision to manufacture watches. The watches were first placed on the market in 1885. They were 18S, open face, stem wind, ¾ plate, and the escapement was between the plates. The compensating balance was set well below the normal. They were 11J, 16,000 bpm train, but soon went to 18,000 or quick train. In 1886, the company started to make higher grade watches and produced four grades: 7J, 11J, 15J, and 17J. That year the output was 100 watches a day.

SETH THOMAS ESTIMATED SERIAL NUMBERS
AND PRODUCTION DATES

Date	Serial No.	Date	Serial No.	Date	Serial No.	Date	Serial No.
1885	5,000	1893	510,000	1901	1,230,000	1909	2,500,000
1886	20,000	1894	600,000	1902	1,320,000	1910	2,725,000
1887	40,000	1895	690,000	1903	1,410,000	1911	2,950,000
1888	80,000	1896	780,000	1904	1,500,000	1912	3,175,000
1889	150,000	1897	870,000	1905	1,700,000	1913	3,490,000
1890	235,000	1898	960,000	1906	1,900,000	1914	3,600,000
1891	330,000	1899	1,050,000	1907	2,100,000		
1892	420,000	1900	1,140,000	1908	2,300,000		

S. Thomas movement, 18 size, 7 jewels, model 9, serial number 574,714.

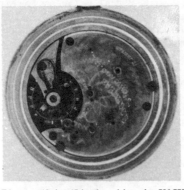

Edgemere, 18 size, 17 jewels, serial number 786,773.

18 SIZE

Grade or Name — Description	Avg	Ex-Fn	Mint
Century, 7J, OF	$50	$75	$125
Century, 7J, HC	75	100	150
Century, 15J, OF	50	75	125
Century, 15J, HC	75	100	150
Chautauqua, 15J, GJS, M#5	125	150	225
Eagle Series, No. 36, 7J, OF	50	75	125
Eagle Series, No. 37, 7J, HC	75	100	150
Eagle Series, No. 106, 11J, OF	50	75	125
Eagle Series, No. 107, 11J, HC	75	100	150
Eagle Series, No. 206, 15J, OF	50	75	125

Liberty, 18 size, 7 jewels, hunting or open face, eagle on movement.

Maiden Lane, 18 size, 28 jewels, gold jewel settings, Adj5p, dated 8,1.99. No serial number.

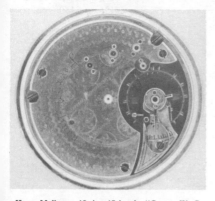

Henry Molineux, 18 size, 17 jewels, "Corona W. Co. USA" on dial, open face, serial number 54,951.

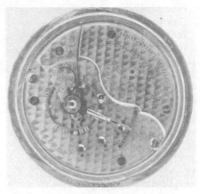

Seth Thomas, 18 size, 23 jewels, gold jewel settings, adjusted, serial number 298,333.

Grade or Name—Description	Avg	Ex-Fn	Mint
Eagle Series, No. 207, 15J, HC	$100	$125	$175
Eagle Series, No. 210, 17J, OF	75	100	150
Eagle Series, No. 211, 17J, HC	150	175	225
Eagle Series, 17J, NI, ¾, OF...........................	75	100	150
Edgemere, 11J	50	75	125
Edgemere, 17J	75	100	150
Keywind M#4, 7J, 11J, & 15J,¾	250	300	375
Lakeshore, 17J, GJS, ADJ, NI	200	250	300
Liberty, 7J, ¾, eagle on back plate	75	100	125
Maiden Lane, 17J, GJS, DR, Adj.6P, NI, marked ... ★ ★	900	1,100	1,400
Maiden Lane, 19J, GJS, DR, Adj.6P, NI, marked . ★ ★ ★	1,000	1,200	1,500
Maiden Lane, 21J, GJS, DR, Adj.6P, NI, marked ..... ★	1,000	1,200	1,500
Maiden Lane, 24J, GJS, DR, Adj.6P, marked ..... ★ ★ ★	1,500	1,700	2,000
Maiden Lane, 25J, GJS, DR, Adj.6P, NI, marked ... ★ ★	2,400	2,500	3,000
Maiden Lane, 28J, GJS, DR, Adj.5P, NI, marked ★ ★ ★ ★	15,000	18,000	25,000
Henry Molineux, M#3, 17J, ¾, GJS, ADJ .... ★ ★	500	550	650
Henry Molineux, M#2, 17J, GJS, ADJ .... ★ ★	500	550	650
Henry Molineux, M#2, 20J, GJS, ADJ .... ★ ★ ★	1,000	1,200	1,500
Monarch Watch Co., 7-15J, 2-tone	75	100	150
Republic USA, 7J, OF	50	75	125
S. Thomas, 7J, ¾, multi-color dial....................	150	200	275
S. Thomas, 7J, ¾	50	75	125
S. Thomas, 11J, ¾, HC	75	100	150
S. Thomas, 11J, ¾, OF................................	50	75	125
S. Thomas, 15J, ¾, HC	100	125	175
S. Thomas, 15J, ¾, gilded, OF	50	75	125
S. Thomas, 15J, ¾, OF................................	50	75	125
S. Thomas, 16J, ¾	75	100	150
S. Thomas, 17J, ¾, OF, nickel	100	125	175

Grade or Name—Description	Avg	Ex-Fn	Mint
S. Thomas, 17J, ¾, 2-Tone	$125	$150	$200
S. Thomas, 17J, ¾, OF, gilded	75	100	150
S. Thomas, 17J, ¾, HC	125	150	175
S. Thomas, 21J, GJS, DR, Adj.5P	275	325	400
S. Thomas, 23J, GJS, DR, Adj.5P .... ★★	800	1,000	1,300
20th Century (Wards), 11J	75	100	150
20th Century (Wards), 11J, 2-Tone	100	125	175
Wyoming Watch Co., 7J, OF.........................	125	150	200
33, 7J, ¾, gilded, OF	50	75	125
37, 7J, ¾, NI, HC	75	100	150
44, 11J, ¾, gilded, OF	50	75	125
47, 7J, gilded, FULL, OF	50	75	125
58, 11J, FULL, gilt, OF	50	75	125
70, 15J, ¾, gilded, OF	50	75	125
80, 17J, ¾, gilded, ADJ, HC.......................	75	100	150
101, 15J, ¾, gilded, ADJ, OF	50	75	125
149, 15J, gilded, FULL, OF	50	75	125
159, 15J, NI, FULL, OF	50	75	125
169, 17J, NI, FULL, OF	75	125	150
170, 15J, ¾, NI, OF	50	75	125
179, 17J, ¾, NI, ADJ, OF	75	125	150
180, 17J, ¾, NI, HC	75	125	150
182, 17J, DR, NI, FULL, OF	100	125	175
201, 15J, ¾, NI, ADJ, OF	75	100	150
245, 19J, GJS, 2-Tone, HC.........................	1,000	1,200	1,500
260, 21J, DR, Adj.6P, NI, FULL, OF.................	225	275	350
281-282, 17J, OF, LS, FULL, DR, Adj.3P, OF, 2-tone ...	150	175	225
382, 17J, OF, LS, FULL, DR, Adj.5P, OF, 2-tone.......	150	175	225

Centennial, 16 size, 7 jewels, three-quarter nickel plate.

Grade 36, 16 size, 7 jewels, open face, three-quarter nickel plate.

16 SIZE
(OF Only)

Grade or Name — Description	Avg	Ex-Fn	Mint
Centennial, 7J, ¾, NI, OF	$50	$60	$75
Locust, 7J, NI, ¾, OF	50	60	75
Locust, 17J, NI, ADJ, ¾, OF	75	100	175
Republic USA, 7J, OF	50	60	75
25, 7J, BRG, OF	50	60	75
26, 15J, BRG, GJS, OF	50	60	75
27, 17J, BRG, GJS, OF	50	60	75
28, 17J, BRG, Adj.3P, GJS, OF	75	100	150
326, 7J, ¾, NI, OF	50	60	75
328, 15J, ¾, NI, OF	50	60	75
332, 7J, ¾, NI, OF	50	60	75
334, 15J, NI, ADJ, ¾, DMK, OF	75	100	150
336, 17J, ADJ, ¾, DMK, OF	100	125	150

Seth Thomas, 12 size, 7 jewels, open face, pendant set.

Seth Thomas, 12 size, 17 jewels, gold jewel settings, gold center wheel, open face, Adj3p.

12 SIZE
(OF Only)

Grade or Name — Description	Avg	Ex-Fn	Mint
Republic USA, 7J, OF	$40	$50	$65
25, 7J, BRG, OF	40	50	65
26, 15J, BRG, GJS, OF	45	55	70
27, 17J, BRG, GJS, OF	50	60	75

Grade or Name—Description	Avg	Ex-Fn	Mint
28, 17J, OF, BRG, Adj.3P, GJS	$55	$65	$80
326, 7J, OF, ¾, NI	40	50	65
328, 15J, OF, ¾, NI	45	55	70

Example of a basic **Seth Thomas** movement, 6 size, 7 jewels, serial number 441,839. Sometimes appears in a 12 size case.

Grade 45, 6 size, 7 jewels, open face, three-quarter nickel plate.

6 SIZE
(Some 6 Size were used to fit 12 Size cases)

Grade or Name — Description	Avg	Ex-Fn	Mint
Century, 7J, NI, ¾	$45	$50	$65
Eagle Series, 7J, No. 45, ¾, NI, DMK, OF	55	60	75
Eagle Series, 7J, No. 205, ¾, HC	75	100	150
Eagle Series, 15J, No. 35, ¾, NI, DMK, OF	65	70	85
Eagle Series, 15J, No. 245, ¾, HC	75	100	150
Republic USA, 7J	45	50	65
Seth Thomas, 7J, ¾, HC, 14K, 26 DWT	250	275	325
Seth Thomas, 11J, ¾, HC	75	100	150
Seth Thomas, 11J, ¾, OF	45	55	65
35, 7J, HC, NI, DMK, ¾	45	55	65
119, 16J, HC, GJS, NI, DMK, ¾	100	125	175
205, 15J, HC	75	100	150
320, 7J, OF, NI, DMK, ¾	50	65	85
322, 15J, OF	55	60	70

NOTE: Add $25 for HC.

0 SIZE

Grade or Name — Description	Avg	Ex-Fn	Mint
Seth Thomas, 7J, OF, No. 1	$60	$70	$85
Seth Thomas, 7J, HC, No. 1	75	100	150
Seth Thomas, 15J, OF, GJS, No. 3	60	70	85
Seth Thomas, 15J, HC, No. 3	75	100	150
Seth Thomas, 17J, OF, GJS, PS, No. 9	60	70	85
Seth Thomas, 17J, HC, GJS, PS, No. 9	75	100	150

NOTE: Add $25 for HC.

SETH THOMAS WATCH CO.
IDENTIFICATION OF MOVEMENTS
BY MODEL NUMBER

How to Identify Your Watch: Compare the movement of your watch with the illustrations in this section. Upon matching the movement exactly, the model number and size can be determined. While comparing, note the location of the balance, jewels, screws, gears, and type of back plate (Full, ¾, Bridge) which will be clues in identifying the movement you have. Having determined the size and model number, you can now find your watch in the main price listing by name or number (which is engraved on the movement).

Model 1, 18 size, Open Face

Model 2, 18 size, Hunting

Model 3, 18 size, Open Face

Model 4, 18 size, Key Wind

Model 5, 18 size, Maiden Lane Series, Open Face.

Model 6, 18 Size, Open Face

Model 7 & 9, 18 size

Model 8, 18 size

Model 10, 18 size, Open Face

Model 11, 18 size, Hunting

Model 13, 18 size, Hunting   16 Size

16 Size, Open Face   12 Size, Open Face

6 Size, Open face   Model 14, 6 size   Model 16 & 17, 6 size

TREMONT WATCH CO.
Boston, Massachusetts
1864 - 1866

In 1864 A. L. Dennison thought that if he could produce a good movement at a reasonable price, there would be a ready market for it. Dennison went to Switzerland to find a supplier of cheap parts, as arbors were too high in America. He found a source for parts, mainly the train and escapement and the balance. About 600 sets were to be furnished. In 1865, the first movements were ready for the market. They were 18S, key wind, fully jeweled, and were engraved "Tremont Watch Co." In 1886, the company moved from Boston to Melrose. Another 18S was made, and the company made its own train and escapement. The watches were engraved "Melrose Watch Co., Melrose, Mass." The Tremont Watch Co. produced about 5,000 watches before being sold to the English Watch Co.

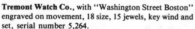

Tremont Watch Co., with "Washington Street Boston" engraved on movement, 18 size, 15 jewels, key wind and set, serial number 5,264.

Example of a basic Tremont movement, 18 size, 15 jewels, key wind & set, serial number 8,875.

Grade or Name — Description		Avg	Ex-Fn	Mint
18S, 7J, KW, KS	★ ★	$250	$275	$350
18S, 11J, KW, KS	★ ★	250	275	350
18S, 15J, KW, KS, Silveroid, recased	★	100	150	200
18S, 15J, KW, KS, gilded	★	250	275	350
18S, 15J, KW, KS, HC, 14K	★	650	675	750
18S, 15J, KW, KS, gilded, Washington Street	★ ★	350	375	450
18S, 17J, KW, KS, gilded	★	300	325	400
18S, 15J, KW, KS from back, ¾ plate	★ ★ ★	1,500	1,700	2,000

NOTE: Watches listed in this book are priced at the retail level, as complete watches having an original 14k gold-filled case, an original white enamel single sunk dial, and with the entire original movement in good working order with no repairs needed, unless otherwise noted.

TRENTON WATCH CO.
Trenton, New Jersey
1885 - 1908

Trenton watches were marketed under the following labels: Trenton, Ingersoll, Fortuna, Illinois Watch Case Company, Calumet U.S.A., Locomotives Special, Marvel Watch Co., and Reliance Watch Co.

Serial numbers started at 2,001 and ended at 4,100,000. Total production was about 1,934,000.

CHRONOLOGY OF THE DEVELOPMENT OF TRENTON WATCH CO.:
New Haven Watch Co., New Haven, Conn. — 1883-1887
Trenton Watch Co., Trenton, N. J. — 1887-1908
Sold to Ingersoll — 1908-1922

TRENTON MODELS AND GRADES
With Years of Manufacture and Serial Numbers

Date	Numbers	Size	Model	Date	Numbers	Size	Model
				1900-1903	2,000,001-2,075,000	6	2
1887-1889	2,001- 61,000	18	1	1902-1905	2,075,001-2,160,000	6	3 LS
1889-1891	64,001- 135,000	18	2			12	2 LS
1891-1898	135,001- 201,000 *1	18	3	1905-1907	2,160,001-2,250,000	6	3 PS
1899-1904	201,001- 300,000	18	6			12	2 PS
1891-1900	300,001- 500,000	18	4	1899-1902	2,500,001-2,600,000	3/0	1
1892-1897	500,001- 600,000	6	1	ca. 1906	2,800,001-2,850,000	6	3 PS
1894-1899	650,001- 700,000	16	1			12	2 PS
1898-1900	700,001- 750,000	6	2	1900-1904	3,000,001-3,139,000	16	2
1900-1904	750,001- 800,000 *2	18	4	1903-1907	3,139,001-3,238,000	16	3 OF
1896-1900	850,001- 900,000	12	1	1903-1907	3,500,001-3,600,000	16	3 HC
1898-1903	900,001-1,100,000	18	5	1905-1907	4,000,001-4,100,000	0	1
1902-1907	1,300,001-1,400,000	18	6				

1 *7 jewel grades made only during 1891; 9 jewel chronograph made 1891-1898.*
2 *A few examples are KWKS for export to England.*

Trenton movement, 18 size, 4 jewels, serial number 4,744.

Trenton movement, 18 size, 7 jewels, 4th model, serial number 788,313.

18 SIZE

Grade or Name — Description	Avg	Ex-Fn	Mint
M#1-2, gilded, OF .... ★	$150	$175	$250
M#3, 7J, ¾	50	75	125
M#3, 9J, ¾	50	75	125
M#4, 7J, FULL	50	75	125
M#4, 11J, FULL	50	75	125
M#4, 15J, FULL	50	75	125
M#4-5, FULL, OF, NI	50	75	125
New Haven Watch Co. style, M#1, 4J .... ★ ★ ★	250	325	450
Trenton, 7J, KW, KS .... ★	225	300	425

Note: Add $25 to value of above watches in hunting case.

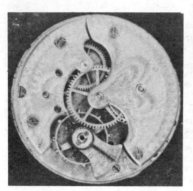 

Trenton movement, 18 size, 7 jewels, serial number 148,945.

Chronograph, 16 size, 9 jewels, third model; start, stop & fly back, sweep second hand.

16 SIZE

Grade or Name — Description	Avg	Ex-Fn	Mint
M#1-2, 7J, ¾, NI, OF	$50	$75	$125
M#3, 7J, 3F BRG	50	75	125
M#3, 11J, 3F BRG	50	75	125
M#3, 15J, 3F BRG	50	75	125
7,11,15J, 3F BRG, NI	50	75	125
Chronograph, 9J, start, stop, & fly back	150	175	225
Convertible Model, 7J, OF	100	125	175
Grade #30 & 31, 7J	50	75	125
Grade #35, 36 & 38, 11J	50	75	125
Grade #45, 16J	75	100	150
Grade #125, 12J	50	75	125
Ingersoll Trenton, 7J, 3F BRG	50	75	125

Ingersoll Trenton movement, 16 size, 19 jewels, three-fingered bridge, adjusted, serial number 3,419,771.

Ingersoll Trenton movement, 16 size, 12 jewels; "Edgemere" engraved on movement.

Grade or Name—Description	Avg	Ex-Fn	Mint
Ingersoll Trenton, 15J, 3F BRG, NI, ADJ	$75	$100	$150
Ingersoll Trenton, 17J, 3F BRG, NI, ADJ	75	100	150
Ingersoll Trenton, 19J, 3F BRG, NI, Adj.5P	150	175	225
Peerless, 7J, SW, LS	50	65	80
Reliance, 7J	50	65	80

Note: Add $25 to value of above watches in hunting case.

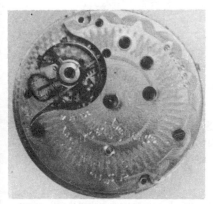

Reliance, 16 size, 7 jewels, serial number 241,265.

Trenton movement, convertible model, 16 size, 7 jewels.

12 SIZE

Grade or Name — Description	Avg	Ex-Fn	Mint
"Fortuna," 7J, BRG	$40	$50	$65

Grade or Name—Description	Avg	Ex-Fn	Mint
M#1, 7J, ¾	$40	$50	$65
Monogram, 7J, SW	30	40	55

Note: Add $25 to value of above watches in hunting case.

Example of a basic **Trenton Watch Co.** movement, 6 size, 7 jewels, open face & hunting, nickel damaskeened.

6 SIZE

Grade or Name — Description	Avg	Ex-Fn	Mint
7J, ¾, NI	$30	$40	$55
7J, 3F BRG	30	40	55
15J, 3F BRG	40	50	65

Note: Add $25 to value of above watches in hunting case.

0 SIZE

Grade or Name — Description	Avg	Ex-Fn	Mint
7J, 3F BRG	$40	$50	$65
15J, 3F BRG	50	60	75

Note: Add $25 to value of above watches in hunting case.

UNITED STATES WATCH CO.
Marion, New Jersey
1865 - 1877

The United States Watch Company was chartered in 1865, and the factory building was started in August 1865 and was completed in 1866. The first watch, called the "Frederic Atherton," was not put on the market until July 1867. It was America's **first** mass-produced stem winding watch. This first grade was 18S, 19J, full plate and a gilt finish movement. A distinctive feature of the company's full plate movements was the butter-fly shaped patented opening in the plate which allowed escapement inspection. That same year a second grade called the "Fayette Stratton" was introduced. It was also a gilt finish, full plate movement. Most of these were 15J, but some of the very early examples have been noted in 17J. In 1868 the "George Channing," "Edwin Rollo," and "Marion Watch Co." grades were introduced. All were 18S, 15J, full plate movements in a gilt finish. In February 1869 the gilt version of the "United States Watch Co." grade was introduced. It was 18S, 19J, full plate and was the company's first entry into the prestige market. Later that year the company introduced their first nickel grade, a 19J, 18S, full plate movement called the "A. H. Wallis." About this same time, in December 1869, they introduced America's most expensive watch, the first nickel, 19J, 18S, full plate "United States Watch Co." grade. Depending on case weight, these prestige watches retailed between $500 and $600, more than the average man earned in a year at that time. The company also introduced damaskeening to the American market; first on gilt movements and later on the nickel grades. The United States and Wallis 19J prestige grades were beautifully finished with richly enameled engraving including a variety of unique designs on the balance cock. It is significant to note that **no** solid gold trains have been seen with these prestige items in the extant examples presently known.

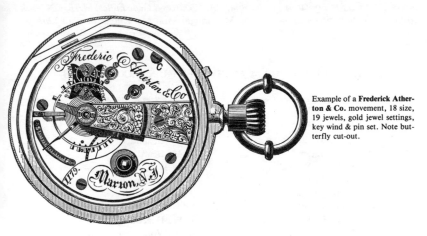

Example of a **Frederick Atherton & Co.** movement, 18 size, 19 jewels, gold jewel settings, key wind & pin set. Note butterfly cut-out.

In 1870 the company introduced their first watch for ladies, a 10S, 15J, ¼ plate, cock & bridge movement which was made to their specifications in Switzerland. This model was first introduced in two grades, the "R. F. Pratt" and "Chas. G. Knapp," both in a 15J, gilt finish movement. Later it was offered in a high grade, 19J "I. H. Wright" nickel finish movement. During 1870 and 1871 several other full plate grades in both gilt and nickel finish were introduced. In 1871 development on a new line of full plate, ¾ plate, and ¼ plate & bridge was started but not introduced to the market until late in 1872 and early in 1873. The 10S and 16S new grades in ¼ plate and bridge were probably delayed well into 1873 and were not available long before the "Panic of 1873" started in September; this explains their relative scarcity.

By July 1874 the "Panic" had taken its toll and it was necessary for the company to reorganize as the Marion Watch Company, a name formerly used for one of their grades. At this time jewel count, finish standards, and prices were lowered on the full plate older grades, but this proved to be a mistake. That same year they introduced a cased watch called the "North Star," their cheapest watch at $15 retail. The year of 1875 hit the watch industry the hardest; price cutting was predatory and the higher priced watches of the United States Watch Co. were particulary vulnerable. Further lowering of finish standards and prices did not help and in 1876 the company was once again reorganized into the Empire City Watch Co. and their products were displayed at the Centennial that year. The Centennial Exhibition was not enough to save the faltering company and they finally closed their doors in 1877. The Howard brothers of Fredonia, New York (Independent and Fredonia Watch Co.) purchased most of the remaining movement stock and machinery. In the ten year period of movement production, current statistical studies indicate an estimated production of only some 60,000 watches, much smaller than the number deduced from the serial numbers assigned up to as high as 289,000.

NOTE: *The above historical data and estimated production figures are based on data included in the new NAWCC book* **MARION, A History of the United States Watch Company** *by William Muir and Bernard Kraus. This definitive work is available from NAWCC, Inc., 514 Poplar St., Columbia, PA. (Courtesy, Gene Fuller, MARION book editor.) This book is recommended by Mr. Shugart and Mr. Engle for your library.*

EMPIRE CITY W. CO. & EQUIVALENT U.S.W.CO. GRADES

Empire City W. Co.	United States W. Co.
W. S. Wyse	A. H. Wallis
L. W. Frost	Henry Randel
Cyrus H. Loutrel	Wm. Alexander
J. L. Ogden	S. M. Beard
E. F. C. Young	John W. Lewis
D. C. Wilcox	George Channing
Henry Harper	Asa Fuller
Jesse A. Dodd	Edwin Rollo
E. C. Hine	J. W. Deacon
New York Belle	A. J. Wood
The Champion	G. A. Read
Black Diamond	Young America

NOTE: *Courtesy Gene Fuller, NAWCC "MARION" book editor.*

United States Watch Co. movement, 18 size, 19 jewels, gold jewel settings, key wind. Their highest grade watch.

United States Watch Co. double sunk dial, hunting, note pin setting at 4 o'clock.

MARION
18 SIZE
(All with Butterfly Cutout
Except for ¾ Plate)

Grade or Name — Description	Avg	Ex-Fn	Mint
Wm. Alexander, 15J, NI, KW, HC....................	$275	$350	$425
Wm. Alexander, 15J, NI, KW, OF	200	250	325
Wm. Alexander, 15J, NI, SW, OF	225	275	350
Frederic Atherton & Co., 15J, SW, gilded..............	250	325	400
Frederic Atherton & Co., 17J, KW, gilded, HC..........	300	350	425
Frederic Atherton & Co., 17J, KW, gilded, OF	250	300	375
Frederic Atherton & Co., 17J, SW, gilded, HC	300	350	425
Frederic Atherton & Co., 17J, SW, gilded, OF	250	325	400

U.S. Watch Co., dial and movement, 18 size, 20 jewels, hunting case, ¾ plate, engraved on movement "N.D. Godfrey," serial number 72,042. Painted on the dial "New York 1873." The dial consists of day-date-month and moon phases.

Grade or Name—Description	Avg	Ex-Fn	Mint
Frederic Atherton & Co., 19J, SW, gilded, ... ★★★★	$800	$1,000	$1,300
Frederic Atherton & Co., 19J, KW, gilded .... ★★	600	700	850
BC&M R.R., 11J, KW........................ ★★★★	1,600	1,800	2,100
BC&M R.R., 15J, gilded, KW .... ★★★★	1,600	1,800	2,100
S. M. Beard, 15J, KW, NI, OF	250	300	375
S. M. Beard, 15J, SW, NI, OF	250	300	375
S. M. Beard, 15J, SW or KW, HC	300	350	425
Centennial Phil., 11-15J, SW or KW, NI........ ★★★★	1,800	2,000	2,300
George Channing, 15J, KW, NI.......................	250	300	375
George Channing, 15J, KW, gilded	225	275	325
George Channing, 15J, KW, NI, ¾ Plate .... ★★	350	400	475
George Channing, 17J, KW, NI.......................	275	325	400
J. W. Deacon, 11-13J, KW, gilded	175	225	300
J. W. Deacon, 15J, KW, gilded	175	225	300
J. W. Deacon, 11-15J, KW, ¾ Plate .... ★	275	325	400
Empire City Watch Co., 11J, SW, no cutout	175	225	300
Empire City Watch Co., 15J, SW, NI, no cutout	200	250	325
Empire Combination Timer, 11J, FULL, time & distance on dial..	400	500	650
Empire Combination Timer, 15J, ¾, time & distance on dial..	600	750	1,000
Fellows, 15J, NI, KW	400	450	525
Benjamin Franklin, 15J, KW	400	450	525
Asa Fuller, 7-11J, gilded, KW	200	225	275
Asa Fuller, 15J, gilded, KW	200	225	275
Asa Fuller, 15J, gilded, KW, ¾ Plate .... ★★	300	325	350
N. D. Godfrey, 20J, NI, ¾ plate, day date month, moon phases, c. 1873, HC, 18K .... ★★★★	4,000	5,000	6,000
John W. Lewis, 15J, NI, KW.........................	225	275	350
John W. Lewis, 15J, NI, SW	250	300	375

Edwin Rollo, 18 size, 15 jewels, gilded, key wind & set, note butterfly cut-out, serial number 110,214.

Marion Watch Co. personalized Watch, 18 size, about 15 jewels, pin set, note butterfly cut-out, serial number 106,761.

Empire City Watch Co. on movement, **U.S. Marion Watch Co.** on dial, 18 size, 15 jewels, note no butterfly cut-out on this model.

United States Watch Co., 18 size, 19 jewels, gold jewel settings, key wind & pin set, serial number 24,054.

Grade or Name—Description		Avg	Ex-Fn	Mint
John W. Lewis, 15J, NI, ¾ Plate	★★	$350	$400	$475
Marion Watch Co., 11J, KW, gilded		200	250	325
Marion Watch Co., 15J, KW, gilded		200	250	325
Marion Watch Co., 15J, SW, gilded, ¾ Plate	★★	300	350	425
Marion Watch Co., 17-19J, KW, gilded	★	300	350	425
N.J. R.R.&T. Co., 15J, gilded, KW		1,200	1,400	1,700
Newspaper Special Order, 11-15J, gilded, SW or KW		325	375	450
North Star, 7J, KW, NI case		300	350	425
North Star, 7J, SW, KS		300	350	425
North Star, 7J, ¾ Plate		325	375	450
Pennsylvania R.R., 15J, NI, KW	★★★★	2,500	2,800	2,900
Personalized Watches, 7-11J, KW, ¾ Plate	★	250	300	375
Personalized Watches, 11J, KW, gilded	★	250	300	375
Personalized Watches, 15J, KW, gilded	★	250	300	375
Personalized Watches, 15J, KW, NI	★	275	325	400
Personalized Watches, 15J, KW, ¾ Plate	★	300	350	425
Personalized Watches, 19J, KW, Full Plate	★	400	450	525
Henry Randel, 15J, KW, NI		250	300	375
Henry Randel, 15J, SW, NI		250	300	375
Henry Randel, 15J, ¾ Plate	★★	350	400	475
Henry Randel, 17J, KW, NI	★	275	325	400
G. A. Read, 7J, gilded, KW		200	250	325
G. A. Read, 7J, ¾ Plate		300	350	425
Edwin Rollo, 11J, KW, gilded		200	250	325
Edwin Rollo, 15J, KW, gilded		200	250	325
Edwin Rollo, 15J, SW, gilded		200	250	325
Edwin Rollo, 15J, ¾ Plate	★	300	350	425
Royal Gold, 11J, KW		200	250	300
Royal Gold, 15J, KW		300	350	425
Royal Gold, 15J, ¾ Plate	★★	400	450	525

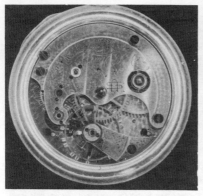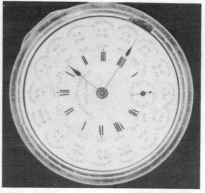

A.H. Wallis on movement, **Empire City Watch Co.** on dial, 18 size, 19 jewels, three-quarter plate, hunting. This combination timer has listed on the dial, 16 cities showing the time of day and distance in comparison with New York City, serial number 54,409.

Grade or Name—Description	Avg	Ex-Fn	Mint
Rural New York, 15J, gilded	$250	$300	$375
Fayette Stratton, 11J, gilded	250	300	375
Fayette Stratton, 15J, KW, gilded	250	300	375
Fayette Stratton, 15J, SW, gilded	250	300	325
Fayette Stratton, 17J, KW, gilded	275	325	400
Fayette Stratton, 17J, SW, gilded	300	350	425
Union Pacific R.R., 15J, KW, gilded ★★★★	1,800	2,000	2,300
United States Watch Co., 15J, NI, KW	500	550	625
United States Watch Co., 15J, NI, SW	600	650	725
United States Watch Co., 15J, ¾ Plate, NI	600	650	725
United States Watch Co., 15J, ¾ Plate, gilded	600	650	725
United States Watch Co., 19J, GJS, Adj.5P, 18K HC, dial mvt. & case all marked, Pin Set, SW ★★★	3,500	4,000	4,500
United States Watch Co., 19J, NI, KW ★★	750	950	1,200
United States Watch Co., 19J, NI, SW ★★	900	1,100	1,350
A. H. Wallis, 15J, KW, NI	250	300	375
A. H. Wallis, 15J, SW, NI	250	300	375
A. H. Wallis, 17J, KW, NI	275	325	400
A. H. Wallis, 17J, SW, NI	300	350	425
A. H. Wallis, 19J, KW, NI ★★★	600	650	725
A. H. Wallis, 19J, SW, NI ★★★	650	700	775
D. C. Wilcox, 15J, SW, no butterfly cutout	250	300	375
I. H. Wright, 11J, KW, gilded	225	275	350
I. H. Wright, 15J, KW, gilded	225	275	350

Note: 18S, ¾ plate are scarce. Add $25 to $50 for listed open face watches with hunting cases.

NOTE: Watches listed in this book are priced at the retail level, as complete watches having an original 14k gold-filled case, an original white enamel single sunk dial, and with the entire original movement in good working order with no repairs needed, unless otherwise noted.

Left: Herman Von Der Heydt. Approximately thirty-five of these self winding watches were made using only the tools from his shop in Chicago. The gilt-lever movement is jeweled throughout with gold chatons. Note the crescent shape weight that swings between the end of a leaf spring to stop and buffer the winding mechanism; patented Feb. 19, 1884. Right: Geo. A. Bowen, Boston, MA. This pocket chronometer employs a spring detent escapement and fusee movement. George Bowen made watches during the mid 19th century.

Left: H. Mitchell, New York. This gilt movement uses a verge escapement and chain-driven fusee. Note the disc regulator under the hand-pierced cock; serial #548, ca. 1790. Right: Hamilton, 36 size, 21 jewels, pocket chronometer with up-and-down, 56-hour power reserve wind indicator. Note pin set next to the pendant stem; *U.S. NAVY* engraved on the sterling silver case, ca. 1912.

Left: Classic enamel scene depicting a lady in a chariot drawn by two white stallions on a deep blue background; ornamental paste stones outline the chariot, ca. 1800, valued at $6,000. Right: 18k gold Swiss enamel watch signed "*L. EPINE*." Multicolored enamel grouping of musical instruments and detailed flowers and leaves; the outer edge is painted with light turquoise-blue coloration, ca. 1850, valued at about $2,800.

Left: Harry Potter, London, ca. 1790. This 20k gold case is skeletonized between the characters and chased with repoussé-style work, featuring five detailed figures, flowers, and scrolls, valued at $5,500. Right: Large, enamel, 18k gold verge fusee watch, ca. 1815. Deep blue enamel background and numerous golden crescent shape forms in an interesting mosaic pattern with bright emerald green tulip shapes within a crescent; gold and green leaves and flowers painted in the center, valued at $3,000.

Left: Swiss, 18k gold, quarter hour repeater chronograph with unique, secret, hidden erotic automatons. The finely painted multicolored enamel erotic scene features a man and woman in a country kitchen, ca. 1900, valued at $2,500. Right: 18k gold Swiss repeater with two automatons. The 175-year-old white porcelain center dial and dark blue porcelain outer ring with multicolored 18k gold Roman soldiers, one with a harp, the other with a horn of plenty, striking on two bells hours and quarters on request, 54mm, valued at about $6,000.

Left: Royal blue, enamel guilloched pattern on front and back, using large rose-cut diamonds, on an 18k gold hunter case, 26 jeweled Swiss minute repeater, ca. 1910, valued at about $12,000. Right: Swiss, 18k, full-color enamel portrait of a maharaja. Around the outer edge perimeter, the case is carved fine with lines in a swirl pattern, ca. 1890, valued at about $3,500.

Left: Patek Philippe & Co., 18k gold, thin dress model with genuine blue lapis inserts at each side and 18k gold strap, ca. 1970s, valued at about $15,000. Right: Lucien Piccard 14k gold rope bezel with gold lace picture frame, antique style case, made by PAUL DITISHEIM, 25mm x 30mm, ca. 1950s.

Left: H. Moser & Cie. Swiss, "signal corps U.S.A.," hinged center wire lugs, 35mm, ca. 1920s. Right: Bulova Accutron, heavy, heart shape 14k case, "space-view," waterproof, see-through tuning fork movement, 32mm, ca. 1970s.

Left: Corum 18k white gold "ROLLS ROYCE" auto grill style watch, 28mm x 30mm, ca. 1980s. Right: Rolex "DAYTONA" stainless steel "COSMOGRAPH" chronograph with round pushers, oyster, black enamel dial with three subsidiary registers, 35mm, ca. 1986.

Left: Vacheron & Constantin 18k gold textured case and dial with center seconds, 35mm. Right: Hamilton "POLARIS" electric model 14k gold case, ca. 1960.

Left: Patek Philippe & Co. 18k gold chronograph, two registers, 23 jewels, made April 1949. Right: Patek Philippe & Co. 18k flared case, faceted glass crystal, ca. 1940s.

Left: International Watch Co. Schaffhausen "DA VINCI." Very complicated wristwatch, round pushers (water resistant), automatic chronograph, perpetual calendar with day, date, month, moonphase, and year, three registers for chronograph, huge 3 oz. 18k gold case, 50mm, ca. 1980s. Right: Rolex 14k rose gold bubble-back style case, oyster perpetual with center seconds, ca. 1940.

Left: Waltham multicolored dial and Riverside movement; 18k watch is case designed, cast and finished by Rolland Fischer, Boulder Co. Right: Hamilton "FLINTRIDGE" 14k gold hunter style case. The lid covering is opened by a spring-loaded lug in upper right-hand corner, 19 jewels, model #979 and 17j. 987, ca. 1935.

Left: Cartier "Santos" stainless steel case and bracelet with 18k gold features, automatic and date, 28mm, ca. 1980. Right: Rolex 18k gold moonphase perpetual with day and month windows and date chapter, 35mm, ca. 1950s.

Left: Violin form, 18k gold enamel watch, 65mm top to bottom and 32mm wide, deep red wood grain finished enamel work with gold accents and black musical notation; golden wire strings are suspended above a black enamel neck, ca. 1820, valued at $7,000. Right: Scarab form enamel watch, length 55mm, 25mm across. The enameled gold, deep red wings are hinged to open and reveal the dial; wings are ornately encrusted with numerous large diamonds, and eyes are accented by small emeralds with a larger emerald on top head area, ca. 1850, valued at $8,500.

Left: Leaf form, enamel, 18k gold cased watch, 37mm long. The heart shape, deeply carved case is shaded with various colors of green and brown, ca. 1840, valued at $3,500. Right: 18k gold, enamel basket form pendant watch. The upper heart shape case is finished in multicolored enamel roses, flowers, and leaves; the basket is featured with a fancy, twisted gold style handle, 30mm long, ca. 1850, valued at $3,500.

16 SIZE
¼ Plate

Grade or Name — Description	Avg	Ex-Fn	Mint
S. M. Beard, 15J, NI, KW, ¼ Plate............ ★ ★ ★	$400	$450	$525
John W. Lewis, 15J, ¼ Plate, NI, KW......... ★ ★ ★ ★	400	450	525
Personalized Watches, 15J, ¼ Plate, NI, SW.... ★ ★ ★ ★	400	450	525
Edwin Rollo, 15J, ¼ Plate, KW .... ★ ★ ★ ★	400	450	525
United States Watch Co., 15J, ¼ Plate, NI, SW. ★ ★ ★ ★	600	700	850
A. H. Wallis, 19J, NI, SW, ¼ Plate .... ★ ★ ★ ★	600	700	850

Note: 16S, ¼ plate are the scarcest of the U.S.W.Co.-Marion watches.

Asa Fuller, 16 size, 15 jewels, stem wind, one-quarter plate, serial number 280,018.

United States Watch Co., 14 size, 15 jewels, three-quarter plate, engraved on movement "Royal Gold American Watch, New York, Extra Jeweled."

14 SIZE
¾ Plate

Grade or Name — Description	Avg	Ex-Fn	Mint
Centennial Phil., 11J, KW, ¾ Plate, gilded	$400	$500	$750
J. W. Deacon, 11J, ¾ Plate...........................	250	300	375
Asa Fuller, 15J, ¾ Plate......................... ★ ★	350	400	475
John W. Lewis, 15J, ¾ Plate, NI................. ★ ★	300	350	400
North Star, 15J, ¾ Plate.............................	250	300	375
Personalized Watches, 7-11J, ¾ Plate .... ★ ★	350	400	475
Edwin Rollo, 15J, ¾ Plate......................... ★	300	350	425
Royal Gold, 15J, ¾ Plate.......................... ★	350	400	475
Young America, 7J, ¾ Plate, gilded...................	300	350	425

10 SIZE
¼ Plate

Grade or Name — Description	Avg	Ex-Fn	Mint
Wm. Alexander, 15J, KW, NI	$200	$250	$325
S. M. Beard, 15J, KW, NI, ¼ Plate...................	200	250	325
Empire City Watch Co., 15J, KW.....................	200	250	325
Chas. G. Knapp, 15J, Swiss, ¼ Plate, KW..............	100	150	225
Personalized Watches, 11-15J, ¼ Plate	200	250	325
R. F. Pratt, 15J, Swiss, ¼ Plate, KW	100	150	225
Edwin Rollo, 11-15J, ¼ Plate .... ★	250	300	375
A. H. Wallis, 17-19J, KW, ¼ Plate	225	275	350
A. J. Wood, 15J, ¼ Plate, KW .... ★ ★ ★ ★	300	350	425
I. H. Wright, 19J, Swiss, NI, ¼ Plate, KW ...... ★ ★ ★	500	550	625

S. M. Beard, 10 size, 15 jewels, key wind, quarter plate, serial number 248,407.

Chas. G. Knapp, 10 size, 15 jewels, Swiss, quarter plate, key wind.

U. S. WATCH CO.
OF WALTHAM
Waltham, Massachusetts
1884 - 1905

The business was started as the Waltham Watch Tool Co. in 1879. It was organized as the United States Watch Co. in 1884. The first watches were 16S, ¾ plate pillar movement in three grades. They had a very wide mainspring barrel (the top was thinner than most) which was wedged up in the center to make room for the balance wheel. These watches are called dome watches and are hard to find. The fork was made of an aluminum alloy with a circular slot and a square ruby pin. The balance was gold at first, as was the movement which was a slow train, but the expansion balance was changed when they went to a quick train. The movement required a special case which proved unpopular. By 1887, some 3,000 watches had been made. A new model was then produced, a 16S movement that would fit a standard case. These movements were quick train expansion balance with standard type lever and ¾ plate pillar movement. The company had a top production of ten watches a day. It was sold to the E. Howard Watch Co. in 1903. The United States Watch Co. produced some 802,000 watches total. Its top grade watch was the "President."

U. S. WATCH CO. OF WALTHAM
ESTIMATED SERIAL NUMBERS
AND PRODUCTION DATES

Date	Serial No.	Date	Serial No.
1887	3,000	1896	300,000
1888	6,500	1897	350,000
1889	10,000	1898	400,000
1890	30,000	1899	500,000
1891	60,000	1900	600,000
1892	90,000	1901	700,000
1893	150,000	1902	750,000
1894	200,000	1903	800,000
1895	250,000		

U.S. Watch Co. of Waltham, The President, 18 size, 17 jewels, hunting, serial number 150,000.

U.S. Watch Co. of Waltham, The President, 18 size, 17 jewels, open face, 2-tone, adj., note regulator, serial number 150,350.

18 SIZE

Grade or Name — Description	Avg	Ex-Fn	Mint
Express Train, 15J, OF, ADJ	$275	$325	$400
Express Train, 15J, HC, ADJ	375	425	500
The President, 17J, HC ★ ★	500	550	625
The President, 21J, GJS, Adj.6P, DR, 14K ★ ★	900	950	1,025
The President, 17J, GJS, Adj.6P, DR, NI, DMK, OF ★	500	550	625
U. S. Watch Co., 15J, OF, 2-tone, stem attached ★	250	300	375
Washington Square, 15J, HC	150	200	275
39 (HC) & 79 (OF), 17J, GJS, ADJ, NI, DMK, Adj.5P, BRG	100	125	175
40 (HC) & 80 (OF), 17J, GJS	100	125	175
48 (HC) & 88 (OF), 7J, gilded, FULL	100	125	175
48 (HC) & 88 (OF), 7J, gilded, FULL, Silveroid	50	60	75
52 (HC)	125	150	200
92 (OF), 17J, Silveroid	50	60	75

Grade or Name—Description	Avg	Ex-Fn	Mint
52 (HC) & 92 (OF), 17J	$100	$125	$175
53 (HC) & 93 (OF), 15J, NI, FULL, DMK	100	125	175
54 (HC) & 94 (OF), 15J	100	125	175
56 (HC) & 96 (OF), 11J	100	125	175
57 (HC) & 97 (OF), 15J	100	125	175
58 (HC) & 98 (OF), 11J, NI, FULL, DMK	100	125	175

(Prices are with gold filled cases except where noted; add $25 to value of above watches with hunting case.)

NOTE: Some grades are not included. Their values can be determined by comparing with similar models or grades listed.

U.S. Watch Co. of Waltham, 16 size, 7 jewels, guilded, note raised dome on center of movement, engraved on movement "Chas. V. Woerd's Patents," serial number 3,564.

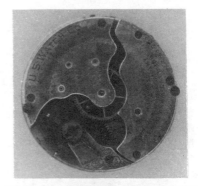

U.S. Watch Co. of Waltham, 16 size, 7 jewels, "A New Watch Company At Waltham, Est'd 1885" on movement, serial number 770,771.

16 SIZE

Grade or Name — Description	Avg	Ex-Fn	Mint
Dome Plate Model, 7J, gilded	$125	$150	$200
Early KW-KS, 7J, S# below 100	500	700	1,000
103, 17J, NI, ¾, ADJ	50	75	125
104, 17J, NI, ¾	50	75	125
104, 17J, NI, ¾, Silveroid	40	50	65
105, 15J, NI, ¾, HC	125	150	200
105, 15J, NI, ¾, OF	50	75	125
105, 15J, NI, ¾, Silveroid	40	65	115
106, 15J, gilded, ¾, Silveroid	40	65	115
106, 15J, gilded, ¾	50	75	125
108, 11J, gilded, ¾	50	75	125
109, 7J, NI, ¾	50	75	125
110, 7J, ¾, HC	50	75	125
110, 7J, ¾, OF	40	50	65

Note: Add $20 to value of above watches in hunting case.

U.S. Watch Co., 16 size, 15 jewels, three-quarter plate.

6 SIZE

Grade or Name — Description	Avg	Ex-Fn	Mint
60, 17J, GJS, NI, ¾, Adj.3P	$40	$60	$85
60, 17J, GJS, NI, ¾, Adj.3P, HC, 14K	225	275	350
62, 15J, NI, ¾	40	60	85
63, 15J, gilded	40	60	85
64, 11J, NI	40	60	85
65, 11J, gilded	20	30	40
66, 7J, gilded	20	30	40
66, 7-11J, NI, ¾	40	60	85
68, 16J, GJS, NI, ¾	50	75	125
69, 7J, NI, HC	75	100	150
69, 7J, NI, OF	20	30	40

Note: Add $10 to value of above watches in hunting case.

Grade 64, 6 size, 11 jewels

U.S. Watch Co. of Waltham, 0 size, 7 jewels, serial number 808,231.

0 SIZE

Grade or Name — Description	Avg	Ex-Fn	Mint
Betsy Ross, HC, GF case..............................	$125	$150	$200
U. S. Watch Co., 15J, HC, GF case...................	100	125	175
U. S. Watch Co., 7-11J, HC, GF case	100	125	175

THE WASHINGTON WATCH CO.
Washington, D. C.
1872 - 1874

J. P. Hopkins, though better known as the inventor of the Auburndale Rotary Watch, was also connected with the Washington Watch Co. which made about 50 watches. They were 18S, key wind, ¾ plate and had duplex escapements. Before Hopkins came to Washington Watch Co. he had handmade about six fine watches. Most of the materials used to produce the watch movements were purchased from the Illinois Watch Co. The company had a total production of 45 movements with duplex escapements.

Grade or Name — Description		Avg	Ex-Fn	Mint
18S, 15J, ¾, KW, KS .... ★ ★ ★		$2,500	$3,000	$3,700

Waterbury Watch Co., skeletonized movement; "A poor man's tourbillon," c. 1890.

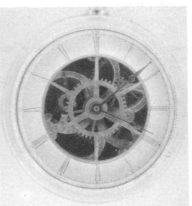

Waterbury Watch Co., long wind movement. Note six spokes on dial.

WATERBURY WATCH CO.
Waterbury, Connecticut
1880 - 1898

The Waterbury Watch Co. was formed in 1880, and D. A. Buck made its first watch. The watches were simple and had only 50 parts. The mainspring was about nine feet long and coiled around the movement. It had a two-wheel train rather than the standard four-wheel train. The Waterbury long wind movement revolved once every hour and had a duplex escapement. The dial was made of paper, and the watch was priced at $3.50 to $4. Some of these watches were used as giveaways.

CHRONOLOGY OF THE DEVELOPMENT OF THE WATERBURY WATCH CO.:

Waterbury Watch Co., Waterbury, Conn. — 1880-1898
New England Watch Co. — 1898-1912
Purchased Ingersoll — 1914
Became U. S. Time Corp. (maker of Timex) — 1944

Example of a basic **Waterbury Watch Co.** movement, Series C.

Series L, Waterbury W. Co. Duplex Escapement, about 16 size.

18 TO 0 SIZES

Grade or Name — Description	Avg	Ex-Fn	Mint
35S, 1890-1891, back wind	$100	$150	$200
Long wind, skeletonized, 3 spokes.................... ★	350	400	550
Long wind, skeletonized, 4 spokes................. ★ ★	600	750	1,000
Long wind, skeletonized, 6 spokes.................. ★	350	400	550
Series A, long wind, skeletonized..................... ★	350	400	550
Series B, long wind.................................	200	225	300
Series C, long wind.................................	200	225	300
Series D, long wind.................................	225	250	350
Series E, long wind (discontinued 1890)	250	275	350
Series F, Duplex escapement	75	85	100

Series I, The Trump, about 18 size, no jewels, pin lever escapement.

Series T, Oxford Duplex Escapement, about 18 size, no jewels.

Grade or Name—Description	Avg	Ex-Fn	Mint
Series G, ¾ lever escapement . . . . ★	$200	$225	$300
Series H, Columbian Duplex . . . . ★ ★	250	275	350
Series I, Trump, ¾	85	95	110
Series J, Americus Duplex	85	95	110
Series K, Charles Benedict Duplex	100	125	150
Series L, Waterbury W. Co. Duplex	85	100	125
Series N, Addison Duplex	60	80	95
Series P, Rugby Duplex	80	90	120
Series R, Tuxedo Duplex	70	80	100
Series S, Elfin	65	75	85
Series T, Oxford Duplex	65	75	85
Series W, Addison	65	75	85
Series Z	65	85	95
Oxford	55	80	95
The Trump	50	75	90
Waterbury W. Co., 7J, ¾, low Serial No.	300	375	500

NOTE: Dollar watches must be in running condition to bring these prices.

E. N. WELCH MFG. CO.
Bristol, Connecticut
1834 - 1897

    Elisha Welch founded this company about 1834. His company failed in 1897, and the Sessions Clock Co. took over the business in 1903. E. N. Welch Mfg. Co. produced the large watch which was displayed at the Chicago Exposition in 1893. This watch depicted the landing of Columbus on the back of the case.

E.N. Welch Mfg. Co., 36 size, back wind & set, made for the Chicago Exposition in 1893. Die debossed back depicting the landing of Columbus in America, Oct, 12th, 1492.

Grade or Name — Description	Avg	Ex-Fn	Mint
36S, Columbus exhibition watch	$200	$225	$300

WESTCLOX

United Clock Co.
Westclox & Western Clock Co.
General Time Corp.
Athens, Georgia
1899 - Present

The first Westclox pocket watch was made about 1899; however, the Westclox name did not appear on their watches until 1906. In 1903 they were making 100 watches a day, and in 1920 production was at 15,000 per day. This company is still in business today in Athens, Georgia.

Grade or Name — Description	Avg	Ex-Fn	Mint
M#1, SW, push to set, GRO	$75	$100	$125
M#2, SW, back set, GRO	50	60	75
18S, Westclox M#4, OF, GRO	50	60	75
1910 Models to 1920, GRO	35	45	60
Anniversary	35	45	60
Antique	20	30	45
Boy Proof	35	45	60
Bingo	30	40	55
Bulls Eye (several models)	15	20	25
Country Gentleman	40	50	60
Dax (many models)	10	15	20

Boy Proof Model, about 16 size, designed to be tamper proof.

Example of a basic **Westclox** movement, stem wind, back set.

Grade or Name—Description	Avg	Ex-Fn	Mint
Elite	$25	$35	$40
Everbrite (several models)	15	20	30
Explorer	200	250	300
Farm Bureau	65	85	100
Glo Ben	65	85	100
Ideal	30	35	40
Lighted Dial	25	30	40
Mark IV	35	45	55
Maxim	30	40	50
Military Style, 24 hour	65	75	95

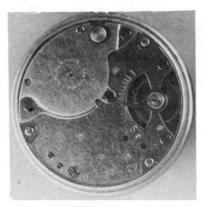

Example of a basic **Westclox** movement, about 16 size, stem wind, lever escapement.

Explorer, back of case and dial, "Wings Over The Pole, The Explorer" on back of case.

Example of a basic Westclox movement, stem wind & set.

Zep, about 16 size with radiant numbers and hands, c. 1929.

Grade or Name—Description	Avg	Ex-Fn	Mint
Mustang	$40	$45	$60
NAWCC, ETP 1,000	40	45	50
Pocket Ben (many models)	20	35	60
Ruby	25	30	45
Scotty (several models)	15	20	25
Smile	25	30	40
Sun Mark	30	35	40
Team Mate (various major league teams)	25	35	40
Tele Time	25	35	45
Texan	35	45	65
Tiny Tim	150	200	275
Victor	80	100	130
Vote	25	35	45
Westclox	15	20	25
Zep	200	250	325

WESTERN WATCH CO.
Chicago, Illinois
1880

Albert Trotter purchased the unfinished watches from the California Watch Co. Mr. Trotter finished and sold those watches. Later he moved to Chicago and, with Paul Cornell and others, formed the Western Watch Company. Very few watches were completed by the Western Watch Co.

Grade or Name — Description	Avg	Ex-Fn	Mint
Western Watch Co., 18S, FULL .... ★ ★ ★	$2,500	$3,000	$4,000

Example of a **Western Watch Co.** movement, 18 size, 15 jewels, key wind & set.

WICHITA WATCH CO.
Wichita, Kansas
July, 1887 - 1888

This company completed construction of their factory in Wichita, Kansas in June 1888, and only a half dozen watches were produced during the brief period the company was in operation. The president was J. R. Snively. These watches are 18S, half plate, adjusted, 15 jewels.

Grade or Name — Description	Avg	Ex-Fn	Mint
18S, 15J, ½ plate, ADJ......................... ★ ★ ★	$2,500	$3,000	$4,000

NOTE: Watches listed in this book are priced at the retail level, as complete watches having an original 14k gold-filled case, an original white enamel single sunk dial, and with the entire original movement in good working order with no repairs needed, unless otherwise noted.

COMIC AND CHARACTER WATCHES

Note: To be mint condition, character watches must have unfaded dials, and boxes must have all inserts. *(PW = Pocket Watch; WW = Wrist Watch)*

Babe Ruth, by Exact Time, ca. 1948.

Betty Boop, by Ingraham, ca. 1934.

Style or Grade—Description	Avg	Ex-Fn	Mint	Mint + Box
Alice in Wonderland, WW, c. 1951, by U.S. Time .	$15	$25	$45	$300
Alice, Red Riding Hood, & Marjory Daw, WW, c. 1953, by Bradley	20	30	55	150
Alice in Wonderland, WW, c. 1958, by Timex	10	20	35	250
Alice in Wonderland & Mad Hatter, WW, c. 1948, by New Haven	25	30	75	150
Annie Oakley, WW, "Action Gun," c. 1951, by New Haven	50	100	200	350
Babe Ruth, WW, c. 1948, by Exact Time, box baseball pledge card	45	95	250	650
Bambi, WW, c. 1949, by U.S. Time	20	60	200	400
Barbie, WW (blue dial)	35	65	125	200
Batman, WW, c. 1970 by Gilbert (band in shape of bat)	45	65	100	250
Batman, WW, c. 1978, by Timex	10	20	35	120
Betty Boop, PW, c. 1934, by Ingraham (with die-debossed back)	350	500	750	1,200
Big Bad Wolf & 3 Pigs, PW, c. 1936, by Ingersoll .	300	350	500	800
Big Bad Wolf & 3 Pigs, WW, c. 1936, by Ingersoll.	200	300	400	700
Buck Rogers, PW, c. 1935, by Ingraham (lightning bolt hands)	250	300	500	750
Bugs Bunny, WW, c. 1951, by Ingersoll (carrot-shaped hands)	100	125	150	350
Bugs Bunny, WW, c. 1951, by Ingersoll (without carrot hands)	45	65	100	200
Bugs Bunny, WW, c. 1949, by Exact Time	100	125	175	250

Big Bad Wolf & 3 Pigs, Ingersoll, ca. 1936.

Buck Rogers, Ingraham, ca. 1935.

Bugs Bunny, Exact Time, ca. 1949.

Buster Brown, Ingersoll, ca. 1925.

Dick Tracy, New Haven, ca. 1948.

Dick Tracy, New Haven (six shooter action arm), ca. 1952.

Style or Grade—Description	Avg	Ex-Fn	Mint	Mint + Box
Buster Brown, PW, c. 1928, by Ingersoll	$125	$175	$250	$300
Buster Brown, PW, c. 1928, by Ingersoll (Buster inside circle)	125	175	270	400
Buzz Corey, WW, c. 1952, by U.S. Time	20	45	95	250
Captain Liberty, WW, c. 1950, by U.S. Time.	35	70	150	250
Captain Marvel, PW, c. 1945, by New Haven	100	200	300	500
Captain Marvel, WW, c. 1948, by New Haven (small watch, plastic box)	75	150	175	350
Captain Marvel, WW, c. 1948, by New Haven (larger size watch)	70	100	170	250
Captain Marvel, WW, c. 1948, Swiss made.	75	125	200	300
Captain Midnight, PW, c. 1948, by Ingraham	250	300	350	400
Cinderella, WW, c. 1950, by U.S. Time (slipper box)	15	25	60	250
Cinderella, WW, c. 1955, by Timex (box with imitation cel)	15	25	60	250
Cinderella, WW, c. 1958, by Timex (box with plastic statue)	15	25	60	250
Cinderella, WW, c. 1958, by Timex (box with porcelain statue)	15	25	60	200
Coca Cola, PW, c. 1948, by Ingersoll	125	150	200	350
Daisy Duck, WW, c. 1947, by Ingersoll (tonneau style)	100	135	200	300
Daisy Duck, WW, c. 1955, by U.S. Time (fluted bezel, bithday series)	75	100	150	200
Dale Evans, WW, c. 1949, by Bradley (western style leather band)	50	60	75	250
Dale Evans, WW, c. 1949, by Bradley (metal band)	15	25	55	200
Dan Dare, PW, c. 1950, by Ingersoll Ltd. (made in England) (action arm).	150	200	285	400
Davy Crockett, WW, c. 1951, by Bradley (round dial)	30	50	90	250
Davy Crockett, WW, c. 1955, by U.S. Time (came with powder horn).	15	25	55	300
Davy Crockett, WW, c. 1956, by Bradley (watch barrel shaped dial).	30	65	100	300
Dennis the Menace, WW, c. 1970, by Bradley	20	35	55	75
Dick Tracy, WW, c. 1948, by New Haven (round dial)	75	100	125	250
Dick Tracy, WW, c. 1948, by New Haven (small tonneau)	75	100	150	250
Dick Tracy, PW, c. 1948, by Ingersoll	200	250	350	500
Dick Tracy, WW, c. 1950, by New Haven (large) . .	75	100	175	400
Dick Tracy, WW, c. 1952, by New Haven (six shooter action arm)	150	200	275	300
Dizzy Dean, PW, c. 1935, by Ingersoll.	150	225	400	700
Dizzy Dean, WW, c. 1938, by Ingersoll	200	250	400	700

Dizzy Dean, Ingersoll, ca. 1935.

Donald Duck, Ingersoll, ca. 1940.

	Avg	Ex-Fn	Mint	Mint + Box
Donald Duck, PW, c. 1939, by Ingersoll (Mickey on back)	$200	$300	$450	$700
Donald Duck, WW, c. 1939, by Ingersoll (Mickey on second hand)	200	335	600	850
Donald Duck, WW, c. 1948, by U.S. Time (tonneau style, silver tone)	100	150	250	350
Donald Duck, WW, c. 1948, by U.S. Time (tonneau style, gold tone)	150	200	300	450
Donald Duck, PW, , c. 1954, Swiss made	35	45	65	150
Donald Duck, WW, c. 1948, by Ingersoll (fluted bezel, birthday series)	150	175	250	450
Donald Duck, WW, c. 1955, by U.S. Time, (plain bezel, pop-up in box)	25	40	75	250
Dopey, WW, c. 1948, by Ingersoll (fluted bezel, birthday series)	100	125	175	400
Dudley Do-Right, WW, 17J (Bullwinkle & Rocky)	55	75	150	225
Flash Gordon, c. 1939, by Ingersoll	250	375	500	650
Gene Autry, WW, c. 1936, by Ingersoll (Gene and Champion on dial)	75	100	220	350

Donald Duck, Ingersoll, ca. 1947.

Gene Autry (Swiss made), ca. 1956.

Above: **Hopalong Cassidy**, U.S. Time, ca. 1950s.
Left: **Hopalong Cassidy**, Ingersoll, ca. 1958.

Style or Grade—Description	Avg	Ex-Fn	Mint	Mint + Box
Gene Autry, WW, c. 1939, by Ingersoll	$75	$100	$150	$300
Gene Autry, WW, c. 1950, by New Haven, (six shooter watch)	150	175	225	450
Gene Autry, WW, c. 1956, Swiss made	45	55	75	200
Goofy, WW, c. 1972, by Helbros, 17J (watch runs backward)	350	400	550	675
Hopalong Cassidy, WW, by U.S. Time (metal watch, box with saddle)	15	25	45	200
Hopalong Cassidy, WW, by U.S. Time (plastic watch, box with saddle)	5	20	35	200
Hopalong Cassidy, WW, by U.S. Time (small watch, leather Western band, flat rectangular box)	25	45	75	300
Hopalong Cassidy, WW, by U.S. Time (regular size watch, black leather cowboy strap)	15	35	65	300
Hopalong Cassidy, PW, c. 1950, by U.S. Time (rawhide strap and fob)	150	200	275	400
Howdy Doody, WW, c. 1954, by Ingraham (with moving eyes)	100	125	175	400
Howdy Doody, WW, c. 1954, by Ingraham (with friends)	75	100	150	550
Jamboree, PW, c. 1951, by Ingersoll, Ltd.	75	100	250	425

Howdy Doody, Ingraham, ca. 1954.

Li'l Abner, New Haven, waving flag, ca. 1948.

Lone Ranger, New Haven, ca. 1939.

Lone Ranger, New Haven, ca. 1939.

Mickey Mouse, Ingersoll, ca. 1933.

Mickey Mouse, Ingersoll, ca. 1933.

Mickey Mouse, Ingersoll, birthday series, ca. 1948.

Mickey Mouse, Ingersoll (U.S. Time), ca. 1950.

Style or Grade—Description	Avg	Ex-Fn	Mint	Mint + Box
James Bond 007, WW, c. 1972, by Gilbert	$25	$50	$80	$100
Jeff Arnold, WW, c. 1952, by Ingersoll (English watch with moving gun)....................	150	200	275	335
Joe Carioca, WW, c. 1952, by U.S. Time (fluted bezel, birthday series)	100	125	200	400
Joe Palooka, WW, c. 1948, by New Haven	100	125	200	400
Li'l Abner, WW, c. 1948, by New Haven (waving flag)	150	175	200	400
Li'l Abner, WW, c. 1948, by New Haven (moving mule)	150	175	200	400
Little King, WW, c. 1968, by Timex..............	35	45	60	75
Lone Ranger, PW, c. 1939, by New Haven (with fob)	150	175	200	325
Lone Ranger, WW, c. 1938, by New Haven (large).	125	150	175	400
Lone Ranger, WW, c. 1938, by New Haven (small)	100	125	150	300
Mary Marvel, WW, c. 1948, by U.S. Time (paper box)	35	65	100	300
Mary Marvel, WW, c. 1948, by U.S. Time (plastic box)	35	65	100	300
Mickey Mouse, PW, c. 1933, by Ingersoll, #1&2 (tall stem)	250	300	400	600
Mickey Mouse, PW, c. 1936, by Ingersoll, #3&4 (short stems)...............................	200	225	300	400
Mickey Mouse, PW, c. 1936, by Ingersoll (Mickey decal on back)	250	300	400	700
Mickey Mouse, PW, c. 1933, by Ingersoll Ltd. (English)	200	300	550	850
Mickey Mouse, PW, c. 1976, by Bradley (bicentennial model)	15	20	30	55
Mickey Mouse, PW, c. 1974, by Bradley (no second hand)	15	20	30	55
Mickey Mouse, PW, c. 1974, by Bradley ("Bradley" printed at 6)	15	20	30	55

Mickey Mouse, Ingersoll. Model no. 3 on the left. Model no. 4 is shown with lapel button.

Style or Grade—Description	Avg	Ex-Fn	Mint	Mint + Box
Mickey Mouse, WW, c. 1933, by Ingersoll (metal band with Mickey)	$75	$150	$275	$400
Mickey Mouse, WW, c. 1936, by Ingersoll (one Mickey for second hand)	100	150	200	550
Mickey Mouse, WW, c. 1936, by Ingersoll (girl's watch, 1 Mickey for second hand)	175	200	250	650
Mickey Mouse, WW, c. 1948, by Ingersoll (fluted bezel, birthday series)	150	175	200	450
Mickey Mouse, WW, c. 1946, by U.S. Time (10k gold plated)	100	125	200	250
Mickey Mouse, WW, c. 1947, by U.S. Time (tonneau, plain, several styles)	50	75	150	350
Mickey Mouse, WW, c. 1947, by U.S. Time (same as above, gold tone)	50	75	150	250
Mickey Mouse, WW, c. 1950s, by U.S. Time (round style)	25	35	55	300
Mickey Mouse, WW, c. 1958, by U.S. Time (statue of Mickey in box)	15	25	45	250

Mickey Mouse, Bradley, ca. 1955.

Mickey Mouse, with wide bezel, Ingersoll, ca. 1948.

Style or Grade—Description	Avg	Ex-Fn	Mint	Mint + Box
Mickey Mouse, WW, c. 1965, by Timex (Mickey Mouse electric)	$100	$125	$155	$250
Mickey Mouse, WW, c. 1965, Timex (manual wind)	35	55	75	200
Mickey Mouse, WW, c. 1970s, by Bradley	10	15	35	80
Mickey Mouse, WW, c. 1980, by Bradley (colored min. chapter)	50	65	85	200
Mickey Mouse, WW, c. 1983, by Bradley (limited commemorative model)	100	125	150	200

Left: Mary Marvel, Swiss made, ca. 1948. **Center: Minnie Mouse**, U.S. Time, ca. 1961. **Right: Orphan Annie**, New Haven, ca. 1939.

Orphan Annie, New Haven, ca. 1940.

Popeye, New Haven, ca. 1938.

Popeye, New Haven (with friends), ca. 1935.

Popeye, New Haven, ca. 1940.

Style or Grade—Description	Avg	Ex-Fn	Mint	Mint + Box
Mickey Mouse, WW, c. 1985, by ETA (clear plastic bezel and band)	$15	$20	$35	$75
Minnie Mouse, WW, c. 1958, by U.S. Time (statue of Minnie in box)	25	35	50	250
Moon Mullins, PW, c. 1930, by Ingersoll	250	300	450	500
Orphan Annie, WW, c. 1939, by New Haven (fluted bezel)	100	125	160	300
Orphan Annie, WW, c. 1940, by New Haven (large style)	100	125	155	400
Orphan Annie, WW, c. 1948, by New Haven smaller model)	100	125	155	350
Orphan Annie, WW, c. 1968, by Timex	35	45	65	95
Peter Pan, PW, c. 1948, by Ingraham	100	150	200	300
Pinocchio, WW, c. 1948, by Ingersoll (fluted bezel, birthday series)	125	160	200	325
Pinocchio, WW, c. 1948, by U.S. Time (Happy Birthday cake box)	125	150	200	450
Pluto, WW, c. 1948, by U.S. Time	75	125	200	300
Popeye, PW, c. 1935, by New Haven (with friends on dial)	200	250	350	475
Popeye, PW, c. 1940, by New Haven (plain dial)	180	235	300	400
Popeye, WW, c. 1936, by New Haven (tonneau style, with friends on dial)	150	175	250	450
Popeye, WW, c. 1952, by U.S. Time (round style)	100	125	165	300
Porky Pig, WW, c. 1948, by Ingraham (tonneau)	100	125	150	350
Porky Pig, WW, c. 1949, by U.S. Time (round)	75	100	135	250
Puss-N-Boots, WW, c. 1959, by Bradley	100	175	250	400
Robin, WW, c. 1978, by Timex	25	35	50	75
Robin Hood, WW, c. 1955, by Bradley (tonneau style)	75	100	150	300
Robin Hood, WW, c. 1958, by Viking (round)	75	100	150	250
Rocky Jones Space Ranger, WW, c. 1955, by Ingraham	100	125	150	300
Roy Rogers, WW, c. 1954, by Ingraham (Roy and rearing Trigger)	50	75	100	250

Robin Hood, Bradley, ca. 1955.

Roy Rogers, Ingraham, ca. 1954.

Roy Rogers, Ingraham, ca. 1960.

Roy Rogers, Ingraham (large), ca. 1951.

Roy Rogers, Ingraham, ca. 1951.

Skeezix, Ingraham, ca. 1936.

Left: Smitty, New Haven, ca. 1936. **Center: Superman**, New Haven, ca. 1939. **Right: Superman**, New Haven, ca. 1939.

Style or Grade—Description	Avg	Ex-Fn	Mint	Mint + Box
Roy Rogers, WW, c. 1954, by Ingraham (Roy and Trigger)	$50	$75	$100	$250
Roy Rogers, WW, c. 1954, by Ingraham (expansion band)	50	75	100	250
Roy Rogers, WW, c. 1956, by Ingraham (round dial)	50	75	100	200
Rudy Nebb, PW, c. 1930, by Ingraham	100	150	200	400
Skeezix, PW, c. 1936, by Ingraham	125	150	200	400
Smitty, PW, c. 1936, by New Haven	100	125	200	450
Smitty, WW, c. 1936, by New Haven	100	125	200	450
Smokey Stover, WW, c. 1968, by Timex	35	45	60	75
Snoopy, WW, c. 1958 (tennis racket)	20	30	45	75
Snoopy, WW, c. 1958 (Woodstock)	20	30	45	75
Snow White, WW, c. 1938, by Ingersoll (tonneau) .	100	125	200	400
Snow White, WW, c. 1952, by U.S. Time (round) .	25	35	50	350
Snow White, WW, c. 1956, by U.S. Time (statue in box)	25	35	50	250
Snow White, WW, c. 1962, by U.S. Time (plastic watch)	25	35	50	250
Superman, PW, c. 1956, by Bradley	150	200	250	450
Superman, WW, c. 1938, by New Haven	150	200	250	450
Superman, WW, c. 1946, by Ingraham (lightning bolt hands)	150	175	200	400
Superman, WW, c. 1978, by Timex (large size)	35	50	75	100
Superman, WW, c. 1978, by Timex (small size)	35	50	75	100
Three Little Pigs, PW, c. 1936, by Ingersoll	350	400	500	850
Tom Corbett, WW, c. 1954, by New Haven	75	100	150	450
Tom Mix, PW, c. 1936, by Ingersoll (with fob)	200	400	675	1,050
Tom Mix, WW, c. 1936, by Ingersoll	175	300	500	950
Woody Woodpecker, WW, c. 1948, by Ingersoll (town)	75	100	175	300
Woody Woodpecker, WW, c. 1952, by Ingraham (round dial)	75	100	150	300
Yogi Bear, WW, c. 1964, by Bradley	15	20	35	65
Zorro, WW, c. 1956, by U.S. Time	25	35	50	250

Left: Tom Corbett, Space Cadet, New Haven, ca. 1936. **Center: Tom Mix,** Ingersoll, ca. 1936. **Right: Woody Woodpecker,** U.S. Time, ca. 1948.

EUROPEAN POCKET WATCHES

EARLY ANTIQUE WATCHES

The early antique watches looked quite similar to small table clocks. These drum-shaped watches were about two inches in diameter and usually over one-half inch thick. The drum-shaped watch lost popularity in the late 1500s. The earliest portable timepieces did not carry the maker's name, but initials were common. The cases generally had a hinged lid which covered the dial. This lid was pierced with small holes to enable ready identification of the position of the hour hand. They also usually contained a bell. The dial often had the numbers "I" to "XII" engraved in Roman numerals and the numbers "13" to "24" in Arabic numbers with the "2" engraved in the form of a "Z." Even the earliest of timepieces incorporated striking. The oldest known watch with a date engraved on the case was made in 1548. A drum-shaped watch with the initials "C. W.," it was most likely produced by Casper Werner, a protege of Henlein.

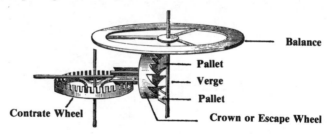

Early pocket watches were designed to run from 12 to 16 hours. The pinions usually bore five leaves, the great wheel 55 teeth, the second wheel 45 teeth, the third wheel 40 teeth, and the escape wheel 15 teeth. With one less pinion and wheel the escape wheel ran reverse to a standard four-wheel watch. During the 1500s, 1600s, and much of the 1700s, it was stylish to decorate not only the case and balance cock but all parts including the clicks, barrel, studs, springs, pillars, hands, and stackfreed. The plates themselves were decorated with pierced and engraved metal scrolls, and in some instances the maker's name was engraved in a style to correspond with the general decoration of the movement. During these periods the most celebrated artists, designers, and engravers were employed. The early watches were decorated by famous artists such as Jean Vauquier 1670, Daniel Marot

1700, Gillis l'Egare 1650, Michel Labon 1630, Pierre Bourdon 1750, and D. Cochin 1750. Most of the artists were employed to design and execute pierced and repouse cases.

THE MID-1700s

In the mid-1700s relatively minor changes are noticed. Decoration became less distinctive and less artistic. The newer escapements resulted in better timekeeping, and a smaller balance cock was used. The table and foot became smaller. The foot grew more narrow, and as the century and the development of the watch advanced, the decoration on the balance cock became smaller and less elaborate. About 1720 the foot was becoming solid and flat. No longer was it hand pierced; however, some of the pierced ones were produced until about 1770. Thousands of these beautiful hand pierced watch cocks have been made into necklaces and brooches or framed. Sadly, many of the old movements were destroyed in a mad haste to cater to the buyers' fancy.

THE 1800s

As the 1800s approached the balance cocks became less artistic as the decoration on movements gradually diminished. Breguet and Berthoud spent very little time on the beauty or artistic design on their balance cocks or pillars. But the cases were often magnificient in design and beauty, made with enamels in many colors and laden with precious stones. During this period the movements were plain and possessed very little artistic character.

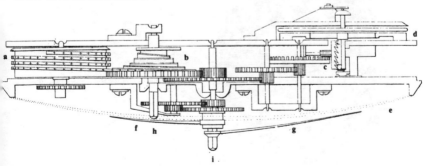

Exposed illustration of an early watch movement, c. 1800-1850. Note that movement is key wind and set from the dial side. The illustrated example is a chain driven fusee with a verge escapement: **a**-Main spring barrel and chain. **b**-Fusee. **c**-Verge escapement. **d**-Balance wheel. **e**-Dial. **f**-Hour hand. **g**-Minute hand. **h**-Winding arbor. **i**-Setting arbor.

As early as 1820 three-quarter and one-half plate designs were being used with the balance cock lowered to the same level as the other wheels. The result was a slimmer watch.

CLUES TO DATING YOUR WATCH

To establish the age of a watch there are many points to be considered. The dial, hands, pillars, balance cock and pendant, for example, contain important clues in determining the age of your watch. However, no one part alone should be considered sufficient evidence to draw a definite conclusion as to age. The watch as a whole must be considered. For example, an English-made silver-cased watch will have a hallmark inside the case. It is quite simple to refer to the London Hallmark Table for hallmarks after 1697. But this hallmark will reveal the age of the case only. This does not fix the age of the movement. Many movements are housed in cases made years before or after the movement was produced. An informed collector will note that a watch with an enamel dial, for instance, could not have been made before 1635. A pair of cases indicates it could not have been made prior to 1640. The minute hand was introduced in 1687. The presence of jewels would indicate it was made after 1700. A dust cap first appeared in 1774. Keyless winding came into being after 1820 but did not gain widespread popularity until after 1860. All of these clues and more must be considered before accurately assessing the age of a watch.

Example of an early pocket watch with a stackfreed design to equalize power much as a fusee does. Note dumbbell shaped foliot which served as a balance for verge escapement, and the tear shaped cam which is part of the stackfreed.

PILLARS

Pillars are of interest and should be considered as one of the elements in determining age. Through the years small watches used round pillars, and the larger watches generally used a square type engraved pillar.

(Illus. 1) This pillar is one of the earliest types and used in the 1800s as well. This particular pillar came from a watch which dates about 1550. It is known that this type pillar was used in 1675 by Gaspard Girod of France and also in 1835 by James Taylor of England.

(Illus. 2) This style pillar is called the tulip pattern. Some watchmakers preferred to omit the vertical divisions. This style was popular between 1660 and 1750 but may be found on later watches. It was common practice to use ornamentation on the tulip pillar.

(Illus. 3) The ornament shown was used by Daniel Quare of London from 1665 to 1725 and by the celebrated Tompion, as well as many others.

(Illus. 4) This type pillar is referred to as the Egyptian and dates from 1630 to the 1800s. The squared Egyptian pattern was introduced about 1630 and some may be found with a wider division with a head or bust inserted. This style was used by D. Bouquet of London about 1640 and by many other watchmakers.

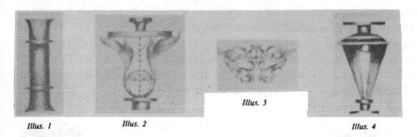

Illus. 1   *Illus. 2*   *Illus. 3*   *Illus. 4*

(Illus. 5) This pillar was used by Thomas Earnshaw of London about 1780. The plain style was prominent for close to two hundred years—1650 to 1825.

Illus. 5   *Illus. 6*   *Illus. 7*   *Illus. 8*

(Illus. 6) This style was popular and was used by many craftsmen. Nathaniel Barrow of London put this in his watches about 1680.

(Illus. 7) This pillar may be seen in watches made by Pierre Combet of Lyons, France, about 1720. It was also used by many others.

(Illus. 8) This style pillar and the ornament were used by John Ellicott of England and other watchmakers from 1730 to 1770.

These illustrations represent just a few of the basic pillars that were used. Each watchmaker would design and change details to create his own individual identity. This sometimes makes it more difficult to readily determine the age of watches.

BALANCE COCKS OR BRIDGES

The first balance cocks or bridges used to support the balance staff were a plain "S" shape. The cocks used on the old three-wheel watches were very elaborate; hand-pierced and engraved. At first no screws were used to hold the cock in place. It is noteworthy that on the three-wheel watch the regulator was a ratchet and click and was used on these earlier movements to adjust the mainspring. About 1635 the balance cock was screwed to the plate and pinned on its underside, which helped steady the balance. The first cock illustrated is a beautifully decorated example made by Josias Jeubi of Paris about 1580. Note that it is pinned to a stud which passes through a square cut in the foot of the cock. Next is a balance cock made by Bouquet of London about 1640. The third balance cock is one made by Jean Rousseau and dates around 1650. The fourth one dates around 1655.

The next two bridges are supported on both sides of the balance cock by means of screws or pins. They are strikingly different and usually cover much of the plate of the movement. This style of balance cock was used around 1675 and was still seen as late as 1765.

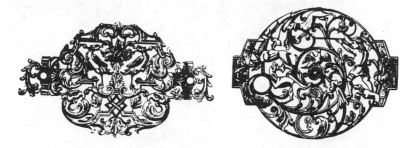

The beautiful balance cock below at left, with the ornate foot, dates about 1660. The next illustrated balance cock with the heavy ornamentation was used from about 1700 to 1720 or longer. By 1720 a face was added to the design. The face shows up where the table terminates on most balance cocks.

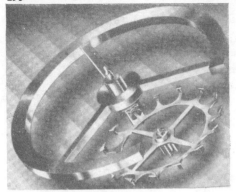

Cylinder escapement

Invented in 1695

Virgule Escapement

Rack and lever escapement

Invented in 1722

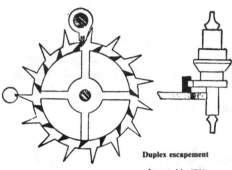

Duplex escapement

Invented in 1750

EARLY EUROPEAN WATCHMAKERS

Note abbreviations used:
enamel = enamel case painter or artist
pat. = patent or inventor
ca. = circa or about
since = founded to present

Achard, J. Francois (Geneva, ca. 1750)
Addison, J. (London, 1760-1780)
Adamson, Gustave (Paris, 1775-1790)
Alfred, W. Humphreys (London, ca. 1905)
Alibut (Paris, ca. 1750s)
Allier, Bachelard & Teron Co. (French, ca. 1830)
Amabric, Abraham (Geneva, ca. 1750-1800)
Amabric, Freres (Geneva, ca. 1760-1795)
Amon (Paris, 1913)
Andre, Jean (enamel) (Geneva, 1660-1705)
Anthony, Willams (London, 1785-1840)
Antram, J. (London, ca. 1700-1730)
Appleby, Edward (London, ca. 1675)
Appleby, Joshua (London, ca. 1720-1745)
Ardin, Coppet (ca. 1710)
Arland, Benjamin (London, c. 1680)

Arlaud, Louis (Geneva, ca. 1750)
Arnold & Frodsham, Charles (London, 1845)
Arnold, Henery (London, ca. 1770-1780)
Arnold, John (London, ca. 1760-1790)
Arnold, John Roger (London, ca. 1800-1830)
Arnold, Nicolas (ca. 1850)
Arnold & Lewis, Lote Simmons (Manchester, ca. 1860)
Arnold & Son (London, ca. 1787-1799)
Assman, Julius (Glasshutte, 1850-1885)
Auber, Daniel (London, ca. 1750)
Aubert, D. F. (Geneva, ca. 1825)
Aubert, Ferdinand (1810-1835)
Aubert & Co. (Geneva, ca. 1850)
Aubry, Irenee (Geneva, 1885-1910)
Audebert (Paris, 1810-1820)

Audemars, Freres (Swiss, 1810 until company splits in 1885)
Audemars, Louis-Benjamin (Swiss, 1811-1867)
Aureole (Swiss, 1921)
Auricoste, Jules (Paris, ca. 1910)
Bachhofen, Felix (Swiss, 1675-1690)
Badollet, Jean-Jacques (Geneva, 1779-1891)
Baillon, Jean-Hilaire (Paris, ca. 1727)
Baird, Wm. (London, 1815-1825)
Balsiger & Fils (ca. 1825)
Barberet, J. (Paris, ca. 1600)
Barbezat, Bole (Swiss, 1870)
Baronneau, Jean-Louis (France, 1675-1700)
Barraud & Lunds (1812-1840)
Barraud, Paul-Philip (London, 1752-1820)
Barrow, Edward (London, ca. 1650-1710)
Barrow, Nathaniel (London, 1653-1689)
Barry, M. (French, ca. 1620)
Bartholony, Abraham (Paris, 1750-1752)
Barton, James (London, 1760-1780)
Barwise (London, 1800)
Bassereau, Jean-Hilaire (Paris, ca. 1800-1810)
Bautte, Jean-Francois (Geneva, 1800-1835)
Bautte & Moynier (Geneva, ca. 1825)
Beaumarchais, Caron (Paris, 1750-1795)
Beauvais, Simon (London, ca. 1690)
Beckman, Daniel (London, 1670-1685)
Beckner, Abraham (London, ca. 1640)
Beliard, Dominique (Paris, ca. 1750)
Bell, Benj. (London, 1650-1668)
Bennett, John (London, 1850-1895)
Benson, J. W. (London, 1825-1890)
Benson, J. W. (London, 1850-1900)
Bergstein, L. (London, ca. 1840)
Bernard, Nicholas (Paris, 1650-1690)
Bernoulli, Daniel (Paris, 1720-1790)
Berrollas, J. A. (Denmark, 1800-1830)
Berthound, Augusta-Louis (Paris, ca. 1875)
Berthound, Ferdinand (Paris, 1750-1805)
Beihler & Hartmann (Geneva, ca. 1875)
Blanc, Henri (Geneva, ends 1964)
Blanc, Jules (Geneva, 1929-1940)
Blanc & Fils (Geneva, 1770-1790)
Bock, Johann (German, 1700-1750)
Bockel (London, ca. 1650)
Bolslandon, Metz (ca. 1780)
Bolviller, Moise (Paris, 1840-1870)
Bommelt, Leonhart (Nuremburg, Ger., ca. 1690)
Bonney (London, ca. 1790)
Bonniksen, Bahne (England, 1890-1930)
Booth, Edward (name change to Barlow)
Bordier, Denis (France, ca. 1575)
Bordier, Freres (Geneva, 1787-1810)
Bordier, Jacques (enamel) (ca. 1670)
Bornand, A. (Geneva, 1895-1915)
Boubon (Paris, 1810-1820)
Bouquet, David (London, ca. 1630-1650)
Bovet, Edouard (Swiss, 1820-1918)
Bovier, G. (enamel painter) (Paris, c. 1750)
Brandt, Iacob (Swiss, ca. 1700)
Brandt, Robert & Co. (Geneva, ca. 1820)
Breitling, "Leon" (Swiss, since 1884)
Brockbank (London, 1776-present)
Brocke (London, ca. 1640)
Brodon, Nicolas (Paris, 1674-1682)

Bronikoff, a Wjatka (Russia, 1850 "watches of wood")
Bruguier, Charles A. (Geneva, 1800-1860)
Bull, Rainulph (one of the first British) (1590-1617)
Burgis, Eduardus (London, 1680-1710)
Burgis, G. (London, 1720-1740)
Burnet, Thomas (London, ca. 1800)
Busch, Abraham (Hamburg, Ger., ca. 1680)
Buz, Johannes (Augsburg, Bavaria, ca. 1625)
Cabrier, Charles (London, ca. 1690-1720)
Capt, Henry Daniel (Geneva, 1802-1880)
Caron, Augustus (Paris, ca. 1750-1760)
Caron, Francois-Modeste (Paris, 1770-1788)
Caron, Pierre (Paris, ca. 1700)
Caron, Pierre Augustin (Paris, 1750-1795) (pat. virgule escapement)
Carpenter, William (London, 1750-1800)
Carte, John (England, 1680-1700)
Champod, P. Amedee (enamel) (Geneva, 1850-1910)
Chapponier, Jean (Geneva, 1780-1800)
Charman (London, 1780-1800)
Charrot (Paris, 1775-1810)
Chartiere (enamel) (France, ca. 1635)
Chaunes (Paris, ca. 1580-1600)
Chavanne & Pompejo (Vienna, 1785-1800)
Cheneviere, Louis (Geneva, 1710-1740)
Cheneviere, Urbain (Geneva, 1730-1760)
Cheriot or Cherioz, Daniel (ca. 1750-1790)
Cheuillard (Blois, France, ca. 1600)
Chevalier & Co. (Geneva, 1795-1810)
Cisin, Charles (Swiss, 1580-1610)
Clark, Geo. (London, 1750-1785)
Clerc (Swiss, ca. 1875)
Clouzier, Jacques (Paris, 1690-1750)
Cochin, D. (Paris, ca. 1800)
Cocque, Geo. (ca. 1610)
Cogniat (Paris, ca. 1675)
Coladon, Louis (Geneva, 1780-1850)
Cole, James Ferguson (London, 1820-1875)
Cole, Thomas (London, 1820-1864)
Collins, Clement (London, ca. 1705)
Collins, John (London, ca. 1720)
Collins, R. (London, ca. 1815)
Colondre & Schnee (ca. 1875)
Combet, Pierre (Lyons, France, ca. 1610-1625)
Cotton, John (London, ca. 1695-1715)
Coulin, Jaques & Bry, Amy (Paris & Geneva, 1780-1790)
Court, Jean-Pierre (ca. 1790-1810)
Courvosier, Freres (Swiss, 1810-1852)
Courvoisier & Houriet (Geneva, ca. 1790)
Cox, James (London, 1760-1785)
Csacher, C. (Prague, Aus., ca. 1725)
Cumming, Alexander (London, 1750-1800)
Cummins, T. (London, 1820)
Cuper, Barthelemy (French, 1615-1635)
Curtis, John (London, ca. 1720)
Cusin, Charles (Geneva, ca. 1587)
Darling, William (British, ca. 1825)
De Baghyn, Adriaan (Amsterdam, ca. 1750)
Debaufre, Peter (French, 1690-1720) (Debaufre escapement)
Debaufre, Pierre (Paris, London, Geneva, 1675-1722)
De Bry, Theodore (German, 1585-1620)

De Charmes, Simon (London, France, 1690-1730)
De Choudens (Swiss & French, 1760-1790)
Decombaz, Gedeon (Geneva, 1780-1820)
Degeilh & Co. (ca. 1880-1900)
De Heca, Michel (Paris, ca. 1685)
De L Garde, Abraham (Paris, "Blois," ca. 1590)
Delynne, F. L. (Paris, ca. 1775)
Dent, Edward John (London, 1815-1850)
Derham, William (English, ca. 1677-1730)
Deroch, F. (Swiss, 1730-1770)
Des Arts & Co. (Geneva, 1790-1810)
Desquivillons & DeChoudens (Paris, ca. 1785)
Destouches, Jean-Francois-Albert (Holland, ca. 1760)
Devis, John (London, 1770-1785)
Dimier & Co. (Geneva, 1820-1925)
Dinglinger (enamel) (Dresden, Ger., ca. 1675)
Ditisheim & Co. "Maurice" (Swiss, 1894)
Ditisheim, Paul (Swiss, 1892)
Dobson, A. (London, 1660-1680)
Droz, Daniel (Chaux-de-Fonds, Sw., ca. 1760)
Droz, Henri (Chaux-de-Fonds, Sw., ca. 1775)
Droz, Pierre Jacquet (Chaux-de-Fonds, Sw., 1750-1775)
Droz, Pierre (Swiss, 1740-1770)
Droz & Co. (Swiss, ca. 1825)
Dubie (enamel) (Paris, ca. 1635)
Dubois & Fils (Paris, ca. 1810)
Duchene & Co. "Louis" (Geneva, 1790-1820)
Ducommun, Charles (Geneva, ca. 1750)
Duduict, Jacques (Blois, France, ca. 1600)
Dufalga, Philippe (Geneva, 1730-1790)
Dufalga, P. F. (Geneva, ca. 1750)
Dufour, Foll & Co. (Geneva, 1800-1830)
Dufour, J. E. & Co. (ca. 1890)
Dufour & Ceret (Ferney, Fr., ca. 1770-1785)
Dufour & Zentler (ca. 1870)
Duhamel, Pierre (Paris, ca. 1680)
Dupin, Paul (London, 1730-1765)
Dupont (Geneva, ca. 1810-1830)
Dupont, Jean (enamel) (Geneva, 1800-1860)
Duru (Paris, ca. 1650)
Dutertre, Baptiste (ca. 1730) (pat. duplex escapement)
Dutton, William (London, 1760-1840)
Earnshaw, Thomas (London, 1760-1842)
East, Edward (London, 1630-1670)
Edmonds, James (London to U.S.A., 1720-1766)
Edward, George & Son (London, ca. 1875)
Ekegren, Henri-Robert (Geneva, 1860)
Ellicott, John (London, 1728-1810)
Emery, Josiah (Geneva, 1750-1800)
Esquivillon & De Choudens (Paris, 1710-1780)
Ester, Jean Henry (Geneva, 1610-1665)
Etherlington, George (London, 1680-1730)
Etienne Guyot & Co. (Geneva, ca. 1880)
Facio De Duillier, Nicholas (British, 1665-1710)
Fallery, Jacques (Geneva, ca. 1760)
Farmer, G. W. (wooden watches) (Germany, ca. 1650-1675)
Fatio, Alfred (Geneva, 1920-1940)
Fatton, Frederick Louis (London, ca. 1822)
Favre Marius & Fils (Geneva, 1893)
Fenie, M. (ca. 1635)
Ferrero, J. (ca. 1854-1900)
Fiacre, Clement (Paris, ca. 1700)

Fitter, Joseph (London, ca. 1660)
Fontac (London, ca. 1775)
Forfaict, Nicolas (Paris, 1573-1619)
Fowles, Allen (Kilmarnock, Scot., ca. 1770)
French (London, 1810-1840)
Fureur (Swiss, 1910)
Gallopin "Henri Capt" (Geneva, 1875)
Gamod, G. (Paris, ca. 1640)
Garnier, Paul (Paris, 1825) (pat. Garnier escapement)
Garrault, Jacobus (Geneva, ca. 1650)
Garty & Constable (London, ca. 1750)
Gaudron, Antoine (Paris, 1675-1707)
Gaudron, Pierre (Paris, 1695-1740)
Geissheim, Smod (Augsburg, Ger., ca. 1625)
Gent, James & Son (London, 1875-1910)
Gerbeau, V. (Paris, 1900-1930)
Gerrard (British, 1790-1820)
Gibs, William (Rotterdam, ca. 1720)
Gibson & Co., Ltd. (Ireland, ca. 1875-1920)
Gidon (Paris, ca. 1700)
Gillespy, Charles (Ireland, 1774-1171)
Girard, Perregaux (Swiss, 1856)
Girard, Theodore (Paris, 1623-1670)
Girardier, Charles (Geneva, 1780-1815)
Girod, B. (Paris, ca. 1810)
Girod, Gaspard (Paris, ca. 1670-1690)
Godod, E. (Paris, ca. 1790)
Godon, F. L. (Paris, ca. 1787)
Golay, A. Leresche & Fils (Geneva, 1844-1857)
Golay, H. (Swiss, 1969-1911)
Golay, Stahl & Fils (1878-1914)
Gollons (Paris, ca. 1663)
Gounouilhou, P. S. (Geneva, 1815-1840)
Gout, Ralph (London, 1790-1830)
Graham, George (London, 1715-1750)
Grandjean, Henri (Swiss, 1825-1880)
Grandjean, L. C. (Swiss, 1890-1920)
Grant, John & Son (English, 1780-1867)
Grantham, William (London, ca. 1860)
Grasset, Isaac (Geneva, ca. 1896)
Gray & Constable (London, ca. 1750)
Grazioza (Swiss, ca. 1901)
Grebauval, Hierosme (ca. 1575)
Gregory, Jermie (London, ca. 1652-1680)
Gregson, Jean P. (Paris, 1770-1790)
Griblin, Nicolas (French, 1650-1716)
Griessenback, Johann G. (Bavaria, ca. 1660)
Grignion "family" (London, 1690-1825)
Grignion, Daniel & Thomas (London, 1780-1790)
Grosclaude, Ch. & Co. (Swiss, ca. 1865)
Grosjean, Henry (French, ca. 1865)
Gruber, Hans (Nurnberg, Ger., ca. 1520-1560)
Gruber, Michel (Nurnberg, Ger., ca. 1605)
Gruet (Geneva, Sw., ca. 1664)
Gubelin, E. (Lucern, Switzerland, ca. 1832)
Guillaume, Ch. (pat. Invar, Elinvar)
Haas Nevevx & Co. (founder B. J. Haas) (Geneva, 1828-1925)
Hagen, Johan (German, ca. 1750)
Haley, Charles (London, 1781-1825)
Hallewey (London, 1695-1720)
Hamilton & Co. (London, 1865-1920)
Harper, Henry (London, ca. 1665-1700)
Harrison, John (England, 1710-1775) (pat. comp. balance)
Hasluck Brothers (London, ca. 1695)

Hautefeuille, Jean (Paris, 1670-1722)
Hautefeuille, John (Paris, 1660-1700)
Hawley, John (London, ca. 1850)
Hebert, Juliette (enamel) (Geneva, ca. 1890)
Helbros (Geneva, since 1918)
Hele or Henlein, Peter (Nurnberg, 1510-1540)
Heliger, J. (Zug, Sw., ca. 1575)
Henner, Johann (Wurtzburg, Ger., ca. 1730)
Henry, F. S. (Swiss, ca. 1850)
Hentschel, J. J. (French, ca. 1750)
Hess, L. (Zurich, Sw., ca. 1780)
Hessichti, Dionistus (ca. 1630)
Higgs & Evans (London, 1775-1825)
Hill, Ben. (London, 1640-1670)
Hoguet, Francois (Paris, ca. 1750)
Hooke, Robert (England, 1650-1700)
Hoseman, Stephen (London, ca. 1710-1740)
Houghton, James (England, ca. 1800-1820)
Houghton, Thomas (Chorley, England,
  ca. 1820-1840)
Houriet, Jacques Frederic (Paris 1810-1825)
Huaud, Freres (enamel) (Geneva, ca. 1685)
Huber, Peter (German, ca. 1875)
Hubert, David (London, 1714-1747)
Hubert, Oliver (London, ca. 1740)
Hubert, Etienne (French, 1650-1690)
Hues, Peter (Augsburg, Ger., ca. 1600)
Huguenin, David L. (Swiss, 1780-1835)
Humbert-Droz, David (Swiss, ca. 1790)
Huygens, Christian (Paris, 1657-1680)
Iaquier or Jacquier, Francois (Geneva,
  1690-1720)
Ilbery, William (London, 1800-1835)
Ingold, Pierre-Frederic (Swiss, Paris, London,
  1810-1870)
Invicta ("R. Picard") (Swiss, 1896)
Jaccard, E. H. & Co. (Swiss, ca. 1850)
Jacot, Charles-Edouard (Swiss, 1830-1860)
  (pat. Chinese duplex)
Jaeger, Edmond (Paris, 1875-1920)
Jaeger Le Coultre & Co. (Swiss, since 1833)
Jamison, Geo. (London, 1786-1810)
Janvier, Antide (Paris, 1771-1834)
Japy, Frederic & Sons "family" (French, Swiss,
  ca. 1776)
Jaquet, Pierre (Swiss, 1750-1790)
Jean Richard, Daniel (Swiss, 1685-1740)
Jean Richard, Edouard (Swiss, 1900-1930)
Jeannot, Paul (ca. 1890)
Jefferys & Gildert (London, 1790)
Jesop, Josias (London, 1780-1794)
Jeubi, Josias (Paris, ca. 1575)
Joly, Jacques (Paris, ca. 1625)
Jovat (London, ca. 1690)
Jones, Henry (London, ca. 1665-1690)
Jump, Joseph (English, ca. 1827-1850)
Junod, Freres (Geneva, ca. 1850)
Jurgensen, Urban & Jules (Copenhagen, Swiss,
  1745-1912)
Just & Son (London, 1790-1825)
Juvet, Edouard (Swiss, 1844-1880)
Juvet, Leo (Swiss, 1860-1890)
Keates, William (London, ca. 1780)
Keely, W. (London, ca. 1790)
Kendall, Larcum (London, ca. 1786)
Kendall, James (London, 1740-1780)
Kessels, H. J. (Holland, 1800-1845)
Kirkton, R. (London, ca. 1790)
Klein, Johann Heinr (Copenhagen, Den., ca.

1710)
Klentschi, C. F. (Swiss, 1790-1840)
Koehn, Edward (Geneva, 1860-1908)
Kreizer, Conard (German, 1595-1658)
Kuhn, Jan Hendrik (Amsterdam, 1775-1800)
Kullberg, Victor (Copenhagen to London,
  1850-1890)
Lamy, Michel (Paris, 1767-1800)
Lang & Padoux (ca. 1860)
Larcay (Paris, ca. 1725)
Lardy, Francois (Geneva, ca. 1825)
Larpent, Isacc & Jurgensen (Copenhagen,
  1748-1811)
Laurier, Francois (Paris, 1654-1675)
Le Baufre (Paris, ca. 1650)
Lebet (Geneva, ca. 1850)
Lebet & Fils (Swiss, 1830-1892)
Le Coultre, Ami (Geneva, ca. 1887)
Le Coultre, Eugene (Geneva, ca. 1850)
Leekey, C. (London, ca. 1750)
Leeky, Gabriel (London, ca. 1775-1820)
Lepaute, Jean-Andre (Paris, 1750-1774)
Lepine, Jean-Antoine (Paris, 1744-1814)
Le Puisne, Huand (enamel) (Blois, Fr., ca. 1635)
Leroux, John (England, 1758-1805)
Le Roy & Co. (Paris, ca. 1853)
Le Roy, Charles (Paris, 1733-1770)
Le Roy, Julien (Paris, 1705-1750)
Le Roy, Pierre (French, 1710-1780)
  (improved duplex escapement)
Levy, Hermanos (Hong Kong, "Swiss,"
  1880-1890)
L'Hardy, Francois (Geneva, 1790-1825)
Lichtenauer (Wurzberg, Ger., ca. 1725)
Lindesay, G. (London, ca. 1740-1770)
Lindgren, Erik (England, 1735-1775) (pat. rack
  lever)
Litherland, Peter (English, 1780-1876)
Loehr, (Von) (Swiss, ca. 1880)
Long & Drew (enamel) (London, ca. 1790-1810)
Losada, Jose R. (London, 1835-1890)
Lowndes, Jonathan (London, ca. 1680-1700)
MacCabe, James (London, 1778-1830)
Maillardet & Co. (Swiss, ca. 1800)
Mairet, Sylvain (Swiss, 1825-1885) (London,
  1830-1840)
Malignon, A. (Geneva, ca. 1835)
Marchand, Abraham (Geneva, 1690-1725)
Margetts, George (London, 1780-1800)
Markwick Markham, "Perigal" "Recordon"
  (London, 1780-1825)
Marshall, John (London, ca. 1690)
Martin (Paris, ca. 1780)
Martin, Thomas (London, ca. 1870)
Martineau, Joseph (London, 1765-1790)
Martinot, "family" (Paris, 1570-1770)
Martinot, James (London, ca. 1780)
Mascarone, Gio Batt (London, ca. 1635)
Massey, Edward (England, 1800-1850)
Massey, Henry (London, 1692-1745)
E. Mathey-Tissot & Co. (Swiss, 1886-1896)
Matile, Henry (Swiss, ca. 1825)
Maurer, Johann (Fiessna, Ger., ca. 1640-1650)
May, George (English, 1750-1770)
Mayr, Johann Peter (Augsburg, Ger., ca. 1770)
McCabe, James (London, 1780-1710)
McDowall, Charles (London, ca. 1820-1860)
Meak, John (London, ca. 1825)

Mecke, Daniel (ca. 1760)
Melly, Freres (Geneva, Paris, 1791-1844)
Mercier, A. D. (Swiss, 1790-1820)
Mercier, Francois David (Paris, ca. 1700)
Meuron & Co. (Swiss, ca. 1784)
Meylan, C. H. "Meylan W. Co." (Swiss, ca. 1880)
Michel, Jean-Robert (Paris, ca. 1750)
Miller, Joseph (London, ca. 1728)
Milleret & Tissot (ca. 1835)
Miroir (London, ca. 1700-1725)
Mistral (Swiss, ca. 1902)
Mobilis (Swiss, ca. 1910)
Modernista (Swiss, ca. 1903)
Moillet, Jean-Jacques (Paris, 1776-1789)
Molina, Antonio (Madrid, Spain, ca. 1800)
Molinie (Swiss, ca. 1840)
Molyneux, Robert (London, ca. 1825-1850)
Montandon, Chs. Ad. (Swiss, 1800-1830)
Morand, Pierre (Paris, ca. 1790)
Moricand & Co. (Swiss, ca. 1780)
Moricand & Desgranges (Geneva, 1828-1835)
Moricand, Christ (Geneva, 1745-1790)
Morin, Pierre (English, French & Dutch style, ca. 1700)
Morliere (enamel) (Blois, Fr., ca. 1636-1650)
Moser, George Michael (London, ca. 1716-1730)
Motel, Jean Francois (French, 1800-1850)
Moulineux, Robert (London, 1800-1840)
Moulinier, Aine & Co. (Swiss, 1828-1851)
Moulinier, Freres & Co. (Swiss, ca. 1822)
Mudge, Thomas (London, 1740-1790)
Mulsund (enamel) (Paris, ca. 1700)
Munoz, Blas (Madrid, Spain, ca. 1806-1823)
Mussard, Jean (Geneva, 1699-1727)
Musy Padre & Figlo (Paris, 1710-1760)
Myrmecide (Paris, ca. 1525)
Nardin, Ulysse (Swiss, ca. 1846)
Nelson, W. (London, 1777-1818)
Nocturne (ca. 1920)
Noir, Jean-Baptiste (Paris, 1680-1710)
Norris, J. (Dutch, 1680-1700)
Nouwen, Michael (1st English, 1580-1600)
Noyean (ca. 1850)
Oldnburg, Johan (German, ca. 1648)
Oudin, Charles (Paris, 1807-1900)
Owen, John (English, ca. 1790)
Palmer, Samuel (London, ca. 1790-1810)
Panier, Iosue "Josue" (Paris, ca. 1790)
Papillon (ca. 1690)
Papillon, Francesco (Florence, ca. 1705)
Parr, Thomas (London, ca. 1735-1775)
Payne, H. & John (London, ca. 1735-1775)
Pellaton, Albert (Swiss, ca. 1873)
Pellaton, James (Swiss, 1903) (Tourbillon)
Pendleton, Richard (London, 1780 1805)
Pennington, Robert (English, 1780-1816)
Perigal, Francis (English, 1770-1790)
Pernetti, F. (Swiss, ca. 1850)
Perrelet, Abram (Swiss, 1780) (self wind)
Perret, Edouard (Swiss, 1850)
Perrin, Freres (Swiss, 1810)
Phillips, Edouard (Paris, ca. 1860)
Phleisot (Dijon, Fr., ca. 1540)
Piaget, George (Swiss, ca. 1881)
Picard, James (Geneva, ca. 1850)
Piguet & Capt (Geneva, 1802-1811)

Piguet & Meylan (Geneva, 1811-1828)
Piguet, Victorin-Emile (Geneva, 1870-1935)
Plairas, Solomon (Blois, Fr., ca. 1640)
Plumbe, David (ca. 1730)
Poitevin, B. (Paris, 1850-1935)
Poncet, J. F. (Dresden, 1750)
Poncet, Jean-Francois (Swiss, 1740-1800)
Potter, Harry (London, 1760-1800)
Pouzait, Jean-Moise (Geneva, 1780-1800)
Poy, Gottfrey (London, ca. 1725-1730)
Prest, Thomas (English, 1820-1855)
Prevost, Freres (ca. 1820)
Prior, Edward (London, 1825-1865)
Prior, George (London, 1800-1830)
Pyke, John (English, 1750-1780)
Quare, Daniel (London, 1700-1724)
Quarella, Antonio (ca. 1790)
Racine, Cesar (Swiss, ca. 1902)
Racine, Charles Frederic (Chaux-de-Fonds, Sw., ca. 1810-1832)
Raillard, Claude (Paris, 1662-1675)
Raiss (1890-1910) (enamel)
Rait, D. C. (German, ca. 1866)
Ramsay, David (Scotland, France, London, 1590-1654)
Ramuz, Humbert U. & Co. (Swiss, ca. 1882)
Ratel, Henri (Paris, 1850-1900)
Recordon, Louis (London, 1778-1824)
Redier, Antoine (Paris, 1835-1883)
Renierhes (London, ca. 1850)
Rey, Jn. Ante, & Fils (Paris, 1790-1810)
Reynaud, P. & Co. (1860)
Rich, John (Geneva, London, 1795-1825)
Richard, Daniel Jean (1685-1740)
Richter, Jean Louis (enamel) (Geneva, 1786-1840)
Rigaud, Pierre (Geneva, 1750-1800)
Rigot, Francois (Geneva, ca. 1825)
Robert & Courvoisier & Co. (Paris, 1781-1832)
Robin, Robert (Paris, 1765-1805)
Robinet, Charles (Paris, ca. 1640)
Robinson, Olivier & Fredmahn (Naples, 1727-1790)
Rogers, Isaac (London, 1770-1810)
Romilly, Sieur (Geneva, ca. 1750-1775)
Rooker, Richard (London, 1790-1810)
Rose, Joseph (London, 1752-1795)
Rosier, John (Geneva, ca. 1750)
Roskell, Robert (London, 1798-1830) (rack-lever)
Roskopf, G. (German to Swiss, 1835-1885)
Rosselet, Louis (Geneva, 1855-1900) (enamel)
Rousseau, Jean (Paris, 1580-1642)
Roux, Bordier & Co. (Geneva, ca. 1795)
Ruegger, Jacques (ca. 1800-1840)
Ruel, Samuel (Rotterdam, ca. 1750)
Rugendas, Nicholas (Augsburg, Ger., ca. 1700-1750)
Rundell & Bridge (London, ca. 1772-1825)
Sailler, Johann (Vienna, Aus., ca. 1575)
Sanchez, Cayetano (Madrid, Spain, c. 1790-1800)
Sandoz, Henri F. (Tavannes W. Co.) (ca. 1840)
Savage, George (London, 1808-1855) (Inv. pin lever)
Savage, William (London 1800-1850)
Savile, John (London, ca. 1656-1679)
Schatck, Johann Engel (Prague, ca. 1650)

Schultz, Michael (ca. 1600-1650)
Schuster, Caspar (Nunburg, ca. 1570)
Sermand, J. (Geneva, ca. 1640)
Sherman De Neilly (Belfort, ca. 1910)
Sherwood, J. (London, ca. 1750-1775)
Solson (London, 1750)
Soret (Geneva, ca. 1810)
Soret, Frederic II (1735-1806)
Soret, Isaac & Co. (1690-1760)
Spencer & Perkins (London, 1790-1808)
Stadlin, Francois (Swiss, 1680-1735)
Staples, James (1755-1795)
Stuffer, M. T. (Swiss, 1830-1855)
Stauffer "Stauffer Son & Co." (London, 1880)
Strasser & Rohde (Glashutte, 1875)
Sudek, J. (ca. 1850)
Sully, Henry (French, London, 1700-1725)
Swift, Thomas (London, ca. 1825-1865)
Tavan, Antoine (Geneva, 1775-1830)
Tavernier, Jean (Paris, 1744-1795)
Tempor Watch Co. (1930) (Masonic watch)
Terond, Allier & Bachelard (ca. 1805-1830)
Terrot & Fazy (ca. 1767-1775)
Terrot, Philippe (Geneva, ca. 1732)
Terroux (ca. 1776)
Theed & Pikett (ca. 1750)
Thierry, J. (London, ca. 1760)
Thierry, Niel (ca. 1810)
Thiout, Antoine (Paris, 1724-1760)
Thorne, Robert (London, 1850)
Thoroton, James (London, 1860)
Thuret, Jacques (Paris, ca. 1695)
Thompion, Thomas (English, 1671-1713)
Timing & Repeating W. Co. (Geneva, 1900)
Tonkin, Tho. (London, ca. 1760)
Toutaia, Henri (French, 1650) (enamel)
Toutin, Jean (enamel) (Blois, Fr., ca. 1630)
Treffler, Sebastain (ca. 1750)
Tregent, J. (English, 1765-1800)
Truitte, Louis & Mourier (Geneva, ca. 1780)
Tyrer, Thomas (London, ca. 1782)

Uhren Fabrik Union (Glashutte, 1893-1970)
Ullman, J. & Co. (Swiss, 1893)
Ulrich, Johann (London, 1820-1870)
Upjohn, W. J. (London, 1815-1824)
Vacheron, Abraham Girod (German, 1760-1843)
Valere (Paris, 1860)
Vallier, Jean (Lyons, Fr., ca. 1630)
Valove, James (London, ca. 1740)
Vanbroff, James (Germany, ca. 1600)
Van Ceule, J. (ca. 1799-1725)
Vandersteen (ca. 1725)
Vaucher, C. H. (Geneva, ca. 1835)
Vaucher, Daniel (Paris, 1767-1790)
Vaucher, Freres (Swiss, 1850)
Vauquer, Robert (French, ca. 1650) (enamel)
Veigneur, F. I. (ca. 1780)
Vernod, Henriette (Paris, ca. 1790)
Vigne, James (London, ca. 1770)
Vrard, L., & Co. (Pekin, 1860-1872)
Vulliamy, Justin (London, ca. 1830-1854)
Vully, Jaques (ca. 1890-1900)
Vuolf (Swiss, ca. 1600)
Waldron, John (London, 1760)
Wales, Giles & Co. (Swiss, ca. 1870)
Waltrin (Paris, ca. 1820)
Weston, D. & Willis (enamel) (London, ca. 1800-1810)
Whitthorne, James (Dublin, since 1725)
Willats, John (London, ca. 1860)
Williamson, Timothy (London, 1770-1790)
Wilter, John (London, ca. 1760)
Winckles, John (London, 1770-1790)
Winnerl, Joseph Thaddeus (Paris, 1829-1886)
Wiss, Freres & Menu (Swiss, ca. 1787-1810)
Wiss, G. (Geneva, ca. 1750)
Wright, Charles (London, 1760-1790)
Wright, Thomas (English, ca. 1770-1790)
Young, Richard (London, 1765-1785)
Zech, Jacob (Prague, Aus. 1525-1540)
Zolling, Ferdinand (Frankfurt, Ger. ca. 1750)

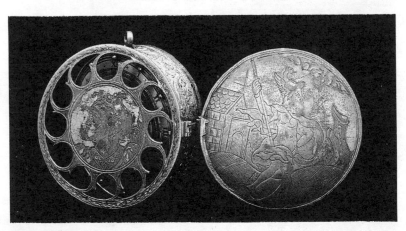

Tambour style case, probably Nuremburg, ca. 1575, hinged cover, pierced to reveal engraved Roman chapter I-XII and Arabic 13-24 Central chapter, 60mm.

HALLMARKS OF LONDON

Hallmarks were used on gold and silver cases imported from England. These marks, when interpreted, will give you the age of the case and location of the assay office.

The date-marks used 20 letters of the alphabet, A-U, never using the letters W, X, Y, or Z. The letters J & I or U & V, because of their similarity in shape, were never used together within the same 20-year period. A total of four marks can be found on English cases, which are:

The Maker's Mark   The Standard Mark

The Assay Office Mark   The Date Letter Mark

1822-up   1478 to 1821

The **Maker's Mark** was used to denote the manufacturer of the case.

The **Standard Mark** was used to denote a guarantee of the quality of the metal.

The **Assay Office Mark** (also known as the town mark) was used to denote the location of the assay office.

The **Date Letter Mark** was a letter of the alphabet used to denote the year in which the article was stamped. The stamp was used on gold and silver cases by the assay office.

SWISS HALLMARKS

18k .750   14k .585   Platinum

Sterling Silver   Silver .800

LONDON HALLMARKS

Letter	Year		Letter	Year		Letter	Year
◊	1551		M	1589		k	1627
P	1552		N	1590		l	1628
Q	1553		O	1591		m	1629
R	1554		P	1592		n	1630
S	1555		Q	1593		o	1631
T	1556		R	1594		p	1632
V	1557		S	1595		q	1633
a	1558		T	1596		r	1634
b	1559		V	1597		s	1635
C	1560		A	1598		t	1636
d	1561		B	1599		U	1637
e	1562		C	1600		A	1638
f	1563		D	1601		B	1639
g	1564		E	1602		C	1640
h	1565		F	1603		D	1641
i	1566		G	1604		E	1642
k	1567		h	1605		F	1643
l	1568		I	1606		G	1644
m	1569		K	1607		H	1645
n	1570		L	1608		I	1646
o	1571		M	1609		K	1647
p	1572		N	1610		L	1648
q	1573		O	1611		M	1649
r	1574		P	1612		N	1650
s	1575		Q	1613		O	1651
t	1576		R	1614		P	1652
u	1577		S	1615		Q	1653
A	1578		T	1616		R	1654
B	1579		V	1617		S	1655
C	1580		a	1618		T	1656
D	1581		b	1619		V	1657
E	1582		C	1620		W	1658
F	1583		d	1621		X	1659
G	1584		e	1622		Y	1660
H	1585		f	1623		Z	1661
I	1586		g	1624		E	1662
K	1587		h	1625		F	1663
L	1588		i	1626		G	1664
						H	1665

Letter	Year		Letter	Year		Letter	Year
J	1666		◊	1709		r	1752
K	1667		◊	1710		◊	1753
L	1668		◊	1711		t	1754
M	1669		◊	1712		u	1755
N	1670		◊	1713		a	1756
O	1671		◊	1714		b	1757
P	1672		b	1715		c	1758
Q	1673		A	1716		d	1759
R	1674		B	1717		e	1760
S	1675		C	1718		f	1761
T	1676		D	1719		g	1762
V	1677		E	1720		h	1763
a	1678		F	1721		i	1764
b	1679		G	1722		k	1765
c	1680		H	1723		l	1766
d	1681		I	1724		m	1767
e	1682		K	1725		n	1768
f	1683		L	1726		o	1769
g	1684		M	1727		p	1770
h	1685		N	1728		q	1771
i	1686		O	1729		r	1772
k	1687		P	1730		s	1773
l	1688		Q	1731		t	1774
m	1689		R	1732		u	1775
n	1690		S	1733		a	1776
o	1691		T	1734		b	1777
p	1692		V	1735		c	1778
q	1693		a	1736		d	1779
r	1694		b	1737		e	1780
s	1695		c	1738		f	1781
t	1696		d	1739		g	1782
v	1697		d	1739		h	1783
u	1698		e	1740		i	1784
w	1699		f	1741		k	1785
x	1700		g	1742		l	1786
y	1701		H	1743		m	1787
z	1702		I	1744		n	1788
b	1703		K	1745		o	1789
c	1704		I	1746		p	1790
k	1705		m	1747		q	1791
l	1706		n	1748		r	1792
m	1707		o	1749		s	1793
n	1708		P	1750		t	1794
			q	1751		u	1795
						A	1796

Letter	Year		Letter	Year		Letter	Year
B	1797		f	1841		I	1884
C	1798		g	1842		K	1885
D	1799		h	1843		L	1886
E	1800		j	1844		M	1887
F	1801		k	1845		N	1888
G	1802		l	1846		O	1889
H	1803		M	1847		P	1890
I	1804		N	1848		Q	1891
K	1805		O	1849		R	1892
L	1806		P	1850		S	1893
M	1807		Q	1851		T	1894
N	1808		R	1852		U	1895
O	1809		S	1853		a	1896
P	1810		T	1854		b	1897
Q	1811		U	1855		c	1898
R	1812		a	1856		d	1899
S	1813		b	1857		e	1900
T	1814		c	1858		f	1901
U	1815		d	1859		g	1902
a	1816		e	1860		h	1903
b	1817		f	1861		i	1904
c	1818		g	1862		k	1905
d	1819		h	1863		l	1906
e	1820		i	1864		m	1907
f	1821		k	1865		n	1908
g	1822		l	1866		o	1909
h	1823		m	1867		p	1910
i	1824		n	1868		q	1911
k	1825		o	1869		r	1912
l	1826		p	1870		s	1913
m	1827		q	1871		t	1914
n	1828		r	1872		u	1915
o	1829		s	1873		a	1916
p	1830		t	1874		b	1917
q	1831		u	1875		c	1918
r	1832		A	1876		d	1919
s	1833		B	1877		e	1920
t	1834		C	1878		f	1921
u	1835		D	1879		g	1922
E	1836		E	1880		h	1923
B	1837		F	1881		i	1924
C	1838		G	1882		k	1925
D	1839		H	1883		l	1926
e	1840						

EUROPEAN WATCHES
COLLECTED IN AMERICA

Auguste Agassiz of Saint Imier and Geneva started manufacturing quality watches in 1832. They later became interested in making a flat style watch which proved to be very popular. Some of these movements can be fitted inside a $20 gold piece.

The company was inherited by Ernest Francillion who built a factory called Longines. The Longines factory continued the Agassiz line until the Great Depression.

Agassiz, 43mm, 17 jewels, stem wind, 14 carat case, open face, serial number 39,863.

Julius Assmann began producing watches with the help of Adolf Lange in 1852. His watches are stylistically identical to those produced by Lange. Later on he adopted his own lever style. Assmann made highly decorative watches for the South American market which are highly regarded by German collectors.

Audemars, Piguet & Cie. was founded in 1875 by Jules Audemars and Edward Piguet, both successors to fine horological families. This company produced many fine high grade and complicated watches, predominantly in nickel and, with a few exceptions, fully jeweled. Their complicated watches are sought after more than the plain timepieces. They also produced some very handsome wrist watches.

The Swiss company of **Blancpain** was founded in 1735 by **Jean-Jacques Blancpain**. The company still produces mechanical watches of the greatest craftsmanship, but does not make a quartz-type watch.

Abraham-Louis Breguet, one of the worlds most celebrated watchmakers.

Abraham-Louis Breguet was born at Neuchatel in 1747 and died in 1823. He was perhaps the greatest horologist of all time in terms of design, elegance, and innovation. He is responsible for the development of the tourbillion, the perpetual calendar, the shock-proof parachute suspension, the isochronal overcoil, and many other improvements. It is difficult to include him in this section because of the complexity surrounding identification of his work which was frequently forged, and the fact that so many pieces produced by his shop were unique. Suffice it to say that the vast majority of watches one encounters bearing his name were either marketed only by his firm or are outright fakes made by others for the export market. Much study is required for proper identification.

As early as 1884 **Leon Breitling** made chronographs using his own name. The Swiss company made chronographs during World War I for different governments, gaining important acceptance in this field. One such model is the "Chronomat."

Breitling Watch Co., about 16-18 size, 16 jewels, open face, stem wind, chronograph.

Henry Daniel Capt of Geneva was an associate of Isac Daniel Piguet for about 10 years from 1802 to 1812. Their firm produced quality watches and specialized in musicals, repeaters, and chronometers. By 1844 his son was director of the firm, and around 1880 the firm was sold to Gallopin.

Cartier was a famous artisan from Paris who first made powder flasks. By the mid-1840s the family became known as the finest goldsmiths of Paris. Around the turn of the century the Cartier firm was designing watches and in 1904 the first wrist watches were being made. In 1917 Cartier created a watch design that was to become known as the tank-style case. The tank-style case was made to look like tank caterpillars of the U. S. This style is still popular today.

The **Chopard** family made and crafted many fine watches as early as 1860 and by the 1920s were making watches for the Swiss Railway. The company was sold to a German company in 1960 and still produces very fine watches.

Edward John Dent worked with Vulliamy and Barraud separately before joining J. R. Arnold in 1830. After 10 successful years in that association, he established his own firm, **E. Dent & Co.**, which continued after his death in 1853. His name is associated with Big Ben, although his successor is responsible for the execution of that contract. Dent's chronometers and complicated watches are particularly desirable, whereas the later products of the company are less so.

Paul Ditisheim founded his company in 1892 at La Chaux de Fonds in Switzerland. He made extremely small watches, some as small as 6.75 millimeters. The company later became Vulcain et Volta, Ditisheim & Co.

Henry Robert Ekegren, a Swiss maker of quality watches, started in business around 1870. The firm specialized in flat watches, chronometers, and repeaters. Ekegren became associated with F. Koehn in 1891.

John Ellicott, an Englishman, made watches from 1706 to 1772. One of his most notable developments was the cylinder escapement. After Ellicott's death the company was named John Ellicott & Son.

J. Girard and A. Schild started a small company in the mid-1800s making movements only, and by 1906 the name was changed to **Eterna**. The company was well known for its precision pocket watches. By 1930 the company decided to make a small wrist watch, which they call the "baguette," and an eight-day alarm. Both proved to be very popular. A movement named the "Eterna-Matic" was being produced by 1948, and their first electronic watch was made in 1974, followed by the quartz "Kontiki" produced in 1976. This Swiss company still produces quality watches, both jeweled and electronic.

Charles Frodsham followed in the footsteps of his father William, whose father was close with Earnshaw. Charles became the most eminent of the family, producing very fine chronometers and some rare tourbillions and complicated watches. He died in 1871. The following code was used to denote the year in which the watch was made:

F R O D S H A M Z   Thus, FMHZ = 1860
1 2 3 4 5 6 7 8 0

Charles Frodsham, 55mm, jeweled through center wheel, engraved on movement "By appointment to the king, A.D. FMSZ" ⁵ 1850. Note Karrusel at top of movement. Included within the Karrusel are the balance and escape wheel. The whole mechanism revolves about once every 60 minutes.

In 1856 the Constant Girard and Henry Perragaux families founded the Swiss firm of **Girard-Perregaux**. About 1880 the firm made a tourbillion with three golden bridges. A replica of this watch was made in 1982. Both were a supreme expression of horological craftsmanship. In 1906 the company purchased the Hecht factory in Geneva. Girard-Perregaux has been recognized many times and still makes prestigious quartz and mechanical watches.

Jacques Edouard Gubelin joined the firm of Mourice Brithschmid in Lucerne around 1854. By 1919 Edouard Gubelin headed the firm. In 1921 they opened an office in New York and produced fine jewelry and watches for five generations.

The founder of the prestigious Swiss **International Watch Co.** was an American engineer F. A. Jones from Boston. The company began in 1868 and in 1879 was sold to Mr. J. Rauschenbach. The company today is still making precision, handcrafted watches. IWC is well known for its super-light watch constructed of titanium.

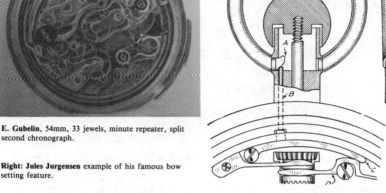

E. Gubelin, 54mm, 33 jewels, minute repeater, split second chronograph.

Right: Jules Jurgensen example of his famous bow setting feature.

The firm of **Jules Jurgensen** was an extension of the earlier firm of Urban Jurgensen & Sons, which was located, at various times, in Copenhagen and Le Locle. Jules ultimately established his firm in Le Locle after his father's death in the early 1830s. From that time forward the company produced, generally speaking, very fine watches that were high grade and complicated. It appears that by 1850 the company had already established a strong market in America, offering beautiful heavy 18k gold watches of exemplary quality. Until around 1885 most stem-winding watches exhibited the bow-setting feature. Almost any collectable Jurgensen watch will be fully signed on the dial and movement, with an impressively embossed "JJ" stamping on all covers of the case. Watches not so marked should be examined carefully; and untypical or inelegant stampings should be viewed suspiciously, as there has been some forgeries of these fine watches. Frequently one finds the original box and papers accompanying the watch, which exhances the value. After 1885, as the firm started to buy movements from other companies, we begin to see variations in Jurgensen watches. By 1930, Jurgensen watches barely resembled the quality and aesthetics of the early period, and they are not particularly desirable to the collector.

Jules Jurgensen, 17 jewels, rectangular 14k case.

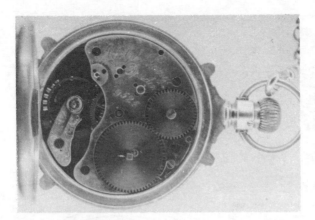

Adolf Lange, 49mm, jeweled through the center wheel, gold escape and pallet, gold jeweled settings, gold train, diamond end stones, 14k hunting case, serial number 9,524.

A. Lange & Sohne was established with the aid of the German government at Glashutte, Germany in 1845. Lange typically produced ¾ plate lever watches in gilt finish for the domestic market, and in nickel for the export market. High grade and very practical, these watches had a banking system for the pallet that was later used briefly by E. Howard in America. Lange complicated watches are scarce and very desirable.

Le Coultre and Co. was founded by Antoine Le Coultre in 1833. A fine clockmaker, he created a machine to cut pinions from solid steel as well as other machines for manufacturing clocks and watches. By 1900 they were making flat or thin watches. They made parts for Patek Philippe & Co., Tissoy, Vacheron & Constantin, Omega, Paul Ditisheim, Agassiz, Longines and others.

Le Coultre round 18k gold case with sweep center second and date.

Le Roy et Cie. was the final product of a dynasty of great watch-makers, starting with Julien Le Roy and his son Pierre, whose credits are numerous in the development of horology in the 18th century. There is, however, much confusion and hooplah over "Le Roy" watches. Frequently you will see watches signed "Le Roy" that have nothing to do with the original family. These watches are unimportant. You have to distinguish between the works of Julien, of Pierre, of Charles; and of their contemporary namesakes. The modern firm, Le Roy et Cie., established in the late 19th century, contracted and finished some very fine and, in some cases, extremely important complicated watches, using imported Swiss ebauches.

The beautiful **Fabrique des Longines** is situated in St. Imier, Switzerland. The company was founded by Ernest Francillon in 1866. They manufacture all grades of watches.

Meylan Watch Co., founded by C. H. Meylan in 1880, manufactured fine watches, with complications, in Le Brassus, Switzerland.

Movado pocket watch, 42mm, 15 jewels, 8 day with alarm.

L. A. Ditisheim & Freres founded their company in 1881 and the name **Movado** ("always in motion") was adopted in 1905. The Swiss company invented a system of watch making which they called "Polyplan." This was an arrangement of three different angles to the watch movement which produced a curve effect to the case so as to fit the curvature of the arm. Another unusual watch produced by this company in 1926 was the "Ermeto." This watch was designed to be protected while inside a purse or pocket, and each time the cover was opened to view the time, the watch was partially wound.

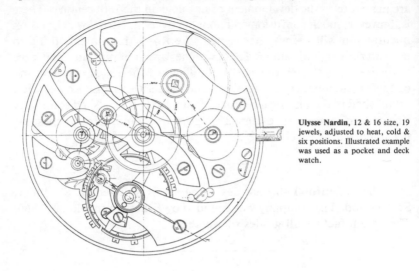

Ulysse Nardin, 12 & 16 size, 19 jewels, adjusted to heat, cold & six positions. Illustrated example was used as a pocket and deck watch.

Ulysse Nardin was born in 1823. The company he started in 1846 produced many fine timepieces and chronometers, as well as repeaters and more complicated watches. This firm, as did Assmann, found a strong market in South America as well as other countries. Ulysse's son Paul David Nardin succeeded him, as did Paul David's sons after him. The firm also made wrist watches.

Omega Watch Co. was founded by Louis Brandt in 1848. They produced watches of different grades. By 1920 Omega had manufactured about 5,000,000 watches; by 1923, 6,000,000; and by 1931, 10,000,000.

Patek, Philippe & Cie. has produced some of the world's most desirable factory-made watches. Antoine Norbert de Patek began contracting and selling watches in the 1830s, later became partners with Francois Czapek, and generally produced lovely decorative watches for a high class of clientel. In 1845 Adrien Philippe, inventor of the modern stem-winding system, joined the firm of Patek & Cie., and in 1851 the firm established its present name. Between Philippe's talent as a watch-maker and Patek's talent as a businessman with a taste for the impec-cable, the firm rapidly established an international reputation which lasts to this day.

Patek, Philippe & Co., 39 jewels, self wind movement, 18k case.

Early Patek, Philippe & Cie. watches are generally signed only on the dust cover, but some are signed on the dial and cuvette. It was not until the 1880s that the practice began of fully signing the dial, move-ment and case—perhaps in response to some contemporary forgery, but more likely a necessity to conform to customs' regulations for their growing international market. Many early and totally original Patek watches have suffered from the misconception that all products of this company are fully signed. Nevertheless, collectors find such pieces more desirable. It requires more experience, however, to determine the originality of the earlier pieces. As with Vacheron & Constantin, some watches were originally cased in America, but this lowers their value in general.

The Swiss company **Piaget** was founded by Georges Piaget who has a history of employing master goldsmiths. They have always pro-duced watches in limited amounts, and watch collectors seek out these watches of *D'art*.

Rolex was founded by Hans Wilsdorf in 1919. In 1926 they made the first real waterproof wrist watch and called it the "oyster." In 1931, Rolex introduced a self-wind movement which they called "perpetual." In 1945 they introduced the "datejust" which showed the day of the month. The "submariner" was introduced in 1953 and in 1954 the "GMT Master" model. In 1956 a "day-date" model was released which indicates the day of the month (in numbers) and the day of the week (in letters).

In 1837 **Charles Lewis Tiffany** opened a store with John P. Young. They enlarged this operation in 1841, with the help of J. L. Eliss, and imported fine jewelry, watches and clocks from Europe. They incorporated as **Tiffany & Co.** in 1853. Tiffany made clocks, on special order, in New York around the mid-1880s. About 1874 Tiffany & Co. started a watch factory in Geneva but with little success. Four years later Patek, Philippe & Co. assumed the management of their Geneva watch business. The watch machinery was returned to America. Tiffany, Young & Ellis had been a client of Patek, Philippe & Co. since 1849. Tiffany & Co. introduced Patek, Philippe to the American market in 1851. Audemars, Piguet and International Watch Co. also made watches for this esteemed company. Tiffany & Co. sell watches of simple elegance as well as watches with complications such as chronographs, moonphases, repeaters, etc.

Vacheron & Constantin, about 38-39mm, 21 jewels, nickel bridge movement, wolf tooth wind, 18k case, serial number 386,637.

The firm of **Vacheron & Constantin** was officially founded by Abraham Vacheron in 1785, but the association bearing the name today did not come into being until 1819. In these early periods, different grades of watches produced by Vacheron & Constantin bore different names. The firm produced several hundred thousand watches. The association with Leschot, around 1840, catapulted the firm into its position as a top quality manufacturer. Before that time, their watches were typical of Genevese production. Vacheron & Constantin exported many movements to the United States to firms such as Bigelow, Kennard & Co., which were cased domestically, typically in the period 1900-1935. In its early period the firm produced some lovely ladies' enameled watches, later it produced high grade timepieces and complicated watches, and to this day produces fine wrist watches.

Zenith Watch and clock factory was founded in 1865 by George Farvre Jacot. They mass produced watches of different grades in large quantities. By 1920 they had manufactured 2,000,000 watches.

Example of **Split Second & Fly-Back Movement** with a minute repeater, c. 1890.

Example of **English Clock Watch**, 20 size, jeweled through hammers, minute repeater. Note two train movement.

REPEATING WATCHES

Repeating watches or repeaters are those watches which will sound the time at the wish of the user. The repeating mechanism is operated by either a slide, plunger, or button in the case of the watch. There are basically five types of repeating mechanisms, some more common than others:

(1). QUARTER REPEATERS—The quarter repeater strikes the previous hour and quarter hour. In the older watches—usually verge— the striking is on a single bell attached to the inside of the case and the hour and quarter striking uses the same tone. There is first a series of hammer blows on the bell to indicate the hours, followed, after a short pause, by up to three twin strikes to denote the number of quarters elapsed. In later watches the striking is on wire gongs attached to the movement itself. The hours are struck on a single deep gong and the quarters on a higher-pitched gong followed by the deeper gong, producing a "ting-tang" sound.

(2). HALF-QUARTER REPEATERS—These strike the hours, the last quarter (ting-tang) and the previous half-quarter; i.e., seven and a half minutes. Half-quarter repeaters are mostly all verge escapement watches and are rarely seen by the average collector.

(3). FIVE-MINUTE REPEATERS—These fall into two types. One system is similar to the half-quarter repeater but follows the quarter "ting-tang" by a single higher-pitched strike for each five minute interval elapsed since the last quarter. The other system strikes the hours on a deep gong and follows this with a single higher note for each five minute period after the hour, omitting a quarter striking.

(4). MINUTE REPEATERS—This is the most complicated of the repeating mechanisms and is similar to the quarter repeater with the addition of the minutes being struck on the higher-pitched gong after the quarters.

(5). CLOCK WATCHES—The clock watch is essentially a repeater with the features of a striking clock. Whereas the above-mentioned repeaters are all operated by a plunger or slide which winds the repeating function and which runs down after the last strike, the clock watch is wound in the same way as the going train—usually with a key—and is operated by the touch of a button in the case. The repeat function can be operated many times before the watch needs to be rewound. The "clock" part of the name comes from the watch also striking the hours and sometimes the quarters or half hour in passing. The clock watch is easily recognizable by the two winding holes in either the case or the dial.

In addition to the five types described above, the features of striking are sometimes found with not only two but three and even four gongs, this producing a peal of notes. These repeaters are known as "carillons."

At the other end of the scale from the carillon is the "dumb" repeater. This strikes on a block of metal in the case or on the movement and is felt rather than heard. It is said that the idea was to produce a watch that would not embarrass its owner when he wished to know when to slip away from boring company. Although the dumb repeater is less desirable for the average collector, it certainly should not be avoided—Breguet himself made dumb repeaters.

A BIT OF HISTORY

Now that we have seen what repeaters are supposed to do, it might be in order to look briefly at their origins.

Before the days of electric light, it was a major project to tell the time at night, since striking a tinderbox was said to have taken up to fifteen minutes to accomplish. Clocks, of course, had striking mechanisms, but they tended to keep the occupants of the house awake listening for the next strike. The repeating addition to the clock meant that the master of the house could silence the passing strike at night and, at his whim, simply pull a cord over his bed to activate the striking in another part of the house and thus waking everyone. To silence those members of the household who did not appreciate a clock booming out in the early hours of the morning, the horologists of the day turned their thoughts to the idea of a repeating watch.

The first mention of repeating watches is in the contest between Daniel Quare (1649-1724) and the Rev. Edward Barlow (1639-1719) to miniaturize the repeating action of a clock. Barlow, who for some reason had changed his name from Booth, was a theoretical horologist of outstanding ability. Barlow's design—made for him by Thomas Tompion—and Quare's watch were both submitted to King James II and the Privy Council for a decision as to whom should be granted a patent. The King chose Quare's design because the repeating mechanism was operated by a single push-button, whereas Barlow's required two. Quare was granted a patent in 1687. Barlow had had his share of fame earlier, however, with the invention of rack-striking for clocks in 1676.

Quare went into production with his new repeater watches, but changed the design to replace the push-button in the case with a pendant that could be pushed in. The first of these watches showed a fault that is still found on the cheaper repeaters of this century—that is, if the pendant was not pushed fully in, then the incorrect hours were struck. To overcome this problem, he invented the so-called ''all-or-nothing'' piece. This is a mechanism whereby if the pendant was not pushed fully home, then the watch would not strike at all.

The half-quarter appeared shortly after the all-or-nothing piece, and then by about 1710 the five-minute repeater was on the market. Some five years after this, a ''deaf-piece'' was often fitted to the watch. This was a slide or pin fitted to the case which, when activated, caused the hammers to be lifted away from the bell and had the same effect as a dumb repeater.

Sometime around 1730, Joseph Graham decided to dispense with the idea of a bell and arranged for the hammers to strike a dust-cover, thus making the watch slimmer and preventing dust from entering the pierced case.

About the middle of the century, the French master Le Roy carried the idea a stage further and dispensed with both bells and dust-covers, and used a metal block which revolutionized the thickness of the repeating watch and introduced the dumb repeater. Breguet used wire gongs around 1789 and the pattern for the modern repeater was set. The minute repeater came into more common use after 1800, and earlier examples are definitely very rare, although it is known that Thomas Mudge made a complicated watch incorporating minute repeating for Ferdinand VI of Spain about 1750.

By the last quarter of the 1700s, Switzerland had gone for the repeater in a big way and the centre of fine craftsmanship for complicated watches was in the Valley of Joux. Here the principle of division of labour was highly refined and whole families were hard at work producing parts for repeating and musical watches. Since one person concentrated only on one part of the watch, it is hardly surprising that parts of excellent quality were turned out. The basic movements were then sold to watchmakers/finishers all over the Continent and even to England, where the principle of one man, one watch, among the stubborn majority eventually led to the downfall of what had once been the greatest watchmaking nation in history.

The greatest popularity of the repeater came, however, in the last quarter of the 1800s, when Switzerland turned them out in the tens of thousands. Although there were many different names on the dials of the watches, most seem to have been produced by the company "Le Phare" and only finished by the name on the dial. The production of repeaters in quantity seems to have ground to a finish in about 1921 due to (a) the invention of luminous dials and universal electric or gas lighting, and (b) a lack of watchmakers willing to learn the highly demanding skills. The interest in horology over the past decade has, however, revived the idea of the repeater and several companies in Switzerland are now producing limited editions of expensive models.

BUYING A REPEATER

Since so many repeaters seem to have been repaired at some time in the past by incompetent watchmakers, it is often too expensive a purchase if the buyer does not know what he is doing.

Rule One should be: if it does not work perfectly, avoid it like the plague unless a competent repairer first gives you an estimate which suits your pocket. All too often in the past the repairer was under the impression that metal grows with age and he has filed the teeth of a rack in order to get the full striking to work again. When it dawned on him that the problem was a worn bearing, the tooth was stretched with a punch and refiled, making it weak. It was then goodbye to a fine piece of craftsmanship.

A better quality repeater is usually one which is "jewelled to the hammers." This simply means that the hammers have jewelled bearing—which can be seen by searching the movement for the hammers, locating the pivots around which they swing, and looking for the jewelled bearing in which they sit.

All repeaters have some system for regulating the speed of the repeating train. On the older fusee types, there was usually a rather primitive arrangement of a pinion in an eccentric bushing which could be turned to increase or decrease the depth of engagement of the pinion with the next wheel. Another system, a little better, uses an anchor and a toothed wheel as in an alarm clock. This system is usually located under the dial but can be detected by the buzzing sound it makes when the train is operated. The far superior system is the centrifugal governor which can be seen whizzing around in the top plate of the watch when the repeating action is operated. On the whole, the watch with the centrifugal governor is more desirable, although it must be mentioned that the Swiss turned out some inferior watches with this system.

If possible—and it should be possible if you are investing a lot of money—have a watchmaker look under the dial to see if the watch is jewelled throughout. Many are only jewelled in the places the owner can see and leave much to be desired in the "blind" places.

Test the watch by operating the repeating train over a full hour, seeing that the quarters and minutes function correctly, then test each individual hour. Finally, set the hands to just before 1 o'clock and test the striking. Any defect due to dirt or worn bearings will show up by the final blow(s), being either sluggish or not striking at all. If there is incorrect striking, have an expert look at it before you buy.

Try a partial operation of the slide or push-piece. If the watch has an all-or-nothing piece (as a reasonable grade movement should have), then the watch will not strike. Partial striking indicates either a low-grade watch or a non-functioning all-or-nothing piece.

Additional features such as chronograph functions, calendar, moon phase, etc., will obviously affect the price of the watch and one must be guided by current price listings from reputable dealers.

Remember Rule One, though—if any function does not work, BEWARE!

Example of a 33 minute karrusel by **Russell & Son**, makers to the Queen (London), 55mm, 16 jewels, open face.

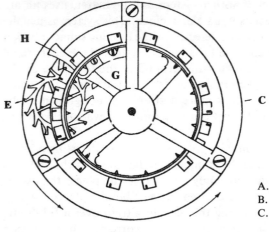

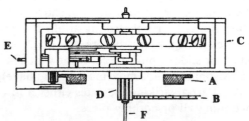

Tourbillon

A. Fixed fourth wheel
B. Third wheel
C. Carriage (one revolution per minute)
D. Carriage pinion
E. Escape Wheel & pinion
F. Arbor for seconds hand
G. Escape cock
H. Lever & pallets

TOURBILLON

Breguet invented the tourbillon in 1795. A tourbillon is a device designed to reduce the position errors of a watch. This device has the escape wheel, lever and balance wheel all mounted in a carriage of light frameworks. This carriage makes one complete turn every minute. The fourth wheel is fixed and is concentric with the carriage pinion and arbor. The escape wheel pinion meshes with the fourth wheel and will roll around the fixed fourth wheel. The escape wheel and lever are mounted on the carriage, and the third wheel drives the carriage pinion, turning the carriage once every minute. This rotation of the escapement will help reduce the position errors of a watch. One of the major objections is that the carriage and escapement weight mass must be stopped and started at each release of the escapement. The tourbillon design requires extreme skill to produce and is usually found on watches of high quality. Somewhat similar to the tourbillon is the karrusel, except it rotates about once per hour and the fourth wheel is not fixed. It also takes less skill to produce.

MUSICAL WATCHES

(Three basic types)

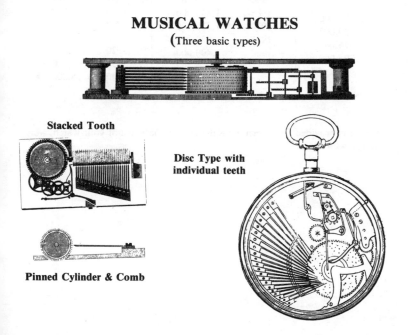

Stacked Tooth

Disc Type with individual teeth

Pinned Cylinder & Comb

PRODUCTION TOTALS

PATEK PHILIPPE

1840	100
1845	1,200
1850	3,000
1855	8,000
1860	15,000
1865	22,000
1870	35,000
1875	45,000
1880	55,000
1885	70,000
1890	85,000
1895	100,000
1900	110,000
1905	125,000
1910	150,000
1915	175,000
1920	190,000
1925	200,000
1950	700,000
1955	725,000
1960	750,000
1965	775,000
1970	795,000

1920	800,000
1925	805,000
1930	820,000
1935	824,000
1940	835,000
1945	850,000
1950	860,000
1955	870,000
1960	880,000
1965	890,000
1970	895,000
1940	900,000
1945	915,000
1950	930,000
1955	940,000
1960	960,000
1965	975,000
1970	995,000
1960	1,100,000
1965	1,130,000
1970	1,250,000
1975	1,330,000
1980	1,400,000

A. LANGE

1870	5,000
1875	10,000
1880	20,000
1885	25,000
1890	30,000
1895	35,000
1900	40,000
1905	50,000
1910	60,000
1915	70,000
1920	75,000
1925	80,000
1930	85,000
1935	90,000
1940	100,000

LONGINES

1870	20,000
1880	200,000
1890	600,000
1900	1,200,000
1910	2,000,000
1920	3,000,000
1930	5,000,000
1940	6,000,000

The above list is provided for determining the approximate age of your watch. Match serial number with date.

EUROPEAN POCKET WATCH LISTINGS
Pricing at Retail Level
(Complete Watches Only)

Unless otherwise noted, watches listed in this section are priced at the retail level and as complete watches having an original 14k gold-filled case with an original white enamel single sunk dial, and the entire original movement in good working order with no repairs needed. Watches listed as 14k and 18k are solid gold cases. Coin or silveroid-type and stainless steel cases will be listed as such. Keywind and keyset pocket watches are listed as having original coin silver cases. Dollar-type watches, or low cost production watches, are listed as having a base metal type case and a composition dial.

Many of the watch manufacturers were commissioned to put jewelers' or jobbers' names on their movements in place of their own. Because of this practice, the true manufacturers of these movements are difficult to identify. These watch models are listed under the original manufacturer and can be identified by comparison with the model sections under each manufacturer. See "Personalized Watches" for more detailed information.

The prices shown were averaged from dealers' lists just prior to publication and are an indication of the retail level or what collectors will pay. Prices are provided in three categories: average condition, extra fine, and mint condition, and are shown in whole dollar amounts only. The values listed are a guide for the retail level and are provided for your information only. Dealers will not necessarily pay full retail price. Prices listed are for watches with **original** cases and dials.

Note: Descriptions and serial number ranges listed for early watches cannot be considered 100 percent accurate due to the manner in which records were kept by these companies.

INFORMATION NEEDED—This price guide is interested in any facts and information you might have that should possibly be considered for future editions. Documented facts are needed. Please send photo or sources of information to Cooksey Shugart, 780 Church Street N.E., Cleveland, Tennessee 37311.

AGASSIZ
Swiss

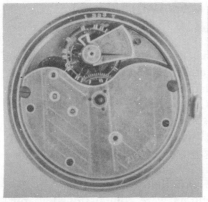

Agassiz, 43mm, 18 jewels, serial number 44,844.

Agassiz, 43mm, 21 jewels, ¾ plate, serial number 39,863.

Size and Description	Avg	Ex-Fn	Mint
52mm, split sec. chronograph, 14K, OF, register	$750	$900	$1,100
50mm, art deco, "Cartier," 1925, 19J, Adj.5P, 18K......	1,000	1,400	1,800
43mm, 17J, nickel mvt., 14K, OF	375	475	575
43mm, 21J, nickel mvt., 18K, OF, WI, 8 day............	700	850	1,050
40mm, 19J, World Time, 32 Cities, 14K, OF	3,600	4,250	5,000
40mm, 19J, World Time, 32 Cities, 18K, OF	4,250	5,000	5,800
37mm, 21J, 8 day, wind indicator, OF, 18K	650	775	950
Lady's, 40mm, HC, 18K, white enamel dial	300	350	475

Agassiz, 43mm, 17 jewels, World Time, 42 towns, ca. 1940.

Assmann, 44mm, 21 jewels, serial number 19,539, ca. 1914.

ASSMANN
GLASSHUTTE

Size and Description	Avg	Ex-Fn	Mint
44mm, elaborate chasing, fancy dial, for South American market, 18K, HC	$3,400	$4,200	$4,900
42mm, SW, Timepiece, OF, 18K	1,900	2,350	2,850

Assmann, 50mm, 19 jewels, diamond cap jewels, gold jewel settings, gold lever escapement, serial number 3,086, ca. 1855.

Assmann, 50mm, 19 jewels, diamond cap jewels, gold jewel settings, gold lever escapement, serial number 3,739, ca. 1857.

AUDEMARS, PIGUET
SWISS

Size and Description	Avg	Ex-Fn	Mint
46mm, OF, min. repeater, chronograph, register, 18K	$3,500	$4,250	$4,800

Audemars, Piguet, 46mm, 20 jewels, minute repeater. Note governor at right-hand side of balance bridge.

Audemars, Piguet, 48mm, 30 jewels, minute repeater, serial number 4,155, ca. 1890.

Size and Description	Avg	Ex-Fn	Mint
46mm, OF, min. repeater, split chronograph, register, 18K	$4,600	$5,250	$6,000
46mm, min. repeater, 18K, HC	3,500	4,200	5,000
46mm, 20J, ¼ repeater, OF, 18K	1,800	2,200	2,600
44-45mm, OF, timepiece, 18K	650	750	950
44mm, OF, min. repeater	2,800	3,400	4,000
44mm, OF, 5-min. repeater..........................	2,200	2,800	3,200
40mm, 31J, min. repeater, 18K, OF, c. 1875	3,000	3,600	4,500

Audemars, Piguet, 46mm, 36 jewels, minute repeater, split-second chronograph, serial number 3853, ca. 1888.

Audemars, Piguet, about 16 size, 18 jewels, adj.6P, jumping hour, day-date-month windows, ca. 1925.

J. W. BENSON
LONDON

Size and Description	Avg	Ex-Fn	Mint
58mm, Grande & Petite Sonnerie, min. repeater, perpetual calendar, moonphases	$54,000	$62,000	$70,000
40mm, KW, KS, fusee, lever, wind indicator, free sprung, 18K, HC................................	1,500	1,800	2,250

ABRAHAM LOUIS BREGUET
PARIS

Date	Serial No.	Date	Serial No.
1795	150	1815	2700
1800	600	1820	3500
1805	1600	1825	4500
1810	2000	1830	5000

Example of a typical Breguet souscription style face and movement. Gilt movement with central winding arbor, gilt balance with parachute suspension, ruby cylinder escapement. White enamel dial with secret signature at 12 o'clock.

Size and Description	Avg.	Ex-Fn	Mint
61mm, ruby cylinder, souscription, enamel dial, gold case .	$6,500	$8,000	$10,000
60mm, ruby cylinder, souscription, secret signature	7,500	8,500	10,500
60mm, ruby cylinder, souscription, back wind, gold case recased..	5,000	6,000	7,000
58mm, clock watch, verge, ting-tang on ½ hour, silver case signed Breguet & Fils but is a ebauche by F. Japy....	2,000	2,500	3,500
56mm, two train ruby cylinder, ¼ repeater, 18K gold case	3,000	4,000	5,000
55mm, ruby cylinder, parachute suspension, gold case	8,000	9,000	10,000
55mm, jacquemarts ¼ repeater, 2 automatons, gold case .	4,000	5,000	6,000
55mm, jacquemarts ¼ repeater, verge escapement, push pendant	3,500	4,500	5,500

Example of a typical souscription style Breguet movement. Dial side shown. Note the ruby cylinder escapement below finger bridge.

Abraham Breguet ¼ repeater, 55mm; a verge repeating watch with two jacquemarts with push pendant to repeat, serial number 23,592.

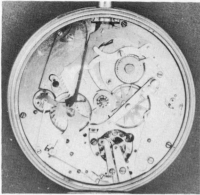

Abraham Louis Breguet, ¼ repeating, ruby cylinder watch. **Left:** gilt movement with standing barrel. Note jeweled parachute suspension. **Right:** Dial side of movement, repeating train with exposed springs.

Size and Description	Avg	Ex-Fn	Mint
55mm, montre simple, secret signature on enamel dial	$3,500	$4,000	$5,000
54mm, ruby cylinder, ¼ repeater, standing barrel, gold dial	10,000	12,000	15,000
54mm, ¼ repeater, verge escapement, push pendant, gold case	1,500	1,800	2,200
54mm, horologer de la marine royale, ¼ repeater, gold case	15,000	18,000	22,000
53mm, min. repeater, split sec. chronograph, two tone gold case, c. 1948	18,000	20,000	24,000
52mm, ruby cylinder, ¼ repeater, push pendant, gold case	10,000	12,000	15,000
52mm, ruby cylinder, ¼ repeater, push piece, gold case ..	10,000	12,000	15,000
51mm, min. repeater, chronograph, WI, day, month, moon phase, 18K case, c. 1932	40,000	45,000	50,000
49mm, ruby cylinder, parachute suspension, gold case	8,000	9,000	10,000
47mm, thin, perpetual calendar, moon ph., platinum case .	10,000	12,000	15,000

Important ¼ repeater Horloger De La Marine by Breguet. **Left:** Guilloche silver dial with roman numberals and typical Breguet hands. **Right:** Gilt brass movement with ruby cylinder escapement and triple arm balance.

Breguet hunting watch, 36mm. Case embellished with 12 pearls for tactile hours (Braille style watch). The arrow on case revolves. Souscription movement with 6 jewels, central barrel, ruby cylinder escapement.

Size and Description	Avg	Ex-Fn	Mint
45mm, thin digital watch, perpetual calendar, 18K case ...	$10,000	$12,000	$16,000
43mm, thin art deco, jump hours & rotary window, 18K ..	4,000	5,000	8,000
36mm, pearls tactile braille watch, 18K enamel case	25,000	30,000	35,000
18mm, small keyless watch, platinum balance, gold case ..	20,000	25,000	32,000

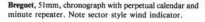

Breguet, 51mm, chronograph with perpetual calendar and minute repeater. Note sector style wind indicator.

Breguet, 53mm, minute repeating, split-second chronograph. Chronograph activated by crown and button on band. Repeater activated by slide.

BULOVA
SWISS AND U.S.A.

Size and Description	Avg	Ex-Fn	Mint
40mm, 18J, "Phantom," c. 1920, OF platinum case ★ ★ ★	$650	$850	$1,050

HENRY CAPT
GENEVE

Size and Description	Avg	Ex-Fn	Mint
52mm, min. repeater, perpetual calendar, moon phases, 18K hunting case	$22,000	$26,000	$32,000
Lady's, OF, 1 min. repeater, 18K	3,000	3,400	4,000

Henry Capt, 52mm, 32 jewels, minute repeater, serial number 34,711, ca. 1900.

Cartier, 52mm, 40 jewels, triple complicated-perpetual calendar, minute repeater, split-second chronograph

CARTIER
PARIS

Size and Description	Avg	Ex-Fn	Mint
52mm, 40J, triple complication moon phase astronomical min. repeater, perpetual calendar, day-date-month, split sec. chron, with min. recorder, signed European Watch & Clock Co., 18K case, c. 1930	120,000	130,000	150,000
49mm, 19J, art deco, black onyx, gold, enamel & diamonds on case	3,200	4,200	5,500

H. R. EKEGREN
GENEVE

Size and Description	Avg	Ex-Fn	Mint
55mm, min. repeater, jeweled to hammers, 18K case, OF	$3,300	$3,750	$4,500

H.R. EKEGREN (continued)

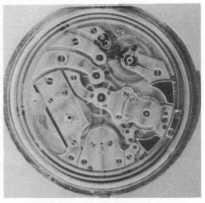

H.R. Ekegren, 39mm, minute repeater, slide activated, jeweled through hammers, open face, serial number 78,268.

H.R. Ekegren, 43mm, minute repeater, jeweled through hammers, hunting case.

Size and Description	Avg	Ex-Fn	Mint
43mm, min. repeater, 18K, HC, jeweled to hammers	$3,400	$3,800	$4,500
42mm, 18K, OF, fully jeweled, SW, LS	600	750	1,000
39mm, min. repeater, jeweled to hammers, OF, 18K	2,800	3,200	3,800

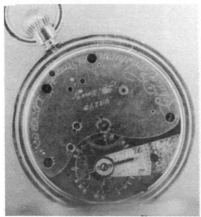

Frodsham, 44mm, jeweled through center wheel. Movement shows coded date under serial number. He used his name 'Frodsham' for numbers 1-8, and Z for 0. For example "AD. FMSZ" means the year 1850, serial number 04172.

Frodsham, 55mm, 60 minute karrusel, 15 jewels, stem wind, open face, 18k gold case, c. 1850.

FRODSHAM
LONDON

Size and Description	Avg	Ex-Fn	Mint
55mm, min. repeater, jeweled thru hammers, DES, 18K, HC	$4,600	$5,250	$6,250
55mm, 16J, 59 min., Karrusel, 18K case	4,600	5,200	5,800
54mm, one min., tourbillon, ¾ plate, signed, 18K, OF ...	26,000	32,000	38,000
44mm, detent escapement, 18K, HC	2,200	2,600	3,200
42mm, 17J, ¾ plate, GJS, DES, 18K, HC	1,000	1,200	1,500
42mm, KW, KS, wind indicator, free sprung, 18K, OF ...	1,300	1,500	1,750
35mm, ¼ & 5 min. repeater, by Thomas Frodsham, 18K, HC	4,700	5,200	6,000

GIRARD PERRAGAUX
SWISS

Size and Description	Avg	Ex-Fn	Mint
55mm, 3 gold bridges, c. 1884, silver case	$5,000	$6,000	$7,000

Girard Perragaux, 55mm, three golden bridge movement, patented March 25th, 1884.

GRUEN
SWISS AND U.S.A.

Size and Description	Avg	Ex-Fn	Mint
45mm, 14K, HC, by D. Gruen & Son, 21J, GJS, gold escape wheel, "Dresden," by Assman	$1,100	$1,300	$1,600
44mm, made for R.R. Service, GF	155	200	285
40mm, 19J, "Precision," SW, LS, YGF	100	120	145
40mm, 50th Anniversary, 21J, including 2 diamonds, 18K, OF	2,600	3,000	3,500
40mm, "Detrich Gruen," marked Extra Precision, 31J, min. repeater, 18K, OF	2,800	3,000	3,500
38mm, 17J, pentagon case, veri thin style, YGF..........	75	85	95
38mm, 17J, pentagon case, veri thin style, 14K	250	325	400
38mm, 17J, pentagon case, veri thin style, 18K	325	400	475

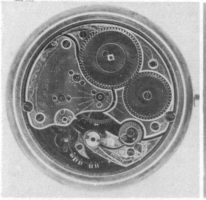

D. Gruen & Son, 44mm, jeweled through center wheel, made for railroad service, serial number 62,428.

Gruen 50th Anniversary Watch, 10 size, 21 jewels, (two diamonds) placed in a five-sided pentagon case, solid gold bridges.

Size and Description	Avg	Ex-Fn	Mint
38mm, 21J, RGJ, GT, Adj.5P, YGF	$75	$110	$145
38mm, 19J, GT, Adj.5P	65	95	110
38mm, 15J, ADJ.....................................	50	60	75
36mm, 17J, ultra veri thin, GF	50	60	75

E. GUBELIN
SWISS

Size and Description	Avg	Ex-Fn	Mint
54mm, min. repeater, 33J, split sec. chronograph, GT	$3,600	$4,200	$5,000
54mm, 28J, min. repeater, OF, 18K	2,600	2,900	3,400
50mm, min. repeater, chronograph, day-date-month, moon phase, 18K, HC.................................	5,000	5,800	6,800
38mm, 21J, deco style, Adj.5P, perpetual calendar, 18K, OF	5,000	5,800	6,800

E. Gubelin, 50mm, 29 jewels, minute repeater, chronograph, day-date-month-moon phase.

C.L. Guinand, 50mm, split-second chronograph, serial number 44,109.

C. L. GUINAND
SWISS

Size and Description	Avg	Ex-Fn	Mint
50mm, 34J, min. repeater, split sec. chronograph, 18K, OF	$3,200	$3,700	$4,400

HAAS, NEVEUX & CO.
SWISS

Size and Description	Avg	Ex-Fn	Mint
42mm, 18K, HC, cover wind	$2,200	$2,600	$3,200
40mm, 31J, min. repeater, 18K hunting case	3,000	3,400	4,200
40mm, 31J, min. repeater, 18K, OF	2,600	3,000	3,600
34mm, $20 gold piece form watch	1,250	1,550	2,000

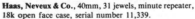

Haas, Neveux & Co., 40mm, 31 jewels, minute repeater, 18k open face case, serial number 11,339.

Hebdomas novelty watch, 8-day movement, balance can be seen from dial side.

HEBDOMAS
SWISS

Style or Grade—Description	Avg	Ex-Fn	Mint
50mm, 7J, 8 day, balance seen from dial	$100	$125	$165

INTERNATIONAL WATCH CO.
SWISS

Size and Description	Avg	Ex-Fn	Mint
54mm, 17J, lever escapement, GJS, 14K, HC	$475	$550	$650
42mm, early mvt., 18K, HC	550	750	950
42mm, OF, 14K case	375	450	550

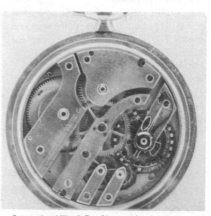

International Watch Co., 42mm, 18 size, 15 jewels, serial number 7,609.

International Watch Co., 54mm, 17 jewels, adj.6P, serial number 741,073.

JULES JURGENSEN
SWISS

Size and Description	Avg	Ex-Fn	Mint
55mm, OF, detent chronometer, KW, 18K	$3,200	$3,600	$4,200
55mm, OF, detent chronometer, SW, 18K..............	5,500	6,500	8,000
55mm, HC, detent chronometer, SW, 18K	6,000	7,200	8,500
50mm, OF, timepiece, enamel dial, 18K.................	1,800	2,200	2,800
49mm, ¼ repeater, c. 1880, nickel lever mvt., gold train, 18K HC...	2,400	2,800	3,400
46mm, OF, min. repeater, chronograph, register, 18K	4,800	5,400	6,200
46mm, OF, min. repeater, split chrono., register, 18K	6,000	6,800	7,800
46mm, HC, min. repeater, 18K	4,800	5,500	6,500
46mm, HC, min. repeater, chronograph, 18K............	5,200	6,000	7,000
46mm, HC, min. repeater, split chronograph, register, 18K	8,000	9,500	11,500
46mm, OF, chronograph, timepiece, register, 18K	2,400	2,800	3,600

Jules Jurgensen, 1 minute repeater, popular bow set, triple signed case, movement & dial, 18k hunting case, serial number 13,824.

Jules Jurgensen, 46mm, 21 jewels, hand-setting by inclination of pendant ring, serial number 14,492, ca. 1890.

Size and Description	Avg	Ex-Fn	Mint
46mm, OF, split chronograph, timepiece, register	$3,200	$3,800	$4,600
46mm, HC, chronograph, timepiece, register	2,800	3,250	4,000
46mm, HC, split chronograph, timepiece, register	3,800	4,400	5,200
45mm, OF, timepiece, enamel dial.....................	1,800	2,200	2,600
45mm, HC, timepiece, enamel dial	2,000	2,500	3,000
45mm, OF, KW, timepiece, enamel dial................	750	950	1,200
45mm, OF, min. repeater, enamel dial	3,800	4,400	5,200
44mm, OF, 5-min. repeater..........................	3,200	3,800	4,400
40mm, OF, timepiece, enamel dial....................	1,200	1,500	1,950
40mm, HC, timepiece, enamel dial	1,600	1,900	2,400

A. LANGE
GERMANY

Size and Description	Avg	Ex-Fn	Mint
55mm, min. repeater, 18K, HC, jeweled thru hammers, GJS, NI, GT, gold escape & pallet, DES, 1st quality mvt. .	$18,000	$20,000	$24,000
55mm, ¼ repeater, NI, DES, 1st quality mvt., HC.......	8,500	9,500	11,000
54mm, ¼ repeater, DES, jeweled thru hammers, OF	6,800	7,800	9,000
53mm, 18K case, c. 1885, GJS, GT, DES, gold pallet and escape wheel....................................	2,400	2,900	3,400
52mm, World War II model, WI, OF, silver case	1,200	1,400	1,800

A. **Lange & Sohne**, 52mm, wind indicator, World War II model, open face.

A. **Lange & Sohne**, 48mm, three-quarter plate, engraved on movement "Deutsche Uhren Fabrikation Glashutte," serial number 58,398.

Size and Description	Avg	Ex-Fn	Mint
49mm, 18K case, 17J, GJS, GT, gold escape wheel & pallet, c. 1914, OF....................................	$1,650	$2,000	$2,400
49mm, 18K case, HC, gild mvt., 17J, GJS, DES, gold lever and escape wheel................................	1,850	2,200	2,600
49mm, min. repeater, 3rd grade mvt., gilt, 14K, triple sized HC.......................................	8,500	9,500	11,500
48mm, ¾ plate, Deutsche Uhren Fabrikation, silver	450	550	700

LE COULTRE & CO.
SWISS

Size and Description	Avg	Ex-Fn	Mint
57mm, 32J, min. repeater, slide repeat, 14K, HC	$2,700	$3,200	$3,800
57mm, 32J, min. repeater, slide repeat, 18K, HC	2,400	2,750	3,250
55mm, 31J, min. repeater, day-date-month, moon phase, 18K, HC	4,200	5,000	6,000
55mm, 30J, min. repeater, 2 automatons, c. 2900, 18K case	7,000	8,000	9,000
54mm, min. repeater, gilt, lever escapement, 14K, HC	1,800	2,200	2,700

Le Coultre & Co., 57mm, 32 jewels, minute repeater, exposed winding gears, 14k hunting case.

Le Coultre & Co., 55mm, 31 jewels, day, date, month and moon phases, 18k hunting case, minute repeater.

Style or Grade—Description	Avg	Ex-Fn	Mint
52mm, ¼ repeater, double dial, calendar, moon phase, 18K, HC	$3,200	$3,700	$4,300
49mm, nickel mvt., 18K, OF	500	650	800

Le Coultre, 55mm, 30 jewels, minute repeater, two automatons.

Le Phare, 56mm, minute repeater, chronograph & calendar with moon phases.

LE PHARE
SWISS

Size and Description	Avg	Ex-Fn	Mint
56mm, min. repeater, day-date-month, moon phase, 18K case	$2,800	$3,200	$3,600

LE ROY
SWISS

Size and Description	Avg	Ex-Fn	Mint
55mm, musical, plays on demand, repeater, 18K	$2,500	$3,000	$3,600
20mm, ¼ repeater, exposed repeat work on back plate, pearl bezel, 18K...............................	3,200	3,800	4,500

Leroy, 50mm, minute repeater, two train, tandem winding wheels, jump center seconds.

LONGINES
SWISS

Size and Description	Avg	Ex-Fn	Mint
59mm, 30J, min. repeater, chronograph, calendar & moon moon phases, 18K HC	$3,600	$4,400	$5,500
59mm, 26J, min. repeater, chronograph, 2 registers, 18K..	2,000	2,500	3,000
55mm, OF, 18K, split chronograph, 2 registers	1,400	1,650	2,000
50mm, chronograph with register, nickel mvt., silver	200	225	295
50mm, 8 day, wind indicator, 15J, Adj.3P, silver	325	425	550
46mm, 21J, "Express Monarch," R.R. approved, Adj.5P.	175	195	235
46mm, rectangular case, 30 small diamonds on case, 15J..	700	900	1,200
44mm, 15J, 3 ADJ, 8 day, WI, 14K....................	500	600	750
44mm, "U. S. Army," sweep sec. hand, WI, Adj.5P.....	300	350	425
26mm, lady's pendant, 18K, OF, enamel & diamonds.....	600	700	850

Longines, 44mm, 21 jewels, U.S. Army AC, adjusted to temp. & 5 positions, World War II model, serial number 5,939,626.

Longines, 59mm, 26 jewels, minute repeater, chronograph, two registers, ca. 1910.

MATHEY-TISSOT
SWISS

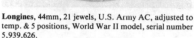

Size and Description	Avg	Ex-Fn	Mint
52mm, ¼ jump sec. chronograph, tandem wind, 2 train, 18K	$2,800	$3,200	$3,800
48mm, min. repeater, 14K, OF	2,000	2,400	2,800

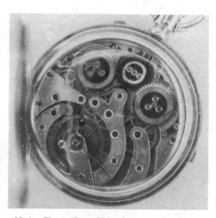

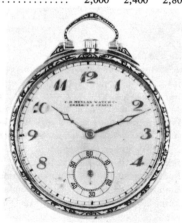

Mathey-Tissot, 52mm, 27 jewels, quarter jump sweep-second chronograph, two train, 18k hunting case.

C.H. Meylan, 44mm, 21 jewels, straight line lever escapement.

C. H. MEYLAN
SWISS

Style or Grade — Description	Avg	Ex-Fn	Mint
50mm, min. repeater, OF, 18K, jeweled to hammers	$2,500	$2,800	$3,500

Style or Grade—Description	Avg	Ex-Fn	Mint
50mm, min. repeater, HC, 18K, chronograph, fully jeweled	$3,000	$3,400	$4,000
48mm, split sec. chronograph, register, OF, 18K	1,000	1,250	1,600
48mm, chronograph, register, OF, 14K	650	800	1,000
46mm, platinum & sapphire dress watch, c. 1925	1,200	1,600	2,050
44mm, min. repeater, 14K, OF........................	2,000	2,450	2,950
44mm, timepiece, 18K, thin model	350	450	550

Ulysse Nardin, 53mm, 52½ minute karrusel, free sprung balance, ca. 1905.

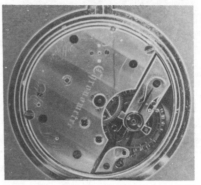

Ulysse Nardin Chronometer, 55mm, 21 jewels, ultra-high grade movement, c. 1878, serial number 7,685.

ULYSSE NARDIN
SWISS

Size and Description	Avg	Ex-Fn	Mint
Deck chronometer w/mahogany box, detent mvt., silver dial	$1,200	$1,400	$1,800
53mm, 17J, 52½ min. karrusel, free sprung regulator, silver	3,000	4,000	5,000
50mm, 15J, made for Corps of Engineers, U.S.A., WWI .	195	245	295
50mm, min. repeater, jeweled thru hammers, HC, 18K ...	3,250	3,800	4,400
45mm, split chronograph, 2 registers, 14K, OF	950	1,150	1,400
45mm, detent chronometer, KW, KS, 18K..............	550	675	825
45mm, SW, timepiece only, 18K, OF	550	675	800
45mm, SW, timepiece only, 14K	350	400	475
42mm, perpetual calendar, moon phases, OF, 18K	5,800	6,800	8,000
42mm, moon phases, perpetual calendar, 18K, HC	7,500	9,500	11,500
40mm, 29J, min. repeater, Adj.5P, 18K, OF	2,600	3,000	3,600

NICOLE, NIELSEN & CO.
SWISS
(Made ebauche for Dent, Frodsham, Smith)

Size and Description	Avg	Ex-Fn	Mint
64mm, tourbillon min. repeater, made for Frodsham, free sprung, c. 1918, 18K case	$70,000	$80,000	$90,000

Nicole, Nielsen, 52mm, minute repeater & split-second chronograph, made for Dent.

Nicole, Nielsen, 64mm, minute repeater, split-second chronograph tourbillon, free sprung escapement.

Size and Description	Avg	Ex-Fn	Mint
52mm, half ¼ repeater, chronograph, slide repeat, 18K case	$4,000	$4,500	$5,000
52mm, min. repeater, split sec. chronograph, made for Dent, 1882, 18K case	6,000	7,000	8,500
50mm, min. repeater, chron., made for Dent, c. 1885, 18K	4,000	4,500	5,250

OMEGA
SWISS

Size and Description	Avg	Ex-Fn	Mint
45mm, 15J, lever escapement, silver	$55	$75	$95
45mm, 17J, OF, 14K	275	325	375
45mm, 17J, HC, 14K	325	375	450
38mm, 15J, OF	55	75	95

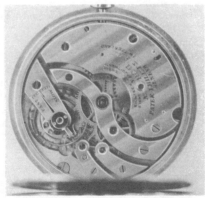

Omega pocket watch, 38mm, 15 jewels, serial number 9,888,934.

Patek Philippe & Co., 38-39mm, 18 jewels, deco bridge movement, 8 adj., 18k open face case, serial number 196,051.

Patek, Philippe dial and movement, minute repeater, 29 jewels, perpetual calendar, day, date, month, moon phase, adjusted to 5 positions, 18k solid gold case.

PATEK, PHILIPPE & CO.
SWISS
(All must be triple signed—case, dial, movement, Patek Philippe)

Size and Description	Avg	Ex-Fn	Mint
56mm, 22J, "Chronometro Gondolo," 24 hr. dial, 18K, OF, c. 1890s	$2,000	$2,600	$3,000
55mm, astronomic, perpetual calendar, min. repeater, 1897, white enamel dial, 3 registers, split sec. chronograph, moon phases, 38J, slide repeat, original box and papers	100,000	110,000	120,000
54mm, split sec. chronograph, 18K, HC	5,000	6,000	7,000
52mm, split sec. chronograph, 18K, OF, Tiffany & Co., register	4,000	5,000	6,000
51mm, 22J, independent dead seconds, 2 train, heavy 18K HC, c. 1890 ★★★★	20,000	26,000	35,000
51mm, 18K, HC, gilt, lever mvt.	2,000	2,500	3,000
50mm, 25J, pulsometer chronograph, c. 1923, 18K case	4,000	5,000	6,000
50mm, 22J, "Chronometer Gondolo," c. 1890, 18K, OF	1,600	1,800	2,200
48mm, 18J, chronometer with one min. tourbillon, awarded first prize 1933-34, platinum case	110,000	130,000	160,000
48mm, 18K, HC, nickel mvt.	2,200	2,700	3,200
48mm, early chronograph, fly back sec. hand, 18K, OF, wolf's teeth winding	2,500	3,000	3,500
47mm, 1 min. tourbillon, by James Pellaton, c. 1920, 18K case ★★★	80,000	90,000	110,000
46mm, OF, timepiece, enamel dial	1,400	1,600	2,000
46mm, two train, min. repeater, Tiffany & Co.	10,000	12,000	15,000
46mm, "Gondolo," OF, timepiece, enamel dial	1,600	1,800	2,200
46mm, 18K, OF, 18J, Adj.5P, cam regulator	1,400	1,600	2,000
46mm, OF, min. repeater, split chronograph, registers	15,000	18,000	22,000

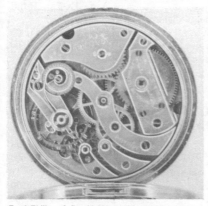

Patek Philippe & Co., 38-39mm, 18 jewels, nickel bridge movement, wolf tooth wind, cam regulator, serial number 124,348.

Patek, Philippe & Co., 50mm, 25 jewels, Chronograph & Pulsometer, ca. 1923.

Size and Description	Avg	Ex-Fn	Mint
46mm, HC, min. repeater, split chronograph, reg.	$17,000	$20,000	$24,000
46mm, HC, min. repeater, split chronograph, perpetual calendar, moon phase...........................	100,000	110,000	120,000
45mm, 18J, 18K, OF, Tiffany & Co.	1,400	1,600	2,000
45mm, 18K, HC, 1860, SW & set, wolf tooth wind	2,500	3,000	3,500
45mm, OF, split chronograph, timepiece, register	4,000	5,000	6,000
45mm, OF, perpetual calendar, timepiece, metal dial	20,000	25,000	30,000
45mm, OF, perpetual calendar, timepiece, enamel dial	25,000	30,000	35,000
45mm, OF, timepiece, gilt dial, 18K	1,400	1,600	1,800
45mm, HC, min. repeater, chronograph.................	14,000	16,000	18,000
45mm, HC, chronograph, timepiece, register	3,500	4,000	4,500
45mm, HC, split chronograph, timepiece, register	5,000	6,000	7,000
45mm, HC, min. repeater, split chronograph, perpetual calendar, register + moon phases	100,000	110,000	120,000
44mm, OF, timepiece, gilt, enamel dial, 18K	1,200	1,400	1,600
44mm, OF, timepiece, nickel, enamel dial, 18K	1,400	1,600	1,800
44mm, HC, min. repeater	14,000	16,000	18,000
44mm, OF, 5 min. repeater...........................	5,000	6,000	7,000
44mm, OF, 5 min. repeater, chronograph	7,000	8,000	9,000
44mm, OF, min. repeater	8,000	10,000	12,000
44mm, OF, min. repeater, chronograph.................	12,000	14,000	16,000
44mm, OF, min. repeater, split chrono., register	15,000	18,000	22,000
42mm, 14K, OF, chronometer on dial, USA cased	800	900	1,000
39mm, 18J, wolf tooth wind, 14K, OF, BRG, nickel mvt. USA cased	800	900	1,000
39mm, 18J, Adj.5P, enamel on bezel & back	1,800	2,000	2,200
38mm, "Gondolo," OF, timepiece, enamel dial, 16 Size ..	1,600	1,800	2,000
35mm, 29J, min. repeater, very thin, 18K, OF	8,000	9,000	10,000
32mm, 18K, HC, early bridge mvt., Tiffany & Co........	2,200	2,500	3,000
30mm, lady's, 18K, gold & enamel + diamonds, lapel watch	4,000	5,000	6,000

Style or Grade—Description	Avg	Ex-Fn	Mint
30mm, lady's, 18K, multi color gold, enamel & diamonds, matching chain & pin, OF, art nouveau	$6,000	$7,000	$8,000
29mm, lady's, 18K, OF	1,000	1,200	1,500
26mm, lady's, 18K, OF, gold, seed pearls & enamel, lapel watch, matching pin	5,000	6,000	7,000

ALBERT H. POTTER & CO.
GENEVA

Style or Grade—Description	Avg	Ex-Fn	Mint
45mm, 29J, min. repeater, 18K, HC	$5,500	$6,500	$8,000
43mm, 22J, helical hairspring, detent chronometer escapement, 18K, HC	4,000	5,000	6,500
33mm, 21J, ¼ repeater, 18K, HC	3,000	3,500	4,500

Albert Potter, 22 jewels, hunting case, helical hair spring, detent escapement.

Rolex, 42-43mm, 17 jewels, three adjustments, cam regulator, exposed winding gears.

ROLEX
SWISS

Size and Description	Avg	Ex-Fn	Mint
43mm, 3 ADJ, cam regulator, 14K, OF	$850	$1,050	$1,250

THOMAS RUSSEL & SONS
ENGLAND

Size and Description	Avg	Ex-Fn	Mint
52mm, ½ ¼ repeater, rachet tooth escapement, 18K, OF	$2,800	$3,200	$3,800
46mm, min. repeater, ¾ plate, 18K, HC	3,800	4,350	5,000
46mm, karrusel, 59 min., chronometer, free sprung, 18K, OF	4,500	5,000	6,500

TIFFANY & CO.
U.S.A.

Size and Description	Avg	Ex-Fn	Mint
49mm, 5 min. repeater, c. 1900, 18K, HC...............	$3,500	$4,000	$4,700
49mm, 1 min. repeater, 18K, OF.......................	3,600	4,100	4,800
49mm, 1 min. repeater, 18K, HC	4,000	4,500	5,200
48mm, nickel mvt., wolf's tooth wind, 18K, OF	850	975	1,150
48mm, nickel mvt., chronograph, 18K, OF	900	1,100	1,350
48mm, nickel mvt., split sec. chronograph, 18K, OF......	1,200	1,400	1,800
48mm, min. repeater, split sec. chronograph, day-date-month, moonphase, perpetual, 18K, OF, mvt. by Vacheron & Constantin	28,000	33,000	38,000
48mm, min. repeater, split sec. chronograph, day-date-month, moonphase, 18K, OF, mvt. by Patek Philippe	75,000	85,000	95,000
48mm, timepiece, 18K, HC, enamel dial	1,250	1,400	1,650
48mm, timepiece, 18K, OF, by Patek, Philippe & Co.	1,000	1,200	1,400
47mm, 5 min. repeater, 18K, OF.......................	3,400	3,900	4,600
45mm, 18K, OF, by Longines..........................	400	525	675
44mm, 18K, HC, timepiece	950	1,000	1,200
42mm, OF, 18K, timepiece	575	650	750

NOTE: Watches listed in this book are priced at the retail level, as complete watches having an original 14k gold-filled case, an original white enamel single sunk dial, and with the entire original movement in good working order with no repairs needed, unless otherwise noted.

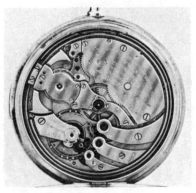

Tiffany & Co., 50mm, 25 jewels, split-second chronograph, made by Ekegren.

Tiffany & Co., flat minute repeater, 45mm, 29 jewels, made by Patek, Philippe & Co., ca. 1911.

Touchon & Co., 47mm, 29 jewels, minute repeater, open face, jeweled through hammers.

Touchon & Co., 47mm, 29 jewels, split-second chronograph and minute repeater, ca. 1910.

TOUCHON & CO.
SWISS

Size and Description	Avg	Ex-Fn	Mint
47mm, 29J, min. repeater, thin model, 1925, 18K, OF....	$2,200	$2,600	$3,200
46mm, min. repeater, jeweled thru hammers, wolf tooth wind, 18K, HC	2,500	2,900	3,500
45mm, 23J, min. repeater, 14K, OF	2,000	2,200	2,450
44mm, OF, 18K, timepiece	375	450	550
40mm, 28J, min. repeater, 14K, OF	1,900	2,100	2,400

50 pesos 24k gold coin with **Vacheron & Constantin** watch inside. The left view shows the movement inside the coin which was hollowed out to receive the Vacheron & Constantin watch.

VACHERON & CONSTANTIN
SWISS

Size and Description	Avg	Ex-Fn	Mint
59mm, chronometer escapement, with silver deck case, c. 1920	$1,450	$1,650	$1,900
55mm, min. repeater, 18K, OF, ultra high grade, nickel mvt.	3,800	4,250	4,800
51mm, 14K, HC, nickel mvt., c. 1890	700	850	1,100
50mm, min. repeater, chronograph mvt., 18K, OF, gilt	3,800	4,400	5,200
47mm, 14K, OF, c. 1900, nickel mvt.	450	550	700
43mm, 18K, OF, c. 1920, nickel lever mvt., Adj.5P	575	700	850
42mm, 14K, OF, 17J, Adj.5P, c. 1915	400	475	600

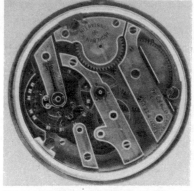

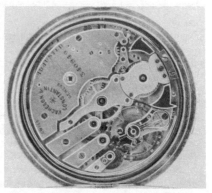

Vacheron & Constantin , 40mm, wolf tooth winding, 18k open face.

Vacheron & Constantin, 40mm, 29 jewels, minute repeater, slide repeat, wolf tooth wind, 18k open face, serial number 340,949.

Style or Grade—Description	Avg	Ex-Fn	Mint
41mm case size, 24mm mvt. size, skeletonized, c. 1930, 18J	$2,200	$2,600	$3,200
40mm, 21J, NI, BRG, wolf tooth wind, 18K, OF	550	650	800
40mm, 19J, high quality mvt., 14K, OF	400	500	650
40mm, 17J, wolf tooth wind, GF, HC	125	175	285
40mm, min. repeater, slide repeat, jeweled thru hammers, OF	2,800	3,200	3,800
40mm, 31J, min. repeater, 18K, OF, slide activated	2,500	2,900	3,400
40mm, 21J, observatory time trial, 3rd place winner, 18K	1,400	1,800	2,400
30mm, lady's, jeweled to center wheel, 18K, OF	300	400	550

MISC. ENGLISH

Size and Description	Avg	Ex-Fn	Mint
120mm, ¼ repeating coach watch with alarm, verge, fusee, by Charles Clay, c. 1730, silver response case	$5,500	$6,500	$7,500
70mm, silver & horn triple cased, for Turkish market, by G. Charles, c. 1810, verge, & pierced cock, enamel dial	750	900	1,100

Quarter repeating coach watch, with alarm, 13 cm diameter, verge fusee, silver mounted shagreen case, ca. 1740.

Size and Description	Avg	Ex-Fn	Mint
60mm, pair cased, silver c. 1800, hand painted battle scene on dial	$550	$650	$775
60mm, ¼ repeater, pair cased, push repeat, pierced cock, 18K, repousse case	1,850	2,250	2,850
56mm, by Robert Roskell, pair cased, 18K, full plate, dust cover, rack & lever escapement	800	1,100	1,400
55mm, min. repeater, by John Barwise, jeweled thru hammers, duplex escapement, heavy 18K case	4,400	5,000	5,600
55mm, reversible case, KW, KS, cylinder escapement, 18K	1,000	1,200	1,600
55mm, fusee, lever escapement, KW, KS, by W. Chance & Sons, 18K pair cased, repousse case	1,000	1,300	1,700
54mm, min. repeater, by H. C. Boddington, 18K, ¾ plate, HC	2,700	3,100	3,600

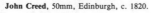

John Creed, 50mm, Edinburgh, c. 1820.   English watch, 55mm, with repousse case.

Size and Description	Avg	Ex-Fn	Mint
52mm, full plate, 14K, HC, by Johnson	$400	$475	$650
52mm, by Arnold & Dent, chronometer, fusee, KW, KS, OF, silver	1,400	1,700	2,000

Size and Description	Avg	Ex-Fn	Mint
52mm, demi-hunter, by Robert Roskell, resilient lever, silver case	$750	$800	$1,000
52mm, gold & enamel + pearls, by John Page, c. 1800, cylinder	2,500	2,900	3,400
51mm, by Dent, OF, lever movement, 18K	500	600	750
50mm, c. 1872, WI, with resilient banking, KW, KS, 18K, HC	1,250	1,500	1,800

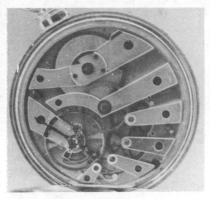

Cooper, 48mm, bar detached lever movement, key wind & set, parachute system at end stone, 18k open face, serial number 6631.

Wm. Hopetown, 48mm, chain driven fusee, verge escapement, dust cover, c. 1842, made in London, pair case, serial number 3865.

Size and Description	Avg	Ex-Fn	Mint
50mm, by William Jones, pierced cock, chain driven fusee, c. 1842, pair cased	$100	$135	$200
50mm, ¼ repeater, silver & enamel, by Weill & Harburg, c. 1886	650	750	900
50mm, gold & enamel + pearls, by John Page, c. 1800, cylinder	2,000	2,400	2,800
50mm, gold & gems, set in OF watch, by James McCabe, c. 1820, cylinder, pierced cock, DES, gold dial, 18K, diamond on back	2,800	3,200	3,700
50mm, by Robert Gellatly, of Edinburgh, 18K, OF, free sprung, c. 1870	800	1,000	1,200
50mm, ¼ repeater, 18K, OF, by John Barwise, c. 1830, ¾ plate	1,200	1,400	1,800
50mm, 11J, lever escapement, fusee, gold balance, by Yates, 16K case	500	600	800
50mm, pair cased, by Creed, Edinburgh, AD1820, silver case	125	145	200
48mm, bar movement, by Cooper, KW, KS, 18K, OF, with parachute, gold dial	325	400	500
48mm, pair case, verge, fusee, pierced cock, silver	100	150	200
48mm, by M. I. Tobias & Co., Liverpool, lever, fusee, KW, KS, 18K, OF, multi-color gold dial	550	750	1,000
48mm, by William Hopetown, London, silver pair case, chain driven, fusee, verge escapement	125	150	200

Berthoud, 58mm, ¼ repeater, center seconds, musical watch striking hours on request, ca. 1820.

Musical watch with 25 vibrating blades showing dial side of movement.

Size and Description	Avg	Ex-Fn	Mint
48mm, 18K, OF, c. 1896, ¾ plate, GJS................	$400	$475	$575
46mm, KW, KS, c. 1865, by McPherson, lever gilt mvt., silver case	55	75	95
46mm, KW, KS, fusee, dust cover, pinned plates.........	55	75	95
46mm, KW, KS, fusee, dust cover, Scotland.............	65	85	110
45mm, KW, KS, c. 1865, dust cover, lever, gilt	45	55	65
45mm, KW, KS, c. 1880, fusee, dust cover, HC	65	75	85
44mm, KW, KS, silver case, lever movement	45	55	65
44mm, fusee, lever, KW, KS, 18K, OF	400	475	575
44mm, repousse, 18K, by Williamson, pierced cock, enamel dial...	1,250	1,600	2,200
23mm, small triple case, 18K & enamel, for Turkish market, by Edward Prior, c. 1815, pierced cock, translucent pink enamel	6,000	7,500	8,500

MISC. FRENCH

Size and Description	Avg	Ex-Fn	Mint
58mm, ¼ repeater, musical 23 vibrating blades, signed "Berthound," c. 1880, 18K........................	$6,000	$7,000	$8,500
55mm, 2 figure automaton, min. repeater, 18K, HC......	4,200	4,800	5,600
55mm, 3 figure automaton, ¼ repeater, 18K, c. 1830.....	3,800	4,200	5,500
54mm, 2 figure automaton, ¼ repeater, 18K	2,800	3,200	3,800
50mm, 1 figure automaton, ¼ repeater, silver	1,600	1,800	2,200
50mm, ¼ repeater, repeat on bell, c. 1780, 18K	1,250	1,500	1,800
50mm, ¼ repeater, by L'Epine, parachute, cylinder escape, gold & enamel, champleve........................	1,650	1,950	2,400
47mm, by La Cloche, ultra thin, 18K, OF, gilt movement .	350	450	575

Father & Baby Time, automated minute repeater, 54mm, note animated bell striking by father and baby time, 18k hunting case.

French made movement, 50mm, chain driven fusee, verge escapement, note hand pierced two-footed cock attached on both sides.

Size and Description	Avg	Ex-Fn	Mint
46mm, time, calendar & mobile sunrise & sunset, virgule escapement, c. 1795, silver	$600	$800	$1,000
45mm, gold champleve enamel, by LeRoy, c. 1840, cylinder escapement	1,400	1,600	1,800
44mm, by Robin, gold enamel portrait, parachute suspension, KW, KS....................................	3,000	3,500	4,000
42mm, musical and ¼ repeater, KW, OF	2,500	2,900	3,500
41mm, ¼ repeater, c.1820, cylinder escapement, KW,KS silver	450	575	750
39mm, skeletonized, 18k gold with diamonds, ca. 1790 ...	2,000	2,400	2,800
38mm, gold & champleve enamel, by A. Verdiere, c. 1830, cylinder	1,000	1,200	1,500
36mm, ¼ repeater, ladies, by LeRoy et Fils, HC.........	1,600	1,800	2,400
32mm, gold enamel, "acorn form," by Ch. Oudin, Palais Royal, c. 1880, cylinder	3,000	3,600	4,200

Time, calendar, mobile sunrise & sunset, virgule escapement, ca. 1795.

French watch, 42mm, musical, plays music on the hour or on demand.

Swiss minute repeater, 54mm, jeweled through hammers, 18k case.

Skeletonized watch with diamond bezel, 39mm, ca. 1780.

Size and Description	Avg	Ex-Fn	Mint
32mm, ¼ repeater, 18K, lever mvt., slide to repeat, KW ..	$1,000	$1,200	$1,500
29mm, gold & enamel with pearls, by Bovet Flevrier, c. 1810, duplex movement	1,800	2,000	2,450

MISC. SWISS

Size and Description	Avg	Ex-Fn	Mint
62mm, min. repeater, calendar & moon phases, split sec., chronograph, 30 min. register, GJS, 18K, HC	$4,800	$5,700	$6,700
60mm, heavy 14K HC, spring detent, by Ulysse Breting, c. 1880, nickel mvt., gold train & escape wheel	1,500	1,800	2,300
56mm, ¼ repeater, chronograph, by R. Picard, 18K, HC .	1,400	1,650	2,000
56mm, ¼ repeating musical, 2 barrels, music on hour or at will, c. 1820, 18K case.........................	3,500	4,200	5,200
55mm, min. repeater, by Paul Henri Mathey, 18K, heavy HC, gold train	2,600	3,000	3,600
55mm, detent, chronometer, by Emile Perret, KW, KS, 18K, HC, nickel mvt....................................	900	1,200	1,500
55mm, split sec. chronograph, by James Picard, fully jeweled, 18K, HC, min. repeater	2,800	3,100	3,600
54mm, min. repeater, moon phases, day-date-month, 18K, HC..	3,500	4,000	4,700
54mm, min. repeater, jeweled thru hammers, 18K, HC ...	2,500	2,800	3,300
54mm, by Piguet & Meylan, ¼ musical repeater, c. 1815, 18K...	3,500	4,000	4,750
54mm, min. repeater, 18K, HC, chronograph with calendar and moon phases................................	3,500	4,000	4,700
54mm, automated min. repeater, Father & Cherub, 18K, HC	4,200	4,800	5,400
54mm, visible so called 1 min. tourbillon, c. 1905, silver ..	1,200	1,500	2,000
53mm, 35J, min. repeater, 1900, 18K, HC, "Zenith"	2,600	3,000	3,600
52mm, moon phase, triple date, massive 18K OF case, by Henri Grandjean	$2,250	$2,750	$3,400

Record Watch Co. Sector style watch, dial and movement, hour and minute hand moves to the right, then returns to home.

World Time Watch, giving time in London, Singapore, Madras, Rangoon, Bombay & Calcutta.

Size and Description	Avg	Ex-Fn	Mint
52mm, captain's watch, KW, KS, OF, 18K, 2 train, independent sec., gold dial	$1,050	$1,350	$1,750
52mm, Time Zone or Captain's watch, KW, KS, 18K, HC	750	850	1,050
52mm, by L'Epine, c. 1869, cylinder escapement, KW, KS, 18K, OF	450	550	750
52mm, min. repeater, by J. Barth, 14K, HC	1,800	2,200	2,600
52mm, min. repeater, by Ernest Duval, 18K, OF	1,900	2,200	2,600
52mm, musical ¼ repeater, KW, KS	2,300	2,600	3,000
50mm, ¼ repeater, by Leresche & Fils, c. 1900, 18K, OF, slide repeat	1,000	1,200	1,500
50mm, 18K, OF, by Duchene Peyrot & Co., c. 1840, gilt, lever, parachute	450	550	750
50mm, min. repeater, Carillon chime, 18K, HC, top grade	3,200	3,600	4,200
50mm, world time, 6 time zones, c. 1900, silver	500	600	800
49mm, 18K, pocket chonometer, by Breting, Frers, c. 1840, spring detent, 15J	1,200	1,400	1,600
49mm, OF, c. 1820-30, by common maker, pierced cock, etc., silver case	85	125	175
45mm, 15J, OF, HCl4P	55	60	75
45mm, 21J, LS, SW, Railway Special, OF	85	95	110
44mm, Waltham Swiss mvt., 17J, "Incabloc"	55	65	75
44mm, 7J, SW, gold filled	50	55	60
44mm, multi-color, verge, pierced cock	1,000	1,200	1,500
44mm, ¼ repeater, 28J, by Bernard Reber, multi-color dial, gold train, 14K, HC	1,350	1,550	2,000
43mm, Automaton, blacksmith with hammered gun metal, pen set	400	500	695
42mm, gold & enamel, 18K, HC	650	700	950
42mm, self wind by Von Loehr, wind indicator, silver	700	800	1,050
42mm, 21J, "Dueber" chronometer, helical hairspring, OF	800	1,000	1,400
41mm, gold champleve enamel, floral design, 18K, c. 1830	800	1,000	1,400

Swiss, self wind, 36mm, cylinder escapement with wind indicator, gun metal case.

Swiss, One minute "so called Tourbillon," center seconds silver watch with decentred dial & visible system.

Size and Description	Avg	Ex-Fn	Mint
40mm, self wind, by Von Loehr, gun metal	$500	$650	$900
40mm, 15J, moon phase, day, date, month, calendar, gunmetal	165	225	350
40mm, 31J, min. repeater, split sec. chronograph, register.	2,400	2,800	3,200
40mm, gilt metal & enamel, verge	300	400	550
40mm, 18K, gold & enamel + diamonds, HC, KW, KS ..	1,000	1,400	1,800
40mm, 18K, HC, enamel landscape scene on each side, c. 1860	1,100	1,400	1,800
40mm, ¼ repeater, gold enamel + diamonds, verge, fusee movement	2,600	3,000	3,500
38mm, 15J, ¾ plate, c. 1930, YGF.	50	70	95
37mm, 20K gold skeleton, entirely pierced, verge, fusee, c. 1770	5,000	6,000	7,000
36mm, self wind, cylinder escapement, gun metal case	250	350	450
30mm, 18K, enamel, OF, blue & white champleve enamel, cylinder movement	400	550	650

Centennial Watch, 55mm, Chronograph, 17 jewels, engraved on movement "Henry O. Stauffer, Ponts-Martel, pat. May 9th, 1882."

A gilt metal verge oignon watch with false pendulum, ca. 1720.

Size and Description	Avg	Ex-Fn	Mint
25mm, gold & enamel watch, matching enamel chain	$1,200	$1,450	$1,750
25mm, 18K gold & enamel, ladies, 17J, lever mvt.	700	900	1,200
25mm, 18K, OF, gold & 7 pearls, lapel watch	400	500	650
21mm, min. repeater, by Henri Grand Jean	2,250	2,850	3,450
21mm, 5 min. repeater, by James Freres, c. 1890, 18K, HC slide repeat	1,800	2,200	2,800

OTHER MISC. WATCHES

Size and Description	Avg	Ex-Fn	Mint
58mm, gilt metal verge oignon, with false pendulum, c. 1720	$1,000	$1,200	$1,500
56mm, 14K, HC, min. repeater, chronograph, calendar & moon phases.....................................	3,600	4,000	4,600
56mm, 18K, HC, by Union Watch Co., GJS, DES, gold pallet & escape wheel	800	900	1,000
53mm, 14K, ¼ repeater, chronograph, "Invicta," c. 1900, push button repeat, HC.........................	1,200	1,500	1,800
50mm, ¼ hour repeater, by J. R. Losada, c. 1870, 18K, slide repeat, HC.................................	1,500	1,700	2,000
50mm, scarab form watch, by Goering Watch Co., enamel & diamond	3,400	4,000	4,800

German Dollar Watch, 50mm, no jewels, 3 adjustments, "Gebruder, thiel, Ruhla Germany" engraved on back plate.

Chronometer, 38mm, 44 diamonds on bezel, platinum case.

Size and Description	Avg	Ex-Fn	Mint
50mm, German dollar watch..........................	$30	$40	$55
46mm, musical ¼ hour repeater, KW, KS, 18K	2,600	2,800	3,100
46mm, min. repeater, by J. Ullman & Co., 14K, slide repeat, c. 1900, OF.......................................	1,500	1,700	2,000

Size and Description	Avg	Ex-Fn	Mint
45mm, min. repeater, 18K HC, case very fancy	$2,200	$2,600	$3,200
45mm, chronometer, 15J, 14K, OF	400	450	550
45mm, lever, bar, Geneve, by Gilbert, 18K	275	325	475
44mm, ¼ repeater, 21J, recased	250	350	450
43mm, 15J, 9K, demi-hunter case	200	250	450
42mm, ¼ repeater, by Denand, 14K, OF	600	725	900
38mm, square-cut corners case, 44 diamonds on bezel, chronometer, platinum	1,200	1,600	2,200

Time Zone or Captain's Watch, 58mm, key wind & set, note separate registers for two time zones, 18k hunting case.

Swiss Quarter Repeater, 50mm, cylinder escapement, note parachute shock for end stone on balance bridge.

SPECIALIZED & TECHNICAL WATCHES

Size and Description	Avg	Ex-Fn	Mint
65mm, world time, double dial in multi-color, 14K, OF ...	$2,200	$2,800	$3,500
60mm, calendar, day-date-month, moon phase, gun metal .	150	200	250
58mm, 2 train, captain's watch, Courvoisier & Co., c. 1860	1,600	1,800	2,400
58mm, min. repeater, perpetual calendar, moon phases, day-date-month, chronograph, 18K, HC	14,000	16,000	19,000
55mm, 52 min. karussel, c. 1920, ¾ plat., signed T. A. Pimblett, 18K, OF................................	3,600	4,000	4,800
55mm, 40J, grand sonnerie clockwatch, carillion strike, 2 train, min. repeater, 18K, HC	7,500	8,200	9,500
55mm, grand & petite sonnerie clockwatch, min. repeater, 2 train, jeweled thru hammers, exposed tandem winding wheels, signed Marcks & Co., 18K, HC	8,500	9,500	12,000
54mm, musical ¼ repeater, Piguet & Meylan, c. 1815, 18K	3,600	4,000	4,600
54mm, musical watch, with pinned cylinder, c. 1800, 18K .	4,000	4,650	5,200
53mm, virgule escapement, by Lepine (inventor), c.1780, 18K	1,400	1,600	2,000
53mm, 2 train, clockwatch, hour repeater, signed Bourguin Le Jeune, c. 1800, 18K, OF	1,400	1,800	2,400
53mm, 13J, visible tourbillon system, c. 1920, silver	1,000	1,200	1,450

Perpetual Calendar Watch, Swiss, 60mm, day-date-month-moon phases, gold hands, gun metal case.

Eight Day Watch, Swiss, 52mm, with exposed escapement, gun metal case.

Size and Description	Avg	Ex-Fn	Mint
52mm, duplex with trapelozoidal weights, c. 1830, KW, KS, deck box, silver case	$1,100	$1,400	$1,750
52mm, deck watch, resilient lever, free sprung, c. 1880 . . .	800	1,000	1,250
51mm, 15J, helical mainspring, by Isaac Gasset & Co., Geneva, 1910 (unusual winding)	1,000	1,600	2,200
50mm, detent escapement, helical hairspring, 17J, gilt mvt., 14K, HC	800	1,000	1,250
50mm, ruby duplex, min. repeater, signed J. R. Lund, 18K OF, 4 color of gold	4,000	4,500	5,500
50mm, ¼ repeater, cylinder escapement, parachute shock, c. 1800, 18K, OF	800	950	1,200
50mm, carillon chimes, triple repeat gongs, ¼ repeater, chronograph, 14K, HC	2,500	2,800	3,400
48mm, gold digital repeater, parachute shock, c. 1820	1,600	1,800	2,250
45mm, detent escapement, gold escape wheel, GF case, OF	225	275	350
45mm, chronometer escapement, wind indicator, by A. P. Walsh, 18K, OF	3,200	3,800	4,500

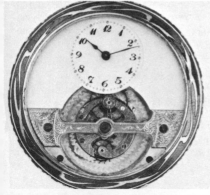

Visible Tourbillon, 53mm, 13 jewels, tourbillon system is visible from dial side, ca. 1920.

Helical Mainspring, 51mm, 15 jewels, unusual winding system, cylindrical spring replaces standard mainspring.

Size and Description	Avg	Ex-Fn	Mint
44mm, reverse fusee, helical hairspring, detent escapement, by J. Penlinston..................................	$1,800	$2,100	$2,400
44mm, circuit breaker, made by Nardin.................	350	400	495
41mm, 2 train, min. repeater, 18K (Wittnauer)..........	3,200	3,600	4,200

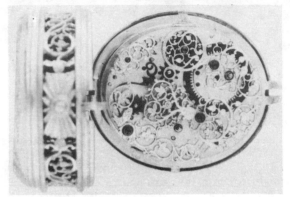

Early **French** watch movement with hour and minute hand, striking bell each hour, fluted case & gilt brass movement, catgut fusee, c. 1600s.

EARLY WATCHES

Size and Description	Avg	Ex-Fn	Mint
172mm, 4 train, coach watch, grand sonnerie, alarm, repeat, repousse case, c. 1700	$12,000	$14,000	$18,000
103mm, 3 train, coach watch, with alarm, by Higgs Evans, c. 1790...	3,500	4,000	4,800
60mm, pair case, by Richard Vick, champleve dial, c. 1700	1,200	1,300	1,500
50mm, pair case, verge fusee, by Clayton, silver, c. 1730..	250	300	425
50mm, rack & lever, fusee, by Ganthony of London, KW, KS	200	250	350
50mm pair case, verge fusee, pierced cock, by J. A. Freeman, c. 1790, silver	125	165	200
50mm, ¼ repeater, pair case, silver repousse scene	800	1,000	1,200
50mm, detached lever, fusee, DES, compensating balance by Marshall, 18K	850	950	1,100
48mm, pair case, repousse, by Robert Allan, c. 1760, 20K	1,500	1,800	2,500
47mm, pair case, verge, pierced cock, Benjamin Lamb, silver	400	485	600
46mm, pair case, verge fusee, by Hallifax, c. 1785, 18K, repousse...	1,200	1,600	2,200
45mm, repousse, fancy matchine chatelaine, pierced cock, by Grantham, c. 1750, 18K..........................	2,500	3,500	4,600
45mm, multi-color enamel case watch, by Berthoud, c. 1780, 18K..	1,800	2,400	2,950
45mm, multi-color gold, verge, KW, KS, by Louis Roch ..	1,800	2,200	2,600
43mm, pair cased, chatelaine, tortoise shell pique, by Cornelius Horbert, London, c. 1695, silver	1,600	2,400	3,400

Chinese Duplex, 59mm, made for Chinese market with Chinese symbols, key wind & set.

Mysterieuse on watch, 51mm, note hands are set with finger, silver case.

Size and Description	Avg	Ex-Fn	Mint
41mm, multi-color gold case, verge, pierced cock, by Romilly, KW, KS	$700	$1,000	$1,400
40mm, 3 colors gold, portrait of lady, diamonds, c. 1760 .	1,800	2,000	2,400
40mm, 3 colors gold & diamonds, ¼ repeater, by Mallet .	2,500	2,800	3,500
40mm, pearls & enamel on gold, verge, pierced cock	2,800	3,000	3,200
39mm, pair cased, Freres Esquivillons, porcelain back	1,400	1,500	1,600
39mm, pair cased, adjustable hour dial, for Japanese market, silver	3,200	3,800	4,000

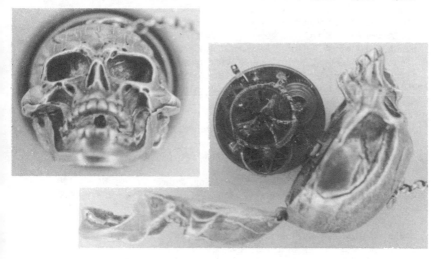

Miniature skull form watch, 30-32mm, cylinder escapement, chain driven fusee, skeletonized movement, silver skull case, popular in the mid-nineteenth century.

NOVELTY WATCHES

Size and Description	Avg	Ex-Fn	Mint
67mm, barometer watch, silver case	$400	$500	$650
60mm, bar movement, day, date, month, moon phase, gun metal, pin set	95	150	225

Rare wooden works by Bronnikoff of Russia, 60-50mm, wooden wheels, balance bridge and movement, no jewels, cylinder type escapement, c. 1890.

Masonic, triangle shaped watch, by Pempor W. Co., 15 jewels, adj.3P.

Size and Description	Avg	Ex-Fn	Mint
50-60mm, wooden works, no jewels	$1,000	$1,200	$1,500
59mm, Chinese duplex, for Chinese market, silver case ...	175	225	295
55mm, 17J, "Commemorative 1776," chronograph dial, American, 14K HC	1,600	1,800	2,250
52mm, 8 day watch, balance seen from dial, GF OF	95	125	185
51mm, "Mysterieuse," mystery watch, crescent mvt.	900	1,100	1,450
51mm, "Mysterieuse," mystery watch, min. repeater, crescent mvt., silver	3,500	4,000	4,500
51mm, repeater, slide repeat, gun metal	250	300	400
50mm, digital jump hour & min., silver	150	225	300
50mm, 15J, visible tourbillon style escapement, c. 1915, gun metal	1,050	1,200	1,600
49x34mm, sector watch (fan shaped), fly back hour & min., by Record W. Co., GF	1,000	1,100	1,350
46mm, gambling devices (roulette, horse racing, & dice)...	85	120	175
46mm, blinking eye, silver case	250	300	375
46mm, blinking eye, gun metal case	175	225	275
45mm, double time watch, single train, OF, silver	250	300	425
44mm, skeletonized, open numbers, open back plates, 18K	550	650	850
42mm, plates in form of bird, 22J, KW, KS, silver	95	110	150
40mm, "Shell" watch, 7-17J, skeletonized, (Girard-Perregaux).......................................	100	125	175
40mm, grasshopper alarm, (cricket sound), silver case	700	900	1,100
40mm, digital watch, engraved dial, silver, c. 1900	225	300	395
40mm, compass watch, KW, KS, silver case	125	175	225

Blinking Eyes, 46mm, pin set, animated eyes.

Lock Form Watch, cylinder escapement, 18k case.

Size and Description	Avg	Ex-Fn	Mint
30mm, ball form watch, silver & enamel, c. 1870	$200	$300	$450
25mm, ball form watch, rim wind & set, small diamonds, 18K...	900	1,000	1,200
25mm, skull form watch, miniature, cylinder escapement, silver	800	875	950
20mm, ball form watch, Juvenia W. Co., silver & enamel, c. 1900..	175	195	275
Lock form watch, cylinder escapement, 18K & enamel	1,500	1,800	2,250
Masonic, triangular shape, by Tempor W. Co., 15J, Adj.3P, Swiss....................................	600	800	1,100

Ball Lapel Watch, rim wind & set, 18k with diamonds & sapphires.

Shell, 40mm, made for Shell Oil Co. as advertising premium.

NOTE: Watches listed in this book are priced at the retail level, as complete watches having an original 14k gold-filled case, an original white enamel single sunk dial, and with the entire original movement in good working order with no repairs needed, unless otherwise noted.

ENAMELLED WATCHES

Floral enamel watch. Bouquet of flowers within a champleve border of scrolls enclosing panels of flowers.

Floral enamel watch. Finely painted floral enamel panel within border of seed pearls, signed Bovet.

Size and Description	Avg	Ex-Fn	Mint
58mm, gold fine harbor scene enamel, duplex, c. 1790	$25,000	30,000	$35,000
57mm, gold fine floral enamel, duplex, (Bovet), pearls....	10,000	12,000	15,000
56mm, transfer painted lovers, c. 1761, gilt case	500	600	700
55mm, gold fine floral enamel, pearl set, ¼ repeating musical, (Piguet-Meylan)	25,000	30,000	35,000
55mm, finely painted floral and seed pearls, (Bovet), gold case	3,000	3,500	4,000
53mm, ¼ repeater, enamel portrait of Napoleon, gold case	4,500	5,500	6,500
52mm, gold enamel portrait, ¾ plate lever mvt., c. 1910..	1,500	1,700	2,000
52mm, gold fine enamel chatelaine, three formed plaques bordered in seed pearls...........................	10,000	12,000	15,000
48mm, painted transfer of man & women, painted border, gilt case	250	300	400
47mm, gold fine enamel ¼ repeater, by Le Roy, with a brequet style ruby cylinder	12,000	15,000	18,000
47mm, gold enamel ¼ repeater, with chatelaine of pierced gold links & enamel plaques with enamel key & fob seals...	4,000	5,000	6,000
46mm, flowers & scrolls on green & white ground, gilt case	500	600	700

Painted floral garlands.

Transfer painted with scene of shepherd.

Painted with scrolls and fans.

Painted with flowers within border of scrolls

Transfer painted scene of boy and lamb.

Transfer painting with couple before altar.

Floral enamel watch, 57mm, bouquet of flowers within a gold case set with split pearls.

Enamel scene watch, 58mm, finely painted scene of ships in harbor.

Size and Description	Avg	Ex-Fn	Mint
45mm, painted boy & lamb, gilt case	$600	$700	$800
43mm, gold basket form champleve enamel, verge, c. 1800	1,800	2,200	2,800
42mm, champleve border, finely painted flowers, (Le Roy), gold case & chain	2,500	3,000	3,500
37mm, rose gold guilloche enamel demi-hunter..........	400	500	600
36mm, gold enamel & champleve enamel, verge, c. 1800 ..	1,800	2,200	2,800
35mm, gold champleve enamel, (L'Epine), cylinder	800	900	1,000
35mm, gold enamel & seed pearls, rose cut diamonds.....	400	500	600
35mm, painted flowers & painted border, gilt case	300	400	500
34mm, gold egg-shaped form enamel, verge, (Austrian) ...	2,000	2,200	2,500
30mm, painted fans & scrolls, gilt case..................	200	300	400
30mm, gold miniature enamel, verge, sea pearls, c. 1800 ..	2,000	2,400	2,800
27mm, gold enamel lapel brooch with seed pearls & rose cut diamonds, c. 1890	700	800	900
27mm, gold fine enamel lapel brooch with cut diamonds (C. H. Meylan)	1,200	1,400	1,800

Enamel gold form basket. Tapered, oval basket with rising rope handle inhanced with panels of flowers.

A chased enamelled gold lady's pendant watch. Enamel portrait of a lady.

AMERICAN & EUROPEAN
WRIST WATCHES

ROMANCING THE WRIST WATCH

The wrist watch is considered by many watch collectors to be "today's collectable." This phenomenon is due, in part, to the development of the quartz movement which began about 20 years ago and virtually revolutionized the watch market. Although these quartz watches are quiet, accurate timekeepers, and are inexpensive to manufacture, the watches of the past hold a special fascination in the heart of the collector. They enjoy collecting the timepieces with jeweled and moving parts that produce a rhythmic heartbeat inside their gold cases.

The watch collector has seen the prices of wrist watches soar in the past 10 years, as wrist watches have become more and more in demand as an object of fashion, function and jewelry. Prices have climbed highest in just the last two or three years. This year a Patek, Philippe man's platinum minute repeater wrist watch sold for the record price of 345,000 Swiss francs, about $250,000 U.S. Not far behind this record-setting sale was a Patek, Philippe "Calatrava" that brought $198,000. A Patek, Philippe enameled white gold "World Time" man's wrist watch sold for about $130,000. Some collectors have seen the values of their wrist watches double and, in many cases, triple in recent years. For example, in the early 1980s, a Patek, Phillipe perpetual calendar chronograph watch would have sold for $10,000. In 1987, the same watch would have sold for $50,000, and in 1988 for $80,000. In 1989, the price could conceivably be $100,000. Such dramatic increases in values have brought about a feverish demand for wrist watches. The Swiss wrist watch has the attention of the wealthiest collectors, with Patek, Philippe & Co. at the top of their list and Audemars Piguet, Cartier, Rolex, and Vacheron & Constantin close behind. Other wrist watches showing appreciable value are Ebel, A. Lange, Gubelin, International Watch Co., Le Coultre, Ulysse Nardin, and Piaget. Next are Jules Jurgensen, Baume & Mercier, Gerard Perregaux, Movado, and Omega; then Benrus, Bulova, Agassiz, Elgin, Gruen, Hamilton, Illinois, Longines, and Waltham, the character watches, chronographs, and complicated watches.

Many wrist watch collectors have focused on fashion and take pride in wearing their unique watches. Women have been buying high fashion men's watches to wear, making women candidates for collecting. Young men appear to enjoy collecting wrist watches rather than pocket watches. The intense competition within their increasing numbers has influenced the rising prices. European and Japanese collectors are making the biggest impact on the wrist watch market with their volume of buying, as well as the higher prices being paid. The American collector has been inspired by the heated market which has been, in part, fueled by the weakened U.S. dollar. The general appearance of a wrist watch seems to be the main factor in the price of the watch, but high mechanical standards, along with the various functions of the watch, also determine the price. Some of these features include repeaters, chronographs, duo-dials, bubble backs, curvex, flip-up tops, reverso, day-date-month moon phase, jump hour, diamond dial, world time, sector, skeletonized, character, first versions as early autowinds, very early electronics, unusual shapes, and enamel bezels.

Ebel Watch Co., chronograph with day-date-month & moon phases, outside chapter shows tachymetre, 18k gold.

Today's watches are a "mixed bag," ranging from gold luxury watches priced at $10,000, and mid-priced watches at $1,000, to the low-end plastic quartz watches at $30, and all keep time equally well. The gold watch is still a status symbol today; a mark of affluence and of appreciation for the finer things in life. The Swiss control about 85 percent of the luxury watch market, while the Japanese have about the same percentage of the market for more moderately-priced watches. The predominant companies producing the "top of the line" watches are Patek, Phillipe & Co., Cartier, Gubelin, Audemars Piguet, Piaget, Vacheron Constantin. Just below in price, but higher in volume, are names like Rolex, International Watch Co., Girard Perregaux, and Le Coultre. Collectors are also wearing high grade new watches by Ebel, Blancpain, Gerald Genta, Hublot, Raymond Weil, and watches produced for and bearing the names of Chanel, Christian Dior, and Dunhill. Prices of Ebel watches start at about $1,000 and go upward to $24,000. This company also manufactures watches for Cartier. Patek, Philippe watches range in price from $3,000 to $100,000. Audemars

Piguet produces a tourbillon wrist watch that retails for about $28,000. Blancpain, owned by Omega, produces only about 100 ultra-thin hand-made watches per year. Rolex is the most recognizable name in today's luxury wrist watch market. The Rolex 18k gold President with fluted bezel, champagne cabochon dial, and 18k gold bracelet, sells for $9,400, while the same watch with diamond bezel and dial sells for $14,400. Rolex makes the Oyster Quartz day-date, 18k gold, pave diamond dial with sapphire, bezel case, and bracelet set with 107 diamonds totaling 8.06 carats, which bears a price tag of $100,000.

The Warhol collection, which included about 200 watches, was sold on April 27, 1988 at Sotheby's for a reported price of $461,000. The artist collected watches of various styles and types. A set of three vinyl quartz character watches brought the price of $2,400. A stainless steel Gene Autry watch listed and pre-determined to bring about $100 sold for $1,700. The so-called "heavy weight" wrist watches such as Patek Philippe, Cartier, Rolex, and Vacheron Constantin sold for two to three times the estimated prices.

The trend or vogue for older watches has motivated some watch companies to reproduce favorite watches from their past models. Companies have searched their archives to find older models that sold well, and are now marketing replicas of those watches. Hamilton Classics—Authentic Reproductions From America's Past—include the Ventura (1957), Wilshire City (1939), Cabot (1935), and Ardmore (1934). Jaeger-LeCoultre's Reverso has been reintroduced, as well as Longines' hour angle watch developed and worn by Charles Lindbergh. Also, the Lorus Company has marketed a close look-a-like to the Mickey Mouse wrist watch first sold by Ingersoll in the early 1930s.

The romancing of the wrist watch is moving at a steady upward pace. Price adjustments may be needed, but should hold for a few more years. The quality American movements may still be undervalued, and the novelty or comic character wrist watches may still be a good value for the investor.

Ebel Watch Co., time only, waterproof, self winding, date, white enamel dial, bracelet and case made of stainless steel and 18k gold.

A SHORT HISTORY OF WRIST WATCHES

In the late 1700s, Queen Elizabeth adorned her wrist with a watch heavily decorated with jewels and gold. While no one is sure who invented the wrist watch Queen Elizabeth was wearing, or even the first wrist watch ever, as few appeared around 1790. Small miniature watches had been made earlier than this, however. David Rosseau made a watch which was about 18mm in diameter (the size of a dime) in the late 1600s.

Miniaturized wrist watch by Waltham. Model number 400. Note size comparison to dime.

Miniaturization was a great challenge to many of the famous watchmakers including Louis Jaquet, Paul Ditisheim, John Arnold and Henri Capt. The smallest watch in semi-mass production was 12mm by 5mm. In early 1930, the American Waltham Watch Co. made a 9mm by 20mm Model 400 watch.

Wrist watches were at first thought to be too small and delicate to be practical for men to wear. However, during World War I a German officer was said to have strapped a small pocket watch to his wrist with a leather webbed cup. This arrangement freed both hands and proved to be most useful. After the war, the wrist watch gained in popularity. Mass production of wrist watches was started around 1880 by the Swiss industry. The Swiss introduced them to the United States around 1895, but they did not prove to be very popular at first. Around 1907 the Elgin and Illinois watch companies were manufacturing wrist watches and by 1912 Hampden and Waltham had started. By 1920 the

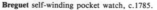

Breguet self-winding pocket watch, c.1785. **Rotor** for self winding wrist watch. **Harwood** self-winding wrist watch, c. 1928.

round styles were being replaced with square, rectangular and tonneau shapes and decorated with gems. By 1928 wrist watches were outselling pocket watches, and, by 1935, over 85 percent of the watches being produced were wrist watches.

Self-wind pocket watches were first developed by Abraham Louis Perrelet in 1770 and by Abraham Louis Breguet about 1777. Louis Recordon made improvements in 1780, but is was not until 1923 that the principle of self-winding was adapted to the wrist watch by John Harwood, an Englishman who set up factories to make his patented self-wind wrist watches in Switzerland, London, France, and the United States. His watches first reached the market about 1929. The firm A. Schild manufactured about 15,000 watches in Switzerland. Mr. Harwood's watch company removed the traditional stem or crown to wind the mainspring, but in order to set the hands it was necessary to turn the bezel. The Harwood Watch Co. failed around 1931 and the patent expired.

Early in 1930 the Rolex Watch Co. introduced the Rolex Oyster Perpetual, the first waterproof and self-winding wrist watch. By 1940 wrist watches came in all shapes and types including complicated chronographs, calendars, and repeaters. Novelties, digital jump hour and multi-dial were very popular, as well.

A dramatic change occurred in 1957 when the Hamilton Watch Co. eliminated the mainspring and replaced it with a small battery that lasted well over one year. In 1960 the balance wheel was removed in the Accutron by Bulova and replaced by a tuning fork with miniature pawls.

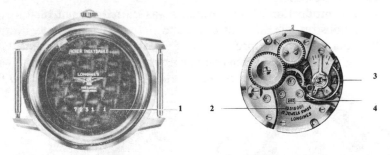

1. Case number. 2. Movement serial number. 3. Caliber number. 4. Caliber number.

Some wrist watches have a grade or caliber number engraved on the movement. For example, Patek, Phillipe & Co. has a caliber number 27-460Q. The '27' stands for 27mm; the '460Q' is the grade; the 'Q' designates Quantieme (Perpetual calendar and moon phases).

AUTOMATIC WINDING

The self-winding watch uses the movements of the body in order to wind up the mainspring slowly and nearly continuously. The first pocket self-winding watches were executed by a watchmaker from Le Locle, Abraham-Louis Perrelet, around 1770.

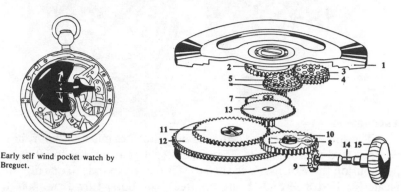

Early self wind pocket watch by Breguet.

Eterna-Matic Automatic Winding Mechanism. 1—Oscillating weight. 2—Oscillating gear. 3—Upper wheel of auxiliary pawl-wheel. 4—Lower wheel of auxiliary pawl-wheel. 5—Pawl-wheel with pinion. 6—Lower wheel of pawl-wheel with pinion. 7—Transmission-wheel with pinion. 8—Crown-wheel yoke. 9—Winding pinion. 10—Crown-wheel. 11—Ratchet-wheel. 12—Barrel. 13¢Driving runner for ratchet-wheel. 14—Winding stem. 15-Winding button.

They were improved soon after by Abraham-Louis Breguet. In the case of the pocket watch, the movements causing the winding of the watch were essentially the result of walking. This system of winding was never widely adopted. The watch was a fancy model and not a really useful one. Herman von der Heydt was the only maker in America to work with the self-winding pocket watch. However, inventors always kept the idea of the self-winding watch in mind.

In 1923, the British firm Harwood took up once again the solution of the problem of automatic winding, for wrist watches. This was the spark which rapidly resulted in research to improve and simplify this type of mechanism. A company was formed in London to manufacture Harwood's watch, and before long over 500 jewelers in the United Kingdom were selling his automatic watch. A second company was formed in France, and a third in the United States. The business flourished about two and one-half years. Then, in 1931, these companies were liquidated.

HOW TO READ THE TACHY-TELEMETER DIAL

Tachometer

The spiral scale around center of dial indicates miles per hour, based on a trial over one mile. It indicates speeds from 400 to 20 miles per hour on three turns. Each turn of spiral corresponds to one minute (scale for first 8 seconds being omitted), the outer turn from 400 to 60 (0 to 1 minute) and the center turn from 30 to 20 miles per hour (2 to 3 minutes).

When passing the first marker of mile zone, start chronograph hand by pressing push piece. When passing following mile marker, press push piece again. The chronograph hand now indicates the speed in miles per hour on the spiral. If a mile has been made in less than one minute the speed will be indicated on outside turn of spiral; from 1 to 2 minutes on middle turn and 2 to 3 minutes on center turn.

EXAMPLE: If a mile has been made in 1 minute and 15 seconds the chronograph hand indicates 48 miles per hour on middle turn of spiral.

Telemeter

The Telemeter scale around margin of dial is based on the speed of sound compared with the speed of light. Each small division is 100 meters. The scale is read in kilometers and hundreds of meters. Approximately 16 divisions equal 1 mile.

TO DETERMINE THE DISTANCE OF A STORM: When you see the flash of lightning press push piece of chronograph. When hearing thunder press again, the chronograph hand will indicate on the Telemeter scale the distance in kilometers and hundreds of meters. One kilometer equals 5/8 of a mile.

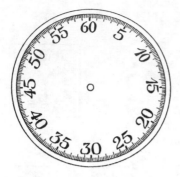

Dial No. 1 is a simple stop watch dial. Graduated into fifths of seconds.

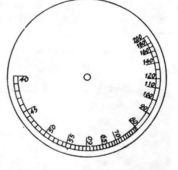

Dial No. 2 is used to time a car over a quarter-mile track and read the numbers of miles per hour directly from dial.

Dial No. 3 is used to measure speed in kilometers per hour over a course of one fifth of a kilometer.

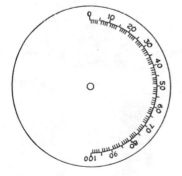

Dial No. 4 used by physicians to count the pulse beats of a patient.

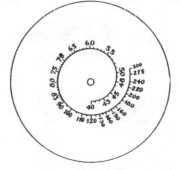

Dial No. 5 is used by artillery officers for determining distance by means of sound in kilometers.

Dial No. 6 shows a tachometer: many watches are made with several scales on the same dial in order to cover a greater range of functions. The figures are sometimes grouped in a spiral form or in several circles, thus the hand may make more than one complete revolution.

368

WRIST WATCH CASE AND DIAL STYLES

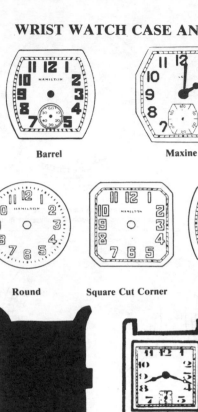

Barrel

Maxine

Square

Round

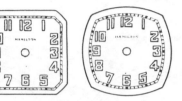

Square Cut Corner

Cushion

Rectangle

Flared

Tank

Round
(Ladies style; converts to lapel or wrist)

Curved or Curvex

**Rectangle
Cut Corner**

Tonneau

Baguette

Oval

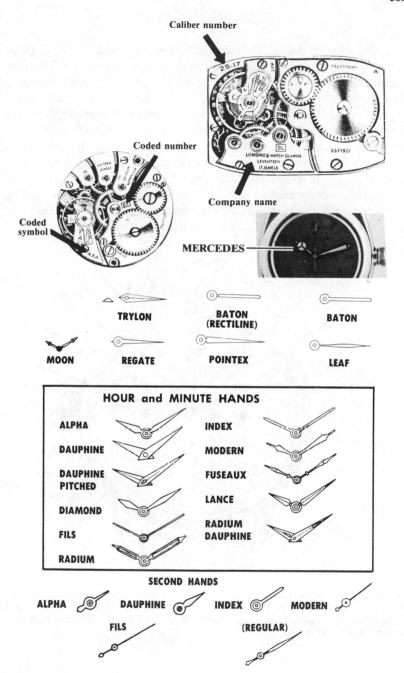

Caliber number

Coded number

Coded symbol

Company name

MERCEDES

TRYLON **BATON (RECTILINE)** **BATON**

MOON **REGATE** **POINTEX** **LEAF**

HOUR and MINUTE HANDS

ALPHA **INDEX**

DAUPHINE **MODERN**

DAUPHINE PITCHED **FUSEAUX**

DIAMOND **LANCE**

FILS **RADIUM DAUPHINE**

RADIUM

SECOND HANDS

ALPHA **DAUPHINE** **INDEX** **MODERN**

FILS **(REGULAR)**

CHRONOGRAPH

The term chronograph is derived from the Greek words *chronos* which means "time" and *grapho* which means "to write." The first recording of intervals of time was around 1822 by the inventor Rieussec. His chronograph made dots of ink on a dial as a measure of time. Around 1862 Adolph Nicole introduced the first chronograph with a hand that returned to zero. The split second chronograph made its appearance around 1879. Today a chronograph can be described as a timepiece that starts at will, stops at will, and can return to zero at will. A mechanical chronograph had a sweep or center second hand that will start, stop, and fly back to zero. The term chronometer should not be confused with chronograph. A chronometer is a timepiece that has superior timekeeping qualities at the time it is made.

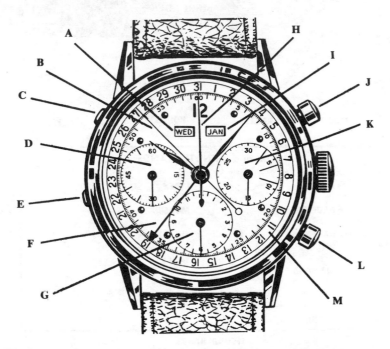

A. Day window. B. Split second hand. C. Calendar pusher. D. Register for seconds. E. Calendar pusher. F. Date hand. G. Register for total hours. H. Sweep center second hand. I. Month window. J. Start/stop pusher. K. Register for total minutes. L. Return pusher. M. Day of month.

SWISS CODE INITIALS

Some Swiss watches have three initials on the balance bridge. These initials are **not** model identification but are for house identification. Following is a list of import initials with the name of the Swiss company maker.

AOC—Roamer
AOL—Adolph Schwarcz &
   Son
AOX—Alstate W. Co.
AXA—Wittnauer
AXZ—Benrus
BOL—Bernard S. Lipman
BXC—Avia
BXJ—Midland
BXN—Benrus
BXP—Imperial, Bayer,
   Pretzfelder & Mills
BXW—Bulova
COC—Crawford
COW—Croton
CXC—Concord
CXD—Cypres
CXH—Clinton
CXV—Cort
CXW—Central; Benrus
DOB—Dreffa W. Co.
DOW—Deauville
EOE—Elrex
EON—Avalon
EOP—Harvel
EOT—Lavina
EXC—Everbrite
FXE—Provis
FXU—Louis Aisenstein &
   Bros.
FXW—Louis
GXC—Gruen
GXI—Gotham (Ollendorff)
GXM—Girard-Perregaux
GXR—Grant
GXW—Gothic
HOM—Homis
HON—Tissot; A. Hirsch

HOR—Lanco; Langendorf
HOU—Oris
HOX—Patek, Philippe
HXF—Harman
HXM—R. H. Macy & Co.
HXN—Harvel
HXO—Harold K. Oleet
HXW—Helbros
JXE—Normandie
JXJ—Jules Jurgensen
KOT—Landau
KXJ—Wm. J. Kappel
KXV—Louis
KXZ—Kelton; Benrus, Central
LOA—Emil Langer
LOD—Latham
LOE—Packard
LXA—Laco, Winton, Elbon
LXE—Evkob
LXJ—LeCoultre
LXW—Longines
MOG—Mead & Co.;
   Boulevard
MOU—Tower; Delbana
MXE—Monarch
MXH—Seeland
MXI—Movado
MXT—Mathey-Tissot
NOS—Heritage
NOU—Louvic
NXJ—National Jewelers Co.
NXO—Oris
OXG—Omega
OXL—Wyler
OYT—Shriro (Sandoz)
POY—Camy; Copley
PXA—Pierce
PXP—Patek, Philippe

PXT—Paul Breguette
PXW—Parker
PYS—Langel
QXO—Kelbert
ROC—Raleigh
ROL—Ribaux
ROP—Rodania
ROW—Rolex
RXG—R. Gsell & Co.
RXM—Galmor
RXW—Rima
RXY—Liengme
RYW—Ritex
SOA—Felca
SOE—Semca
SOW—Seeland
SOX—Cortebert, Orvin
SXE—Savoy; Banner
SXK—S. Kocher & Co.
SXS—Franco
UOA—Actua
UOB—Aero
UOW—Universal
UXM—Medana
UXN—Marsh
UYW—Stanley W. Co.
VOS—Sheffield
VXN—Vacheron & Constantin
VXT—Kingston
WOA—Tower
WOB—Wyler
WOR—Creston
WXC—Buren
WXE—Welsbro
WXW—Westfield
ZOV—Titus
ZYV—Hampden (new
   company)

Coded number

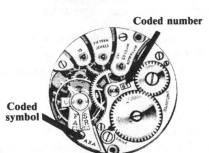

**Coded
symbol**

WRIST WATCH LISTINGS
Pricing at Retail Level
(Complete Watches Only)

Unless otherwise noted, wrist watches listed in this section are priced at the retail level and as complete watches having an original 14k gold-filled case with an original dial, and the entire original movement in good working order with no repairs needed. They are also priced as having a watch band made of leather except where bracelet is described. Watches listed as 14k and 18k are solid gold cases. Coin or silveroid-type and stainless steel cases will be listed as such. Dollar-type watches, or low cost production watches, are listed as having a base metal type case and a composition dial.

Many of the watch manufacturers were commissioned to put jewelers' or jobbers' names on their movements in place of their own. Because of this practice, the true manufacturers of these movements are difficult to identify. These watch models are listed under the original manufacturer and can be identified by comparison with the model sections under each manufacturer. See "Personalized Watches" and "Swiss Code Initials" for more detailed information.

The prices shown were averaged from dealers' lists just prior to publication and are an indication of the retail level or what collectors will pay. **Prices** are provided in three categories: **average condition, extra fine,** and **mint condition**, and are shown in whole dollar amounts only. The values listed are a guide for the retail level and are provided for your information only. Dealers will not necessarily pay full retail price. Prices listed are for watches with **original** cases and dials.

Note: Descriptions and serial number ranges listed for early watches cannot be considered 100 percent accurate due to the manner in which records were kept by these companies.

WARNING: There are currently fake wrist watches being sold on the worldwide market. These watches have the appearance of authenticity but are merely cheap imitations of prestigious companies such as Rolex (all types), Gucci, Cartier, and Piaget.

INFORMATION NEEDED—The authors are interested in any facts and information you might have that should possibly be considered for future editions. Documented facts are needed, so please send photo or sources of information. (Please send a self addressed, stamped envelope). Send to Cooksey Shugart, 780 Church St. N.E., Cleveland, TN 37311.

Abercrombie & Fitch Co., 17 jewels, "Sea Farer," chronog., waterproof
s. steel..........................$100 $125 $150

Accro W. Co., 17 jewels, hinged back,
18k..........................$800 $900 $1,000

Admes, 17 jewels, self wind, waterproof, center sec.,
gold filled..........................$25 $30 $40

Agassiz, 17 jewels, World Time,
18k $12,000 $14,000 $16,000

Agassiz, 17 jewels, fancy bezel,
18k $2,000 $2,500 $3,000

Agassiz, 18 jewels, for Tiffany & Co., 48mm,
18k   **$1,700 $1,800 $2,000**

Agassiz, 18 jewels, barrel shaped dial, 40mm,
18k $1,200 $1,300 1,500

Agassiz, 17 jewels, for Tiffany & Co., 45mm
18k $1,500 $1,600 $1,800

Alpina, 15 jewels, sweep sec. hand
gold filled..........................$50 $60 $70

Alpina, 15 jewels, automatic, water proof, center sec.
gold filled..........................$30 $40 $50

Alpina, 17 jewels, automatic, water proof, aux. sec.
18k $200 $250 $300

Alsta, 17 jewels, wrist alarm
gold filled.......................$200 $225 $250

Altus, 17 jewels, ref. 827
18k $200 $225 $250

Am. Waltham, 17 jewels, barrel shaped dial, c. 1920
14k $500 $550 $600

Am. Waltham, 17 jewels, "Cromwell"
gold filled........................$75 $100 $125

Am. Waltham, 17 jewels, "Oberlin"
gold filled........................$75 $100 $125

Am. Waltham, 15 jewels, engraved bezel
gold filled........................$65 $80 $110

Am. Waltham, for Tiffany & Co.
14k $400 $450 $500

Am. Waltham, 17 jewels, wire lugs
14k $300 $400 $500

Am. Waltham, 21 jewels, curved back
14k $300 $350 $425

Am. Waltham, 17 jewels, "Duxbury"
gold filled........................$75 $100 $125

Am. Waltham, 17 jewels, wandering sec., c. 1930
gold filled........................$200 $250 $300

Am. Waltham, 17 jewels, "Fairmont"
gold filled........................$100 $150 $200

Am. Waltham, 17 jewels, "Stan Hope"
gold filled.....................$75 $100 $125

Am. Waltham, 17 jewels, "Winfield"
gold filled.....................$75 $100 $125

Am. Waltham, wandering min., jumping hr., c. 1933
gold filled $700 $900 $1,200

Am. Waltham, 21 jewels, "Albright"
14k $100 $125 $150

Am. Waltham, 21 jewels, "Sheraton"
14k $125 $150 $175

Am. Waltham, 17 jewels, center sec.
gold filled......................$40 $50 $65

Am. Waltham, 15 jewels, wire lugs, c. 1916
silver $200 $250 $300

Am. Waltham, 15 jewels, center lugs, enamel dial
silver $250 $300 $350

Am. Waltham, 15 jewels, in protective grill, c. 1928
silver $400 $500 $600

Am. Waltham, 15 jewels, "Depollier," early water
proof, (tin can style), c. 1917
silver $400 500 $600

Am. Waltham, 15 jewels, protective grill, c. 1907
14k $1,200 $1,300 $1,500

Am. Waltham, 17 jewels, military with hack set
s. steel............................$50 $60 $75

Am. Waltham, 17 jewels, cut-corner dial
14k $300 $400 $500

Am. Waltham, 17 jewels, luminus dial
14k $300 $400 $500

Am. Waltham, 17Jewels, wire lugs,
silver $150 $200 $250

Am. Waltham, 17 jewels, "Allen"
gold filled $75 $100 $125

Am. Waltham, 17 jewels, "Penton"
gold filled........................$65 $80 $100

Am. Waltham, 9-17 jewels, "side-wrist"
gold filled.....................$125 $150 $200

Am. Waltham, 17 jewels, center lugs
14k $125 $150 $175

Am. Waltham, 17 jewels, curvex, 52mm
14k $500 $600 $700

Am. Waltham, 17 jewels, curvex, 42mm
14k $300 $350 $400

Am. Waltham, 17 jewels, curvex, 42mm
gold filled......................$125 $150 $175

Am. Waltham, 17-21 jewels, curved
14k $200 $250 $300
gold filled........................$75 $85 $125

Am. Waltham, 17 jewels, curved, aux. sec.
gold filled........................$75 $100 $125

Am. Waltham, 17 jewels, "Jeffrey"
gold filled........................$75 $100 $125

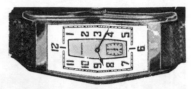

Am. Waltham, 17 jewels, curved
gold filled.........................$65 $75 $95

Am. Waltham, 21 jewels, "Tulane"
gold filled.........................$40 $50 $60

Am. Waltham, 17 jewels, curved
gold filled.........................$60 $70 $80

Am. Waltham, 17 jewels, curved
gold filled.........................$65 $75 $95

Am. Waltham, 17 jewels, triangular, masonic symbols,
fancy hands, c. 1950
gold filled..................$1,800 $2,000 $2,500

Am. Waltham, 17 jewels, enamel bezel
14k $1,000 $1,200 $1,500
14k (w).........................$600 $800 $1,000
gold filled $300 $350 $400

Americus, 17 jewels, 8 day movement, c. 1933
18k $1,000 $1,200 $1,500
gold filled $400 $500 $600

AMERICAN WALTHAM WATCH CO. IDENTIFICATION BY MOVEMENT

Model 1900, 0 size

Model 1907, 0 size

Jewel Series

Model 1900, 0/3 size,
open face

Model 1907, 0/3 size,
hunting

Model 1898 & 1912,
0/6 size, hunting

Model 1898 & 1912,
0/6 size, open face

10½ ligne

10 ligne

7½ ligne

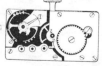

5¼ ligne

Model 400

Model 450

Model 650

Model 675

Model 750

Angelus, 17 jewels, chronog., 2 reg., c. 1943
18k $700 $900 $1,100
14k $400 $500 $600
gold filled $150 $200 $250

Arbu, 17 jewels, triple date, moon phase
18k $800 $1,000 $1,200
s. steel $300 $350 $400

Angelus, 17 jewels, chrono., 2 reg., water proof
s. steel...........................$200 $250 $300

Arbu, 17 jewels, chronog., 3 reg., day-date-month
s. steel...........................$200 $250 $300

Angelus, 27 jewels, quarter repeater
s. steel.....................$2,500 $2,700 $3,000

Arbu, 17 jewels, split sec. chronog.
18k $3,000 $3,500 $4,000

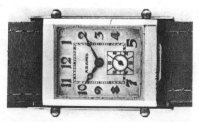

Aramis, 15 jewels, early self wind, lug action winding
by back & forth motion of watch case, c. 1933
s. steel...........................$600 $700 $900

Aristo, 17 jewels, chronog., water proof
s. steel...........................$150 $175 $225

Aristo, 17 jewels, day-date-month, moon phase
s. steel..........................$100 $135 $185

ARSA, 17 jewels, day-date-month, moon phase
18k $900 $1,000 $1,200
s. steel $300 $350 $400

ARSA, 15 jewels, day-date-month, moon phase
18k $900 $1,000 $1,200
s. steel $300 $350 $400

Asprey, 16 jewels, curved hinged back
9k $300 $400 $500

Asprey, 15 jewels, duo dial
18k $1,500 $1,800 $2,200

Asprey, 17 jewels, enamel dial, articulated lugs
9k $200 $250 $300

Audemars Piguet, 29 jewels, min. repeater, repeats on gongs, c. 1907
18k $100,000 $110,000 $120,000

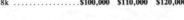

Audemars Piguet, 29 jewels, min. repeater, c. 1925
platinum.............$120,000 $130,000 $140,000

Audemars Piguet, 19 jewels, tourbillon, self-winding tourbillon can be seen from dial side
18k $15,000 $16,000 $18,000

Audemars Piguet, 36 jewels, octogonal shaped case, triple date, moon phase
18k C&B $15,000 $18,000 $22,000

Audemars Piguet, 18 jewels, day-date-month, moon phase
18k $10,000 $12,000 $14,000

Audemars Piguet, 36 jewels, gold rotor, day-date-month, moon phase
18 C&B................. $15,000 $16,000 $18,000

Audemars Piguet, 18 jewels, "Le Brassus," chronog. skeletonized
18k C&B $20,000 $22,000 $25,000

Audemars Piguet, 17 jewels, chronog., 3 reg., c. 1945
18k $25,000 $30,000 $35,000

Audemars Piguet, 18 jewels, skeletonized
18k $7,000 $8,000 $10,000

Audemars Piguet, 22 jewels, chronog., 2 reg.,
18k $20,000 $25,000 $30,000

Audemars Piguet, 17 jewels, thin skeletonized
18k $5,000 $6,000 $7,000

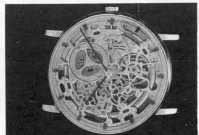

Audemars Piguet, 36 jewels, skeletonized
18k $5,500 $6,500 $8,000

Audemars Piguet, 17 jewels, center lugs, skeletonized
18k $7,000 $7,500 $8,500

Audemars Piguet, 17 jewels, Dodecagonal, black dial
18k $1,500 $1,800 $2,200

Audemars Piguet, 17 jewels, diamond dial, c. 1970
18k $3,000 $3,500 $4,000

Audemars Piguet, 17 jewels, sapphire dial
18k (w) $1,200 $1,300 $1,500

Audemars Piguet, 36 jewels, self-winding
18k $1,400 $1,600 $1,800

Audemars Piguet, 17 jewels, adj. to 5 positions
18k C&B $1,200 $1,400 $1,600

Audemars Piguet, 17 jewels, rope style bezel
18k C&B $2,000 $2,200 $2,500

Audemars Piguet, 17 jewels, diamond bezel, ctr. lugs
18k $2,500 $2,800 $3,000

Audemars Piguet, 20 jewels, "Le Brassus," c. 1970
18k C&B $3,000 $3,500 $4,000

Audemars Piguet, 17 jewels, fancy bezel, c. 1950
18k $1,500 $2,000 $2,500

Audemars Piguet, 36 jewels, self-winding
18k $1,800 $2,000 $2,400

Audemars Piguet, 17 jewels, unusual hour hand
18k $2,200 $2,500 $2,800

Audemars Piguet, 36 jewels, lazuli dial
18k C&B $2,200 $2,400 $2,800

Audemars Piguet, 20 jewels, thin model
18k $900 $1,000 $1,200

Audemars Piguet, 17 jewels, thin style
18k C&B $2,000 $2,200 $2,500

Audemars Piguet, 17 jewels, wide bezel, thin model
14k C&B $1,500 $1,600 $1,800

Audemars Piguet, 21 jewels, auto wind, center sec.
18k $1,500 $1,600 $1,800

Audemars Piguet, 18 jewels, gold train
18k $3,000 $3,500 $4,200

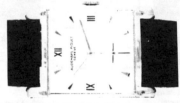

Audemars Piguet, 18 jewels, adj. to 8 pos., c. 1940
18k $1,500 $1,600 $1,700

Audemars Piguet, 18 jewels, aux. sec. c. 1940
18k $2,000 $2,200 $2,500

Audemars Piguet, 17 jewels, for Tiffany & Co.
18k C&B $1,500 $1,600 $1,800

Audemars Piguet, 18 jewels, aux. sec.
18k $2,000 $2,400 $2,800

Audemars Piguet, 18 jewels, tank style, c. 1960
18k (w) $1,500 $1,600 $1,800

Audemars Piguet, 18 jewels, hooded lugs
18k $2,500 $2,800 $3,200

Audemars Piguet, 18 jewels, curved back, c. 1940
18k $2,200 $2,500 $2,800

Audemars Piguet, 18 jewels, center sec., c. 1950
18k $1,500 $1,800 $2,200

Audemars Piguet, 18 jewels, straight line lever escape.
18k $1,200 $1,400 $1,700

Audemars Piguet, 18 jewels, screw back, waterproof
18k $1,600 $1,800 $2,000

Audemars Piguet, 17 jewels, mid-size
18k $500 $600 $700

Audemars Piguet, 18 jewels, auto wind, waterproof
18k $1,600 $1,800 $2,000

Audemars Piguet, 18 jewels, enamel dial, c. 1970
18k $800 $900 $1,100

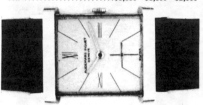

Audemars Piguet, 18 jewels, aux. sec., c. 1950
platinum $5,000 $6,000 $7,000

Audemars Piguet, 17 jewels, gold train, 2 tone case in
platinum & gold
18k (w) C&B $2,500 $2,700 $3,000

Audemars Piguet, 21 jewels, 18k gold rotor
18k $1,700 $1,900 $2,300

Audemars Piguet, 17 jewels, gold train
18k $1,000 $1,200 $1,500

Audemars Piguet, 17 jewels, gold train
14k C&B **$1,600 $1,800 $2,200**

Autorist, 15 jewels, lug action, enamel dial
s. steel **$1,000 $1,200 $1,400**

Audemars Piguet, 18 jewels, textured bezel, c. 1950
18k **$2,000 $2,200 $2,600**

Autorist, 15 jewels, lug action, c. 1930
s. steel **$1,000 $1,200 $1,400**

Audemars Piguet, 17 jewels, gold train, c. 1960
18k (w) **$1,500 $1,600 $1,800**

Autorist, 15 jewels, lug action, c. 1930
gold filled **$1,100 $1,300 $1,500**

Audemars Piguet, 18J, curvex, large bezel, c. 1950
18k **$2,000 $2,200 $2,500**

Autorist, 15 jewels, lug action (lady's)
s. steel **$400 $450 $575**

Audemars Piguet, 18 jewels, tank style
18k **$2,000 $2,200 $2,500**

Ball W. Co., 25 jewels, adj. to 5 pos., E.T.A.
10k **$300 $325 $375**

Ball W. Co., 25 jewels, adj. to 5 pos., E.T.A.
gold filled.....................$200 $225 $275

Ball W. Co., 25 jewels, adj. to 5 pos., E.T.A.
s. steel.........................$175 $200 $225

Baume & Mercier, 18 jewels, triple date, moon phase
s. steel.........................$400 $450 $500

Baume & Mercier, 18 jewels, chronog., 3 reg. & dates
s. steel.........................$500 $600 $700

Baume & Mercier, 18 jewels, chronog., 3 reg. & dates
18k $1,400 $1,600 $1,800

Baume & Mercier, 18 jewels, tachymeter, c. 1960
s. steel.........................$500 $600 $700

Baume & Mercier, 18 jewels, chronog., fancy lugs
18k $1,800 $2,200 $2,600

Baume & Mercier, 17 jewels, chronog., triple date
18k $1,200 $1,400 $1,600

Baume & Mercier, 18 jewels, triple date, moon phase
18k $1,200 $1,400 $1,600

Benrus, 18 jewels, mystery-diamond dial
18k $500 $600 $700
gold filled.......................$200 $225 $250

Baume & Mercier, 17 jewels, 2 dials, 2 time zones &
2 movements
18k $700 $800 $1,000

Benrus, 15 jewels, date, c. 1948
s. steel............................$50 $60 $70

Baume & Mercier, 18 jewels, gold dial, date
14k C&B $400 $450 $500

Benrus, 15 jewels, quick change date
gold filled..........................$60 $75 $90

Baume & Mercier, 18 jewels, thin model
14k C&B $400 $450 $500

Benrus, 15 jewels, date, fancy lugs, c. 1950
14k $100 $150 $200

Benrus, 15 jewels, jumping hour, wandering min.
gold filled.........................$100 $120 $140
s. steel............................$60 $70 $85

Benrus, 15 jewels, fancy lugs, c. 1948
14k $100 $150 $200
gold filled.........................$60 $75 $90

Benrus, 15 jewels, fancy bezel, cal. BB14
14k $100 $120 $140
gold filled.........................$60 $75 $90

Benrus, 15 jewels, enamel bezel, c. 1930
14k (w)..........................$125 $150 $175

Benrus, 15 jewels, 26 diamond bezel
14k (w).........................$400 $500 $600

Benrus, 15 jewels, flip-top case, c. 1940
gold filled.......................$150 $200 $250

Benrus, 15 jewels, hooded lugs
gold filled.........................$75 $95 $125

Benrus, 15 jewels, cal. AX, fancy bezel
14k $200 $250 $350

Benrus, 17 jewels, curved back, large hooded lugs
14k $200 $250 $350

Benrus, 15 jewels, curved back, c. 1942
gold filled............................$60 $75 $90

Benson, 15 jewels, enamel dial, tank style case
9k $300 $400 $500

Benson, 15 jewels, enamel dial, flared case
9k $400 $450 $600

Blancpain, 23 jewels, day-date-month, moon phase
18k $3,000 $4,000 $5,000

Boillat Freres, 17 jewels, "Blita," waterproof
s. steel..............................$30 $40 $50

E. Borel, 17 jewels, chronometer, aux. sec.
18k $300 $400 $500
gold filled........................$75 $85 $100

E. Borel, 17 jewels, auto wind, date
gold filled.........................$80 $90 $110

Bovet, 17 jewels, chronog., 2 reg., c. 1940
s. steel..........................$100 $150 $200

Bovet, 17 jewels, chronog., triple date & 3 reg.
14k $300 $450 $550
gold filled.......................$125 $150 $225

Breguet, 21 jewels, skeletonized
18k C&B $7,000 $7,500 $8,000

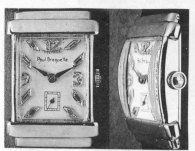

P. Breguette, 17 jewels, diamond dial, c. 1940
14k $250 $300 $400

Breguet, 17 jewels, chronog., triple date, moon phase
s. steel....................$8,000 $9,000 $10,000

Breitling, 17 jewels, "Chronomat," slide rule bezel
18k $1,500 $1,600 $1,700
gold filled $300 $400 $500
S. steel $250 $350 $450

Breguet, 17 jewels, silver dial, thin model
18k $1,200 $1,400 $1,600

Breitling, 17 jewels, chronog., "Navitimer," 3 reg.
18k $3,000 $3,300 $3,600
s. steel $500 $600 $700

Breguet, 17 jewels, curvex
platinum...................$3,000 $4,000 $5,000

Breitling, 17 jewels, split sec. chronog., 2 reg.
s. steel....................$2,000 $2,500 $3,000

Breitling, 17 jewels, chronog., "Navitimer," date
s. steel..........................$500 $600 $700

Breitling, 17 jewels, chronog., "Cosmonaute," date
s. steel..........................$500 $600 $700

Breitling, 17 jewels, chronog., "Chronomat," 3 reg.
s. steel..........................$250 $350 $450

Breitling, 17 jewels, telemeter, 1 button, hinged lugs
s. steel..........................$700 $800 $900

Breitling, 17 jewels, tachymeter, wire lugs
s. steel..........................$1,00 $1,100 $1,200

Breitling, 17 jewels, chronog., pulsations
s. steel..........................$500 $600 $700

Breitling, 17 jewels, telemeter, hinged lugs, 1 button
s. steel..........................$800 $900 $1,000

Breitling, 17 jewels, chronog., 2 reg.
s. steel......................$1,000 $1,100 $1,200

Breitling, 17 jewels, chronog., "Premier," 3 reg.
s. steel..........................$400 $500 $600

Breitling, 178 jewels, tachymeter, hinged lugs
s. steel..........................$700 $800 $900

Breitling, 17 jewels, chronog., day-date-month, 3 reg.
18k $1,800 $2,000 $2,400
s. steel....................$1,000 $1,200 $1,400

Breitling, 17 jewels, chronog., "Toptime,"
s. steel..........................$400 $500 $600

Breitling, 17 jewels, chronog., 2 reg.
s. steel..........................$200 $250 $300

Breitling, 17 jewels, chronog., 2 reg.
18k $500 $600 $700

Breitling, 17 jewels, chronog., 2 reg.
s. steel..........................$200 $250 $300

Breitling, 17 jewels, split sec. chronog., "Duograph"
18k $4,000 $5,000 $6,000
s. steel.....................$2,000 $2,500 $3,000

Bueche-Girod, 17 jewels, day-date-month, moon ph.
s. steel.....................$600 $700 $800

Bucherer, 17 jewels, 1 button chronog., 21 reg.
18k $1,000 $1,200 $1,500

Bueche-Girod, 17 jewels, tank style case
18k $600 $700 $850

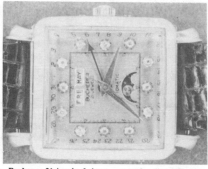

Bucherer, 21 jewels, 3 dates, moon ph., diamond dial
18k $2,500 $3,000 $3,500

Bueche-Girod, 17 jewels
18k C&B $600 $700 $800

P. Buhre, 17 jewels, aux. sec.
gold filled.....................$70 $80 $100

Bucherer, 15 jewels, 8 day movement
18k $1,500 $2,000 $2,500
gold filled $800 $900 $1,000

Bulova, Accutron, "Spaceview"
s. steel.....................$125 $150 $175

Bulova, Accutron, "Spaceview," c. 1960
14k $400 $450 $500
gold filled........................$125 $150 $175
s. steel...........................$100 $125 $150

Bulova, Accutron, "Spaceview," Alpha, waterproof
14k $500 $600 $700
gold filled........................$200 $300 $400
s. steel...........................$150 $200 $250

Bulova, Accutron, "Spaceview"
s. steel...........................$100 $125 $150

Bulova, Accutron, "Spaceview," center lugs
s. steel...........................$150 $175 $200

Bulova, Accutron, "Spaceview"
18k $600 $700 $800

Bulova, Accutron, cal. 214, c. 1966
14k $400 $450 $500

Bulova, Accutron, "Spaceview," c. 1967
s. steel...........................$150 $200 $250

Bulova, Accutron, cal. 214, diamond dial
14k $500 $600 $700

Bulova, Accutron, sweep sec. hand
gold filled......................$100 $125 $150

Bulova, Accutron, masonic dial
14k $400 $450 $500

Bulova, Accutron, asymmetric
14k $600 $700 $800

Bulova Accutron Astronaut, 24 hour dial
14k C&B $1,000 $1,100 $1,200

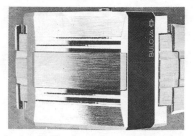

Bulova, digital
s. steel..........................$75 $100 $135

Bulova, enamel bezel
s. steel..........................$100 $125 $150

Bulova, 16 jewels, military style
s. steel..........................$200 $250 $300

Bulova, self winding, c. 1960
gold filled..........................$40 $50 $60

Bulova, 23 jewels, waterproof
14k $110 $120 $140

Bulova, cal. 700, tin can style, c. 1946
s. steel.........................$200 $300 $400

Bulova, 23 jewels, date, 6 adj., c. 1951
gold filled.........................$75 $85 $110

Bulova, early auto wind, by Champ, c. 1930
gold filled.......................$500 $600 $700

Bulova, 17 jewels, center sec., c. 1935
gold filled...........................$40 $50 $65

Bulova, diamond dial, c. 1939
14k (w) $250 $300 $350

Bulova, 21 jewels, hidden lugs, diamond dial, c. 1935
14k $225 $250 $275

Bulova, fancy long lugs, c. 1942
gold filled.........................$50 $60 $75

Bulova, hidden lugs, diamond dial, c. 1945
14k $200 $225 $250

Bulova, 21 jewels, diamond dial, long lugs, c. 1941
14k (w) $200 $235 $270

Bulova, 17 jewels, curved, cal. 7AP, c. 1939
14k $250 $300 $350

Bulova, 17 jewels, curved, c. 1939
gold filled.......................$100 $125 $150

Bulova, 21 jewels, curved, c. 1939
gold filled.......................$100 $125 $165

Bulova, 17 jewels, duo dial, c. 1935
s. steel.........................$300 $350 $400

Bulova, 17 jewels, 2 tone duo dial
s. steel.........................$300 $350 $400

Bulova, 17 jewels, 2 tone dial, fancy bezel
s. steel.........................$75 $85 $100

Bulova, 17 jewels, stepped case, wandering sec., c. 1942
gold filled.......................$200 $250 $300

Bulova, 17 jewels, cal. 10GM, fancy lugs, c. 1953
14k $200 $225 $250

Bulova, 21 jewels, hooded lugs, cal. 8AC, c. 1952
14k $250 $300 $350

Bulova, 17 jewels, fancy long lugs, c. 1942
14k $300 $350 $400

Bulova, 17 jewels, aux. sec.
14k $200 $225 $275

Bulova, 15 jewels, engraved bezel, c. 1925
gold filled......................$125 $150 $175

Bulova, 17 jewels, fancy bezel
gold filled......................$100 $120 $140

Bulova, 17 jewels, cal. 8AC, c. 1940
14k $175 $200 $225

Bulova, 17 jewels, bell shaped lugs
14k $300 $350 $400

Bulova, 15 jewels, wandering hr. min. sec., c. 1928
s. steel..........................$125 $150 $175

Bulova, 17 jewels, fancy lugs
14k $200 $225 $250

Bulova, 17 jewels, cal. 8AZ, c. 1938
14k $300 $400 $500

Bulova, 17 jewels, "The Governor"
14k $225 $250 $300

Bulova, 17 jewels, "The Ambassador"
gold filled..........................$50 $60 $75

Bulova, 17 jewels, "The Curtis," tank style
gold filled.....................$100 $125 $150

Bulova, 15 jewels, "The Athelete"
gold filled.....................$100 $115 $125

Bulova, 17 jewels, "The Lone Eagle," fancy bezel
gold filled.....................$280 $300 $350

Buren, 17 jewels, day-date-month, moon phase
s. steel........................$150 $185 $245

Buren, 17 jewels, long lugs
14k $150 $170 $200

Carlton, 15 jewels, stepped case, c. 1939
14k $200 $250 $300

Cartier, 18 jewels, sapphire crown & bezel, c. 1970
18k $2,000 $2,200 $2,500

Cartier, 18 jewels, 8 day movement, tank style, signed
European W. Co.
18k $40,000 $45,000 $50,000

Cartier, 18 jewels, curved, tank style
18k $7,000 $8,000 $9,000

Cartier, 18 jewels, curved, European W. Co.
18k $5,000 $6,000 $7,000

Cartier, 18 jewels, tank style, platinum case & band
platinum C&B $20,000 $22,000 $24,000

Cartier, 18 jewels, tank style case
18k $1,200 $1,400 $1,600

Cartier, 20 jewels, tank style case, c. 1950
18k $1,000 $1,100 $1,200

Cartier, 18 jewels, tank style, European W. Co.
18k C&B $6,500 $7,000 $8,000

Cartier, 18 jewels, by Mavado
14k $1,200 $1,600 $2,200

Cartier, 18 jewels, duo plan, European W. Co.
18k C&B $5,000 $6,000 $7,000

Cartier, 18 jewels, aux. sec., long lugs
18k $900 $1,000 $1,100

Cartier, 18 jewels, curved, hidden lugs
18k $4,000 $5,000 $6,000

Cartier, 18 jewels, by Universal, c. 1960
18k $1,200 $1,400 $1,600

Cartier, 18 jewels, center lugs, c. 1930
18k $800 $900 $1,000

Cartier, 18 jewels, reversible to view 2nd dial & 2nd
time zone
18k $12,000 $15,000 $18,000

Cartier, 18 jewels, c. 1960
18k $1,000 $1,100 $1,200

Cartier, 18 jewels, lady's watch by European W. Co.
18k $800 $900 $1,000

Cartier, 18 jewels, jump hr. & min., European W. Co.
c. 1930
platinum $30,000 $35,000 $40,000

Cartier, 18 jewels, "Santos," 18k & s. steel case, band
platinum & 18k C&B $12,000 $14,000 $16,000
18k & s. steel C&B $1,000 $1,200 $1,400

Cartier, 18 jewels, "Santos," date
18k & s. steel C&B..........$1,200 $1,300 $1,500

Cartier, 18 jewels, "Santos," octogonal, date
18k & s. steel C&B..........$1,100 $1,200 $1,300

Cartier, 18 jewels, "Santos," lady's, date
18k & s. steel C&B $800 $900 $1,000

Cartier, 25 jewels, chronog., European W. Co.
18k $70,000 $80,000 $90,000

Cartier, 29 jewels, min. repeater, c. 1925
18k $175,000 $225,000 $275,000

Cartier, 18 jewels, c. 1925
18k $4,000 $4,500 $5,000

Cartier, 18 jewels, asymmetric, E. W. Co., c. 1928
18k $11,000 $12,000 $13,000

Cartier, 18 jewels, self winding, by Le Coultre
18k $2,000 $2,500 $3,000

Cartier, 29 jewels, min. repeater, by Le Coultre, c. 1930
platinum $100,000 $130,000 $160,000

Cartier, 18 jewels, date chapter, by Le Coultre
14k $1,000 $1,200 $1,400

Chevrolet, 6 jewels, in form of car radiator, c. 1927
silver $400 $500 $600

Chopard, 18 jewels, skeletonized, diamond dial & hands
18k $4,000 $4,500 $5,000

Clebar, 17 jewels, chronog., c. 1938
s. steel............................ $75 $85 $100

Concord, 17 jewels, center sec.
14k $125 $150 $175

Cortebort, 15 jewels, c. 1941
gold filled.......................... $60 $70 $85

Cortebort, 17 jewels, "Sport," triple date, moon phase
18k $1,000 $1,200 $1,400
gold filled $200 $240 $300

Corum, 21 jewels, gold dial
18k $400 $500 $600

Cortebort, 17 jewels, center sec.
s. steel...............................$40 $45 $60

Corum, 17 jewels, in form of Rolls-Royce car radiator
18k $1,800 $2,000 $2,200

Croton, 17 jewels, diamond bezel & dial
14k (w) $700 $800 $900

Corum, 17 jewels, peacock feather dial
18k $700 $800 $900

Croton, 17 jewels, chronog., c. 1946
s. steel...........................$100 $125 $150

Corum, 17 jewels, in form of book
18k $600 $700 $900

Cyma, 17 jewels, aux. sec.
18k $200 $250 $300
14k $175 $200 $250
gold filled $65 $75 $85

Daynite, 7 jewels, 8 day movement, c. 1925
s. steel..........................$250 $300 $400

P. Ditisheim, 17 jewels, "Solvil," diamond dial, c. 1947
platinum.......................$700 $800 $900

P. Ditisheim, 17 jewels, "Solvil," diamond dial, c. 1948
platinum.......................$700 $800 $900

P. Ditisheim, 17 jewels, "Solvil," curved, diamond dial
platinum...................$1,000 $1,200 $1,500

P. Ditisheim, 17 jewels, diamond dial, curved
platinum...................$1,000 $1,200 $1,500

P. Ditisheim, 17 jewels, baguette diamonds, fancy bezel
platinum...................$1,200 $1,400 $1,600

P. Ditisheim, 17 jewels, hinged lugs, enameled bezel
14k............................$800 $900 $1,000

Dome, 25 jewels, triple dates, auto wind
18k............................$500 $600 $700

Doxa, 17 jewels, center sec.
14k............................$100 $135 $165

Doxa, 17 jewels, chronog., fancy lugs
s. steel..........................$100 $125 $165

Doxa, 17 jewels, center sec., fancy lugs
14k $100 $125 $150

Doxa, 17 jewels, chronog., triple dates, moon phase
14k $1,100 $1,200 $1,500

Doxa, 17 jewels, center sec., c. 1949
gold filled......................$100 $125 $150

Doxa, 17 jewels, chronog., cal. 1220, c. 1940
s. steel..........................$125 $150 $175

Driva, 15 jewels, ¼ repeater, repeats on gong, repeater wound by bolt above hand, c. 1930
s. steel......................$5,000 $6,000 $7,000

Duodial, 15 jewels, c. 1934
9k $1,000 $1,200 $1,500

Doxa, 17 jewels, chronog., 2 reg., c. 1942
gold filled......................$200 $250 $300

Ebel, 21 jewels, chronog., self winding, perpetual cal.
18k $7,000 $8,000 $9,000

Ebel, 18 jewels, applied gold numbers, c. 1950
18k $400 $450 $500

Ebel, 17 jewels, chronog., 3 reg., c. 1941
s. steel............................$450 $550 $650

Ebel, 17 jewels, slide open to wind
silver $200 $250 $300

Eberhard, 18 jewels, split sec. chronog., 3 reg.
18k $6,000 $8,000 $10,000

Ebel, 17 jewels, chronog., 2 reg., enamel dial
s. steel............................$400 $500 $600

Eberhard, 17 jewels, tele-tachymeter, enamel dial, c. 1930
18k $2,500 $3,000 $3,500

Ebel, 17 jewels, chronog., c. 1955
s. steel............................$400 $500 $600

Eberhard, 17 jewels, chronog., 2 reg.
18k $1,500 $1,700 $2,000

Eberhard, 17 jewels, chronog., center lugs, 1 button
s. steel...........................$400 $500 $600

Ekegren, 17 jewels, jumping hr., min. hand, c. 1920
platinum...............$15,000 $17,000 $20,000

Ekegren, 18 jewels, jumping hr., c. 1920
18k....................$12,000 $14,000 $16,000

Electra W. Co., 17J, chronog., 1 button, hinged back
silver............................$500 $600 $700

Elgin, 17 jewels, raised numbers
14k............................$250 $300 $350

Lord Elgin, 21 jewels, curved, raised numbers
14k............................$225 $250 $275

Elgin, 17 jewels, embossed dial
14k............................$175 $200 $250

Lord Elgin, 21 jewels, curved
gold filled......................$100 $120 $140

Elgin, 17 jewels, curved, "Streamlined"
gold filled......................$100 $120 $140

Elgin, 17 jewels, raised numbers
gold filled......................$100 $120 $140

Elgin, 15 jewels, curved, fancy bezel
gold filled......................$100 $120 $140

Lord Elgin, 21 jewels, curved
platinum.........................$500 $600 $700

Lord Elgin, 21 jewels, curved
14k $200 $250 $275

Elgin, 17 jewels, curved
gold filled.........................$100 $120 $140

Elgin, 17 jewels, curved
gold filled.........................$125 $150 $175

Elgin, 17 jewels, "Ristflo"
gold filled.........................$250 $300 $350

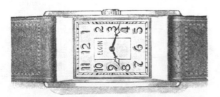

Elgin, 17 jewels
gold filled.........................$100 $110 $125

Elgin, 17 jewels, embossed dial
gold filled.........................$100 $110 $125

Elgin, 17 jewels, hidden lugs
gold filled.........................$100 $110 $120

Elgin, 17 jewels, curved, thin model
gold filled.........................$100 $110 $120

Elgin, 17 jewels, stepped case
gold filled.........................$100 $110 $120

Elgin, 15 jewels, "William Osler"
gold filled.........................$150 $200 $250

Elgin, 7 jewels, center sec.
gold filled.........................$125 $150 $200

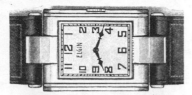

Elgin, 15 jewels, center lugs
gold filled.........................$80 $90 $100

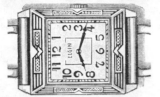

Elgin, 7 jewels, fancy bezel
s. steel.............................$50 $60 $70

Elgin, 7 jewels, fancy bezel
gold filled.........................$60 $70 $80

Elgin, 17 jewels, "Crusade"
gold filled.........................$100 $120 $140

Elgin, 7 jewels
gold filled.........................$40 $50 $60

Elgin, 7 jewels, stepped bezel
s. steel.............................$60 $70 $80

Elgin, 17 jewels, raised numbers
gold filled.........................$80 $90 $100

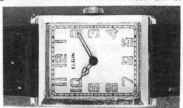

Elgin, 17 jewels, c. 1927
14k $175 $225 $275

Lord Elgin, 21 jewels, diamond dial
14k (w).............................$135 $155 $185

Elgin, 19 jewels, c. 1947
14k $125 $150 $175

Lord Elgin, 21 jewels, diamond dial
14k (w).............................$125 $150 $200

Lord Elgin, 21 jewels, aux. sec., fancy lugs
14k $175 $200 $250

Elgin, 15 jewels, enamel dial, wire lugs, c. 1915
silver $150 $175 $200

Lord Elgin, 21 jewels, flared case
14k $200 $250 $300

Elgin, 19 jewels, fancy lugs
14k $175 $200 $250

Elgin, 15 jewels, center lugs
gold filled......................$175 $200 $225

Elgin, 15 jewels, "Official Boy Scout" model
s. steel.........................$100 $125 $175

Elgin, 15 jewels, center lugs, c. 1922
silver $175 $200 $225

Elgin, 7 jewels, "Official Boy Scout" model
s. steel.........................$50 $65 $85

Elgin, 15 jewels, center lugs, c. 1928
silver $175 $200 $225

Elgin, 23 jewels, "B. W. Raymond," R.R. approved
14k $300 $350 $400
gold filled........................$150 $200 $250
s. steel............................$125 $150 $175

Lord Elgin, 21 jewels, diamond dial, c. 1958
14k (w) $250 $300 $400

Lord Elgin, 21 jewels, mystery dial, c. 1957
14k (w).........................$150 $200 $250

Elgin, 17 jewels, in form of golf ball, rotating hr. & min.
gold filled........................$250 $300 $350

Lord Elgin, 21 jewels, applied numbers, c. 1946
14k $200 $250 $300

Lord Elgin, 21 jewels, curved, applied numbers
14k $300 $350 $450

Lord Elgin, 21 jewels, diamond dial, faceted crystal
14k $350 $400 $475

Elgin, 17 jewels, hinged back
14k (w) $250 $300 $375

Elgin, 17 jewels, enamel bezel
14k (w) $700 $800 $900

Elgin, 15 jewels, Art Deco bezel, c. 1935
gold filled........................$100 $125 $150

Elgin, 15 jewels, 2 tone, c. 1930
gold filled.........................$80 $100 $120

Elgin, 15 jewels, enamel bezel, c. 1920
14k (w) $700 $800 $900

Elgin, 17 jewels, raised numbers
gold filled.........................$80 $100 $120

Elgin, 21 jewels, enamel bezel, 2 tone, c. 1931
14k $800 $900 $1,000

Elgin, 7 jewels, fancy bezel
s. steel.........................$50 $60 $70

Elgin, 7 jewels, engraved bezel
s. steel.........................$35 $40 $50

Elgin, 17 jewels, curved
gold filled.........................$90 $100 $110

Elgin, 17 jewels, aux. sec., curved
gold filled.........................$100 $120 $140

Elgin, 17 jewels, curved
gold filled.........................$90 $100 $110

Elgin, 21 jewels, enamel bezel, c. 1920
14k $1,500 $1,700 $1,900

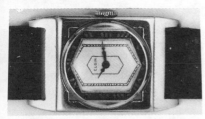

Elgin, 21 jewels, enamel bezel
18k $1,800 $2,000 $2,200

Lord Elgin, 21J, model 670, large lugs, anniversary of
50,000,000th watch (small run of watches prod.), c. 1953
18k $1,600 $2,000 $2,400

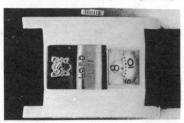

Lord Elgin, 21 jewels, wandering hr. & min., curved
gold filled.....................$200 $250 $300

Elgin, 17 jewels, double dial
gold filled.....................$500 $600 $700

Lord Elgin, 21 jewels, hooded lugs, c. 1952
14k $225 $250 $275

Lord Elgin, 21 jewels, curved, c. 1957
14k $200 $250 $300

Lord Elgin, 21 jewels, hooded lugs
14k $200 $225 $250

Elgin, 15 jewels, waterproof
s. steel.....................$30 $40 $50

Elgin, 15 jewels, center sec.
gold filled.....................$35 $45 $55

Elgin, 7 jewels, aux. sec.
gold filled.....................$25 $30 $40

Lord Elgin, 21 jewels, stepped case
18k $400 $450 $500

Lord Elgin, 21 jewels, stepped case, curved
14k $250 $300 $350

Elgin, 17 jewels, curved
gold filled........................$100 $120 $140

Elgin, 17 jewels, stepped case
14k $200 $225 $250

Elgin, 19 jewels, stepped case
gold filled........................$100 $120 $140

Lord Elgin, 21 jewels, curved
gold filled........................$110 $120 $135

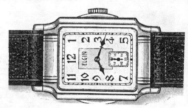

Elgin, 15 jewels
gold filled.........................$80 $90 $100

Elgin, 17 jewels, curved, fancy bezel
gold filled........................$100 $120 $140

Elgin, 7 jewels, fancy bezel
s. steel............................$40 $45 $50

Elgin, 17 jewels, curved, stepped case
gold filled........................$100 $120 $140

Elgin, 17 jewels, curved, stepped case
gold filled........................$100 $120 $140

Elgin, 7 jewels, fancy bezel
gold filled.........................$80 $90 $100

Elgin, 15 jewels, fancy bezel
gold filled.......................$100 $110 $120

Lord Elgin, 21 jewels, curved
14k $200 $225 $300

Elgin, 21 jewels, curved
gold filled.......................$100 $120 $140

Lord Elgin, 21 jewels, aux. sec.
gold filled.......................$100 $120 $140

Lord Elgin, 21 jewels, raised numbers
14k $200 $250 $300

Elgin, 17 jewels, curved
gold filled.......................$100 $120 $140

Lord Elgin, 21 jewels, curved, c. 1938
14k $250 $300 $350

Lord Elgin, 21 jewels, curved
14k $200 $275 $300

Lord Elgin, 21 jewels, curved
14k $225 $250 $275

Elgin, 17 Jewels, raised numbers
14k $200 $225 $250

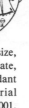    

Model 3, 3-0 size, three-quarter plate, open face, pendant set, first serial number 18,179,001, Grade 414, March, 1915.

Model 1, 5-0 size, three-quarter plate, hunting, pendant set, first serial number 14,699,001, Grade 380, Feb., 1910.

Model 2, 5-0 size, three-quarter plate, open face, pendant set, first serial number 17,890,001, Grade 399, Feb., 1914.

Model 2, 8-0 size, Grade 532, 539, sweep second.

Model 7, 8-0 size, Grades 554, 555, 556.

Model 20, 8-0 size, Grades 681, 682.

Model 1, 10-0 size, three-quarter plate, open face, pendant set, first serial number 8,752,001, Grade 255, Apr., 1902.

Model 2, 15-0 size, Grades 623, 624, 626.

15-0 Size, movement, Grades 670, 672, 673.

15-0 size, movement. Grade 674.

15-0 size, movement, Grades 557, 558, 559.

Model 2, 21-0 size, Grade 541, 533, 535.

Model 3, 21-0 size, Grade 547, sweep second.

Model 4, 21-0 size, Grades 617, 617L, 619, 619L.

Model 9, 21-0 size, Grades 650, 651.

Model 9, 21-0 size, Grades 655, 656.

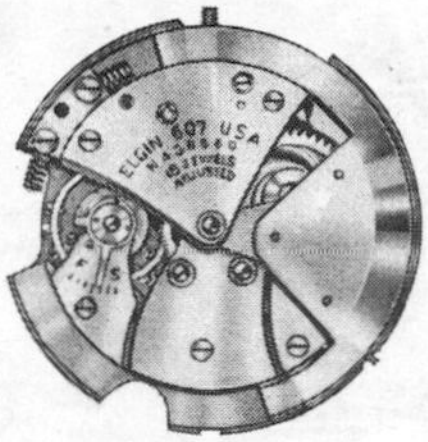

Grade 607, self wind.

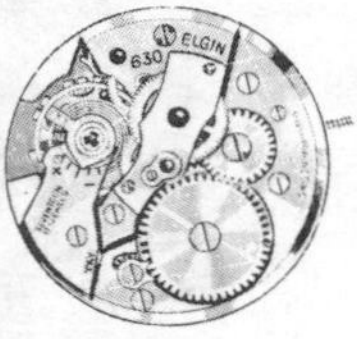

Grade 630, sweep second.

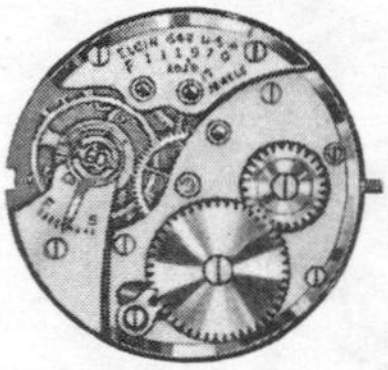

Grade 641, 642

Grade 643, self wind.

Grades 644, 645, self wind.

Grade 647, sweep second.

Grade 661

Grade 666, sweep second.

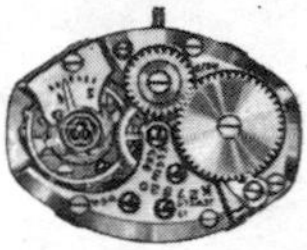

Grade 668, sweep second.

Grade 685

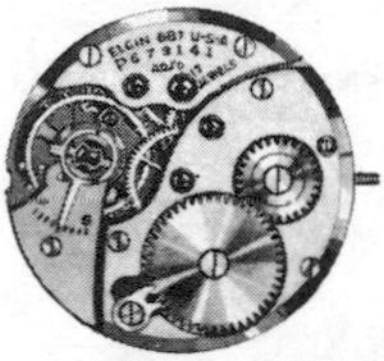

Grade 687

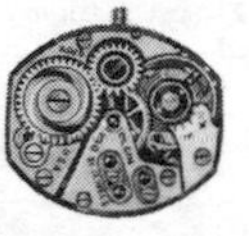

Grade 700

Grade 710

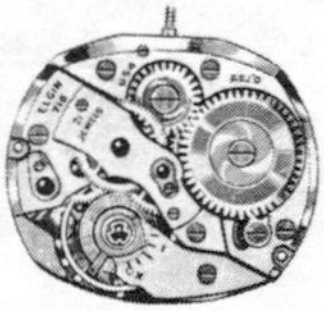

Grade 716

Enicar, 17 jewels, center sec.
s. steel...............................$30 $40 $50

Eska, 17 jewels, chronog., 2 reg., c. 1940
s. steel......................$1,500 $1,700 $2,000

Enicar, 17 jewels, triple date, moon phase
gold filled......................$150 $200 $250

Eska, 17 jewels, multi-colored enamel dial
18k $3,000 $3,500 $4,000

Enicar, 15 jewels, egg shaped with compass, c. 1918
silver $400 $450 $500

Eterna, 19 jewels, day-date-month
18k $350 $400 $450

Eska, 17 jewels, chronog., triple date, moon phase
gold filled.................$1,200 $1,400 $1,600

Eterna, 17 jewels, chronog., triple date, 3 reg.
18k $2,500 $3,000 $3,500

Evans, 17 jewels, chronog., 2 reg., c. 1940
18k $300 $400 $500

Exactus, 17 jewels, chronog., day-date-month, moon ph.
s. steel...........................$500 $600 $700

Excelsior, 17 jewels, chronog., 2 reg.
gold filled.......................$150 $200 $250

Excelsior, 17 jewels, chronog.
s. steel...........................$200 $225 $250

Felca, 17 jewels, auto wind
18k $250 $300 $350

Fontainemelon, S. A., 17 jewels, gold train, digital
14k $1,500 $1,600 $1,800

Friedli, 17 jewels, auto wind, center sec.
18k $250 $300 $350

Gallet, 15 jewels, waterproof, auto wind
s. steel...........................$50 $60 $70

Gallet, 17 jewels, chronog., 3 reg., c. 1945
s. steel..........................$300 $350 $400

Gallet, 17 jewels, chronog., 2 reg.
s. steel..........................$100 $150 $200

Gallet, 17 jewels, chronog., 3 reg., c. 1942
s. steel..........................$300 $350 $400

Gallet, 17 jewels, chronog., waterproof
s. steel..........................$200 $250 $300

Gallet, 17 jewels, chronog., 3 reg., c. 1955
s. steel..........................$300 $350 $400

Gallet, 17 jewels, chronog., 2 reg.
s. steel..........................$100 $150 $200

Gallet, 17 jewels, day-date-month, c. 1941
gold filled..........................$350 $400 $450

Gallet, 17 jewels, chronog., 2 reg.
s.steel $100 $135 $165

Gallet, 17 jewels, chronog., 2 reg.
gold filled......................$125　$175　$225

Gallet, 17 jewels, chronog., 2 reg.
s. steel..........................$100　$150　$200

Gallet, 17 jewels, chronog., 2 reg., c. 1939
s. steel..........................$135　$185　$235

Gallet, 17 jewels, chronog.
s. steel..........................$125　$150　$200

Geneve, 15 jewels, dual dial, c. 1939
s. steel..........................$300　$350　$400

Geneve, 15 jewels, dual dial, c. 1937
s. steel..........................$300　$350　$400

Germinal, 15 jewels, early auto wind, lug action, c. 1933
s. steel..........................$600　$800　$1,000

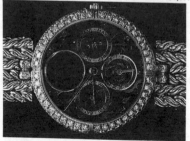

Gerald Genta, 29 jewels, skeletonized, auto wind
18k C&B...............$20,000　$25,000　$30,000

Girard-Perregaux, 39 jewels, center sec.
14k..............................$300　$350　$400

Girard-Perregaux, 39 jewels, date-center seconds
14k $300 $350 $400

Girard-Perregaux, 17 jewels, aux. sec., fancy lugs
14k $400 $450 $500

Girard-Perregaux, 39 jewels, auto wind, c. 1960
18k $300 $350 $400

Girard-Perregaux, 17 jewels, chronog., 3 reg., c. 1952
s. steel...........................$350 $400 $500

Girard-Perregaux, 17J, chronog., triple date, moon phase
18k $1,200 $1,400 $1,600

Girard-Perregaux, 17 jewels, aux. sec.
gold filled.......................$125 $135 $150

Girard-Perregaux, 17 jewels, tank style, c. 1948
14k $200 $250 $300

Girard-Perregaux, 17 jewels, date, stepped case, aux. sec.
14k $600 $700 $800

Glycine, 17 jewels, curved, c. 1938
18k $350 $400 $500

Glycine, 17 jewels, aux. sec., c. 1934
14k (w).......................$125 $150 $175

Glycine, 18 jewels, faceted crystal & bezel
gold filled.......................$90 $100 $130

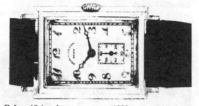

Golay, 18 jewels, aux. sec., c. 1928
18k & platinum.............$2,500 $3,000 $3,500

Golay, 32 jewels, min. repeater, adj. to 5 positions
18k $60,000 $70,000 $80,000

Gruen, 17 jewels, curvex, extremely curved, driver's watch
gold filled.......................$600 $700 $800

Gruen, 17 jewels, curvex, flexible long lugs
gold filled.......................$700 $800 $900

Gruen, 17 jewels, curvex, c. 1949
gold filled.......................$250 $275 $300

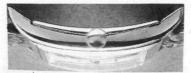

Gruen, 17 jewels, curvex, 35mm long
gold filled.......................$300 $400 $500

Gruen, 17 jewels, curvex, 55mm long, ca. 1937
14k $800 $900 $1,000

Gruen, 17 jewels, curvex, c. 1937
gold filled.......................$300 $400 $500

Gruen, 17 jewels, curvex, c. 1945
gold filled.......................$300 $350 $400

Gruen, 17 jewels, curvex, 50mm long, c. 1937
gold filled.......................$400 $500 $650

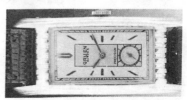

Gruen, 17 jewels, curvex, c. 1937
s. steel..........................$200 $225 $250

Gruen, 17 jewels, curvex, aux. sec.
gold filled.........................$300 $400 $500

Gruen, 17 jewels, curvex
gold filled.........................$225 $250 $300

Gruen, 17 jewels, curvex
gold filled.........................$200 $225 $250

Gruen, 17 jewels, curvex
gold filled.........................$200 $225 $250

Gruen, 17 jewels, curvex, fancy lugs
14k $300 $350 $400

Gruen, 17 jewels, double dial, c. 1935
gold filled.........................$700 $750 $800

Gruen, 17 jewels, curvex, long lugs
14k $350 $400 $450

Gruen, 17 jewels, jumping hr., double dial
14k $2,000 $2,500 $3,000

Gruen, 17 jewels, double dial
gold filled.........................$500 $600 $700

Gruen, 17 jewels, aux. sec., c. 1932
gold filled.........................$400 $450 $550

Gruen, 17 jewels, double dial, curved
gold filled.........................$400 $450 $550

Gruen, 17 jewels, curved, c. 1938
gold filled.......................$400 $450 $550

Gruen, 15 jewels, in form of car radiator, curved
nickel..........................$800 $900 $1,000

Gruen, 17 jewels, double dial
gold filled.......................$500 $550 $600

Gruen, 17 jewels, curvex, diamond dial, c. 1946
14k $300 $400 $500

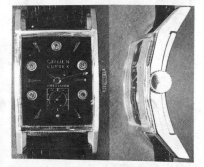

Gruen, 17 jewels, curvex, diamond dial, faceted crystal
14k $400 $450 $500

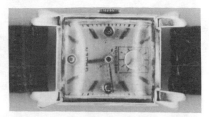

Gruen, 17 jewels, diamond dial, fancy lugs
14k $500 $550 $600

Gruen, 17 jewels, curvex, precision
gold filled.......................$300 $400 $500

Gruen, 17 jewels, auto wind, cal. 840, c. 1952
18k $350 $400 $450

Gruen, 17 jewels, curvex, fancy lugs
14k $350 $400 $450

Gruen, 21 jewels, diamond dial, fancy center lugs
14k $500 $550 $600

Gruen, 21 jewels, fancy lugs, c. 1945
14k $400 $450 $500

Gruen, 17 jewels, curvex, diamond dial, fancy lugs
14k (w) $300 $350 $400

Gruen, 17 jewels, curvex, c. 1943
14k $350 $400 $450

Gruen, 17 jewels, diamond dial
14k(w)...........................$600 $700 $800

Gruen, 17 jewels, curved, diamond dial
14k $500 $600 $700

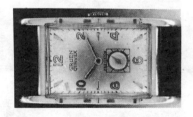

Gruen, 17 jewels, curvex
14k $500 $600 $700

Gruen, 17 jewels, curvex, diamond dial, c. 1945
14k $500 $600 $700

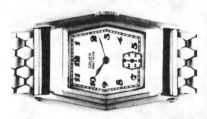

Gruen, 19 jewels, precision, c. 1920
14k $500 $600 $700

Gruen, 17 jewels, curvex, c. 1951
14k $350 $400 $450

Gruen, 17 jewels, curved
gold filled......................$175 $200 $250

Gruen, 17 jewels, curvex
14k $500 $600 $700

Gruen, 17 jewels, curvex, c. 1943
14k $350 $400 $450

Gruen, 17 jewels, curvex, c. 1936
gold filled.....................$300 $350 $400

Gruen, 17 jewels, precision, fancy lugs
14k $400 $500 $600

Gruen, 17 jewels, curvex, c. 1947
14k $350 $400 $450

Gruen, 17 jewels, curvex, c. 1937
gold filled.....................$175 $200 250

Gruen, 17 jewels, curvex, fancy lugs
14k $400 $450 $500

Gruen, 17 jewels, curvex, c. 1939
gold filled.....................$400 $450 $500

Gruen, 17 jewels, curvex, fancy lugs, c. 1961
14k $550 $600 $700

Gruen, 17 jewels, rope style bezel with diamonds
14k $300 $350 $400

Gruen, 17 jewels, physicians chronog., screw back
18k $1,500 $1,700 $2,000

Gruen, 17 jewels, day-date-month, c. 1948
s. steel.............................$70 $80 $95

Gruen, 17 jewels, veri thin model, fancy lugs
14k $300 $350 $400

Gruen, 17 jewels, jumping dial, c. 1960
gold filled.........................$200 $250 $300

Gruen, veri thin model, 24 hour dial
14k $400 $500 $600

E. Gubelin, 19 jewels, chronog. 3 reg., c. 1950
18k $1,200 $1,400 $1,600

E. Gubelin, 29 jewels, min. repeater
18k C&B $50,000 $60,000 $70,000

E. Gubelin, 25 jewels, ipso-matic, triple date, moon ph.
18k $2,000 $2,500 $3,000

E. Gubelin, 19 jewels, 18k case, 14k band
18k & 14k C&B $500 $700 $900

E. Gubelin, 19 jewels, hunter style pop-up lid, c. 1930
18k (w) $7,000 $8,000 $9,500

E. Gubelin, 17 jewels, jumping hr., c. 1924
14k $10,000 $12,000 $15,000

E. Gubelin, 25 jewels, triple date, moon phase, c. 1950
18k 3,000 $4,000 $5,000

E. Gubelin, 19 jewels, fancy bezel, enamel dial
18k $2,200 $2,500 $3,000

E. Gubelin, 19 jewels, fancy lugs, center sec.
18k $500 $600 $800

E. Gubelin, 19 jewels, fancy hooded lugs
18k $400 $500 $600

E. Gubelin, 19 jewels, curvex, 2 tone
18k $2,000 $2,500 $3,000

E. Gubelin, 19 jewels, center sec., flared case, c. 1950
18k $350 $450 $550

E. Gubelin, 21 jewels, center sec.
18k $300 $325 $375

E. Gubelin, 17 jewels, by Vacheron & Constantin
18k $3,000 $3,500 $4,000

E. Gubelin, 18 jewels, curved, stepped case, c. 1940
18k $5,000 $6,000 $7,000

Guinand, 17 jewels, chronog., day-date-month, 3 reg.
18k.............................$800 $900 $1,000
s. steel $300 $350 $400

Guinand, 17 jewels, chronog., triple date, moon phase
18k $2,000 $2,500 $3,000
s. steel $700 $800 $900

Hallmark, 17 jewels, day-date-month, auto wind
gold filled.......................$150 $175 $200

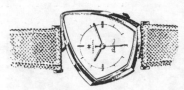

Hamilton, electric, "Altair"
gold filled.......................$500 $600 $700

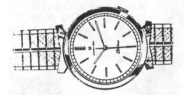

Hamilton, electric, "Aquatel
gold filled.......................$100 $125 $150

Hamilton, electric, "Clearview"
s. steel...........................$125 $150 $175

Hamilton, electric, "Converta"
gold filled.......................$100 $125 $150

Hamilton, electric, "Everest"
gold filled.......................$125 $150 $17

Hamilton, electric, "Meteor," c. 1959
gold filled.......................$200 $250 $30(

Hamilton, electric, "Nautilus"
14k $150 $200 $250
gold filled.......................$50 $60 $70

Hamilton, electric, "Saturn"
14k $500 $600 $700
gold filled.......................$150 $200 $250

Hamilton, electric, "Pacer," 2 tone
gold filled.......................$150 $200 $250

Hamilton, electric, "Savitar"
14k $350 $400 $450

Hamilton, electric, "Polaris
14k $300 $350 $400

Hamilton, electric, "Sea-Lectric I"
s. steel..........................$100 $125 $150

Hamilton, electric, "Regulus"
s. steel..........................$100 $125 $150

Hamilton, electric, "Sea-Lectric II"
s. steel..........................$100 $125 $150

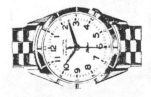

Hamilton, electric, "R. R. Special"
14k $125 $150 $185
gold filled.......................$75 $100 $125
s. steel..........................$60 $75 $95

Hamilton, electric, "Skip Jack"
gold filled.......................$70 $80 $90

Hamilton, electric, "Spectra"
14k $400 $500 $600
gold filled.........................$100 $150 $200

Hamilton, electric, "Summit"
10k $150 $175 $200,
gold filled.........................$100 $125 $150

Hamilton, electric, "Taurus"
gold filled.........................$100 $125 $150

Hamilton, electric, "Titan II"
gold filled.........................$100 $125 $150

Hamilton, electric, "Titan III"
gold filled.........................$100 $125 $150

Hamilton, electric, "Uranus"
gold filled.........................$125 $150 $175

Hamilton, electric, "Vantage
gold filled.........................$150 $200 $250

Hamilton, electric, "Vega"
14k $350 $400 $450
gold filled.........................$150 $175 $200

Hamilton, electric, "Victor II"
gold filled.........................$150 $200 $250

Hamilton, electric, "Ventura"
18k $1,500 $1,800 $2,500
14k $900 $1,000 $1,200
14k diamond dial $1,100 $1,300 $1,500

Hamilton, 17 jewels, "Seckron," dual dial
gold filled......................$500 $600 $700

Hamilton, 17 jewels, dual dial
gold filled......................$500 $600 $700

Hamilton, 17 jewels, "Flint Ridge," flip top
14k $2,000 $2,200 $2,500

Hamilton, 17 jewels, "Cross Country," c. 1962
14k $300 $350 $400

Hamilton, 17 jewels, "Flight II"
14k $1,500 $1,700 $2,000
gold filled $500 $600 $700

Hamilton, 19 jewels, "Otis," reversible, c. 1946
gold filled.................$1,200 $1,400 $1,600

Hamilton, 19 jewels, "Coronado," black enamel bezel
14k $1,200 $1,400 $1,600

Hamilton, 19 jewels, "Piping Rock," enamel bezel
14k $1,200 $1,300 $1,400

Hamilton, 19 jewels, blue enamel bezel, grade 986
14k $1,200 $1,400 $1,600

Hamilton, 19 jewels, "Spur," enamel bezel
14k $3,000 $3,500 $4,000

Hamilton, 19 jewels, "Andrews"
14k $300 $350 $400

Hamilton, 17 jewels, "Alan"
gold filled.......................$100 $150 $200

Hamilton, 19 jewels, "Allison"
14k $350 $450 $550

Hamilton, 17 jewels, "Bagley," applied numbers
gold filled.......................$100 $150 $200

Hamilton, 19 jewels, "Boulton"
gold filled.......................$100 $150 $200

Hamilton, 17 jewels, "Brandon"
gold filled.......................$100 $125 $150

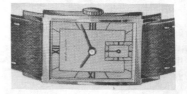

Hamilton, 19 jewels, "Brock"
gold filled.......................$125 $150 $175

Hamilton, 19 jewels, "Brock"
gold filled.......................$125 $150 $175

Hamilton, 19 jewels, "Byrd"
14k $400 $500 $600

Hamilton, 19 jewels, "Cameron"
14k $300 $400 $500

Hamilton, 17 jewels, "Ericsson"
14k $300 $400 $500

Hamilton, 17 jewels, "Dodson"
gold filled.......................$150 $175 $200

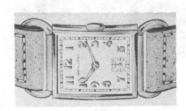

Hamilton, 17 jewels, "Emerson"
gold filled.......................$125 $150 $175

Hamilton, 19 jewels, "Dunkirk"
14k $300 $350 $400

Hamilton, 17 jewels, "Endicott
gold filled.......................$100 $125 $150

Hamilton, 15 jewels, "Dyson"
gold filled.......................$100 $125 $150

Hamilton, 17 jewels, "Essex"
gold filled.......................$125 $150 $175

Hamilton, 17 jewels, "Eric"
gold filled.......................$100 $120 $140

Hamilton, 17 jewels, "Forbes"
gold filled.......................$125 $150 $175

Hamilton, 19 jewels, "Foster"
14k $400 $500 $600

Hamilton, 19 jewels, "Gilman"
14k $300 $400 $500

Hamilton, 19 jewels, "Glenn Curtis"
14k $400 $500 $600

Hamilton, 17 jewels, "Grant"
gold filled. $100 $125 $150

Hamilton, 17 jewels, "Greenwich"
gold filled. $125 $150 $175

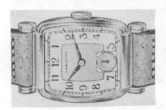

Hamilton, 19 jewels, "Judson"
gold filled. $100 $150 $200

Hamilton, 17J, "Lange," 14k; "Langdon," gold filled
14k $150 $175 $200
gold filled. $100 $125 $150

Hamilton, 17 jewels, "Langley"
14k . . . . ★ ★$600 $700 $800

Hamilton, 17 jewels, "Lee"
gold filled. $125 $150 $175

Hamilton, 19 jewels, "Linwood"
gold filled. $150 $175 $200

Hamilton, 19 jewels, "Livingston"
14k $300 $350 $450

Hamilton, 19 jewels, "Oakmont"
14k $400 $450 $550

Hamilton, 17 jewels, "Martin"
gold filled......................$100 $125 $150

Hamilton, 19 jewels, "Paige"
gold filled......................$100 $110 $120

Hamilton, 19 jewels, "Midas," hidden lugs
14k $300 $350 $400

Hamilton, 17 jewels, "Perry"
gold filled......................$100 $125 $150

Hamilton, 17J, "Norde," 14k; "Nordon," gold filled
14k $200 $225 $250
gold filled......................$100 $125 $150

Hamilton, 17 jewels, "Putnam"
14k $200 $225 $250

Hamilton, 19 jewels, "Norman"
14k $150 $200 $250
gold filled......................$100 $125 $150

Hamilton, 17 jewels, "Putnam"
gold filled......................$100 $125 $150

Hamilton, 17 jewels, "Reagan"
gold filled.....................$100 $150 $200

Hamilton, 19 jewels, "Ross"
gold filled.....................$100 $125 $150

Hamilton, 17 jewels, "Russell
gold filled.....................$150 $200 $250

Hamilton, 19 jewels, "Rutledge"
platinum $800 $900 $1,000

Hamilton, 17 jewels, "Stanford"
gold filled.....................$150 $175 $200

Hamilton, 19 jewels, "Stanley"
gold filled.....................$125 $150 $175

Hamilton, 17 jewels, "Sentinel," hack setting
gold filled.....................$100 $120 $140

Hamilton, 17 jewels, "Sidney"
gold filled.....................$125 $175 $225

Hamilton, 17 jewels, "Steeldon"
s. steel.....................$50 $60 $70

Hamilton, 19 jewels, "Sutton"
gold filled.....................$125 $150 $175

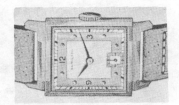

Hamilton, 19 jewels, "Touraine"
14k $175 $200 $225

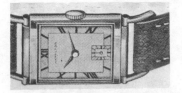

Hamilton, 19 jewels, "Wilshire"
gold filled.......................$175 $200 $225

Hamilton, 17 jewels, "Vincent"
gold filled.......................$125 $150 $175

Hamilton, 17 jewels, "Winthrop"
14k $200 $250 $300

Hamilton, 17 jewels, "Webster"
gold filled.......................$150 $200 $250

Hamilton, 17 jewels, "Yorktown"
gold filled.......................$150 $175 $200

Hamilton, 17 jewels, "Whitman"
gold filled.......................$150 $175 $200

Hamilton, 17 jewels, "Cushion B"
gold filled.......................$80 $100 $120

Hamilton, 17 jewels, "Whitney"
gold filled.......................$125 $150 $175

Hamilton, 17 jewels, cushion style case
14k $200 $250 $300
gold filled.......................$100 $125 $150

Hamilton, 17 jewels, tonneau
14k $200 $250 $300
gold filled.......................$100 $120 $140

Hamilton, 17 jewels, long lugs
14k $250 $300 $350

Hamilton, 17 jewels, 2 tone dial, engraved fancy
14k $200 $250 $300
gold filled.......................$100 $125 $150

Hamilton, 17 jewels, engraved bezel, c. 1920
14k $300 $350 $400

Hamilton, 17 jewels, 2 tone dial, aux. sec.
14k $150 $175 $225

Hamilton, 17 jewels, "Hamilton Illinois" on dial
gold filled.......................$100 $150 $225

Hamilton, 17 jewels, engraved bezel, hinged back
18k $500 $600 $700

Hamilton, 19 jewels
platinum $800 $900 $1,100

Hamilton, 17 jewels, hidden lugs
14k $350 $450 $550

Hamilton, 19 jewels
platinum C&B.............$1,000 $1,100 $1,300

Hamilton, 19 jewels, applied numbers
platinum $800 $900 $1,100

Hamilton, 19 jewels, "Gordon," masterpiece
18k $500 $600 $700

Hamilton, 17 jewels, curved, c. 1938
14k $350 $450 $550

Hamilton, 19 jewels, "Chattam"
14k $250 $300 $375

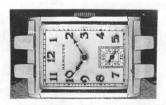

Hamilton, 15 jewels, center lugs
14k $175 $200 $225

Hamilton, 19 jewels, "Barton," hidden lugs
14k $475 $575 $675

Hamilton, 17 jewels, "Mount Vernon," c. 1932
gold filled.......................$100 $125 $150

Hamilton, 15 jewels, military frogman style, waterproof
(USN Buship on dial), tin can style
s. steel...........................$200 $300 $400

Hamilton, 17 jewels, Top Hat, diamond dial
14k $1,000 $1,100 $1,250

Hamilton, 17 jewels, diamond dial, hooded lugs
14k $350 $450 $550

Hamilton, 17 jewels, diamond dial
14k (w) $300 $400 $500

Hamilton, 17 jewels, diamond dial, c. 1945
14k $350 $400 $500

Hamilton, 17 jewels, diamond dial
14k (w) $300 $400 $500

Hamilton, 17 jewels, diamond dial, hooded lugs
14k $350 $450 $550

Hamilton, 17 jewels, diamond dial, curved
14k $1,000 $1,100 $1,250

Hamilton, 17 jewels, diamond dial, hooded lugs
14k $350 $450 $550

Hamilton, 17 jewels, diamond dial, c. 1940
14k $1,000 $1,100 $1,250

Hamilton, 17 jewels, diamond dial, c. 1948
14k (w) $1,100 $1,200 $1,300

Hamilton, 17 jewels, diamond dial
14k $250 $300 $350

Hamilton, 17 jewels, diamond dial
14k (w) $250 $300 $350

Hamilton, 17 jewels, diamond dial, hooded lugs
14k (w) $300 $400 $500

Hamilton, 17 jewels, diamond dial
14k (w) $250 $300 $350

Hamilton, 17 jewels, mystery dial with diamonds
18k $500 $600 $750
14k $400 $500 $600

Hamilton, 17 jewels, diamond dial, long lugs
14k (w) $200 $250 $300

Hamilton, 17 jewels, diamond dial
14k $250 $300 $350

Hamilton, 17 jewels, diamond dial, hooded lugs
14k $350 $450 $550

Hamilton, 17 jewels, diamond dial
14k (w) $250 $300 $350

Hamilton, 17 jewels, diamond dial
14k(w)........................$200 $235 $275

Grade 986A, 6/0 size
Open face, ¾ plate movt., 17 jewels, double roller

Grade 987, 6/0 size
Hunting, ¾ plate movt., 17 jewels, double roller

Grade 987A, 6/0 size
Open face, ¾ plate movt., 17 jewels, double roller

Grade 987S, 6/0 size
Hunting, ¾ plate movt., 17 jewels, double roller

Grade 747, 8/0 size
Open face, ¾ plate movt., 17 jewels, double roller

Grade 980, 14/0 size
Open face, ¾ plate movt., 17 jewels, double roller

Grade 982, 14/0 size
Open face, ¾ plate movt., 19 jewels, double roller

Grade 982M, 14/0 size
Open face, ¾ plate movt., 19 jewels, double roller

Grade 989, 18/0 size
Open face, ¾ plate movt., 17 jewels, double roller

Grade 997, 20/0 size
Open face, ¾ plate movt., 17 jewels, double roller

Grade 721, 21/0 size
Open face, ¾ plate movt., 17 jewels, double roller

Grade 995, 21/0 size
Open face, ¾ plate movt., 17 jewels, double roller

Grade 911, 22/0 size
Open face, ¾ plate movt., 17 jewels, double roller

Grade 911M, 22/0 size
Open face, ¾ plate movt., 17 jewels, double roller

Grade 780, 21/0 size
17 jewels

Grade 770, 12/0 size
22 jewels

Grade 761, 21/0 size
22 jewels

Grade 757, 21/0 size
22 jewels

Grade 753, 12/0 size, 19 jewels
Grade 752, 12/0 size, 17 jewels

Grade 754, 12/0 size, 19 jewels
Grade 770, 12/0 size, 17 jewels

Grade 750 & 751, 21/0 size
17 jewels

Grade 748, 8/0 size
18 jewels

Grade 747, 8/0 size
17 jewels

Grade 735, 8/0 size
18 jewels

Grade 730, 8/0 size
17 jewels

Grade 679, 17 jewels
Grade 692, 694 - calendar

Grade 666 & 663, 17 jewels
Grade 668 - calendar

Grade 658, 661, 667, 17 jewels
Grade 665, 23J, Grade 664, 25J
Grade 662, 690 - calendar, 17J

Grade 623 & 624, 17 jewels

Grade 505, electric, 11 jewels

Hampden, 17 jewels, double dial, c. 1930
gold filled....................**$125** **$150** **$175**

Hampden, 15 jewels
14k **$150** **$175** **$200**
gold filled......................**$60** **$70** **$80**

Hampden, 15 jewels
14k **$150** **$175** **$200**
gold filled......................**$50** **$60** **$70**

Harvard, 17 jewels, chronog., tach-telemeter
s. steel..........................**$100** **$125** **$150**

Harvard, 17 jewels, 1/5 sec. chronog.
s. steel............................**$50** **$60** **$70**

Harwood, 15 jewels, early self winding, c. 1928
18k (w) **$700** **$800** **$900**
14k **$600** **$650** **$700**
gold filled......................**$300** **$350** **$400**
s. steel..........................**$200** **$250** **$300**

Harwood, 15 jewels, rim set by turning bezel clockwise
9k **$500** **$550** **$600**

Harwood, 15 jewels, back set, c. 1925
18k **$600** **$700** **$800**

Harvel, 17 jewels, date-o-graph
s. steel............................$50 $60 $70

Heuer, 17 jewels, chronog., 3 reg., 3 dates, moon phase
18k $2,000 $2,500 $3,000
s. steel $700 $800 $1,000

Hebdomas, 7 jewels, visible escapement, 8 day movement
s. steel............................$500 $700 $900

Heuer, 17 jewels, chronog., 3 reg.
s. steel............................$300 $350 $425

Helbros, 17 jewels
14k $200 $250 $300

Helvetia, 21 jewels, auto wind
gold filled..........................$50 $60 $80

Heuer, 17 jewels, chronog., 3 dates, 3 reg.
s. steel............................$200 $225 $250

Heuer, 17 jewels, "Carrera," chronog., 2 reg.
s. steel...........................$150 $175 $200

Heuer, 17 jewels, day-date-month, moon phase
s. steel...........................$100 $135 $175

Heuer, 17 jewels, day-date-month
s. steel...........................$100 $125 $150

Howard, 17 jewels, engraved on movement, (Howard
Watch USA, Lancaster, PA, HW138, 17J. H980)
gold filled...........................$600 $700 $800

E. Huguenin, 17 jewels, "Black Star," c. 1940
14k $1,000 $1,100 $1,200

Hydepark, 17 jewels, flip up top
14k $400 $500 $600

Illinois, 17 jewels, "Aviator"
gold filled...........................$150 $200 $250

Illinois, 19 jewels, "Beaubrummell"
gold filled...........................$200 $250 $300

Illinois, 17 jewels, "Champion"
gold filled........................$125 $150 $200

Illinois, 15 jewels, "Ensign"
gold filled........................$200 $250 $300

Illinois, 15 jewels, "Chatham"
gold filled........................$150 $175 $200

Illinois, 17 jewels, "Jolly Roger"
gold filled........................$200 $250 $300

Illinois, 17 jewels, "Chieftain"
gold filled........................$300 $400 $500

Illinois, 17 jewels, "Major"
gold filled........................$175 $225 $275

Illinois, 19 jewels, "Consul"
14k $300 $400 $500

Illinois, 19 jewels, "Major"
gold filled........................$175 $225 $275

Illinois, 21 jewels, "Consul"
14k $300 $400 $500

Illinois, 19 jewels, "Marquis"
gold filled........................$200 $250 $300

Illinois, 17 jewels, 'Mate''
gold filled.....................$150 $200 $250

Illinois, 17 jewels, "Prince"
gold filled.......................$150 $175 $200

Illinois, 17 jewels, "New Yorker"
14k $275 $325 $400

Illinois, 15 jewels, "Rockingham"
gold filled........................$75 $85 $100

Illinois, 17 jewels, "Piccadilly"
gold filled...................★ ★$500 $600 $700

Illinois, 15 jewels, "Sangamon"
gold filled........................$75 $85 $100

Illinois, 17 jewels, "Speedway"
gold filled.......................$200 $250 $300

Illinois, 17 jewels, "Pilot"
gold filled......................$150 $200 $250

Illinois, 15 jewels, "Standish"
gold filled........................$75 $85 $100

Illinois, 15 jewels, "Urbana"
gold filled........................$150 $175 $200

Illinois, 17 jewels, engraved bezel, grade 807, c. 1920
14k $300 $350 $425

Illinois, 17 jewels, wandering sec., c. 1926
gold filled........................$150 $175 $200

Illinois, 15 jewels, aux. sec. at 9 o'clock, c. 1925
gold filled........................$125 $150 $175

Illinois, 17 jewels, engraved bezel
gold filled........................$90 $100 $125

Illinois, 15-17 jewels, lady's watch
14k $100 $120 $140
gold filled........................$30 $40 $50

Illinois, rectangular, Grade 207, 12/0 size, 17 jewels.

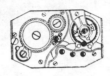

Illinois, rectangular, 18/0 size, 1st, 2nd & 3rd model.

Ingersoll, 7 jewels
base metal $5 $10 $15

Ingersoll, 7 jewels, radiolite dial
base metal $10 $20 $30

Ingersoll, 7 jewels, military style, protective grill cover
base metal $50 $60 $70

Ingraham, 7 jewels, "Wristfit"
base metal $5 $10 $15

International W. Co., 17 jewels, c. 1920
18k $600 $700 $800

International W. Co., 17 jewels, curved
14k $1,000 $1,200 $1,500

International W. Co., 17 jewels, c. 1925
18k $1,600 $1,800 $2,100

International W. Co., 17 jewels
14k $500 $600 $800

International W. Co., 21 jewels, center sec., c. 1920
18k $800 $1,000 $1,200

International W. Co., 21 jewels, auto wind, date
18k $600 $800 $1,000

International W. Co., 17 jewels
14k C&B $900 $1,000 $1,200

International W. Co., 17 jewels, c. 1940
18k $1,500 $1,600 $1,800

International W. Co., 17 jewels, hidden lugs
14k $800 $1,000 $1,200

International W. Co., 17 jewels, engraved on dial "Yard"
18k $1,500 $2,000 $2,500

International W. Co., 17 jewels, curved, "Yard"
platinum...................$2,000 $2,500 $3,000

International W. Co., 17 jewels, hinged back
14k $500 $600 $700

International W. Co., 17 jewels, curved
14k $700 $800 $900

International W. Co., 17J, date, auto wind, waterproof
18k $1,200 $1,400 $1,600

International W. Co., 21 jewels, auto wind, date
18k $900 $1,000 $1,200

International W. Co., 17 jewels, center sec.
18k $600 $700 $800

International W. Co., 17 jewels, center sec.
18k $600 $700 $800

International W. Co., 18 jewels, center sec.
18k $600 $700 $800

International W. Co., 17 jewels, center sec.
18k $600 $700 $800

International W. Co., 17 jewels, winds at 12 o;clock
s. steel.............................$400 $450 $500

International W. Co., 17 jewels
18k $350 $450 $550

International W. Co., 17 jewels, c. 1953
18k $350 $450 $550

International W. Co., 36 jewels, "Da Vinci," chronog.
auto wind, day-date-month, moon phase, center lugs
18k **$6,000 $7,000 $8,500**

International W. Co., 17 jewels, aux. sec.
18k $400 $450 $500

International W. Co., 17J, Royal Navy model, c. 1950
s. steel.............................$400 $500 $600

International W. Co., 17 jewels, c. 1948
18k $600 $700 $800

INTERNATIONAL WATCH CO.
MOVEMENT IDENTIFICATION

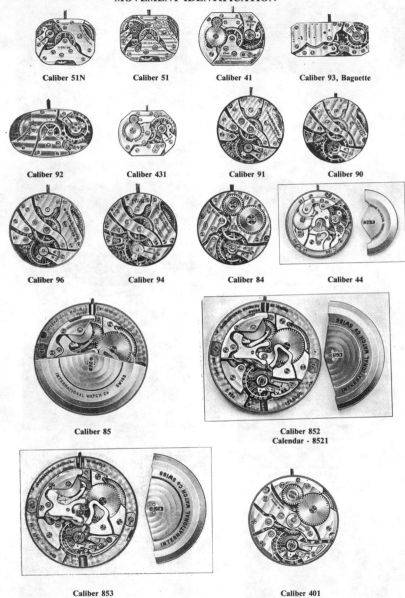

Caliber 51N

Caliber 51

Caliber 41

Caliber 93, Baguette

Caliber 92

Caliber 431

Caliber 91

Caliber 90

Caliber 96

Caliber 94

Caliber 84

Caliber 44

Caliber 85

Caliber 852
Calendar - 8521

Caliber 853
Calendar - 8531

Caliber 401

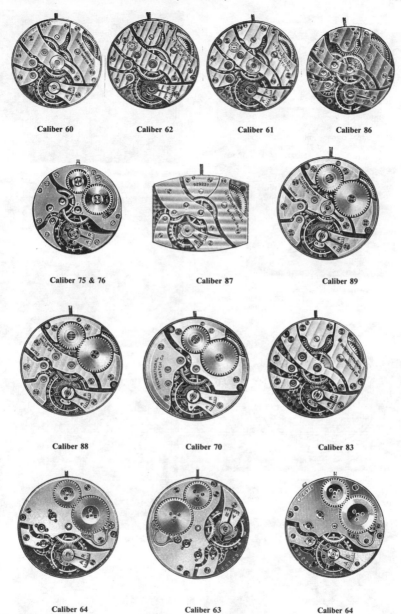

Caliber 60   Caliber 62   Caliber 61   Caliber 86

Caliber 75 & 76   Caliber 87   Caliber 89

Caliber 88   Caliber 70   Caliber 83

Caliber 64   Caliber 63   Caliber 64

Invicta, 15 jewels, chronog., min. reg. at 6 o'clock, decimal aperture for sec. at 12 o'clock
18k .... ★★$5,000 $6,000 $7,500

Invicta, 17 jewels, date, center sec.
18k $300 $350 $400
s. steel...........................$75 $100 $125

Invicta, 17 jewels, day-date, waterproof
18k $150 $175 $225
s. steel...........................$60 $70 $80

Invicta, 17 jewels, day-date-month
18k $200 $250 $300
s. steel...........................$70 $80 $95

Invicta, 17 jewels, day-date-month, moon phase
18k $300 $350 $400
s. steel...........................$100 $120 $140

Invicta, 17 jewels, waterproof
18k $150 $200 $250
s. steel...........................$40 $50 $60

Invicta, 17 jewels, auto wind, waterproof
18k $150 $200 $250
s. steel...........................$50 $60 $70

Jean Louis, 17 jewels, double dial, c. 1930
14k $300 $350 $425

J. Jurgensen, 31J, 5 min. repeater, enamel bezel, c. 1906
18k $40,000 $50,000 $60,000

J. Jurgensen, 15J, jumping hr., revolving min., c. 1930
18k $8,000 $9,000 $10,000

J. Jurgensen, 17 jewels, fancy lugs
14k $300 $400 $500

J. Jurgensen, 17 jewels, extra fancy lugs, c. 1946
18k $500 $600 $700

J. Jurgensen, 17 jewels, c. 1950
18k $300 $400 $500

J. Jurgensen, 17 jewels
18k $175 $200 $225

Jewel, 15 jewels, dual dial, c. 1938
gold filled........................$200 $250 $300

Johnson-Matthey, 15 jewels, 5 gram ingot 24k gold
24k $200 $250 $300

Junenia, 21 jewels, gold movement
18k $400 $450 $600

Kelbert, 17 jewels, fancy lugs, c. 1949
gold filled........................$70 $80 $100

Kelton, 7 jewels, curved, stepped case
gold filled..........................$30 $35 $40

Kelton, 7 jewels, "Drake"
gold filled..........................$30 $35 $40

Kingston, 17 jewels, day-date-month, moon phase
gold filled........................$100 $150 $200

Kurth, 17 jewels, "Certina"
gold filled..........................$30 $40 $50

Lange, 17J, (Glashutte), date, auto wind, waterproof
18k $1,500 $1,600 $1,800

Langendorf, 17 jewels, "Lanco-Matic," waterproof
gold filled..........................$50 $60 $70

Le Coultre, 19 jewels, alarm
18k $700 $800 $900
gold filled......................$200 $275 $350
s. steel..........................$100 $125 $150

Le Coultre, 19 jewels, alarm, c. 1950
18k $700 $800 $900
gold filled......................$200 $275 $350
s. steel..........................$100 $125 $150

Le Coultre, 19 jewels, "Memovox," date, c. 1959
18k $900 $1,000 $1,200
gold filled $300 $350 $400
s. steel $125 $150 $175

Le Coultre, 17 jewels, center lugs, c. 1960
18k $300 $350 $400

Le Coultre, 19 jewels, alarm, date, c. 1950
18k $900 $1,000 $1,200
gold filled $300 $350 $400
s. steel $125 $150 $175

Le Coultre, 15 jewels, wire lugs, c. 1919
silver $200 $225 $250

Le Coultre, 17 jewels, fancy lugs, c. 1950
14k $500 $600 $700

Le Coultre, 17 jewels, auto wind, wind indicator
14k $300 $350 $425

Le Coultre, 17 jewels, fancy lugs, c. 1952
14k $300 $400 $500

Le Coultre, 17 jewels, screw back
18k $500 $600 $700

Le Coultre, 17 jewels, fancy bezel & lugs
14k $500 $600 $700

Le Coultre, 17 jewels, auto wind, textured bezel, c. 1950
18k $250 $350 $450

Le Coultre, 17 jewels, mystery dial, c. 1955
14k $300 $350 $400

Le Coultre, 17 jewels, center sec., c. 1949
18k $250 $300 $350

Le Coultre, 17 jewels, diamond mystery dial, waterproof
14k $900 $1,000 $1,200

Le Coultre, 17 jewels, alarm, date, auto wind
14k $600 $700 $800

Le Coultre, 17J, diamond dial, textured bezel, c. 1962
14k (w) $300 $350 $400

Le Coultre, 17 jewels, chronog., 3 reg.
18k $4,000 $4,500 $5,000

Le Coultre, 15 jewels, day-date-month, c. 1945
s. steel............................$200 $300 $400

Le Coultre, 17J, astronomic w/moon phase, c. 1940s
18k $2,000 $2,500 $3,000

Le Coultre, 17 jewels, triple date, moon phase, fancy lugs
gold filled.................$1,600 $1,800 $2,200

Le Coultre, 17 jewels, "Futurematic"
18k $600 $650 $800
14k $500 $550 $650

Le Coultre, 17J, auto wind w/power reserve indicator
gold filled......................$125 $150 $200
s. steel.........................$125 $150 $175

Le Coultre, 17 jewels, "Reverso," c. 1930
18k $6,000 $7,000 $8,000
s. steel....................$2,000 $2,200 $2,500

Le Coultre, 17 jewels, "Reverso," c. 1940s
18k $6,000 $7,000 $8,000
s. steel....................$2,000 $2,200 $2,500

Le Coultre, 17 jewels, fancy hooded lugs, c. 1952
14k $600 $650 $700

Le Coultre, 17 jewels, fancy lugs
14k $700 $800 $900

Le Coultre, 17 jewels, fancy lugs
14k $800 $900 $1,000

Le Coultre, 17 jewels, long lugs, c. 1944
18k $300 $350 $400

Le Coultre, 17 jewels, uniplan, c. 1938
14k (w) $600 $700 $800

Le Coultre, 15 jewels, duoplan, c. 1940
14k $2,000 $2,400 $2,800

Le Coultre, 17 jewels, fancy lugs, c. 1948
14k $500 $600 $700

Le Coultre, 17 jewels, fancy lugs
14k $600 $700 $800

Le Coultre, 17 jewels, diamond dial, fancy lugs
14k $800 $900 $1,000

Le Coultre, 17J, triple date, moon ph., engraved bezel
18k .... ★ ★ ★$5,000 $6,000 $7,000
gold filled...................$1,800 $2,000 $2,300

Le Coultre, 17 jewels, c. 1945
18k $300 $350 $400

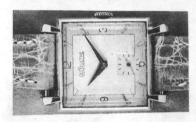

Le Coultre, 17 jewels, fancy lugs, c. 1948
14k $400 $500 $600

Le Coultre, 17 jewels, center lugs, c. 1945
14k $400 $500 $600

Le Coultre, 17 jewels, center lugs, c. 1945
14k $400 $500 $600

Le Coultre, 17 jewels, c. 1950s
14k $500 $600 $700

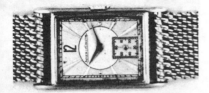

Le Coultre, 17 jewels, 18k case & band
18k C&B $1,200 $1,500 $1,800

Le Coultre, 17 jewels, date cal. 810, c. 1952
14k $600 $700 $800

Le Coultre, quartz, date, waterproof, c. 1960s
18k $400 $500 $600

Le Coultre, 17 jewels, c. 1953
14k $500 $600 $700

Le Coultre, 17 jewels, small, c. 1953
14k $300 $350 $400

Le Coultre, electric, digital calendar
silver & gold $300 $400 $500

Lemania, 17 jewels, auto wind
s. steel............................$50 $60 $70

Lemania, 17 jewels, chronog., c. 1950
18k $600 $700 $900

Leonidas, 17 jewels, triple date, 3 reg.
18k $1,000 $1,200 $1,400
s. steel $600 $700 $800

Le Phare, 17 jewels, chronog., 2 reg.
18k...........................$800 $900 $1,100
14k...........................$600 $700 $800
s. steel $200 $250 $300

Leonidas, 17 jewels, auto wind, triple date, moon phase
s. steel...........................$200 $250 $300

Le Phare, 17 jewels, triple date, moon phase, waterproof
18k $1,200 $1,400 $1,600
gold filled $250 $300 $350

Leonidas, 17 jewels, chronog., 2 reg.
s. steel...........................$200 $250 $300

Lip, electric, bulbous crown
s. steel...........................$200 $250 $335

Le Phare, 17 jewels, chronog., triple date, 3 reg.
18k $3,000 $4,000 $5,000

Longines, 17 jewels, small Lindberg model, c. 1930s
18k ....★ ★$15,000 $18,000 $20,000
s. steel....................$2,000 $2,500 $3,000

Longines, 17 jewels, large Lindberg model, moveable bezel & center dial, c. 1930s

18k	★ ★ ★ $35,000	$40,000	$45,000
silver	$8,000	$9,000	$10,000
nickel	$6,000	$7,500	$8,500

Longines, 15 jewels, Weems U.S. Patent 200B734, c. 1940
s. steel............................$150 $200 $250

Longines, 17 jewels, chronog., 1 button, c. 1923
silver $1,000 $1,100 $1,200

Longines, 17 jewels, chronog.
s. steel............................$400 $500 $650

Longines, 17 jewels, chronog., ref. 1333, enamel dial
silver $1,000 $1,100 $1,200

Longines, 17 jewels, chronog., 2 reg.
18k $1,200 $1,400 $1,600

Longines, 17 jewels, chronog., 2 reg.
18k $1,000 $1,200 $1,400

Longines, 17 jewels, chronog.
14k $400 $500 $600

Longines, 15 jewels, c. 1940s
18k $400 $450 $500
14k $300 $350 $400
s. steel.........................$100 $125 $150

Longines, 21 jewels, "Grand Prize," c. 1946
s. steel..........................$100 $125 $150

Longines, 17 jewels, c. 1950
14k $300 $400 $500

Longines, 17 jewels, center seconds
14k $200 $250 $350

Longines, 17 jewels, fancy lugs, c. 1954
14k $350 $400 $450

Longines, 17 jewels
14k $125 $150 $200

Longines, 17 jewels, "Ultra Chrono," date, auto wind
14k $300 $350 $425

Longines, 17 jewels, "Flagship"
14k $200 $250 $300

Longines, 17 jewels, mystery hand, 12 diamond dial
14k $600 $700 $800

Longines, 17 jewels, fancy lugs, c. 1949
14k $350 $400 $450

Longines, 17 jewels, "Ultra Chrono," diamond dial
14k $250 $300 $475

Longines, 17 jewels, diamond dial, center lugs
14k $600 $700 $800

Longines, 17 jewels, diamond dial, c. 1944
14k $400 $450 $500

Longines, 17 jewels, diamond dial, c. 1938
s. steel..........................$300 $400 $500

Longines, 17 jewels, hidden lugs, diamond dial
14k (w)..........................$500 $600 $700

Longines, 17 jewels, diamond dial, c. 1944
14k $400 $450 $500

Longines, 17 jewels, diamond dial, c. 1949
14k $450 $500 $550

Longines, 17 jewels, diamond dial, c. 1935
14k $450 $500 $550

Longines, 17 jewels, 18 diamond dial
14k (w)..........................$300 $350 $425

Longines, 17 jewels, flared, 6 diamond dial
14k $600 $700 $800

Longines, 17 jewels, diamond bezel, c. 1960
14k.............................$800 $900 $1,000

Longines, 17 jewels, 4 diamond dial
14k $250 $300 $350

Longines, 17 jewels, 12 diamond dial
14k (w) $300 $350 $425

Longines, 17 jewels, 12 diamond
s. steel...........................$300 $400 $500

Longines, 17 jewels, c. 1923
gold filled.......................$200 $250 $300

Longines, 17 jewels, curved, fancy lugs, c. 1939
14k $350 $400 $500

Longines, 17 jewels, fancy lugs, c. 1943
14k $300 $350 $400

Longines, 17 jewels, torpedo shaped numbers
14k $250 $300 $350

Longines, 17 jewels, center lugs, c. 1937
14k $200 $250 $300

Longines, 17 jewels, flared, c. 1959
14k $350 $400 $450

Longines, 17 jewels, flared
14k C&B $600 $700 $800

Longines, 17 jewels, hooded lugs
14k $400 $450 $525

Longines, 17 jewels, diamond dial, fancy lugs
14k $500 $600 $700

Longines, 17 jewels, diamond dial, c. 1944
14k $300 $400 $500

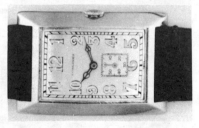

Longines, 17 jewels, c. 1930
18k............................$800 $900 $1,000
14k............................$500 $600 $700
gold filled $250 $300 $350

Longines, 17 jewels, fancy lugs
14k $500 550 $600

Longines, 17 jewels, fancy lugs
14k $500 $600 $700

Longines, 17 jewels
14k (w) $300 $400 $500

Longines, 17 jewels, c. 1939
14k $400 $500 $600

Longines, 17 jewels, fancy lugs, c. 1942
14k $500 $600 $700

Longines, 17 jewels, fancy lugs, c. 1947
14k $350 $400 $450

Longines, 17 jewels, curvex, slanted lugs
14k (w) $250 $300 $375

Longines, 17 jewels, curved, flared
14k $350 $400 $475

Longines, 15 jewels, chased bezel
14k $600 $700 $900

Longines, 15 jewels, engraved bezel, c. 1928
14k (w) $400 $450 $500

Longines, 17 jewels, enameled bezel, c. 1928
14k $400 $450 $500

Longines, 17 jewels, formed case
14k $350 $400 $450

Lorton, 17 jewels, chronog., c. 1950
s. steel..........................$150 $200 $250

Lucien Picard, 17 jewels, movement by P. Ditisheim
14k $600 $700 $800

Lucerne, 17 jewels, 14k case & band
14k C&B $400 $500 $600

Lucien Picard, 17 jewels, gem set bezel
gold filled......................$300 $400 $500

Lucien Picard, 17 jewels, "Seahawk," auto wind
18k C&B $500 $600 $700

Lucien Picard, 17 jewels, skeletonized
18k $1,800 $2,000 $2,300

Lucien Picard, 17 jewels, wind indicator, c. 1958
s. steel............................$75 $85 $100

Lusina, 17 jewels, aux. sec., fancy lugs
gold filled............................$50 $60 $70

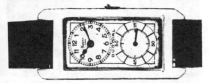

Mappin, 15 jewels, duo dial, c. 1930
9k $1,000 $1,200 $1,500

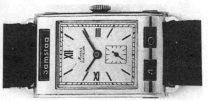

Mars, 17 jewels, "Dateur," hinged back, c. 1934
gold filled........................$300 $400 $500

Meylan, 17 jewels, c. 1940s
18k $800 $1,000 $1,200

Meylan, 18 jewels, jumping hr., c. 1920
18k $15,000 $17,000 $19,000

Meylan, 16 jewels, wire lugs
14k $1,000 $1,200 $1,500

Meylan, 27 jewels, 1 button chronog., 2 reg.
18k $800 $900 $1,000

Mido, 15 jewels, in form of car radiator, c. 1940s
silver $2,000 $2,500 $3,000

Mido, 17 jewels, diamond dial
14k $250 $300 $350

Mido, 17 jewels "Multifort," diamond dial
s. steel..........................$175 $200 $250

Mido, 17 jewels, fancy lugs, c. 1945
14k $250 $300 $350

Mido, 15 jewels, mystery dial, c. 1935
s. steel..........................$250 $300 $350

Mido, 17 jewels, chronog., multi-center chrono
s. steel..........................$500 $600 $700

Mido, 17 jewels, chronog., c. 1952
s. steel..........................$500 $600 $700

Mildia, 17 jewels
s. steel.............................$40 $50 $60

Mimo, 15 jewels, date
gold filled......................$200 $225 $250

Mimo, 17 jewels, jumping hr., wandering min. & sec.
gold filled......................$300 $400 $500

Mimo, 17 jewels, 8 day, 6 gear train, c. 1950s
gold filled....................$800 $900 $1,000

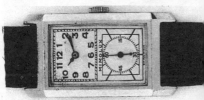

Mimo, 17 jewels, duo dial
s. steel..........................$200 $300 $400

Mimo, 15 jewels
gold filled.........................$40 $50 $60

Mimo, 15 jewels, "Mimomatic," c. 1932
s. steel...........................$40 $50 $60

Minerva, 29 jewels, min. repeater, repeats on 2 gongs
18k $40,000 $50,000 $60,000

Minerva, 17 jewels, chronog., 2 reg.
s. steel........................$175 $200 $225

Minerva, 17 jewels, 2 reg.
18k $1,000 $1,200 $1,400

Minerva, 17 jewels, waterproof, c. 1950s
s. steel........................$300 $350 $400

Minerva, 17 jewels, chronog., c. 1942
s. steel........................$175 $200 $225

Minerva, 19 jewels, chronog., 3 reg.
s. steel........................$300 $350 $400

Minerva, 17 jewels, chronog., day-date-month, 3 reg.
18k $1,700 $1,800 $2,000

Minerva, 17 jewels, center sec., auto wind
gold filled..........................$70 $80 $100

Misc. Swiss, 17 jewels, jump hr., wandering min., c. 1930
9k.............................$700 $800 $1,000

Misc. Swiss, 17 jewels, wandering min., hr. by red mark
s. steel..........................$125 $150 $200

Misc. Swiss, 17 jewels, fancy bezel
14k..............................$400 $500 $600

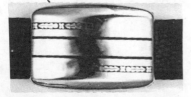

Misc. Swiss, 17 jewels, hunter "Flip Top"
18k.......................$1,000 $1,200 $1,500

Misc. Swiss, 17 jewels, masonic symbols, c. 1950s
s. steel & gold filled........$1,800 $2,000 $2,400

Misc. Swiss, 15 jewels, early auto wind, c. 1930s
s. steel..........................$800 $900 $1,000

Misc. Swiss, 17 jewels, digital hr., min., sec.
s. steel..........................$500 $600 $700

Misc. Swiss, 15 jewels, 8 day movement
silver............................$300 $400 $500

Misc. Swiss, 17 jewels, chronog.
s. steel..........................$250 $300 $400

Misc. Swiss, 29 jewels, ¼ repeater, 2 jacquemart
18k $4,000 $4,500 $5,000

Misc. Swiss, 18 jewels, chronog., c. 1930s
18k $600 $700 $900

Misc. Swiss, 17 jewels, chronog., 1 button, 2 reg.
s. steel........................$400 $500 $600

Misc. Swiss, 17 jewels, early auto wind, c. 1930s
14k $400 $500 $600

Misc. Swiss, 17J, chronog., triple date, moon ph., c. 1945
s. steel........................$300 $350 $400

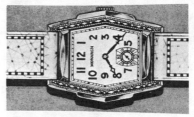

Monarch, 7 jewels, stepped case
gold filled.........................$40 $50 $60

Monarch, 7 jewels
gold filled.........................$40 $50 $60

Misc. Swiss, 17 jewels, split sec. chronog., 2 reg.
s. steel....................$1,500 $1,600 $1,700

Monarch, 7 jewels, engraved bezel, curved
gold filled.........................$50 $60 $70

Monarch, 7 jewels, curved
gold filled............................$60 $70 $80

H. Moser & Co., 17J, "Signal Corps USA", ctr. lugs
silver............................$500 $600 $700

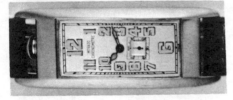

Movado, 17 jewels, polyplan, winds at 12 o'clock, 46mm,
curved, c. 1910
18k $8,000 $9,000 $10,000

Movado, 17 jewels, polyplan, winds at 12 o'clock, c. 1910
14k $5,000 $6,000 $7,000

Movado, 50mm long, Calendarmeto
leather............................$600 $700 $800

Movado, 17 jewels, day-date-month, c. 1945
18k $700 $800 $900
gold filled........................$300 $350 $400
s. steel............................$250 $300 $350

Movado, 15 jewels, day-date-month, center sec.
18k $700 $700 $900

Movado, 17 jewels, auto wind, waterproof
14k $1,000 $1,200 $1,400

Movado, 15 jewels, center lugs, c. 1930
18k............................$600 $800 $1,000

Movado, 15 jewels, aux. sec.
14k C&B $300 $400 $500

Movado, 15 jewels, c. 1929
18k $500 $600 $700

Movado, 17 jewels, aux. sec., center lugs
14k $400 $500 $600

Movado, 17 jewels
14k $400 $500 $600

Movado, 17 jewels, date at 12 o'clock
14k C&B $400 $500 $600

Movado, 17 jewels, automatic, tank style
18k $1,400 $1,600 $1,800

Movado, 15 jewels, fancy lugs
18k $1,000 $1,200 $1,400

Movado, 17 jewels, fancy lugs, c. 1947
14k $400 $500 $600

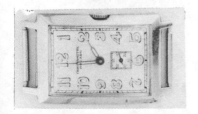

Movado, 15 jewels, curved
14k $600 $700 $800

Movado, 17 jewels
18k $800 $900 $1,000

MOVADO MOVEMENT IDENTIFICATION

Caliber 35

Caliber 65

Caliber 575

Caliber25, 27-Sweep Second

Caliber 28

Caliber 575, Ermeto-Baby

Caliber 578, Ermeto Calendine

579, Calendoplan Baby

Caliber 5

Caliber 15

Caliber 50SP

Caliber 105, 107-Center Second

Caliber 190

Caliber 375, 377-Center Second

Caliber 440, 443-Center Second

Caliber 510

Caliber 260M, 261

Caliber 150MN, 157-Sweep Second

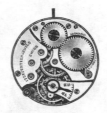

Caliber 155, Calendermeto   Caliber 470, 477-Center Second   Caliber 473, 473SC-Calendar/Moon phase

Caliber 475, 475SC-Center Second   Caliber 225, 255M

Caliber 115   Caliber 118   Caliber 220, 220M

Caliber 221, 226   Caliber 223, 228   Caliber 224, 224A

U. Nardin, 29 jewels, "Astrolabium," self wind, waterproof, local time, equinoctial time, months, signs of zodiac, elevation & azimuth of sun & moon, aspect in which sun & moon stand to each other
18k $6,000 $7,000 $9,000

U. Nardin, 17 jewels, split sec. chronog., c. 1910
silver $12,000 $14,000 $16,000

U. Nardin, 17 jewels, chronog., c. 1950s
18k $2,500 $2,700 $3,000

U. Nardin, 17 jewels
14k $400 $500 $600

U. Nardin, 17 jewels, chronog., "Pulsations," c. 1920
18k $3,000 $3,500 $4,000

U. Nardin, 25 jewels, date
14k $300 $350 $400

U. Nardin, 17 jewels, chronog., 3 reg. c. 1940s
18k $3,000 $3,500 $4,000

U. Nardin, 17 jewels, auto wind, c. 1952
14k $300 $350 $400

U. Nardin, 17 jewels, faceted crystal & bezel
s. steel...........................$200 $250 $325

U. Nardin, 17 jewels, c. 1920
18k $700 $750 $800

U. Nardin, 17 jewels, WW I military style
s. steel...........................$300 $350 $400

National, 15 jewels
gold filled..........................$40 $50 $60

National, 17 jewels, day-date-month
gold filled..........................$100 $110 $125

National, 17 jewels, center sec., waterproof
s. steel.............................$30 $40 $50

National, 17 jewels, auto wind, center sec., waterproof
gold filled..........................$35 $45 $60

New Haven, 7 jewels, engraved bezel
base metal $10 $15 $20

New Haven, 7 jewels, stepped case
base metal $10 $15 $20

New Haven, 7 jewels
base metal $10 $15 $20

New York Standard, 7 jewels
gold filled..........................$10 $15 $20
base metal $5 $10 $15

Nivada, 25 jewels, waterproof, c. 1940
gold filled.......................$300 $400 $500

Normandie, 17 jewels, compass, c. 1945
s. steel............................$50 $60 $70

Ogival, 17 jewels, auto wind
gold filled..........................$50 $60 $70

Ollendorff, 17 jewels, fancy lugs
14k $400 $450 $500

Ollendorff, 17 jewels, gold movement
14k $600 $700 $800

Olympia, 15 jewels, double dial, c. 1938
s. steel............................$200 $250 $300

Omega, 17 jewels, center sec.
14k $225 $275 $350

Omega, 17 jewels, chronog., "Seamaster," 3 reg.
14k $1,500 $1,800 $2,200

Omega, 17 jewels, chronog., c. 1935
18k $2,500 $3,000 $3,500

Omega, 17 jewels, chronog., "Seamaster," c. 1963
s. steel $800 $900 $1,000

Omega, 17 jewels, chronog., "Flightmaster," 3 reg.
18k $6,000 $7,000 $8,000

Omega, 17 jewels, day-date-month, moon phase
18k $1,500 $1,800 $2,200
14k $1,200 $1,400 $1,600

Omega, 17 jewels, day-date-month, moon phase, c. 1940
14k $1,300 $1,500 $1,700

Omega, 17 jewels, day-date-month, moon phase, c. 1950s
18k $3,000 $3,500 $4,000

Omega, electronic, "F300," c. 1950s
18k C&B $1,600 $1,800 $2,000

Omega, 17 jewels, "Constellation," auto wind, date
gold filled........................$150 $200 $250

Omega, 24 jewels, "Constellation," auto wind
18k C&B \$1,200 \$1,400 \$1,600

Omega, 24 jewels, "Constellation," c. 1959
18k \$350 \$450 \$550

Omega, 17 jewels, "Seamaster," date, waterproof
18k \$350 \$450 \$550

Omega, 17 jewels, automatic, date
14k \$200 \$225 \$275

Omega, 17 jewels, aux. sec.
14k C&B \$600 \$700 \$800

Omega, 17 jewels, hidden lugs
14k \$300 \$400 \$500

Omega, 17 jewels
14k \$350 \$450 \$550

Omega, 17 jewels, sculptured lugs
14k \$400 \$500 \$600

Omega, 17 jewels, c. 1938
14k \$250 \$300 \$350

Omega, 17 jewels, c. 1948
14k $300 $350 $400

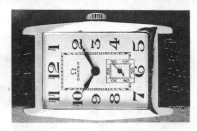

Omega, 15 jewels, c. 1935
14k $275 $300 $350

Omega, 17 jewels, aux. sec.
18k $350 $450 $550

Omega, 17 jewels, c. 1937
s. steel.........................$175 $200 $225

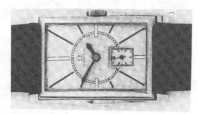

Omega, 17 jewels
14k $250 $300 $350

Omega, 15 jewels, hidden winding stem, c. 1930
s. steel...................$1,500 $1,750 $2,000

Omega, quartz, marine chronometer
s. steel.........................$500 $550 $600

Opel, 21 jewels, waterproof
gold filled......................$75 $100 $125

Orator, 17 jewels, auto wind
s. steel.........................$50 $60 $70

Orfina, 17 jewels, triple date, moon phase
gold filled.........................$200 $250 $300

Orfina, 17 jewels, triple date, moon phase
gold filled.........................$200 $250 $300

Orfina, 17 jewels, day-date-month
gold filled.........................$70 $80 $100

Orfina, 17 jewels, date
s. steel.............................$50 $60 $70

Orvin, 17 jewels, day-date, c. 1945
s. steel.............................$70 $80 $90

Patek Philippe, 29 jewels, min. repeater, c. 1920
platinum...............$200,000 $225,000 $250,000

Patek Philippe, 29 jewels, min. repeater, 30 x 34mm
18k $170,000 $190,000 $210,000

Patek Philippe, 29 jewels, min. repeater, six watches
finished by E. Gublin, 18k case & band
18k C&B $100,000 $110,000 $120,000

Patek Philippe, 29 jewels, min. repeater, made by Piguet
18k .... ★ ★$200,000 $215,000 $230,000

Patek Philippe, 18J, designed by Gilbert Albert, c. 1958
18k $40,000 $45,000 $50,000

Patek Philippe, 50 sec. tourbillon, 57 hr. power reserve
5 gear train, 28 x 38mm
18k $150,000 $170,000 $190,000

Patek Philippe, 18 jewels, asymmetric case designed by
Gilbert Albert, c. 1958
18k $40,000 $45,000 $50,000

Patek Philippe, 18 jewels, horizontal hood case, 2 tone
18k $20,000 $22,000 $24,000

Patek Philippe, 18 jewels, polished fluted hooded lugs
18k $12,000 $14,000 $16,000

Patek Philippe, 18 jewels, extremely horizontal case
18k $16,000 $18,000 $20,000

Patek Philippe, 18 jewels, asymmetric, diamond set case
platinum C&B $25,000 $30,000 $35,000

Patek Philippe, 18 jewels, asymmetric, c. 1960
18k $20,000 $22,000 $26,000

Patek Philippe, 18 jewels, asymmetric, platinum case
diamond set
platinum...............$30,000 $35,000 $40,000

Patek Philippe, 18 jewels, M. 9, hinged back, c. 1920s
18k $8,000 $9,000 $10,000

Patek Philippe, 18J, M. 9, curved, hinged back, c. 1926
18k $8,000 $9,000 $10,000

Patek Philippe, 18 jewels, M. 9, curved, c. 1926
18k $8,000 $9,000 $10,000

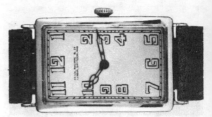

Patek Philippe, 18 jewels, M. 10, hinged back, c. 1920s
18k $8,000 $9,000 $10,000

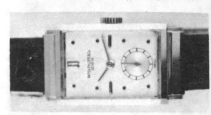

Patek Philippe, 18 jewels, M. 9, c. 1940s
18k $6,000 $7,000 $8,000

Patek Philippe, 18 jewels, M. 9, c. 1950s
18k $5,000 5,500 $6,000

Patek Philippe, 18 jewels, M. 9, c. 1940s
18k $4,500 $5,000 $5,500

Patek Philippe, 18 jewels, c. 1950s
18k $3,500 $4,000 $4,500

Patek Philippe, 18 jewels, M. 9
18k $5,000 $6,000 $7,500

Patek Philippe, 18 jewels
18k $5,000 $5,500 $6,000

Patek Philippe, 18 jewels, M. 9
18k $5,000 $6,000 $7,500

Patek Philippe, 18 jewels, M. 9, c. 1960s
18k $6,000 $6,500 $7,000

Patek Philippe, 18 jewels, c. 1940s
18k $4,000 $4,500 $5,000

Patek Philippe, 18 jewels, M. 9
18k $6,000 $7,000 $8,000

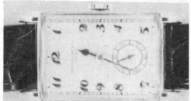

Patek Philippe, 18 jewels, c. 1943
18k $6,000 $6,500 $7,000

Patek Philippe, 18 jewels, decorated enamel case, c. 1920s
18k $10,000 $11,000 $12,000

Patek Philippe, 18 jewels, c. 1930s
18k $5,500 $6,000 $6,500

Patek Philippe, 18 jewels, hidden lugs, c. 1930s
18k $4,000 $4,500 $5,000

Patek Philippe, 18 jewels, c. 1945
18k $5,500 $6,500 $7,500

Patek Philippe, 18 jewels, c. 1940s
18k $6,000 $6,500 $7,000

Patek Philippe, 18 jewels, hinged back, c. 1920s
18k **$8,000** **$8,500** **$9,000**

Patek Philippe, 18 jewels, M. 9, hooded lugs
18k **$6,000** **$7,000** **$8,000**

Patek Philippe, 18 jewels, applied gold numbers
18k **$10,000** **$12,000** **$14,000**

Patek Philippe, 18J, engraved bezel, hinged back, c. 1920s
18k **$8,000** **$9,000** **$10,000**

Patek Philippe, 18 jewels, M. 9, fancy lugs
18k **$14,000** **$16,000** **$18,000**

Patek Philippe, 18 jewels, large lugs, c. 1960s
18k **$8,000** **$9,000** **$10,000**

Patek Philippe, 18 jewels, curved, hooded satin lugs
18k **$10,000** **$12,000** **$14,000**

Patek Philippe, 18 jewels, M. 9, c. 1930s
platinum **$10,000** **$12,000** **$14,000**

Patek Philippe, 18 jewels, "Staybrite," curved case
s. steel **$800** **$900** **$1,000**

Patek Philippe, 18 jewels, curved
18k **$8,000** **$9,000** **$10,000**

Patek Philippe, 18 jewels, c. 1930s
18k **$8,000** **$9,000** **$10,000**

Patek Philippe, 18 jewels, c. 1940s
18k $6,000 $6,500 $7,000

Patek Philippe, 18 jewels, M. 9, center lugs, c. 1940s
18k $5,000 $5,500 $6,000

Patek Philippe, 18 jewels, curved, c. 1940s
18k $5,000 $5,500 $6,000

Patek Philippe, 18 jewels, triple lugs
18k $16,000 $18,000 $20,000

Patek Philippe, 18 jewels, M. 9, c. 1940s
18k $8,000 $10,000 $12,000

Patek Philippe, 18 jewels, curved, c. 1950s
18k $8,000 $9,000 $11,000

Patek Philippe, 18 jewels, M. 9, c. 1940s
18k $4,500 $5,000 $5,500

Patek Philippe, 18 jewels, moveable lugs
18k $10,000 $12,000 $14,000

Patek Philippe, 18 jewels, c. 1940s
18k $8,000 $8,500 $9,000

Patek Philippe, 18 jewels, M. 9, c. 1920s
18k $6,000 $6,500 $7,000

Patek Philippe, 18 jewels, hinged back, stepped case
18k $7,000 $8,000 $9,000

Patek Philippe, 18 jewels, M. 9, extended lugs
18k C&B $18,000 $20,000 $22,000

Patek Philippe, 18 jewels, M. 9, concave lugs
18k $10,000 $12,000 $14,000

Patek Philippe, 18 jewels, lapidated lugs
18k $9,000 $10,000 $11,000

Patek Philippe, 18 jewels, fancy lugs
18k $9,000 $10,000 $11,000

Patek Philippe, 18 jewels, stylized hooded lugs
18k $8,000 $10,000 $12,000

Patek Philippe, 18 jewels, M. 9, c. 1940s
18k $8,000 $9,000 $10,000

Patek Philippe, 18 jewels, 2 tone, hooded & stepped lugs
18k $15,000 $18,000 $20,000

Patek Philippe, 18 jewels, "Reverso"
18k $30,000 $35,000 $40,000
s. steel.................$10,000 $12,000 $14,000

Patek Philippe, 18 jewels, top hat style, c. 1940s
platinum $9,000 $10,000 $11,000
18k $7,000 $8,000 $9,000

Patek Philippe, 18 jewels, top hat style, 18k case & band
18k C&B $8,000 $9,000 $10,000

Patek Philippe, 18 jewels, hooded & fluted lugs
18k $12,000 $14,000 $16,000

Patek Philippe, 18 jewels, M. 9, curved, tank style
18k $12,000 $14,000 $16,000

Patek Philippe, 18 jewels, c. 1960s
18k $6,000 $7,000 $8,000

Patek Philippe, 18 jewels, Adj. to 8 positions
18k $7,000 $8,000 $9,000

Patek Philippe, 18 jewels, curvex, c. 1940s
18k $7,000 $8,000 $10,000

Patek Philippe, 18 jewels, converted to jump hr., recased
18k $4,000 $4,500 $5,000

Patek Philippe, 18 jewels, flared case, c. 1940s
18k $8,000 $9,000 $10,000

Patek Philippe, 18 jewels, M. 9, c. 1950s
platinum $15,000 $16,000 $18,000

Patek Philippe, 18 jewels, massive flared case
18k $16,000 $18,000 $20,000

Patek Philippe, 18 jewels, M. 9, flared case, c. 1950s
18k $8,000 $9,000 $10,000

Patek Philippe, 18 jewels, Eiffel Tower style, c. 1945
18k $16,000 $18,000 $20,000

Patek Philippe, 18 jewels, M. 9, curved, flared case
18k $16,000 $18,000 $20,000

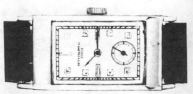

Patek Philippe, 18 jewels, diamond dial, c. 1935
platinum.................$8,000 $9,000 $10,000

Patek Philippe, 18 jewels, flared case
18k $10,000 $12,000 $14,000

Patek Philippe, 18 jewels, diamond dial, c. 1945
187k $8,000 $8,500 $9,000

Patek Philippe, 18 jewels, flared case, c. 1950s
18k $8,000 $9,000 $10,000

Patek Philippe, 18 jewels, diamond dial & bezel
platinum.................$10,000 $12,000 $14,000

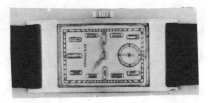

Patek Philippe, 18 jewels, diamond dial
platinum...................$6,000 $6,500 $7,000

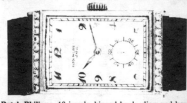

Patek Philippe, 18 jewels, hinged back, diamond bezel
18k $8,000 $9,000 $10,000

Patek Philippe, 18 jewels, diamond dial, flared case
18k $13,000 $14,000 $15,000

Patek Philippe, 18 jewels, c. 1950s
18k $10,000 $12,000 $14,000

Patek Philippe, 18 jewels, c. 1940s
18k $5,500 $6,000 $6,500

Patek Philippe, 18J, M. 9, diamond dial, starbrite steel
s. steel....................$4,000 $5,000 $6,000

Patek Philippe, 18 jewels, M. 9, c. 1963
18k $1,800 $2,000 $2,200

Patek Philippe, 18 jewels, 18k band & case, c. 1950s
18k C&B $4,000 $4,500 $5,000

Patek Philippe, 18 jewels, c. 1947
18k $1,800 $2,000 $2,200

Patek Philippe, 18 jewels, textured bezel, c. 1940s
18k $4,000 $4,500 $5,000

Patek Philippe, 18 jewels, c. 1960s
18k $1,800 $2,000 $2,200

Patek Philippe, 18 jewels, ogival lugs, thick crystal
18k $5,000 $5,500 $6,000

Patek Philippe, 18 jewels, oval lugs
18k $5,000 $5,500 $6,000

Patek Philippe, 18 jewels
18k $2,800 $3,000 $3,300

Patek Philippe, 18 jewels
18k $3,000 $3,500 $4,000

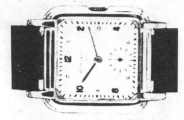

Patek Philippe, 18 jewels, M. 9, c. 1948
18k $5,000 $5,500 $6,000

Patek Philippe, 18 jewels, M. 9, c. 1970s
18k C&B $3,500 $3,800 $4,300

Patek Philippe, 18 jewels, diamond bezel
platinum $12,000 $13,000 $14,000

Patek Philippe, 18 jewels
18k (w) $3,500 $4,000 $4,500

Patek Philippe, 18 jewels, curved, diamond dial
platinum $10,000 $12,000 $14,000

Patek Philippe, 18 jewels
18k C&B $4,000 $4,500 $5,000

Patek Philippe, 18 jewels, M. 9, hidden dial, gold & plat.
18k & platinum $20,000 $22,000 $24,000

Patek Philippe, 18 jewels, textured dial & bezel
18k $3,500 $4,000 $4,800

Patek Philippe, 18 jewels, M. 9, c. 1980s
18k C&B $5,000 $5,500 $6,000

Patek Philippe, 18 jewels, c. 1950s
18k $3,000 $3,500 $4,000

Patek Philippe, 18 jewels, center sec., c. 1960s
18k C&B **$5,000 $5,500 $6,000**

Patek Philippe, 18 jewels, M. 9, c. early 1910s
18k C&B **$8,000 $9,000 $10,000**

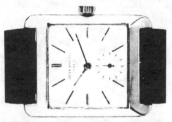

Patek Philippe, 18 jewels, c. 1950s
18k **$3,000 $3,500 $4,000**

Patek Philippe, 18 jewels, c. 1950s
18k **$5,000 $5,500 $6,000**

Patek Philippe, 18 jewels, c. 1950s
18k **$3,500 $4,000 $4,500**

Patek Philippe, 18 jewels, c. 1960s
18k **$3,000 $3,500 $4,000**

Patek Philippe, 18 jewels, guilloche bezel, thick lugs
18k **$5,000 $5,500 $6,000**

Patek Philippe, 18 jewels, hidden lugs, c. 1945
18k **$4,000 $4,500 $5,000**

Patek Philippe, 18 jewels, fluted cylindrical hooded lugs
18k **$10,000 $12,000 $14,000**

Patek Philippe, 18 jewels, hidden lugs
18k **$2,400 $2,600 $2,800**

Patek Philippe, 18 jewels, hooded lugs, c. 1940s
18k $4,000 $4,500 $5,000

Patek Philippe, 18 jewels, large bezel
18k $3,000 $3,500 $4,000

Patek Philippe, 18 jewels, blue sapphire bezel
platinum.................$12,000 $13,000 $14,000

Patek Philippe, 18 jewels, c. 1940s
18k $3,000 $3,500 $4,000

Patek Philippe, 18 jewels, overhanging lugs
18k $10,000 $11,000 $12,000

Patek Philippe, 18 jewels, c. 1910
18k $6,000 $7,000 $8,000

Patek Philippe, 18 jewels, fluted dropped lugs
18k $10,000 $11,000 $12,000

Patek Philippe, 18 jewels, c. 1920s
18k $5,000 $6,000 $7,000

Patek Philippe, 18 jewels, c. 1940s
18k $5,000 $5,500 $6,000

Patek Philippe, 18 jewels, c. 1920s
18k $6,000 $7,000 $8,000

Patek Philippe, 18 jewels, c. 1920s
18k $5,000 $5,500 $6,000

Patek Philippe, 18 jewels, M. 9, c. 1910
platinum.................$8,000 $9,000 $10,000

Patek Philippe, 18 jewels, c. 1930s
18k $4,000 $5,000 $6,000

Patek Philippe, 18 jewels, c. 1930s
18k $6,000 $7,000 $8,000

Patek Philippe, 18 jewels
18k (w) $4,000 $5,000 $6,000

Patek Philippe, 18 jewels, M. 9, c. 1925
18k $6,000 $7,000 $8,000

Patek Philippe, 18 jewels, M. 9, c. 1920s
18k $6,500 $7,500 $8,500

Patek Philippe, 18J, diamond dial, curved, 42mm, c. 1919
platinum................$15,000 $17,000 $20,000

Patek Philippe, 18 jewels
18k $5,000 $6,000 $7,500

Patek Philippe, 18 jewels, made for E. Gublin
18k $7,000 $8,000 $9,000

Patek Philippe, 18 jewels, "Chronometro Gondolo"
18k $7,000 $8,000 $9,000

Patek Philippe, 18 jewels, "World Time," cloisonne polychrome enamel map on dial, 41 cities
18k $160,000 180,000 $200,000

Patek Philippe, 18 jewels, "World Time," 41 cities
18k $12,000 $14,000 $16,000

Patek Philippe, 18 jewels, landscape cloisonne polychrome enamel dial
18k $20,000 $25,000 $30,000

Patek Philippe, 18 jewels, 2 hands, 2 time zones
18k $20,000 $25,000 $30,000

Patek Philippe, 18 jewels, traveling man's watch, hr. hand moves forward or backward to time zone, steps 1 hr. at a time
18k $20,000 $25,000 $30,000

Patek Philippe, 18 jewels, chronog., 1940s
18k $28,000 $30,000 $32,000

Patek Philippe, 18 jewels, chronog.
18k $30,000 $32,000 $35,000

Patek Philippe, 18 jewels, chronog., 2 reg., c. 1940s
18k $22,000 $24,000 $26,000

Patek Philippe, 32 jewels, split sec. chronog.
18k .... ★ ★ ★ $170,000 $190,000 $210,000

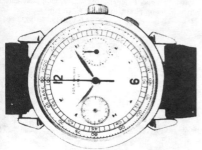

Patek Philippe, 18 jewels, chronog., 2 reg., fancy lugs
18k $26,000 $28,000 $30,000

Patek Philippe, 18 jewels, split sec. chronog., c. 1958
18k $160,000 $180,000 $200,000

Patek Philippe, 18 jewels, chronog., 2 reg., c. 1943
18k $30,000 $32,000 $34,000

Patek Philippe, 18 jewels, chronog., waterproof
18k $35,000 $40,000 $45,000

Patek Philippe, 18 jewels, chronog., 2 tone
18k & s. steel............$30,000 $32,000 $35,000

Patek Philippe, 18 jewels, chronog., pulsometer, c. 1965
18k $30,000 $35,000 $40,000

Patek Philippe, 18 jewels, chronog., triple date, moon ph.
18k $110,000 $120,000 $140,000

Patek Philippe, 18 jewels, split sec. chronog., day-date-month, moon phase, made for E. Gublin
18k C&B $100,000 $110,000 $120,000

Patek Philippe, 18 jewels, chronog., triple date, moon ph.
18k $60,000 $70,000 $80,000

Patek Philippe, 18 jewels, date, mid-sized
platinum $9,000 $10,000 $11,000

Patek Philippe, 18 jewels, chronog., triple date, moon ph.
platinum $100,000 $110,000 $120,000

Patek Philippe, 18 jewels, auto wind, date, c. 1970s
18k C&B $3,500 $4,000 $4,500

Patek Philippe, 18 jewels, chronog., triple date, moon ph.
18k $60,000 $70,000 $80,000

Patek Philippe, 37 jewels, triple date, moon ph. ref. #3448
platinum $40,000 $45,000 $50,000

Patek Philippe, 18 jewels, day-date-month, moon phase, waterproof, perpetual date
18k $30,000 $35,000 $40,000

Patek Philippe, 15 jewels, enamel dial, c. 1910
18k $13,000 $15,000 $17,000

Patek Philippe, 18 jewels, triple date, moon ph., c. 1962
18k $50,000 $60,000 $70,000

Patek Philippe, 18 jewels
18k $2,000 $2,200 $2,500

Patek Philippe, 18 jewels, winding stem at 12 o'clock
18k $2,000 $2,500 $3,000

Patek Philippe, 18 jewels
18k $3,000 $3,200 $3,500

Patek Philippe, 15 jewels, enamel dial, c. 1910
18k $8,000 $9,000 $10,000

Patek Philippe, 18 jewels, aux. sec.
18k $2,500 $2,800 $3,200

Patek Philippe, 18 jewels, aux. sec., c. 1940
18k $2,500 $2,800 $3,200

Patek Philippe, 18 jewels, aux. sec., c. 1950s
18k $3,000 $3,200 $3,500

Patek Philippe, 18 jewels, c. 1955
18k $2,200 $2,400 $2,600

Patek Philippe, 37 jewels, self winding
18k $2,800 $3,000 $3,200

Patek Philippe, 18 jewels, man's half size, c. 1920
18k $4,000 $4,500 $5,000
s. steel....................$2,600 $2,800 $3,000

Patek Philippe, 18 jewels, aux. sec., c. 1950s
18k $2,000 $2,200 $2,400

Patek Philippe, 18 jewels, c. 1950s
18k $1,600 $1,800 $2,000

Patek Philippe, 18 jewels, aux. sec., c. 1950s
18k $2,000 $2,200 $2,400

Patek Philippe, 18 jewels, "Calatrava," c. 1950s
18k $3,000 $3,200 $3,500

Patek Philippe, 18 jewels, aux. sec., c. 1950s
18k $2,200 $2,400 $2,600

Patek Philippe, 18 jewels, auto wind, waterproof, c. 1950s
18k $4,000 $4,500 $5,000

Patek Philippe, 18 jewels, waterproof, c. 1940s
18k $2,200 $2,400 $2,600

Patek Philippe, 18 jewels, "Calatrava," c. 1950s
18k $4,500 $5,000 $5,500

Patek Philippe, 18 jewels, waterproof, c. 1950s
18k $2,500 $3,000 $3,500

Patek Philippe, 18 jewels, extra long lugs, c. 1950
18k $2,300 $2,500 $2,700

Patek Philippe, 18 jewels, waterproof
18k $2,500 $3,000 $3,500

Patek Philippe, 30 jewels, auto wind, gold rotor
18k $2,200 $2,400 $2,600

Patek Philippe, 18 jewels, "Calatrava," waterproof
platinum...................$5,000 $6,000 $7,000

Patek Philippe, 18 jewels, "Calatrava," c. 1950s
18k $2,800 $3,000 $3,200

Patek Philippe, 18 jewels, fancy lugs, c. 1940s
18k $4,000 $4,500 $5,000

Patek Philippe, 18 jewels, "Calatrava," c. 1950s
18k $3,800 $4,000 $4,200

Patek Philippe, 18 jewels, curled lugs
18k $3,800 $4,000 $4,200

Patek Philippe, 18 jewels, aux. sec.
18k C&B $6,000 $6,500 $7,000

Patek Philippe, 18 jewels, "Calatrava," c. 1950s
18k $3,200 $3,400 $3,600

Patek Philippe, 18 jewels, "Calatrava," c. 1940s
18k **$3,200 $3,400 $3,600**

Patek Philippe, 18 jewels, center sec., waterproof
s. steel.....................**$2,000 $2,500 $3,000**

Patek Philippe, 18 jewels, "Calatrava," waterproof
18k **$4,000 $4,500 $5,000**

Patek Philippe, 18 jewels, center sec., c. 1950s
18k **$2,500 $2,700 $2,900**

Patek Philippe, 21 jewels, "Calatrava," c. 1950s
18k **$3,500 $4,000 $4,500**

Patek Philippe, 18 jewels, conical lugs, center sec.
18k **$5,000 $6,000 $7,000**

Patek Philippe, 18 jewels, center sec., c. 1950s
18k **$1,800 $2,000 $2,200**

Patek Philippe, 20 jewels, center sec.
18k **$2,500 $2,700 $2,900**

Patek Philippe, 18 jewels, textured dial & bezel
18k $2,500 $2,700 $2,900

Patek Philippe, 18 jewels, center sec., c. 1950s
18k $3,000 $3,200 $3,500

Patek Philippe, 18 jewels, center sec., c. 1952
18k $2,400 $2,600 $2,800

Patek Philippe, 18 jewels, center sec., c. 1960s
18k C&B $4,000 $4,500 $5,000

Patek Philippe, 18 jewels, center sec., waterproof
18k $3,500 $3,700 $4,000

Patek Philippe, 18 jewels, auto wind
18k $3,000 $3,500 $4,000

Patek Philippe, 20 jewels, center sec.
18k $2,500 $2,700 $2,900

Patek Philippe, 18 jewels
18k $2,500 $2,800 $3,200

Patek Philippe, 18 jewels, date-month
18k $2,800 $3,000 $3,200

Patek Philippe, 18 jewels, "Calatrava," c. 1940s
18k $2,800 $3,000 $3,200

Patek Philippe, 18 jewels, "Calatrava," c. 1940s
18k $2,000 $2,200 $2,400

Patek Philippe, 18 jewels, unusual shape, c. 1940s
18k   .$10,000 $12,000 $15,000

Patek Philippe, 36 jewels, c. 1970s
18k $2,800 $3,000 $3,200

Patek Philippe, 36 jewels, "Nautilus," date
s. steel.....................$1,800 $2,000 $2,200

Patek Philippe, 18 jewels
18k C&B $4,000 $4,500 $5,000

Patek Philippe, 36 jewels, "Nautilus," diamond bezel
18k $7,000 $8,000 $9,000

Patek Philippe, 36 jewels, diamond dial & bezel
18k $4,000 $4,500 $5,000

Patek Philippe, 18J, "Calatrava," mid-sized, dia. dial
platinum $9,000 $10,000 $11,000

Patek Philippe, 18 jewels, c. 1980s
18k C&B $3,700 $3,900 $4,500

Patek Philippe, quartz, c. 1980s
18k C&B $3,000 $3,200 $3,500

Patek Philippe, 18 jewels, c. 1960s
18k C&B $3,000 $3,200 $3,500

Patek Philippe, 18 jewels, c. 1980s
18k C&B $3,200 $3,400 $3,600

Patek Philippe, 18 jewels, massive lugs
18k $3,800 $4,000 $4,200

Patek Philippe, 18 jewels, concave & hooded lugs
18k $5,000 $5,500 $6,000

Patek Philippe, 18 jewels, mid-sized, 2 tone
18k (y & w) $15,000 $20,000 $25,000

Patek Philippe, 18 jewels, lady's watch, c. 1950s
18k $3,000 $3,500 $4,000

Patek Philippe, 18 jewels, extended lugs, 2 tone
18k (y & w) $16,000 $18,000 $20,000

Patek Philippe, 18 jewels, lady's watch, c. 1940s
18k C&B $3,500 $4,000 $4,500

Patek Philippe, 18 jewels, lady's watch
18k $1,800 $2,000 $2,200

Patek Philippe, 18 jewels, lady's watch, min. repeater
18k $80,000 $90,000 $100,000

Patek Philippe, 18J, lady's, hinged lid set in diamonds
18k $3,500 $4,000 $4,500

Patek Philippe, 18 jewels, lady's watch, c. 1950s
18k $3,000 $3,500 $4,000

Patek Philippe, 18 jewels, lady's watch
18k C&B $2,500 $3,000 $3,500

Patek Philippe, 18 jewels, lady's watch, c. 1940s
18k $1,000 $1,200 $1,400

Patek Philippe, 18 jewels, lady's watch, diamond bezel
platinum $3,000 $3,500 $4,000

Patek Philippe, 18 jewels, lady's watch, c. 1950s
18k $1,800 $2,000 $2,200

PATEK, PHILIPPE
MOVEMENT IDENTIFICATION

Caliber 6¾, no. 60
S.no. 865000-869999
(1940-1955)

Caliber 7, no. 70
S.no. 943300-949999
(1940-1960)

Caliber 8, no. 80
S.no. 840000-849999
(1935-1960)

Caliber 8, no. 85
S.no. 850000-859999
(1935-1968)

Caliber 9, no. 90
S.no. 833150-839999
S.no. 970000-979999
(1940-1950)

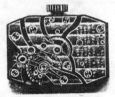

Caliber 9, no. 90a
830000-833149
(1940-1950)

Caliber 10, no. 105
S.no. 900000-909999
(1940-1945)

Caliber 10, no. 110
S.no. 910000-919999
(1940-1950)

Caliber 10, no. 200
S.no. 740000-759999
(1952-1965)
S.no. 950000-959999
(1945-1955)

Caliber 23, no. 300
S.no. 780000-799999
(1955-1965)

Caliber 12, no. 600AT
S.no. 760000-779999
(1952-1960)

Caliber 12, no. 400
S.no. 720000-739999
(1950-1965)

Caliber 12, no. 120
826900-829999 (1935-1940)

Caliber 12, no. 120A
92000-929999 (1940-1950)
960000-969999 (1946-1952)
938000-939999 (1952-1954)

Caliber 13, no. 130A **Caliber 13, no. 130B** **Caliber 13, no. 130C**
Chronograph, no. 862000-863995 (1940-1950); no. 867000-869999 (1950-1970)

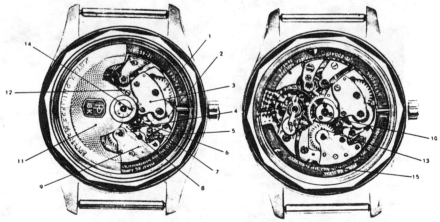

Caliber 12-600 AT, S.no. 760,000-779,999 (1960-1970)

Patria, 7 jewels, enamel dial, compass
s. steel...........................$400 $450 $500

Perfine, 17 jewels, chronog., 2 reg.
gold filled......................$100 $125 $150
s.steel $45 $65 $85

Perpetual W. Co., 15 jewels, rim wind & set
14k $600 $700 $800
gold filled......................$300 $350 $400
s. steel..........................$125 $150 $175

Perpetual W. Co., 15 jewels, c. 1930s
14k $600 $700 $800
gold filled......................$350 $400 $450

Perpetual W. Co., 15 jewels, fancy bezel
gold filled......................$350 $400 $450

Perpetual W. Co., 15 jewels, diamond bezel, c. 1930s
silver $700 $800 $900

Piaget, 18 jewels, 1904 20 dollar gold piece, flip top
22k $2,000 $2,200 $2,400

Piaget, 18 jewels, center sec., auto wind
18k $600 $700 $800

Piaget, 18 jewels, ref. #8177, auto wind
18k $600 $700 $800

Piaget, 18 jewels, gold train, center lugs, thin model
18k $500 $600 $700

Piaget, 18 jewels
18k $500 $600 $700

Piaget, 18 jewels
18k C&B $400 $450 $550

Piaget, 30 jewels, auto wind, gold rotor
18k $650 $750 $850

Piaget, 18 jewels
18k $400 $450 $500

Piaget, 18 jewels, textured bezel
18k $700 $800 $900

Piaget, 18 jewels, 18k case, 14k band
18k & 14k C&B $800 $900 $1,000

Piaget, 18 jewels, textured bezel
18k $700 $800 $900

Piaget, 30 jewels, textured bezel
18k $700 $800 $900

Piaget, 18 jewels, tank style
18k $500 $550 $650

Pierce, 17 jewels, early auto wind, "Parashock," c. 1930s
gold filled.......................$500 $600 $700

Pierce, 17 jewels, auto wind, c. 1948
gold filled..........................$40 $50 $60

Pierce, 17 jewels, chronog.
s. steel..............................$70 $80 $95

Pierce, 17 jewels, chronog., c. 1940s
s. steel...........................$100 $125 $150

Pierce, 17 jewels, day-date-month, moon phase
gold filled.......................$150 $200 $250

Pontifa, 17 jewels, chronog. day-date-month, 3 reg.
s. steel.....................$1,200 $1,500 $2,000

Prexa, 17 jewels, auto wind
gold filled...........................$40 $50 $60

Pronto, 17 jewels, triple date, auto wind, waterproof
s. steel.................................$60 $70 $85

Record, 17 jewels, split sec. chronog.
s. steel....................$2,200 $2,500 $3,000

Record, 17 jewels, triple date, moon phase, c. 1940s
18k...........................$800 $900 $1,000

Record, 17 jewels, day-date-month, moon phase
s. steel...........................$125 $135 $185

Pulsar, L.E.D. (light emitting diode)
18k $400 $450 $500
14k $300 $375 $450
gold filled......................$125 $150 $185
s. steel...........................$75 $95 $125

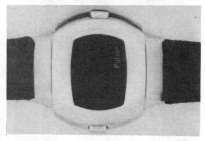

Record, 17 jewels, split sec. chronog., date, moon phase
18k $5,000 $5,500 $6,000

Record, 17 jewels, triple date, moon phase, auto wind
18k $1,200 $1,400 $1,600

Roamer, 17 jewels, date, auto wind
gold filled............................$40 $50 $60

Roamer, 17 jewels, auto wind, aux. sec.
gold filled............................$25 $30 $35

Roamer, 23 jewels, ref. #4346
gold filled............................$40 $50 $60

Roamer, 17 jewels, hidden lugs
gold filled............................$30 $40 $50

Rolex, 15 jewels, enamel dial, flip top, c. 1918
silver $1,000 $1,100 $1,200

Rolex, 17 jewels, ref. #4035
14k C&B $1,600 $1,800 $2,000

Rolex, 26 jewels, "Milgauss," oyster, perpetual
s. steel...........................$400 $450 $550

Rolex, 17 jewels, "¼ Century Club," c. 1960s
14k $1,800 $2,000 $2,200

Rolex, 17 jewels, center sec., large lugs
18k $1,200 $1,400 $1,700

Rolex, 17 jewels, "Precision," center sec.
18k $400 $450 $650

Rolex, 17 jewels, ref. #9659
14k C&B $1,600 $1,800 $2,000

Rolex, 15 jewels
9k..............................$800 $900 $1,000

Rolex, 17 jewels, "Precision"
gold filled......................$300 $350 $400

Rolex, 17 jewels, "Precision"
18k $1,000 $1,200 $1,500

Rolex, 17 jewels, oyster, center sec.
18k $3,000 $3,400 $3,800
14k $2,200 $2,600 $3,000
9k $1,400 $1,600 $1,800
silver.......................$900 $1,000 $1,200
s. steel $800 $900 $1,000

Rolex, 15 jewels, early waterproof, pair of cases (case
within a case)
silver $1,600 $1,800 $2,000

Rolex, 17 jewels
14k C&B $1,600 $1,800 $2,000

Rolex, 17 jewels, oyster, c. 1934
18k $3,000 $3,200 $3,400
14k $2,200 $2,500 $2,800
9k $1,600 $1,800 $2,000
silver.......................$800 $900 $1,000
s. steel $600 $700 $800

Rolex, 17 jewels, oyster, c. 1927
s. steel.........................$400 $500 $700

Rolex, 17 jewels, oyster, ref. #4547
s. steel.........................$500 $600 $800

Rolex, 17 jewels, oyster, ref. #2081
gold filled.......................$600 $700 $900

Rolex, 15 jewels, oyster, c. 1929
s. steel.........................$600 $700 $800

Rolex, 17 jewels, oyster, center sec.
18k $2,500 $2,700 $3,000
14k $2,000 $2,200 $2,500
9k $1,400 $1,500 $1,700
s. steel $600 $700 $800

Rolex, 17 jewels, oyster, c. 1930s
18k $2,500 $2,800 $3,400
14k $2,200 $2,400 $2,600

Rolex, 17 jewels, graduated bezel, c. 1928
silver $800 $950 $1,100

Rolex, 17 jewels, oyster, "Viceroy," 2 tone, c. 1943
14k & s. steel.............$1,300 $1,500 $1,700

Rolex, 17 jewels, oyster, extra prima
18k $1,200 $1,400 $1,600

Rolex, 17 jewels, chronog., mid-sized, c. 1950s
18k $12,000 $14,000 $18,000
14k $10,000 $12,000 $15,000

Rolex, 17 jewels, chronog., flat, tachometer, c. 1940s
18k $20,000 $25,000 $35,000

Rolex, 17 jewels, chronog., 3 reg.
s. steel $800 $900 $1,000

Rolex, 17 jewels, chronog., 2 reg., curved back
18k $35,000 $40,000 $45,000

Rolex, 17 jewels, chronog., 3 reg.
14k $7,000 $8,000 $10,000

Rolex, 17 jewels, chronog., center lugs, c. 1940s
18k $9,000 $10,000 $12,000
14k $6,000 $7,000 $9,500
9k $4,000 $5,000 $6,500
s. steel....................$3,000 $3,500 $4,500

Rolex, 17 jewels, chronog., day-date-month
18k $28,000 $30,000 $34,000
14k $22,000 $25,000 $28,000
s. steel...................$9,000 $10,000 $12,000

Rolex, 17 jewels, chronog., pulsations, 3 reg., c. 1960s
18k $10,000 $12,000 $14,000

Rolex, 17 jewels, day-date-month, 3 reg.
s. steel....................$2,200 $2,800 $3,200

Rolex, 17 jewels, chronog., 3 reg., c. 1950s
18k $10,000 $12,000 $14,000

Rolex, 17 jewels, "Daytona," chronog., waterproof
18k $10,000 $12,000 $14,000
14k $8,000 $9,000 $12,000
s. steel....................$1,800 $2,000 $2,500

Rolex, 17 jewels, chronog., 3 reg., tear drop lugs, c. 1940s
18k $14,000 $16,000 $18,000
14k $12,000 $14,000 $16,000
s. steel....................$7,000 $8,000 $9,500

Rolex, 17 jewels, tachometer, 3 reg. c. 1960s
18k $10,000 $12,000 $14,000
14k $8,000 $9,000 $12,000
s. steel....................$1,800 $2,000 $2,500

Rolex, 17 jewels, day-date-month, moon phase, oyster
18k $20,000 $22,000 $24,000
14k $14,000 $15,000 $17,000
s. steel...................$6,000 $7,000 $8,500

Rolex, 17 jewels, day-date-month, moon phase, c. 1945
18k $22,000 $24,000 $28,000

Rolex, 15 jewels, jumping hr., duo dial, c. 1930s
platinum $14,000 $16,000 $19,000
18k $12,000 $14,000 $16,000
14k $10,000 $11,000 $12,000
9k $7,000 $8,000 $9,000
silver $6,000 $7,000 $8,000
gold filled.............$4,000 $5,000 $6,500
s. steel...................$5,000 $6,000 $7,500

Rolex, 17 jewels, day-date-month, moon phase, oyster
s. steel C&B................$6,000 $7,000 $8,000

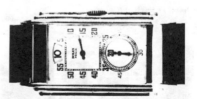

Rolex, 17 jewels, jumping hr., duo dial, c. 1930s
18k 2 tone $15,000 $18,000 $22,000
18k $12,000 $14,000 $16,000
14k $9,000 $10,000 $12,000
9k $7,000 $8,000 $10,000
s. steel...................$6,000 $7,000 $8,000

Rolex, 17 jewels, stars on dial, triple date, c. 1945
18k $25,000 $28,000 $32,000

Rolex, 17 jewels, "Prince," duo dial
18k C&B $6,000 $7,000 $8,000

Rolex, 17 jewels, flared, duo dial, c. 1930s
9k $1,800 $2,000 $2,400

Rolex, 17 jewels, "Prince," duo dial, stepped case
18k $6,000 $7,000 $8,000
14k $4,500 $5,000 $6,000
9k $3,500 $4,000 $4,500
silver $3,500 $4,000 $4,500
s. steel....................$3,000 $3,500 $4,000
gold filled.................$2,800 $3,200 $3,500

Rolex, 17 jewels, 2 tone case
18k $12,000 $14,000 $16,000

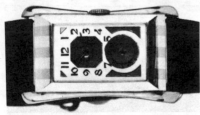

Rolex, 17 jewels, 2 tone case, Adj. to 6 pos.
18k $12,000 $14,000 $16,000
14k $10,000 $11,000 $12,500
9k $7,000 $7,500 $8,500

Rolex, 15 jewels, extra prima, 2 tone
9k $2,000 $2,200 $2,500

Rolex, 15 jewels, flared, duo dial, Adj. to 6 pos.
9k $3,000 $3,200 $3,500

Rolex, 15 jewels, "Prince," duo dial, c. 1930s
s. steel....................$2,500 $3,000 $3,600

Rolex, 15 jewels, chronometer, duo dial, c. 1930s
s. steel....................$3,000 $3,500 $4,000

Rolex, 15 jewels, "Railway," stepped case, c. 1930s
18k 2 tone $15,000 $16,000 $18,000
18k $12,000 $13,000 $15,000
14k 2 tone $10,000 $11,000 $12,500
14k $7,000 $8,000 $9,000
9k 2 tone $5,000 $6,000 $7,000
9k $4,000 $4,500 $5,500
s. steel.................$4,000 $4,500 $5,000

Rolex, 15 jewels, "Prince," center sec., c. 1930s
18k $10,000 $12,000 $15,000

Rolex, 15 jewels, "Prince," c. 1935
platform $10,000 $11,000 $12,000
18k $6,000 $7,000 $8,000
14k $5,000 $5,500 $6,500
gold filled $3,000 $3,200 $3,500

Rolex, 15 jewels, stepped case
18k $6,000 $7,000 $8,000

Rolex, 17 jewels, oyster, perpetual, date
14k $1,500 $1,700 $2,000

Rolex, 17 jewels, center sec., date just
18k C&B $4,000 $5,000 $6,000

Rolex, 17 jewels, ref. #4325
14k $1,200 $1,300 $1,400

Rolex, 17 jewels, oyster, perpetual
14k C&B $2,500 $2,700 $3,000

Rolex, 17 jewels, oyster, perpetual, date, c. 1940s
14k $1,500 $1,700 $2,000

Rolex, 17 jewels, auto wind, center sec., c. 1950s
14k $1,000 $1,200 $1,500

Rolex, 17 jewels, "Speed King"
s. steel $300 $350 $400

Rolex, 25 jewels, "Explorer"
s. steel.........................**$400** **$500** **$600**

Rolex, 19 jewels, center sec., c. 1960s

18k	**$2,000**	**$2,300**	**$2,600**
14k	**$1,800**	**$2,000**	**$2,200**
9k	**$1,500**	**$1,600**	**$1,800**
s. steel	**$500**	**$600**	**$700**

Rolex, 17 jewels, oyster, manual wind

18k	**$1,000**	**$1,100**	**$1,250**
14k	**$800**	**$900**	**$1,000**
9k	**$500**	**$550**	**$700**
gold filled	**$300**	**$350**	**$400**
s. steel	**$250**	**$300**	**$350**

Rolex, 17 jewels, center sec., c. 1945

18k	**$2,000**	**$2,200**	**$2,500**
14k	**$1,000**	**$1,200**	**$1,500**
9k	**$900**	**$1,000**	**$1,100**
s. steel	**$350**	**$450**	**$550**

Rolex, 25 jewels, ref. #6593
14k **$1,000** **$1,200** **$1,500**

Rolex, 26 jewels, bubble back, center sec., c. 1945
14k **$2,500** **$2,800** **$3,200**

Rolex, 17 jewels, center sec.
18k & s. steel.............**$1,200** **$1,400** **$1,700**

Rolex, 26 jewels, bubble back, hooded lugs

18k	**$6,000**	**$6,500**	**$7,500**
14k	**$5,000**	**$5,500**	**$6,500**
9k	**$3,000**	**$3,500**	**$4,000**
s. steel	★ ★ **$5,000**	**$6,000**	**$7,000**

Rolex, 26 jewels, bubble back, hooded lugs, 2 tone
18k & s. steel..............$6,000 $7,000 $8,000

Rolex, 26 jewels, bubble back, c, 1940s
18k	$3,000	$3,500	$4,000
14k	$2,500	$3,000	$3,500
9k	$1,800	$2,000	$2,500
gold filled	$1,000	$1,100	$1,200
s. steel	$600	$700	$850

Rolex, 26 jewels, bubble back, hooded scalloped lugs
18k & s. steel..............$5,000 $6,500 $8,000

Rolex, 26 jewels, bubble back, graduated bezel
14k $2,500 $3,000 $3,500

Rolex, 26 jewels, bubble back, mercedes hands, c. 1940s
18k	$3,800	$4,000	$4,400
14k	$2,800	$3,000	$3,300
9k	$2,000	$2,200	$2,400
gold filled	$800	$900	$1,000
s. steel	$700	$750	$850

Rolex, 19 jewels, bubble back, 2 tone
18k & s. steel..............$3,400 $3,600 $4,000

Rolex, 26 jewels, bubble back, mercedes hands, c. 1930s
18k	$3,200	$3,400	$3,800
14k	$2,400	$2,600	$3,000
9k	$1,800	$1,900	$2,200
gold filled	$800	$850	$950
s. steel	$600	$700	$800

Rolex, 26 jewels, bubble back, Arabic & Roman numbers
18k $3,400 $3,700 $4,000

Rolex, 26 jewels, bubble back, center sec.
9k $2,800 $3,000 $3,300

Rolex, 26 jewels, bubble back, marked bezel, c. 1940s
18k $4,000 $4,200 $4,500
14k $3,500 $3,700 $4,000
9k $2,800 $3,000 $3,300
gold filled $900 $1,000 $1,200
s. steel $700 $800 $900

Rolex, 26 jewels, bubble back, c. 1940s
14k $2,800 $3,000 $3,300

Rolex, 26 jewels, bubble back, 2 tone, c. 1940s
18k & s. steel...............$1,000 $1,200 $1,500

Rolex, 26 jewels, bubble back, c. 1940s
s. steel..........................$600 $700 $800

Rolex, 19 jewels, bubble back, center sec.
18k $3,200 $3,400 $3,800
s. steel $700 $800 $900

Rolex, 26 jewels, bubble back
18k $3,200 $3,400 $3,800
s. steel $600 $700 $850

Rolex, 26 jewels, bubble back, c. 1945
14k $2,800 $3,000 $3,300

Rolex, 26 jewels, bubble back, c. 1940s
18k $3,000 $3,300 $3,800
14k $2,500 $2,800 $3,200
s. steel $600 $700 $800

Rolex, 18 jewels, bubble back, c. 1940s
s. steel..........................$600 $700 $800

Rolex, 18 jewels, bubble back, c. 1942
18k $3,200 $3,400 $3,800
14k $2,800 $3,000 $3,300
s. steel $700 $750 $850

Rolex, 18 jewels, bubble back, gold & s. steel band
14k & s. steel C&B..........$1,000 $1,200 $1,500

Rolex, 18 jewels, bubble back, date, winds at 9 o'clock
18k case & s. steel band $3,000 $4,000 $5,000

Rolex, 26 jewels, "Presidential," 44 diamonds on dial
& bezel, day-date, oyster, perpetual
18k C&B $7,000 $8,000 $9,000

Rolex, 21 jewels, day-date, 10 diamond dial
18k C&B $5,000 $6,000 $7,000

Rolex, 26 jewels, "Presidential," diamond dial, day-date,
perpetual, oyster
18k C&B $5,500 $6,000 $6,500

Rolex, 26 jewels, "Presidential," (Tridor), oyster, day-
date, diamond dial, perpetual, oyster
18k (y & w) $8,000 $8,500 $9,000

Rolex, 26 jewels, "Presidential," bark finish, day-date
18k C&B \$4,500 \$5,000 \$6,500

Rolex, 26 jewels, "Presidential," day-date, perpetual,
oyster, diamond bezel
18k C&B \$7,000 \$7,500 \$8,500

Rolex, 26J, "Presidential," day-date, perpetual, oyster
18k C&B \$6,000 \$7,000 \$8,000

Rolex, quartz, diamond dial & bezel add \$1,200-\$1,500
18k \$4,000 \$5,000 \$6,000
14k \$3,000 \$4,000 \$5,000

Rolex, 26 jewels, jubilee band, 10 diamond dial, date
18k C&B \$4,500 \$5,500 \$6,500
14k C&B \$3,500 \$4,000 \$5,000
gold & s. steel C&B \$2,000 \$2,500 \$3,000

Rolex, 26 jewels, date, perpetual, oyster
18k \$2,500 \$2,700 \$3,000
14k \$1,600 \$1,800 \$2,200
s. steel \$450 \$550 \$650

Rolex, 21 jewels, date, center sec., c. 1965
18k \$3,500 \$4,000 \$5,000

Rolex, 26 jewels, date, oyster, mid-size
s. steel C&B....................\$500 \$600 \$700

Rolex, 26 jewels, perpetual, oyster, date just
18k $4,000 $4,500 $5,500
18k & s. steel..............$1,400 $1,600 $2,000
14k $2,800 $3,200 $4,000
14k & s. steel...............$1,200 $1,400 $1,600
s. steel $500 $600 $800

Rolex, 26 jewels, oyster, date, ref. #1625
14k & s. steel C&B.........$1,000 $1,200 $1,500

Rolex, 26 jewels, perpetual, oyster, date, graduated bezel
14k $2,400 $2,600 $2,800
s. steel $600 $700 $850

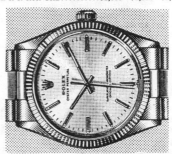

Rolex, 21 jewels, perpetual, oyster
18k $1,800 $1,900 $2,000
18k & s. steel $700 $800 $900
14k $1,400 $1,500 $1,600
14k & s. steel $600 $700 $800
s. steel $300 $400 $500

Rolex, 21J, "Thunderbird," perpetual, oyster, date just
18k $3,000 $3,200 $3,400
s. steel $400 $500 $700

Rolex, 26 jewels, "Explorer," perpetual, oyster
s. steel..........................$400 $500 $600

Rolex, 26 jewels, perpetual, oyster
s. steel..........................$300 $400 $500

Rolex, 17 jewels, "Luminor Paneral," for military diving
s. steel.....................$2,500 $3,000 $3,500

Rolex, 26 jewels, "GMT-Master," perpetual, oyster, date
ruby & diamond dial
18k $4,000 $5,000 $6,000

Rolex, 21 jewels, "Sea-Dweller," up to 4,000 ft., date
s. steel $900 $1,000 $1,200

Rolex, 26J, "GMT-Master II," perpetual, oyster, date
18k $3,200 $3,700 $4,200
s. steel $500 $600 $800

Rolex, 21 jewels, "Explorer II," date
s. steel..........................$450 $550 $650

Rolex, 26 jewels, "Submariner," perpetual, oyster, date
18k C&B $6,000 $7,000 $8,000
18k & s. steel C&B.........$2,000 $2,200 $2,500
s. steel $700 $900 $1,200

Rolex, 26 jewels, "Submariner," perpetual, oyster
s. steel..........................$600 $700 $850

Rolex, 17 jewels, "Precision"
18k $1,500 $1,700 $2,000

Rolex, 17 jewels, curvex
18k C&B $6,000 $7,000 $8,000

Rolex, 17 jewels, curved, c. 1940s
gold filled.........................$600 $700 $800

Rolex, 17 jewels, "Ultra Prima," gold train
18k $1,800 $2,000 $2,400

Rolex, 17 jewels, "Standard," c. 1939
14k $2,000 $2,500 $3,000

Rolex, 17 jewels, hooded lugs, 2 tone
rose & white gold $3,000 $4,000 $5,000

Rolex, 17 jewels, "Benvenuto Cellini," thin model
18k $1,500 $1,600 $1,700

Rolex, 21 jewels, perpetual, oyster, c. 1945
18k $2,500 $2,800 $3,200

Rolex, 17 jewels, "Precision," c. 1940s
18k $1,200 $1,400 $1,600
14k $1,000 $1,200 $1,400

Rolex, 17 jewels, "Precision," tank style, faceted bezel
18k $2,000 $2,200 $2,500

Rolex, 17 jewels, extra flat, c. 1950s
18k $2,200 $2,400 $2,700

Rolex, 21 jewels, "Cellini"
18k $900 $1,000 $1,200

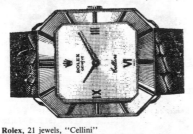

Rolex, 21 jewels, "Cellini"
18k $1,000 $1,100 $1,300

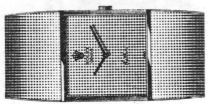

Rolex, 21 jewels, "Cellini"
18k C&B $1,500 $1,800 $2,200

Rolex, 21 jewels, "Cellini," diamond bezel
18k C&B $2,500 $2,800 $3,200

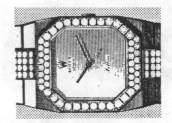

Rolex, 21 jewels, "Benvenuto Cellini," diamonds on bezel & band
18k $12,000 $14,000 $16,000

Rolex, quartz, "Tudor," (Prince)
s. steel...........................$150 $175 $200

Rolex, quartz, "Tudor," chronog., date
s. steel...........................$300 $350 $400

Rolex, quartz, "Tudor," date, 2 tone
18k & s. steel....................$250 $300 $400

ROLEX PERPETUAL WATCHES
Of Caliber Numbers
1030, 1035, 1036
1040, 1055, 1065

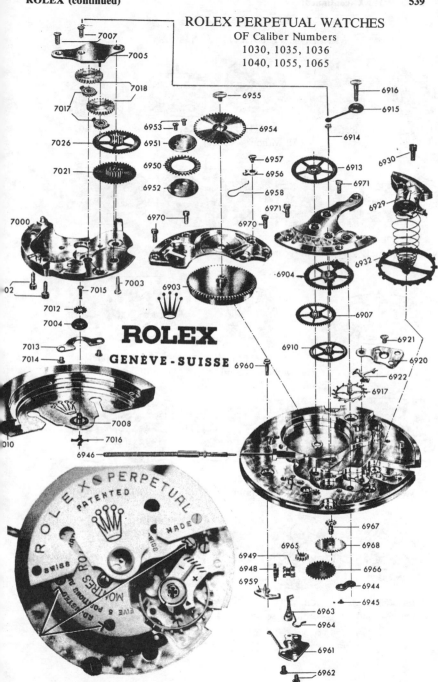

ROLEX
MOVEMENT IDENTIFICATION

Ref. 90   Ref. 100   Ref. 150   Ref. 160   Ref. 161

(All without seconds)

Ref. 170   **Ref. 180**   **Ref. 200**   **Ref. 210**
without seconds   without seconds   without seconds   sweep seconds

Ref. 250   **Ref. 270**   **Ref. 300**
without seconds   without seconds   ordinary seconds

Ref. 310   **Ref. 350**   **Ref. 360**
sweep second   jump hour   ordinary second

Ref. 400   **Ref. 420**   **Ref. 420**   **Ref. 500**
ordinary seconds   ordinary seconds   rotor   ordinary seconds

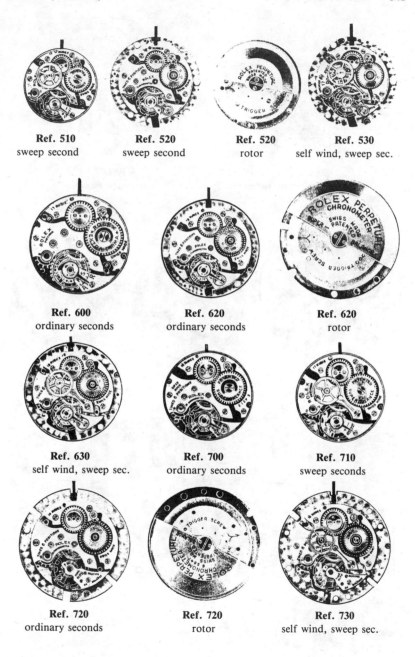

Ref. 510
sweep second

Ref. 520
sweep second

Ref. 520
rotor

Ref. 530
self wind, sweep sec.

Ref. 600
ordinary seconds

Ref. 620
ordinary seconds

Ref. 620
rotor

Ref. 630
self wind, sweep sec.

Ref. 700
ordinary seconds

Ref. 710
sweep seconds

Ref. 720
ordinary seconds

Ref. 720
rotor

Ref. 730
self wind, sweep sec.

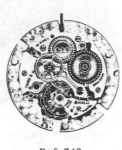

Ref. 740
self wind, calendar, sweep sec.

Ref. 800
ordinary seconds

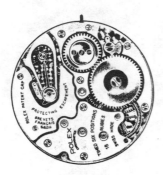

Ref. 850
ordinary seconds

Ref. 72
chronograph, 3 registers

Ref. 23
chronograph, 2 registers

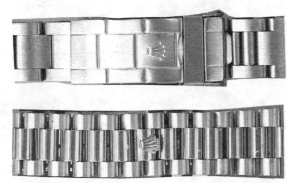

Above: Oyster style bracelet. **Below:** Presidential style band with hidden clasp.
Right: Jubilee style bracelet.

Rolls, 15 jewels, early auto wind, by Leon Hatot, movement inside case moves back & forth to wind, c. 1920s
s. steel..........................$600 $700 $900

Rolls, 15 jewels, early auto wind, c. 1920s
s. steel $700 $800 $1,000

Rolls, 15 jewels, "ATO," flip top
s. steel..........................$600 $700 $900

Semca, 17 jewels, day-date-month, moon phase, c. 1950s
18k $1,400 $1,600 $1,800

Semca, 17 jewels, day-date-month, moon phase, c. 1950s
18k $1,400 $1,600 $1,800

Sperina, 7 jewels, day & date on lugs
s. steel............................$60 $70 $80

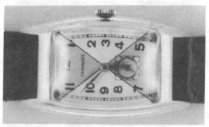

Tavannes, 17 jewels, hour glass dial, curved
14k $350 $400 $450

Tavannes, 15 jewels, "334," c. 1939
14k (w) $200 $250 $300

Tavannes, 17 jewels, aux. sec.
14k $225 $250 $275

Tiffany & Co., 17J, curved, mvt. by P.P. & Co., c. 1910
18k $9,000 $10,000 $12,000

Tiffany & Co., 26J, min. repeater, automaton, 40mm
18k **$8,000 $10,000 $12,000**

Tiffany & Co., 15 jewels, c. 1926
18k **$1,200 $1,400 $1,600**

Tiffany & Co., 17 jewels, chronog., day-date-month
14k **$1,800 $2,000 $2,200**

Tiffany & Co., 21 jewels, mvt. by P.P. & Co., c. 1950
18k **$800 $900 $1,000**

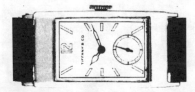

Tiffany & Co., 17 jewels, c. 1935
18k **$1,200 $1,400 $1,600**

Tiffany & Co., 17 jewels, fancy bezel, c. 1942
14k **$900 $1,000 $1,100**

Tiffany & Co., 17 jewels, sculptured lugs, c. 1948
14k **$1,000 $1,200 $1,400**

Timecraft, 17 jewels, c. 1950
s. steel. **$125 $150 $175**

Tissot, 21 jewels, world time, 24 hr. dial, 24 cities
18k **$3,000 $3,500 $4,500**

Tissot, 21J, world time, 24 hr. dial, 24 cities, mid-size
18k $2,500 $3,000 $3,500

Tissot, 17 jewels, chronog., triple date, moon phase
14k $2,000 $2,200 $2,600

Tissot, 17 jewels, 1898 USA 20 dollar gold piece
24k $2,000 $2,200 $2,400

Tissot, 17 jewels, day-date-month, moon phase, ctr. sec.
18k $2,000 $2,200 $2,500

Tissot, 17 jewels, chronog., 3 reg., c. 1956
s. steel...........................$400 $450 $500

Tissot, 17 jewels, auto wind, aux. sec.
s. steel.............................$60 $70 $85

Tissot, 17 jewels, chronog., 3 reg., c. 1940s
14k $1,000 $1,200 $1,400

Titus, 17 jewels, chronog., 2 reg.
18k $300 $450 $500
14k $200 $300 $400
s. steel...........................$100 $150 $200

Touchon, 17 jewels, jump hr., wandering min., c. 1930s
18k $10,000 $12,000 $15,000

Turler, 17 jewels, chronog., triple date, 3 reg.
18k $700 $900 $1,200

Tourneau, 17 jewels, triple date, 3 reg., moon ph., c. 1952
s. steel $350 $450 $550

Uhrenfabrik Glashutte, 17 jewels, chronog., c. 1940s
18 . . . .$3,000 $3,500 $4,000

Trebex, 15 jewels, c. 1940
gold filled $50 $60 $70

Unitas, 17 jewels, triple date, moon phase, c. 1948
s. steel $250 $300 $375

Trebex, 15 jewels, c. 1940s
gold filled $30 $40 $50

Urania, 15 jewels, military style grill, c. 1915
silver $300 $400 $500

Universal, 17 jewels, chronog., triple date, moon phase
14k $2,000 $2,200 $2,400

Universal, 17 jewels, chronog., aero compax, 4 reg.
18k $2,200 $2,600 $3,200

Universal, 17 jewels, chronog., tri-compax, moon phase
18k $2,400 $2,600 $2,900

Universal, 17 jewels, chronog., compax, massive case
18k $2,500 $2,700 $3,000

Universal, 17J, chronog., aero compax, diff. meridian
14k $1,800 $2,000 $2,400

Universal, 17 jewels, c. 1952
14k $125 $150 $175

Universal, 17 jewels, chronog., M. #281, c. 1950s
18k $2,200 $2,500 $2,800

Universal, 17 jewels, day-date-month
14k $125 $150 $175

Universal, 17 jewels, chronog., dato-compax, c. 1950s
14k $1,200 $1,400 $1,600
s. steel $400 $600 $800

Universal, 17 jewels, auto wind, c. 1955
gold filled........................$100 $120 $140

Universal, 17 jewels, triple date, moon phase, c. 1940s
18k $1,200 $1,400 $1,600

Universal, quartz, day-date, center sec., c. 1960s
18k $400 $500 $600

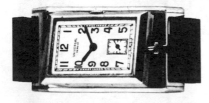

Universal, 17 jewels, "Cabriolet," reverso, c. 1930s
s. steel.....................$2,000 $2,500 $3,000

Universal, 17 jewels, auto wind
gold filled........................$80 $90 $100

Universal, 17 jewels, auto wind, date
18k $200 $300 $400

Vacheron, 36 jewels, skeletonized, triple date, moon phase, gold rotor
18k $10,000 $12,000 $14,000

Vacheron, 36 jewels, diamond bezel, triple date, moon phase, gold rotor
18k C&B $8,000 $9,000 $10,000

Vacheron, 17J, triple date, fancy lugs, moon ph., c. 1940s
18k $16,000 $18,000 $22,000

Vacheron, 17 jewels, triple date, moon phase, c. 1947
18k $25,000 $28,000 $32,000

Vacheron, 17 jewels, triple date, fancy lugs, c. 1940s
18k $5,000 $5,500 $6,500

Vacheron, 17 jewels, triple date, moon phase, c. 1945
18k $15,000 $16,000 $18,000

Vacheron, 17 jewels, day-date-month, c. 1940s
18k $5,000 $5,500 $6,500

Vacheron, 17 jewels, triple date, moon phase, c. 1950s
18k $12,000 $14,000 $16,000

Vacheron, 29 jewels, gold rotor, date
18k $1,800 $2,200 $2,600

Vacheron, 29 jewels, waterproof, c. 1960s
18k $3,000 $3,200 $3,500

Vacheron, 17 jewels, chronog., 2 reg.
18k $18,000 $20,000 $24,000

Vacheron, 29 jewels, auto wind, c. 1960s
18k $2,600 $2,700 $2,900

Vacheron, 17 jewels, 1 button chronog., c. 1910s
18k $40,000 $45,000 $50,000

Vacheron, 36 jewels, gold rotor, date
18k $1,500 $1,800 $2,200

Vacheron, 19 jewels, chronog., 2 reg., c. 1950s
18k C&B $22,000 $24,000 $28,000

Vacheron, 29 jewels, center sec., auto wind, date
18k $3,000 $3,200 $3,500

Vacheron, 17 jewels, chronog., 2 reg., c. 1945
18k $18,000 $20,000 $24,000

Vacheron, 29 jewels, min. repeater, slide repeat, c. 1950
18k **$70,000 $80,000 $110,000**

Vacheron, 17 jewels, textured bezel
18k **$1,200 $1,400 $1,700**

Vacheron, 17 jewels, mystery dial w/diamonds
18k C&B **$1,400 $1,600 $2,000**

Vacheron, 18 jewels, fancy graduated bezel, c. 1950s
18k **$7,000 $8,000 $10,000**

Vacheron, 17 jewels, skeletonized
18k **$5,000 $5,500 $6,500**

Vacheron, 18 jewels, center sec., c. 1940s
18k **$1,800 $2,000 $2,400**

Vacheron, 17 jewels, skeletonized, c. 1960s
18k **$4,000 $4,500 $5,000**

Vacheron, 18 jewels, auto wind, center sec.
18k **$1,500 $1,800 $2,200**

Vacheron, 18 jewels, center sec.
18k $1,800 $2,000 $2,400

Vacheron, 18 jewels, center sec.
18k $2,000 $2,200 $2,400

Vacheron, 18 jewels, center sec.
14k $1,500 $2,000 $2,800

Vacheron, 18 jewels, center sec., waterproof, c. 1950s
18k $2,800 $3,000 $3,500

Vacheron, 21 jewels, gold rotor, center sec.
18k $1,500 $1,700 $2,000

Vacheron, 29 jewels, center sec., auto wind, c. 1950s
18k $2,500 $2,800 $3,200

Vacheron, 29 jewels, center sec., auto wind, c. 1949
18k $3,000 $3,200 $3,500

Vacheron, 29 jewels, textured dial, c. 1948
18k $3,500 $3,800 $4,200

Vacheron, 29 jewels, center sec.
18k $1,000 $1,100 $1,200

Vacheron, 29 jewels, center sec., c. 1950s
18k $1,600 $1,800 $2,000

Vacheron, 29 jewels, 2 tone dial, center sec.
18k $1,400 $1,600 $1,800

Vacheron, 17 jewels, aux. sec., fancy lugs
18k $1,000 $1,200 $1,400

Vacheron, 17 jewels, aux. sec.
18k $1,000 $1,100 $1,200

Vacheron, 17 jewels, aux. sec., stepped lugs
18k $1,000 $1,200 $1,400

Vacheron, 17 jewels, 2 tone dial, aux. sec.
18k $1,500 $1,800 $2,400

Vacheron, 17 jewels, aux. sec.
18k $1,500 $1,700 $2,000

Vacheron, 17 jewels, aux. sec.
s. steel $800 $900 $1,000

Vacheron, 17 jewels, aux. sec.
14k C&B $1,000 $1,200 $1,400

Vacheron, 17 jewels, aux. sec.
18k $1,300 $1,400 $1,600

Vacheron, 17 jewels, aux. sec., c. 1940s
18k $1,500 $1,700 $2,000

Vacheron, 17 jewels, aux. sec.
18k $1,200 $1,300 $1,400

Vacheron, 17 jewels, aux. sec., c. 1940s
18k $1,600 $1,800 $2,100

Vacheron, 17 jewels, aux. sec., c. 1940s
18k $1,500 $1,700 $2,000

Vacheron, 17 jewels
18k C&B $1,100 $1,200 $1,400

Vacheron, 17 jewels, aux. sec., large lugs, c. 1950s
18k $3,000 $3,200 $3,500

Vacheron, 17 jewels
18k $1,000 $1,100 $1,200

Vacheron, 17 jewels, extra thin model
18k $1,000 $1,100 $1,200

Vacheron, 15 jewels
18k C&B $2,800 $3,300 $4,200

Vacheron, 17 jewels
18k $3,000 $3,200 $3,500

Vacheron, 36 jewels, auto wind
18k C&B $1,200 $1,500 $1,800

Vacheron, 17J, with shutters, crowns at 3 & 9 o'clock
18k ....★★$25,000 $30,000 $36,000

Vacheron, 17 jewels, hinged back
18k $2,500 $2,800 $3,200

Vacheron, 17 jewels, aux. sec.
14k $2,000 $2,200 $2,400

Vacheron, 17 jewels, flat & thin model, c. 1960s
18k $1,400 $1,500 $1,600

Vacheron, 18 jewels, c. 1950s
18k $2,500 $3,000 $3,500

Vacheron, 17 jewels
18k C&B $5,000 $5,500 $6,000

Vacheron, 18 jewels, textured bezel
18k **$2,000** **$2,200** **$2,600**

Vacheron, 17 jewels, applied gold numbers
18k **$2,000** **$2,200** **$2,500**

Vacheron, 18 jewels, aux. sec., c. 1940s
18k **$2,500** **$3,000** **$3,500**

Vacheron, 15 jewels, c. 1920s
18k **$2,200** **$2,400** **$2,700**

Vacheron, 17 jewels, aux. sec., c. 1950s
18k **$1,800** **$2,000** **$2,300**

Vacheron, 17 jewels, 2 tone, 24mm, c. 1920s
18k **$3,000** **$3,500** **$4,000**

Vacheron, 17 jewels, applied gold numbers, c. 1940s
18k **$2,800** **$3,000** **$3,500**

Vacheron, 17 jewels, 68 diamond bezel
18k **$3,000** **$3,200** **$3,500**

Vacheron, 17 jewels, aux. sec., c. 1945
18k **$2,600** **$2,800** **$3,200**

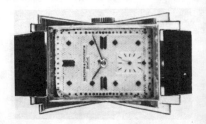

Vacheron, 17 jewels, flared, curvex, c. 1940s
18k **$8,000** **$9,000** **$11,000**

Vacheron, 17 jewels, flared, aux. sec., c. 1948
platinum.................$10,000 $12,000 $15,000

Vacheron, 22 jewels, lady's watch, c. 1970s
18k $2,500 $3,500 $4,500

Vacheron, 17 jewels, flared, c. 1948
18k $5,000 $6,000 $7,500

Vacheron, 17 jewels, aux. sec., ruby dial
18k $3,200 $3,600 $4,000

Vacheron, 17 jewels, flared, c. 1940s
18k $5,000 $6,000 $8,000

Vacheron, 21 jewels, center sec., c. 1950s
18k $5,000 $6,000 $7,500

Vacheron, 17 jewels, "Chronoscope," jumping hr.,
revolving ruby min. indicator, c. 1930s
18k ....★★$14,000 $16,000 $18,000

Vacheron, 17 jewels, aux. sec., fancy lugs, c. 1947
18k $4,000 $4,500 $5,000

Vacheron, 20 jewels, Adj. to 5 Pos., c. 1970s
18k $3,500 $4,000 $5,000

Vacheron, 17 jewels
14k $2,200 $2,500 $3,000

Vacheron, 17 jewels, fancy lugs
18k $3,000 $3,500 $4,500

Vacheron, 17 jewels, c. 1950s
18k $2,800 $3,100 $3,500

Vacheron, 17 jewels, fancy lugs
14k $2,000 $2,200 $2,600

Vacheron, 17 jewels, stars on dial
18k C&B $3,500 $4,000 $4,500

Vacheron, 17 jewels, 14k $2,000 $2,400 $2,800

Vacheron, 17 jewels, aux. sec.
14k $2,000 $2,200 $2,400

Vacheron, 17 jewels, aux. sec., c. 1946
18k $3,000 $3,500 $4,000

Vacheron, 18 jewels, aux. sec.
18k C&B $3,000 $3,500 $4,500

Vacheron, 17 jewels, aux. sec.
18k $3,000 $3,500 $4,200

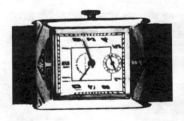

Vacheron, 17 jewels, Art Deco bezel, c. 1925
18k $10,000 $11,000 $12,000

Vacheron, 17 jewels, long lugs, applied numbers
18k $3,000 $3,500 $4,000

Vacheron, 15 jewels, c. 1925
18k C&B $3,500 $3,800 $4,200

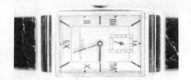

Vacheron, 17 jewels, curved, hooded lugs, c. 1930s
18k $3,000 $3,500 $4,000

Vacheron, 17 jewels, heavy bezel
18k $2,400 $2,700 $3,200

Vacheron, 17 jewels, lady's watch, c. 1960s
18k C&B $1,800 $2,000 $2,400

Verno, 15 jewels, chased bezel
gold filled (w) $150 $175 $200

Vulcain, 17 jewels, "Cricket," alarm
s. steel.........................$100 $125 $150

Vulcain, 17 jewels, "Cricket"
14k $150 $175 $200

Vulcain, 17 jewels, "Minstop"
s. steel...........................$40 $50 $80

Wakmann, 17 jewels, chronog., 3 reg., c. 1958
s. steel.........................$300 $400 $550

West End, 17 jewels, "Keepsake," c. 1925
silver $125 $150 $175

West End, 17 jewels, center lugs
18k $500 $600 $700

Whittnauer, 17 jewels, chronog., c. 1948
s. steel..........................$125 $150 $

White Star, 17 jewels, triple date, moon phase, c. 1948
s. steel..........................$200 $250 $300

Whittnauer, 17 jewels, auto wind, sector, date
s. steel $700 $800 $1

Whittnauer, 17 jewels, fancy lugs
14k $250 $300 $375

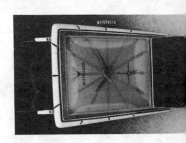

Whittnauer, 17 jewels, c. 1950s
14k ....$200 $230 $

Whittnauer, 17 jewels, chronog., day-date-month
s. steel..........................$175 $200 $250

Whittnauer, 17 jewels, fancy lugs, c. 1950s
14k $200 $250

Wig Wag, 15 jewels, early auto wind, c. 1932
s. steel $800 $1,000 $1,200

Wyler, 17 jewels, chronog., c. 1940s
s. steel.......................... $125 $150 $175

Wyler, 17 jewels, early auto wind, watch winds by using
the muscular movement of the wrist, back set
gold filled...................... $600 $700 $800

Yale, 15 jewels, calendar, c. 1939
gold filled...................... $100 $125 $175

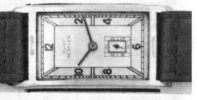

Wyler, 17 jewels, early auto wind, back set
gold filled...................... $600 $700 $800

Zelia, 17 jewels, chronog.
18k $500 $600 $700

Wyler, 17 jewels
s. steel.......................... $40 $50 $70

Wyler, 17 jewels, diamond dial, c. 1946
s. steel.......................... $60 $70 $100

Zenith, 19 jewels, 33mm, c. 1950s
gold filled...................... $100 $125 $150

Zenith, 17 jewels, chronog.
18k $1,000 $1,200 $1,500

Zodiac, 17 jewels, ref. #8088
14k $125 $150 $175

Zenith, 36 jewels, chronog., auto wind, c. 1969
s. steel...........................$450 $500 $600

Zodiac, 17 jewels, auto wind with reserve power gauge
14k $175 $200 $250
gold filled........................$85 $100 $120

Zenith, 36 jewels, "El Primero," chronog., triple date
moon phase, c. 1970s
18k $2,400 $2,600 $2,800

Zodiac, 17 jewels, day-date-month, moon phase, c. 1957
14k $225 $250 $300

Zenith, 17 jewels, fancy bezel
18k $250 $350 $500

WATCH TERMINOLOGY

ADJUSTED—Adjusted to compensate for temperature, positions, and isochronism.

ALARM WATCH—A watch that will give an audible sound at a pre-set time.

ANCHOR ESCAPEMENT—Also called the recoil escapement.

ANNEALING—Heating and cooling a metal slowly to relieve internal stress.

ANTI-MAGNETIC—Not affected by magnetic field.

Arbor

ARBOR—The mechanical axis of a moving part; on the balance it is called the "staff," on the lever it is called the arbor.

ASSAY—Analyzing a metal for its gold or silver content.

AUTOMATON—Animated mechanical objects and figures; actuated by the going, striking or repeating train.

AUXILIARY COMPENSATION—Additional temperature compensators found on marine chronometers.

Balance Cock

BALANCE COCK—The bridge that holds the upper jewels and the balance.

Balance Spring

BALANCE SPRING—Also called the hairspring; the spring governing the balance.

Balance Staff

BALANCE STAFF—The shaft of the balance wheel.

Balance Wheel

BALANCE WHEEL—A device shaped like a wheel that does for a watch what a pendulum does for a clock.

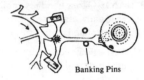
Banking Pins

BANKING PINS—The two pins which limit the angular motion of the pallet.

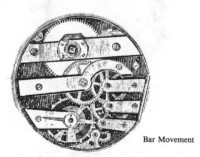
Bar Movement

BAR MOVEMENT—A type of movement employing about six bridges to hold the train.

Barrel

BARREL—Drum-shaped container that

houses the mainspring. A going barrel has teeth around the top or bottom and drives the gears.

BEAT—Refers to the tick or sound of a watch; about 1/5 of a second. The sound is produced by the escape wheel striking the pallets.

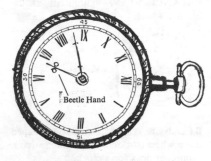

Beetle Hand

BEETLE HAND—Hour hand resembling a stag beetle; usually associated with the poker-type minute hand.

BELL METAL—Four parts copper and one part tin used for metal laps to get a high polish on steel.

O S. Htg. Bezel,

BEZEL—The rim that covers the dial (face) and retains the crystal.

BI-METALLIC BALANCE—A balance designed to compensate for changes in temperature; made of a strip of brass and steel usually.

BISEAUTAGE—The grinding of a crystal to size it to fit a bezel.

BLIND MAN'S WATCH—A Braille watch; also known as a tact watch.

BLUING—By heating steel to about 540 degrees, the color will change to blue.

Bow

BOW—The ring that is looped at the pendant to which a chain or fob is attached.

BOX CHRONOMETER—A marine or other type chronometer in gimbals so the movement remains level.

BOX JOINTED CASE—A heavily hinged decorative case with a simulated joint at the top under the pendant.

BREGUET KEY—A watch key permitting winding in one direction only.

BREGUET SPRING—A type of hairspring that improves timekeeping (see Overcoil).

BRIDGE—A metal bar which carries the pivot for the balance or other pivot-bearing gears.

BULL'S EYE CRYSTAL—Used on old watches; the center of the crystal was polished which achieved a bull's eye effect.

CALENDAR WATCH—A watch that shows the date, month and day.

CAP JEWEL—Also called the endstone, the flat jewel on which the staff rests.

CENTER WHEEL—The second wheel; the arbor for the minute hand; this wheel makes one revolution per hour.

CHAIN (Fusee)—Looks like a miniature bicycle chain connecting the barrel and fusee.

CHAMPLEVE—An area hollowed out and filled with enamel and then baked on.

CHRONOGRAPH—A movement that can be started and stopped to measure short time intervals and return to zero; also called a stop watch, but a stop watch does not keep the time of day.

CHRONOMETER ESCAPEMENT—A detent escapement used in marine chronometers.

CLICK—A name given to a part that permits the gear to move in one direction; a pawl and ratchet mechanism; a click can be heard as the watch is wound.

CLOCK WATCH—A watch that strikes the hour but not on demand.

CLOISONNE—Enamel set between strips of metal and baked onto the dial.

Club Tooth

CLUB TOOTH—Some escape wheels have a special design which increases the impulse plane; located at the very tip of the tooth of the escape wheel.

COARSE TRAIN—16,000 beats per hour.

COCK—the metal bar that carries the balance wheel; a bridge.

CYLINDER ESCAPEMENT—A type of escapement used on some watches.

DAMASKEENING—The art of producing a design, pattern, or wavy appearance on a metal.

COMPENSATION BALANCE—A balance wheel designed to correct for temperature.

DEMI-HUNTER—A hunting case with the center designed to allow the position of the hands to be seen without opening the case.

COMPLICATED WATCH—A watch with complicated works; other than just telling time, it may have a perpetual calendar, moon phases, equinoxes, up and down dial, repeater, musical chimes or alarms.

DETENT ESCAPEMENT—A detached escapement. The balance is impulsed in one direction; used on watches to provide great accuracy; found on marine chronometers.

CONTRATE WHEEL—A wheel with its teeth at a right angle to plane of the wheel.

CONVERTIBLE—Made by Elgin; a means of converting from a hunting case to an open-face watch or vice-versa.

CRAZE (Crazing)—A minute crack in the glaze of enamel watch dials.

DIAL—the face of a watch. Some are enameled and hand-painted; some are made of gold or silver with diamonds for numbers, etc.

DISCHARGE PALLET JEWEL—The left jewel.

Crown

Crown Wheel

CROWN—A winding button.

CROWN WHEEL—The escape wheel of a verge escapement; looks like a crown.

DOLLAR WATCH—Watches that sold for a dollar or close to a dollar ("the watch that made the dollar famous").

Curb Pin

CURB PINS—The two pins that change the rate of a watch; these two pins, in effect, change the length of the hairspring.

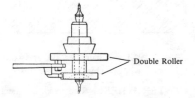

Double Roller

DOUBLE ROLLER—A watch with one impulse roller table and a safety roller, thus two rollers.

DRAW—The inclined position of the locking face of the pallet jewel; this causes the pallet to be drawn toward the escape wheel and the fork toward the banking pin where it is in position to receive the roller jewel.

DROP—The space between a tooth of the escape wheel and the pallet from which it has just escaped.

DUMB REPEATER—One that strikes the hour on the case or block rather than a bell or gong.

DUPLEX ESCAPEMENT—An escape wheel with two sets of teeth, one for locking and one for impulse.

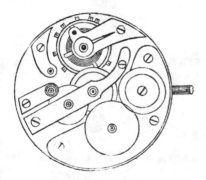

EBAUCHE (i-bo-she)—A movement not completely finished or "in the grey;" in the rough; not detailed; a movement made up of two plates or bars with pillars, barrel and train, and assembly screws. These parts were roughly filed and did not include a dial, case, or escapement.

ECCENTRIC—Non-concentric; usually a cam.

ELECTRONIC WATCH—Newer type watch using quartz and electronics to produce a high degree of accuracy; accurate within a few seconds a month and accurate to within a minute a year.

ELINVAR—A hairspring made of a special alloy that does not vary at different temperatures and is not affected by magnetism: nickel, steel, chromium, manganese and tungsten.

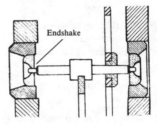

Endshake

ENDSHAKE—The up and down play of an arbor between the plate and bridge or between the jewels.

END STONE—The jewel or cap at the end of the staff.

ENGRAVING—Cutting away to form a pattern.

EPHEMERIS TIME—The time calculated for the Earth to orbit around the sun.

ESCAPE WHEEL—The last wheel in a going train; works with the fork or lever and escapes one pulse at a time.

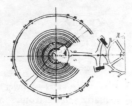

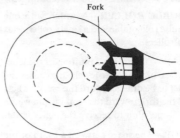

Fork

ESCAPEMENT—The device in a watch by which the motion of the train is checked and the energy of the mainspring communicated to the balance. The escapement includes the escape wheel, lever, and balance complete with hairspring.

FARMER'S WATCH—A large pocket watch with a verge escapement and a farm scene on the face or dial.

FIVE-MINUTE REPEATER—A watch that denotes the time every five minutes, and on the hour and half hour, by operating a slide.

FLINQUE—Enameling over hand engraving.

FLY BACK—The hand return back to zero on a timer.

FOB—A decorative short strap or chain.

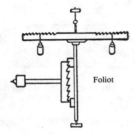

Foliot

FOLIOT—A straight-armed balance with weights on each end used for regulation; found on the earliest clocks and watches.

FORK—The part of the lever that engages with the roller jewel.

FREE SPRUNG—A balance spring free from the influence of curb pins. Curb pins tend to destroy isochronism.

FULL PLATE—A plate (or disc) that covers the works and supports the wheel pivots. There is a top plate, a bottom plate, half plate, and ¾ plate. The top plate has the balance resting on it.

FUSEE—A spirally grooved, truncated cone used in some watches to equalize the power of the mainspring.

GENEVA STOP WORK—(See Maltese Cross)

GILT (or Gild)—To coat with gold leaf or a gold color.

GOING BARREL—The barrel houses the mainspring; as the spring uncoils, the barrel turns, and the teeth on the outside of the barrel turn the train of gears.

GOLD-FILLED—Sandwich-type metal: a layer of gold, a layer of base metal, another layer of gold—then the metals are soldered to each other to form a sandwich.

GOLD JEWEL SETTINGS—In high-grade watches the jewels were mounted in gold settings.

GREAT WHEEL—The main wheel of a fusee type watch.

HACK-WATCH—A watch with a balance that can be stopped to allow synchronization with another timepiece.

HAIRSPRING—The spring which vibrates the balance.

HALLMARK—The British silver or gold assay marker stamp. It gave the place (town), quality marks, maker's mark, and year.

HEART-PIECE—A heart-shaped cam which causes the hand on a chronograph to fly back to zero.

HELICAL HAIRSPRING—A cylindrical spring used in marine chronometers.

HOROLOGY (pronounced Haw-RAHL-uh-jee)—The study of timekeeping or the science of time.

HUNTER CASE—A pocket watch case

with a covered face that must be opened to see the watch dial.

IMPULSE—The force transmitted by the escape wheel to the pallet by gliding over the angular or impulse face of the pallet jewel.

IMPULSE PIN (Ruby pin)—A pin on the balance which keeps the balance going (roller pin).

INCABLOC—A shock absorbing device which permits the endstone of the balance to "give" when the watch is subjected to an impact or jolt.

INDEX—A regulator that can alter the length of the hairspring through means of a lever that moves two curb pins.

ISOCHRONISM—"Isos" means equal; "chronos" means time—occurring at equal intervals of time. The balance should not vary in its swing. The watch will not run any faster one hour after it is wound than it will 24 hours later.

JEWEL—A bearing made of a ruby or other type jewel; the four types of jewels include: cap jewel, hole jewel, roller jewel or ruby pin, pallet jewel or stone.

KARRUSEL (Kar-oo-zell)—A style or type similar to a tourbillon; the escapement rotates its position in an effort to solve the error of positions.

KEY SET—Older watches that had to be set with a key.

KEY WIND—A key used on earlier watches to wind the watch (crank).

LEAVES—The teeth of the pinion gears.

LEVER ESCAPEMENT—Invented by Thomas Mudge in 1760.

Lever

LEVER SETTING—The lever used to set some watches.

LOCKING—Holding the escape wheel (lock) while the balance swings around.

MAINSPRING—A flat spring coiled or wound to supply power to the watch. If it were not for the mainspring the watch would not be portable. The unbreakable main is made of iron, nickel, chromium, cobalt, molybdenum, manganese, and beryllium. The non-magnetic mainspring was introduced in 1947.

MAIN WHEEL—The first driving wheel, part of the barrel.

MALTESE CROSS—The part of the stop works preventing the barrel from being overwound.

Marine
Chronometer

MARINE CHRONOMETER—An accurate timepiece; has a dent escapement and sets in a box with gimbals which keep it in a right position; may have up and down dial.

MEAN TIME—Also equal hours; average mean solar time; the time shown by watches; hours shown by sundials vary in length. When time was averaged into equal hours, this was called mean time.

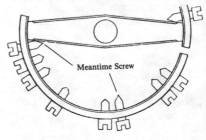

Meantime Screw

MEANTIME SCREWS—Balance screws used for timing, usually longer than other balance screws; when turned away from or toward the balance pin, they cause the balance vibrations to become faster or slower.

MICROMETRIC REGULATOR—A regulator used on railroad grade watches to adjust for gain or loss in a very precise way.

MICROSECOND—A millionth of a second.

MILLISECOND—A thousandth of a second.

MINUTE REPEATER—A watch that strikes or sounds the hours, quarter hours, and minutes on demand by moving a slide.

MOVEMENT—The works of a watch without the case or dial.

MUSICAL WATCH—A watch that plays a tune on demand or on the hour.

MULTI-GOLD—Different colors of gold—red, green, white, blue, pink, yellow, and purple.

NANOSECOND—One billionth of a second.

NATIONAL ASSOCIATION OF WATCH AND CLOCK COLLECTORS—Formed in 1943 to stimulate interest in the study and collecting of timepieces. Mailing address: N.A.W.C.C., P. O. Box 33, Columbia PA 17512.

NON-MAGNETIC—Resistant to magnetism; not affected by magnetic forces.

NUREMBERG EGG—Nickname for a German watch that was oval-shaped.

OIL SINK—A small well around a pivot which retains oil.

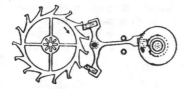

OVERBANKED—A lever escapement error; the roller jewel passes to the wrong side of the lever notch, causing one side of the

pallet to rest against the banking pin and the roller jewel to rest against the other side, thus locking the escapement and stopping the motion of the balance.

PAIR-CASE WATCH—An extra case around a watch—two cases, hence, a pair of cases. The outer case kept out the dust. The inner case could not be dustproof because it provided the access to winding the watch.

PALLET—The part of the lever that works with the escape wheel—jewelled pallet stones, entry pallet and exit pallet.

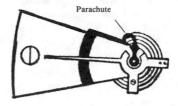

Parachute

PARACHUTE—An early shockproofing system designed to fit as a spring on the endstone of balance.

Pendant

PENDANT—The neck of the watch; attached to it is the bow (swing ring) and the crown.

PILLARS—The rods that hold the plates

apart. In old watches they were fancy.

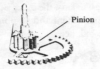

Pinion

PINION—The large gear is called a wheel. The small solid gear is a pinion. The pinion is made of steel in some watches.

PLATE—A watch has a front and a back plate or top and bottom plate. The works are in between.

POISE—A term meaning "in balance;" to equalize the weight of the balance.

PONTILLAGE—The grinding of the center of a crystal to form a concave.

POSITION—As adjusted to five position; a watch may differ in its timekeeping accuracy as it lays in different positions. Due to the lack of isochronism, changes in the center of gravity, a watch can be adjusted to six positions: dial up, dial down, stem up, stem down, stem left, and stem right.

QUICK TRAIN—A watch with five beats per second or 18,000 per hour.

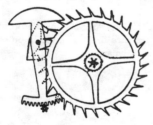

RACK LEVER ESCAPEMENT—Developed by Abbe de Hutefeuille in 1722 and by Petter Litherland in 1791; does not use a roller table, but a pinion.

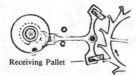

Receiving Pallet

RECEIVING PALLET—Also called "R" stone; the first of two pallet jewels with which a tooth of the escape wheel comes into engagement.

REPEATER WATCH—A complicated pocket watch that repeats the time on demand with a sounding device.

REPOUSSE—A watch with a decorative design embossed on the case.

ROLLED GOLD—Thin layer of gold soldered to a base metal.

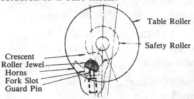

Table Roller

Safety Roller

Crescent
Roller Jewel
Horns
Fork Slot
Guard Pin

ROLLER JEWEL—The jewel seated in the roller table, which receives the impulse from the pallet fork.

ROLLER TABLE—The part of the balance in which the roller jewel is seated.

SAFETY PINION—A pinion in the center wheel designed to slip if the mainspring breaks; this protects the train from being stripped by the great force of the mainspring.

SAFETY ROLLER—The smaller of the two rollers in a double roller escapement.

SIDEREAL TIME—The time of rotation of the Earth as measured from the stars.

SIDE-WINDER—A mismatched case and movement; a term used for a hunting movement that has been placed in an open face case and winds at the 3 o'clock position. With an open face movement the pendant should be at the 12 o'clock position.

SILVEROID—A type of case composed of various metals.

SINGLE ROLLER—The safety roller and the roller jewel are one single table or roller.

SIZE—Systems used to size the movement to the case.

SKELETON WATCH—A watch made so the viewer can see the works. Plates are pierced and very decorative.

SKULL WATCH—A pendant watch that is hinged at the jaw to reveal a watch.

SLOW TRAIN—A watch with four beats per second or 14,000 per hour.

SNAILING—Ornamentation of the surface of metals by means of a circle design; sometimes called damaskeening.

SOLAR YEAR—365 days, 5 hours, 48 minutes, 49.7 seconds.

SPOTTING—Decoration used on a watch movement and barrels of movements.

SPRING RING—A circular tube housing a coiled type spring.

STACKFREED—Curved spring and cam to equalize the uneven pull of the mainspring.

STAFF—Name for the axle of the balance.

SUN DIAL—A device using a gnomon or style that casts a shadow over a graduated dial as the sun progresses, giving solar time.

SWIVEL—A hinged spring catch with a loop of metal that may be opened to insert a watch bow.

TOP PLATE—The metal plate in the back of a movement that houses the gears. This plate usually contains the name and serial number.

TORSION—A twisting force.

TOURBILLON—A watch with the escapement mounted on a platform which revolves once a minute. This is to compensate for various errors in positions. Also called a revolving carriage.

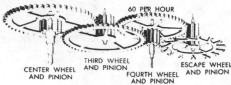

CENTER WHEEL AND PINION THIRD WHEEL AND PINION 60 PER HOUR FOURTH WHEEL AND PINION ESCAPE WHEEL AND PINION

TRAIN—A series of gears that form the works of a watch. The train is used for other functions such as chiming. The time train carries the power to the escapement.

TRIPLE CASE WATCH—An early watch with three cases.

UP AND DOWN DIAL—A dial that

shows how much of the mainspring is spent and how far up or down the mainspring is.

VERGE ESCAPEMENT—Early type of escapement with wheel that is shaped like a crown.

VIRGULE ESCAPEMENT—Early escapement introduced in the mid 1700s.

WATCH PAPER—A disc of paper with the name of the watchmaker or repairman printed on it; used as a form of advertising and found in pair-cased watches.

WIND INDICATOR—A dial that shows how much of the mainspring is spent.

WOLF TEETH—A winding wheel's teeth, so named because of their shape.

ABOUT THE AUTHORS

Mr. Shugart, who compiled and published the highly successful first edition in 1980, was joined by Tom Engle as a co-author in the second edition. Mr. Engle is a widely known watch dealer and authority in the field. Each edition contains updated and revised information and prices, and has become the accepted standard reference work of the watch market.

Both authors have been avid watch collectors for the past three decades, and both have been vitally interested in seeing a reliable and accurate watch guide produced. "We see this book as an extension of the information we have been gathering for years and take great pride in sharing it with other fans who have a deep and abiding interest in watches," the authors stated.

The authors have been long-time members of the National Association of Watch and Clock Collectors and have been students of horology for many years. Both have specialized in early American and Railroad-type pocket watches. They are also well informed in the field of European pocket and wrist watches, especially in the high-grade watches such as Patek, Philippe & Co. Both have enjoyed broadening their knowledge in horology while traveling in Europe.

The co-authors travel extensively throughout the United States to regional meets and shows and keep an up-to-date pulse of the pocket watch market. They continually expand their horological reference library and their extensive selection of watch photographs.

Because of the unique knowledge of the market these two co-authors possess, this volume should be considered one of the most authoritative watch references on the market today.

Mr. Shugart resides in Cleveland, Tennessee, and Mr. Engle lives in Louisville, Kentucky.

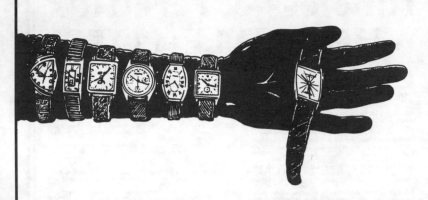

ADVERTISE IN THE GUIDE

ATTENTION DEALERS: This book will receive world-wide bookstore distribution, reaching thousands of people buying and selling pocket watches. It will also be sold directly to the collector's market as well. We will be offering limited advertising space in our next edition. Consider advertising with us. Since the Guide is an annual publication, your ad will pull all year long. Unlike monthly or quarterly publications, your ad will stay active for a much longer period of time at a cost savings to y o u .

PRINTED SIZES AND RATES

FULL PAGE—7½" long x 4¾" wide.
HALF PAGE—3½" long x 4¾" wide.
FOURTH PAGE—3½" long x 2¼" wide.
EIGHTH PAGE—1¾" long x 2¼" wide.

Ad rates are set in the late summer prior to each edition's release. Write at that time for rates (between August and September).

NOTE: Submit your ad on white paper in a proportionate version of the actual printed size. We must ask that all ads be neatly and professionally finished, camera ready. **Full payment must be sent with all ads**. Your ad will be run as received.

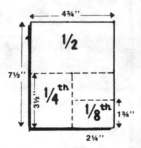

Ad deadline next edition — October 15

This comprehensive **GUIDE** is the **STANDARD REFERENCE WORK** in the field and is distributed to thousands of collectors thoughout the world. Don't miss this opportunity to advertise in the Guide.

NOTICE: All advertisements are accepted and placed in the Guide in good faith. However, we cannot be held responsible for any losses incurred in your dealings with the advertisers. If, after receiving legitimate complaints, and there is sufficient evidence to warrant such action, these advertisers will be dropped from future editions.

OVERSTREET PUBLICATIONS, INC.
780 Hunt Cliff Drive, N.W.
Cleveland, Tennessee 37311
(615) 472-4135

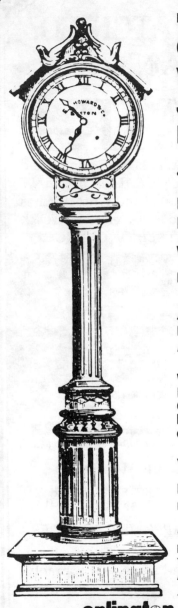

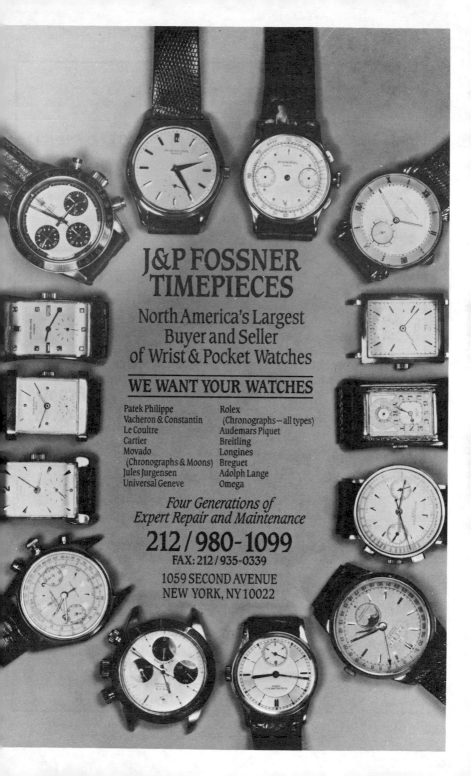

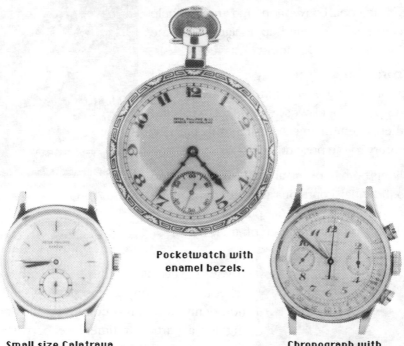

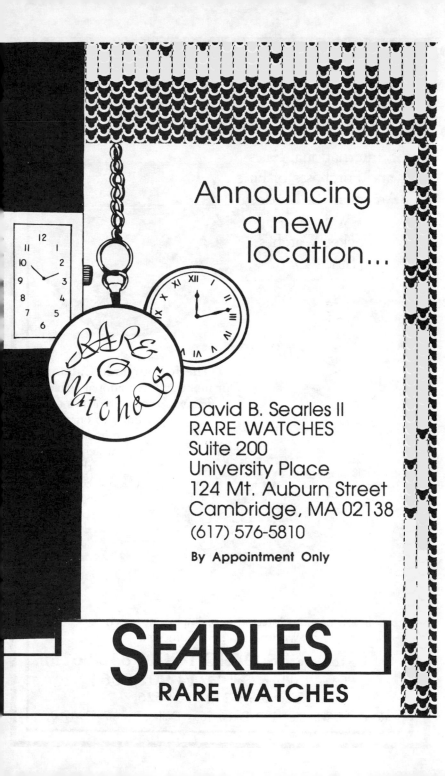

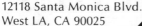

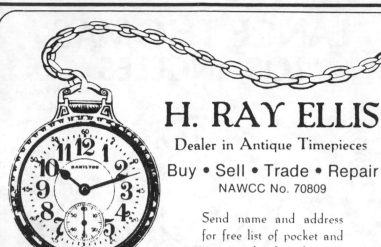

SILVER: ELEGANT *AND* COLLECTIBLE!

Expert JERI SCHWARTZ, writer for *Country Living* magazine, brings us *The Official® Identification and Price Guide to Silver and Silverplate*, which, for the first time, includes American *and* European pieces. From English Georgian tea services to Russian snuffboxes to American hollowware, there is *no other* comparable source!

※ Over 150 photos... eight pages of stunning color... fully indexed!

THIS BOOK REALLY SHINES!

THE BLACKBOOKS!

The leading authorities on U.S. coins, paper money, and postage stamps!

All national bestsellers, these dynamic books are the *proven* annual guides for collectors in these fields for more than two decades!

COINS—Every U.S. coin evaluated...features the American Numismatic Association Official Grading System!

PAPER MONEY—Every government-issued note covered!

POSTAGE STAMPS—Every U.S. stamp detailed...features a full-color, fast-find photo index arranged by the Scott numbering system!

DON'T LEAVE HOME WITHOUT THEM!

BESTSELLING GUIDE TO ANTIQUE JEWELRY!

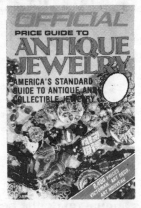

An invaluable reference, *The Official® Price Guide to Antique Jewelry* gives important tips on how to determine the value of your jewelry!

Expert ARTHUR KAPLAN details every type, style, and period of jewelry, from Georgian and Victorian to Art Nouveau and Art Deco, from brooches and bracelets to rings and watches.

♦ Over 4,000 photos... eight pages of vibrant color... fully indexed!

THIS BOOK IS A GEM!